THE WORLD
IS A GHETTO

THE WORLD
IS A GHETTO

Race and Democracy Since
World War II

HOWARD WINANT

BASIC
BOOKS

A Member of the Perseus Books Group

Designed by Bookcomp, Inc.

FIRST EDITION

A CIP catalog record of this book is available from the Library of Congress.

ISBN 0-465-04340-2
01 02 03 04 / 10 9 8 7 6 5 4 3 2 1

To

Johanna,
Carmen,
and Gabriel Winant:

THINKERS, DOERS, DREAMERS.

HAITI

Quando você for convidado pro subir no
    adro da Fundação Casa de Jorge
    Amado
Pra ver do alto a fila de soldados, quase
    todos pretos
Dando porrada na nuca de malandros
    pretos
De ladrões mulatos e outros quase
    brancos
Tratados como pretos
Só pra mostrar aos outros quase pretos
(E são quase todos pretos)
E aos quase brancos pobres como pretos
Como é que pretos, pobres e mulatos
E quase brancos quase pretos de tão
    pobres são tratados
E não importa se olhos do mundo
    inteiro
Possam estar por um momento voltados
    para o largo
Onde os escravos eram castigados
E hoje um batuque um batuque
Com a pureza de meninos uniformizados
    de escola secundária
Em dia de parada
E a grandeza épica de um povo em for-
    mação
Nos atrai, nos deslumbra e estimula
Não importa nada: nem o traço do
    sobrado
Nem a lente do fantástico, nem o disco
    de Paul Simon
Ninguém, ninguém é cidadão
Se você for ver a festa do Pelo, se você
    não for
Pense no Haiti, reze pelo Haiti
O Haiti é aqui—o Haiti não é aqui

E na TV se você vir um deputado em
    pánico mal dissimulado
Diante de qualquer, mas qualquer
    mesmo, qualquer qualquer
Plano de educação que pareça fácil
Que pareça fácil e rápido
E vá representar uma ameaça de democ-
    ratizaçao

HAITI

When you are invited up on the terrace
Of the Casa de Jorge Amado
    Foundation
To watch from above the row of soldiers,
    almost all black
Beating on the necks of the black good
    for nothings
Of mulato thieves and other almost white
    ones
Treated like the black ones
Just to show the other almost black ones
(And they are almost all black)
How it is that blacks, poor men and
    mulattoes
And almost white ones, so poor they're
    almost black are treated
And it doesn't matter if the eyes of the
    whole world
Might be for a moment turned to the
    square
Where the slaves were punished
And today the pounding of drums
    pounding of drums
With the purity of boys in secondary
    school uniforms
On parade day
And the epic grandeur of a people in for-
    mation
Attracts us, astonishes us and stimulates
    us
Not one thing matters: not the trace of
    the mansion's architecture
Not the camera lens from Fantastico, not
    Paul Simon's record
No one, no one is a citizen
If you go to the party there at Peló, and if
    you don't go
Think about Haiti, pray for Haiti
Haiti is here—Haiti is not here

And on TV, if you see a congressman in
    barely concealed panic
When faced by any, absolutely any any
    any
Plan for education that seems easy
That seems fast and easy

Do ensino de primeiro grau
E se esse mesmo deputado defender a
    adoção de pena capital
E o venerável cardeal disser que vé tanto
    espírito no feto
E nenhum no marginal
E se, ão furar o sinal, o velho sinal
Vermelho habitual
Notar um homen mijando na esquina da
    rua
Sobre um saco brilhante de lixo do
    Leblon
E quando ouvir o siléncio sorridente de
    São Paulo
Diante da chacina
111 presos indefesos, mas presos são
    quase todos pretos
Ou quase pretos, ou quase brancos quase
    pretos de tão pobres
E pobres são como podres e todos sabem
    como se tratam os pretos
E quando você for dar uma volta no
    Caribe
E quando for trepar sem camisinha
E apresentar sua participação inteligente
    no bloqueio a Cuba
Pense no Haiti, reze pelo Haiti
O Haiti é aqui, o Haiti não é aqui
—Caetano Veloso (1994)

And will represent a threat to democra-
    tize
Primary school education
And if this same congressman should
    defend
The adoption of capital punishment
And the venerable cardinal should
    declare
That he sees so much soul in the fetus
And none in the criminal and if,
When you run a red light, the old famil-
    iar red light
You should notice on the street corner a
    man pissing
On a shiny bag of garbage from Leblon
And when you hear the smiling silence of
    São Paulo
In response to the massacre
One hundred and eleven defenseless
    prisoners
But prisoners are almost all blacks
Or almost blacks, or almost whites so
    poor they're almost black
And poor men are rotten, and everyone
    knows
How blacks are treated
And when you go on holiday in the
    Caribbean
And when you have sex without a con-
    dom
And participate intelligently in the block-
    ade of Cuba
Think about Haiti, pray for Haiti
Haiti is here, Haiti is not here
—Caetano Veloso (1994)

IF WE ARE TO HOPE TO UNDERSTAND THE OFTEN VIOLENT WORLD IN WHICH WE LIVE (AND UNLESS WE TRY TO UNDERSTAND IT, WE CANNOT EXPECT TO BE ABLE TO ACT RATIONALLY IN IT AND ON IT), WE CANNOT CONFINE OUR ATTENTION TO THE GREAT IMPERSONAL FORCES, NATURAL AND MAN-MADE, WHICH ACT UPON US. THE GOALS AND MOTIVES THAT GUIDE HUMAN ACTION MUST BE LOOKED AT IN THE LIGHT OF ALL THAT WE KNOW AND UNDERSTAND; THEIR ROOTS AND GROWTH, THEIR ESSENCE, AND ABOVE ALL THEIR VALIDITY, MUST BE CRITICALLY EXAMINED WITH EVERY INTELLECTUAL RESOURCE THAT WE HAVE. THIS URGENT NEED, APART FROM THE INTRINSIC VALUE OF THE DISCOVERY OF TRUTH ABOUT HUMAN RELATIONSHIPS, MAKES ETHICS A FIELD OF PRIMARY IMPORTANCE. ONLY BARBARIANS ARE NOT CURIOUS ABOUT WHERE THEY COME FROM, HOW THEY CAME TO BE WHERE THEY ARE, WHERE THEY APPEAR TO BE GOING, WHETHER THEY WISH TO GO THERE, AND IF SO, WHY, AND IF NOT, WHY NOT.

—Isaiah Berlin (1990)

[T]O RETHINK SOCIALISM IN THESE NEW CONDITIONS COMPELS US TO UNDERTAKE TWO STEPS. THE FIRST IS TO ACCEPT, IN ALL THEIR RADICAL NOVELTY, THE TRANS-FORMATIONS OF THE WORLD IN WHICH WE LIVE—THAT IS TO SAY, NEITHER TO IGNORE THEM NOR TO DISTORT THEM IN ORDER TO MAKE THEM COMPATIBLE WITH OUTDATED SCHEMAS SO THAT WE MAY CONTINUE INHABITING OLD FORMS OF THOUGHT WHICH REPEAT THE OLD FORMULAE. THE SECOND IS TO START FROM THIS FULL INSERTION IN THE PRESENT—IN ITS STRUGGLES, ITS CHALLENGES, ITS DANGERS—TO INTERROGATE THE PAST: TO SEARCH WITHIN IT FOR THE GENEALOGY OF THE PRESENT SITUATION; TO RECOGNIZE WITHIN IT THE PRESENCE—AT FIRST MARGINAL AND BLURRED—OF PROBLEMS THAT ARE OURS; AND, CONSEQUENTLY, TO ESTABLISH WITH THAT PAST A DIALOGUE WHICH IS ORGANIZED AROUND CONTINUITIES AND DISCONTINUITIES, IDENTIFICATIONS AND RUPTURES.

—Ernesto Laclau and Chantal Mouffe (1990)

THE BIRTH OF A NEW PARADIGM, EXPANDING DEMOCRACY BY RENDERING VISIBLE NEW IDENTITIES WHICH DEMAND CONSIDERATION OF THEIR ASPIRATIONS, IS THE CONCERN OF RADICAL SOCIAL MOVEMENTS. . . . [D]EMOCRACY IS NOT A SPHERE TO BE MANAGED OR ENLARGED. IT IS A CONTINENT TO BE DISCOVERED, FROM ONE CENTURY TO THE NEXT.

—Alain Lipietz (1994)

Contents

Preface

THIS BOOK IS AN EFFORT to explain why race is such an important social fact. I wrote it because I wanted to situate race at the turn of the twenty-first century, the start (according to Western, Christian-inflected calendars, anyway) of a new millennium. I wanted to understand our racial history, our collective, world-wide racial history: how did we get to this racial present?

This huge agenda came, of course, from my personal as well as my intellectual trajectory. For many years, when asked about my background and my interests, I would reply that like so many others I was a child of "the movement." I was an adolescent in the early 1960s, and a university student in the later years of that decade. I was politically active in youth groups and especially in college; I was drawn into anti-racist activities when I was still quite young; and I have remained so ever since. So my response to such questions would run.

But actually the sources of my political and intellectual commitments, and thus of this book, go deeper than that. They involve fascism and the primordial racism it represented: anti-semitism.

My parents were refugees, Jewish refugees from Nazism. My late father Karl Weininger (1918–91) grew up in Vienna, and experienced the *Anschluss* of March 1938 (he was twenty years old that same month). Soon after, knowing that Jewish men and boys were being rounded up and sent off to forced labor or worse, he went to the train station and took the first train he could out of town. He was determined to escape, but escape was not so easy. The train took him to Berlin! And there, in the Nazi capital, he encountered far less anti-semitism than he had in Vienna. Berlin, then as now, was a relatively "progressive" city. He went to the museums, and swam in the Wannsee (of course prohibited to Jews). He was in Berlin on the night of June 22, 1938, when Joe Louis knocked out Max Schmeling in New York (many Berliners, he said, welcomed Schmeling's defeat). As the news of the "brown bomber's" triumph came through—it was already the morning of the 23rd—my dad determined to make it to the United States. Through a complex series of maneuvers he finally arrived there, sick and broke but young and safe, before war began in Europe.

So I grew up in the shadow of the Holocaust. I was born in 1946. My parents were not tremendously political, but they hated fascism and knew racism when they saw it. (My mom Dé Haagens was a refugee too, from the Netherlands; she had had an easier time getting out of Europe.) Who were the fascists in America? In their view: Joe McCarthy, J. Edgar Hoover, the young Richard Nixon, James Eastland, Strom Thurmond. I remember my dad watching the Army–McCarthy hearings on our new and then-rather-miraculous TV in 1953. "Watch this, Howard," he told me. "This is what fascism looks like." I was seven years old.

My intellectual work flows from these two places, then: from "the movement," and from a childhood framed by the Holocaust, shaped by refugee parents and by a secular Jewish, New York milieu. I have been working on race for a long time. My initial interests were very movement-driven, very North American. I still retain that set of concerns, but as my knowledge and experience has broadened, so too has my awareness of the globality of race.

This book is an extended essay, not a work of primary research. It is an attempt to clarify the world-historical dimensions of race, but its primary focus is trained on the contemporary era, the period that extends from World War II to the present day. It is also an effort to sound a political alarm: *all around the world the momentum of the struggle against racism is stalemated.* The successes of anti-racist and anti-colonial movements in recent decades are being transformed into new patterns of racial inequality and injustice. The "new world racial system," in sharp contrast to the old structures of explicit colonialism and state-sponsored segregation, now presents itself as "beyond race," "color-blind," multicultural, and post-racial. It seeks to render racism invisible: it attempts to dismiss race as a holdover from a benighted past, something now well on the way to being transcended. It presents race as a "problem" that is finally being "solved." Ironically enough, these claims are asserted at a moment when the disparities between the world's North (more white than not) and its South (more dark than not) are intensifying, and when northern fears of "swamping" by immigrants are very much present once again.

That race is still largely perceived as a problem, rather than as a flexible dimension of human variety that is valuable and permanent, is itself an indication of the continuing danger that the "new world racial system" embodies. I have addressed this theme in an earlier work, *Racial Conditions* (1994), but in this book I seek to expand and deepen our awareness of it. Our effort must not be to "do away" with race, to "get beyond" race; this is no more possible than it is to "do away" with other forms of human variety. Rather we must renew our quest to reduce racial inequality, racial hierarchy, racial subjugation. This is not the first "world racial system" we have ever experienced; it will not be the last.

I've talked and corresponded with a great many people about this work. Some of those listed below read and commented on large sections of the manuscript. Others furnished me with materials or references. And others took walks or tea with me. In more ways than I can enumerate, the people listed below helped me keep my perspective on the material covered or the arguments offered here.

I can hardly name everyone who helped me; many did so in ways they could not know and I cannot acknowledge. But those who must be mentioned include: David Anthony, Peter Baehr, Robin Blackburn, Fred Block, David Brundage, Martin Bulmer, Aurora Camacho de Schmidt, Randall Collins, Jim Clifford, Douglas Dowd, Phil Evanson, Adrian Favell, Joe Feagin, George Fredrickson, Paul Gilroy, Eddie Glaude, Linda Gordon, Peter Gran, Michael Hanchard, Chester Hartman, Dienke Hondius, Syd Jeffers, David Kairys, Robin D. G. Kelley, Martin Kilson, Norman Koerner, Michèle Lamont, Magali Sarfatti Larson, Douglas Massey, James O'Connor, Michael Omi, Lucius Outlaw, Bob Perelman, Jan Rath, Lauret Savoy, Jim Shoch, Nikhil Pal Singh, Thomas Skidmore, Chris Smaje, Stephen Small, Bashar Tarabieh, Edward Telles, Daniel Tompkins, France Winddance Twine, Vron Ware, Jonathan Warren, S. Craig Watkins, Robert Vitalis, and Tukufu Zuberi. Of course none of those listed bears any responsibility for the final work, but each deserves thanks for dialogue, debate, and discussion.

This book was begun as a collaboration with Gay Seidman. Although the project did not remain a joint effort, it continues in many ways to be a product of that association. Gay took part in extensive preparations and planning for the book. She and I together gave several talks based on this work, at conferences and university forums. I visited the University of Wisconsin several times at her invitation, enjoying both the opportunity to present preliminary material from this project, and the hospitality of her home and family: Heinz, Ben, and Matthew. She wrote an initial draft of Chapter Eight; that chapter is truly the product of both our hands, although the final responsibility for its content remains with me. Gay continues to be my good friend and admired colleague.

I have had two editors at Basic Books. Tim Bartlett advocated for the book on 53rd St. and provided important criticism and support in the early stages of its preparation. Vanessa Mobley ably took over when Tim moved to another position. The oversight and support of a skilled editor is an enormous gift to both writer and reader. I am grateful to both. I also greatly appreciate the skilled copyediting and book production efforts of Maria and David den Boer, and Christine Marra.

I have had the benefit of material and logistical support from several institutions. Temple University granted me a year's leave from my teaching responsibilities, which made a lot of reading and writing possible. I found a great deal of support at the University of Pennsylvania, where Doug Massey, chair of the Department of Sociology, not only provided me with an office and a visitor's title, but facilitated the availability of various essential resources. At the University of California, Santa Cruz, a "second home" for me and as near to an earthly paradise as I am likely to discover, my colleagues and old friends Nancy

Stoller and Michael Rotkin organized working space and technical support for me. Other crucial assistance came from Don Hartman at Temple and Melessa Hemler at UCSC; their administrative backup and good will often turned difficult logistics into smooth sailing. The Common Counsel Foundation made writing time and space available to me at the Mesa Refuge. I am grateful to all these organizations, friends, and colleagues.

Librarians too numerous to mention by name helped me out at the Paley Library of Temple University, the Van Pelt Library of the University of Pennsylvania, the McHenry Library of the University of California, Santa Cruz, and the Firestone Library of Princeton University. Thank you, bookhounds, document specialists, and internauts one and all.

Preliminary versions of these texts were presented in talks at the University of Amsterdam, Brown University, the University of Chicago, Columbia University, the University of Maryland, the University of Michigan, Northwestern University, the University of Pennsylvania, the Russell Sage Foundation, Rutgers University, Swarthmore College, the University of Southern California, the University of Sussex, the University of Washington, and the University of Wisconsin.

The book's title samples Brian Cutler's song "The World is a Ghetto." The mixture of tenderness and reproach contained in that cut has moved me since 1972, when it first appeared on an album by the band War (Avenue Records 1972; R2 71043).

One

INTRODUCTION

RACE HAS BEEN fundamental in global politics and culture for half a millennium. It continues to signify and structure social life not only experientially and locally, but nationally and globally. Race is present everywhere: it is evident in the distribution of resources and power, and in the desires and fears of individuals from Alberta to Zimbabwe. Race has shaped the modern economy and nation-state. It has permeated all available social identities, cultural forms, and systems of signification. Infinitely incarnated in institution and personality, etched on the human body, racial phenomena affect the thought, experience, and accomplishments of human individuals and collectivities in many familiar ways, and in a host of unconscious patterns as well.[1]

Only a few decades ago—let us say before World War II—the "social fact" of racial inequality and thoroughgoing racial difference was taken for granted. Although there was always both small- and large-scale resistance, this was widely seen as exceptional, anomalous, or at least containable. In the ruling circles—the metropoles, the world's capitals both imperial and peripheral—it was taken for granted as natural, ineluctable, an "objective" reality, that to be white (however that is defined) conferred a *deserved* advantage on those so identified, while a dark skin *properly* signified inferiority. The name for this set of beliefs, this racial ideology, is white supremacy.

Within the past two generations, however, the world has witnessed an accelerated challenge to the continuity of worldwide white supremacy. It has seen the Holocaust and the massive population shifts accompanying and succeeding World War II. There have been powerful movements for decolonization, civil rights, and the end of official apartheid. And we have lived through the "twilight struggle" that neo-colonialism and the Cold War brought to the jungles and deserts of the world's South.

In the aftermath of these, as well as countless other manifestations of the worldwide rupture of the racial status quo, the ironic view has emerged that we are now in a post-racial, color-blind world. At present, serious arguments are being made that the race-concept is outmoded, atavistic, a relic of earlier times. The very idea of race has come in for deprecation. And what remains of racial discourse has a new tone, as evidenced in claims about "color-blindness" and "multiculturalism." Race-talk today presents itself as egalitarian, respectful of "cultural difference," and, above all, humane. The appearance and consolidation of such post-racial sentiments is a recent phenomenon; it has reshaped contemporary understanding and debates over race.

This post-racial view is at odds with the central claims of this book: that racial hierarchy lives on; that it correlates very well with worldwide and national systems of stratification and inequality; that it corresponds to glaring disparities in labor conditions and reflects differential access to democratic and communicative instrumentalities and life chances. My view is that the race-concept is anything but obsolete and that its significance is not declining. We are not "beyond race."

What is obsolete, however, are traditional or parochial ways of analyzing the matter of race. At the beginning of the twenty-first century, at the dawn of a new millennium, there is a pressing need for a new *global* approach to race that takes into account the new, "cleaned-up" racial ideologies or post-racial perspectives I have mentioned. Adequately to understand the importance of race—historical and contemporary—requires us to reconsider many of our ideas and assumptions about modernity, development, labor, democracy, identity, culture, and indeed, our concepts of social action and agency. Taken as a whole, these are the coordinates of all social theory. We need a new, racially more adequate, theoretical compass if we want to navigate properly in the twenty-first-century world.

My thesis is that the upsurge of anti-racist activity since World War II constitutes a fundamental and historical shift, a global rupture or "break," in the continuity of worldwide white supremacy. Throughout this book I use the term *break* to refer to the mid-century challenge to the continuity of world racial rule over the *longue duree* of the modern epoch. The origins and contours of that shift are at the center of this work.

PART I. FROM THE ABYSS: RACE AND MODERN HISTORY

The first section of the book examines the historical sociology of race. In Chapters Two through Five I consider the ways that race has been a key force driving world development, one of the central pillars of the edifice of modernity. The book locates the foundations of race, both conceptually and social structurally, at the dawn of the modern epoch around the year 1500. It then traces the world that race built, from the appearance of Columbus's sails on the Atlantic horizon to the post–World War II break.

These four chapters outline the racial dimensions of the rise of the modern world system. The fifteenth century, when the planet was first circumnavigated, first knitted together into a single and finite entity, first subjected, albeit unevenly and imperfectly, to the rule of a core group of nation-states, was also when racial rule first appeared in something approximating modern form. Through Part I of the book I trace out this historical sociology of race, culminating with the crucial ruptural moment of World War II.

Chapter Two specifically frames the outlines of a historical *theory* of race, which sees the phenomenon as a key factor in the creation of the modern world. Here I argue that the foundation of modern nation-states, the construction of an international economy, and the articulation of a unified world culture were all deeply racialized processes. The chapter documents the ways that development occurred in complex interaction with a series of different modes of racial domination, racially based resistances, and racial significations. It shows how the problematic of race came to permeate most of the formative struggles of the modern age, shaping debates and conflicts over labor regimes, democracy, national independence and identity, and citizenship.

This chapter also introduces the argument that I have linked to Myrdal's theory of circular and cumulative causation (Myrdal 1963): the racialization of the world is both the cause and consequence of modernity. It is important to bear in mind, as one ventures deeper into this text, the *centrality* I claim for race, both historically and in the present day. Race must be grasped as a fundamental condition of individual and collective identity, a permanent, although tremendously flexible, dimension of the modern global social structure. The epochal phenomenon of race has been the basis for the most comprehensive systems of oppression and injustice ever organized, and simultaneously the foundation for every dream of liberation, at least since the inception of the modern world. The theory presented in Chapter Two is that race "accumulated" in all the fissures and faultlines of modern society.

Chapter Three, "Learning to Catch Hell," follows the rise and consolidation of the world racial system from the late fifteenth to the early nineteenth centuries. Here I highlight the relationship of conquest and slavery to the origins of modernity. I first consider precursors to racial modernity, exploring the creation of Europe as a racial project. The foundation and consolidation of nation-states along the European Atlantic raised crucial questions about the tension between peoplehood (the "national") and the structure of domination ("statism"), questions that were never more than partially resolved by intra- and extra-European imperial initiatives.

Next I address the two principal regions in which Europe found its modern "others": Africa and the Americas.[2] Both these vast regions underwent extensive mutations as their fates were linked to the global system of exploitation and stratification. These social relationships were comprehensively racialized, a reality that flew back to Europe as well as hierarchizing the periphery. Thus the lower strata at home were increasingly ruled by techniques perfected in the colonies, and indeed found their cultural traits (including their resistance to exploitation and absolutism) equated to those of colonial subjects (Cooper and Stoler 1997). The chapter concludes by considering the dawning of obstacles to imperial rule, the increasing tensions brought about by slavery, and the impact of these factors on democratization.

From the standpoint of racial theory, the categorization employed in these chapters, and more generally in Part I of this book—that of Europe and its modern "others"—has some decided limitations. In its fundamental bipolarity it neglects the highly divergent patterns of historical encounter among various peoples and indeed continents. In other writings I have criticized bipolar concepts of race.[3] Although I do not reduce race in this book to a matter of black and white, there are certainly points at which I verge on a similar error in my attempts to explain the historical intersection between the modern world's racialization and its explosive development as a capitalist, statist, and secularizing planet. In any case, there were certainly many "others": not white, not black, not Native American (how inadequate these classifications seem in world-historical perspective!). Indeed there were many European identities as well as the myriad of "others." There were many localized racial systems too. In the Americas systems of racial classification varied, schematically speaking. Some sought to distinguish as absolutely as possible between whites and "others," employing for this purpose a hypodescent (Harris 1964) or one-drop rule system of racial categorization. Others relied on a racial continuum concept that admitted more intermediate positions (*mestizo, mulato, moreno*, and a large variety of other hybridized identities). Predominance of the former scheme has been linked to British- (and Protestant-) based systems of enslavement and colonization, particularly (but not exclusively) in the Americas, while the latter variants have been linked (again, especially in the Americas) with Latin European- (and Catholic-) based systems. While particularities were significant, they were by no means clear-cut: there was a lot of overlap between the "two variants in race relations" identified by Hoetink (1971; see also Davis 1991). Most telling: throughout the Americas and indeed across the merging world racial system, racial hierarchy prevailed.

All these peoples, all these concepts, would ultimately be employed in the complex project of knitting together the modern world; all would inescapably be involved in fracturing world society too. No writer I know could adequately delineate this vast panorama of multiple connections and faultlines. I have already mentioned my decision to focus in general on the Atlantic complex as the central locus of modernization; I acknowledge my relative neglect of Asia and Asian peoples, and of their particular rendezvous with modernity. But this is just the most telling of the many oversights I have committed in my quest to present the world of today as possessing a racial lineage, a racialized gestation, a genealogy of racial formation.

In Chapter Four, "The Empire Strikes Back," the historical focus shifts to the *praxis* of the subjugated. Here I consider the dynamics and consequences of resistance to conquest and enslavement, looking at everyday hindrance and strife, slave rebellion and *marronage,* and finally arriving at abolitionism, revolution, and anti-colonialism. Resistance and opposition, like racial rule itself, traversed successive historical stages, in general moving from what Gramsci (1971, 229–235) called "war of maneuver" to "war of position." The chapter begins with the early stages of racial resistance, when enslaved subjects lacked virtually all rights and were effectively deprived of personhood (not to mention citizenship); in such circumstances resistance logically focused on subversion, escape, and, where possible, on revolt. As racial rule evolved in worldhistorical (and national-political) terms, the forms of resistance and opposition shifted as well. Slowly and unevenly, political and cultural conflict became more possible. Opponents of racial rule found themselves gradually or intermittently acquiring leverage and allies. They were now able to press some claims on the state, and even to operate in the transnational political system. The chapter concludes by examining the first global social movement, abolitionism, comparing its North American, British, and Brazilian manifestations.

Chapter Five, "Nineteenth-Century Nightmares, Twentieth-Century Dreams," explores the aftermath of slavery and the emergence of contemporary antiracism and anti-colonialism. With the general obsolescence of slavery and the success/incorporation of abolitionist demands, the world racial system entered a new, twilight phase of racial subjugation. The destruction of slavery occupied the entire nineteenth century, although its crucial battle was the U.S. Civil War. With chattel-based forms of coerced mass labor on the wane, colonial and plantation-based labor demand gave rise to systems of peonage based in primary goods-exporting economies and racial policies of segregation (aka demarcation of "native reserves"). This situation combined unevenly with massive new waves of migration (both coerced and "free"), expanding industrialization and urbanization of labor (both white and non-white), and military mobilization, particularly that occasioned by World War I. As a significant population of ex-slaves and former colonials (or their progeny) made their way to the cities, they formed political and cultural movements that would barely have been conceivable a century earlier: anti-colonialism, civil rights, pan-Africanism. They sought to express and encompass, to lead or at least to aid, the hosts remaining "down home," whom Du Bois characterized in 1900 as "the millions of black men (sic) in Africa, and the Islands of the Sea, not to speak of the brown and yellow myriads everywhere" (Du Bois 1995 [1900], 639). Often linking their fortunes with Marxist and socialist currents (as well as with such other alternatives as existed: Wilsonian self-determination, negritude, etc.), these movements paved the way for the massive upsurges of World War II and after. This chapter details these developments and shows how they laid the groundwork for the break.

Part I thus concludes by arriving at the contemporary period, the mid-twentieth century. This brings the analysis to the threshold of Part II of this book. There the optic shifts, so to speak, from the diachronic to the synchronic, from the genealogy of the world racial system to the comparison of some of that system's main present-day instances.

But first a final word on the historical sociology of race. My presentation of that subject in Part I is more than an effort to set the stage for contemporary studies of race, although it is that as well. It is an effort to *reclaim the centrality of race*, both historically and in the present day. This argument links to the pressing political agenda of the present age, which once more I take to be a racial matter. To say that race endures is to recognize that both the range of "social problems" associated with racial stratification—inequality, exclusion, bigotry, indeed disdain and ignorance—endure. But it is also to recognize something more, something racial that is not a "problem" but is the opposite of a problem: the dream of liberation endures, the goal of democracy endures. The epochal phenomenon of race has been both the basis for the most comprehensive system of oppression and injustice ever organized, and simultaneously the foundation for every dream of liberation, at least since the inception of the modern world. Why is the concept of race subject to such continual conflict and reinterpretation? Not because it is a social problem, but because it is a fundamental social fact! To say that race endures is to say that the modern world endures.

PART II. THE CONTEMPORARY SOCIOLOGY OF RACE

The post–World War II break was at best a partial shift away from formally avowed white supremacy. The demolition of the racial subjugation that created the modern world is far from complete. Rather, we are in a racial interregnum: we are on a voyage between the discredited but undead racial past and the much anticipated but far from realized racial future.

The World War II rupture resulted in a worldwide stalemate, an unstable equilibrium between the old and the new world racial orders. Since that time, two openly contradictory world-historical racial *projects* have coexisted: deeply rooted and dearly held attachments to white supremacy on the one hand, and fierce and implacable and partially institutionalized legal and social commitments to racial justice, universalism, pluralism, and democracy on the other.

The second section of the book is a comparative sociological study that tracks the process of this transition in four distinct settings. It traces the vicissitudes of the race-concept and of the various national and global experiences of race (or racialized social structures), thus elucidating how the break—a massive shift away from *official* white supremacy—operated in different global and national contexts. Separate chapters on the United States, South Africa, Brazil, and the European Union seek to shed light on how the break has played itself out in the world's North and South, in its "developed" and "less developed" countries, in its post-colonial northern metropoles and its newly emancipated southern settings.

Controversy over the meaning and significance of race was greatly heightened after World War II. The war itself had significant racial dimensions, and left a legacy of revulsion at racism[4] and genocide. The social movements and revolutionary upsurges that succeeded the war and brought the colonial era to an end also raised the question of race to a new level of moral and political prominence. The civil rights movement in the United States and the anti-apartheid struggle in South Africa are but the most prominent examples. As it gained its independence, the post-colonial world quickly became embroiled in the competition of the Cold War, a situation that placed not only the legacy of imperial rule but also the racial policies of the superpowers (especially those of the United States) under additional scrutiny. Another consequence of the war was enormous migratory flows from the world's rural South to its metropolitan North; in these demographic shifts "the empire struck back," pluralizing the former "mother-countries" (Centre for Contemporary Cultural Studies 1982). All these developments raised significant questions about the meaning of race.

The five chapters of Part II focus on the contemporary sociology of race, taking the break as their point of departure. After an initial discussion of my approach to these studies, which frames and explains the political-sociological method, these chapters concentrate on selected national cases. The nation-state is a necessary unit of analysis for any comparative political sociology. Yet at the same time country-specific studies of global racial dynamics—even those concerned most centrally with the political dimensions of race—have clear limitations. In the contemporary period, the years since the postwar break, racial themes, which have been global in scope ever since their first appearance on the world-historical stage, have become in many ways even more planetary, even more transnational.[5]

A further problem in the political sociology of race concerns the non-statist dimensions of racial politics: the sphere of civil society, and indeed that of personal politics, or the "micro-level." As I have detailed in other work (Omi and Winant 1994; Winant 1994a), racial politics can hardly be grasped merely as matters of state management or of contention within established political institutions (courts, legislatures, etc.). One must also consider the extent and dynamics of the "public sphere" (Habermas 1989; Calhoun, ed. 1992), the emergence and "political process" of social movements (McAdam et al, eds. 1996), and the whole matter of "cultural politics" (Axford 1995; Beverley 1996; Bhabha 1994; Lowe and Lloyd, eds. 1997). At the "micro-level," race is "signifying action"

(Perinbanayagam 1985), a kind of politics best theorized through the pragmatist tradition of Mead (1938; see also Joas 1993, 1996), through Blumer's
symbolic interactionism (1958; 1969), and through Du Bois's thought (West
1989, 138–150).

So, as the world lurches forward into the next millennium, widespread confusion and anxiety remain about race: about its political significance and even
its meaning. Around the world, a kind of split or dualistic mentality has developed on the subject. On the one hand, there is continuing concern to oppose
racism and undo the weighty legacy of racial inequality left by centuries of colonialism, slavery, and white supremacy. On the other hand, there is a prominent,
indeed growing, tendency to consider this task as largely accomplished: to
operate, in other words, as if racial oppression had *already* been largely overcome, as if the errors of white supremacy had *already* been corrected. To sort
out and analyze the variations of this new racial dualism is the aim of this part
of the book.

The term *racial dualism* echoes the double consciousness and veil concepts
so central in W. E. B. Du Bois' analysis of race. A full century after he introduced them these ideas may still be applied, not only to U.S. racial conditions
but to the world racial situation. Or so I argue here: the race-concept is at once
denied and affirmed. As a colossal impediment to democracy and equality it is
studiously ignored or consigned to the dead past; while as an effective means
of allocating resources, shaping power relations, and configuring identity it
remains as essential as ever.

Racial dualism takes on very different forms in distinct national settings at
the turn of the twenty-first century. In the United States, the increasingly popular view is that with the enactment of civil rights legislation and the formal
repudiation of state-sponsored racial discrimination, the country has at last
moved "beyond race." The talisman of the current "color-blind" discourse about
race in the United States has been the resurgence of faith in doctrines of individualism and meritocracy. Thus there has been a heightened effort to repeal
affirmative action policies, for example, on the grounds that they are no longer
necessary and may even constitute a new kind of discrimination in reverse.[6]

Elsewhere in the world too, or just about everywhere, parallel instances of
racial dualism can be cited. Debates simmer—and occasionally rage—about
whether or not racial injustice perseveres, and about how it can best be confronted. Should racial matters be publicly addressed through the continuation
or even expansion of reform legislation and open public debate? Or should
they be ignored as atavisms, relics of the "bad old days" that will disappear of
their own weight over time and with the passing of older, more racially "dam-
aged," generations? Around the world, not just in the United States, such questions are raised.

In most of the Americas, for example, the *mestizaje*, racial democracy, and color continuum that in the past were invoked to distinguish Brazil, Mexico, or Cuba from their muscular northern neighbor's policies of segregation and color-line, are now being celebrated anew. Yet for all their echoes of earlier ideologies of racial exceptionalism—the theory of *luso-tropicalismo* (Freyre 1986 [1933]) in Brazil, the alternative image of *nuestro América* (Martí 1977) in Cuba, and the idea of *la raza cosmica* (Vasconcelos 1966 [1924]) in Mexico would be some good examples[7]—new generations of racial activists have arisen to denounce these meliorist visions as embodying racial hierarchies of their own.

In southern Africa the successors to the apartheid system and Portuguese colonial rule are laboring to fulfill the African National Congress's (ANC's) 1955 pledge of non-racialism. Yet South Africa is still haunted by demons left over from those "ignoble and unhappy regimes." Nor has the rest of Africa escaped continued racialization, notably in the genocidal conflicts in Angola/Rwanda/Burundi/Uganda/Congo and so on,[8] in the civil wars and continuing slavery of the Sudan and Mauretania (Cotton 1998; Bales 1999), and elsewhere. Throughout Africa, but especially in South Africa under the leadership of the ANC, these debates continue to rage.[9]

In a Europe pluralized by years of immigration, contemporary experiences of racialized heterogeneity call previous concepts of national identity and the role of the state into question, as well as meshing with other forms of economic and social crisis. Efforts to guarantee human and political rights to postwar immigrants and their children in European countries have produced some fascinating political and theoretical debates. Many in Europe are unable fully to accept their relatively new condition of racial heterogeneity; yet at the same time memories of World War II remain strong, and present-day echoes—in the form of "ethnic cleansing," anti-immigrant demagogy, and neo-fascism—are loud indeed. Simultaneously Europe is also experiencing the discipline of the international market and the inexorable process of European integration, pressures that render racial exclusionism increasingly unworkable (Soysal 1994; Bourdieu 1998; Hollifield 1994).

Even in Asia, in regions long thought to be largely free of racial conflict (in both South Asia and East Asia, for example), the situation looks quite different today as divisions on the Indian subcontinent undergo racial articulation (Baber 1999) and as Yamato and Han supremacy in Japan and China come under review from more racially tuned-in analysts (Dikötter 1997).

Part II, "The Comparative Sociology of Race," examines this global situation, or at least some of its highlights. This section of the book begins with a discussion in Chapter Six ("Notes on the Postwar Break") that seeks to frame the potentialities and pitfalls of a comparative case study approach to race in the post–World War II period. In this chapter I first situate the break in its historical context. I make the case that a worldwide rupture with the long-established traditions, conventions, and social structures of white supremacy did indeed occur after the war. The break can thus be seen as a worldwide *crisis of racial formation.*

Chapter Six also presents the case study approach used in Part II. This part of the book focuses on four national/regional cases: the United States (Chapter Seven), South Africa (Chapter Eight), Brazil (Chapter Nine), and the European Union (Chapter Ten). In Chapter Six I explain why these particular cases were selected: each of these four countries/regions has particular characteristics that qualify it for intensive reflection here. The postwar racial break occurred in a unique and exemplary way in each setting. Each of these four national/regional cases arrived at the point of postwar racial crisis—the racial "breaking-point," one could say—by a quite different route. Some were or had been dominant world powers; others had been peripheral. Some had important racial counter-traditions and social movements seeking justice and liberation. Others had more effectively incorporated and defused racially based opposition. Each was linked in a different way to the challenge to white supremacy that was developing as a global phenomenon in the postwar years. Four central dimensions of that challenge were, however, present in all the case study settings: *demographic change, movement mobilization, reform of state racial policies,* and *interaction with global racial networks.* These themes provide a broad comparative framework for the chapters that follow. Yet for a number of reasons I set out in Chapter Six, the comparative analysis proposed here cannot effectively be carried out within the parameters of conventional sociological methods. An important task of this chapter is thus to clarify and justify the unique methodology I utilize in this part of the book.

The United States

In Chapter Seven ("United States: The End of the Innocence") I note that the United States entered the postwar era as the leading superpower and culturally hegemonic society. But it also carried its racial baggage and contradictions: it was a settler society, a society created by African slavery, and yet the pioneering anti-colonial and democratic, indeed revolutionary, society as well. The United States was the only "developed"/core/metropolitan country whose national identity had been *internally* defined by these elemental racial experiences. So the United States could not unproblematically don the mantle of leader of what it called the "free world" while systematically denying political and human rights to a substantial proportion of its citizens. It could not revert to its earlier policies of segregation and disenfranchisement of its racially defined minorities. Those groups and their allies, ever more mobilized and politically engaged, would not permit this; but neither would the rest of the international community, which watched with unflagging interest as the

United States sought to overcome, or at least manage more effectively, its historical reliance upon a racist and anti-democratic system of rule.

In this chapter I trace the course of postwar racial politics in the United States, beginning with the background conditions and "rehearsals," so to speak, that had occurred in the period before the break. I consider the emergence of the civil rights vision, the partial victories won by its movement adherents, and the brief glimpses they were permitted of radical alternatives to the mere gaining of "rights." The enduring significance of race in the ambiguous and unresolved racial stalemate of the post–civil rights era, I suggest, points to the long-term ineffectiveness of state racial policy reforms achieved in the 1960s. These measures turned out to be rather more symbolic than serious efforts to move U.S. society in the direction of racial justice. Yet state-based reform policies that seek to incorporate opposition—the essence of what Gramsci called "hegemony"—can accomplish nothing if the state does not offer real concessions to those insurgents whom it seeks to control and co-opt. The outcome of the movement/state dialectic of the postwar years was thus itself contradictory or dualistic in the United States. While racial opposition was certainly muted by concessions and reforms, the underlying tensions of a deeply racialized social structure were not addressed.

South Africa

Chapter Eight, "South Africa: When the System Has Fallen," considers what until recently was the world's most unabashedly racial state. The country accepted the inevitability of the break very late, and only after exhausting nearly the entire toolkit of reactionary racial intransigence. White intractability in the face of the determination of a substantial African majority to achieve full democracy and inclusion led South Africa to the brink of impasse, or perhaps to the doorstep of revolution, before the irrationality of white supremacy was recognized at last. The very lateness of the coming of the break, of the beginning of the passage toward a democratic and inclusive society, makes South Africa a crucial case study. But beyond this question of timing, the extremity of the racial inequality fostered by apartheid, and the legacy of the abysmal racial differentiation and stratification left floating in its wake, also impel intellectual interest and practical concern.

Opposition to racial hierarchy in South Africa was to a significant extent an international movement, a virtually global anti-racist consensus. And the democratic government that succeeded the white supremacist regime in 1994 had for many decades nurtured a vision of "non-racialism" deep in its adherents' hearts. How would that government, and the movement/political party that led it (the African National Congress) come to terms with the continuing salience of race in the post-apartheid era? With all this taken into consideration, the country still bears terrible racial burdens, although it has entered a promising but difficult transition from apartheid to multiracialism.

Brazil

Chapter Nine, "Brazil: Back to the Future," examines recent racial dynamics in Brazil. In many ways the country has been the opposite case from South Africa. South Africa only acknowledged the inevitability of the break at the latest possible moment, while Brazil *anticipated* the break. From the 1930s on, Brazil has at least professed allegiance to a model of racial democracy, once again markedly distinguishing itself from the South African model. By proclaiming itself a racial democracy, although hardly instituting the major social reforms that would have been required to realize this in practice, Brazil was able to defuse much of the racial mobilization that other societies encountered during the postwar years. Indeed in the early postwar years the United Nations Educational, Scientific, and Cultural Organization (UNESCO) sponsored an important series of social scientific studies on Brazilian racial themes, informed by the perception (which these studies largely disproved) that Brazil offered a model of racial harmony other countries might emulate.

The myth of racial democracy still endures, although it has been attacked as little more than a figleaf covering widespread racial inequality, injustice, and prejudice. It is more properly characterized as a racial ideology that still carries out important explanatory tasks. Even though its integrative capacity is slowly diminishing, the Brazilian racial system, with its color continuum (as opposed to the more familiar color-line of North America), still tends to dilute democratic demands. Many other factors also contribute to Brazil's seeming racial exceptionalism: the tradition of *cordialidade* (cordiality), the widespead acceptance of *miscigenação*, the absence of a traumatic transition from slavery to emancipation, the roughly even demographic balance between black and non-black populations (depending upon how one defines "black"), and the existence of a long (1964–85) military dictatorship that made *all* social movement activity very perilous and difficult to sustain.

The European Union

Chapter Ten, "Europe: The Phantom Menace," considers the racial pluralization of the European Union (EU). Western Europe is no longer a congeries of competitive mother-countries, imperial metropoles driven by global economic competition and fiercely militarized rivalry. As the region entered the post-imperial era over the first decades after World War II, as it rebuilt and began to contemplate federation, it also welcomed—or at least received—vast numbers of ex-colonial subjects, as well as refugees, from all around the world. As a result most of Europe, especially former imperial powers like the United Kingdom, the Netherlands, France, and Spain, but also Germany, Italy, the Scandinavian countries, and to some extent even the East, are now far more racially hetereogeneous places than they were before the war. The influx of substantial numbers of non-whites during the post-colonial period has deeply altered a dynamic in which the racial order and the imperial order had been one, and in which the racialized "other" was largely—if not totally—kept outside the walls of the mother-countries. As a stroll around London, Frankfurt, Paris, or Madrid quickly reveals, those days are now gone forever.

Yet the response to the new situation often takes repressive and anti-democratic forms, focusing attention on the "immigrant problem" (or the "Islamic problem"), seeking not only to shut the gates to Maghrebines or sub-Saharan Africans, Turks or Slavs (including Balkan refugees), but often to define those "others" who are already present as threats to the national culture, as inimical to the "ordinary German" (or English, or French, etc.) way of life. This is the so-called new racism (Taguieff 2001 [1988]; Wieviorka 1995; Balibar 1991; Barker 1981) that may be Europe's most prominent contribution to the fin-de-siècle racial stalemate.

Why have I presented the European Union, as distinct from, say, France or Germany, as a case study? Although European national identities and differences are not about to be transcended, they are eroding under the pressure of integration. Many of the most crucial dimensions of racial politics and policy are increasingly handled at the regional level: immigration policy is being coordinated, and citizenship policies regularized (under the principle of *jus soli*), to pick the two most prominent examples. For these and many other reasons as well, to focus attention on the EU is to address very centrally the question of the globalization of race. But beyond that it is to consider the aftermath of empire, the post-colonial question, not in the periphery or the South (which I do elsewhere), but in the core, the metropolitan heartland of the old imperial racial system, the headquarters of Eurocentrism. If race persists here, if it takes on new meanings and appears newly problematic here and now, after the last vestiges of empire have been liquidated, that will be particularly revealing, I suggest, of the new dynamics of the twenty-first-century world racial system.

Chapter Eleven, "Millennium Arrives?" is a concluding essay that interprets and applies the analysis developed in the historical and comparative sections of the book. I argue that the break that began with movement activity during and after World War II, and was contained from the late 1960s on by political reforms, has not been completed. It is properly characterized as a stalemate, an unstable equilibrium. Just as earlier stages of modern racial history failed to resolve many issues, so too does the present epoch. At the beginning of the twenty-first century, the world as a whole, and the national/regional cases examined here, are far from overcoming the tenacious legacies of colonial rule, apartheid, segregation, and racial injustice. Even as reform policies have ame- liorated some of the worst abuses of the past, and as mainstream political lead- ers and intellectuals contend that the race problem has finally been resolved, confusion, anxiety, and conflict over race are still experienced all around the world. The legacies of the epochal struggles for racial freedom and democracy, and for human rights in general, persist as well. I evaluate the transition to a new world racial order in comparative and historical perspective, keeping in view the continuing racial conflicts that have shaped our entire epoch.

Despite the enormous vicissitudes that demarcate and distinguish national conditions, historical developments, roles in the international economy, polit- ical tendencies, and cultural norms, racial differences often operate as they did in centuries past: as a way of restricting the political influence, not just of racially subordinated groups, but of all those at the bottom end of the system of social stratification. This is true both globally and locally.

But in the contemporary era, racial beliefs and practices have become far more contradictory and complex. The old world racial system, the "bad old days," have not disappeared, but the white supremacy that shaped them and that went virtually unquestioned has been identified and challenged. The legacy of democratic, racially oriented movements such as the U.S. civil rights movement, anti-apartheid struggles, *SOS-Racisme* in France, the *Movimento Negro Unificado* in Brazil, and anti-colonialist initiatives throughout the world's South, is thus a force to be reckoned with. My aim in this work is to explore the results of this situation.

It is impossible to address worldwide dilemmas of race and racism by ignor- ing or transcending these themes, for example, by adopting so-called color- blind policies or seeking (in the multiculturalist approach so much in fashion) to "celebrate diversity" or "preserve cultural differences." In the past the cen- trality of race deeply determined the economic, political, and cultural config- uration of the modern world; although recent decades have seen a tremendous efflorescence of movements for racial equality and justice, the legacies of cen- turies of racial oppression have not been overcome. Nor is a vision of racial jus- tice fully worked out. Certainly the idea that such justice has largely been achieved already—as seen in the color-blind paradigm in the United States, the non-racialist rhetoric of the South African Freedom Charter, the Brazilian rhetoric of racial democracy, or the emerging racial differentialism of the Euro- pean Union—remains problematic.

What would a more credible vision entail? The pressing task today is not to jettison the concept of race, but instead to come to terms with it as a form of flexible human variety. What does this mean in respect to *racism*? Racism has been crucial to the global reproduction of capital for five hundred years; it remains so today. Yet it has been called into question, indeed discredited and forced to reorganize, by the massive social movements that have taken place in recent decades. These movements were international in scope and influence. They were deeply interwoven with democratizing and egalitarian trends, such as labor politics and feminism. They were able to mobilize around the injustices and exclusion experienced by racially subordinated groups, and simultaneously to sustain alliances across racial lines. This is background; such experiences cannot simply recur. Yet the massive mobilizations that created the global break of World War II and its aftermath have certainly reshaped the contemporary world. Were these movements fated to be the last popular upsurges, the last egalitarian challenges to white supremacy, to racial hierarchy? Surely not. In all the national/regional case studies presented here, and in transnational ties among these countries, the influence of these earlier precedents persists today, sparking new attempts to challenge racism.

The World Is a Ghetto questions the racial status quo. The comparative and historical analysis presented here also strongly suggests that contemporary racial politics remain unstable and conflictual, both globally and locally. Perhaps presumptuously, I attempt in "Millennium Arrives?" the book's concluding chapter, to identify some of the main racial issues that confront us at the start of the twenty-first century. As will already be clear, these issues are not "merely" racial, but also fundamental to the emerging planetary social order.

To think about race at the global level is to adopt a planetary perspective. It is to reject the division of the world between "the West and the rest" (Hall 1996a; Holt 1995; Huntington 1993). That division, imposed by Europe on the world's "others," evolved with the race-concept. This very division has been significantly eroded, but not yet overturned, after the post–World War II racial break. As the split between "the West and the rest" was called into question—politically, economically, culturally—the race-concept was also problematized. For example, the West has prided itself on its democratic commitments, on its respect for the rule of law, and on its extension of social citizenship through the welfare state. Yet the implementation of these commitments across racial lines has always been limited and problematic.[10]

The problem goes far deeper than that: for the West attained its prosperity and invented its democracy at the expense of those whom it exploited and excluded. The West therefore owes a substantial debt to the world's "others." This "external debt" parallels on a global level the debt owed by the United States to the descendants of African slaves. The failure to provide emancipated slaves with "forty acres and a mule" after the Civil War's end, the resistance to demands for reparations for the theft of life and labor that was slavery (Robinson 2000), can readily be seen as operating on a planetary level.

What if the present movement for "Jubilee" were to succeed? What if the demand that the International Monetary Fund (IMF), the World Bank, and the "developed" nations forgive the external debt of the poor nations of the world (or less developed countries [LDCs])—all of which fall in the category of the "others"—were to be met?[11] This would be a valuable first step in the direction of restitution for the historical debt that the West, it may be argued, really owes to these peoples.[12] The analysis offered here suggests that the global issue of "underdevelopment" is in fact a racial issue. In a socially just and historically conscious world the West would not only forgive the debt of the world's "others"; it would seek their forgiveness; it would seek to make good on their losses, to make them whole in the legal sense. Such an event—difficult even to imagine today, but a pressing world-historical requirement—would go a long way toward destroying the racial hierarchy built into the contemporary global political economy.[13]

At the cultural level as well, the tropological character of race needs to be undone. European rule and white supremacy proceeded in large part from assumptions of cultural superiority that were already evident in the key texts of the Enlightenment (Eze 1997; Count 1950). These assumptions were embedded in virtually all systems of social signification and representation: in literary forms, for example, in music, and in painting (Said 1993). So the comprehensive racialization of *identity* in the modern world was also built upon a tremendous debt.

The "borrowing" from the non-European world of cultural forms of all types—musical, literary, imagistic, and so on—although extensive, was not the central dimension of this debt. Rather, it was the use made of the "other" to define the self, *the reliance on difference to produce identity*, that constituted the cultural dimensions of modernity on the foundation of racial hierarchy. By relegating most of the world's population to the derogatory status of lesser and indeed "other" beings, by using them to represent identities antithetical to those of the "civilized" West, Enlightenment culture and its sequelae performed spectacular acts of symbolic violence. These practices extended well beyond the mere articulation and justification of racial hierarchy on the "high" cultural plane. Indeed their most crucial applications were arguably to be found at the level of the quotidian, of everyday life, of popular culture.

Making this situation whole is also almost unimaginable. But we may take heart from its continuing contradictions and irresolution, from the determined efforts on the part of the "others" to reconceive themselves and their world. The cultures of resistance that have arisen over the centuries, that such theoretical approaches as subaltern studies (among many schools of thought) have explored in depth, have laid the groundwork, if not for the elimination of hierarchies of racial signification, at least for their discrediting and delegitimation.

PART ONE

FROM THE ABYSS:
RACE AND MODERN HISTORY

Two

THE HISTORICAL SOCIOLOGY OF RACE

Race has been a constitutive element, an organizational principle, a *praxis* and structure that has constructed and reconstructed world society since the emergence of modernity, the enormous historical shift represented by the rise of Europe, the founding of modern nation-states and empires, the *conquista*, the onset of African enslavement, and the subjugation of much of Asia. To explain how race came to play this part in the making of modernity, and to trace the general pathways through which the relationship between race and the modern world system have developed down to our own time, is the task of Part I of this book.

In this chapter I present the outline of a *historical sociological theory of race*. To do so presents a profound intellectual challenge. The vast literature on race generally treats it in a reductionist fashion: it is frequently considered a manifestation of some other, supposedly more profound or more "real" social relationship.[1] The task here is to rethink that logic, to resituate the development of the race-concept in a historically grounded framework. This enables an alternative view of race to emerge, one that sees it as a key causative factor in the creation of the modern world. Imperialism's creation of modern nation-states, capitalism's construction of an international economy, and the Enlightenment's articulation of a unified world culture, I argue, were all deeply racialized processes.[2]

Why undertake this complex historical argument? Because I wish to demonstrate the continuing significance of race. Of course the flexibility of race must also be recognized: its meaning is always subject to reinterpretation, just as racial practices and racialized social structures are subject to reform and reorganization (Omi and Winant 1994). Racialized identities and social structures coexist with all other dimensions of social organization. Although arguing for the importance of race, I am not a racial determinist. The crucial point is that these racial dynamics, so characteristic of contemporary society both local and global, arrived in the present only through a profound gestation, a genealogy that eventually embraced the entire modern world.

The question of how race operated in the making of the modern world is of more than historical interest. To answer it is also to explain much about the present. It is to put in context the concept—central to this work—that after World War II a break from the long-established verities of race occurred. This break, significant as it is, is not a full-scale repudiation of the past. It is one of many reorganizations and rearticulations of the meaning of race that have occurred throughout the centuries. Have the momentous changes in racial awareness experienced in the latter half of the twentieth century finally laid to rest the invidious racial legacy of centuries past? No, they have not. To what extent do these changes permit the present continuation of racial hierarchy? To a great extent indeed. These points, which receive central attention in Part II of this book, are historically grounded and contextualized in Part I.

How can we understand, how can we theorize, the multiple effects of race in shaping the transition to modernity? What Myrdal (no stranger to racial matters) called a logic of circular and cumulative causation was at work here (Myrdal 1963; see also Wallerstein 1991, 80–103). There is obviously no one "event" that marks the onset of modernity, no single chasm lying between the remote past and the start of the modern epoch in which we live. All the elements that were unevenly accumulated and accreted to create the modern world had their earlier incarnations: proto-capitalist systems for extraction of surpluses, for the organization and exploitation of labor; imperialisms with their states, their metropoles and hinterlands; and cultural logics of identity and meaning, can readily be found in the ancient and middle ages. Early forms of racial distinction can be identified throughout these precursive forms of sociohistorical organization.

Yet there is something different about the modern world system, as Wallerstein has argued extensively. This difference lies in its combination of global reach and lack of unified authoritative rule.[3] This system is a form of world-historical organization that came into being gradually, repeating organizational elements and social categories that had gone before, for example, slavery (here is Myrdal's "circularity"), yet combining and transforming these components in new ways, and achieving some sort of synergy (Myrdal's "cumulation") in the process.

Into the account of the origins and development of the modern world system—from which I have learned a great deal—I want to insert the theme of race. This account is not really a negation of other macro-historical sociologies; rather, it is an attempt to give race its due as *both* cause and effect in such accounts. I am especially opposed to relegation of race to an effect, an epiphenomenon, an outcome of, say, capitalist development, the emergence of the nation-state, the rise of Europe, or the onset of modernity.

Modernity, then, is a global *racial formation* project. In making this claim I draw not only on Myrdal and Wallerstein but on my earlier work with Michael Omi, which proposed that racial formation takes place in the national context through the clash of racial projects. In this approach, the key element in racial formation is the link between signification and structure, between what race means in a particular discursive practice and how, based upon such interpretations, social structures are racially organized. The link between meaning and structure, discourse and institution, signification and organization, is concretized in the notion of the racial project. To interpret the meaning of race in a particular way at a given time is at least implicitly, but more often explicitly, to propose or defend a certain racial policy, a specific racialized social structure, a racial order. By studying the range of racial projects in given historical contexts it becomes possible to study given racial formation processes in detail, giving particular attention to the ways in which projects intersect (Omi and Winant 1994, 55–61).

That argument was framed in a largely national and comparative context that overlaps with the present work. The task here is to develop the racial formation approach in a world-historical perspective:[4] global racial formation. Indeed, historical time could well be interpreted in terms of something like a racial *longue durée*. Does not the rise of Europe, the onset of African enslavement, the *conquista*, and the subjugation of much of Asia represent an epochal sociohistorical transformation, an immense planetary metamorphosis? I take the point of much post-structural scholarship on these matters to be quite precisely an effort to explain Western or colonial time as a huge project demarcating human "difference," or more globally (as Todorov, say, would argue) of framing partial collective identities in terms of externalized "others" (Todorov 1984). Just as, for example, the writers of the *Annales* school sought to locate the deep logic of historical time in the means by which material life was produced—diet, shoes, and the like[5]—so we might usefully think of a racial *longue durée* in which the slow inscription of phenotypical signification took place upon the human body, in and through conquest and enslavement to be sure, but also as an enormous act of expression, of narration.[6]

The claim that race was one of the central ingredients in the circular and cumulative causation of modernity hinges on the presence of racial dynamics, key processes of racial formation, in all the main constitutive relationships that structured the origins and development of the modern world system. These crucial relationships involved the making of new forms of *empire and nation*; the organization of new systems of *capital and labor*; and the articulation of new concepts of *culture and identity*. Because these are circular and cumulative processes, they must be understood as thoroughly intertwined; there is no need or possibility of proposing one of these three as primary or causative. Nor is it desirable (or even possible) to offer any comprehensive theorization of these massive themes here. I simply indicate the presence of racial dimensions within each. Having suggested how in each area world-historical developmental and racial formation processes were intertwined, I trace the genealogy of the racial system of our own time. This is the task of the subsequent chapters of Part I:

to show how, from the dawn of the modern world to the middle of the twentieth century, the ongoing dilemmas of democratization, economic equality, and the recognition of human distinctiveness continue to be deeply shaped by racial logic.

EMPIRE AND NATION

An important part of the transition to modernity was nation-building (Eisenstadt and Rokkan 1973; Bendix 1964), a process inextricable in Europe from conquest, exclusion, and the beginnings of empire. In becoming modern nations, in challenging their legacies of fragmentation and subordination to early empires, the countries on the Atlantic fringe of Europe both made themselves into racially/nationally homogeneous entities (with assorted tendentious and uncertain elements remaining, to be sure, but in much reduced and suppressed form) and sought new peoples to subordinate. They formed stronger, more centralized states (Tilly 1975); began the transition to capitalism, passing along various paths through plunder and mercantilism on the way; and sought adequate discursive representations of these undertakings in religious, philosophical, and political terms. All this was intertwined with the emergent racial projects of conquest and enslavement.

Only nation-states could tackle the immense efforts of restructuring the world economy (Polanyi 1980 [1944]). Yet nation-states themselves had to be created, both through internal unification and differentiation from peripheral "others"—whether local rivals, however recognizable, or distant and different peoples, however unknown and unrecognized.

Nation-building was a complex process. Within the local or regional context it involved expelling some of those viewed as "different" and incorporating others whose identities had to be amalgamated or subordinated in a greater, nascent, national whole. In the larger imperial sense, the transoceanic context, let us say, the process of nation-making entailed distinguishing the nation *en bloc* from other nations. There were two dimensions to this distinction: rivalry and "othering." Rivalry came from developing inter-imperial competition, which could be more or less ferocious and sanguinary. "Othering" came not from national, but from supranational distinctions, nascent regional distinctions between Europe and the rest of the world, between "us," broadly conceived, and the non-Christian, "uncivilized," and soon enough non-white "others,"[7] whose subordination and subjugation was justified on numerous grounds—religious and philosophical as much as political and economic.

Thus nascent states constructed their key instrumentalities, institutions,

and capabilities for action, particularly their own political and military apparatuses. Thus they worked out the beliefs and collective identities that would
allow imperial activities to be launched and organized. The emergence of early
concepts of race was integral in these processes. With the initiation of transatlantic conquest and African slavery, race begins to appear as an important
tool in the advancement and interpretation of these activities.

The suggestion that the modern nation has ethnic or racial origins is a
familiar one (Smith 1987). Certainly the nations of imperial Europe only
forged themselves into racially/ethnically homogeneous entities through prolonged processes combining both amalgamation (Weber 1976) and exclusion
(Hroch 1985; Hroch 1993; Gellner 1983). In part this process unified nation-
states internally, while separating them more definitively from one another and
indeed pitting them against each other. All this made the endeavors of conquest
and enslavement more vital, thus helping to constitute the imperial mission. By
evolving systems of enslavement and conquest that differentiated their "nationals" (soldiers, settlers)[8] from the proto-racial "others" who were the conquered
and enslaved, imperial nations also consolidated themselves. They were not
only the French, the Portuguese, the Dutch, the British; they were also the
whites, the masters, the true Christians. A distinction crystallized between rulers
and ruled that was readily "phenotypified," corporealized. This duality, complicated eventually by creolism, *mestizaje,* and the sometimes ambiguous status of
workers, soldiers, and peasants (in both the mother-countries and the colonies),
nevertheless laid out the national-political axes of the modern racial order and,
as I have begun to suggest, of the modern world system.

Intermediate strata necessarily arose as colonization advanced and the slave
system grew. Both class and status distinctions multiplied in colonies and
metropoles, generated by burgeoning economic, political, and social contacts
and conflicts among imperial enterprises: rivalries and competition, colloquy
and debate, as well as outright warfare. As creole status-groups developed in
the colonies, national rivalries with the colonial powers emerged (for example,
criollos versus *peninsulares* throughout *Nueva España*). Often differentiated by a
range of racial signifiers from the "true whites" of the mother-country, the
creole (or planter, or settler, or *mestizo*) elites sought to establish their own
national/political rights in various ways. Some wished only to administer their
own slave systems, others to embark on a separate path of national independence, and still others to implement a new American version of the Declaration of the Rights of Man. Since such desires generally required armed revolt,
it was often necessary to emancipate slaves, enfranchise *mestizos,* and redistrib-
ute land and wealth in order to raise a revolutionary army and thus win independence. So at later stages of what was a long process, nation-building took
place through upheavals in racially determined social status.

There were, of course, many forms of upheaval, many types of resistance.

Native peoples who were able to do so challenged their would-be conquerors and masters militarily, and took flight where possible. But confusion and division also characterized the subjugated. Amid the Africans and African-Americans of the New World, for example, many (intra-racial) divisions emerged from differences in national origin and the temporal/generational dimensions of exile from the African motherland.[9] That these particularities would have important consequences for the success of uprisings or patterns of escape and *marronage* is clear. Divisions between Afro-Creoles and native Africans are well recognized as crucial to the unfolding of the Haitian revolution, for example (Thornton 1991; Thornton 1993; Nicholls 1996).

Parallel complexities and social divisions emerged throughout the imperial world in respect to social class. These too had racial dimensions. In the earliest stages of American conquest there was not yet African enslavement. Native peoples were the first modern racial "others," and some Africans were among the *conquistadores*. African slavery only developed as a result of labor shortages of natives and indentured servants. Indigenous people were killed en masse, worked to death, fled, or occasionally went to war, none of which rendered them available for ongoing toil. Early imported labor (generally bonded and, although multiracial, largely poor and European) could not be had in sufficient quantity, nor degraded comprehensively enough, to produce profits from early mines or plantations (Morgan 1995; Rout 1976; Cope 1994; Russell-Wood 1998). Turning to Africa for exploitable labor meant creating a class of free persons, usually (although not always) white, usually (although not always) not slaveholders, and destined to be (or already perceiving themselves to be) competitors with Africans, both enslaved and emancipated. Since this situation involved a range of potential political alignments (both labor versus planters and whites versus blacks were possible lines of conflict), nation-building meant steering away from class conflict and toward race conflict, or at least entrenched social hierarchy based on racial status (Breen and Innes 1980).

Thus, while we must note the tremendous variations within this process of national ontogeny, it is equally important to recognize the centrality of racial dynamics in forging both imperial nations and colonies, and ultimately in sundering those identities and bonds.

CAPITAL AND LABOR

The subjugation of the Americas and the enslavement of Africa financed the rise of the European empires, as the classical political economists including Adam Smith and Karl Marx recognized (Smith 1994 [1776]; Mill 1994 [1848]); Marx 1965–67 [1867]; Mintz 1985). Vast flows of treasure were shipped to Europe; millions came under the lash of planters and mine-owners (Williams

1994 [1944]).[10] The transition from an insular, regionally contained, and mechanically solidaristic social order to an integrated, global society with an increasingly complex division of labor demanded the creation of a worldwide racial division between Europe and the "others." Through slavery and colonialism, through the extraction of immense quantities of natural resources, and most particularly through the institutionalization and elaboration of techniques for the exploitation of mass labor at a hitherto inconceivable level, the apparatus was synthesized for the accumulation of wealth on a grand scale.

Slavery became "a massive global business" (Walvin 1986, 20), the first fully worked-out system of multinational capitalism.[11] An intense debate has taken place over how capitalist African slavery in the Americas actually was. That slavery, particularly in sugar production and milling, was the first capitalist industrial enterprise (preceding the "dark satanic Mills" of Britain), is an argument most closely associated with C. L. R. James' work (James 1989 [1938]).[12] Here there is no need to resolve the controversy over the relationship between capitalism and slavery; it is enough to specify that slavery served the developing capitalist system that traversed the Atlantic, that it provided the exploitable mass labor nascent capitalism required.

But what about *forms* of mass labor? What distinguishes its enslaved, peonage, and waged variants? Between slavery and peonage,[13] and between peonage and "free labor," there was in practice (and remains today) a continuum, a spectrum, rather than a clear-cut, formal distinction. This was evident in the ambiguities and conflicts among the legal and social statuses of lifelong/hereditary enslavement on the one hand, and fixed-term indentured servitude on the other. Throughout the developing Atlantic "mass labor market," uncomfortable convergences arose among these three different forms, and their political, moral, religious, and economic significance.[14]

In the developing empires, as has been amply documented, this tension rather quickly came to be seen in racial terms: it obtained among the statuses of enslaved blacks, free blacks, and free whites.[15] Resolving the ambiguities in law, politics, and common sense among these social positions was at most a gradual and partial process in the colonies and the early United States (Morgan 1995; Berlin 1998; Fields 1985; Davis 1966; Davis 1975; Moura 1990; Russell-Wood 1998). Similar variations among hemispheric slave systems—over manumission, "hiring out," religious and recreational practices, and a host of other regulatory systems—confirm that it was slavery's contribution to the accumulation of capital, not its legal-rational legitimacy (much less its "natural," Aristotelian state) that justified the enormous economic and ideological investments made in American slave systems from the sixteenth to the nineteenth centuries. This is hardly news.

The metropolitan working classes, too, were complexly affected by the developing system of world racial hierarchy: as systems of imperial regulation developed through slavery and peonage, the nascent working classes often found themselves equated with colonized or even enslaved subjects. Political technologies used to regulate their status were applied in the colonies, and vice versa. The relative merits and moralities of "free" and slave labor systems were continually discussed. Elites critical of the lack of discipline and absence of ascetism among their various "natives" often discovered these same defects in the working classes at home (Cooper and Stoler 1997). Yet in other respects the white workers of the mother-countries were insulated by their race and nationality from the full rigors of imperial domination. Thus they became ambivalent allies, or only partial critics, of the imperial order. They too were regulated by race.

No matter how much overlap between statuses may have existed in practice, these three categories of exploitable labor—worker, peon, and slave—can certainly be analytically (ideal-typically) distinguished, and doing so will help us understand their varied relationships to the processes of production that modern empires organized. Use of this Weberian methodological notion—ideal-typical categories of analysis—can also help bring into focus the racial distinction between types of workers, a distinction vital to the accumulation of capital throughout the entire history of the modern age. The threat of enslavement effectively provoked enmity and hostility toward (black) slaves among free (white) workers, thus helping to ground racial antagonism in popular culture (Roediger 1991; Saxton 1990). The promise of emancipation, of property rights in one's own person and in land, cemented the loyalties of intermediate groups and "middleman" minorities, in both slavery and debt-based systems of labor. In fact, in the Americas slavery, bonded labor, and free labor could coexist for centuries, so long as accumulation processes were largely uninterrupted.

What about other developing relationships between race and accumulation? Europe relied upon slavery and other forms of coerced labor to provide the raw materials, agricultural produce, and precious metals that were needed at home, in the colonies, and eventually across the entire world market. Particularly in the early capitalist period, slavery furnished the material inputs necessary to create the modern capitalist economy. Over time slavery shaped the European internal markets for both production and consumption of goods, creating both the mass commodification and the labor market characteristic of mature industrial capitalism.

Slavery-produced commodities reached the developing world market in a variety of forms, as both primary products and processed goods. Sugar, for example, was generally milled on or near the plantations where it was produced (Moreno Fraginals 1976; Mintz 1985), arriving by sea in varieties available for consumption or for further processing. Tobacco was harvested and dried before shipping, but usually processed after landing, at Bristol, for example.

Cotton was first cleaned by hand (that is, by African hands) in a labor process so difficult and slow that it seriously impeded cultivation and bred excessive brutality.[16] Only when ginning was introduced at the end of the eighteenth century did cotton begin to replace wool as the primary material of British textile manufacture, the leading edge of the industrial revolution. The cotton gin allowed the processing of this commodity to take place in successive stages on opposite sides of the Atlantic, with enslaved Africans serving as the cultivators and initial processors, and wage laborers in England functioning as secondary and relatively skilled industrial workers, who produced both textiles and sewn products. By the early nineteenth century New England factory workers would also be occupied in these tasks.

As this brief exposition already demonstrates, what slavery chiefly offered to developing capitalism was massive inputs of coercible labor, where, in the Americas, other sources were largely unavailable.[17] In later capitalist periods, the place of slavery in colonial or otherwise dependent settings was largely supplanted by peonage. Here the contribution to accumulation was generally equivalent, with the added advantage that the exploited were held responsible for the costs of their own reproduction (Luxemburg 1951 [1923]; Wallerstein 1979).

How profitable were slavery and peonage? Debates in the literature about the costs (and thus the profitability) of Atlantic slavery are long-standing.[18] Today it seems clear that, although the profitability varied, slavery was the linchpin, the core activity, in the creation of the modern world economy. Of course by the twentieth century slavery had been reduced in scope; peonage, however, still constitutes the principal form of labor worldwide. Although its gradual replacement by both agricultural and industrial waged labor[19] seems to be proceeding, this southern form of labor is still by and large distinguished from its northern counterparts by the criterion of race. As Du Bois could write in 1935:

> That dark and vast sea of human labor in China and India, the South Seas and all Africa; in the West Indies and Central America and in the United States—that great majority of mankind, on whose bent and broken backs rest today the founding stones of modern industry—shares a common destiny; it is despised and rejected by race and color; paid a wage below the level of decent living; driven, beaten, prisoned, and enslaved in all but name; spawning the world's raw material and luxury—cotton, wool, coffee, tea, cocoa, palm oil, fibers, spices, rubber, silks, lumber, copper, gold, diamonds, leather—how shall we end the list and where? All these are gathered up at prices lowest of the low, manufactured, transformed, and transported at fabulous gain; and the resultant wealth is distributed and displayed and made the basis of world power and universal dominion and armed arrogance in London and Paris, Berlin and Rome, New York and Rio de Janeiro. (Du Bois 1977 [1935], 15)

CULTURE AND IDENTITY

The enormous social transformations of conquest and enslavement demanded a lot of explaining; they occasioned fierce debates. In the early stages of empire the crucial question of human variation, of "difference," was widely addressed, both informally, for example, in literary work,[20] and officially. A good example of the latter process was the famous debate between Sepulveda and las Casas, held in Valladolid at the behest of the Spanish Crown in 1630. Here as elsewhere in the early moments of encounter between Europe and the "others," the terms of discussion were religious, as might be expected: Did the Americans have souls? Were they, then, humans to whom their conquerors would have obligations, or animals who could be subjugated without limit, indeed harvested? Should they be converted to the true faith? Were they, perhaps, humans of an inferior type, naturally suited for slavery (Todorov 1984)?[21]

Later in the imperial process, the terms of discourse expanded. Enlightenment thought evinced a deep preoccupation with racial difference, whose meaning was continuously interpreted as setting limits on "natural rights" and thus justifying systems of rule founded in profound commitments to inequality and exclusion. The great philosophers and statesmen of the eighteenth and nineteenth centuries, from Kant and Hume to Jefferson and Napoleon, all endorsed the hierarchical division of humanity into superior and inferior races (Eze 1997; Count 1950). Artistic meditations upon the nature of "the other" were constant.[22]

Racial themes received ever-increasing intellectual and scientific attention as colonialism advanced to the moment when, at the end of the nineteenth century, it encompassed the entire world. The triumphant age of empire (Hobsbawm 1987) and the French revolutionary and Napoleonic legacies had generated substantial political motives for thinking racially, for "inventing traditions" that were often explicitly racial, in other words, for finding an ancient racial unity at the bottom of emergent national identities (Hobsbawn and Ranger 1983). Numerous examples of this device exist, for example, Scott's *Ivanhoe*, or the Abbe Sieyès's (Pasquino 1998; Rooy 1990) interpretation of the Revolution as the triumph of an ancestral Gallic people over a usurping Frankish aristocracy.[23]

It is not surprising to find many disparate racial beliefs and practices melding into one broad stream of white supremacist common sense as modernity advanced. I have already noted that the philosophical foundations for this confluence were laid down across Europe and the Americas as early as the Enlightenment and throughout the age of revolution. By the end of the eighteenth century, Blumenbach had applied the principles of Linnaean taxonomy to humans. As more modern science arose, elaborate racial "knowledge" was created and widespread interchange took place among its practitioners: taxonomists, craniologists and phrenologists, criminologists, evolutionists, and so on

(Gould 1981; Mosse 1978; Chase 1977; Breman et al. 1990). The biological sciences, of course, were matched by contributions from the emerging social sciences: history, anthropology, psychology, and sociology also presented themselves as racially focused disciplines, especially in the aftermath of Darwin's *On the Origin of Species*, which was published in 1859 (Darwin 1988 [1859]). Consider here the work of Herbert Spencer, the rise of social Darwinism in both Europe and the United States, and the development of eugenics, a term coined by Francis Galton, Darwin's cousin (Stepan 1991; Kevles 1985; Chase 1977; Barkan 1992; Hofstadter 1959 [1955]).

Reactionary and romantic analyses also surfaced for the first time in the nineteenth century. Portraying race as the fundamental world-historical conflict, such work—particularly that of Arthur de Gobineau[24]—would leave a terrifying legacy, not merely through its legitimation of racial hierarchy, but through the link it forged between white supremacy on the one hand, and opposition to democracy and the legacy of the French Revolution on the other.

Nor was the interpretation of racial themes strictly a highbrow affair. Popular media, for example, the vastly important phenomenon of minstrelsy in the nineteenth-century United States, effectively diffused racial common sense among the subordinate strata, chiefly white male workers (Lott 1993; Roediger 1991; Rogin 1996). Institutionalized popular cultural forms reinforced racial divisions and eroded working class solidarity at both the national and global levels.

Even Marxism and socialism were affected by these tendencies, which had reached a high volume by the nineteenth century. The International Working Men's Association, founded by Marx in 1864, had an ambivalent relationship to the wave of racial belief that swept the nineteenth century. Its opposition to slavery and efforts to restrict European (particularly British) support for the Confederacy in the U.S. Civil War were laudable. But Marxian socialism *as a doctrine* was still ambivalent about race and imperialism. The romantic view of Darwin taken by Marx (and even more by Engels) is well known. Deterministic views about evolution tended to be equated with deterministic views about history, so that in early Marxian accounts the "higher," more evolved social formations turned out to be not only the industrial capitalist ones, but also the northern, western, European countries, and so on. Thus the white mothercountries, the slave powers and their legatees, could be viewed (at times) as the pitiless sources of progress.[25] Marx and Engels' views of the development of capitalism, of the role played by the backward hinterlands, and of the necessity and even "revolutionary" character of the penetration of these areas by capital in the form of conquest and colonialism, have been extensively criticized, but not generally seen in racial terms.[26]

What role did this panoply of cultural developments play in the making of modernity? Of course no uniform or even consistent understanding of race can be drawn from such a varied collection of discursive and practical encounters with racial themes. But neither can there be any doubt that the complex of

racial signifiers attained unprecedented comprehensiveness and ubiquity as
the imperial order, the world capitalist system, the modern pattern of nation-
states, first hove into historical view and then, as it were, dropped anchor. Cultural factors—understood here as ways of representing and assigning meaning
to the varieties of human identity—must be seen as causative in this developmental process in two ways. First, they allowed and indeed necessitated the
emerging global social structure to ascribe identities to all actors, individual
and collective, consistent with the emerging new world social order aka
"modernity." Second, only by ordering the social world along racial lines, only
by assigning racial identities to all beings, only by generalizing a racial culture
globally, was the new world order able to constitute itself as a social structure
at all. It was a system of accumulation and unequal exchange, a set of world-
embracing institutions of domination, rule, and authority, only to the extent
that it was racialized.

This is but another way of saying that modernity itself was among other
things a worldwide racial project, an evolving and flexible process of racial
formation, of structuration and signification by race. To the extent that it
deployed cultural instrumentalities—of interpretation, of representation, of
identification that made use of racial discourse—modernity was a culturally
based racial project as much as it was an economically or politically based one.
To identify human beings by their race, to *inscribe* race upon their bodies, was
to locate them, to subject them, in the emerging world order. Here it avails to
invoke Kafka's "The Penal Colony" once again.

TOWARD THE TWENTIETH CENTURY

These epochal, convergent processes, racial formation and political economic
development, constructed the modern world. As a result, democracy—a revolutionary, northern invention—encountered its most profound limitations.
From its earliest modern, popular appearance (as opposed to its classical,
Greek and Roman, patrician forms) democracy found itself tied up with the
logic of race—not only in North America and France but throughout the world
(Davis 1966; Du Bois 1977 [1935]); James 1989 [1938]). That the popular
classes of the North generally abandoned the impoverished, the enslaved, and
the superexploited of the South, is not difficult to explain. Powerful material
and political forces, deep-seated cultural logics, impelled this.

Yet in the long run the price that the popular strata paid for this abandonment, even in the North, in the "developed" world, would be very high. "Democracy for some" is not a viable proposition; at best, it is a recipe for thoroughgoing social and political conflict, and often for open warfare. Yet this formula
ruled for centuries, and in many respects continues to characterize the world
today. Why? The denial of rights to large classes of people permits their *super-*

exploitation. Slavery and peonage throughout the world's South furnished to the metropoles virtually all necessary raw materials, and most of the manufactured ones as well—and provided them cheaply, at the point of a bayonet. What need had these workers, then, for schools, housing, health, even life? And as long as dark-skinned workers were available for sale or rent at well below the cost of their reproduction, sociopolitical arrangements not essentially different from those of the eighteenth century still obtained.

In this sense the racial history of the twentieth century can be seen as the general effort on the part of dark-skinned people to raise the cost to the metropoles (both for capital and, to a lesser extent, for northern labor) of doing business as usual. Nationalist movements and national liberation wars, as well as anti-racist and civil rights movements, contested the terms upon which racialized labor would be available for exploitation in the colonies and neo-colonies of the South, as well as in the "internal colonies" of the North. They were accompanied by vast population movements as "the south moved north" and the countryside flowed toward the city. This also tended to raise the political stakes, as the docility of the hinterlands gave way to the savvy of the metropoles.

The combined effects of these various struggles were not only to create new difficulties for capital and privileged sectors of the working classes, but also to problematize the forms of rule and cultural norms for states and social systems where hegemony was organized (as it almost universally was) along racial lines. By the mid-twentieth century, the challenges posed for power-holders by the mobilizations in various forms of their ex-colonials and former slaves had grown severe enough to dismantle most official forms of discrimination and colonial rule.

But with these developments—decolonization, the enactment of formally egalitarian "civil rights" laws, and the adoption of cultural policies of a universalistic and/or pluralistic character—the global racial order has apparently reached a new, if unstable, equilibrium. The concession of formal equality and sovereignty, perhaps paradoxically, means that the achievement of substantive equality is less likely. Certainly political and cultural reforms are not unimportant, and their conquest has represented a series of real gains for oppositional movements of natives and racial minorities. Yet nowhere have these gains resulted in the large-scale redistribution of resources. Perhaps that goal too will be achieved in the coming years, but at this point it seems that without a new wave of racially based resistance, the political momentum necessary for such a gain will be lacking.

THE BREAK

Thus the world racial order evolved with and gave rise to modernity, inventing and instituting white supremacy as a global norm quite early on, and advancing over centuries to a point at which that racial rule, while extensively questioned, still endures. To be sure there was always resistance. Racial rule was never unquestioningly accepted; it always had to be enforced. No system of subordination, however ubiquitous or well-entrenched, can expect to meet no resistance. Yet once well-established, white supremacy was also common sense. That is, worldwide racial rule, having moved from the particular to the general, having developed through a quasi-millennial process that displayed increasingly convergent tendencies over time, attained a state of normalization by, let us say, the turn of the twentieth century. The moment used to locate the apotheosis of this state of affairs can only be arbitrary. Certainly by this time significant challenges to racial rule had already appeared, in the forms of near-universal abandonment of slavery, for example, and of a budding if still preliminary critique of imperialism.

But by the end of World War II, not too many decades after Du Bois' famous 1903 diagnosis that "the problem of the Twentieth Century is the problem of the color-line," white supremacy had begun to experience an unprecedented crisis.[27] The color-line was not about to disappear from the world scene. But it began to be altered—by sustained political conflict, by massive population movement, by the unbridled globalization of capital, by tectonic cultural shifts.

What were the forces that contributed to the profound transformation in the global logic of race that began in earnest with the end of World War II? Among them were new anti-colonial pressures springing from the "liberation" of numerous countries from Axis occupation (and these countries' subsequent reluctance to embrace anew the Allied colonialists of the past). Then there was a need to reintegrate former soldiers who had become used to bearing arms, and who had been politically tempered by wide-ranging international experience. There was a (not unjustified) celebratory atmosphere surrounding the global victory over the horrors and racisms of the Nazis and the Japanese. There was the onset of new global competition between the "free world" and the Soviet Union, that is, the Cold War. All these factors (and others too numerous to list) contributed to the problematization of the traditional, racialized forms of rule that had shaped the world order in crucial ways for half a millennium or so.

For roughly a quarter century, from the war's end to about 1970 (another somewhat arbitrary date), these new, more progressive racial tendencies demanded dramatic amendments in the global sociopolitical constitution. They insisted upon the formal decolonization—often only as the result of ferocious armed struggles—of the great European imperial holdings in Africa, the Caribbean, Asia, and the Pacific. They challenged, sometimes successfully and sometimes not, the neo-colonial arrangements put in place by the new world hegemon, the United States, which sought to impose a new (let us call it northern) order after the old European powers had been compelled to lower their flags. They set in motion other, deeply related tendencies: the old empires struck back as former colonial subjects—East and West Indians, Caribeños, Maghrebines and sub-Saharans, Filipinos and Moluccans, Koreans and Chinese—set off in unprecedented numbers for the northern metropoles, often locating themselves in the heart of their former mother-countries, indeed often recruited as *gastarbeiter*. As a result of these migrations the face of Europe was forever changed, Yamato supremacy in Japan was for the first time at all challenged, principally after the Korean War; and the United States became a far browner and yellower country (to use the vernacular terms) than it had ever been before.

Speaking of the United States, its postwar racial developments were perhaps the most remarkable of any nation, both because it was now the leading superpower and culturally hegemonic society, and because of its unique racial dementia, its centuries-long, convoluted complicity with both the conquest/deracination of its native population, and with African enslavement and its permanent consequences. It was indeed the only northern country whose national identity had been *internally* defined by these elemental experiences. Thus in the postwar period, as had been foretold by many—Du Bois and Myrdal among others—it underwent an internal, and of course unique, version of the whole international dynamic presented here. In this period the country experienced, for example, massive migration, intense mobilization of racially subordinate subjects demanding their political and social rights, and widespread reform of state institutions where racial matters were at stake. It also underwent serious and sophisticated "backlash," or "racial reaction" (Edsall and Edsall 1992; Omi and Winant 1994).

The peculiar state of racial affairs in which the postwar world found itself, then, a few decades after the surrender of the Axis, was *dualistic*. The old white supremacy had been challenged, wounded, and changed. A new, countervailing framework had emerged after centuries of lonely and isolated gestation in many varied settings, and had gained considerable ground. Reforms had occurred, populations had moved, democracy was at least widely espoused in racial matters. Yet white supremacy, although perhaps weakened, had hardly died. Indeed, it could be said to have gained some real new strength from the very racial reforms that it had been forced to initiate.

THE STAKES TODAY

This is the situation that exists today, then. Colonialism is finished; apartheid, in both its South African and U.S. forms, has been discredited; the northern, post-industrial countries are all permanently polyracial; in the world's South, an ostensibly color-blind transnational capital seeks labor and markets without recourse to racialism, not to mention explicit white supremacy. Yet beneath the surface, below the commonsense understanding from which nefarious racism has been banished, a global racial order remains: transformed, but not transcended; revivified by decades of battle with (and yes, concessions to) the menial laborers and peasantries of the world, the darker peoples it formerly held in contempt.

At the same time those once-excluded peoples—ex-colonials, descendants of slaves, indigenes—confront the present from a greatly altered position. Many millions of them are long gone from the hinterlands, the *sertões*; they are to be found today in the metropolitan centers, of both the South and the North. They have achieved some measure of political inclusion and democratic rights that would have been inconceivable only a few years ago. Limited and uneven as their oppositional victories were over the past half century or so, the scope of their postwar challenge to white supremacy still dwarfs the accomplishments of any other movement of resistance to the world racial order that took center stage from about the fifteenth century on.

More yet: a variety of solidarities—let us call them southern or diasporic— has flowered in the last decades, both fulfilling and obviating earlier dreams of resistance. Pan-Africanism as a movement lost much of its rationale as the sun finally set on the British (and French, and Belgian, and Portuguese) empires, yet Afro-diasporic solidarity continues to flourish, impelled as in the past by cultural as well as political interchange, conscious as in the past of the necessity, as well as the perils, of black self-determination. Indigenous movements have probably reached new heights in the present, giving rise to hemispheric congresses of native peoples in the Americas and movements for reparations in such unexpected spots as New Zealand (Farnsworth 1997). Meanwhile, communities with origins in the sending regions of the world's South—such as Turkey, the Philippines, India, and China—are also experiencing new (if sometimes uncertain) diasporic impulses.

Undoubtedly one factor generating such transcontinental ties is simply the vastly reinforced presence of racialized minorities in the former imperial homelands; another is the relative freedom and ease of communication and travel, which in the past was the preserve largely of Europeans. But undoubtedly most important in the gestation of diasporae are the political achievements of the "others" since World War II's end. These gains—of voice, vote, and (sometimes) democratic inclusion; of the means of communication and cultural production; and here and there of the attainment of material wellbeing and the progressive redistribution of income and wealth—serve as models and resources across borders and beyond oceans.

Diasporic tendencies and movements call into question the nation-state. They are thus linked, as were their predecessors slavery and peonage, with capital's forms of accumulation and rule. Their presence, both within various national political scenarios and globally as circuits of labor, culture, and political influence, suggests that a new racial order is emerging. Without making predictions, it is possible to identify the world racial dynamics that will shape the twenty-first century: in the near-term future the color-line will not be superseded, but will operate in a far more contradictory and contested way.

Hegemony works by incorporating opposition. Thus global racial dynamics will reflect the unstable equilibrium, the uneasy tension, between the centuries-long legacy of white supremacy and the post–World War II triumphs—ambiguous and partial but nevertheless real—of the movements of the colonized and racially excluded. The world racial system will therefore simultaneously incorporate and deny the rights, and in some cases the very existence, of the "others" whose recognition was only so recently and incompletely conceded. In short, we are witnessing the dawn of a new form of racial hegemony. In the twenty-first century, race will no longer be invoked to legitimate the crucial social structures of inequality, exploitation, and injustice. Appeals to white superiority will not serve, as they did in the bad old days. Law, political and human rights, as well as concepts of equality, fairness, and human difference will therefore increasingly be framed in "race-neutral" terms.

Yet the race-concept will continue to work at the interface of identity and inequality, social structure and cultural signification. The rearticulation of (in)equality in an ostensibly color-blind framework emphasizing individualism and meritocracy, it turns out, preserves the legacy of racial hierarchy far more effectively than its explicit defense (Crenshaw et al. 1995). Similarly, the reinterpretation of racialized differences as matters of culture and nationality, rather than as fundamental human attributes somehow linked to phenotype, turns out to justify exclusionary politics and policy far better than traditional white supremacist arguments can do (Taguieff 2001 [1988]).

These are merely some early indications of what the world racial system will look like in the twenty-first century, when it will have to operate under the contradictory (or dualistic) conditions that tend toward the development of a variety of "anti-racist racisms." Contemporary world racial dynamics are unique, most notably because they have had to adapt for the first time in half a millennium to a relatively comprehensive opposition to racial inequality and injustice. If the opposition that has developed since World War II has not achieved the elimination of racial injustice and inequality, it has at least succeeded to an unprecedented degree in legitimizing the struggle against these patterns. This alone is a great achievement, one that would not be intelligible without a comprehensive account of the evolution of the world racial order to the present day. Yet the reordering of world racial dynamics over the past decades does not suggest that we are in any way "beyond race," or that comprehensive patterns of racial inequality and injustice are no longer fundamental to the global social structure. It only means—and this is important enough—that world racial formation continues.

Three

LEARNING TO CATCH HELL:
RACE AND MODERNITY

IN WHAT SENSE was the creation of the modern world system a *racial* project? Certainly twentieth-century concepts of race did not yet exist as Europe was consolidated regionally and nationally in the fifteenth and sixteenth centuries, as the early dawn of capitalism occurred and the imperial age began. Yet some early notion of race did operate: some division of the world along the familiar axis of "Europe and its others" was coming into being. This was the first appearance of what Du Bois would call "the problem of the color-line."

Nor did the world system change overnight from a condition largely oblivious to racial divisions to one deeply structured by them. The invention of race took longer than that. In fact, large-scale social constructs like the concept of race cannot be *invented* at all. They are developed, interpreted in new ways, and imported from other times and places. They are *re*invented, more properly put.

This chapter traces some of the elemental origins of modernity in the relationships of conquest and slavery. It describes in racial terms the historical trajectory the modern world system has followed, focusing on its rise and consolidation from the late fifteenth to the early nineteenth centuries. The account first considers *precursors* to racial modernity, reviewing the antecedents and prefigurations of the racial concepts on which the emerging world racial order drew. Next it explores *Europe at the threshold of modernity*, focusing particularly on the creation of nation-states along the European Atlantic and the origins of the tension between peoplehood (the "national") and the structure of domination ("statism") that would prove so problematic at later stages of European imperialism. Then it contemplates the transformative impact of modernity on the two principal regions in which Europe found its modern "others": the transformation of what had been an *African Africa to a colonial Africa*, and the "discovery" and rising significance of the *world's other hemisphere*, the Americas. Both these vast regions underwent comprehensive mutations as their fates were linked to the global system of exploitation and stratification; these social relationships were comprehensively racialized. Plunder, unequal exchange, and imperial rule played the greatest parts in forging and perpetuating these linkages, although

by the nineteenth century themes of independence and abolition were beginning to appear as well. The chapter concludes by considering *the limits to growth*,
by which I mean the dawning of obstacles to imperialism, the increasing tensions between state/civil society-based views of slavery, and the impact of these
factors on democratization. The issues of resistance and democratization
become central concerns in Chapter Four.

PRECURSORS

The historical origins of the concept of race are extremely diverse. Some type
of group identity seems universal and primordial. The group's idea of itself may
take many forms—tribal, spatial, linguistic, religious—all serving to distinguish
between members and outsiders. Some form of ethnocentrism may even characterize all human society. The articulation of this concept in terms of the
body—in corporeal, "phenotypic" terms[1]—is also found in early texts.

It is a big jump, however, from this tendency to modern notions of race.
Although the concept is perhaps prefigured by ethnocentrism, and takes preliminary form in ancient concepts of civilization versus barbarity (Snowden
1983), or citizen (or *zoon politikon*) versus outsider/slave (Hannaford 1996;
Finley 1983), it is only in the past few centuries, under the tutelage of various
European imperialisms, that the world's peoples have been classified relatively
systematically along racial lines. In terms of scale and inexorability the race-
concept only began to attain its familiar meanings at the end of the Middle
Ages. Religion, science, philosophy, and politics were all implicated in the gestation of racial logic. Probably the most significant rehearsals for that classification—the fierce anti-Islamic and anti-Jewish campaigns of the Crusades and
the Inquisition—drew their inspiration from religious sources. The consolidation of nation-states, notably on the Atlantic margins of Europe, was in large
measure accomplished in tandem with the launching of transoceanic imperial
ventures and the takeoff of the African slave trade. Accumulation of natural
resources, at first largely the result of plunder, fueled this process, signaling the
end of feudalism and the transition to capitalism.[2]

The rise of Europe was a multidimensional process. It involved the onset of
capitalism, of course: the slow development of more effective means of accumulation that vastly outstripped the limitations of feudalism. Beginning with
the plunder of outlying regions, then developing extensive trade, and finally
evolving the system of industrialization, this economic development, this accumulative leap, "combined and uneven," was in turn dependent on a series of
political and cultural institutions that regulated and protected it.

Beliefs in a global human hierarchy of natural and ineluctable provenance came to play a central supporting role in the imperial order as the immense historical rupture represented by the rise of Europe, the onset of African enslavement, the *conquista,* and the subjugation of much of Asia proceeded. Myrdal's insight about circular and cumulative causation can be used to make sense of the importance of race in the organization of the modern world (Myrdal 1963). Employing this perspective facilitates an account of modernity as an "overdetermined" process, a complex evolution and interaction that gradually linked appropriation, coercion, and common sense from approximately 1500 on. The interaction (and tension) among processes of capital accumulation, techniques of state-building and political rule, and general understandings that explained (or rationalized) the conflicts this emerging system entailed, were all deeply shaped by race.

EUROPE AT THE THRESHOLD OF MODERNITY

The Europe that could "take off" into capitalism was far from consolidated regionally or nationally. European elites—noble, mercantile, and religious— began to seek the benefits of predatory adventure overseas, the benefits of proto-capitalist accumulation, in the fifteenth century, largely building on Italian experiences (which involved slavery as well) in the Mediterranean. Portuguese sugar cultivation on Madeira, and Portuguese/Spanish plantations on the Canaries, were early models for the Brazilian and Caribbean enterprises to follow. The Portuguese made the first recorded capture of Africans to be sold as slaves (probably to Madeira or the Algarve), on the Guinean coast in 1441.

Centralizing states also benefited from imperial initiatives. The effort to consolidate fractious or even warring peoples, provinces, ethnic groups, or even nations (take your pick among these terms) into a unified nation ruled by a central state was dear to the heart of many a monarch, court, or even *parlement.* The prospect of state-building based on the plunder of external resources was especially opportune, if only because it required lesser degrees of coercion—of nobility, burghers, or peasants. The financing of imperial ambitions, the strengthening of the central state by infusions of precious metals plundered abroad (Cole 1985; Bakewell 1984; Bakewell 1971; Ladurie et al. 1990),[3] the assembly of armed forces both land- and sea-borne, and the formation of alliances among traders, nobility, and military fortune-seekers—all tendentially converged in early imperial projects, and all tended to formalize and institutionalize racial hierarchy and classification.

The development of imperial/state-building projects depended, especially in their early moments, on the overcoming of challengers, both internal and external. Regionally, competition was fiercest with the Islamic powers. The

Turkish Empire to the southeast had a foothold in Europe and a history of armed clashes in the Middle Ages with the feudal predecessors of these same western European powers.[4]

To the south were Maghrebine or Levantine Muslims. These "Moors" had been a presence in Spain and Portugal for five hundred years. The two Islamic powers—Turkish and Moorish—were themselves rivals, and another Christian domain also existed in Europe: the Orthodox realms that survived after Byzantium in Greece, the Slavic regions, and Russia. Of the two Christian worlds and the two Islamic ones, only in northern and western Europe did the resources and motives exist for imperial adventure. The chief reason for this was the fragmentation and conflict[5] of the Holy Roman Empire into a series of potential nation-states, whose rivalry itself propelled imperial expansion. The rise in western Europe of nation-states bent on (and capable of) expansion distinguished that area from other, more quiescent zones. The consolidation of these realms combined with the decline of feudalism under the pressures of initial and tentative experiments with capitalism. It overlapped with the *reconquista*, the centuries-long process of re-Christianizing southern (and particularly Iberian) Europe.[6] It also informed early imperialist impulses, as these newly assertive nation-states sought to constitute their power and wealth by subduing and plundering others, particularly in areas hitherto unexplored (Kiernan 1969; Abu-Lughod 1989; Blaut 1993; Patterson 1997; Wolf 1982).

Thus nation-building and proselytism were characteristic of early imperial ventures. That early imperialists understood their errands in religious terms, that they saw them in part as missions to propagate the faith, was understandable for many reasons, among them the need to combat the antagonistic worldviews perceived in rival religious orientations, particularly Islamic ones. Add to this the quest for wealth and the drive to open trade routes in a world becoming less insular. Figure in as well the developing intra-European rivalries among states and aspirant empires not yet even fully nationalized, much less internationalized, in their collective identities. So early imperialisms balanced their accumulative economic aspirations—both as states and as a range of protocapitalist enterprises[7]—with politically and culturally regulatory agendas. Principal objectives, especially at first, were the suppression of internal others—notably Muslims and Jews in the Iberian peninsula, but also elsewhere—and consolidation: territorial, political, economic. These projects also worked by religious means to compel greater cohesion both in the emerging European nations and in their respective spheres of influence.

In all these formative moments of imperialism—in the quest for plunder and trade, the project of nation-building, and the religious order demanded by the state—we can detect proto-racial dimensions, early impulses to draw fundamental lines of distinction between Europeans and "others." Initial versions of these demarcations varied, to be sure. In many cases they were "merely" doctrinal, ethnocentric, accumulative. It would have required extensive experience and much debate to consolidate concepts of race that throroughly naturalized, indeed biologized, the European/"other" boundary. Yet precursors to the race-concept certainly emerged, driven foward by early colonial efforts and by nation-building itself.

Most of the imperial nations only consolidated themselves in sharp relation to the quest for colonies, and often in respect to simultaneous internal as well as external "ethnic cleansing" (to employ the familiar genocidal phrase anachronistically). England, France, Spain, even little Holland and Portugal had either to subdue various fractious internal "nations" (the Scots, the Bretons, the Galicians, etc.), or to break free from the imperial ambitions of other European powers. Both Portugal and Holland had to shake off the toils of Spanish rule, for example. In the Iberian case, the legacy of Moorish rule and its sequelae (after the thirteenth century) weighed heavily on the imperial ambitions of both Castile and Lisboa, first within the peninsula and then beyond it. English determination to master Ireland has often been seen as the proto-racial rehearsal par excellence for broader imperial efforts.[8] But everywhere in Atlantic Europe, early exercises in racial "othering" furnished precedents for the coming depredations of conquest and enslavement. Consider the following brief illustrations: the experiences of those two paradigmatic early European "others," Muslims and Jews, in the centuries preceding the onset of empire.

The Moors ruled Portugal from 711 to 1249. While this rule was ended well before the onset of Portuguese empire-building, what were its effects on the racial logic imposed by the Portuguese in their colonies such as Brazil? Gilberto Freyre and others have seen this long-lasting experience, this intermingling of Portugal and North Africa, as one of the sources of a supposedly more tolerant and benign Portuguese form of slavery and colonialism.[9] Other writers have stressed that the intense conflict that characterized this regime was the source of a particular Portuguese hostility to things African (Moura 1988). Similar questions can be raised about Spain, where the expulsion of Muslims was only completed in 1609.

Whether the Iberian contact with North Africa was salutary[10] or harmful for future regimes, there can be no doubt that these early experiences played a decisive role in initiating the Portuguese and Spanish entrances into conquest and slavery, both African and Native American. By translating slavery from the Italian colonies of the Mediterrean to the islands of Madeira, São Tomé, and the Canaries; by experimenting there with the development of plantation-style cultivation of sugar and other labor-intensive crops; by importing greater numbers of enslaved Africans both there and into their home territories[11] than did the other imperial powers; indeed by learning some of the skills of slave-trading from Maghrebine Arabs who brought their slaves north across the

Sahara from Mali and Mauretania, the Portuguese and Spanish became the first European slave traders, the first to consume the labor and lives of proto-racial "others." The northern European imperial powers would enter into the Americas, and into the slave trade, almost a century later, in the early to mid-1600s.

The Jews were the other early "outsiders" of premodern Europe. In the Crusades Jews were as fiercely assaulted as Muslims, and a series of expulsions drove the survivors from most of the later imperial powers as they were consolidated as nation-states (in the fourteenth and fifteenth centuries), and as imperial ambition dawned. The Inquisition, founded in 1229, came by the sixteenth century to embody a fairly racial anti-semitism with its renewal of persecutions against *conversos* or *novos cristões*. Now it was no longer the Jew's beliefs, but his or her essence, as depicted in the doctrine of *limpieza de sangre*, that was seen as unredeemable; thus even conversion was not acceptable: only expulsion or extirpation would generally suffice (Poliakov 1977; Mosse 1978; Arendt 1973; Netanyahu 1995).

FROM AFRICAN AFRICA TO COLONIAL AFRICA

Although European raiding and kidnapping of Africans for enslavement was pioneered in the fifteenth century, the transformation of European outposts in Africa into enclaves for the export of humans to the western hemisphere was a gradual and conflictual process. During the fifteenth and sixteenth centuries, Portuguese raiding and kidnapping along the Gulf of Guinea sometimes produced human captives, but often met resistance as well (Thornton 1998). Trading and even exchanges of envoys between Lisbon and the Senegambian and Congolese coasts were instituted quite early on—during the fifteenth century. These arrangements, although far from stable, began to lay the groundwork for meeting the future massive demands of the slave trade.

Still, it took a long time to replace the traditional system of acquiring slaves—banditry or piracy—with a relatively organized market. The reasons for this were many. The demand for mass labor grew only gradually as transatlantic conquest expanded. Not until the turn of the seventeenth century would a deeper demand for slave labor begin to emerge. African resistance was continuous and not infrequently successful. Competition and warfare among the European powers vying for access to the West African coast was severe. But perhaps the most formidable obstacles to the slave trade's gestation were the difficulties involved in creating a "supply-side" for human chattels in the African interior. Obtaining a steady flow of coerced persons depended on the ability to confer trading advantages (for example, manufactures, notably weapons and textiles) on African trading partners and agents. It demanded the translation of traditional slaving practices—generally unpleasant, but hardly genocidal—into far more brutal and thoroughgoing routines of regional intervention and domination. It involved fomenting rivalries and warfare among African peoples, and overcoming opposition of many types. Warfare among peoples, some suborned by the slavers, some jealous of their independence, was a major source of slave supply. Armed bands engaged in widespread kidnapping. Already-captured Africans revolted repeatedly. Movements of resistance to slave trading, often religiously based, appeared intermittently.

Mass slave labor was tried out in island sugar cultivation, as we have seen, and also in mining and placer operations,[12] but it was not until large-scale sugar cultivation was instituted in the Brazilian Northeast (beginning in the seventeenth century and expanding rapidly toward the turn of the eighteenth) that the demand for African slaves seriously increased. Struggles between the Portuguese and the Dutch expanded from the African coast to Brazil, and by the early 1700s the British were able to impose their rule by virtue of their naval power and their own burgeoning need for slaves in the Caribbean. I discuss the American features of these shifts in a moment, but first it must be recognized that in Africa these developments led beyond the creation of entrepôts and coastal fortresses (themselves much fought over by the Europeans, and also the scenes of frequent slave revolts) to the establishment of proto-colonial spheres of influence. More serious attempts to impose colonial regimes, notably British ones but also French and Portuguese efforts, eventually succeeded and solidified these arrangements.

Why was this? Above all, the demand for enslaved Africans increased dramatically, beginning in the seventeenth century and continuing until the nineteenth. To furnish those human supplies required a more substantial European presence in Africa, a more effective set of coercive instrumentalities, for one thing, and a more developed legitimating rationale, for another. After all, was this not "the dark continent," the region of the world which, from Hegel to Trevor-Roper, was seen (from Europe) as "having no history"?[13]

To provide a steady and reliable flow of slaves, and to support an ever-more intrusive colonial enterprise, entailed huge costs. Thus as slavery developed, an extensive network of Africa-related trade exfoliated as well. Sugar became a commodity accessible to the popular classes in Europe, not just to the elites. The interplay of sugar and tea trading (not to mention other agricultural products dependent on mass labor and plantation systems of cultivation), and hence the interconnection of Asia and the Americas under European imperial auspices, was a major integrative step. African colonies too became huge markets, as multilateral trading circuits and mercantilist economic regimes took hold.[14] Through the eighteenth and nineteenth centuries extractive enterprise in Africa developed prodigiously: mining and cultivation took various forms using both enslaved labor and peonage systems. Latecomers to the colonial racket, notably the Belgians and the Germans, implemented genocidal means of extraction as late as the nineteenth and early twentieth centuries.

THE WORLD'S OTHER HEMISPHERE

Demand for enslaved African labor in the western hemisphere began its prolonged tendential increase during the seventeenth century. The first major importer of slaves was Brazil, and the engine of that growth was sugar production in the Brazilian northeast.

Both Portugal and Spain had by this time laid waste the native populations of their American colonies, through a combination of disease and rapacious labor practices, notably in mining (Stannard 1992; Stavenhagen and Iturralde 1990). Spanish extraction of gold and silver, based on enslaved indigenous labor, was largely a sixteenth-century phenomenon.[15] It had been these practices, among others, which had drawn the condemnation of las Casas and other erstwhile protectors of the Indians.[16]

Spanish booty, largely in the form of American gold and silver extracted from the limitless toil of native peoples, greatly facilitated the consolidation of European imperial states. As noted, these riches appeared in royal treasuries without coercive patrimonial extraction from nobles, and without similarly unwelcome levies on nascent bourgeoisies or potentially restive peasants. Thus the rise of imperial states (as distinct from gestating capitalist classes) is attributable in significant measure to colonial, racially interpretable, plunder.

The other side of the imperial enterprise was commercial. Here trade in many products, among them pepper and spice, lumber, and tobacco, was involved. But it was sugar that became, along with the slaves themselves who produced it, the first truly extensively traded global commodity.

Sugar was Portuguese for a good while. Early Portuguese predominance in sugar production can be traced to the experience gained in the Atlantic islands and the Algarve, but mostly it derived from the head start Portuguese navigators and slave traders had established in Atlantic Africa. Brazil, first reached by Europeans in the expedition of Cabral (1500), was far more accessible from the slave-exporting ports of West Africa, and indeed from Iberia itself, than were the Caribbean or the other mainland colonies. After searching for gold for a while (prematurely as it turned out) and doing their best with *pau-do-Brasil* (the wood for which the country was named), the Portuguese introduced Madeira-style sugar production in the mid-sixteenth century, largely in the northeastern areas of Pernambuco and Bahia,[17] known as the Reconcavo.

By the end of the sixteenth century European rivalries were extremely intense. The Spanish Habsburgs held on to Portugal from 1580 to 1640, but had substantially lost control of the Low Countries by 1610. The Dutch financed much of the Portuguese sugar trade, but also slugged it out with the Portuguese: at stake was seventeenth-century imperial hegemony, in West Africa, Brazil, and for that matter Asia. Dutch assaults on Portuguese fortresses and coastal outposts, and on the Brazilian Northeast, did not ultimately succeed, although they did hold on to some Caribbean and Guyanese territory and of course bested the Portuguese in the Malacca Straits (Indonesia) region. Because of their far more advanced commercial capitalism and the seafaring/ trading advantages it conferred, the Dutch became the largest slave traders of the seventeenth century, and the chief importers and distributors of Brazilian sugar.[18] Unlike the Spanish, from whose toils they had finally broken free, and in some contrast to the Portuguese as well, the Dutch were more capitalist than statist in their imperialism. This meant operating through "companies," the West Indian Company (founded in 1621) and the earlier East India Company (founded in 1602). Citing Sombart, Blackburn labels these entities as "proof of the emergence of a new type of aggressive and plundering bourgeoisie" (Blackburn 1997, 187; Sombart 1967, 75). But even if the Dutch balance between state and civil society tended to favor the latter more than the Iberian powers' arrangements did (and thus also resembled more closely the British approach of the succeeding imperial period), it still required a massive state involvement, at least to provide the coercive apparatus—the military and naval might—that was necessary to carve out an internationally competitive strategy. One other thing the Dutch shared with their Portuguese friends/enemies, their combined political rivals/business partners, was a solid appreciation for the utility of African slavery in reaping enormous trading profits across multiple markets, oceans, and continents.

By the later seventeenth century, though, the British had come to play the central role. By allying themselves with Portugal, they were able to outmaneuver all their other European rivals. Sugar production techniques learned from Brazil were employed on the widest of scales in the Caribbean, and the slave trade to that region burgeoned. The 1713 Treaty of Utrecht—a very complex series of European agreements centered on Spain—included the *Asiento,* an accord through which the British received exclusive license to import African slaves into *Nueva España.* The traffic in African flesh burgeoned after the treaty, with Britain in the lead, and French, Portuguese, and Dutch traders following behind. Brazil and the Caribbean were now the most significant receiving areas for the traffic, and sugar production the most central activity in which slave labor was engaged.

During the eighteenth century roughly half of the 6 million Africans Curtin enumerates as exported to the Americas went to the Caribbean. About one-third still went to Brazil, and something like one-sixth arrived in North America (Curtin 1969, 265). Although figures are in permanent dispute here, it is certain that over the century's course at least a million Africans died in the middle passage and prior to embarcation (Curtin 1969; Solow 1991).

The production of a wide variety of goods depended on slave labor. Of these commodities sugar was by far the most important, but by no means the only product that British-owned African slaves produced. Exported from the primary producing areas not only to Britain, but through it to the rest of the world—Britain having replaced Holland as the world's central trading post by the early 1700s—slave-produced goods were the chief sources of national revenues. Furthermore, British trade with the colonies, both slaveholding and slave-exporting (that is, both American and African, speaking generally) was crucially shaped by these provinces' demand for manufactured goods, whose export drove the development of British industry to rapid rates of increase. As British colonies and home industries increased their productive capacities in response to the demand for exports, both of primary goods like sugar and tobacco and of manufactured goods like textiles, various "multiplier" effects developed. For example, the interplay of sugar and tea (largely a South Asian product) has often been noted. Solow writes:

> The total production of sugar and much of the production of tobacco, their cheapness, and their elasticity of supply were dependent upon the continuing flow of the productive labor of slaves to the colonies. The 18th century saw the full fruition of this trade reorientation. Total trade increased greatly, and the Atlantic was crisscrossed by British ships carrying manufactured goods to Africa, the West Indies, Brazil, Portugal, and British North America. The Atlantic islands were exporting wine, Africa slaves, Brazil gold, and the West Indies sugar and molasses. Some of the British North American colonies were sending rice and tobacco to Britain; others were sending fish, lumber, horses, and flour to the West Indies and were buying British manufactures with the proceeds. Every one of these flows depended on the product of slave labor. (Solow 1991, 71)

In the seventeenth century the slave trade had already increased markedly, particularly the trade to Brazil and (after mid-century when *Pernambucano* technologies of sugar production were brought there), the trade to the Caribbean as well. This was in itself remarkable, because during this century a significant slowdown—what some see as the first capitalist depression—affected most other economic activities (Hobsbawm 1987). But by the eighteenth century, as I have noted, the apogee of slave-trading was attained. Here too the multiplier effects of slavery upon trade in general—and thus the development of capitalism in its mercantile phase—must be appreciated:

Shortly before the American Revolution sugar by itself accounted for about a fifth of all English imports and with the addition of tobacco, coffee, cotton, and rum, the share of slave-produced commodities in England's imports was about 30%. The impact of slavery on world trade did not end there. Much of England's shipping was engaged in transporting either sugar to Europe, slaves from Africa to the New World, or manufactured goods from England to the slave colonies. Toward the end of the eighteenth century more than half of England's exports were bound for one or another of the slave colonies. It was not just Britain but also France, Spain, Portugal, Holland, and Denmark that thrived on buying from or selling to slave colonies. (Fogel 1989, 21–22)

Investment in slaves was the first and largest-scale capital investment of the early industrial era. Because slavery was so central to economic growth and offered a seemingly unlimited labor supply, because at least in the eighteenth century slave-exploiting commodity production was relatively impervious to the business cycle (which in any case was still poorly understood), the ownership of African slaves represented a different type of investment than any other form of capital. It embodied a certain hubris, shall we say, above and beyond its moral degeneracy and religious hypocrisy: an unbounded economic privilege, an almost godlike immunity to risk,[19] a "license to steal," an unbounded luxury—especially for the absentee owner.

Indeed in the Caribbean, as earlier in Brazil, many owners were absent. Enslaved African populations exceeded whites by significant numbers. Interestingly, this was not the usual case in British North America, where large inflows of immigration took place during the eighteenth century. Even where the North American colonies were not primarily engaged in exploiting slave labor, though, there was "dependence" on slavery. To quote Solow again:

> Their land was suited to agricultural commodities which could not easily bear the cost of transport to Britain. They could import British manufactures only by shipping their surplus food and raw materials to the slave colonies of the West Indies and earning there the foreign exchange that enabled them to meet their balance of payments deficits in Britain. Thus, the international trade of the Northern colonies depended on slave production as much as did the trade of Virginia and South Carolina. (Solow 1991, 71)

The centrality of African slavery as the "motor" of early capitalist development, especially in the North Atlantic, cannot be overestimated.

Especially during the late eighteenth century, British economic growth was very rapid, despite the strains of the Seven Years and the American Revolutionary

Wars. This growth was export-led and protected, especially in its early stages, by the dependence of the colonies and by Britain's abilities to enforce restrictions on trading with third parties. As mercantilism, having succeeded the booty capitalism of the earlier periods of colonialism, gradually gave way to industrialism,[20] the social structures established by slavery remained in place. They were not merely residual, but fundamental economic, social, and cultural lineaments of the Atlantic world.

Thus the long-running discussion of the degree of capitalist production relations embodied in slave-based, plantation-style agriculture tends to miss the most important points: slave labor created much of the wealth and made possible the circuits of capitalist exchange that transformed and integrated the world economy;[21] this massive subsidization of nascent capitalism could only be provided by "others," by coercing the labor of Africans whose humanity, not to mention survival, did not have to be taken fully into account.[22]

THE LIMITS TO GROWTH

Of the many important arguments that swirl through the literature on the relationship between capitalism and slavery, one seems most telling: the incompatibility in the long term of slavery and capitalist industrial production. As industry developed, the conflicts involved in maintaining two distinct systems of labor, two distinct labor forces, intensified.

Slavery had permitted the superexploitation of what seemed for a long time to be a relatively inexhaustible supply of labor (provided that Africans could be captured and brought alive to the plantations, of course—not an easy matter). It had limited the slaveowner's commitment to the reproduction and maintenance of the slave. It had located slave labor largely at the margins of the national/imperial territory, isolating slave laborers from "free" ones, something of special importance as industry developed, largely in the metropoles, the "home" areas of the imperial nations. In contrast to the growing "free" working classes, the slave system formally afforded no political rights, no citizenship status or even personhood, to slaves; exclusion from the political realm was nearly total: opportunities for collective action were restricted as much as whites could manage (although such opportunities were of course not entirely absent). And, as I have been at pains to argue, a crucial social marker, ubiquitous and evident, demarcated the boundary between the enslaved and the "free," between chattel and person/worker/citizen: racial identity.

None of these distinctions were absolute. Industrial slavery certainly did exist: in the North American colonies and antebellum southern states as well as in the sugar mills of meso-America, and in mines and mills throughout the world. Superexploitation was hardly the fate only of slaves; it was the predominant experience of the early industrial proleteriat, the "free" workers of the "dark satanic mills" of England and New England, as well as elsewhere (Engels 1958 [1845]; Dawley 1976). Despite their primary engagement as plantation laborers, enslaved Africans were not all that remote from the gaze or experience of whites. Nor were slaves utterly without power: denied the right to organize, they still managed to "strike" and "negotiate" with their masters, as Ira Berlin (1998) and George Rawick (1972a), among others, have shown. An important theme of this book, glimpsed here and elsewhere, is that the distinction between "unfree" and "free" cannot be definitive.

Yet with the development of industry, the incompatibilities between slavery-based and "free" labor-based sysems were heightened. Industrial capitalists never had the same (relatively) inexhaustible source of labor supply that plantation slavemasters enjoyed until around the turn of the nineteenth century. Industrial development required more skilled and committed workers than plantation agriculture. The spatial proximity of the social classes at home, and the relatively more accessible means of political mobilization there, impelled notable concessions and reforms of a democratizing type. And as these shifts occurred, the legitimacy of slavery was ever-more called into question.

The incongruous relationship between slavery and industrialism became more obvious as industry developed and slavery was marginalized. This incongruity was not only, perhaps not even principally, economic. In a crucial sense it was primarily political. As will be argued in the next chapter, the odor of absolutism lay heavily upon slavery. Democratization—however partial, however tentative—was not only a transition from exclusion to inclusion, significant as that was. It was also a passage from slave-based to "free" labor, from a labor system deeply dependent upon coercion to one based on consent. The outcome of this transformation was the convergence—although far from complete, to be sure—between the emancipatory interests of the enslaved Africans and the accumulative interests of an increasingly powerful segment of the bourgeoisie. The obsolescence of the slave system also created new mutual interests— although hardly total solidarity—between "free" workers and slaves (or former slaves).

By the early eighteenth century the existence of a divided, racialized world, a world system distinguishing systematically between persons and slaves, between Europeans and "others," between white and non-white, was a generally acknowledged, comprehensive phenomenon.[23] But despite their reliance on depredation and brutality, most systems of imperial rule may be more effectively described as thoroughly stratified by race than as "eliminationist." These systems (or subsystems of a global racial order) were more than racially stratified, more even than racially dualistic. They were *riven* by race: permitting no involvement by native subjects in the exercise of authority; locally consulting only with the settlers, and even with them only in such manner as prescribed by the metropolitan authorities.

Such practices led to predictable consequences: the widespread obliteration of distinctions between the state and such "private enterprise" as existed meant that there would be massive enrichment of favored colonial officers, licensees, and legatees at the expense not only of natives, but also of small settlers. The latter were transformed into overseers, hirelings, and petty entrepreneurs who were in perpetual danger of "going native," and thus came to fear above all the loss of their (white) privileges. For the real natives and slaves, of course, all political involvement was unthinkable. They could occasionally contemplate escape or even armed resistance, but they remained officially voiceless.

Not only was imperial rule forced to confront the distinctions and overlaps between slavery and wage labor; but also the techniques for managing different forms of labor—enslaved and "free," peripheral and metropolitan—tended to converge. Indeed each system of control made what use it could of the experience of the other. The arrogance and superciliousness of white supremacy in all its many forms extended outward to the farthest reaches of empire, while much of its contempt for natives and slaves found echoes in domestic disdain for, and fear of, the working classes, whose physicality itself—whose sexuality, for example (Stoler 1995)—was increasingly equated with that of the alien native or slave who labored at the opposite end of the world. The more effective control of an abject mass of laborers and slaves was the object of continual striving on the part of those in charge. Indeed the development of a sociopolitical "repertoire" adequate to the challenges of organizing national and transnational social orders premised on exclusion, coercion, and cultural deracination was deemed—not without reason—essential to the objectives of imperial expansion and industrial growth (Cooper and Stoler 1997).

In the later stages of slavery, and especially in the later nineteenth century, these patterns underwent still further alterations. Creolization had created divisions among the privileged strata and led to demands for independence. The decolonization of the Americas was the most notable result. The prevalence of *mestizaje,* which (once again in the Americas most notably) overlapped to various degrees with the creole category, tended to undermine and attenuate the political logic of racial rule. Mixed-race figures, *trigueños,* even *mulatos,* appeared among the elites. Independence-minded creoles sought to enlist slaves and landless peons in their rebel armies, bringing abolitionism to (some) Latin American countries in the early nineteenth century (Toplin 1972; Rout 1976), and to all by the dawn of the twentieth.[24] The demolition of colonialism in the Americas prefigured its eventual demise in Africa and Asia during the post–World War II break with which this book is centrally concerned. These interlinked, epochal shifts in the developing modern world system were all deeply racial processes.

Four

THE EMPIRE STRIKES BACK: RESISTANCE TO RACIAL RULE

THE WORLD-HISTORICAL OUTRAGES that plunged natives and kidnapped Africans into chattel status, that casually relegated whole peoples to genocide, gave rise to a wide variety of resistance practices, ranging from small-scale obstruction and sabotage to massive uprisings and revolutions. Of course, racial rule not only spawned resistance; it also bred uncertainty, despair, and self-hatred. Indeed it is something of a marvel that so much resistance was possible: among those who survived the brutalities of slave raiding and transportation, who endured the massacres, epidemics, and forced labor of the *conquista*, it surely required an indomitable spirit to sustain defiance, to contemplate opposition, to organize revolt.

Challenging the slavemasters and colonialists was no easy task. Resources were lacking and understanding difficult to achieve. Native peoples and kidnapped Africans developed their capacities for resistance over a centuries-long journey through the netherworld of human existence. Their "social death" (Patterson 1982) might well be conceived as leading to a "social resurrection" to which the invention of resistance practices was decisive. Developing "the arts of resistance" (Scott 1990) involved a type of experimentation, a kind of *bricolage* (Levi-Strauss 1966), whose significance for social theory remains largely unexplored. But for present purposes, what should be emphasized is the variety and creativity of resistance practices; the necessary interaction between their experiential and structural dimensions (or if one prefers this language, their "micro-macro" linkages) (Alexander et al. 1987; Collins 1987; Huber 1991); and their tendential development toward greater world-historical significance. Each of these elements of resistance to conquest and enslavement contained essential racial components.

Resistance to racial rule—the most fundamental characteristic of modern slavery (and later, colonialism)—also opened the way toward nationalism and self-determination, embattled as those concepts eventually became. Resistance to slavery proved to be the prophetic forerunner of other forms of popular opposition as well: challenging peonage, superexploitation, unequal exchange, and colonial rule. Thus the origins of modern class struggle,[1] nationalism, and many democratic movements may be found in struggles over racial rule.

This chapter examines the emergence and development of resistance to racial rule, noting its sources and logic, and considering its influence on world politics. I do not take the idea that "the empire strikes back" from filmmaker George Lucas or from the cultural studies tradition (Centre for Contemporary Cultural Studies 1982). Instead this figure serves as an important marker of two themes central to the present work. First, it is a reminder that all systems of rule breed opposition; this is manifestly applicable to the global system of imperialism and its crucial component of slavery. Second, the idea that "the empire strikes back" suggests that the conflicts over imperialism have a cyclical or reiterative quality: Myrdal's circular and cumulative causation once again.[2] For example, the resolution of the tension between the domination and resistance involved in slavery—in other words, emancipation—necessarily took on a precursive, prefigurative character, providing a framework for later stages of subordination and emancipation, for later struggles over democracy. Indeed the *idea* of slavery lived on even after the general abolition of slavery by the end of the nineteenth century. It became a trope for anti-democracy in many social spheres—notably in respect to labor. Examples like this can situate the trajectories of anti-slavery and abolitionism as important precedents, rehearsals so to speak, for the post–World War II break in global racial politics that defines our own time.

This chapter aims at a sociohistorically focused, theoretically informed account of resistance to racial rule. It proceeds by stages, beginning with resistance to enslavement and conquest, moving through slave rebellion and *marronage*, and finally considering abolitionism and anti-colonialism. As noted, the development of the forms of racial rule parallels and in some respects underlies the development of modernity, capitalism, and the nation-state.

In what follows, I first discuss *resistance to enslavement and conquest* at the beginning stages of European seaborne empire. I focus on the resources—principally knowledge and power resources—available to Africans and Native Americans in their early encounters with European predation and absolutism. I largely confine myself to an Atlanticist framework here, although early colonial adventures during the period covered in this section (sixteenth to eighteenth centuries) certainly included Asian conquest as well.

From the beginning of the slave trade, and increasing with the proliferation and deepening of the slavery-based world economy, resistance also developed and deepened. It took many forms, including *subversion, escape and* marronage, *revolt and revolution.* These types of resistance, although prefigured and rehearsed from the beginning, augmented their effectiveness and frequency with the rise of modernity. As capitalism, empire, and communication all experienced substantial growth, this growth also fueled emancipatory aspirations and potentialities. By the late eighteenth to early nineteenth centuries local revolts and revolutionary slave uprisings reached their highest moment in the Haitian revolution, a national independence movement in which slaves could intervene en masse. The armed uprising of the "black Jacobins" (James 1989 [1938]) under L'Ouverture and Dessalines, and the "general strike" (Du Bois 1977 [1935]) of North American blacks during the Civil War signaled the end of absolutist racial rule.

Next I discuss *abolitionism.* The emancipatory outbreaks in Haiti and North America not only buoyed democratic aspirations on a global scale, not only sounded the death-knell of slavery, but also realized a series of movement demands. Abolitionism was the first transracial, international social movement in history; it represented a new type of democratic mobilization that had far-reaching consequences throughout and even beyond the Atlantic world. But abolitionism was also a contradictory movement, which tended to justify further modernization, both of capitalism in general and of particular colonial regimes.

Racial rule had largely (though never entirely)[3] dispensed with slavery by the end of the nineteenth century. Yet by then it had also amply demonstrated the resilience of other forms of exploitation. Varieties of peonage, a wide repertoire of oppressive labor regimes, and continuing political exclusion effectively substituted new forms of coercion for formal enslavement, not only in the colonial and post-colonial regimes of the world's South, but also in industrializing settler states like the United States, Australia, and South Africa. In all these settings the racial dimensions of authoritarianism continued to operate. Hence resistance to racial rule continued as well.

This resistance took on new forms once more in the twentieth century: it now moved *toward an anti-colonialist, diasporic direction* (or pan-, or even Third World, non-aligned, or southern) as well as adopting the variety of nationalist and Marxian forms denoted by the phrase *national liberation.* In place of a conclusion to this chapter (for this set of themes is addressed later in the book), a few final sentences are devoted to the world racial situation that succeeded the abolition of slavery.

RESISTANCE TO ENSLAVEMENT AND CONQUEST

Slavery was ubiquitous as the primary source of labor in the premodern world. What "slavery" means, however, has varied enormously across historical periods and in different places. The enslaved may be chattel, subject to being bought and sold like other property, or they may be "bound" to a lord and required to work a certain land, in a relationship more easily understood as feudal than enslavement. In classical Europe and the Middle East chattel slavery was more common than in premodern Africa, where bound forms of service predominated before the coming of the Europeans.[4] Bonded servitude (possibly overlapping with chattel slavery) was occurring in Africa by means of the trans-Sahara trade between the Maghreb and North Central Africa—present-day Chad, Mali, and Sudan.[5] But African chattel slavery only attained world-historical significance after Portuguese seafaring along the west coasts of Africa began in the fifteenth century, overshadowing land-based trade.

In the ancient and classical worlds, in the pre-Columbian Americas, and in world's South and East, slavery was generally a byproduct of conquest. Through warfare grand or petty, through piracy, plunder, and raiding, slaves were captured and transported to their place of service. Slave "trading"—that is, the settlement of political and economic claims of various kinds through the exchange of human captives—was also very widely practiced.[6]

While conquest and reduction to chattel imposed serious status differences between slave and non-slave, differences that logically often took on such recognizable ethnic (that is, cultural) forms as linguistic and religious discrepancy, slavery was only *racialized* in a definitive fashion with the rise of the Atlantic system. This was a system that involved European enslavement, not only of Africans, but of Native Americans as well. With no more than an insignificant number of exceptions, this system attributed *ineffable, permanent, and transgenerational distinctiveness* to the enslaved. Irrespective of ethnic differences, of religious, linguistic, or other cultural overlaps between those viewed as proprietors and those defined as chattel, and notwithstanding the fact that in many instances of the Atlantic system escape from chattel to "free" status was occasionally possible, African or Native American identity converged early on with slave status.

Those who were not European, not white, were presumptively permanently subjected, ineluctably distinguished from those who were "free" (or at most temporarily bonded): the possessors of European-derived identities. The emergence over time of substantial creolized, manumitted, and "miscegenated" populations, the long-run failure—notwithstanding genocidal attempts—to consign entire indigenous peoples to slavery, and the latter-day entrance into the Atlantic system of "other others" who were neither white, black, nor red (to employ a familiar "color" parlance somewhat anachronistically), did not fundamentally alter the deeply racialized social structure imposed by slavery. Europeans—soon enough seen as "whites"—were *persons*, presumptively free. If sometimes bound into servitude, whites were never contracted for life, much less hereditarily bound. Africans and Native Americans, with minor exceptions, were *chattel*: property, animal-like beings, semi-human at best, they were subject to white will and enjoyed few legal protections or rights (Cover 1975).

Resistance to slavery must be understood in this context. From very early on, it confronted a situation of thoroughgoing racialization. The entire complex of Atlantic enslavement was confronted by resistance, uneven and intermittent, but nevertheless substantial. Beginning in Africa with kidnapping, confinement, and forced marches; and then continuing in the middle passage, through "seasoning," sale (and resale), and superexploited labor, the Atlantic system was marked by coercion throughout. Although all slavery is coercive and thus entails resistance, in the great historical panoply of slavery there is no parallel to the racial chasm that Atlantic slavery opened between masters and subjects.

Where slavery was not racial it was generally less onerous. Heritability of slave status, for example, was far less enforceable where no fundamental, phenotypical distinction was made between master and chattel. As much literature documents, slaves in the ancient and southern worlds were often able to intermarry with "free" persons, even within the households of their masters. Sometimes they even rose to positions of considerable power, without shedding their formal situation of enslavement. While such situations were certainly far from the norm of slave oppression and debasement, what must be emphasized here is the uniqueness of Atlantic system racial slavery. It was modern slavery's widespread insistence on the phenotypical demarcation of the enslaved that generated these same enslaved persons' unswerving commitment to rebellion, escape, and indeed freedom.

Another key factor shaping both Atlantic slavery and resistance to it was the complex and contradictory role it assigned to ethnicity. As scholars have come to realize recently, and only with shameful slowness, enslaved Africans *lived in their ethnicity as much as anyone else.* Racial slavery generally worked to efface ethnicity (although there were some exceptions), but African resistance to slavery both sought to preserve ethnicity and to be sustained by it. Due to the innovative efforts of a transnational network of historians and social scientists who have reexamined and indeed reinvented scholarship on the African diaspora, we now have a wealth of studies on the history of the Atlantic slave system as seen "from below." Such work potentializes entirely new treatments of the role played by religion (notably Islam, but also Christianity and animism) in slave resistance (Diouf 1998). It sheds new light on the awareness possessed by slaves of continuities and changes in their African communities of origin.[7] It also highlights the political awareness slaves brought to resistance initiatives of various kinds (Thornton 1998).[8]

The Conquest of the Americas

When Europe came to America, it brought with it comprehensive, fundamental, permanent slavery: *racial* slavery. In the aftermath of Columbus's adventures, the enslavement of indigenous peoples grew precipitously in the Spanish Caribbean, Central American, and Andean regions. The Spanish demand for labor derived chiefly from operations of extraction and plunder: mining in the first place, but also lumbering and the beginnings of plantation agriculture. The early Spanish approach was to enslave all the natives who could be captured, putting to work those who were locally needed and transporting all others to locations where labor demand remained unfulfilled. In many areas, for example, Potosí (in present-day Bolivia—where mining operations were extensive), this meant working slaves (both local and "imported") to death (Cole 1985; Bakewell 1984). In the mainland Caribbean, enslavement meant forced marches to the coast and transport to island colonies where plantation agriculture (at first, largely cacao; sugar came later) was underway. Central Americans were also transported to the mines of Bolivia and Peru in great numbers. Upwards of 500,000 enslaved Native Americans were "exported" from Central America prior to 1550, "contributing to the rapid and severe depopulation" of the area (Bolland 1994). Epidemics of European-borne diseases like typhoid, smallpox, measles, and bubonic plague also surged through the region. "The native population of what is now Nicaragua and Honduras was reduced from more than a million before the conquest to 20,000 or 25,000 by mid-century, and possibly to less than 10,000 by the end of the century" (ibid., 13).

Early Indian resistance throughout the Americas largely took the form of flight. The reasons for this were many. The Spanish *conquistadores* (and in the hemisphere as a whole, Portuguese, British, French, etc. colonists as well) exhibited limitless brutality and callousness; disparities in weaponry were severe; death was omnipresent; and there was usually a nearby hinterland in which pursuit would be difficult.

The totality and brutality of European enslavement of native peoples was surely incomprehensible as well. This may account in part for the relative lack of early resistance and the preference for flight. According to various testimonies, slavery had existed in pre-Columbian times, a fact that the conquerors often emphasized to justify their own practices (Todorov 1984; Adorno 1992). But since pre-Columbian systems of rule were tributary and markets were largely barter-based, slavery before the *conquistadores* was largely of the bonded service or tributary captivity types. Thus indigenous people may have expected that conquest would result in some form of enslavement, but certainly not on so massive a scale as the European *conquista* entailed. Nor was there such a gulf, such a proto-racial chasm, between, say, *Mexica* and *Tlaxcala* societies as there was between *Castellano* and *Indio* ones. Even the greatest early colonial humanitarians, such as las Casas and Vieira, sought to temper their opposition to the enslavement of Native Americans by encouraging the enslavement of Africans instead.

The Onset of African Slavery

The burgeoning significance of the Atlantic slave trade in Africa from its inception in the fifteenth century, through its heyday—circa 1660–1830 (Thomas

1997; Vansina 1990; Rodney 1981a; Davidson 1961; Miller 1988)—meant that the slave-based economy and the duress imposed by slavery-based systems of rule came to dominate a huge proportion of the continent. Arab and European activity coexisted for several centuries—although Arabs predominated—in the East African slave trade, which traversed the Indian Ocean between East Africa and both the Arabian Peninsula and India, and contributed to the Atlantic system as well.

As in the Americas, a limited (by later standards) and "normal" (that is, tributary, quasi-feudal) slavery in the pre-fifteenth century period may have disposed the Africans to minimize the threat that the Atlantic slave complex would become to their societies. Certainly it minimized early resistance.

In the first attempts to capture slaves through direct raids, Europeans (principally the Portuguese in the fifteenth century) were repulsed by Congolese warriors both on the shore and in war canoes, and emissaries were even exchanged between the two courts (Thornton 1998). But soon enough there were *pombeiros* (slave merchants) moving inland, and as demand for slaves developed and trading grew—particularly in textiles and weapons—the capture of people for enslavement became the chief form of economic activity and the principal way force was exercised. Slaving and transport of slaves for export disrupted and subordinated preexisting forms of economic activity: cultivation, husbandry, mining and refining, trade. Regular caravans of armed raiders, and a spreading warfare whose objective was often the capture of people for sale as slaves, became the norm over time:

> The growth in European demand was met mostly by expanding the area affected by the European trade, not by extracting an ever greater number of slaves from the same region. . . . Persons were still first enslaved as prisoners of war or as pawns for debts, including court fines. But in practice, on the forward edge of the trading zone, kidnapping occurred and raids were started to capture slaves. Closer to the coast, existing legal processes were perverted to raise the supply of slaves. Defenseless people were condemned to slavery under the most trifling of pretexts, such as for breaking an imported dish. In many cases, death penalties were commuted to sale into slavery. (Vansina 1990, 207)

There is ample evidence of resistance to such practices in Africa, although only in the past few decades has the African phase of enslavement received the extensive historical study it deserves (Lovejoy 1983; Fisher 1970; Thornton 1998; Rodney 1981a; Manning 1990). Resistance of a spontaneous type certainly characterized these experiences. The general sequence of events involved in capture and enslavement was as follows: slave-raiding (often in consequence of war); capture (often after flight and attempts to escape the slavers, their agents, or the enemies who would trade with them); the ordeals of transport to the point of embarkation (extensive "death marches," frequent sale and resale, deprivation of every sort); followed by confinement in pens or "barracoons"[9] in the coastal cities (under conditions of filth, thirst, malnutrition, and disease rivaling any modern concentration camp—say, Nazi or gulag—equivalent). All this while still in Africa! The horrors of the middle passage (see below) and the auction block, to say nothing of the conditions of plantation life and labor in the Americas, were to follow.

Under such circumstances, resistance was frequent, although often futile. Tremendously high death rates and overwhelming despair were the "normal" state of affairs. But historical work on the slave trade suggests that escape attempts were constant, that maroon communities sprang up throughout the African "exporting" regions, not just in the Americas, and that often right on the outskirts of the entrepôts and ports (near Luanda and Lagos, for example, and in East Africa as well) as well as on the routes of the "way of death" from the interior to the coast, there was constant spontaneous rebellion and flight (Miller 1988, 385–386).[10]

Numerous African states dealt strategically with the intrusive and relentless European demand for slaves. Where there were strong states, accommodation was possible. Coming to some terms with European slavers, however, principally involved displacing the demand for human chattel onto other, more vulnerable peoples—in other words, becoming agents for the Europeans. The case of Dahomey (present-day Benin) is an instructive example. Confronted with the burgeoning slave trade, this West African kingdom increased its military capacity, and was able to avoid enslavement of its own people for several centuries. However, Dahomey "eventually became the classic raiding state of West Africa, after failing to get Europeans to accept any products other than human beings" (Rodney 1981a, 120; see also Law 1977; Manning 1982; Polanyi 1966; Herskovits 1966).

Adjustment to the market for human chattel became the crucial measure of many African states' success at surviving the early phases of European onslaught. While many sold their own people, many more used slave raiding and warfare as the means of acquiring human "produce" to trade. As a byproduct of the commitment to slave-raiding and slave-trading, local/African servitude increased as well. Those captives who were not sold into slavery across the Atlantic were relegated to a type of domestic serfdom. But as I have noted, bound labor within Africa was generally more benignly treated than transoceanic varieties, and generally not heritable.

Although slave-trading was primarily driven forward by economic forces, it was political and religious as well. Successful states regularly sold rebels and political opponents into slavery, for example, sometimes setting the stage for American revolts. A well-known example is that of the *Males*, the Muslim slaves who in 1835 staged a famous rebellion at Salvador da Bahia, then the principal city of Brazil. The central figures in this group were Hausas from the Sokoto Caliphate (roughly, present-day Sokoto and Kebbi states in Nigeria and parts of Niger as well); they had been enslaved as prisoners of war and veterans of an Islamic jihad in Central Africa, and subsequently sold as slaves to Brazil (Reis 1993; Lovejoy 1994; Diouf 1998).

Once aboard the slave ships, resistance sometimes led to mutinies, an occurrence much dreaded by owners and sailors. Numerous measures were taken to prevent shipboard uprisings: limiting access to the deck, training guns on shipboard slaves, frequent floggings, and so on. "Perhaps no more than one slave voyage in ten experienced an actual outbreak," notes Michael Craton, indicating how prevalent such rebellions were.

> But few voyages were ever completed without the discovery or threat of slave conspiracy, and no slaving captain throughout the history of the Atlantic trade ever sailed without a whole armory of guns and chains, plus as many white crewmen as he could recruit and keep alive to act as seaborne jailers. (Craton 1982c, 25; see also Greene 1944)

SABOTAGE AND SUBVERSION, ESCAPE AND *MARRONAGE*, REVOLT AND REVOLUTION

Sabotage and Subversion

Resistance to racial rule, to conquest, enslavement, and peonage, can be classified along a continuum encompassing many types of action: agency can be small or large, and acts of resistance can be performed by individuals or large groups. Resistance may be carefully planned and plotted, or unpremeditated and spontaneous. It may be the product of deep-seated identifications and solidarities among actors, or it may forge unanticipated alliances and antagonisms. The main points to be emphasized are first, the interaction among the many dimensions of resistance, small and large; second, the accretive dimensions of resistance practices;[11] and third, the inevitability of racially based depictions, racial categorizations, of acts of resistance in the context of the developing Atlantic system. Here I concentrate on the larger argument about the varieties of racial resistance.[12]

Racial logic and racial identity were central throughout the many and varied experiences of resistance to conquest and enslavement. Although the racial divide did not guarantee racial solidarity,[13] the rapidly consolidated color-line did provide a very effective practical guidepost for assessing loyalties and affording (or withholding) trust. Just as the whites had resorted to racialized structures in mounting the massive projects of conquest and enslavement, so too did natives and blacks learn to operate within the confines of the color-line in developing strategies of resistance to these social structures.[14]

Resistance practices were largely continuous. Racial solidarity served as a precondition for many types of resistance: from petty and quotidian acts of "foot-dragging," theft, and sabotage, to daring and even occasionally world-historical acts of revolt and revolution. Acts of resistance—individual disobedience, subversion, or escape on one side of the spectrum, to organized uprisings, the creation of fugitive communities, or revolution of national or even transnational scope—overlapped in many respects. In all these initiatives there was a shared purpose, a desire that informed and guided the pursuit of freedom. This was the *racial unity* that generally overrode the myriad differences—ethnic, political, status-based, and so on—among the occupied and enslaved.

Based on this unity the experience of uprising could evoke solidarity across many thousands of miles: consider the case of the Haitian revolution in this regard. When a colony of exploited slaves successfully liberated itself through a sanguinary and prolonged struggle (1791–1804), overcoming repeated invasions and attempts to reinstitute slavery, this was not only a unique case in history, but an inspiration to African peoples throughout the Americas.[15]

Africans in the Americas developed complex repertoires of resistance and subversion. Scholars of African resistance have sometimes seen it as a form of *racialized class struggle.* For example, much resistance consisted in simple efforts to recapture *time* from the slaveowner's control (Hanchard 1999). By seeking to expand the limited amount of "non-working" (certainly not "free") time available to them, enslaved Africans fought for a limited but real autonomy. This type of conflict resembled the early industrial struggles over the length of the working day analyzed by Marx as central to working class formation. The endeavor to create or expand "free" time was but one of many labor struggles: refusing to exert oneself any more than required in a labor process from which "alienation" was total; stealing food and other valuable items from their owners (a way to "get paid" as well as enlarge one's prospects for survival), were other means of resistance. These efforts to operate as laboring subjects, not as docile objects of the lash, continued even after formal emancipation had been achieved, as new forms of exploitation based on peonage and debt servitude supplanted slavery (Jaynes 1986). But even under conditions of slavery, as George Rawick suggests, slaves engaged in frequent "strikes" and other forms of labor slowdowns (Rawick 1972a, 105–107). The "general strike" of the Civil War is of course the most crucial instance of this (Du Bois 1977 [1935], 55–83).

Other forms of resistance are best understood as *gender-based, familial,* and *religious.* Vast literatures have appeared in respect to all three dimensions (but once again, all too recently). Here I can merely enumerate some of these themes. Early racial conflicts concerned such matters as the validity of the spiritual rights of the subordinated; control over the body and sex; and the meaning of practical concepts of time, property, and physical mobility.

A great deal of confusion was exhibited by early colonialists and slavers with respect to the status of their subjects' souls and potential salvation. Many early struggles on the part of the subordinated involved perceived imperatives to preserve their religious and cultural traditions. Practices of concubinage and "breeding" were ubiquitous in slavocratic systems of all sorts. Elaborate legal and regulatory apparatuses were instituted for the surveillance of slaves and (necessarily) of the "social relations of race": the development of pass systems; of organized responses to slave escapes and to the presence of maroons; the recuitment of armed corps dedicated to slave patrolling; the regulation and control of slave-based subsistence activities; the elaboration of conventions for the punishment and manumission, the registration, enumeration, and heritability of slaves. All these and many more "superstructural" systems underwent specification in slavery-based societies throughout the Americas, resulting in the creation of *codes noires* and fugitive slave laws, among many others.

From the earliest moments of the Atlantic encounter the *gendered* character of conquest and enslavement is abundantly evident: the rapes and habitual concubinage that accompany both the advent of Europe in America and the establishment of African slavery are but the most familiar manifestations.[16] During later periods the interaction between ownership of slaves and the residual chattel status of women (Stanley 1998; Ware 1992; Pateman 1998) certainly served as a prompt for abolitionism, which mobilized women in the nineteenth century to an unprecedented degree (Goodman 1998; Midgley 1992), and which became in turn a formidable foundation for feminism. Familial issues combine gender-based and political-economic dimensions of rule and resistance in frequently racialized ways (Malone 1992; King 1995). Looking at U.S. slavery, for example, we find a very wide range of contemporary feminist struggles prefigured by black women's activities. Resistance to rape and refusal of concubinage, insistence on marital rights, defense of children (and themselves) from physical abuse, and struggles over the conditions of work, were but some of the major themes of black women's grievances and action.[17]

The *religious dimensions* of resistance, both African and Native American, are also manifold. A substantial body of scholarly work (Stuckey 1987; Bastide 1978 [1960]; Henry 1990, 60–75; Thompson 1983; Barnes 1997; Mills 1997; Leon-Portilla 1992) explores how religious orientations shaped the complex interactions between Europeans and both native peoples and enslaved Africans. Since the priority interests of invaders and slavers were generally quite predatory, their religious orientations most frequently devolved to the supercilious, the projective, or at best the paternalistic. Before the rise of abolitionism it was only very occasionally that from the ranks of the conquerors and enslavers there emerged a person whose religious commitments impelled a disavowal of slavery. In such cases it was not only the despoliation of the human body and the apparent triumph of human greed that aroused denunciatory ire; rather it was the predatory effects of slavery upon the human spirit, upon the souls of both captives and conquerors, that provoked outrage even from within the ruling ranks. But such religious opposition was rare and for the most part ineffective until the dawning of the abolitionist movement at the turn of the nineteenth century.

For natives and captives, whose efforts merely to comprehend, much less to survive or resist the seizure of their bodies and lands (plus their impending or already well-established exploitation), would have required herculean mental feats, the invocation of religious interpretations and solutions to the dilemmas of slavery and conquest, the reliance on religious resources for resistance, was obviously ubiquitous. No mere syncretism, but a channeling of fundamental spiritual substance, was involved.[18]

Violence was a recurrent form of slave resistance. Native peoples mounted military resistance wherever possible.[19] Slaves fought back against the overseers and "pattyrollers" in numerous ways: from tripping their horses with ropes tied across the roads to confronting them in individual and group battles.[20] Arson, self-defense, and premeditated murder are all documented in the records and narratives that have been preserved throughout the Americas from slavery times.[21]

Escape and Marronage

Escape was a constant, but took many forms depending on the regime of white control, the motivation of the fugitives, and the presence or absence of safe havens. Under more ferocious systems of surveillance and punishment, flight and capture could result in mutilation, torture, and execution. Yet *marronage* is an ongoing and universal feature of slave systems in the Americas (and, as noted, within African slaving systems as well). Communities of escaped slaves appeared in the sixteenth century at the latest, and sometimes resulted in long-lasting free rebel quasi-nations: self-sufficient, armed, and on occasion approaching sovereign status. Jamaica (Patterson 1970), Brazil, and Surinam are the most extensively researched locations of maroon communities, but they are known to have existed everywhere that African slavery was practiced: Ecuador and Colombia (Whitten 1974), Mexico (Carroll 1991), the entire Caribbean—both the islands and the mainland—and the northern colonies and later the independent United States, were all sites for *marronage*. Some maroon communities were never defeated: as the Prices have documented most extensively in respect to Surinam, the upland Saramaka maroons were never subdued by the Dutch, developed "miscegenated" ties with local indigenous groups, and were able to negotiate various treaties with the Europeans who ran slave plantations in the coastal lowlands (Price 1983; Price 1990).[22] In other cases, maroon communities maintained a tense modus vivendi with lowland slave regimes. Here I can only comment on a few instances of this complex and varied set of resistance practices.

Maroon communities (*quilombos*) were widespread throughout Portuguese Brazil (and independent pre-1888 Brazil), existing not only in the Northeast, which was the prime slave plantation/sugar zone, but also extending into the various *sertoes* (backland regions) that abutted other, later, regions of slave exploitation: in Minas Gerais, for example, where the Brazilian gold boom of the eighteenth century occurred,[23] and even in the more developed parts of the southeast, site of the *carezais* (coffee plantations) that first flourished in the nineteenth century.

Many black communities scattered throughout rural Brazil, especially in the Northeast, trace their origins back to *quilombos*, and contemporary efforts to conduct archeological research, as well as to organize black movement pilgrimages to these places, proceed apace.[24] As a final note on Brazilian *quilombismo*: the contemporary black nationalist current in the anti-racist movement in Brazil, whose long-established intellectual leader is the poet, playwright, activist, and sometime senator Abdias do Nascimento, assigns that name ("*Quilombismo*") to its political philosophy, taking its inspiration from the Palmares *quilombo* of the seventeenth century, which withstood four military assaults before finally succumbing to a Portuguese expeditionary force in 1695.[25]

Nor was the North American mainland immune from *marronage*. Although largely lacking a highly mountainous region like Jamaica, or a relatively inaccessible upland or jungle zone like Surinam or Brazil, the principal plantation area, the U.S. Southeast, did possess numerous swamplands, plus a semi-impenetrable peripheral area in Florida, which was also home to an unsubdued Indian nation, the Seminole. Throughout the eighteenth century (when Florida was still a Spanish-controlled territory), and to some extent after it was annexed to the United States, enslaved Africans escaped to Florida, formed maroon communities, and mixed ("miscegenated") with the Indians. As late as the mid-nineteenth century a group of maroons joined with a force of Seminoles under the leadership of the Seminole chief John Horse in a "long march" from Florida to northern Mexico in an effort to escape from slavery. Successfully reaching Mexico, they later provided military service to both the Mexican and U.S. military.[26]

And what was the "underground railroad" but an apparatus in service to *marronage*, a means to assist escaping slaves both to "get away" and to "settle down" safely somewhere, in the northern states or in Canada? Organized chiefly by free blacks (helped in abolition times by anti-slavery whites, notably Quakers and Methodists), the "railroad" carried human cargo that not only "stole itself" (that is, slaves who escaped on their own), but that also "stole others" (or was liberated), from time to time, for example, by armed guerrillas like Harriet Tubman. But like other maroons, once away, once "settled down," these maroons were not truly free, since the U.S. Congress authorized their capture and reenslavement in the fugitive slave laws, attempting to override the abolition of slavery in northern states by federal intervention on behalf of the slave states.[27] Thus in 1851 at Christiana, Pennsylvania (in a "free" state), a group of "settled down" escaped slaves led by William Parker confronted an armed group of southern slave catchers in the employ of Edward Gorsuch, who had come from Maryland to recapture his escaped slave Samuel Thompson under the terms of the Fugitive Slave Act. In an exemplary armed confrontation, a group of free blacks (that is, maroons) defeated the slave-raiders. Frederick Douglass wrote of the Christiana battle and other similar confrontations:

> [T]he thing which more than all else destroyed the fugitive slave law was the resistance made to it by the fugitives themselves. A decided check was given to the execution of the law at Christiana, Pennsylvania. . . . This inflicted fatal wounds on the fugitive slave bill. It became thereafter almost a dead letter, for slaveholders found that not only did it fail to put them in possession of their slaves, but that the attempt to enforce it brought down odium upon themselves and weakened the slave system. (Forbes 1998)

Revolt and Revolution

Revolt, like *marronage* with which it is deeply interconnected, was a feature of the entire system of conquest and slavery. From the earliest moments after the arrival of the Europeans at the turn of the sixteenth century until the achievement of emancipation at the end of the nineteenth century (and even after this in some cases), enslaved Africans and indigenous people who faced enslavement, removal, and confinement in many combinations, staged armed revolts.

The number of these uprisings grew steadily with the scale of European incursion, the intensity of the slave trade, and an ever-increasing awareness on the part of the oppressed regarding the scale and stakes of the enterprise in which they were immured. The Arawaks and Caribs who in the fifteenth century first witnessed the appearance of Columbus's sails, or the Akan and Asante who fifty years before had first beheld the arrival of the Portuguese at the Bight of Benin, were understandably unaware of what these events portended. But the same cannot be said of Indians throughout the Americas who by a century later had begun to experience the seizure of their lands, the slaughter and enslavement of much of their peoples, and the ravages of diseases that in some cases wiped out 90 percent of their populations. The same cannot be said of Africans who a century later were undergoing the march to the Atlantic coast, the middle passage, and the auction block.

From the first outbreaks of armed revolt of which we have records—perhaps the rebellion against Columbus's nephew Diego in 1522 Hispaniola (Segal 1995, 89)—to the Saint Domingue revolution of 1791–1804 and the Jamaican war of emancipation in the 1830s, there was a steady augmentation, an escalation of resistance. By the nineteenth century a few slave revolts had attained the status of full-fledged revolutions. These conflicts were marked by fervent calls for liberation from agitators and rebel leaders (Walker 2000 [1829]), widespread destruction and enormous brutality, complex international alliances and expeditionary interventions, and tallies of casualties that rivaled any "ordinary" war of the time.

Yet considerably earlier, for example in the seventeenth-century Palmares *quilombo* I have already discussed, many revolutionary elements were already present. The whole social organization of the *Palmarinhos* suggests the pattern of "war of maneuver." From its beginnings as a refuge for runaway slaves located deep in the remote and heavily forested Bahia/Pernambuco *sertao*, Palmares is generally agreed to have evolved into a kingdom of Congolese/Angolan structure.

Can Palmares be properly understood simply to have undertaken a life in collective exile? Hardly. Although its longevity attests to its degree of mobilization and self-sufficiency,[28] Palmares was also an insurgent entity, a little "Yenan" or "Sierra Maestra," so to speak. The *Palmarinhos* steadily sought new adherents through armed incursions against colonial plantations on the edges of the Reconcavo, the sugar-cultivation/plantation zone in the Brazilian Northeast. Some enslaved blacks, eager to escape, they immediately recruited. Others they kidnapped and removed to Palmares against their will, only granting these reluctant recruits their freedom if they engaged in military service. In this fashion the ranks of the maroon community, the kingdom, the insurgency, grew to include tens of thousands.[29]

Thus Palmares was from its beginnings around 1612 until its downfall in 1695 a proto-revolutionary entity. As noted, it was in a perpetual state of war with the colonial and slavocratic powers that surrounded it. It represented a threat to these same powers, which could hardly expect to maintain their slave-based system of cultivation in the nearby Reconcavo with a "liberated zone," an explicitly African sociopolitical entity, on their doorstep. Both the Portuguese and the Dutch (who competed in this part of Brazil with the Portuguese during the seventeenth century) mounted numerous expeditions against the *quilombo*. All were repelled until in 1695, by a combination of force and treachery, Palmares was finally subdued.

The nineteenth-century age of revolution is usually understood as the period in which absolutism definitively passed away from the historical stage, to be replaced by bourgeois and at least tendentially democratic regimes (Markoff 1996). Only a few radical accounts have suggested that race played a central role in shaping the age of revolution. That, however, is precisely what I argue here.

Beginning with the American and French Revolutions, and then moving through the Haitian revolution and the extended period of decolonization of the Americas, the problem of slavery and the prospect of abolition repeatedly played a role in shaping the destiny of the Atlantic complex, the world center of gravity in this era. Toward the end of this period, too, the "closing" of the world's frontier was taking place, not only in the American hinterlands of the U.S. West or the Amazonian jungles, but also in the "scramble for Africa" (Lewis 1987). Areas in which there had been long-standing colonial domination—founded in large part on slavery—sought independence, as "creolized" elites chafed under restrictive trade rules and overbearing administration from mother-countries they saw as increasingly remote. As these struggles sharpened, the popular classes as well as the excluded slaves and natives grew restive, and attempted to leverage both elite rulers and elite insurgents, who needed them not only to labor, but also to bear arms. While all this was occurring, reform movements, notably democratization and abolitionism, were on the rise in Europe and the newly independent American countries as well.

All these tendencies interacted, unevenly and episodically, from empire to empire and nation to nation. To inventory such processes, much less to analyze them in detail, would obviously be a very different project than the present one. Indeed, even to catalogue the huge number of slave revolts that furnished but one element of the race-related social transformations with which we are directly concerned, would be well beyond the scope of this chapter.[30] Instead, I consider the role of race in some of the early anti-colonial revolutions that created the independent nations of the Americas, and thus played a crucial part in the invention of the modern world.

The North American Revolution of 1776–81 has been seen as the debut of a revolutionary age, of the democratic transition that occupied the "long" nineteenth century (Palmer 1959; Morgan 1988; Hobsbawm 1962; Moore 1966). While I cannot engage this large subject here, I take note of the substantial racial dimension that characterized this "age" in all sorts of complex and contradictory ways, operating not only in North America, but throughout the entire hemisphere.

When the British colonies in North America sought their national independence, their demands (and the protracted warfare needed to realize them) already had significant racial implications.[31] The language of the Declaration of Independence, as is well known, derived from Enlightenment doctrines of natural rights. It asserted universal and unalienable rights to human freedom, to consensual government, and even to revolution should those rights be denied. Reconciliation between these lofty principles and the presence in the proposed "United States" of both chattel slavery and settlement by conquest was deeply problematic. These two practices, or rather social structures, were fundamental to the very existence of the new nation, as much as they had been to the colonies. The country's material well-being, indeed the greater proportion of its trade and economy, were intimately bound up with slavery. And the United States was primordially a settler state, occupying in its entirety territory taken by force from subject peoples. Thus at their most foundational level, the principles legitimating the American Revolution were gainsaid where non-Europeans were concerned.

This contradiction was impossible to hide; it was well-known and widely acknowledged both doctrinally and in practice. As they had in colonial days, so too in the early days of the Republic, American leaders sometimes urged the complete destruction—the genocide—of native peoples, describing them as "wild beasts" and rationalizing their wholesale slaughter and expulsion by both religious and philosophical argument (Drinnon 1980; Takaki 1993; Rogin 1975). Racial matters appeared in the Declaration, which contained a brief diatribe against "merciless Indian savages," and in draft form had equated colonial rule with slavery. In the Constitution as well, although the drafters found it impossible to commit to paper the words *slave* or *slave trade*, they managed to incorporate race: through various euphemisms and compromises the document integrated and regulated the practices of enslavement and trafficking in human chattel within the system of law. The Constitution also strictly distinguished Indians from whites, although almost no sovereignty was formally conceded to native peoples.[32]

Race was constitutive of the new nation in practice as well. In innumerable social conflicts, political decisions, and court cases, black freedom and slavery, as well as citizenship rights and enfranchisement, became issues after the Revolution.[33] These disputes and unresolved questions were already ambiguous and contradictory during the revolutionary period. For example: although in large measure they were disenfranchised and excluded from the developing Republic, blacks and Indians also participated in the Revolution, sometimes receiving freedom or land grants in return. Thus the same period that gave rise to the Revolution also laid the groundwork for abolitionism. Although ratifying slavery, the new Republic did not do this unequivocally. Various northern states were taking steps toward abolition shortly after the Revolution. In a pattern to be repeated throughout the Americas, many states allowed blacks, including escaped slaves, to fight in their regiments during the war, granting them freedom in return for military service.[34] British units also mobilized and freed slaves in return for armed service (Foner 1975, 292–344), and the British evacuated some loyal manumitted slaves and free persons of color to Nova Scotia. This group later furnished participants in the repatriation project that created Sierra Leone.

Racial dynamics were also crucial in shaping the new nation's relations with the indigenous population, the Indian nations, of North America. The Revolution was in important respects an anti-Indian war and the Constitution explicitly excluded native peoples from citizenship. Although this is much debated, the writers of the Constitution may have drawn on the federalism of an Indian nation, the Iroquois, in planning the new North American polity. The politics and policy of subjugation of the indigenous peoples of North America ("Indian removal," etc.), laid the foundations for the imperial elements in the development of the United States as a nation-state, elements that were to become central to U.S. national identity as the country achieved great-power, and then hegemonic status (Mintz 1999; Rogin 1975). Thus the early linkage between race and empire in the North American context.

The revolutionary event that most directly challenged the Atlantic slave system was unquestionably the Haitian revolution of 1791–1804.[35] This was an independence struggle of unparalleled importance, not only for that country but for the hemisphere and the emerging world system. Only in Haiti was a black-led revolution successful. Only there did independence and abolition coincide. Only there did black insurgency intersect fully with the dawning revolutionary ideal of popular rule.

The Haitian revolution not only created the second American post-colonial state and first free black nation in the world; it also heralded Latin American and Caribbean independence; and it prefigured the revolutionary anti-colonial upsurges of the twentieth century. News of the revolution inspired opposition to slavery everywhere in the hemisphere, and greatly fueled the abolitionist movement as well.[36] Haiti thus had truly diasporic consequences, prefiguring and inspiring the pan-Africanist and national liberation movements of the twentieth century.

The revolution was largely unanticipated and almost unimaginable (at least to the whites and slaveowners) before its outbreak. Indeed, even after it was an accomplished fact, after slavery had been abolished, independence declared, and the country renamed, the realities of the revolution continued to be denied (Trouillot 1995). Of course, social upheavals are difficult to predict; revolution is often so shattering to established systems of rule that it sparks fear and defensiveness, reactionary intervention, and furious denial as a matter of course.[37] All these phenomena occurred during and after the Haitian events.

The Saint Domingue revolution destroyed slavocracy, instituted Haitian national independence, seriously wounded French imperialism, and inspired the entire African diaspora. It also struck fear into the hearts of slaveholders throughout the Atlantic system. Haiti was the crown jewel in the French Empire, so the revolution there tore away the most lucrative sugar-producing colony in the Americas and the world. Before its outbreak, Haiti had been the source of about one-third of the world's sugar production (Klein 1986, 90). Its independence meant significant disruption in the world's largest commodity market, but also gave a noticeable boost to the competitive positions of other colonial sugar suppliers such as Brazil, Cuba, and Jamaica. The revolution entailed hundreds of thousands of casualties, not only among Haitian combatants but also among French, British, Spanish, and even Polish expeditionary forces who fought in its bloody battles and were struck by disease (particularly yellow fever) while in Saint Domingue. There was also mass slaughter among the general population, groups of which were targeted along racial lines for general butchery at various points.[38]

The Haitian revolution must be interpreted as the result of an extremely unique constellation of determinations. Slave uprisings in Haiti had occurred in 1691, 1697, and 1757 before the final war of independence commenced in the 1790s. But there was nothing so special about that; as we have noted, slave revolts were ubiquitous throughout the American colonies. What was singular about Saint Domingue was the conjuncture, the overdetermined quality of the situation there on the eve of the revolution's outbreak. The revolutionary factors operating in Haiti began with the revolution occurring in the mother-country, the metropole, an uprising imbued with an emancipatory rhetoric and a ruptural ferocity far outstripping its immediate North American precedent. The French events deeply problematized the exploitative and thoroughgoing unfreedom of the slavocratic colony. To this must be added the anti-colonial and anti-slavery dimensions of the Haitian struggle. Although these were not fully comprehended, even in the revolutionary France of the Directory, they tended to radicalize the upsurge in the mother-country as well.[39]

Then there was the significant African connection—a Congolese one—to the revolution: the uprising, therefore, was not merely an offshoot of the French events but an accomplishment of skilled African insurgents as well.[40] There were the deep social divisions cutting across Saint Domingue. The Haitian forces were split among whites, blacks, and mulattoes; and among white slaveowners (French and creole), *gens de couleur* (free people of color, sometimes slaveholders themselves) and blacks, both creolized (i.e., native-born in Saint Domingue) and African (i.e., captured in Africa—most likely in Congo— and "imported" to Haiti). Divisions among both revolutionary and reactionary forces made for a pattern of exceptional fluidity, frequently shifting alliances, and frequent betrayal and perfidiousness.

The ebbing of the French Revolution into the Bonapartist period (the "Napoleonic restoration") further complicated this picture. Napoleon had imperial ambitions in the Americas, was fervently anti-black/racist, and sought to restore slavery in Haiti after its partial abolition by Sonthonax and complete eradication by L'Ouverture.

Mention of Napoleon brings to mind the important international context of the Haitian upheavals. Many powers outside Saint Domingue, and outside the French orbit, perceived their interests to be riding on the outcome of of the Haitian struggle. These included the other main Caribbean slavocratic powers, Britain and Spain, as well as the United States.

The Haitian revolution was possible because this set of cleavages and conflicts aligned in what Althusser would have called a "ruptural unity."[41] Its success stemmed most centrally from two factors in this pattern: the implacable demand of the *noirs* for the eradication of slavery, and the formidable disunion of the slaveowners and colonial powers. It is generally recognized that the Haitian process presaged the breakup of the Atlantic slave complex, inspired black resistance throughout the hemisphere and even beyond (Scott 1986), and gave new strength to nascent abolitionism. Less often understood is that Haiti helped initiate the Latin America anti-colonialism that would soon engulf most of the hemisphere.[42]

Throughout the Americas, revolutionary independence movements, influenced to varying degrees by the U.S. and French Revolutions as well as the Haitian one, abolished (or at least mitigated) racial slavery as an element of their anti-colonial struggles. In 1816 in Venezuela, for example, "Simón Bolívar appealed to Venezuela *pardos*, blacks, and zambos to join his cause. . . . Similarly, he appealed to slaves to join him by promising them freedom in return for their support" (Wright 1990, 27). Bolívar was not an anti-racist; although himself of mixed-raced descent, he was a member of the creole landed elite. Throughout Latin America in the nineteenth century, insurgent *criollos* sought independence from the colonial rule of the *peninsulares* (that is, Spanish administrators and legatees). Like many of his status, Bolívar was quite nervous about abolitionism.[43] Although he recognized the mixed-race and *mestizo* qualities of the Venezuelan population, he also expressed the typical fears of many creole landowners that, once emancipated, blacks would wreak revenge. They might, he said, establish a "pardocracy." Or perhaps, he said, "we shall have more and more of Africa" (Wright 1990, 28). Nevertheless, the creole revolt in which the independence movement was grounded, and the need for insurgent troops, forced him first toward manumission of black slaves, and later toward greater emancipation, not only in the territory that would become Venezuela but throughout the *Gran Colombia* he dreamed of but could not create.[44]

Parallel accounts can be offered for many Latin American countries. In almost every case, anti-colonial insurgencies were led by creole elites and drew upon a mass base composed of *mestizos* and blacks, some *libertos* and many slaves recruited with promises of freedom (Lynch 1986; Domínguez 1980). Although there were some parallels with the North American revolution, these consisted mainly in the political and class alignments of the independence movements. Lacking a significant democratic ideology, the anti-Spanish insurgencies relied on *caudillismo* for leadership, and impoverished peasants and black slaves for adherents and fighters. Slavery was generally weakened by independence, but not abolished immediately. In countries where black populations were particularly high—notably Cuba and Brazil—abolition was considerably retarded, above all by racial unity among the elite. A crude formula here would suggest that where the split between *criollos* and *peninsulares* could be avoided, emancipation was delayed. And the single most important factor in forestalling this division was anti-black racial unity.[45]

ABOLITIONISM

Although there was always resistance to slavery, most of it came from slaves themselves and from "free persons of color" who were united with the enslaved by ties of race. Precious little political or philosophical opposition to slavery existed during the long period from the fifteenth through the eighteenth centuries, while the Atlantic slave complex came into being and developed as the motor of the modern world. In the few cases when audible criticisms of slavery were made during this extended period, they were usually posed by religious figures, such as las Casas and Vieira early on,[46] and by Quakers and Methodists in the eighteenth and nineteenth centuries. Such preliminary expressions of what was to become abolitionism, of what would be a powerful international movement in the nineteenth century, were at first easily countered, ignored, or at most given merely symbolic approval. Only in the late eighteenth century did this situation began to change.

The United States

Early abolitionism was largely a U.S. phenomenon. There, as I have noted, deep contradictions emerged between Enlightenment doctrines of natural rights, embodied in the core principles of the Revolution, on the one hand; and a pressing, indeed still growing, demand for coercible African labor, on the other. It was this labor upon whose "bent and broken backs" (Du Bois 1977 [1935], 15) rested the profit and prosperity, first of the colonies, and then of the independent United States. Not just the profits of the planters depended upon slavery, but those of craftspersons and nascent manufacturers as well; in short, the fates of the whole lot of colonial and then "free" (i.e., white) people, indeed the well-being of all the settlers in this "brave new world," were tied to the slave system.

The sources of North American abolitionism may be found here. The contradiction between slavery and freedom was a systemic problem. It proceeded from the ever-more manifest connections between individual economic activity and the growing world system of trade, of capitalism. It emerged from the political vision of the American Revolution, which challenged the regnant absolutism of the Old World and the British Empire (Davis 1975).

For a century or more—at least since the elaboration of the "slave codes" in colonial Virginia and elsewhere in the South in the later seventeenth century—*the only way to reconcile slavery with freedom had been through race.* The formulation of a system of racial classification, and the divulgation—throughout civil society and the system of law—of racial regulations that extended those classifications into every imaginable human relationship, had been the first American attempt to manage the contradictions of freedom and slavery. In the law of property, contract, and family; in criminal law; in the organization of the franchise and imposition of taxes; a racially based system of regulation and control was elaborated and refined from the seventeenth century on (Morgan 1995; Cover 1975).

Racial classification justified a seemingly comprehensive "exceptionalism" from Enlightenment doctrines of natural rights, rationality, and freedom. The American colonies had been founded in the age of absolutism; thus the Enlightenment-based doctrine of natural rights, and indeed any doctrine save that of divine right, had been of little concern. But with the Enlightenment's advance, with the advent of early mercantile capitalism, with the beginnings of slavery and mass labor, and with the appearance of popular rebellion in late-seventeenth-century Virginia, the colonial elites recognized the need for social and political regulation. The slave codes were created over some decades in response to the organizational pressures imposed by the foundation and growth of new settler societies.

By the revolutionary era a century later, cracks were appearing in the facade of racial regulation. Most centrally, the irreconcilable struggle between slavery and freedom arose from the presence of black people themselves. As the Republic was being founded, black folk in North America were already becoming active and articulate advocates for their freedom, not only demanding an end to slavery, but also seeking equality. Symptoms of the crisis of racial rule proliferated. In one indicative incident of 1787, for example, "free blacks" praying in St. George's Methodist Episcopal Church in Philadelphia "were pulled from their knees . . . and told to go to the seats designated for black folks." The unwillingness of these African Americans to accept segregation within their church led to their withdrawal and the founding of the first black Christian churches in the 1790s:

> We see similar incidents repeated throughout the major cities in the Northeast and along the Atlantic seaboard. As whites refused to share authority with their black members and continued to subject them to various forms of public humiliations (i.e., refusing to christen black babies, serving blacks communion only after all whites were served, and denying blacks access to church burial grounds), many African Americans sought to create institutions where they could worship and fellowship without the burden of white Christian racism. (Glaude 2000, 42–43)

This was not only religiously based resistance, but an early manifestation of African American nationalism (Moses 1996).

As the nineteenth century dawned, abolitionist currents grew in the U.S. northern states, often taking a religiously inflected form. Among free blacks they resonated very strongly; among whites they found their adherents largely in the more egalitarian Protestant sects.[47]

Abolitionism appeared early in the United States, above all, because tendencies toward religious dissent, self-government, and proto-capitalism, and the relative weakness of imperial (in other words: absolutist) authority all combined with a substantial presence of "free persons of color." This community of black folk, largely located in the North where slavery was weaker and the plantation system almost nonexistent, had not ruptured its ties to its enslaved brothers and sisters. Far from it: much of the "free black" community had known slavery. North American blacks who had escaped the toils of slavery— by whatever means—were far less likely to own slaves themselves, far less likely to identify with whites, than, say, the *gens de couleur* in Haiti or *mulato* and "free black" communities elsewhere. Why was this? Because the color-line was different in North America than in much of the rest of the hemisphere, particularly the "Latin" slave societies;[48] because the northern states had become a relatively "free" area by the end of the eighteenth century, when abolitionism was truly beginning; because escape from slavery in North America posed alternatives to a rural maroon existence, which was all that escape in the islands or the less developed Latin American slavocracies could offer; and finally because in the late eighteenth century North America underwent an anti-colonial revolution that offered something more than the rhetoric, if also something less than the reality, of democracy and equality. For all these reasons, then, there was more black unity—between the enslaved and the "free"—in the early United States than elsewhere. For all these reasons too, black commitment to abolitionism would be greater and occur sooner in the United States.

As U.S. abolitionism advanced in the nineteenth century, so too did slavery. The pace and direction of slave-trading as its days grew numbered has been the source of much discussion and debate (as is much of the demographic data on the trade),[49] but for the present I simply note that the increasing deployment of U.S.-based slaves in cotton production, and the rising demand for cotton as industrialization took hold in both England and the United States, was one of the main causes for the rapid increase in the U.S. slave population during the first half of the nineteenth century. Although England (in 1807) and the United States (in 1808) enacted prohibitions on the international slave trade, and although both countries sent naval squadrons over the Atlantic to enforce these bans, these measures only somewhat impeded the trade during this period. Extensive operations continued, by the Portuguese and Spanish, as well as those of a wide variety of clandestine traders, or more properly, smugglers and pirates. Indeed slaving may have been rendered more profitable by price rises that resulted from the British and American interdictions, however ineffectual. Previously less voluminous sending areas, such as Portuguese Mozambique, now increased their exports. Meanwhile the constant influx of Africans into the Americas served to preserve ethnic ties between the two continents, as well as to reinforce abolitionist sentiments, particularly among slaves.

As U.S. abolitionism grew in the early decades of the nineteenth century, the reaction of slavery's defenders stepped up as well. Making the case for slavery in the U.S. context involved adducing a familiar set of arguments: the "backwardness" and "degeneracy" of Africans was asserted once more in the attempt to "whitewash" the institution of slavery itself, whose supposed paternalism was also defended. To claim the superiority of slavery, as against the inhumanity of the wage system, was to make a distinctive sectional argument, as well as to join hands in a peculiar fashion with some of the early socialists of the day.[50]

Although U.S. abolitionism was in many ways a black-initiated and black-led movement, the eventual adherence of thousands of whites to the abolitionist cause cannot be attributed to black leadership, for racism was endemic in the late eighteenth and early nineteenth centuries. The crucial black role was catalytic: it was to make the nation aware of the injustice and horrors of slavery. It was especially to challenge the farce of colonization and to advocate the "immediatist" position (Goodman 1998). Abolitionism broadened its appeal to whites by drawing on religious bases, finding skilled agitators and publicists like William Lloyd Garrison and Wendell Phillips among many others, and carrying forward the radicalism that was a crucial legacy of the Revolution.

Yet like the Revolution as well, abolitionism in the United States was a contradictory phenomenon. It was in part a movement for *equality*; yet it was also embraced by industrializing capital. That it attracted few workers is partially attributable to its equation of freedom with wage labor; more of its adherents were motivated by religious fervor and moral outrage. In contrast to England, where abolitionism had a real working-class base, in the United States most workers were at best uncommitted to the cause, and many opposed it.[51]

In fact, as a wealth of literature shows (Du Bois 1977 [1935], 17–31) white workers greatly feared not only black competition—which they saw as the inevitable consequence of emancipation—but also resisted any equation between their activities and those of slaves or "servants." This "*herrenvolk* republicanism," as David Roediger and Alexander Saxton have labeled it (Roediger 1991; Saxton 1990), expressed itself in anti-abolitionism and racism. It also took the form of white support for African colonization schemes. This was a "moderate" defense of slavery that in some ways anticipated the white liberalism and neo-conservatism of the post–World War II United States. Inspired by the British experiment in Sierra Leone, American proponents of African repatriation sought by adopting such proposals (the most notable of which was the Liberian project) to deflect or co-opt abolitionism's egalitarian orientation onto the *herrenvolk* republican path (Goodman 1998, 11–22). Although these repatriation schemes (or more properly, expulsion schemes) did garner a modicum of black support, blacks by and large rejected them as diversions from the fundamental goals of U.S. abolitionism. Only by hewing fiercely to the project Goodman calls "immediatism"—the demand for immediate and total abolition—were black abolitionists able to exert so significant an influence over the movement (Goodman 1998). Frederick Douglass's role was most notable here.

Because abolitionism, at least in its immediatist and radical currents, was a deeply egalitarian movement, it necessarily brought women's grievances to the fore. The equation of slavery with "the bonds of womanhood" drew many women into abolitionist activism, and planted the seeds of American feminism (Yellin and van Horne 1994; Berg 1978). Such "founding mothers" as Lucretia Mott and Lydia Maria Child, among many others, drew much of their political orientation from the movement (Karcher 1994).

In this respect abolitionism's legacy in the United States was more than its contribution to the anti-slavery cause, central though that was. Because it was an interracial egalitarian movement, it served as the origin of U.S. radicalism. The abolitionist heritage highlights the differences between the origins of "left" or "progressive" movements in the United States and Europe.[52] Abolitionism was a cross-class, multiracial, egalitarian movement at whose center was the theme of race. It was sectionally and religiously strongest in the U.S. Northeast, where Puritan traditions were concentrated, and where it resonated strongly with the nascent pragmatism of thinkers like Emerson and Thoreau, whose ideas lay at the foundations of American radicalism.

Abolitionism's opposition to slavery drew the movement steadily toward a radical egalitarianism as the Civil War approached. The forceful leadership of figures of the caliber of Douglass, Garrison, and Child, plus the radical actions of John Brown and other militants,[53] both mobilized thousands of supporters and left a vital historical legacy. By placing the issue of equality on the nation's political map, the abolitionist movement expanded and revised the American revolutionary legacy of "four score and seven years ago" (Wills 1992).

When emancipation was formally achieved, beginning with Lincoln's Emancipation Proclamation and then continuing with the passage of the Civil War amendments to the Constitution, this was in part a victory for the abolitionist movement. But an even more central aspect of the movement's victory was the uprising of blacks, both slave and free, against the South during the Civil War. The black "general strike," combined with widespread black enlistment in the Union armies, was an abolitionist action par excellence. Here, finally, large numbers of enslaved Africans could act decisively for their own freedom and that of their people. Under the conditions of war, and given the enormous dependence on black labor that existed in the South, blacks could in many ways abolish slavery themselves, emancipate themselves. Emancipation had an implicitly revolutionary character: it continued and radicalized the Revolution of the late eighteenth century (Du Bois 1977 [1935]).

How far away from Haiti was the United States in 1865? Still pretty far, for the country was hardly in the hands of former slaves. The U.S. class system, although greatly altered by emancipation, was still fundamentally intact. The losing side was not sent packing as the Haitian whites and French rulers had been. Nor was land redistributed, although there were tentative initiatives in that direction.[54] In fact, the largest redistribution of wealth that the Civil War achieved was the expropriation of Southern property in the slaves themselves. No small accomplishment this, and very likely the most "socialist" state policy ever carried through in the United States, but it hardly amounted to revolution. The cutting-short of Reconstruction a decade after it began, and the fairly prompt relegation of former slaves to the status of peonage and disfranchisement, meant that even this redistribution would be interrupted before blacks could truly gain control of their own persons, before they could achieve more than the palest semblance of freedom.[55]

Britain

British abolitionism also demands attention. The most notable feature of the British case is its working-class adherents, the sustained grassroots character of the British abolitionist movement. The anti-slavery mobilization of the English working class induced many to fear the disruption that abolition would bring, for slavery was enmeshed in Britain's seafaring and trading hegemony, had struck deep roots in many port cities (Liverpool, Bristol, etc.), and had strong ties to the textile industry and even to the British diet (the English "cuppa," etc.). Yet British abolitionism also had powerful popular roots, notably in the industrial centers of the Midlands (Drescher 1981; Drescher 1987; Thomas 1997). Initially sparked by religious revulsion against the brutalities of the trade (with Quakers and to some extent Methodists once more playing a central part), the British petition drives against slavery are best understood as a central act of working-class political commitment, of participative class formation.

The English abolitionist movement was interwoven (although uneasily so) with Chartism, the great working-class movement of the same period (Saville 1987; D'Anjou, 1996; Jones 1984). The petitions were certainly acts of political protest, yet they were undertaken in non-disruptive form. Carried out by a popular stratum largely excluded from politics, yet on the verge of incorporative reform, the petitions were ostensibly brought on behalf of an entirely other group: enslaved blacks in the colonies. Yet they indirectly worked to advance workers' interests, and served as a rehearsal, so to speak, for the mass mobilizations to follow.

For a good while in the late eighteenth and early nineteenth centuries, the British bourgeoisie was in the majority strongly pro-slavery.[56] This was hardly lost on the organizers of the petitions. In its support for abolition (which even extended to mass boycotting of sugar!) the popular movement was also identifying with the democratic impulses of the American and French Revolutions, and very importantly drawing a firm distinction between their "free" worker status and that of slaves. These allegiances lent strong support to British democratic reform initiatives between the 1830s and 1860s, as well as reinforcing Chartism. There was, in short, a strong link between British democracy and working-class consciousness on the one hand, and popular abolitionism on the other.

But here too abolitionism had a contradictory character. If the dominant sectors of British capital were still oriented to the slavery-based production of the Caribbean (and of the American South's cotton), this had for more than a century been based, not on a commitment to slavery itself, but instead to the complex circuit of trade that slave-based production (particularly of sugar) had anchored. As late as the U.S. Civil War, thirty years after emancipation had come to Britain's own colonies, important figures in the textile industry sought British intervention in the war in favor of the South. Although efforts at military intercession were thwarted (principally by popular—i.e., working-class—opposition), Britain still managed to deliver about $200 million in arms and other supplies (no small sum in the 1860s) to the Confederacy, mainly through Bermuda and the Bahamas.[57]

The British bourgeoisie was still divided over slavery in the mid-nineteenth century. Despite powerful residual interests in the American South, as they advanced into the nineteenth century, the British bourgeoisie were becoming more and more industrialized. Since trade now followed industrial production as much as it ever had done slave-based plantation agriculture, and since working-class pressure was increasing at home, would it not make sense at some point to accede to the demands of enlightened, forward-looking advocates of "free labor" like William Wilberforce and Charles Fox? After all, cheap labor could always be obtained in the colonies, and slave upkeep had been condemned as uneconomical by Adam Smith as early as 1776. So when in 1838 Britain finally accomplished complete emancipation,[58] it was doing more than simply ending slavery. Basing its new orientation upon the years of abolitionist agitation it had undergone, Britain was able to transform itself, within a remarkably short time, into the world's foremost advocate for "free" labor. No pressing conflicts were to be noted for a very long time between this reform (largely aimed at the home market) and widespread English reliance on peonage-based forms of labor in the colonies (where slavery had been "abolished").

The principal distinction between British and U.S. abolitionism was the absence in Britain of a substantial black population. Domestically, slavery was not nearly as significant an issue as in the United States, as the early *Somerset* ruling (1771) had demonstrated. Nor was there a significant number of black British abolitionists. Although not without conflicts and immersed in a political sea roiled by crosscurrents, British abolitionism was at its core a powerful popular movement. Its successes came from its ability to yoke together its deeply moral cause with that of democratic reform; in this way abolitionism consolidated its popular base. But an additional element in its success was its ability to win over to its side a modernizing sector of capitalist class interests. These were industrialists and imperialists, but not planters. They recognized both that slavery was no longer needed to ensure the availability of an exploitable colonial labor force,[59] and that opposition to slavery would afford them (and in some sense, British national interests) a decided advantage as the country approached the apex of its hegemony.

After half a century of British political conflict over abolition, it was still necessary to sweeten the planters' cuppa tea, so to speak, rather substantially: as a final concession to slaveowning interests, in the first bill of abolition (1833), Parliament voted compensation to those British slavemasters "expropriated" by abolition, in the amount of £20 million.

Brazil

Abolition came very late to Brazil. When the *Lei Aurea* (the "golden law" of final emancipation) was signed in 1888, Brazil was the last country in the hemisphere where legal slavery still existed. Slavery persevered there, unlike in almost every other Latin American country, because there was no compelling reason to abolish it. It could be permitted to erode. Brazil had avoided the punishing wars of independence seen elsewhere in the region. Such wars impelled their participants to recruit large numbers of slaves to bear arms, and thus provided strong support to abolitionism.[60] The country also bypassed the late colonial schisms that had engulfed many Latin American regimes in the early nineteenth century, dividing elites and governments (and necessarily, slaveholders) between *criollos* and *peninsulares*. Although elsewhere in Latin America these splits had led to internecine struggles among *caudillos* who, by mobilizing slaves into their armies, had once more sown the seeds of abolition, Brazil had prospered under the conciliatory Emperor Dom Pedro II, who operated as a sort of royal premier in a system of very limited parliamentarism.[61]

There was a very large black population, by far the largest of any single American country. But there was hardly any industry (in the sense of manufacturing), and thus no developed capitalist classes, neither bourgeoisie nor workers (Fernandes 1976; Azevedo 1975). To be sure there was a substantial merchant bourgeoisie, and a significant plantocracy. The latter was composed of a remnant in the Northeast of the once-dominant sugar barons; and (by the later nineteenth century) the more formidable and influential *fazendeiros* of São Paulo and Rio, who dominated the economy and held most of the remaining slaves.

A large and growing proportion of the Afro-Brazilian population was composed of "free" persons,[62] whose racial classification, as is typical of Brazil, varied widely not only by color, but by class, status, party, and even region. Racial mobility could be achieved by various means, and a significant number of blacks and *mulatos* (for example, the engineer Andre Rebouças) became active abolitionists. Centuries of miscegenation had produced a substantial stratum of *mulatos* who were almost entirely free by the time of abolitionism. *Mulato* status was racially intermediate, although still distinct from whites, and there were significant numbers of literate, educated *mulatos*.[63]

Despite numerous manumissions, a series of partial emancipation laws that freed children (in 1871)[64] and those age 60 or more (in 1886), there remained in the 1880s perhaps 3 million enslaved blacks, most of them still toiling on *Paulista* or *Carioca fazendas*, picking coffee. Slave revolts occurred with some frequency in these areas during the late 1870s and early 1880s, notably around the town of Campinas. Outside Santos, the chief port of São Paulo and an abolitionist center, a huge black community called Jabaquara was well-established (Andrews 1991, 37–40). It had developed from a *quilombo* into a diasporic city, tied to the black Atlantic world in much the same way as New Orleans or Liverpool was.

So, in a situation tempered by gradualism and partial reforms of slavery, the Brazilian abolitionists got a late start, developing into a serious movement only in the late 1860s. The movement acquired an urban-based leadership drawn largely from the elite and professional classes. The organized movement was white, black, and *mulato*, although it necessarily relied upon the sympathy and growing mobilization of the country's massive black population. Notable leaders like Joaquim Nabuco and Luis Gama sought to use their bases in the legislature and their access to other public fora for agitation and movement-building (Toplin 1972). Abjuring calls to insurrection or mass escape, they founded newspapers, set up local chapters of abolitionist movement groups in the main towns, gave endless speeches, and agitated in the national and provincial assemblies. They preached the gospel of economic modernization and the immorality of slavery. In the Brazilian context, however, few established voices gave any credence to ideas of racial equality; indeed this notion hardly ever came up among whites.[65] The general sentiment, even among white abolitionists, was nationalist: Brazil was a backward country, in significant ways because it was too black; it needed "whitening," especially via European immigration (Beiguelman 1981); and besides, blacks could not provide the skills and cultural resources needed for a modern workforce, a "free labor" economy (Azevedo 1987). Thus elite abolitionists argued that emancipation, although overdue, must take place in a regulated, disciplined manner. Only in this way could European immigration be promoted; only in this way could the economy be developed beyond its extractive and agricultural basis.

Yet Brazilian abolitionism also had an extensive popular base. It was a proto-democratic movement, with a mass of black adherents, many of them already free by the 1880s (Graham 1999). Since they were entirely excluded from politics, the approach of these *libertos* was necessarily that of "war of maneuver." In 1882 the radical Antônio Bento took over the leadership in São Paulo after the death of Gama; Bento was a white from a *fazendeiro* background, but he favored mass agitation, even revolt:

> Basing his operations in the black church of Nossa Senhora dos Remédios in the provincial capital, Bento and his followers (many of whom were members of the church's lay brotherhood) organized networks of *caifazes*, agents who circulated through the countryside, spreading news of the movement, of the abolition of slavery elsewhere in Brazil (the provinces of Amazonas and Ceará had outlawed slavery in 1884) and Latin America elsewhere . . . , and urging the slaves to rise up against their masters and flee. (Andrews 1991, 38–39)

This was a proto-revolutionary model that would not get very far in Brazil. Still it drew on spontaneous resistance practices that by the 1880s were extremely common among Brazilian blacks. Brazil simply wasn't a very repressive slavocracy by the 1880s. "Free agency," so to speak, was relatively available to slaves, even if politics was off-limits. Millions of blacks were already free. Escape was so frequent that slave-capture was unlikely. The army intervened against uprisings, but refused to carry out slave patrols or pursue escapees. In 1887 there were black protest marches in São Paulo and other cities, terrifying the whites with revolts, mass escapes, and tumultuous demonstrations (Azevedo 1987, 175–211).

When the *Lei Aurea* was finally promulgated on May 13, 1888, there were celebrations all across the country. Abolitionism had become the first national political movement in Brazilian history. That it succeeded at so late a moment implies a good deal of inevitability, but in Brazil as much as elsewhere, abolitionism required organization and mobilization. It is rather easy to suggest in the Brazilian case that capitalist modernization drove slavery off the national stage, and this certainly has its truth. Yet it is also worthwhile to remember that abolitionist mobilization unified and politicized Brazil as never before, and that a little more than a year after emancipation the country was declared a republic.[66] The idea that the destruction of slavery was necessary for the development of capitalism (Fernandes 1976; Azevedo 1975) can be understood in two ways. One account is class-based: here one stage of political-economic development (or mode of production) makes way for another, clearing away the obstacles that impede progress. In my view such an approach is too deterministic; it tends to reduce racial dynamics to merely economic matters. An alternative account of abolition understands it as the product of a complex fusion of interests and actions, the great majority of which are efforts at self-emancipation, manifestations of the energy of resistance. In the Brazilian case this "effervescence" was well-leavened by elite voices who recognized the links between modernization and the end of slavery. That abolition served the interests of capitalist development in Brazil was certainly important, but not in itself decisive, for Brazilian elites remained divided on the question of slavery right up to the *Lei Aurea*. Ultimately abolition was an accomplishment of the blacks themselves.

TOWARD ANTI-COLONIALISM AND DIASPORA

As in the United States and Britain, Brazilian abolitionism was a multiclass political project. In Brazil as in the United States the participation of blacks in their own emancipation was crucial and necessary, while in Britain proper the movement's mass base was furnished for obvious reasons by white workers. In all three settings the destruction of slavery was enormously emancipatory and at least pointed in the direction of democratization. Yet in all three countries abolitionism also proved useful to capital, which could harness anti-slavery logic to equate wage labor with "freedom" as appropriate: notably in Britain proper and in the U.S. North. Capital could also work around the abolition of slavery to develop other highly exploitative forms in which to organize the labor process: notably in the colonies, the U.S. South, and Brazil.

Abolitionism was the worldwide debut of racial *hegemony*. Initiated by resistance that was always present, always at least crepuscular, but that always threatened to explode in subversion, violence, rebellion, and even revolution, abolition was a channeling of revolutionary anti-racism into politics. It was chancy: race-based revolutions happened. Opposition to slavery did intervene in absolutist regimes or exclusionary, *herrenvolk* democracies, and when it did so successfully it at least upset the applecart, turned the tide of wars, pushed class struggle to higher levels. Yet abolitionism also incorporated and thus curtailed revolutionary anti-racism (mostly; not in Haiti). The world would wait the better part of a century before a revolutionary, dark-skinned South would reappear.

As the turn of the twentieth century approached, the great majority of the world's workers still remained without significant political rights in their confrontations with imperial rule and with the tender mercies of capital. In the now industialized North the same waged workers, the same largely white "free labor," continued to endure the labor regime they had already come to know. These northern workers were more organized now, though. In some ways they had been educated by the struggle against slavery, the anti-racist struggle. Yet they were also available for hegemonic incorporation: they could also be placated by an astute combination of reform and northern nationalism, well-brewed with racist, anti-colonial ideology (Du Bois 1995 [1915]).

And in the world's South who did capital find? "That dark and vast sea of human labor" (Du Bois 1977 [1935] 15), no longer slaves, but hardly "free," relegated in large measure to peonage, often confined to labor reserves, segregated, and regulated, but available for work where the demand for mass labor continued, as unchecked as ever, in agriculture and extraction, in primary goods production on plantations, in forests, and in mines.

Here, in the effort to end coercion and institute democracy, in the transition (only just beginning) from violent opposition to politics, in nascent anticolonialism, pan-Africanism, and diasporic consciousness, lay "the problem of the 20th century, the problem of the color-line."

Five

NINETEENTH-CENTURY NIGHTMARES, TWENTIETH-CENTURY DREAMS

THE SYSTEM OF SLAVERY WAS overthrown, the colonial system entered its twilight phase, and democracy became a racial issue over an extended period that took shape throughout the nineteenth century and continued into the twentieth. Because the obsolescence of slavery and the decadence of imperial rule were unevenly recognized and prolonged, colonial and plantation-based demand for mass labor continued. Low-paid or unpaid, coerced or "free," bound or mobile, such labor took on new forms. Since chattel slavery had been largely eliminated, it had to be replaced. Schematically speaking, slavery was supplanted by peonage, although in practice the arrangements that succeeded slavery were extremely diverse. However varied across the globe, the racial demarcation of the division of labor survived abolition quite well. Based in a capricious array of policies, often taking such forms as racial segregation and demarcation of "native reserves," and generally enforced by coercive means (usually state-based although occasionally also privately administered), peonage was a product of the *color-line* that had been forged by conquest and slavery, but that reached its global apogee (as the "problem of the twentieth century") only after abolition.

What about "free" labor? As the turn of the twentieth century came and went, increasing numbers of "colored" workers found their way into industrial workplaces and urban settings. They were also swept up by new waves of military mobilization, particularly during World War I. No system of segregation or exclusion could forestall their entry into the mainstream of economic life, in both the peripheral areas and the metropoles. No color-line, however consolidated or global, could prevent their movement by the millions from plantation to factory, from the backlands to the big cities, from the colonies to the mother-countries. In joining and "colorizing" the massive migratory waves that characterized the late nineteenth and early twentieth centuries, they profoundly transformed the demographic profile of the global working class. A new racial pluralization and stratification of the global working class set in.[1]

The political and cultural consequences of these developments would be enormous. The racialized "others" now prepared to enter the modern world as political subjects, not beasts of burden. This would prove an arduous journey. A few had already made that transition in the fight against slavery and the early decolonizations that had gripped the Americas. Many more remained colonial subjects, though, or even continued in slavery as the nineteenth century approached its end.

Those who could do so now sought to voice the demands of their long-oppressed brothers and sisters, to offer leadership or at least aid to the hosts remaining "down home," whom Du Bois characterized in 1900 as " . . . the millions of black men (sic) in Africa, and the Islands of the Sea, not to speak of the brown and yellow myriads everywhere . . . " (Du Bois 1995 [1900], 639). Democratic and revolutionary aspirations found early expression in trade unionist, socialist, and nationalist forms. The foundation was being laid for the "break" of World War II and after.

At the same time, racial reaction also surged to new levels of commitment, intransigence, and violence. Reaction took many forms: it both found roots in the world's metropolitan centers and was packaged for export to the colonies and backlands. It was a smörgasbord of nationalism and nativism, romanticism and anti-modernism, masculinism and imperialist cant. Its antipathies were extremely diverse: the subhumanity of the racial "others," the emancipation of Jews, the end of slavery, and the threats posed by "race-mixing," egalitarianism, and, democracy were only the most prominent of these. Race was a constant preoccupation of nineteenth-century reaction, whose anti-modernist and romantic orientations were simultaneously "highbrow" and "popular"—manifested in scientific and artistic production on the one hand, and in mass mobilization and mob action on the other. In both Europe and the United States (and for export to the world's South as well), racial reaction combined state-based and mass-based violence, intellectually credible discourse, and the wildest, most hate-filled demagogy. By the turn of the twentieth century, the world racial climate was a bilious mixture of hatred and fear on the one hand, and sanctimony and paternalism on the other. Roiling within it were active programs of genocide in such places as the Congo, southwest Africa, and the Amazon; anti-semitism in theory and practice (Mosse 1978; Gilman and Katz 1991); white supremacist social policies and political programs in almost all "developed" states; biologistic racial theorizing of all types, notably in the eugenics movement (Grant 1970 [1916]; Chase 1977; Haller 1963; Jones 1980; Keith 1919); and frequent upsurges of mob action, for example, in the orgy of lynchings that swept the U.S. South, and in the Dreyfus affair in France. The *Action Français* of Charles Maurras and Maurice Barrès,[2] the broad racist current that had been spawned by Gobineau (Biddiss 1970; Todorov 1993) and Lapouge (1899), Wagner[3] and Houston Stewart Chamberlain, Haeckel (Rooy 1990), and the rise of criminology with Lombroso,[4] all embodying the trend toward romantic racism, reached their apogees during this time.[5]

In the United States the withdrawal of federal troops from the South—as part of the 1877 agreement to allow local elites to reassert their plantocratic power—fomented a confederate irredentism that still survives today. Its immediate consequences were the effective nullification of the post–Civil War constitutional amendments in the South and the onset (or resurgence) of a regime of white racial terrorism that would last for a century. This system of rule was to have several significant upsurges, notably in the 1890s and the 1920s, and to be dominated by a reactionary movement whose initials would come to be known by all: KKK.

In some ways the post-slavery period may be seen as a prolonged rehearsal, a worldwide run-up to the post–World War II break. But to conceive it that way would be to commit a serious historicist error: to read backwards in time, to engage in teleology. I make no attempt to provide such an account here; it would be very difficult to distill the world-historical processes of this long "racial nineteenth century"[6] into so limited a space. Besides, my purpose is different: I want to link the racial present with the racial past thematically, theoretically, sociologically. Most centrally, I want to argue that much of the "great transformation" (*pace* Polanyi—he'll appear shortly) that shook up the greater part of the nineteenth century and the first half of the twentieth too, may be understood racially. This chapter therefore concentrates on the global transition "from slavery to freedom," a profound passage that took a century or more to get underway and that is hardly complete even today.

I begin with a brief reconnaissance of *the aftermath of slavery*. Although the entire nineteenth century was a period of abolitionist advance, slavery was never entirely eliminated. Nevertheless, the (incomplete) breakdown of slavery, the institution that had been central to global patterns of accumulation and domination, was the most momentous event of the age. Abolition would set in motion most of the significant transformations—demographic, economic, political, cultural—of the twentieth century.

The next theme I address is *the post-emancipation economy as an instituted process*. Abolition brought about an economic crisis in those extensive regions of the nineteenth-century world where labor needs were largely met by slavery. Beyond this it ended—or hastened the process of ending—the most important form of trade of the time: the trade in human chattel, upon which most other trade had depended for hundreds of years. The destruction of slavery thus signified *both* that new systems of mass labor would have to be created, *and* that reform of the extractive and agricultural economies that characterized colonialism would have to be undertaken, such that these territories could maintain their trade-based linkages to the world economy. In practice this meant the institution of new forms of labor that continued to be structured by race even though racial slavery was being phased out. These transformations also involved changing patterns of colonial settlement, new systems of coercion and political authority, and the articulation of new interpretations of colonial society and identity. Such matters are discussed in subsequent sections of this chapter.

The key arguments in this section concern the continuity of race as an organizing principle in the newly instituted economy of the post-slavery world. I draw on Polanyi's economic anthropology, his account of economies as "instituted processes," to explain the centrality of race in the colonies, the hinterlands, and the former slave zones of the later nineteenth and early twentieth centuries.

The third topic considered in this section is *the rationalization of rule.* The obsolescence and defeat of slavery called into question the logic of empire and the dynamics of colonial rule. It problematized the mechanisms of labor acquisition and organization. Slavery's retirement weakened the legitimation of rule over what had been seen relatively unproblematically—in London, Paris, and New York, say—as the world's "lesser orders." Thus by the later nineteenth century the economic and political "order of things" required revision and repair. A lot of this work would be cultural production: the formulation of new ideas and images, new representations and interpretations, even new intellectual disciplines (Foucault 1973; Stoler 1995).

On one level this was nothing new. Justifications for empire, and for harsh systems of rule, had always oscillated between a certain taken-for-grantedness that was rooted in the unquestioned hierarchy held to inhere among peoples, on the one hand; and an obligation of uplift and tutelage that the putative superiors felt they owed to their supposed inferiors, on the other. Already among the ancients there were spirited debates between these two stereotypical positions (Aristotle 1959), although these controversies were about human hierarchy in general, not about race.[7] Yet almost never were the intrinsic limits of this perspective—the problematic characterization of vast populations as inherently superior or inferior beings—taken seriously,[8] just as the fact that the outer limits of citizenship did not exceed those of maleness was almost completely unquestioned.

Yet there was a new wrinkle in the cultural work required to fortify or regroove imperial rule and white supremacy in the aftermath of abolition and at the high tide of colonialism. This was the successful harnessing of *science* to the cause of racial hierarchy. Whereas earlier "racial science" had always been speculative and subject to significant "finagling" (Gould 1981), the rise and consolidation of *eugenics* in the later nineteenth century represented a new and ostensibly "harder" scientific outlook on racial matters. This generalization of racial logic to most knowledge disciplines and skilled professions was part of the process Weber was describing around this time as disenchantment and rationalization. It provided both tremendous opportunities and great obstacles for the revision-and-repair effort necessitated by the waning importance of slavery. Thus I have used the term *rationalization* in *petit hommage* to Weber.

The fourth theme considered here is the changing "peripheral" *political structure at the turn of the twentieth century.* Abolitionism itself had been a convergence of heterodox political forces: it had combined the efforts of modernizing elites, both metropolitan and colonial, with those of fervent religious groups, of working-class republicans, of "free persons of color," and of rebellious slaves determined to make an end of their degradation. All these interests had merged uneasily at best, and often clashed. With slavery gone (or in decay) and abolition's aims at least minimally accomplished, significant uncertainties and abuses remained, and a series of new power vacuums and conflicts appeared.

Early opposition to the new forms of rule were necessarily continuations of the "war of maneuver" (Gramsci 1971) that had shaped resistance under slavery: efforts to withdraw from the cash economy and systems of coerced labor and peonage are good examples here, as is the sporadic armed resistance that occurred principally, but not only, in Africa. However, as more urban labor was needed and migration became more possible, as elites formed among colonial subjects and ex-slaves, other forms of opposition—political ones—appeared in the world's colonies and backlands. The early outlines of "war of position" began to emerge: here the subaltern (or their leaders) attained some sort of political standing and voice. This trend would expand progressively, although not without setbacks, into the twentieth century.

The fifth theme of this chapter also has its roots in Gramsci; it is Duboisian as well. This theme is *racial dualism and the crisis of late colonialism.* Here I emphasize the racial dynamics of the "subaltern studies" approach to late colonialism. The term *subaltern* has been imported from Gramsci's work into colonial and post-colonial studies to denote the instability and tension inherent in the later stages of colonial rule (Guha 1997; Guha and Spivak 1988; Beverley 1999; Chakrabarty 1988; Chatterjee 1988; Kelley 1994; Scott 1990; Cooper 1994). The usefulness of the concept is immediately evident in its refusal of the class-race distinction, its insistence on the intertwining of inequality and difference—of class and race (and gender)—in colonial and post-colonial settings. For its mere anti-reductionism, it deserves (as my students might say) "mad props," great respect. The importance of the subalternity concept, however, far exceeds this useful equation. The broad analytical current of subaltern studies attempts a deep reinterpretation of the sociocultural dimensions of late colonial rule and resistance.

The subaltern studies approach permits a better understanding of the limits of rule, particularly late colonial rule and post-slavery racial rule, than more traditional approaches, whether mainstream or radical, allow. Most important for present purposes, such an approach focuses quite intensively on the racial (and gender) dynamics of this epoch. Stressing the combination of increased autonomy and continuing subordination that characterized late colonialism (and, I would add, such post-slavery regimes as U.S. "Jim Crow"), subalternity approaches recognize the contradictory and necessarily limited engagement of the "masses" in political struggle. While it was generally difficult to mount organized, "formal" resistance, ex-slaves, peasants, superexploited workers, and those relegated to various forms of peonage did carry out informal resistance of many kinds. They acted out the "hidden transcripts" often available to the oppressed, even while confronted by ongoing racial oppression carried over (and sometimes intensified) from the days of slavery and earlier colonialism. I argue here that this situation closely corresponds to the one theorized by Du Bois as double consciousness or racial dualism.

Early resistance was logically led by religious and traditional authorities, as well as by warriors. These figures and their initiatives set the stage for the later appearance of such anti-colonial movements as nationalism and socialism. Their activities were rehearsals for the revolutionary and democratic movements (also elite-initiated or -led) that would come later. It was not accidental that more privileged members of the subaltern strata played this role: the extremely difficult tasks of mobilizing against late colonialism and white supremacy demanded knowledge of "the white man's ways." To organize strikes, for example, is a far different matter than invoking traditional religiosity or seeking a return to subsistence farming. Leaders, whether Du Bois' "talented tenth" or the fomenters of the Lagos dock workers' strike of 1897, were necessarily also those who had some knowledge of metropolitan techniques—some education, some cultural hybridity, at a minimum. Since insurgent and accommodationist impulses would vie for their loyalties, subaltern elites were also subject to the antinomies of racial dualism.

The transition from something like emancipation to something like freedom—or at least toward the crucial break of World War II and its aftermath—took place in a prolonged confrontation. White rulers, colonial rulers, faced not only their subaltern subjects, but also the insurgent organizations and ideologies that so fiercely marked the twentieth century: nationalism and socialism in all their variations. As opposition to their rule intensified, colonial and plantocratic elites came to rely upon lower-strata whites (settlers, immigrants, farmers, workers) to furnish the sociopolitical base for their authority. The complexities of conflict and accommodation among these four collective actors—ruling whites, subordinate whites, a nascent subaltern counter-elite, and the subaltern masses—were the transitional racial dynamics that led up to the break of World War II.

In an incomplete, anxiety-ridden, and prefigurative way, this multifaceted encounter anticipated in numerous ways the contemporary racial situation with which this book is primarily concerned. In its early stages, that situation was identified by Du Bois as *racial dualism*, the "peculiar sensation" of simultaneous alienation and identification, opposition and inclusion. This concept effectively locates the contradictory racial dynamics that pervaded the period. It also anticipates the insights of the subaltern studies theorists.

A final section of this chapter, "Toward the Break," considers the first emergence of racial opposition politics after the turn of the twentieth century. The mere fact that a variety of political currents could come into being and acquire some political voice indicates the significance of the transition that the old world racial order was undergoing in the period under review here. The movements and the global and local contexts that gave rise to them—notably World War I—are examined as precursive moments, initial manifestations, of what would become the worldwide racial break of World War II and its aftermath.

THE AFTERMATH OF SLAVERY

The curtailment of slavery was a prolonged process.[9] The emancipatory challenge to slavery during the nineteenth century was largely, although by no means totally, an Atlantic one. Abolitionism's most important advances were made in the western hemisphere. As I have argued, the abolitionist umbrella covered divergent political currents: slavery was ended by revolution (Haiti), by civil war (United States), and by anti-colonial war (Latin America). Slave revolts that were unsuccessful in toppling colonial rule sometimes still impelled emancipatory reform (most notably in the British Caribbean). Slavery hung on for a long time in a few American territories (Brazil and Cuba); these were important exceptions to the abolitionist trend. The overall tendency of the later nineteenth century was to replace chattel slavery with peonage. This process went forward unevenly; it was driven not only by economic interests but by political necessities, and it had to be articulated in culturally acceptable terms. The replacement of slavery by peonage—in whatever form it took—was never an unproblematic transition, never a done deal. On the contrary, it was always contentious, always the subject of political and cultural struggle. Much of this chapter is devoted to the fundamental racial components of that struggle.

In Europe, slavery was challenged by a combination of popular movements linked in Britain to religious and democratic reform, and in France to the Jacobin legacy. Abolition also had powerful elite supporters, principally industrialists who saw no further use in owning slaves. Official British support for the transatlantic slave trade had ended in 1807, but British ability (or willingness) to interdict pirate slave-traders on the high seas was at best uneven. Abolition in the British Caribbean took place in the 1830s, accompanied by generous compensation paid to planters who were considered to have been expropriated. This contrasted rather sharply with Haiti, where land was to some extent redistributed to former slaves, and the United States, which toyed with similar policies (the famous "40 acres and a mule") but then rejected them (Oubre 1978). Slavery was abolished during the French Revolution, not by the Assembly (which was still divided by the issue), but only by the Convention in 1794

(James 1989 [1938], 76–78, 138–142). Napoleon restored it in 1802, and not until the Second Republic did France abolish slavery again, in 1848.

For the rest of the century and even beyond it, European colonial rule teetered between official opposition to slavery and tacit acceptance of it *within* Africa, as long as profits could be made, or as long as colonial rule made sense "for reasons of state."

In nineteenth-century Africa, slavery first turned eastward and inward, and then went underground. For much of the century, colonial rule in the continent's interior was minimal or nonexistent. The effects of Atlantic slave-trading, however, had been felt for a long time in the interior, especially the hinterlands of the west coast of Africa. Slave-raiding and the fomenting of wars, whose chief effects were the production of human captives, had already become extensive during the eighteenth century. As the demand for slaves increased, whole areas of West Africa and its backlands were depopulated. Weapons traded for slaves increased the lethality of warfare and raiding, disease became more prevalent, and subsistence farming became more difficult and dangerous. Thus the indirect consequences of the slave trade, not only the direct ones, also proved deleterious (Vansina 1990).[10]

The export of human cargo to the Americas eroded over the first half of the nineteenth century, a process driven by a range of abolitionist pressures, intermittent enforcement of the ban on slave-trading (primarily by the British navy), and augmented scarcity on the "supply-side" in West Africa. As West African human prey became scarcer, the Atlantic trade began to make greater use of East African sources.[11]

Although the Atlantic trade did not entirely cease until the last bastions of American slavery—Brazil and Cuba—abolished it in the 1880s, a significant trade remained; this activity passed human cargo through North and East Africa to the Ottoman Empire, the Persian Gulf, and South Asia and the Malay Peninsula. All the major East African ports (Mombasa, Djibouti, etc.) were involved. Zanzibar played a central role, as did the Horn region and the Sudan. Even little Réunion and Mauritius, sites of clove, spice, and coconut plantations, took part as importers.

The East African and trans-Sahara slave trades were largely Arab-run, with local suppliers in East or West Africa who were almost entirely Muslim. The volume of this human commerce, which has not received much historical attention until recently, was very high, although it did not attain the levels of the transatlantic trade.[12] While I cannot focus attention on this commerce here, it is interesting to note that the demand for African slaves in the Maghrebine and Ottoman lands was not primarily based on mass labor extraction (as it had been in the Americas). Rather, it was oriented toward military service (Pipes 1981)—notably in the Egyptian and Sudanese zones of the empire under Mehmet Ali (Muhammad Ali), the Albanian-descended ruler who ruled from 1805 to 1848—and domestic service and concubinage (Toledano 1998).[13] This complex and controversial set of practices was not dismantled until the empire itself was destroyed by World War I and by the rise of Ataturk. And even after that slave caravans traveled north across the Sahara to the Maghrebine lands.[14]

Colonial rule was extended into the interior of the continent only in the last half of the nineteenth and indeed beginnings of the twentieth centuries. After the slave trade waned, European economic priorities in Africa shifted. The principal early concerns were the extraction of resources, notably ivory, diamonds, gold, and rubber; the development of a limited number of cash-crop exports, for example, peanuts, Kola nuts, and palm oil; and the management of rivalries with other colonial powers through expeditionary operations and subjugation of natives. A certain amount of infrastructural development and significant amounts of native labor were required for all these activities.

As the chief African economic activity shifted from the export of human beings to the export of natural and agricultural resources, slavery turned (or returned) to an internal African system. In some cases colonial rulers or concessionnaires could ally with or contract with African chiefs or traders for the goods they sought—ivory and rare woods, for example. Enslaved Africans were used extensively for gathering and porterage. The archetype of such a figure was "the almost mythic African ivory-rubber-slave magnate Hamed bin Muhammad bin Juna al-Marjebi, known to history as 'Tippu Tip'" (Lewis 1987, 10). He played an important role both in relation to the Swahili-speaking merchant shipping of East Africa and in his dealings with Henry Morton Stanley, King Leopold's agent in the Congo.[15] But such arrangements operated throughout Central Africa in the latter decades of the century. Manning notes that

> surveys by French officials just after 1900 showed, for vast areas of the Western Sudan, that two-thirds of the population was enslaved, and that the great majority of adult slaves were women. Among such Central African trading peoples as the Chokwe and Bobangi, most of the population was servile. For the territories of francophone sub-Saharan Africa as a whole, one may speculate that as many as ten million people lived in servile status in the late 19th century, and that most of them were female. (Manning 1998, 26)

These sorts of data are highly suspect, both because information-gathering techniques were rudimentary, and because paternalistic colonial officials' claims about the mistreatment of women tended to justify colonial practices as uplifting the backward natives. But even discounting the numbers substantially, the extent of late-nineteenth-century slavery must be reckoned as extensive.

Slaving practices in British-dominated zones were also extensive. In detailed work on the Sokoto caliphate (largely situated in present-day northern Nigeria) Lovejoy and Hogendorn "follow the decline of slavery over the course of four decades, from 1897 to 1936." They argue that "British policy aimed at reforming slavery and thereby protected an otherwise doomed institution for some years" (Lovejoy and Hogendorn 1993, 7).

There are significant debates on the forms taken by African labor during the transition from the primacy of the Atlantic slave trade to the belated abolition of slavery.[16] Few would disagree, however, that in a variety of incarnations, slavery persisted within Africa for many decades after it had ended elsewhere. The irony of European hand-wringing about this—at the great conferences of Berlin (1884–85) and Brussels (1889) that divided Africa among the colonial powers and organized the "scramble" that threatened to destabilize Europe— is that the colonial powers did not hesitate to make use of enslaved or quasi-enslaved labor themselves. Both in their efforts to dominate in practice the territories they had assigned themselves on paper at Berlin, and in their commitment to exploitation of African resources, the colonial powers and their concessionnaires (Cecil Rhodes, the Royal Niger Company, the *Force Publique*, etc.) were dependent on slave labor. The subversion (or conversion) of abolitionist ideals into their practical opposite—the depredations of the Congo, the German slaughters in southwest Africa (Namibia), the mass coercions of labor on the Rand—are but the most familiar examples of this irony. In Africa at least the end of the century of abolition occurred with the transformation of abolitionism into new forms of servile and coerced labor.

Yet even this bitter characterization is inadequate. As colonialism penetrated Africa after the scramble, as it set up or took over numerous export-oriented activities—indigo and rice production, cotton, coffee, and cocoa plantations, numerous rubber, peanut, groundnut, and palm oil operations, lumbering and milling, and most especially, mining of gold and diamonds in southern Africa and copper in Katanga—the labor question became paramount. The production of these goods had previously been carried out by slave labor,[17] but now the tide was beginning to turn away from slavery. The shift from the export of humans to the export of primary goods demanded fundamental economic reorganization. It meant the invention of a new African economy. New modes of labor—new "occupations"—had to be created; the persons who were to occupy such positions had to be located and induced (or more likely, coerced) into their "roles": as porter, miner, tenant farmer, and so on. Both labor and products had to be moved about. Transportation and urban development had to be fostered. Roads and rail linkages had to be built, port facilities constructed, urban populations and workforces first recruited and then housed and fed.

THE POST-EMANCIPATION ECONOMY AS AN INSTITUTED PROCESS

Abolition obviously did not eliminate the need for cheap and coercible labor, but it did problematize the overlap of race and class. The destruction of slavery meant that new systems of mass labor would have to be invented, or more properly exhumed, from the available repertoires of exploitation. The obsolescence of slave labor and the slow death of the slave trade put pressure on colonial states and modernizing elites to reorganize the social relations of production. New means of exploitation had to be established, especially in the colonies and agricultural hinterlands that had previously depended on slavery. Furthermore, new bases of trade had to be created to replace the repressed commerce in human chattel. These were among the central world economic challenges of the nineteenth century.[18]

Although they were hardly unprecedented—for systems of labor coercion that did *not* involve slavery were as ancient as slavery itself—these new systems did initiate massive, indeed worldwide, sociopolitical transformation. They brought issues of social stratification to the fore. Racial categorization was the chief means employed to interpret and enforce developing inequalities within the laboring classes, who of course made up the large majority of the population in both colony and metropole.

As they groped toward and experimented with the reorganization of social systems on a world scale, as the social conflicts over slavery and abolitionism advanced and consolidated, the colonial and modernizing states of the nineteenth century *instituted a new world economy*. Both the impasses and dilemmas of the outmoded slavery-based economy, and the upheavals and strife brought on by its replacement, were primarily racial issues.

In the broad sense, all economic relationships, all economies, are instituted. This point was most forcefully made by Karl Polanyi, who criticized the tendency to "naturalize" market relationships: to treat markets as somehow automatically arising, self-regulating social relationships.[19] In *The Great Transformation* (1980 [1944]) Polanyi sought to demonstrate how much instrumental action, and above all how much state-based organization, legislation, and intervention, was necessary to create modern capitalism in England. In later theoretical work aimed at reframing economic anthropology, he argued that even earlier economic systems—which he somewhat problematically characterized as "archaic" and "primitive"—were also marked by their "instituted," or sociopolitically constituted, character (Polanyi 1957).

The concept of economies as socially instituted processes is very interesting theoretically, but my immediate concerns here are narrower: I seek to interpret the aftermath of abolition as a complex and uneven sociopolitical process. In doing away with an economic system whose most significant trade had been in human chattel, colonial regimes[20] were modernizing the extractive and mercantile relationships that had characterized their economies at earlier moments. They were entering, so to speak, an intermediate period between slave labor- and "free" labor-based systems.

The destruction of slavery meant that new systems of mass labor would have to be created. The developing social structure of peripheral capitalism did not lack a repertoire here: bound and taxed; cheated and confined; kidnapped and "reserved" forms of labor were all resorted to. Ranging from genocidal and exterminationist levels of violence that exceeded even the predations of the slave trade, to arrangements characterized by greater (although still varying) degrees of benignity, the labor systems that succeeded slavery went under many names: indenture, tenancy, sharecropping, and corvée were only a few of these.

What is distinctive about peonage is its "intermediate" character: it is neither full-fledged enslavement nor "free" labor. In its most brutal versions, such as the rubber-gathering of King Leopold's Congo or in the Putumayo region of the Amazon, those consigned to peonage were purely coerced: their families were kidnapped, their villages were destroyed, and torture and maiming were common when production quotas were not met (Hochschild 1998; Taussig 1986). Slavery is too dignified a term to apply to this labor, for these workers were neither paid nor fed. Yet they were not chattel either, nor even "legitimately" ruled. They were simply captured and herded.

Yet such horrific instances are extreme cases: other intermediate forms abounded which, while hardly free of coercion, necessarily incorporated limited but real dimensions of autonomy. Such forms of labor were inevitably racially classified. In the post-slavery period they were common, not only to Africa, but to all the zones of the world where slavery and colonial conquest had existed or continued to exist. Indeed, labeling these types of labor as "*super*exploitation" already implies a tacit recognition of the racial distinction between those who occupied these positions in the global economy and those who, by the later nineteenth century, had consolidated their status as "free" laborers. Thus to differentiate, *grosso modo*, between ex-slaves and colonized workers, and in some cases peasants on the one hand, and "free" waged workers on the other, is obviously problematic. Yet I insist that such a general boundary did exist within the worldwide division of labor at the moment when abolition was being consolidated and incorporated at roughly the turn of the twentieth century. This was the point of Du Bois' famous remark that "the problem of the 20th century is the problem of the color-line."[21]

"Free" labor—in other words, waged labor—too made its belated entrance at this time in the more remote corners of the world. That the realm of "free" labor was being extended did not mean that it was prevalent (or that it was anything like free) as a general rule. In fact much of the operative meaning of the designation *free* stemmed from the renewed emphasis that nineteenth-century capitalism placed on European migration and settlement to the colonies and hinterlands. Stressing (and in many cases inventing) cultural differences among immigrant European labor and settlers on the one hand, and newly emancipated "colored" slaves on the other, capitalism and colonialism defined freedom as a condition (social to be sure, but also fundamentally economic) which slaves and former slaves did not, and could not, share.[22]

The transition away from colonial and hinterlands economies based on slavery not only implied a change in the modes and status of labor. It also involved new conflicts among colonial elites. In a general way, mine-owners and planters who produced for export needed to find abundant sources of cheap labor; even settlers with small farms to maintain were in this position. Such labor had to be coerced, and coercion required the use of the state: law, administration, and military force. But by the late nineteenth century colonial offices in London and Paris, financially pressed because of economic downturns (particularly in the 1890s) and uneven prospects for revenues from the colonies, were restricting outlays for expeditions against the natives. They demanded that local colonists and elites take matters into their own hands: that they raise their own revenues through exports of raw materials, that they operate more self-sufficiently and control their own natives. In Washington, too, the national rulers preferred to leave the southern hinterlands in the hands of local officials. Cotton country experienced a surge in lynchings as the federal government abandoned the Reconstruction amendments to the Constitution and resolved to let the South handle its own affairs. Meanwhile even remote Brazil experienced "rebellion in the backlands" in the 1890s (Cunha 1995 [1902]). Everywhere in the post-slavery system there was economic tension as new means were sought to render colonial and hinterlands economies profitable. To organize new forms of coercive labor extraction was the central component of the new agenda; the solution arrived at, however contradictory and conflictual, was peonage.

How was the post-emancipation economy instituted in particular local situations? In what ways were particular racial regimes, in both colonial and independent national settings, reconfigured once slavery had been abolished? Such questions may be answered by comparing South Africa, the United States, and Brazil. Some brief remarks on the Caribbean are also included.

South Africa

Slave labor had been a pillar of colonialism in South Africa since the arrival of Europeans there in the seventeenth century. Colonial practices under the Dutch East India Company and later, after the arrival of the British, were agrarian of course, but also largely subsistence-oriented (Elphick and Giliomee 1989). The Cape was relatively isolated from the developing capitalist world economy for a long time, although there was some export (for example, of wine). The original settlement at the Cape—in the days of van Riebeeck— had sought to service and provision the seventeenth-century slave trade. Later the Cape Colony was involved in the trade on both the Atlantic and Indian Ocean routes. Internally, both the Dutch and British not only depended continuously on local slavery, but both groups also sporadically imported slaves and indentured labor, first from the East Indies (notably the Malay Pensinsula) and later from China and India.

British abolitionism reached South Africa in the 1820s and 1830s,[23] roughly coincident with the success of campaigns to end slavery in the Caribbean. Its principal antagonists in South Africa were the Boers, for whom slavery was the principal means of extracting labor in agricultural settings both large and small.[24] British advocacy of abolition, notably on the part of Rev. John Philip, a missionary with considerable sponsorship from London, was therefore not merely the formal fulfillment of an imperial commitment, but also a maneuver to assert London's power in the Cape. After some years of struggle between the whites, the response of the outnumbered and less powerful Boers was to withdraw to the interior in the famous Great Trek. The sources of the Trek—subsequently enshrined in Afrikaner national mythology—were complex:

> Major annoyances were the failures of the government to open up new frontiers for pastoralists running short on land and to make life more secure on the ones that existed. But a particular insistent source of complaint was revulsion against *gelystelling*, or the equalization of status between black and white. (Fredrickson 1981, 167)

Another notable study has identified three competing tendencies among the whites: a desire to expand the role of the state—in this case the British colonial state—in the Cape; a settler model, in which a predatory ethnonational group—the Boers—was turned loose in the hinterlands, where it clashed with and subjugated the native peoples it encountered; and a missionary model, in which the vision of abolition was linked to that of colonial uplift and tutelage (Comaroff and Comaroff 1991).

The short-term outcome of this multisided confrontation would be decided in a few decades: the aftermath of the 1880s discoveries of extensive gold deposits in the Transvaal would reinforce British interests and powers in the area substantially, leading eventually to war with the Afrikaners. After the Boer War the entire region fell under British authority. But long before that, the legacy of abolition had been sacrificed to the colonial need for mass labor.

The transition from slavery required labor, but labor was not readily available. By the end of the century there were labor shortages, especially at the prices the colonialists and planters were willing to pay. The importation of other types of subjugated labor began: South Asians and Chinese in particular were brought under indenture arrangements (Sacks 1967).

At the same time a far more varied and complicated social order was being created. As the century wore on and economic crises set in, new waves of settlers arrived, notably in southern Africa and after the French conquest of the Maghreb. European settlers had been in Africa for centuries, but in much smaller numbers and fewer areas. As the colonial project reached closer to its limits, the number of settlers was greatly augmented, and with their presence came a far more complicated and stratified socioeconomic order. Consistent with the tidal wave of European emigration of the period,[25] eastern and southern Europeans, and many Russian and Polish Jews immigrated as white settlers. The old divisions—master and slave, colonist and colonized—became more complicated as well: white workers and even poor whites appeared and took some kind of root; mixed-race categories proliferated as miscegenation and hybridization became more common.

As new forms of labor took shape for both "natives" and immigrants, slavery was replaced, in some regions summarily and by law, in others gradually in a "slow death." For all but "whites"—a somewhat nebulous racial category, to be sure, especially in the early post-slavery years—replacements were to occupy the diverse labor positions I have grouped under the category of *peonage*. White ethnic divisions, as well as non-white, non-black immigrants—"other others"—appeared on the scene. The resulting intricacies of the new racial system could have undermined the colonial social structure upon which it was built; they certainly threatened to do so in various ways. But instead, the danger of breakdown in the system of racial hierarchy served as a warning, principally for those in power, but also for those whose "freedom" was most vulnerable: poor whites, "free" whites, for whom a waged job or a small farm was the most essential guarantee of status and belonging. The compulsion to reinforce and defend white racial privilege was greatly strengthened as the colonial social order became more stratified. The parallels between this developing racial system, in southern Africa most particularly, and post-emancipation social dynamics in the late-nineteenth-century United States, have been a continuous subject of study (Fredrickson 1981; Cell 1982; Greenberg 1980; Marx 1998).

Development of the labor reserve system and forcible recruitment of African miners had substantial precedents. Both in the Cape and in the Orange Free State coercive labor policy had developed well before the "mineral revolution" in the effort to ensure agricultural labor supplies (these went under various names: squatters, servants, tenants, etc., rather than slaves). No sooner was abolition decreed than it was subverted "on the ground" by a series of laws, regulations, and practices designed to obtain and discipline servile black labor: vagrancy and pass laws, coercive native taxation, and systems of "apprenticeship" and debt bondage, created a system that more than one historian has labeled "serfdom" (Wilson 1971; Bundy 1979; Ross 1993; Cell 1982).

But with the takeoff of the mining sector of the economy the whole dynamic of labor changed. Many blacks were forced to abandon subsistence agriculture, squatting, and marginal agricultural labor. They were steadily herded into "Native Reserve" areas. The Native Land Act of 1913 reflected both the need to make African labor more available in the mines and the increasing commercialization of agriculture, which now required a more disciplined rural proletariat and more complete control of arable land. Long before the formal declaration of apartheid as national policy, racial rule had largely hemmed in the African native population through coercive land and labor regulation. On the one hand, the 1913 act (and various attendant measures) sought to reduce if not eliminate native subsistence farming; on the other hand, the urbanization of blacks also had to be curtailed as far as possible, for the success of mining operations depended on the availability of cheap black labor. And while these measures, combined with tax policies and repression, drove blacks (black males) to work in the mines and as farm laborers, those economic niches were restricted as well: as blacks came to work more and more for wages, the color bar was fortified to protect white workers from black competition.[26]

Thus the coercive techniques of labor recruitment that had begun in the 1880s[27] were deployed ever more widely and deeply. Labor was imported from the entire southern African region, up to and beyond the Limpopo River. Nyasaland (present-day Malawi), Rhodesia (Zimbabwe), and Bechuanaland (Botswana) were trolled for workers. Contracts were signed with the Portuguese to organize the inflow of Mozambican sojourners. Arrangements for these labor migrations varied somewhat, but they all partook of the peonage model: they involved various forms of indenture and indebtedness, colonial coercion, and contracts based not so much on the sale, but rather on the long-term rental of cheap labor. Since (male) workers were what was wanted, families (women and children) were prohibited from accompanying their husbands and fathers. This had the effect of reducing labor costs: it dispensed with any residual obligation to pay a family-oriented subsistence wage. "Traditional" (that is, non-market-based) means of reproduction were assumed to permit the alimentation and overall survival of black workers' families, to the extent that the colonial state and mining enterprises concerned themselves with such matters at all.

Thus the groundwork for modern apartheid was laid long before the system was officially made policy (not until 1948). Few would disagree that race played a crucial role in structuring the South African economy as it underwent the dramatic transitions of the "long nineteenth century." South Africa began that period as an agricultural, relatively isolated, slavery-based society in which Dutch and British colonists coexisted uneasily, and where the interior remained to a significant extent native land. Abolition provoked the great schism that would divide the whites. It set up a definitive rupture among the colonial groups; the Great Trek, the 1836 withdrawal of the Afrikaners into the interior, signified both the Boers' unwillingness to give up slavery and their refusal to submit to British colonial *diktat*. The unstable rivalry among the whites—a particularly predatory situation for the blacks—was only resolved by a brutal war between the two white groups.

By the opening decades of the twentieth century the country had been forcibly unified as a British colony. Antagonisms among Anglos and Boers simmered on, but the forging of a common commitment to white supremacy went a long way toward easing intra-white tensions. Meanwhile the consolidation of what would eventually become formal apartheid tended to fragment black solidarity along political, ethnic, and even racial lines. There were significant Asian and coloured[28] populations; differences among African language and tribal groups, as well as disagreements about oppositional strategies, also took their toll. The British slowly disengaged their colonial rule after the Boer War. The Union, established in 1910, linked the provinces under a national constitution and established local autonomy for whites while maintaining overall British control; formal independence was not granted until the 1930s. During and after its political transition of the early twentieth century, South Africa built its mineral-based, export-oriented, core economic institutions through the relentless and rigid superexploitation of blacks. The country's development took place by means of an all-but-comprehensive reduction of blacks to the landless and powerless status of peonage. Its modern economy was politically and culturally constructed *by racial means*—it was *racially* instituted—over a decades-long process around the turn of the twentieth century.[29]

The United States

The United States suffered its great historical trauma in the Civil War, not only through the massive bloodletting the war occasioned, but also because the war's termination involved the ending of slavery, the partial fulfillment of the abolitionist dream. The war therefore definitively wrenched the country away from its backward preindustrialism. As it moved away from the *herrenvolk* republicanism (Roediger 1991) associated with the Jeffersonian and Jacksonian legacies, those traditions also entered into crisis. The expansionist orientation (aka Indian removal) that earlier had been linked to the demand for "free soil" also reached its domestic limits in the decades after the Civil War as the frontier closed. In place of artisanal conceptions of labor, which viewed the worker as an independent producer who depended on no "master" and was thus the opposite of a "servant" (or slave), workers now found themselves regimented into industrial settings—factories and mines and particularly railroads—as the country underwent full-blown capitalist development. A great deal of this industrial expansion occurred as a direct consequence of the war, which had stimulative effects on the northern economy. Industrial development meant labor demand: the latter decades of the nineteenth century saw immense waves of immigration from both Europe and Asia. Industrial and craft unionism of several political tendencies surged and dissipated in epochal battles with the "lords of labor," the great robber barons of industrial America: Carnegie and Frick, Gould and

Rockefeller, Fisk and Pullman. In great waves of hard-fought strikes the grow-ing working class tried to resist reduction to a new type of servile status.

Farmers and settlers too entered a different world after the war. Not only was the Jeffersonian ideal of yeomanry on the wane; not only was "free soil," accomplished at the expense of the Indians, a reality, but the onset of world-wide depressions, first in the 1870s and then again in the 1890s, left U.S. farm-ers and workers vulnerable to the vicissitudes of the global economy in an unprecedented way. Populist movements arose in the agrarian areas of the West and South in an attempt to defend the vulnerable rural population—the former yeomanry of Jacksonian days—against the depredations of national and international capital. The great strikes of the 1870s and 1890s were workers' responses (particularly railroad workers) to wage-cutting. The battle for the eight-hour day also took shape in a context of worldwide capitalist recession.

Abolition itself was a source of transformation. Du Bois' magisterial *Black Reconstruction* (1977 [1935]), as well as a series of other works largely inspired by it, demonstrate how much emancipation was the product, not only of the abolitionist movement, but more centrally of action by the slaves themselves. Their refusal to work for the Confederacy (Du Bois' "general strike"), their mass escapes from the plantations to the Union lines, and their insistence on taking up arms to fight for freedom, transformed the Civil War. What had been an effort on the part of the national government to suppress rebellion—whether or not that suppression involved the end of slavery—was transmuted by black people into a semi-revolution against the slavery-based mode of production.

But a partial revolution, as the saying goes, digs its own grave. In the United States the end of the importation of human commodities for purposes of mass labor and the rise of abolitionism brought to a head not only the conflict over slavery, but also the debate over the economic and political development of the country.[30]

The end of the slave trade (or its tendential diminution after 1807, anyway) also overlapped in important ways with the first mass European immigrations. Irish immigration to the United States (and the Caribbean) before the Civil War was as much a product of the "push" of famine induced by the British colo-nial regime as it was of the "pull" of available land and labor. By the post–Civil War era, global economic crises impelled vast migrations to the United States. Late-nineteenth-century immigrants did not arrive in the United States as bear-ers of greater stores of social capital (or capital of any kind) than those pos-sessed by the emancipated slaves who were contemporaneously being con-signed to peonage in the South (Lieberson 1980). Indeed, immigrants were subject to severe exploitation. Yet the immigrants were assimilable in the "free" (waged) labor system to a far greater extent than were blacks. Other perquisites of citizenship were offered to whites as well (although incompletely): the fran-chise (Keyssar 2000), public schooling, and significantly greater rights of asso-ciation and organization than were available to southern blacks. The contemporary U.S. system of social stratification, with its pronounced emphasis on status derived from both race and ethnicity,[31] was perhaps not founded during this period, but was nevertheless significantly reinforced and deepened by these transformations.

In the aftermath of the northern victory the Union armies, on which emancipated slaves had to depend for protection against their former masters and against lower-status whites, soon proved unreliable. Defeated southern oligarchs and commoners alike, who had been steeped in white supremacism for centuries, fought from the first to reassert their control in the region. Despite attempts on the part of freedpeople and their Radical Republican allies to consolidate the revolution with land reform, the creation of black militias, and other similar measures, whites in the South, backed by numerous political allies on the national scene, successfully reclaimed power when federal troops were withdrawn in 1877.[32]

Indeed the year 1877 is a convenient moment at which to view the institution of a new economy in the post–Civil War United States. In that year, as the last occupying troops were being withdrawn from the South,[33] black voters were already being removed from the electoral rolls, Freedmen's Bureau schools, banks, and labor bureaus were being closed, land under independent black cultivation was being repossessed by whites using coercive means, and white terrorists operating under the sign of the Klan were pillaging and murdering. Although it would require a few decades to complete the transition that Du Bois entitles "Back Toward Slavery," the key elements were put in place rather quickly. Most important of these was the foreclosure of black alternatives to agricultural peonage in the reconstituted plantations of the region. Blacks by the millions became "sharecroppers." This was not a new status; many poor whites had been "cropping" for generations. What happened here, as noted, was the extension of an established repertoire of labor exploitation to include emancipated blacks.

The 1877 railroad strike briefly threatened to become a national general strike. Pay cuts implemented by the major railroad lines as the depression-ridden economy staggered through its fourth year were met by spontaneous walkouts all across the country. The strike also spread beyond rail to other industries, tending to take hold in the more advanced sectors of the economy, but also gaining support from farmers, ministers, and even politicians (particularly Radical Republicans). For a brief moment, the threat of a revolutionary conflagration loomed, as whole cities (for example, St. Louis) were taken over by striking workers and their supporters. Police, private guards, and finally federal troops under the command of the newly installed President Rutherford B. Hayes battled the strikers and ultimately broke the strike. The strike had two crucial racial dimensions. First, the developing labor movement that conducted it was at best divided, and in many ways opposed, to the inclusion of black workers:

Immediately enmeshed in the [1866] founding convention of the National Labor Union was the dilemma of a racially divided labor force. Already in the North, black workers, some of them skilled and many of them veterans of the war, were seeking admission to labor unions. In the South, slaves equal to about one-eighth of the US population had been set free by the Thirteenth Amendment. While most were agricultural laborers, some were skilled or semi-skilled artisans. . . . Given the apparent direction of Republican policies in the early years of Reconstruction, it would have seemed that ex-slaves were about to become free wage laborers with the same rights, presumably including suffrage and geographical mobility, as white workers. (Saxton 1990, 300)

But this was not to be.[34]

A second crucial dimension of the 1877 events was that in California, the strike was transformed into an anti-Chinese working-class movement:

In San Francisco, demonstrations supporting the railroad strikes were taken over by anti-Chinese agitators. Fighting continued for four days. Mobs killed Chinese in the streets and tried to burn the . . . docks where Chinese immigrants frequently came ashore. Anger at the Central Pacific Railroad was transposed into violence against Chinese, of whom the railroad was reputedly the largest employer. Temporarily at least these events shattered the balance of California politics (Saxton 1990, 297; see also Almaguer 1994, 164–174; Saxton 1971; Brundage 1994).

With the defeat of the massive strikes of the 1870s and 1890s, the post–Civil War, post-abolitionism U.S. system of social stratification was consolidated. It was first and foremost a system of *racial stratification.*

The reversal of Reconstruction-era black empowerment had been completed by the 1890s, when segregation policies became universal in the South. Abandonment of the 14th Amendment's egalitarian principles was ratified on a national scale by the 1896 *Plessy* decision, with its absurd insistence that segregation was not inequality. A year before *Plessy*, Booker T. Washington, the preeminent U.S. black leader, had announced his capitulation to the regime of Jim Crow in a famous speech at Atlanta (see below).

The anti-Asian agitation of 1877 also solidified in subsequent decades, giving rise to a permanently split labor market in the West (Saxton 1971; Ong 1981; Chan 1991; Okihiro 1991; Hing 1993). Anti-Chinese pogroms, as well as anti-Japanese (Ichioka 1988) and anti-Filipino agitation (Sobredo 1998), became the central organizing principles of much of the West Coast labor movement,[35] although there were some radical counter-tendencies like the Industrial Workers of the World (IWW), an anarcho-syndicalist organization.

At the national level, a series of exclusionary and restrictive immigration and naturalization policies endorsed and deepened discrimination against and superexploitation of Asians:

> The political issue in 1877 was racial, not financial, and the weapon was not merely the ballot, but also "direct action"—violence. The anti-Chinese agitation in California, culminating as it did in the Exclusion Law passed by Congress in 1882, was doubtless the most important single factor in the history of American labor, for without it the entire country might have been overrun by Mongolian [sic] labor and the labor movement might have become a conflict of races instead of one of classes. (Perlman 1950, 52)

In large measure, indeed, the U.S. labor movement *did* become a conflict of races. Racial inequality and discrimination, enforced by working-class violence and legitimated by state policy, became the foundation of the U.S. class system in the age of industry.

Brazil

Elsewhere in the Americas, roughly parallel situations obtained. Brazil too entered a profound transition as abolition was belatedly completed. Although a large number of Afro-Brazilians had already been freed from slavery by various means before the official decree of emancipation (the *Lei Aurea* or "Golden Law") was promulgated on May 13, 1888, hundreds of thousands of slaves remained (Ianni 1988; Graham 1999). Memories were still fresh of the 1896–97 rebellion in the *sertão* (backlands, "boondocks") of Bahia state, which provoked considerable anxiety among both planters and republicans. Slavery (and free black labor as well) was still concentrated on the plantations—the diminished sugar-producing *fazendas* of the northeast and the *cafezais* (coffee plantations) of the southeast.

Emancipation took place at a moment of great historical transition for Brazil. The shift of the *Lei Aurea* was followed by the proclamation of the republic in November 1899. Athough the end of the monarchy occurred peacefully in a palace coup, the early years of the republic were marked by various conflicts between monarchists and republicans. A naval revolt in 1893 and warfare in the country's South provoked U.S. intervention, and self-proclaimed "Jacobins" demonstrated in the streets in support of the republican president Floriano Peixoto, who ruled under martial law during the 1891–94 period.[36]

Prompted most centrally by these events, the country experienced something of an identity crisis, in which a central element was race. A prolonged and extensive debate took place about Brazilian racial identity and its supposed effects on the country's capacity to modernize (Schwarcz 1987; Azevedo 1987;

Viotti da Costa 1985). Discussion focused in detail on the role of the *libertos* (free blacks); much of it was permeated with the familiar warnings about endemic black laziness (*vadiagem*).[37] Instead of developing either official policies of segregation or programs of integration (in the manner of U.S. Reconstruction efforts), elite consensus settled on the imperative of *branqueamento* (whitening) through the recuitment of European immigrants (Skidmore 1993 [1974]).

Meanwhile, in the Northeast, especially in the old sugar-producing states of Bahia and Pernambuco, paternalism and violence coexisted uneasily. The majority of Afro-Brazilians still inhabited this region, but the sugar-based sector of the Brazilian economy was extremely vulnerable to international competition (Scott 1994; Scott et al. 1988; Eisenberg 1974; Baronov 1994).

The region's backwardness was reinforced by emancipation in 1888 (and by erosion of the slave labor system before that). In the countryside the system of *coronelismo* evolved fairly directly from the old *fazendas*. Impoverished rural workers, largely black and brown, found themselves at the mercy of these authoritarian bosses, who resembled feudal lords more than ranchers (Luna 1983; Pang 1978). Efforts to avoid peonage on the old plantations led to a substantial exodus into the arid backlands, where subsistence farming was almost impossible to sustain. As large numbers of former slaves fled the plantations, they came to comprise an impoverished migrant population that wandered the region in search of food, labor, or land for subsistence farming. Some became *jagunços* (rural riffraff, country gangsters), and gravitated to the massive rural rebellion that erupted in the Bahian *sertão* at Canudos in 1896.

The Canudos community, a messianic religious group, formed a cult-like alternative society, led by the Catholic romantic (and reactionary) Antonio Conselheiro. Comprised of ex-slaves and impoverished rural people, and fed by a continuous stream of migrants, the *jagunços*[38] of Canudos in some ways resembled the old *quilombo* of Palmares, requiring several federal military expeditions to defeat them. Meanwhile, in the heavily black city of Salvador, the largest town in Bahia state (and former capital of the country), drumming could be heard at night on the outskirts of town.[39] There was growing interest in *candomblé*, a syncretic religion tied to Yoruba animism as well as Catholicism. Needless to say, the modernizing elites of the Southeast were less than pleased with the general trend of events in the country's Northeast.

In Rio de Janeiro and São Paulo, where the coffee plantations were located, labor market competition between white immigrants and blacks was on the increase, resulting in large-scale displacement of black wage workers (Holloway 1977a; Holloway 1977b; Holloway 1980). Here black attempts to regularize wage labor arrangements in the post-emancipation years (to negotiate contracts, for example) threatened and offended the coffee planters. In addition, the planters often found that newly arrived white immigrants were so desperate for work that they would underbid even *libertos* (Andrews 1991, 81–89). Labor conditions on the São Paulo coffee plantations at the turn of the century were so exploitative that the Italian government banned further emigration to Brazil in 1902 (Lesser 1999, 85).

Thus the great majority of former slaves and their progeny found themselves in peonage in agricultural settings (often on the same sugar and coffee plantations where they had worked before), marginalized in the most impoverished circumstances imaginable, or relegated to menial and servile jobs in the towns. In large measure this was because the national government had embarked on a policy of replacing them, as completely as possible, with white labor. European immigration was subsidized from 1890 to 1927. Although the ex-slaves' socioeconomic status was generally not all that different from that of the new European immigrants arriving under the whitening policies that were the elite's preferred solution to the "Negro problem," there was a profound difference between the two groups. The immigrants'

> integration occurred to a large degree through the wage labor system that existed in dynamic regions and economic sectors. As a consequence, the initial position of the immigrants, though hardly favorable, allowed them to monopolize the opportunities for social mobility created by the economic system. (Hasenbalg 1979, 166)

Afro-Brazilians, in contrast, were not integrated into the wage system; they were relegated to peonage.

Another interesting Brazilian pattern, parallel to U.S. post-emancipation dynamics as well, was the extensive recruitment of Asian immigrants. In the first years of its whitening policy, Brazil had banned emigration from both Africa and Asia. But as early as 1892 emigration from Japan was being advocated, because the Japanese—as was argued along racial/eugenic lines—were preferable to the Chinese. White labor shortages,[40] combined with reluctance of the São Paulo-based planters to hire blacks, led to negotiations with Japanese authorities,[41] and a treaty was signed in 1895 (Lesser 1999; Reichl 1988; Tsuchida 1978; Saito and Maeyama 1973).

The Caribbean

Although the focus of this book is on other areas, I allow myself some very brief remarks about the post-emancipation Caribbean economy. Here too there was a parallel transition toward peonage. Here too there had been extensive debate (largely in Europe but also in the region) about the suitability of emancipated slaves for "free" labor. Planters and colonists, who had agitated for and received substantial compensation for the "losses" they incurred through emancipation, also argued on racist grounds that gradual and coercive processes of tutelage ("apprenticeship," etc.) would be needed to socialize the workforce to the demands and discipline of "free" labor. The emancipated former slaves desired the least possible continuation of relationships with their former masters (now redefined as their employers), and instead sought the independence of autonomous (and as far as possible, collectively organized) systems of peasant cultivation. This overlapping pattern of race and class conflict led to rebellion and repression in the case of Jamaica (Holt 1992; Heuman 1994). In other Caribbean sugar colonies too, former slaves were unwilling to accept the discipline of the plantation. With limited options to foment immigration and settlement a la the United States or Brazil, the British sought to overcome shortages of low-waged (or unwaged) labor, as well as to counter the rebelliousness of the Afro-Caribbean populations they ruled, by importing workers from the Indian subcontinent.[42] Generally victimized by this highly exploitative indenture system, these new and different peons were recruited to Guyana and Trinidad almost immediately after abolition, first arriving around 1838 (Segal 1995, 186). The resulting fragmentation and lack of solidarity among the working classes in the anglophone Caribbean was probably the main pillar of the peonage system there (Rodney 1981b).

THE RATIONALIZATION OF RULE

The latter half of the nineteenth century was a period of upheaval. The U.S. Civil War announced the terminal condition of the global system of slavery. The establishment of independent nation-states in the Americas was the first wave of decolonization. The triumph of industrial capitalism and the onset of economic crises in the 1870s and 1890s revealed the volatility of a largely unregulated global marketplace. Great processions of migrants marched across the globe, reorganizing and stratifying societies everywhere: in the Old World and the New, in metropole, colony, and ex-colony.

New social theories—new common sense—was needed as systems of rule changed and as different social and political actors appeared on the scene. Both rulers and ruled struggled to grasp the shifting political-economic and cultural mainsprings of the tumultuous world. The political-economic and social theories that would guide the modern era were being worked out at this time, not by coincidence, but because there were desperate needs for new concepts, new guidance, new forms of knowledge. Social theory was born in the aftermath of the French Revolution, especially in the work of Hegel. With the appearance of Marxism and the mainstream's rejoinders to it—marginalist economics and the systematic sociological theory of Weber and Durkheim—[43] the explanatory tools needed for the industrial age were coming into being.

Enlightenment-based accounts of race, systems of human racial classification, and the various proto-anthropologies that had been available from the eighteenth century on were another important source of explanatory resources. Born of explorers' and travelers' accounts and developed in the natural history genre of that century, European understandings of human diversity had become more empirical and proto-scientific in the nineteenth century as Morton, Agassiz, Broca and others developed their methods of anthropometry, cranial capacity measures, and so on (Gould 1981).[44] These early interventions, combining with the rich literature of racial stereotyping and antisemitism long available in Europe (Mosse 1978), were the founding documents of scientific racism. A very important statement about the centrality of race that both drew on this tradition and harked back to its earlier philosophical predecessors was the romantic and conservative work of Count Arthur de Gobineau.[45] In his *Essai sur l'inégalité des races humaines*, published in the 1850s, Gobineau laid the groundwork for anti-modern currents of thought about race; his target was as much the legacy of the French Revolution and the modernizing aspects of Enlightenment culture as it was the racial "mongrelization" of Europe.[46]

But in the latter nineteenth century the demand for social theory was considerably augmented by the pace of sociopolitical and economic change. Detached from the author's reactionary and anti-modernist beliefs, and rearticulated over the decades following the appearance of Darwin's theory of evolution, Gobineau's thought and its successors would furnish the scientific world with an explanation of racial hierarchy that remains highly significant even today. Darwin's *On the Origins of Species* (1859) was not particularly concerned with racial matters, despite its subtitle ("The Preservation of Favored Races in the Struggle for Life"), but in *The Descent of Man* (1871), influenced no doubt by his cousin Francis Galton, whose book *Hereditary Genius* had appeared two years before (Galton 1978 [1869]), Darwin embraced the racial notions of human hierarchy that were the common sense of the time. The synthesis of Gobineau and Darwin was also mediated by Herbert Spencer, who originated the phrase "survival of the fittest" (Spencer 1967; Hofstadter 1959 [1955], 39). Eugenics—the term was Galton's coinage—provided a modern rationalization of racial rule in the aftermath of slavery.[47]

Galton's work and the massive literature of and about eugenics cannot be reviewed here, but it is worthwhile to note that already in 1869, as Reconstruction was underway in the United States and the former slaves of the British colonies were being "disciplined" (or subordinated) into various forms of peonage and superexploitation, Galton was arguing that "the average intellectual standard of the negro race is some two grades below our own" (Galton 1978 [1869], 342). The eugenics "movement"[48] acquired a degree of political credibility that far outstripped earlier efforts to defend racial hierarchy. Eugenics was embraced throughout the world as a modern and indeed practical necessity, something human progress itself demanded. Its assumptions of evident human differences in intelligence, fitness for reproduction, and even beauty were rarely criticized before the 1920s. Its reformulation on ostensibly scientific grounds of the racial stereotypes inherited from earlier periods of colonialism, slavery, and anti-semitism was accepted by diverse political currents. Not only elites anxious to justify low wages and Malthusian anti-welfare policies, not only nativists of all classes threatened by immigration and wage competition, but progressives and socialists too fell under its spell. They understood eugenics as a way of taking control of human development and social evolution across the generations; it resonated with their ideals of emancipation and self-determination.[49] As Barkan notes,

> By the turn of the century, racial theories which contructed a hierarchy of races with the Nordic at the top were considered factual, free of prejudice and generally pertinent to social and political analysis. Scientists were entrusted with the tasks of discriminating between fact and opinion and defining the social and political discourses of race. (Barkan 1992, 2)

But the preponderant effect of eugenics was to reinforce whiteness as the consequences of emancipation and massive immigration made themselves felt. The process of eugenic "reform" was carried out unevenly from country to country and from the world's North to its South; yet the differences within the "movement" were ultimately rather minor. Eugenics had the desired outcome: it rationalized racial rule. The two main U.S. eugenics advocates, Madison Grant and Lothrop Stoddard, were both quite clear in their arguments for white supremacy. In *The Passing of the Great Race* (1970 [1916]), perhaps the most influential statement of the movement's objectives, Grant made defense of whiteness paramount:

> The cross between a white man and an Indian is an Indian; the cross between a white man and a negro is a negro; the cross between a white man and a Hindu is a Hindu; and the cross between any of the three European races and a Jew is a Jew. (Quoted in Marks 1995, 111; see also Nash 1999, 23; Myrdal 1962 [1944], 114)

Stoddard, a somewhat younger man, visited Nazi Germany, met Hitler, took part in a Nazi "eugenics court," and wrote as late as 1940 that

> The relative emphasis which Hitler gave racialism and eugenics many years ago foreshadows the respective interest toward the two subjects in Germany today. Outside Germany, the reverse is true, due chiefly to Nazi treatment of its Jewish minority. Inside Germany, the Jewish problem is regarded as a

passing phenomenon, already settled in principle and soon to be settled in fact by the physical elimination of the Jews themselves from the Third Reich. It is the regeneration of the German stock with which public opinion is most concerned, and which it seeks to further in various ways. (Quoted in Chase 1977, 348; see also Stoddard 1920, which contains an introduction by Grant; Kühl 1994)

Eugenics was to have enormous effects in other ways as well. Its explicit use as a legitimation device for policies of racial discrimination and immigrant exclusion[50] eroded after World War II in consequence of its association with the Nazis (Barkan 1992; Mazumdar 1992).[51] But its effects on the development of social science were enormous and probably irreversible. Modern quantitative analysis—the multivariate analytical techniques taught to graduate students in the social sciences—originated in the eugenics of Galton, and developed much farther in the work of his followers Karl Pearson and Ronald Fisher (Marks 1995, 78–79). In the work of these eugenicists and their followers inferential statistics supplanted descriptive statistics as the state-of-the-art quantitative methodology in the neophyte social sciences.[52]

By making the transition from metaphysical speculation and the fledgling racial "science" of Samuel Morton, Paul Broca, and Louis Agassiz (Gould 1981) to the statistically sophisticated accounts of the turn of the twentieth century, eugenics trumped a great many critical analyses of racial inequality and injustice. Although it was in fact riddled by impressionistic and subjective biases, although it suffered from chronic and blatant (by today's standards) construct invalidity (Marks 1995), although it was no less a pseudo-science than the earlier works it claimed to have supplanted, the superficial scientificity of eugenics seemed far more powerful than the critical objections it encountered, which were at any rate few in number.[53] Eugenics played a vital role at the turn of the twentieth century, both in rationalizing the changing demography of race and in justifying the continuation of racial hierarchy. Its success in attaining global intellectual leadership on matters of racial meaning and racial policy, at a time when significant challenges to the legitimacy of colonialism (not to mention slavery) were on the rise, cannot be overestimated.

POLITICAL STRUCTURE IN THE LATE NINETEENTH CENTURY

Although slavery was dying its "slow death," empire survived. Mass labor was still required: in mines and fields, in public works, even in nascent industry. A vast hinterland still rattled its chains. In place of slavery a new and more uneven system of domination and resistance was evolving. This system was more integrated, more competitive, more industrial, more comprehensively capitalist. It was, however, still mixed, still "combined and uneven," still transitional.

In the aftermath of slavery there was very limited possibility of even the demonstration, much less the consolidation, of political opposition from below. In direct continuity with the period of slavery, withdrawal (or escape) from various coercive labor regimes, and armed conflict, were the only forms of explicit challenge available.[54] The comprehensiveness of racial exclusion from civil society—if such a thing as "civil society" may even be said to have existed—was perhaps the most formidable carryover from the ancien régime of slavery. Lacking recognition and citizenship, opposition was at first largely restricted to warfare and rebellion. Political activity was effectively foreclosed. This is the political logic Gramsci designates as *war of maneuver*. Ideal-typically it is appropriate to societies where the level of popular legitimation (or "consent") is low, and where the ready use of force is the main guarantee of domination.

Yet the effect of abolitionism, for all its combination of wildly diverse political impulses, was also to spur significant incursions from below into the realm of the politically possible. The abolition of slavery foreshadowed and set the stage for a vast *abertura*—a global "opening"—in politics. That opening took many different forms, varying in the colonies and the metropoles, as well as in different regions of the world. It took a long time too: in fact it is far from over even now, as we enter the twenty-first century. From the nineteenth to the twenty-first centuries, though, the symbolic value of the struggle against slavery has remained constant. The delegitimation of slavery definitively breached the most deeply fortified barriers of political exclusion, and heralded the emergence of a new stage in democratization. I treat this hard-won expansion of political access as a transition to *racial war of position*, as a dawning and blooming of the potential of racial democracy. The opening up of political life to the racially subjugated, the subaltern, that was no more than foreshadowed in the struggle against slavery, would take on new forms in the twentieth-century twilight of colonialism and white supremacy.

Schematically speaking, in the first stages of the transition after abolition, the ex-slaves still lacked political "voice" (Hirschmann 1970).[55] Local elites, however, were frequently able to renegotiate the terms of rule in these irregular and disorderly situations. As new forms of colonial rule were being improvised and tested, colonial offices and parliaments (and presidents and congresses too) recognized that they needed the cooperation of power-holders in their imperial and provincial hinterlands. Compromise might now be required; failing that, maneuver of a divide-and-conquer type might achieve the main metropolitan aim: subordination of the colonized territories (Laitin 1986). Thus in the later nineteenth century the metropoles strove mightily to cede nonessential powers to local colonial elites and settlers (for example, in post–Boer War South Africa), to negotiate more workable terms of trade or labor relations with the colonies (Cooper 1987), and to cultivate neo-colonial arrangements with independent yet less-developed peripheral countries.[56]

So even by the late nineteenth century in an uneven way, and more strongly in the twentieth century, the metropolitan powers had to reckon with power structures and conflicts that were entrenched at the edges of their domains and spheres of influence. In Africa and Asia the peculiarities of late colonial politics were setting in. No longer committed to slavery in the main, colonial rule now required labor in different forms, more diversified forms of authority, and alternative means of local collaboration. The state now shrank from the high imperial ambitions of the past: to project power as widely as possible, to play the "great game," to fulfill the responsibilities of cultural uplift, to shoulder the white man's burden, were all called into question. The value of local allies, of traditional structures of authority, of divide-and-rule tactics, was increased when the objectives of rule were the relatively modest ones of profitable export-oriented cash-crop production or mining, rather than the institution and administration of more comprehensive forms of rule.[57] Metropolitan powers operating on other frontiers—the gilded age industrial bourgeoisie confronting the post–Civil War U.S. South, the British in independent Latin America—faced similar limits.

Post-slavery regimes had to deal with colonial, and even independent, elites: creolized, maybe even racially hybridized partners, competitors, or opponents. Because they were willing—or compelled really—to forego their dreams of thoroughgoing domination, colonial rulers and overseers, planters and traders, had to confront their subjects in new ways. Racial issues were thus very much in play during the prolonged transition into the twentieth century. Unlike chattel slaves, whose utter domination, or "natal alienation" as Patterson (1982) calls it, had been the ideal (if not quite attainable) state of subjection, the post-emancipation, post-slavery system of identity was more partial, more ambiguous. As the confrontation between master and slave became one of settler and native, landlord and tenant, boss and worker, the dynamics of rule became a lot more complicated. The master-slave dialectic, which at the time of the French Revolution could effectively figure almost all the salient issues of politics (Hegel 1967 [1807]; Marcuse 1960 [1941])—incorporating inclusion/exclusion, (in)dependence, domination/subordination, even exploitation/alienation/ "species-being"—by a century later had become almost entirely inadequate and anachronistic as a trope of political conflict. At the dawn of the twentieth century the "problem of the color-line" was first recognized as having replaced the problem of slavery as a central world-historical political issue (Du Bois 1989 [1903]). This was but a reflection of the increasing autonomy and subjectivity that the world's "others," its non-white, non-European, non-citizens, had begun to acquire by this time.

Thus, incomplete and uneven as it was, *the assault on slavery launched modern politics.* Beginning with abolitionism, the dominated and excluded of the world embarked on a long journey. They began the continuing effort to put an end to empire and colonialism, to extend political and human rights to the ends of the earth.[58]

The destruction of the worldwide system of human slavery was the point at which race became a proper political issue. Abolitionism was the social movement that first included racially identified subjects—the colonized, the formerly enslaved, the subaltern—on the terrain of the political. Not the fulfillment of abolitionist goals, but the launching and spread of the movement, marked the beginning of the *socialization of the political*, of the extension of political rights toward the universal. There had of course been earlier emancipatory efforts: slaves and peasants have rebelled since slavery and peasant agriculture came into being. The impulse for political inclusion also had earlier incarnations: among the northern countries, and notably in the U.S. and French Revolutions(Shapiro et al. 1998), there had been inklings, initial demands, that the popular strata must be involved in the process of governance. Before the spread of abolitionism there had been, in short, intimations of democracy. But these incursions, these violations of the boundary between rulers and ruled, tended to stop at the edge of national boundaries, the borders of the *volk*, if not always the *herrenvolk*. Yes, there were exceptions—the *gens de couleur* in Haiti or New Orleans, for example (James 1989 [1938]; Hirsch and Logsdon 1992; Davis 1966)—but these are not crucial. Before the successes of abolitionism, non-Europeans could have almost no political standing, no credibility. They were outside the realm of civil society; their mobilizations—as seen in countless slave revolts, in *marronage* and anti-colonial warfare, and in subversion of all sorts—were *wars of maneuver*, to use the Gramscian terminology.[59]

So the global racial formation process had global political consequences. Not only did race shape the modern world in a great many ways: as a fundamental dimension of capitalist development, as a key factor in imperial expansion and conquest, as a corporealizing means of human identification and classification that informed everyday life and culture. But it also established the overall contours, as well as the particular political and cultural legacies, of subordination and resistance. Racial rule meant the restriction or even the foreclosure of the political terrain upon which colonized and enslaved people, subaltern groups, could mobilize within civil society. It thus constituted these groups as *outside* what civil society there was. Racial rule denied the existence of commonalities among colonizers and colonized, Europeans and non-Europeans, whites and "others."

How extensive, how effective, was this denial? The answer to this question is necessarily mixed: never was it possible to cleave the world, or any society, by means of an unbridgeable racial gap: such transracial commonalities and ambiguities as shared economic activities, shared rights (or lack of rights) as citizens or non-citizens, shared familes and children, racially mixed and miscegenated identities, have just about always managed to exist. Yet racial rule, especially before abolitionism and emancipation, tended to construct race, at least ideal-typically, in terms of *all-embracing social difference.* It tended to homogenize distinctions among those whose difference with whites, whose racial "otherness," was considered the most crucial component of their identities. The boundary could be trangressed, but it remained. To remove it, to obliterate it, would be to topple one of the pillars on which the world rested.

Over time, then, this "white versus other" concept of difference created not particular and unchanging racial identities—for these are always in flux—but the potentiality, the social structures, indeed the necessity, of universally racialized identities on a nearly global scale. Over the centuries before the emergence of abolitionism this process of global racial formation created the conditions under which racial war of maneuver would be the only form of political mobilization accessible to the subaltern.

But with abolitionism there were the beginnings—just the beginnings, but they were significant—of the entry into "mainstream" politics of racially defined "others." In some cases, as I have argued (notably in the United States), this transformation took the form of actual entry, on the part of ex-slaves who were almost universally disenfranchised and of dubious citizenship, into the realm of "mainstream" political discourse. Thus arose such figures as Frederick Douglass and André Rebouças,[60] ex-slaves and descendants of slaves who fought their way into the political sphere. But this was difficult. Usually the subaltern lacked political voice, as Spivak (1988) has argued in a quite different context. Abolitionism too was often grounded in arguments made by ("free") citizens, on behalf of the civic inclusion (or partial inclusion) of those held in bondage. As is generally recognized in the historical literature, abolitionist positions varied from explicit advocacy of racial hierarchy (for example, those who argued for recolonization/repatriation of Africans),[61] to those who stood for immediatism: complete equality and full citizenship rights for ex-slaves.[62]

War of position is predicated on some measure of presence and voice within the political system. Such inclusion is achieved only after prolonged exclusion, only after sustained war of maneuver. It is an aftermath of resistance and revolution. War of position implies the possibility of political reform, concessions, and incorporation, even formal representation. It is in short a situation of *hegemony* as opposed to one of domination.[63]

After centuries of subjugation and resistance, after Haiti and Jamaica and the U.S. Civil War, unevenly and incompletely, came emancipation. With the consolidation, often at terrible costs, of racially identified non-European communities—"natives" and ex-slaves, non-white immigrants—whose social and political claims could no longer be summarily dismissed, the terms of racial formation began to be altered. The emergence of racial war of position can be seen in the slow migration of racial resistance to the towns and cities, to the workplaces, to the print media. War of position is visible in the onset of strike

activity, in the overt assertion of religiously grounded claims, and in the articulation of a wide range of culturally based forms of resistance, all on the part
of ex-slaves, the colonized, and the subaltern.

By the second half of the nineteenth century, capitalism had arrived at its first
modern crisis. Not only slavery, but the whole available range of labor regimes
had become problematic. Colonialism—ostensibly the central battlefield of the
great powers—had both crystallized and begun to antiquate by the turn of the
century.[64] Worldwide depressions in the 1870s and 1890s signaled new disruptions in the economic system. Wholesale population movements—particularly
new flows of European emigration—were sparked by the hard times.

Migration reworked the demography of the Americas, as well as such other
areas as Australia, South Africa, and Indonesia, just as the slave trade and conquest had previously done. Meanwhile the legacy of the anti-slavery movement,
the mobilizing experience and lessons of abolitionism, heralded an expansion
of democracy beyond the elites for whom democratic rights had hitherto been
reserved. Here were the beginnings of new political forms, more popular, more
participative.

Not only in the metropoles and industrial areas, but in the empires and the
agrarian backwaters of the system, challenges were brewing. These disruptions
were triggered in part by the decline of slavery. Resistance movements and anti-
colonial warfare were only occasionally successful, but even when they weren't
they still presented colonial rulers with significant impediments to their authority, not to mention unwelcome costs. As difficulties and divisions set in for the
sahibs and massas of the world—obstacles their subjects themselves, both foreign and domestic, had placed in their rulers' path—the subjects increased and
diversified their mobilization. In a variety of collective forms—as ethnonational
groups, religious adherents, and workers—they made early efforts to intervene
in politics. They staged strikes, refused to pay taxes, and where possible reinvented ethnonational states deriving from past formations. Where institution-
alizing resistance was not an option—and it was difficult as best—colonized and
racially subordinated folks experimented with heightened cultural resistance.
By the early twentieth century, too, there were new forms of insurgency—of
socialism and nationalism particularly—afoot among them.

RACIAL DUALISM AND THE CRISIS OF LATE COLONIALISM

The whole idea of "freedom" succeeding slavery in much of the colonial world,
as well as in those areas that had already achieved national independence, is
itself highly problematic. A host of coercive labor arrangements and statuses
followed hard upon slavery. Emancipation was succeeded by labor regimes and
overall systems of rule more akin to what had been abolished than to any form

of "free" labor, much less general democracy. Yet these "intermediate" regimes were necessarily prone to conflicts and contradictions that had barely existed under slavery.

The main colonial economic activity in the late nineteenth and early twentieth centuries remained the extraction of resources, both primary and agricultural. Independent nations too, even industrializing ones like the United States, maintained a rural hinterland, generally organized as a plantation-based agrarian zone. Threats to systems of labor exploitation were central problems in the aftermath of emancipation, but there were plenty of social and political upheavals as well. As I have argued, these disturbances could hardly be confined to the realm of the economic. They acquired increasingly political form as the subaltern began to acquire rights and voice. They also overran the frontier between production and reproduction. That is, they took on greater cultural significance as the old racial barriers that had buttressed slavery eroded: issues of family, health, gender, education, and child-raising became more prominent in public debate and social policy-making. The increasing presence of mixed-race/"colored"/*mestizo* populations, and of miscegenation in all its disruptive configurations (concubinage, rape, the eroticism of the racial "other," marriage, cohabitation, "going native," etc.), worked to undermine the authority and coherence of colonial and hinterland regimes (Stoler 1991; Stoler 1995; Hunt 1997; Colonna 1997; Hodes 1997; Hodes 1999).

Late colonialism should be understood as a complex racial formation process. It should be seen as an extended political confrontation among four groups: (1) colonial/provincial powers or ruling elites; (2) white settlers, small farmers, and industrial workers; (3) emergent nationalist forces, who constituted a nascent and radical counter-elite; and (4) subaltern lower strata, the natives, the ex-slaves and their progeny, the mass laborers. This model both draws upon the subaltern studies paradigm and necessarily puts it to some new and schematic uses.

Racial Dualism and Subalternity

Subalternity was a deeply racialized phenomenon. Subalternity should be seen as a late colonial racial formation process, as well as a post-slavery one. Racial dynamics are always relational: in any given social situation, each group's position overlaps and clashes with that of each other group. Around the turn of the twentieth century and for decades afterward, late colonial and post-slavery societies underwent protracted conflict about race. The principal collective actors in these contests were *colonial and provincial elites* and *lower-strata whites* on the one hand and *racialized subaltern strata* as well as *insurgent counter-elites* on the other. As clashes and maneuvers were taking place *among* these groups, each was also divided *within* itself by issues of racial meaning and identity. This is what I mean by use of the Duboisian term *racial dualism*.

In *The Souls of Black Folk* Du Bois famously described the "peculiar sensation" of "double-consciousness, this sense of always looking at oneself through the eyes of others" (1989 [1903], 5). This duality was a hallmark of the dawning twentieth century, a sign of the transition from slavery to freedom. This analysis, with its central concept of the "veil," was Du Bois' announcement of the importance of the color-line as both a world-historical problem and an intrapsychic one. Du Bois' account of the "peculiar sensation" prefigured the subalternity analysis, extending his account across the world, linking the situation of former slaves to that of the "darker peoples of the world."

Subalternity took this dualistic form in a wide variety of national and sociopolitical contexts. It reflected the relation of *natives and emancipated slaves* to peonage, their continuing disfranchisement, and their experience of the contempt and abjection inherited from slavery. In the United States, as Du Bois himself exhaustively documented, there were significant although brief experiments with redistribution of land to blacks, black capital formation, black public schools, and black enfranchisement and office-holding. But beginning in 1877, these initiatives were rolled back; that process had been largely completed by the turn of the century. Thus "freedmen"/women had had a taste of life on the other side of "the veil." For many it would be their first and last. Terrorism (in the form of lynching) was now the prevalent means used to control "free" blacks, in significant measure because they had experienced a brief alternative to nearly comprehensive subjugation. Although they had to operate within the white rules and offer the proper deference, black people could nevertheless advance their cause incrementally: they could own some property, they had access to money, they had some mobility. Building on the experience of slavery, black racial dualism evolved into what writers as diverse as Scott, Bhabha, and Kelley might call a "hidden transcript" of resistance (or more properly, of subversion and ridicule of the "ways of white folk"). But the very "hiddenness" of resistance practices testified to their limits.

In Africa, somewhat ironically, colonialism advanced much deeper into the continent as emancipation became the official metropolitan value. Only around the turn of the twentieth century was European domination of most of Africa secured. Resistance of the "war of maneuver" type was widespread, as wars swept much of the continent's interior during these years. Religious movements (sometimes millennial), refusals to succumb to the colonial cash economy and peonage-based labor system, flight into the interior, and efforts to sustain subsistence-based farming were the forms these conflicts took, short of outright war. These "primary resistance" strategies have been equated with later nationalist movements (Ranger 1967; Ranger 1986), a point quite consistent with the argument being developed here. But even in their own time and place, these movements suggest a developing dualism, an "art of resistance" that is partial, less than fully effectual, but capable of self-preservation.

The racial dualism of *subaltern elites* also crystallizes at this time. Du Bois famously pinned his hopes upon a "talented tenth": an educated upper stratum that would furnish leadership for the race. Its role was not just exemplary but tutelary: "Above all, the better classes of the Negroes should recognize their duty toward the masses," he wrote.

> [T]hat they do something already to grapple with these social problems of their race is true, but they do not yet do nearly as much as they must, nor do they clearly recognize their responsibilities. (Du Bois 1998 [1899], 392–393; see also Du Bois 1969 [1903])

Much of his early political and agitational work—his struggles with Booker T. Washington, his participation in the founding of the Niagara Movement and then the National Association for the Advancement of Colored People (NAACP)—can be understood as a sustained effort to implement this program. Appeals to the black middle classes have of course become a staple of reformism since this time, and Du Bois himself revised his position in his later, radical years (see Du Bois 1995 [1948]; Gates and West 1996).

The very forms in which resistance to late colonialism and racial segregation first appeared were deeply marked by the legacies and structures of the system of rule it endeavored to overthrow. The "talented tenth's" ambivalence about the black poor was certainly not the same as the nascent African trade unionists' ambivalence about the coerced peasants in the hinterlands; I am thinking here of the Lagos dock workers whose 1897 strike was one of the first instances of native trade unionism in Africa.[65]

Yet these workers' uncertainty about the possibilities and indeed desirability of resistance was also parallel to that of the nascent black bourgeoisie (really a middle class) in Philadelphia, Durham (North Carolina), and Washington. The contradictions experienced by racialized counter-elites would persist into the era of black nationalism and pan-Africanism, and would even characterize socialism and cultural movements such as Negritude. However committed to resistance and self-determination, these leaders had perforce to mediate between the powerful and the powerless. Uniformly led by members of a counter-elite, a subaltern elite, so to speak, these movements would also demonstrate their participants' racial dualism.

Subaltern struggles were therefore riven and paradoxical. On the one hand they were marked by expanded agency as well as augmented political and cultural autonomy. On the other hand they were limited by the continuity of white supremacy and the "curse of the nation state" (Davidson 1992). At the macrolevel these movements channeled resistance toward various insurgencies—notably nationalism but also socialism. At the micro-level these same movements demanded conformity and denied demotic experience and expression.

Perversely and inescapably, then, *as a result of resistance itself,* popular aspirations remained stifled, hidden, indeed "subaltern." Thus the prolonged progression up to and into the twentieth century, the long journey away from slavery and toward the break of World War II, could at best only anticipate the possibilities of democracy and "self-determination." The subaltern studies[66] approach shows us how much these aspirations, these hidden transcripts, remained profoundly coded along racial lines. The subaltern were both "freed" and ruled by racial dualism.

White Racial Dualism at the Elite and Mass Levels

When Du Bois formulated it at the turn of the twentieth century, he meant the concept of racial dualism to apply to blacks in the United States.[67] I extend it here to whites only with caution, for it shifts the focus away from subalternity. But the application of the notion to whites does highlight the metamorphosis that white identities too underwent in the aftermath of emancipation and the later stages of colonialism.

I turn first to *colonial and provincial elites.* These groups were comprised principally of landowners, colonial capitalists, and state officials. Although defined as European and white, they experienced their own racial identities as increasingly threatened. Like all creole ruling groups, late colonial and provincial elites confronted their metropolitan masters (in London, Paris, Washington, etc.) across more than a great geographical distance; there were other distances as well, notably those of politics and culture. Caught between their imperial or national loyalties and their tentative local authority, they struggled to maintain both their power base and their identities. Their positions were replete with contradictory tendencies: colonial elites often lived an *echt* British (or French, or Dutch) lifestyle, all the while experimenting with miscegenation and resenting both their dependence on the metropole and their increasing marginalization (Shaw 1995; Clifford 1988; Young 1995).

Post–Civil War planters in the U.S. South gradually recaptured a measure of national political influence, but remained in charge of a traumatized and marginalized region that had to be ruled by racial dictatorship and terror. Newly republicanized Brazilian elites feared the *irreconciliados* who still supported the monarchy (and whom they had to defeat by force of arms and martial law); they were even more worried, though, that their country might "deteriorate" or "devolve" into a *republica morena* (a "brown republic") if it was not rapidly whitened. South African ruling strata remained oriented toward London, but only at the price of placating the resentful Afrikaners, their white junior partners. Blacks paid for the repressive racial policies that developed in pursuit of this aim. The Boers saw themselves as implacably white: orthodox in their Dutch Reformist Protestantism and explicitly white supremacist; yet they found themselves trapped between the English and the natives. The English sneered at their provincialism

In both the metropoles and the colonies, *lower-strata whites* underwent significant shifts in class and status that were understood in racial terms. Emerging industrialism in the metropoles demanded their subordination; I have already discussed some of the variants of these themes in the later nineteenth century. By the time of World War I Du Bois detected

> a more subtle movement arising from the attempt to unite labor and capital in world-wide freebooting . . . , admitting to a share in the spoils of capital only the aristocracy of labor—the more intelligent and shrewder and cannier workingmen. The ignorant, unskilled, and restless still form a large, threatening, and, to a growing extent, revolutionary group in advanced countries. (Du Bois 1995 [1915], 647)

For the latter there were offered only the dubious satisfactions of a "psychological wage"[68] and the threat of lower-waged native/black/Asian competition. Far from prompting revolutionary mobilizations, these "restless" white workers tended (with some notable exceptions of course) to organize along racially exclusive lines (Saxton 1990; Goldfield 1997; Almaguer 1994).

Indeed the tentative extension of political voice to the racialized "others" produced profound disorientation among whites, especially when "race-mixing" was officially rendered taboo by obdurate segregation, anti-miscegenation laws, and so on.[69] The particular variety of racial dualism experienced by whites in situations where a racial system of hypodescent[70] remained in force, then, was necessarily primitive and focused on the defense of white "purity" and "discipline" (Roediger 1991). This was very clearly manifested in the U.S. South, where in the post–Civil War era (and especially in the post-Reconstruction period) whites embraced an irredentism marked by violent assertion of racial prerogatives. The social-psychological character of lynching—as a barbarous form of white "defense mechanism" against the displacement of racial authority—has been argued extensively in the literature on this practice (Tolnay and Beck 1995; Brundage 1993; McMillen 1989).[71] But this formula, while useful, only begins the detailed work needed. The depths of the insecurities turned loose by the abolition of slavery have yet to be plumbed. The "sexualization of Reconstruction politics," for example (MacLean 1994; Hodes 1997; Williamson 1986), or the cross-class white alliances that lynching consolidated, are only now emerging as crucial historical and sociological vantage-points.

Another major topic related to white racial dualism in the segregated South is its ties to political rule. Southern irredentism, the most active expression of white racial dualism, was placated by the national political system at all levels: the judiciary endorsed it in *Plessy v. Ferguson*; the "solid South" anchored the

Democratic Party electorally and legislatively; national institutions like the military deferred to it. Although many of these practices clearly undermined the Constitution and other laws, they remained in place because they reproduced the "compromise" of 1877: they attempted to resolve the conflict about national identity that the Civil War and Reconstruction had posed.[72]

Race-mixing was a form of racial dualism that was deeply threatening, even where it was commonplace. The system of racial rule had always to contain and regulate this menace: throughout the post-slavery world there was a search for an effective combination of repression and toleration of "race-mixing." But nowhere could the subversive implications of the intersection of race and sex be effectively contained. For example, in Brazil the central distinction was made between white workers on whose discipline and productivity the fate of the nation was thought to rest, and "primitive" black workers considered to be prone to *vadiagem* (laziness, vagrancy) and thought to require authoritarian but paternal treatment (Andrews 1991; Borges 1993). But this distinction always remained tenuous because of the deeply established tradition of *mistura racial* (race-mixing). The threat that white workers too might "go native"—indeed it was more than a threat—linked Brazil to such places as the Dutch and French East Indies (Stoler 1997), and to many areas in the Caribbean as well. In such cases, where the color-line could not be securely defined or easily recognized in ordinary interaction, a variety of intermediate racial categories came into common usage, accompanied by widespread anxiety about downward racial mobility.

TOWARD THE BREAK

As the twentieth century dawned, fledgling political classes stirred among the emancipated and colonized. These nascent leaderships faced a daunting challenge. Small and divided, they confronted an updated and somewhat reformed system of white supremacy that was overwhelmingly more powerful than any conceivable opposition.

Although hardly free of crisis and conflict, late colonial rule and post-slavery systems of racial subordination had been reorganized in an atmosphere that combined repression and paternalism. The African revolts and anti-colonial resistance that had challenged the Europeans during and after the late-nineteenth-century scramble had been largely suppressed by various colonial regimes, in some cases with a modicum of reform, but often through massive bloodletting.[73] In many cases, native workers and peasants had been driven off the desirable lands into reserve labor settings and vagabondage. In the Americas, the system of peonage and superexploitation was securely in place: largely plantation-based, racial rule had graduated from slavery to a system run by planters, overseers, and bosses, *caciques* and *coroneis*. In certain economic sectors (in public works, in construction, in domestic service, even in factories) there were established patterns of waged labor. Obviously there was extensive variation—in the amplitude of coercion applied, the economic options available, and the cultural deference required of subaltern groups. But in general, the system of racial rule at the start of the twentieth century was one of quiescent, if not entirely tranquil, white supremacy.

Under these circumstances it is understandable why political strategies of accommodationism and self-reliance were developed among the racially subjugated. These approaches largely built on the religious and millenarian traditions of earlier African nationalism, and tended to marginalize the revolutionary and resistance legacies of Haiti, David Walker, *quilombismo*, Morant Bay, the Zulu wars, and the like. Since little could be expected in the way of democratic concessions, a significant worldwide tendency toward conservative nationalism developed among racially identified minorities.

The leading practitioner of the difficult political balancing act this situation required was Booker T. Washington, whose influence was not only enormous within the United States, but in the Caribbean and Africa as well.[74] Yet Washington's leadership was merely the most successful of a wide-ranging series of trends and initiatives. The old-style Ethiopianism, the religiously based contacts and missionary orientations of such men as Alexander Crummell, the early pan-Africanism and Liberianism of Edward Wilmot Blyden, various Masonic and fraternal/sororal organizations, the African repatriation movements of Bishop Henry McNeal Turner, and others continued as well. Black awareness and concern for Africa, notably in regard to King Leopold's murderspree in the Congo, was also very intense at this time (Moses 1978, 221–222; Williams 1985 [1890]).

Accommodationism a la Washington was also a more complex movement than is ordinarily acknowledged. In part it was a practical response to the triumph of Jim Crow segregation, in part an effort to stake out the political terms of racial compromise. Washington's Atlanta Exposition speech of September 18, 1895, delivered on the verge of the Supreme Court's *Plessy* decision and in the wake of the Court's 1883 invalidation of the Civil Rights Act of 1875, was more than an acknowledgment that white supremacy was now the law in the South. It was also an attempt to propose limits to white reaction, something initially favored even by Washington's great opponent W. E. B. Du Bois. Upon getting news of the Atlanta speech Du Bois wrote in its praise that

> [H]ere might be the basis of a real settlement between whites and blacks in the South, if the South opened to the Negroes the doors of economic opportunity and the Negroes cooperated with the white South in political sympathy. (Lewis 1993, 175)

That Du Bois would not long after (in *The Souls of Black Folk* [1903]) take a far more critical stance toward Washington's maneuvering indicates just how uncertain black political options still appeared at this time.

Radicals and reformers were appearing as well; so Washingtonian accommodationism did not take up the whole field of emergent black politics. The first Pan-African Congress was held in London in 1900; here Du Bois delivered the address "To the Nations of the World," in which his most-quoted sentence ("The problem of the twentieth century is the problem of the colour line") was first presented. The manifesto continues:

> If, by reason of carelessness, prejudice, greed and injustice, the black world is to be exploited and ravished and degraded, the results must be deplorable, if not fatal, not simply to them, but to the high ideals of justice, freedom, and culture which a thousand years of Christian civilization have held before Europe. (Lewis 1995, 639–640)

Nor were disagreements among various political currents—over democratic demands like the vote, separate development, and even attitudes toward white rule—entirely clear at this point. Indeed Washington himself was involved in the outcry over Belgian atrocities in the Congo (Hochschild 1998, 241).[75] Pan-Africanism was emerging as an ideology of "uplift" and democratic reform as well as separate development, in Africa and the Caribbean as well as in the United States.[76] Du Bois' 1897 talk, "The Conservation of Races," provoked controversy by breaking with the model of assimilation bequeathed by Frederick Douglass and his generation of abolitionists to Washington and Du Bois. Here Du Bois proposed the widespread deployment of "race organizations"; he offered the outlines of a political program that was profoundly far-sighted:

> Here, it seems to me, is the reading of the riddle that puzzles so many of us. We are Americans, not only by birth and by citizenship, but by our political ideals, our language, our religion. Farther than that, our Americanism does not go. At that point we are Negroes, members of a vast historic race that from the very dawn of creation has slept, but half awakening in the dark forests of its African fatherland. We are the first fruits of this new nation, the harbinger of that black to-morrow which is yet destined to soften the whiteness of the Teutonic to-day. We are that people whose subtle sense of song has given America its only American music, its only American fairy-tales, its only touch of pathos and humor amid its mad money-getting plutocracy. As such, it is our duty to conserve our physical powers, our intellectual endowments, our spiritual ideals; as a race we must strive by race organization, by race solidarity, by race unity to the realization of that broader humanity which freely recognizes differences in men, but sternly

deprecates inequality in their opportunities of development. (Lewis 1995, 24–25)

More than a century after its articulation, and notwithstanding the residues of Herderian nationalism that it contains, this statement continues to point to a radical vision of democracy that beckons us from the future, not the past.[77] Du Bois here anticipates the most sophisticated rights-oriented political theory of our own time, the "constructivism" of John Rawls (1993).[78]

Although strategic debate and fledgling political initiatives were most advanced in the United States, where the experiences of the Civil War and Reconstruction were still prominent and recent memories, they were by no means limited to that country. Black and native political organizations, as well as transnational anti-colonial initiatives, were getting underway everywhere as the century turned. The South African Native Congress (SANC) was founded in 1898. Its successor would be the the the South African Native National Congress, started in 1912 and initially headed by John L. Dube, a follower of Booker T. Washington. A "coloured" association, the African Political Organization, was started in 1900; this group also had Washingtonian leanings. In Jamaica the National Club, "a proto-nationalist organization," provided early political orientation for Marcus Garvey, a printer and trade unionist who held a leadership post in the Club before immigrating to the United States in 1910 (James 1998, 50).

In Brazil, explicitly political black organizations did not emerge until the 1920s, but self-help associations, known as *irmandades* (brotherhoods), had been around for centuries and had been active in the struggle for abolition. These groups were uncommitted to the republic, which they (as well as other working-class Brazilians) saw as a creature of the planter elite. Discontented with the government's explicit racism, angered at its denial of their basic social and political rights through its de facto disenfranchisement of blacks and its refusal to support public schooling,[79] and outraged at its policy of *branquea-mento* (whitening) through immigration, blacks gravitated toward the various uprisings and insurgencies of the republic's early years.[80] But it was not until the 1920s that explicitly political black organizations made their appearance, a tardiness that Florestan Fernandes explains as a result of slavery's "racial plun-der" (*espoliacão racial*) and a consequent anomie of Brazilian blacks.[81]

A worldwide black movement was taking shape, beginning at the turn of the century and accelerating greatly after World War I. Its central element was nationalism, African nationalism, pan-Africanism.[82] The movement thus reprised—and of course went far beyond—the earlier nationalism that had informed the resistance, revolutionism, and reformism of the abolition period. The movement also overlapped with the great socialist/communist upsurge that galvanized the world after 1917. In this aspect too, black mobilization revis-ited and reinvented earlier moments of struggle, notably the U.S. Civil War.[83]

In his comparative study of black movements in the United States and

South Africa, George Fredrickson identifies "three distinct varieties" of pan-Africanism that overlapped and competed after World War I. "Pan-Africanism," he says, "was an insurgent force in political thought and expression throughout the black world." It took conservative, liberal reformist, and populist forms (Fredrickson 1995, 145). It is not necessary to recapitulate Fredrickson's incisive account here; in a few brief notes I simply comment on the numerous ways in which this movement's efflorescence anticipated the post–World War II break.

Fredrickson properly associates conservative pan-Africanism with the influence and legacy of Booker T. Washington. Although appropriate for Washington's actual lifetime (he died in 1915), this is something of a stretch for the post–World War I period. An element of Washington's model of self-reliance did carry forward into the anti-colonial and anti-racist mobilizations of the 1920s and beyond, particularly in the Garvey movement. But Washington's accommodationism and strategic refusal of political engagement, although logical responses to the ferocious Jim Crow of the late-nineteenth-century United States (and he was particularly concerned with the United States), made a lot less sense in the aftermath of World War I.

That war and the racial transformations that followed it prefigured the much greater dislocations of white supremacy that succeeded World War II. But the World War I events were hardly minor. Hundreds of thousands of African and African-American soldiers fought in Europe, most for the British, French, and Americans, but some for the Germans as well.[84] On the Entente side, fevered war propaganda highlighted democratic themes while pervasive colonialist and segregationist practices went largely unquestioned.[85] This brewed up an explosive set of contradictions both on military bases and among the Entente general staff. In the war's aftermath those same contradictions led to white race riots and pogroms in the United States, as well as a more restrictive "colour bar" in South Africa. They also had a heightening effect on anti-colonial mobilization (particularly in Africa, the Caribbean, and South Asia).[86]

Another notable feature of World War I was the stimulus it provided for the urbanization of blacks and natives. While migration to the cities was of course uneven, it still heralded an alternative to peonage for many former rural workers and peasants, as well as demobilized veterans. In the metropoles, notably the United States, the great migrations northward and city-bound were drawn on by the prospect of regular, industrial, waged labor.[87] Even in the hinterlands and colonies there were significant urbanizing trends: these "pull" factors had to do with increased demand for export goods, both agricultural and extractive; in addition, there were augmented public works agendas: docks, roads, railways, and all sorts of public facilities needed expansion. The war produced a boom that spread over the world.

At the war's end there were uncertainties and crises, both global and local.

Extensive promises had been issued to black and colonial soldiers: so many Senegalese had been mobilized that blacks in the French army were simply referred to as *les sénégalais*, when not simply called *les noirs*, we may presume (Manning 1998, 67). Du Bois had used his editorship of *The Crisis* to urge black support for the war effort, and had even at one point sought an officer's commission (he was 50 years of age when the United States entered the war). As the most prominent African-African leader of the period, he expected to exercise some influence over postwar reform policies both at home and in Africa. Not only were he and other pan-Africanists—of what Fredrickson labels the "liberal reformist" variety—disappointed, but they felt thoroughly betrayed. They pressed at Versailles for the extension of Wilsonian principle of self-determination to Africa and the Caribbean; they were roundly ignored. Their efforts to hold a Pan-African Congress in Paris at the time of Versailles were subverted by all the Allied governments; a small congress was made possible only by the personal intervention of Blaise Diagne of Senegal, a hero of the war and a loyal colonialist "factotum" of Clemenceau (Lewis 1993, 566–579; Marable 1986, 101–102).

Far worse were the outrages awaiting black soldiers returning to the United States. The "red summer" of 1919 featured white race riots in dozens of cities across the country. Abetted by local authorities and unchecked by any law enforcement, white mobs attacked and destroyed black neighborhoods, killing and burning systematically (Tuttle 1997). The extensive assaults on black communities throughout the country was testimony, if any more was needed, that whatever promises made during the war years of racial reform and inclusion would now be unceremoniously shelved. As uniformed black veterans marched by the thousands through the streets of Harlem, whole black communities elsewhere were being put to the torch, and other uniformed black veterans were being lynched in the South. Du Bois returned to the United States in time to witness the spectacle, and questioned his former support for Wilson.[88]

Disillusionment led Du Bois to move away from the moderate agenda of racial reformism associated with the NAACP, although it was not until 1934 that his conflicts with the organization's reform-oriented agenda led to his resignation as editor of *The Crisis* (Du Bois 1991 [1940], 312–315). The implicit endorsement at Versailles of continuing colonialism in Africa led him, as well as the African anti-colonialists and other insurgent elites with whom he was allied, to abandon hope in the Wilsonian program of self-determination. Thus Fredrickson's label of Du Bois's pan-Africanism as "liberal reformism," although more accurate about his earlier positions, somewhat mischaracterizes his politics at least from the 1920s on. The events of 1919 and their aftermath, combined with the impact of the Russian revolution, explain his move to the left during the 1920s and 1930s. In place of the sham of Wilson's self-determination, Du Bois and radical black counter-elites in the Americas and Africa at least approached, if not fully embracing, the alternative and revolutionary

Leninist version of self-determination that was also a product of World War I. Du Bois had, after all, anticipated much of Lenin's *Imperialism* in his 1915 article, "The African Roots of the War." Back home, organizations such as the African Blood Brotherhood were formed by left-leaning black veterans—many of them Afro-Caribbean immigrants—to defend black neighborhoods against white mobs by force of arms. These groups would shortly be incorporated in the Communist Party.[89]

In fact, the rise of an elective affinity between Marxism and pan-Africanism in the aftermath of World War I would prove to be a major factor shaping the worldwide racial break, now only a few decades off. After the Russian revolution and the Soviet Union's embrace of global anti-colonialist politics in the 1920s, adherence to the communist cause among the black and colonized peoples of the world would grow enormously (Horne 1986; Kelley 1994). The Comintern under Lenin's urging transformed the 1848 slogan of Marx and Engels, "Workers of all countries, unite!" into "Workers and oppressed peoples of all countries, unite!" thereby inviting anti-colonial adherence to the new (Third) International, and offering to support (as well as bidding to control) insurgent movements in Africa, the Americas, and elsewhere (Robinson 1983, 301–310; Eschen 1997).

The third pan-Africanist trend identified by Fredrickson is the "populist" one, exemplified by the Universal Negro Improvement Association (UNIA) of Marcus Garvey, an organization with its greatest following in the United States and Caribbean, but also with some presence throughout the African diaspora.[90] The appellation *populist* is appropriate for a group that was able to mobilize millions of black people in the United States alone, and that profoundly threatened both the reform-oriented (and middle-class) NAACP and the socialist and communist left. There were other reasons that Garveyism attained such a high level of mass support: among these were its continuity with the religiously based nationalism of the nineteenth century[91] and its profound mistrust of whites, white alliances, and even race-mixing.[92] Garvey's early experience as a trade unionist and labor organizer and his hortatory style of pan-Africanism all augmented his appeal.

Although there is a great deal of literature on the Garvey movement, scholars still have difficulties explaining its contradictions and lack of practicality. The UNIA could hardly have attained its organizational successes by mystifying and duping so many members: Garvey appealed largely to urban blacks whose political acuity was fairly high. In one of the best analyses available, Robert A. Hill argues that in its first phase the UNIA was a trade union-oriented, quasi-socialist organization that sought to mobilize the emergent, diasporic black working classes along anti-colonial and anti-white supremacist lines. But in the early 1920s the movement entered a second phase. After harassment by the Justice Department, Garvey grasped the meaning of the bitter anti-immigrant and red-baiting policies of Attorney General A. Mitchell Palmer and his young protégé J. Edgar Hoover. He knew he and his U.S. activities were among those being targeted, so he regrooved his political orientation. After 1921, he abandoned class appeals and toned down his anti-white rhetoric in favor of a racially separatist and self-help ideology more reminiscent of his mentor Booker T. Washington (Hill and Bair 1987; Marable 1986, 117).[93] He could thus offer racial militance without directly confronting white rule on the terrain of the political. His attempted rapprochement with the Klan and the Anglo-Saxon Clubs, his paramilitarism (the uniforms, the parades),[94] his attempts to build a kind of international Tuskegee through a series of shipping businesses and other commercial activities (all of which failed rather dismally), thus appear as efforts to evade the onerous task of political confrontation with colonialism and segregation.

This account deepens our understanding of the logic of Garvey's populism. It was flexible, symbolic, articulable to left or right, aesthetic. Fredrickson's useful idea here, borrowed from George Rudé, is that Garveyism was a "structured" ideology that did not require or even permit rigid adherence (Fredrickson 1995, 156). Populism is perhaps the quintessential example of this phenomenon. Without pushing the theoretical points too far, I want to invoke Laclau's (1977a) account of populism and Gilroy's (1996) examination of fascism as a potentially black phenomenon, not to refute but to deepen Fredrickson's account.

For Laclau, populism becomes an effective form of political mobilization when politics cannot occur through "normal" means. I have noted that after World War I black demands were considerably strengthened as a result of urbanization and the experience of wartime mobilization. But "normal" political alternatives were still foreclosed by the powerful institutions of white supremacy: Jim Crow and colonial rule were not about to be toppled. Although Garveyism sought to evade this confrontation, as a movement it was stuck. On the one hand, the old coercive racial system that had bred Washington's attempts at anti-political synthesis—what Fredrickson calls "accommodationism"—still ruled, although it had been weakened. On the other hand, emergent black political capabilities—what Fredrickson calls "liberal reformism," and we may add, however controversially, communism—were not yet very strong. Garveyism was an attempt to navigate between these shoals. It could only symbolically address the needs of the masses of black people, but even this symbolism was more than the counter-elites of the NAACP or the newly formed Communist Party could do. Of course Garvey's politics were doomed in the longer run: there was no program, "no there there." The result was what Gilroy calls "conservative irrationalism."

For Gilroy Garvey's determination to "purify and standardize our race" is crucial:

> Garvey is saying that racial purity and standardization have to be fashioned. The combined, deadly weight of racial difference, subordination, and oppression is insufficient to generate them spontaneously. The martial technologies of racial becoming: drill, uniforms, medals, titles, massed display have to be set to work to generate these qualities that are not immediately present. Garvey's views were framed and sanctioned by a version of nationalism figured through the familiar masculinist virtues of conquest and military prowess. (Gilroy 1996, 81)

Thus the flirtation with, or collapse into, a form of fascism, which is itself a populist articulation. The pathos of this situation, the defeat already built into his movement's self-restriction to the symbolic, the aesthetic, the mere imposturing of resistance to white supremacy, was emblematic not only of Garvey's failure, but of the inadequacy and insufficiency of political conditions. The time for a significant break with white supremacy was not yet.

During the late nineteenth and early twentieth centuries the preconditions for the break evolved: certainly not in a linear fashion, but fitfully and variably, with advances and setbacks occurring both globally and locally. As the world's "others" groped their way forward, if not toward "freedom," at least toward some degree of self-possession and political autonomy, they were continually constrained by the residual might of the old colonial and plantocratic systems. They were confronted by continuous efforts to deny them political voice, and limited as well by the various insurgent options available to them.

No proper historical account has been given here of the vast changeover that shook the world between the era of slavery and abolition and that of modern anti-colonialism, revolutionary communism, and liberal reformism. Instead I have traced the sociological contours of the emergent twentieth-century racial world, a world in which, unevenly but still inexorably, ex-slaves were becoming workers, asserting their political rights and encountering their identities, their subjectivities, in antagonistic and insubordinate ways.

This transition was, of course, far from complete. Even today, after the break, after colonialism and apartheid and civil rights, world racial hierarchy persists. Certainly at the end of the period I have considered in this chapter, the old world racial order persisted as well.

Yet that system had been massively challenged. I argue throughout this book that the dynamics of race comprehensively shape social structures, both globally and locally. It would be absurd to think that the structural transformations I have considered here—the institutionalization of new economic systems; the acquisition of political voice and the commencement of "war of position"; and the advancement and consolidation of subaltern subjectivity—only affected the racialized "others" of the world.

No. Although ample efforts were made and much blood (and ink) was spilled to stem "the rising tide of color against white world supremacy" (Stoddard 1920) in the extended period following abolition, worldwide racial formation, unsurprisingly, proceeded apace. The new racial dynamics that resulted—racially stratified labor forces, new forms of democratic mobilization, subaltern subversion—confronted the white world once again with uncertainty and turmoil. Socialism and anti-colonialism, not to mention depression, fascism, and war, would soon enough engulf the old world racial order in its most serious crisis ever.

PART TWO

THE CONTEMPORARY SOCIOLOGY OF RACE

Six

NOTES ON THE POSTWAR BREAK

IN THE PERIOD AFTER World War II, opposition to racial stratification and racial exclusion became major political issues. Anti-colonial and civil rights movements fought for national independence and democracy more fiercely than ever before. They challenged the expropriation of southern resources—land, labor, primary goods—by the northern metropoles. They demanded an end to the political domination and exclusion that had characterized colonial rule and racial subjection. They questioned political practices and global social structures that had endured for centuries. These opposition movements were color-conscious, but they were generally not racially homogeneous. Indeed, anti-racist movements could usually count on a heterogeneous assortment of allies. Of course, consciousness of race and racism counted; had not the colonial and slavery-based regimes that spawned movements for racial justice also been color-conscious?

This dawning anti-racist politics took different forms and emphasized different issues in the numerous settings where it emerged. Often anti-racist mobilizations overlapped with labor movements—socialist, communist, or simply trade unionist—in their denunciations of the conditions under which "colored" labor was available for exploitation in the former colonies as well as the metropoles. These anti-racist movements were largely congruent with democratic ones: they condemned the old forms of political exclusion as dictatorial, inconsistent with the libertarian and participative rhetoric that the mother-countries—the winners (in general) of the recent global conflict—had claimed they were fighting to defend. The global anti-racist challenge also called into question a whole panoply of mainstream cultural icons: long-established artistic, linguistic, scientific, and even philosophical verities were revealed to be deeply problematic racially.

And beyond all this, on a purely practical level the anti-racist movements of the postwar world drew on common experiences. Millions could identify with their political demands—most notably those who had undergone military mobilization followed by an embittering return to a segregated or colonized homeland. Movement adherents and activists not only remembered the democratic ideals they had fought for, but also sought to apply those ideals to the anti-colonial and anti-racist norms they encountered at home. Wartime experience gained in resisting the Axis powers translated fairly directly into national liberation and democratic movements as veterans were demobilized: in South Carolina or Vietnam, in South Africa or Indonesia, in Senegal, France, or Trinidad.

The anti-racist and anti-colonial movements that sprang up all over the postwar world attained a newly transnational character, as growing northern labor demand and southern poverty sparked widespread migration to the world's metropoles. The world had been transformed by the war, and was undergoing significant changes in the war's aftermath. The result was a strong motivation, a powerful summons, to complete the democratizing work begun a century before with slavery's abolition. Demographically, socioeconomically, politically, culturally, there was a worldwide break with the customary practices and entrenched institutions of white supremacy.

The racially based democratic movements that arose with this break demanded a series of social and political reforms from national governments around the world. These ranged from decolonization to belated enfranchisement and the granting of formal citizenship rights, from the delegitimation of state-enforced (de jure) racial segregation to the creation and implementation of a "politics of recognition" (Taylor et al. 1992) that attempted to valorize such norms as multiculturalism. These reforms were eventually undertaken, although unevenly; they were implemented, but less than thoroughly. Still, although framed in uncertain and sometimes contradictory ways, a great wave of racial reforms swept over the world in the postwar decades, notably from the 1960s on.

By the end of that tumultuous decade, the descendants of slaves and ex-colonials had forced at least the partial dismantling of most official forms of discrimination and empire. In great numbers they had left their "native reserves" and segregated communities, migrating not only to their countries' urban centers but overseas to the metropoles from which they had been ruled for centuries. They had begun to partake in the limited but real new political and economic opportunities on offer in many national settings (notably in the northern, post-imperial countries). In those countries where implacable racist and dictatorial regimes still held sway, movements for racial equality and inclusion were invigorated by the successes achieved elsewhere, redoubled their activities in the 1970s and after, and eventually won democratic reforms as well.

And yet the break was incomplete. The rupture with the white supremacist past was not—and could not be—total. Despite these epochal developments—decolonization, the enactment of new civil rights laws, the undoing of long-standing racial dictatorships, and the adoption of cultural policies of a universalistic character—the global racial order entered a new period of instability and tension in the last decades of the twentieth century.

How could it have been otherwise? However enigmatic and unjust, the racial classification and racial hierarchization of the world was a deeply established sociohistorical fact. No popular movement, no series of political reforms, no encounter with the moral dereliction implicit in the comprehensive racism of the modern epoch, would have been sufficient to undo or remove it.[1]

Still, reform was preferable to inaction or intransigence, even if it was also inadequate to the task of undoing the diverse legacies of centuries of racial hierarchy, exploitation, and exclusion. With hindsight we can see that the various movements for inclusion and democracy would only be partially satisfied by the reforms they could achieve. We can understand today, better than we could in the heat of political struggle, why these movements found it difficult to sustain their momentum in the aftermath of reform.

Most centrally, racial hegemony was still very much present in the reform process: the various states and elites that had been confronted by anti-racist opposition demonstrated their ability to withstand it by incorporating it, at least in part. In the aftermath of such transformations—which were the very heart and soul of the break—the real meaning of achieving racial "equality," of overcoming the legacy of racism, became controversial. What Du Bois had theorized almost a century earlier as "the veil"—the peculiar membrane of racial division that traversed both societies and individuals—proved difficult to lift (Du Bois 1989 [1903]; Du Bois 1990 [1941]). And was its lifting even desirable? In a situation where substantial racial inequality and injustice continued, where both identities and institutions still bore the indelible mark of centuries of racial oppression, the claim that racism had now at last been remedied would surely ring hollow. The veil might well survive half-hearted, symbolic, or co-optative gestures at removing it.

DIMENSIONS OF THE BREAK

Throughout these comparative case studies, I argue that the post–World War II break is a global backdrop, an economic, political, and cultural context in which these sorts of national racial conflicts were being reworked as the twentieth century drew to its end. With the post–World War II break there was an undermining of the old systems of racial rule. The break can thus be seen as a worldwide *crisis of racial formation*. It was a result of the long gestation of racial tensions that had built up in the modern world over centuries, but that had only reached a "ruptural unity" during and after World War II. Once the incompatibility of the old racial system with the postwar social order—both national and global—was acknowledged, it became clear that widespread social and political transformations would have to occur. Decolonization and civil rights, democratization and political inclusion are some of the terms that can be applied to these shifts.

But the break was not only a *consequence* of long-standing tensions coming to the fore during and after the war; it was also itself a *cause* of new instabilities. It was not an easy task to reconcile long-standing concepts of national identities, forged during centuries of empire and slavery, racial segregation and apartheid, with large waves of immigration and settlement on the part of ex-colonials and formerly excluded and disenfranchised "people of color." It was one thing to grant these former slaves, these indigenous people, and these new immigrants formal citizenship rights (not that this was always forthcoming); but it was quite another to eliminate widespread discrimination and exploitation directed at them. It was one thing to profess tolerance and equality, but it was quite another to adjust to racially based movements demanding radical change and an abrupt end to the long legacy of "normalized" whiteness, not to mention the effective continuity of North–South rule even in a global, postcolonial regime.

So the postwar break expressed in a stronger form than ever the long-standing tensions about the significance of race and the persistence of racial inequality that simmered in each national setting. It also raised to new levels the transnational dimensions of opposition to racial rule. As I argued in Part I of this book, resistance to slavery and conquest, and particularly the rise of abolitionism, represented the first appearance of international social movements on the world-historical stage. Once the twentieth century dawned, new levels of international movement solidarity were achieved as anti-colonial and anti-racist movements gathered strength. The success of the Russian revolution, and the consequently increased appeal of Marxism-Leninism in the colonial world, heighten the pressure on the old empires.[2] But in the aftermath of World War II the transnational significance of anti-racist movements and mechanisms of solidarity increased exponentially.

THE CASE STUDIES

In the chapters that follow, I examine the postwar break as it took place in four distinct settings: the United States, South Africa, Brazil, and the European Union. While I cannot hope to address the full range of variations that overtook the post–World War II world as it finally confronted the momentous legacy of half a millennium of racial rule, these cases have not been selected arbitrarily either. They were chosen not only because they are crucial variants, important "laboratories," where new racial dynamics are being developed; but because they are some of the central national stages on which the world's racial drama is being played out. It is becoming more and more problematic, however, to stress national frameworks of racial formation. The comparative dimensions of this approach are designed to overcome that, to redirect attention to the transnational character of racial formation processes, and to emphasize that not only today, but in historical sociological terms as well, there has been a *world racial system* in place for the past five hundred years.

In the aftermath of World War II and during the decades-long Cold War, the *United States* became the leading superpower and culturally hegemonic society. The end of WW II heralded the start of an "American century" (Henry Luce coined this term) due to the overwhelming economic, military, and cultural prowess of the United States. It was less recognized, however, that the United States was also *racially* emblematic of the epoch. The United States embodied the dawning racial crisis: it was at once *both* the leading imperial power and the avatar of anti-colonialism. Its late-eighteenth-century Revolution had been the first successful challenge to a European empire, the first attempt to create a post-colonial democracy, albeit one still marred by slavery (and limited in other ways as well). The United States, although founded by means of the conquest/deracination of its native population and constructed in significant measure by enslaved Africans, nevertheless presented itself in the post–World War II years as the bastion of democracy and self-determination. A settler society in which white supremacy still operated largely (although not totally) unchallenged, the country drew its founding myths from a revolutionary upsurge whose rhetoric was emancipatory and egalitarian. The United States was not just hegemonic: its national identity was *internally* defined by the same elemental—and fundamentally racialized—contradictions that were now engulfing the entire world. In the years following World War II, then, the country was particularly ripe for a racially driven political crisis.

As leader of what it called the "free world," the United States could hardly uphold its earlier policies of segregation and subjugation of its racially defined minorities. Those groups and their allies, ever-more mobilized and politically engaged, would not permit this. Neither would the rest of the international community, which watched with unflagging interest as the United States sought to overcome, or at least manage more effectively, its historical reliance upon a racist and anti-democratic system of rule.

On the other hand, segregation, systematic discrimination, and white supremacism were not mere atavisms; they served powerful interests, economic and cultural, local and national. They were intrinsic to the national economy, built into the institutions of political rule, and so unquestionably part of popular conceptions of identity that they could not be dismantled. To dispense with these practices, these social institutions, was virtually inconceivable; in many respects it remains so today. Only through sustained political assault could the deep structures of white supremacy be undermined, if not washed away. Only through the slow gestation of powerful political opposition to racial "business as usual" could this racial system even be reformed.

South Africa is an obvious choice as a case study, if only because until recently it was the world's most unabashedly racial state. The apartheid regime clung determinedly, foolishly, nearly suicidally, to its *herrenvolk* democracy—more properly characterized as racial dictatorship—until it had exhausted nearly the entire toolkit of reactionary racial intransigence. White intractability in the face of the determination of a substantial African majority to achieve full democracy and inclusion led the country to international ostracism, not to mention the portals of revolution, before its irrationality was at last recognized. The very lateness of the coming of the break, of the beginning of the passage toward a democratic and inclusive society, makes South Africa a crucial case study.

The destruction of apartheid can be understood as a belated outcome of Cold War conflict in the world's South, similar in some ways to the demise of neo-colonialism in Vietnam. Apartheid's sponsors in the West, the "free world," upheld the South African regime for decades as a supposedly distasteful but necessary anti-communist outpost. The breakup of the Soviet Union made that rationale—flimsy enough in its heyday—completely obsolete. But by that time the ANC-led opposition to the whites-only regime had attained overwhelming popularity and support. The West, and those members of the apartheid elite who retained their balance (political and mental), had to recognize that comprehensive reform was necessary and still possible, even at so late a date. The downfall of the old regime and the attainment of democracy culminated with the inauguration of President Nelson Mandela in 1994.

The extremity of the racial inequality fostered by apartheid, the legacy of the abysmal racial differentiation and stratification left floating in its wake, also impels intellectual interest and practical concern. Just as opposition to racial hierarchy in South Africa was to a significant extent an international movement, a virtually global anti-racist consensus, so too the ANC has been strongly cautioned by the masters of the global financial marketplace to approach its reform agenda cautiously. Thus it must attempt to steer between the Scylla of capital flight and financial sanction on the one hand, and the Charybdis of popular demands for progressive redistribution on the other. In this way the former struggles of the apartheid era persist: these are struggles not only of class, or development, but emphatically struggles of race as well.

And on top of all that: the South African democratic movement had for many decades nurtured a vision of "non-racialism" deep in its adherents' hearts; how would that movement/political party (the ANC), and the government that it led, come to terms with the continuing salience of race in the post-apartheid era? Taken together, all these factors suggest that the country still faces serious racial dilemmas, even as it pursues its transition from apartheid to multiracialism.

Brazil seems to be the opposite case from South Africa. South Africa only acknowledged the inevitability of the break at the latest possible moment, while Brazil *anticipated* the break. From the 1930s on Brazil has at least professed allegiance to a model of racial democracy, although the country's ability even to sustain a formally democratic political system has hardly been secure over that period. Still, by proclaiming itself a racial democracy, Brazil was able to defuse much of the racial mobilization that other societies encountered during the postwar years, although it hardly instituted the major social reforms that would have been required to realize democracy—racial or otherwise—in practice.

In fact, the Brazilian racial system, with its color continuum—as opposed to the more familiar color-line of North America—tends to dilute democratic demands. Many other factors also contribute to Brazil's (partial) racial exceptionalism: the tradition of *cordialidade* (complaisance), the widespead acceptance of *miscigenação*, the absence of a traumatic historical transition from slavery to emancipation, the roughly even demographic balance between black and non-black populations (depending upon how one defines "black"), and the prolonged rule of a military dictatorship (1964–85) that made *all* social movement activity very perilous and difficult to sustain.

The ideology of racial democracy abides. Since the return of political democracy to Brazil in 1985, and indeed during the 1979–85 *abertura* ("opening") that heralded the military's impending exit from power, a more racially conscious Brazil has reappeared. While there has been no movement upsurge to parallel the U.S. or South African cases—as a result of the racial democracy ideology's continuing effectiveness, no doubt—that same ideology has come under new attack as little more than a figleaf covering widespread racial inequality, injustice, and prejudice. Movement activity has continued to percolate, and race-consciousness continues to grow; indeed it flourishes now in such unlikely places as churches and popular culture. Racial policies are undergoing reform as well—nothing drastic, but more than before. Is Brazil, then, continuing its anticipatory style of racial rule, or are the aftershocks of the break only now being felt in this, the largest black nation in the hemisphere?

The European Union: During the years since World War II it has been established that, indeed, "the empire strikes back." Europe today is a racially pluralized region to an extent that would have been inconceivable before the war, during the heyday of colonialism. Indeed the greatest pluralization, which is to say the greatest immigration, the most racially decisive demographic shifts, have occurred especially in former imperial powers like Britain, the Netherlands, France, and Spain. But even in Germany, Italy, and the Scandinavian countries, indeed even to some extent in the East, there has been a substantial influx of non-whites. This post-colonial shift has deeply altered not only demographic patterns, but also sociocultural ones. In the old dynamic the racial order and the imperial order were the same; the racialized "others" were largely outside the borders of the mother-countries; they were in the colonies, where they were wogs, coolies, and kaffirs. That a considerable number of these subalterns are now present throughout metropolitan Europe is not only the result of informal economic processes: indeed many were even recruited! They were *gastarbeiter* ("guest workers"), or ex-colonials—settlers or collaborators—who came to the metropole after they wore out their welcomes; that is, after the empires were dismantled.

Yet however closely the fates of the "colored" populations of Europe are tied to those of their former masters, their presence is now causing discomfort. Political responses to the new pluralism often take on repressive and anti-democratic forms, focusing attention on the "immigrant problem" (or the "Islamic problem"), seeking not only to shut the gates to Maghrebines or sub-Saharan Africans, Turks or Slavs (including Balkan refugees), but often to define those "others" who are already present as enemies of the national culture and threats to the "ordinary German" (or English, or French, etc.) way of life.

Thus the particular racial issue that must be confronted in Europe is the *racial dimension of post-coloniality*: the multiplication of group identities. To what extent can the former mother-countries accept their racial pluralization? Currently there is significant denial that the demographic differentiation of Europe is even a "racial" matter. Analysts and political leaders from across the whole range of the political spectrum—from left to right and from the most die-hard nationalist to the most fervent European integrationist—tend to argue that race is not the issue and that the problem of integration is "cultural" or "ethnic." At the same time explicitly racist and anti-democratic tendencies are widely visible: new right and neo-fascist groups have gained political power in some countries, and popular racial antagonisms are on the rise. At both the state and regional levels the agenda of restriction is threatening citizenship rights, access to mobility of employment or residence, and sometimes even religious or other cultural practices. Conflicts over immigration and hiring policies, over inclusion and equality, have taken on new intensity, with crucial implications for the character of democracy.

Why the European Union, as distinct from, say, France or Germany, as a case study? Although European national identities and differences are not about to be transcended, they are eroding under the pressure of integration. Many of the most crucial dimensions of racial politics and policy are increasingly handled at the regional level: immigration policy is being coordinated, and citizenship policies nationalized (under the principle of *jus soli*), to pick the two most prominent examples. For these and many other reasons as well, to focus attention on the EU is to address very centrally the question of the globalization of race. But beyond that it is to consider the aftermath of empire, the post-colonial question, not in the "periphery" of the South, but in the "core," the metropolitan heartland of the old imperial racial system, the headquarters of Eurocentrism. The resurgence of racial conflict here, as well as the determined effort to incorporate and contain it in the political system, is emblematic of the transcendent importance of regionalism in Europe. Unification, integration, even federalism among the eternally fractious European nation-states, the former empires, obviously cannot be accomplished by currency reform or relaxation of border controls. It requires an internal pluralization that is fundamentally sociocultural and political. The upsurge of racial conflict within the EU, then, is not only symbolic, not merely a symptom of the difficulties of integration; it is also a powerful impetus toward accomplishing the task of building a new and inclusive Europe.

THE METHOD

The break was a global accumulation of sociopolitical forces—demographic, experiential, institutional, ideological—that combined to discredit and finally undo the old world racial system. None of these developments was entirely new or unprecedented: massive migrations had been a regular feature of world history; a wave of decolonization, some of it revolutionary, had swept the Americas more than a century before a similar tide reached Africa and Asia; the abolition of slavery, followed by real efforts (however unsuccessful ultimately) to extend the rights of citizenship to the emancipated, had preceded civil rights and anti-apartheid movements, once again by a full century; indeed even the massive disruptions and mobilizations occasioned by world war and world capitalist-communist rivalry had occurred before, in the period during and following World War I. Not only had all these rehearsals taken place before, but those earlier events had often contained significant racial dimensions, as I have shown in my discussion, for example, of nineteenth-century Latin American decolonization.[3]

What was new about the break, then, was not its ingredients. Rather, two principal facts, two circumstances of the break's occurrence, were unprecedented. First, there was the *centrality of race* in all the major social upheavals that began during the war and ramified around the globe after it, engulfing metropoles, colonies, and ex-colonies alike. And second, there was the striking *synchrony of racial events and experiences*—the massive migrations, combined with the transnational challenges to traditional practices of segregation, Eurocentrism, racial hierarchy, political exclusion, and so on—that lent the break the ruptural unity (or if one prefers, the "overdetermination") needed to call the established national and global racial hierarchies of race into question (Althusser 1969).

So the break is an example of what Myrdal called "circular and cumulative causation": circular because precedents for the main event were recurrent; cumulative because the determinants of the break accreted and combined to rupture the old world racial system (Myrdal 1963).

How to study such a phenomenon? Traditional social scientific methods are not up to the task. A framework of circular and cumulative causation, a process of overdetermination, defies the linear cause-and-effect logic so central to nomothetic social scientific methodology. There is no set of clear-cut independent variables, whose effects upon a group of dependent variables (these don't exist either) can be measured, assessed, or quantified. The convergent determinations I have identified as crucial components of the break—such as military mobilization among the subordinated, say, or great-power rivalry for their loyalties—all occurred unevenly, or more properly, recurred. This was the "circular" part. And then, all these determining factors shaping the break (I refuse to call them "independent variables") interacted with each other. Such phenomena as a Third World group making the transition from anti-Axis to anti-colonial resistance cannot clearly be located in one or another analytical category: is this "Third World nationalism"? response to "Cold War competition"? or extension of the democratic/anti-racist legacy of World War II?

My response to these dilemmas is to locate the account in the tradition of comparative historical sociology, an approach that draws on the idiographic methods of Weber, Du Bois, Polanyi, Moore, and Wallerstein,[4] to be sure. But at the same time I seek to give a structured account of the break, in continuing recognition of the weight of the nomothetic social scientific paradigm with its stress on cause-and-effect logic. This is accomplished by use of three devices: attentiveness to historical background; reiterative recourse to the common, transnational, and relational context of the comparative national case studies; and reliance upon a small group of determining factors (*not* independent variables) that I argue played central roles in shaping the post–World War II racial break on a world scale.

The *historical background* to the break has been surveyed extensively in Part I. I argued there that the existence of a world racial system is a feature of modernity. Important, even earth-shaking as it may be in terms of such substantive issues as global mobility and democratization, the post–World War II break is formally no more than a major shift in world racial systems, part of an epochal transition still very much underway: from a system based on white supremacy to one of greater racial parity and plurality. Part of my task in these comparative case study chapters is to analyze how this transition took form in the national settings under examination, beginning with World War II or the run-up to it.

Having frequent *recourse to the transnational dimension* of these case studies is more than a mere methodological device. The contemporary world racial system is considerably more interactive and diasporic than it was in the past. It is not always easy to acknowledge the transnational dimensions of racial formation processes generally considered to be primarily local or national in nature. But as I have already suggested,[5] the globalizing tendency of racial formation is coextensive with the rise of the modern. And beyond all this, it is also vital to recognize that the transnational interchanges that shaped the break in these case study countries/regions were a two-way street, so to speak: what took place in one country both had effects elsewhere and was in turn produced, at least in part, by occurrences outside national borders. In the United States, for example, national engagement in the "twilight struggle" of the Cold War had dramatic effects on the drive for civil rights; conversely, the U.S. civil rights movement had worldwide influence.

What were the principal determining factors for the post–World War II racial break? Four fundamental postwar racial dynamics were present in all the case study settings: *demographic change, movement mobilization, reform of state racial policies,* and *interaction with global racial networks.* Themselves interacting in complex ways, these four key elements undermined the logic of the previous racial order in each of the national/regional cases. They sparked new tensions and debates about the significance of race and the persistence of racial inequality in each of these settings.

In succeeding chapters of this section, I consider these aspects of the break in greater depth, exploring their configurations in different national settings. But perhaps it is worthwhile to provide brief exegeses of these themes here.

Demographic Change

The demographic and social profile of each the countries/regions studied here was dramatically changed in the postwar period. Demographic change was chiefly brought about by migration, both international and internal, as well as by urbanization and changing patterns of racial stratification. These shifts signaled the arrival of new actors on the political stage, whose presence facilitated the growth of anti-racist social movements. In these case studies I draw upon new approaches to patterns of racial stratification and inequality (Wood and Carvalho 1988; Telles 1999; Oliver and Shapiro 1995; Zuberi and Khalfani 1999) as well as new approaches to migration (Massey et al. 1998; Portes 1995; Light and Bonacich 1988), in order to examine the shifting racial dynamics that characterize the postwar break.

Racially Based Movements

Popular mobilizations, sometimes based in racially defined minority communities and their supporters, and sometimes encompassing large majorities, articulated new political demands for inclusion, plunging many national political systems into serious crises. In general these movements had unprecedented national influence in their postwar incarnations, perhaps because the political assertion of racially defined group identities had previously been prohibited, or because sufficient numbers of racially defined "others" had not previously been present. In other cases, the post–World War II mobilization of racially excluded or subordinated groups was a reassertion of long-standing demands, a resurgence of a venerable movement heritage. Recent advances in the social scientific study of social movements permit new explorations of anti-racist mobilization in structural, organizational, and cultural terms; they enable new "issue evolution" approaches and social psychological perspectives as well (McAdam et al. 1996; Tarrow 1994; Carmines and Stimson 1989).

Alterations in State Racial Policies

National political systems responded to racially based social movement challenges in the period under investigation with programs of reform. These were generally arrived at after initial responses of coercion and repression failed to subdue popular insurgency and democratic agitation. The shift to more incorporative, more adaptive policy responses sometimes happened rather rapidly, and in other cases involved significant latency periods, monumental struggles, prolonged political campaigns, or even international intervention. Long used to the administration of racial inequality and exclusion, states and ruling elites confronted with movements for racial equality and inclusion often reflexively reacted at first with intransigence, repression, and "rejectionism." Such policies also revealed the limited political leverage initially available to emergent movements for racial justice.

At later moments, however, these movements confronted the state from more advantageous positions, having at their disposal substantial domestic and international constituencies, a variety of resources, and well-worked-out political positions and strategic orientations. Faced with substantial political pressure, state administrators, legislatures, electoral systems, and courts, as well as state repressive apparatuses, were compelled to adapt to the new dynamics of racial politics as they consolidated and developed in the postwar years. The defeat of hard-line resistance to democratic reform, as well as the uneven rise of strategies of reform—or of incorporation and co-optation—characterized the later postwar decades. In these chapters I make use of new developments in policy studies that permit more nuanced understandings of those trajectories of incorporation that have proved so crucial to racial reforms (Rueschemeyer and Skocpol 1996; Tilly 1990; Hero 1998; Shapiro et al. 1998).

Global Context, Transnational Pressures

These national cases, however, cannot be understood in isolation. Anti-racist movements often drew on *transnational resources, ideas, and political leverage.* Thus, for example, movements and states were deeply affected by international pressures for democracy and universalism, preventing a full return to the racial dynamics of a previous era. Diasporic perspectives on race, research on political communication, migration and citizenship studies, and new research on the impact of non-governmental organizations (NGOs) in human rights as well as other fields, provide important avenues through which contemporary perceptions of racism can be reframed, placing racism and anti-racism once again in an international context. In a qualified way, this resurgent transnationalism may be seen as a revivification of the abolitionist and pan-Africanist traditions, which expressed an earlier, anti-colonial version of globalism (Keck and Sikkink 1998; Ware 1992; Thompson 1969; Johnson 1998; Fredrickson 1995).

Racial contradictions accumulated over the post–World War II break period. The mounting incongruities and unmanageability of the ancien régimes of colonialism, white supremacy, apartheid, segregation, and racial hierarchy in general brought long-standing grievances to the fore, and revived awareness of old injustices and conflicts. Here again was the circular and cumulative logic of the break. As racial regimes were confronted with growing opposition, they began to contemplate policy reforms. Eventually these reforms were implemented, although obviously at various rates and with different degrees of upheaval.

Yet for all their achievements, the insurgent movements of the break period were unable to realize a full-scale repudiation of the past, were incapable of destroying white supremacy, were inadequate to generate an anti-racist, anti-colonialist revolution. In fact, the product of all this struggle and conflict was "merely" reform—incorporative reform, hegemonic reform. The old systems of racial rule proved capable of withstanding much of the pressure. The reforms won were of course significant, but they were far from total. Indeed, even in the relatively few cases where full-scale armed revolutions were required to put an end to colonial rule (for example, in the Portuguese colonies of Africa) the independent regimes these revolutions constructed were so marginal to the late-twentieth-century political and economic systems that their first priority became reintegration into the established order.

How then to judge the outcome of the post–World War II racial break? If revolution was not possible, if only racial reform was possible, what does that mean for the present political situation, for racial dynamics in the dawning twenty-first century?

I discuss this question more fully in the concluding chapter of this book,[6] but it is important to foreshadow one point here: just as oppression and injustice breeds opposition, oppression *needs* opposition. Without opposition, without resistance, hegemony would not be possible: for not only would there be no need to make concessions to the subjugated and subaltern, but there would be no impetus to modernize, to reinvent, to adapt systems of rule.

The racial reforms achieved in the second half of the twentieth century, although they were certainly momentous, were also *dualistic* in the Duboisian sense. They were contradictory: they expanded democracy and lessened racial hierarchy, but they also allowed white supremacy to survive, to modernize, to adapt to post-colonial and post-apartheid conditions. They gave it a new lease on life.

In the following chapters, the paths taken in the various case study countries toward the postwar racial break are explored and compared. As I consider the various national workings-out of the dynamics just described, I generally adhere to a narrative historical model. Thus in some respects these accounts continue the work undertaken in Part I, specifying particular cases and tracing the unfolding, over recent decades, of a new set of national racial formations, new racial regimes. Throughout I strive to maintain a certain focus on the specific determinants of the break I consider most central for each case study setting. But as I have already made clear, this does not mean that events in each national setting transpired independently from those elsewhere. Indeed, for all their specificity and uniqueness—which are the factors, after all, that inspired these countries' selection as case studies in the first place—it is preeminently clear that their postwar racial experiences, their national racial histories so to speak, are in a sense not national at all. They are parts of an unfolding world-historical shift to a new racial system.

Nor is the break over, by any means. After examining and comparing the case studies in the chapters of Part II, I turn in the concluding chapter of this book to a discussion of the continuing transitional and contradictory state of world racial dynamics.

Seven

UNITED STATES: THE END OF THE INNOCENCE

THE DRAMA OF RACIAL CONFLICT in the post–World War II United States was immeasurably heightened because the country was now the leading super-power and culturally hegemonic society. Its unique racial dementia was now on full display: its centuries-long, convoluted complicity with both the conquest/deracination of its native population and with African enslavement. The United States was the only northern country whose national identity had been *internally* defined by these elemental experiences.

Already during the war, and with sustained intensity after it, anti-racist movements increased and refocused their stuggles for democracy. With a new clarity in the decades following the war, these movements—led by black civil rights organizations already seasoned by decades of experience—moved to consolidate and coordinate their efforts in a variety of political arenas: legislative, judicial, workplace, and community-oriented strategies were developed. Religious and cultural institutions were engaged, and a mass base, a popular base, was built on an unprecedented scale.

Nor were blacks the only insurgents. Other racially defined "minorities," inspired to be sure by black examples, but also influenced by anti-colonial and socialist ideals, joined the fray as well. Progressive whites also recognized that the future of democracy hinged on the battle against racism.

The U.S. population was shifting too; the postwar mobilization of the racially subordinate in search of their political and social rights was a partial result of these demographic shifts. Massive migration took place in the United States, both during and after the war. Coming from outside and from within the nation's borders, millions of migrants, largely racially defined minorities, drastically altered residential and voting patterns, especially in urban settings and in the northern and western regions of the country.

So after World War II the United States became a huge laboratory for social policy reform, as the national state attempted to reorganize long-established racial policies and the sociopolitical norms that underwrote them. Internationally too, the postwar United States underwent a slow geopolitical repositioning that involved many racial dimensions, as the country moved through (and ultimately beyond) the Cold War and as the post-colonial era dawned.

All these developments had profound implications both domestically and globally. At home, deep conflicts over the meaning and supervision of the domestic racial order came to a boil in the 1950s and 1960s. Although racial themes had long been central to U.S. social structure and national identity, far more than "merely" racial issues—racial stratification, domination, or ideology, say—was at stake in the confrontations of those decades. The very future of democracy, the survival of principles of equality and social justice, hung in the balance as the civil rights movement awoke, advanced in all its gallantry, and then was forced to retreat from the battlefield with no more than a partial victory. Fundamental matters of democracy, equality, and social justice were called into question as the United States reformed its immigration laws, which dated from the era of eugenics; as it moved from an urban country with a substantially underdeveloped rural hinterland to a metropolitan country with a substantial, privileged suburbia; and as it abandoned its attempts to succeed European colonialism with a neo-colonialism all its own. All these momentous shifts had profound racial dimensions.

In other words the United States was at the same time a domestic and global racial theater. As it assumed its place as leader of what it called the "free world," the country was forced to face its lack of freedom within. U.S. society confronted anew the anti-democratic and immoral racial subordination upon which it continued to depend. It faced once again the racial limits of its culture, its politics, its economic life. Was the United States really "the land of the free, and the home of the brave"? Were its vaunted "free market" and "free enterprise system" really "free" for all? Due to the political and moral challenges posed by the black movement and its allies in the postwar period, these commonsense beliefs were questioned, not for the first time, but to an unprecedented extent. This was the "end of the innocence."

This chapter begins by reviewing the *background conditions* encountered by the nascent civil rights movement in the early postwar period. The postwar black movement had not only acquired a newly urbanized and working-class base that had been tempered by war; the movement was also the inheritor of a centuries-long struggle for citizenship and generalized racial justice. Yet black insurgents faced new difficulties after the war's end. They were now both persecuted by the right and courted by liberals, whom they needed as allies but also were required to placate.

As prosperity deepened and the Cold War atmosphere was normalized, the black movement became the leading democratizing force in the United States. Its exemplary creativity and political openness permitted an unprecedented degree of popular intervention into North American civil and political life. It attracted and motivated activists and intellectuals concerned with every major social and political issue, inspiring movements among the Latino, Asian American, and Native American communities, as well as deeply galvanizing many whites. As had occurred in slavery days more than a century before, the black movement breathed new life into the feminist project. In addition, it greatly shaped the new waves of peace and anti-imperialist movement activities, a development that also had earlier precedents.

The next section of this chapter examines the *emergence of the civil rights vision* in the postwar years. That vision focused on the long-delayed realization of the promises of democracy and inclusion that had been wrung from a reluctant state—and from recalcitrant whites—over the near-century that had succeeded emancipation and the Union victory in the Civil War. These rights had been extended only in the most limited fashion; they had always been subject to restriction, reduction to mere lip-service, and outright withdrawal. The civil rights vision evolved through a series of early battles and setbacks during World War II and after the war's end. Not until the mid-1950s could that vision be translated into mass mobilization. Only in the 1960s could the movement begin to take on the immense dilemmas of racial politics and white supremacy, which were surfacing not only as national but as global issues by that time.

Therefore, the movement's vision of civil rights had a contradictory character. On the one hand, it constituted a democratic prospect, a political horizon: it represented the most innovative democratic project ever conceived in the U.S. context. On the other hand, the goal of civil rights was an obviously restricted one: the idea that the United States would, or even could, "live out the true meaning of its creed," as Dr. King put it (echoing Gunnar Myrdal), expressed a restricted and overly optimistic understanding of the meaning of race, of the embeddedness of race in the U.S. sociopolitical system.

I consider these *limits of racial reform* in the following section. The very comprehensiveness of the racism the movement sought to overcome served as a practical limit to the movement's demands. The movement was repeatedly forced to choose between radicalism and moderation: the former was a constant temptation, imposed by the embeddedness of race in the social and psychic structures of U.S. life. The latter was a political necessity, a pragmatic imperative in the real situation where (let it be remembered) whites vastly outnumbered blacks. Furthermore, reliance upon and support for racial hierarchy and privilege was largely unconstrained: racially defined minorities had little effective leverage over white racial attitudes and practices. So the movement oscillated between the twin poles of radicalism and moderation, largely hewing to the moderate line, the integrationist and pacific pole.[1] While a wide range of positions were upheld by the many organizations and leaders involved, riots and rebellions happened; confrontations happened. Both mainstream and militants had their say and indeed accomplished a great deal. The radicalism of the movement, although often submerged beneath a political realism that did it credit, was never repudiated. Nor could it be: it was a logical response to the racism built into the U.S. social structure.

The incipient radicalism of the movement was not overlooked by its adversaries, who recognized the implicit connection between racial democracy and comprehensive, indeed proto-revolutionary, societal transformation. Attempts to defeat black insurgency, via a strategy of massive resistance, ended in ignominious defeat for those who sought to perpetuate the most repressive forms of white supremacy. This led to the replacement of such die-hard segregationists by racial moderates who developed a *strategy of incorporation*—or co-optation—of civil rights. In the next section of this chapter I consider the development of this strategy of racial reform within the state. Crucial to this approach was the severing of the radical democratic implications of the movement's vision from its more manageable moderate demands. "Rights" could be accommodated largely, if not entirely, within the status quo, for after all, these rights—like the vote and the ending of formal, state-sanctioned discrimination and exclusion—were grounded in the post–Civil War amendments to the Constitution; they were hardly new demands. But the radical democratic claims of the movement, from "social justice" to "black power"—with their disruptive, redistributive, and participatory content, indeed with their affinities to the socialist and Third Worldist currents afoot on the global scene—these would have to be abandoned.

Equality of opportunity and desegregation, desirable as these were, would have proved inadequate even if realized. The movement drew much of its strength from its radical democratic aspirations: invoking the Old Testament prophet, Dr. King envisioned a time when justice would "rain down like waters, and righteousness as a mighty stream." Movement activists in the Student Nonviolent Coordinating Committee (SNCC) and elsewhere saw themselves as a "beloved community." Indeed, a proto-socialist, redistributive set of political demands became ever-more visible as the movement evolved. In other words, as the movement gained strength, it moved the "horizon" of what was politically possible in the United States. As the movement developed, radical democratic possibilities began to peep over the political horizon as well. No longer could the political system be judged legitimate and representative if it were not also striving for social justice. No longer could equality of "opportunity" suffice as a democratic objective. Now substantive rather than mere formal equality became the movement's goal. Although largely co-opted and incorporated in practice, the movement had succeeded as well: it had both achieved the civil rights agenda and demonstrated the insufficiency of that vision.

The radical democracy bequeathed by the movement remained an important legacy as the century drew to an end. But as the 1960s came to a close it was increasingly confronted by a formidable new antagonist: the neo-conservatism that urged a color-blind approach to issues of racial injustice and indeed denied the very existence of race. This was "soft-core," commonsense racial reaction. The incorporative, moderate tendencies associated with neo-conservatism were its most mainstream and popular. There were also "hard-core" and indeed "hard right" tendencies though, political positions that powerfully overlapped with neo-conservative currents. Willingness to "play the race card" in electoral politics—a distinguishing feature of the new right—went hand-in-hand with the color-blind claims of the neo-cons. And even more extreme voices exhorted the country's violent and reactionary dragons—the substantial cohorts of neo-fascist and Klan sympathizers—to wake from their torpor and take to the streets. Even biological racism, long thought defunct after the discrediting of eugenics and because of its deep association with Nazism, loomed up again on the right as a pseudo-intellectual facet of the reactionary racial complex (Herrnstein and Murray 1994).

The chapter concludes with some notes on the *continuing significance of race*. As the twenty-first century begins, the U.S. racial right is not unified, not coherent, not even free of deep divisions. But despite its residual (sometimes still quite powerful) troglodytic factions that stubbornly maintain their avowed white supremacy, the core strength of the racial right lies in its incorporative currents. These are the tendencies of the racial reaction that most concern me here. They have the greatest influence, both domestic and global. They have learned the most from the civil rights movement they once opposed: indeed, they now mold their ideology by rearticulating the civil rights legacy's moderate agenda of "rights" and "opportunities" in an ideology of individualism and meritocracy. They have largely defused the radical democratic vision that sustained the movement vision, and now claim to have entered a post-racial, indeed color-blind phase.

BACKGROUND CONDITIONS

Considerable discussion had taken place during the war about the momentous racial issues the United States would confront in the war's wake.[2] In this sense the movement upsurge that followed the war had been rehearsed, so to speak, by events that had occurred since the fall of the slave system. As Du Bois showed in *Black Reconstruction*, blacks had already demonstrated the depth of their desire for democracy, for inclusion and self-determination, in their actions during the Civil War and in that war's aftermath. During Reconstruction they mobilized in every possible way to consolidate their newfound freedom. The national state too, finding itself cast in the role of an occupying power, set itself the mission—not without reluctance, of course, but nevertheless seriously—of generating democracy in the defeated South. Hence the Reconstruction policies, chiefly economic and political, but also oriented toward such social welfare issues as education and housing, were important precedents for the post–World War II racial reforms and social policies of a century later (Du Bois 1977 [1935]; Foner 1988; Foner 1983).

Early Migration and Whitening

Similar rehearsals for the shifting racial dynamics of the post–World War II period can be seen when immigration and the impact of World War I are considered. European immigration reached unprecedented levels in the latter decades of the nineteenth century, as the labor demands of the rapidly industrializing Northeast and Midwest surged and the depressions of the 1870s and 1890s set in, both in Europe and elsewhere. As Italians, Jews, Slavs, and others entered the United States by the millions, they restratified the social order, generating a range of racially "intermediate" positions and competing fiercely both with older established white groups and with newly emancipated blacks. These newly arrived peasants experienced their own diasporas, setting up migratory chains that anticipated post–World War II patterns (Thomas and Znaniecki 1984 [1923]). They attracted the attention of Progressive-era reformers and feminists (Addams 1938; Butler 1909); they strove fiercely for economic stability and sociopolitical assimilation; and they sought racial classification as "white," an achievement that could only be gained at the expense of blacks (Saxton 1990; Allen 1974; Lieberson 1980).[3]

Asian and Latin American immigration also expanded, largely for the same reasons. The influx of immigrants surged in the West and Southwest, both because of the "pull" of western industrialization (particularly in railroads and mining), and because of agricultural development. Asian and Latin American "push" factors also played a role: Japanese economic distress around the turn of the century led to a widespread Japanese outflow toward the western hemisphere, as emigrant workers sailed not only to the United States but to Mexico, Peru, and especially Brazil. Chinese immigration to the United States experienced surges as early as the immediate post–Civil War years, when mass Chinese labor was crucial in railroad construction. Immigrant chains were created as "pioneers" and labor contractors sent news home to China or Japan about their circumstances and recruited new immigrants, or where possible requested a bride from home.[4]

U.S. racial composition has always been deeply intertwined with global political-economic conditions. Worldwide economic cycles of boom and bust, tied to shifting levels of technological/industrial development, have structured the flow of immigrants to U.S. shores since the early days of conquest. Because these dynamics have shaped labor demand and supply since the beginning of U.S. development, it has never been possible to separate racial demography from class formation, or indeed from capitalist development. The link between the racialization of the populace and "internal migration" has always been strong, as have the connections between these demographic issues, regional disparities within the United States, and national efforts to make population policy, particularly in such areas as census policy (Anderson and Fienberg 1999; Washington 1997; Nobles 2000), as well as immigration and citizenship policy (Shklar 1991; Smith 1997).

Does this line of argument imply an "economic determinism" in respect to U.S. racial formation or racialization? No, because U.S. racial demography has always been flexible and malleable in terms of racial classification. In respect to "who gets counted as what," the terms and categories of racial classification have undergone tremendous evolution right up to our own time. The reinter-pretation of race, the racial reclassification (or racialization) of group identi-ties, was already proceeding apace during the later nineteenth century. To see the millions of immigrants from southern and eastern Europe who arrived in the United States during the last decades of that century as "white" is to indulge in serious anachronism.

But if they were not white, what racial classification was assigned them?[5] To be sure, European immigrants were "other" in no uncertain terms, potential candidates for racialization as both "white" and "non-white."[6] Even a cursory reading of the vast sociological and progressive movement literature about these immigrants' conditions will confirm this (Thomas and Znaniecki 1984 [1923]; Wirth 1964; Park, Burgess, and McKenzie 1967; Addams 1938; Butler 1909; Greenwald and Anderson 1996; Platt 1969). Furthermore, a good deal of the social Darwinism of the period, not to mention the nascent eugenics "movement," was directed at proving their inferiority.

That their "whiteness" was by no means established upon their arrival sig-nificantly distinguished these immigrants from U.S. "natives" who, whether of elite or low degree, were nevertheless certified White Anglo-Saxon Protestants. Yet at the same time, these "FOB" (Fresh off the Boat) Europeans were clearly different as well from U.S. blacks, from indigenous peoples, and from immi-grants of non-European provenance. In contrast to Africans, whose "immigra-tion" (at least until the latter part of the nineteenth century) had been coerced, and in distinction from Latin Americans whose "immigration" was the product of conquest and annexation, these North Atlantic arrivals had for the most part chosen to immigrate.[7] They were of intermediate racial status, "NQW" (Not Quite White) but potentially so. Jews, Italians, Greeks, Poles, and Slavs certainly faced the contempt, prejudice, and discrimination of the ruling elites and their old nativist mass constituencies,[8] but these groups were able to obtain access to resources—jobs, education, and above all the franchise—at a rate that far outstripped the progress of non-Europeans.

And what of blacks? What of internal migration? Although still concen-trated in the South in the many decades before the post–World War II break, the South had already begun to move north. During the period leading up to World War I, and particularly after the United States had entered that war in 1917, demand for labor in the industries of the North and Midwest (and in southern industrialized cities like Birmingham and Atlanta) had stimulated large-scale internal migration.[9] The onset of World War I largely cut off the flow of European immigrants who had furnished the developing industries of the North and Midwest with a steady supply of low-waged labor. In the aftermath of the war, restrictive immigration legislation (significantly informed and rationalized by racist/eugenicist logic) further curtailed and regulated that flow, again shifting labor demand to the impoverished South. A further factor stimulating migration northward was a severely fluctuating cotton economy: demand for this key southern crop of course rose during the war, leading to plantocratic resentment of the recruiters seeking to lure "their" workers toward the better wages of the industrial North. But after the war the price of cotton dropped severely, and did not recover as the overall economy fell into depression. Not until World War II would demand for cotton soar again. By the time that happened, northern demand for black labor was at an all-time high, and shortly after that war's end (around 1948), mechanized cotton harvesting had begun to push out the remaining plantation labor (Baron 1971; McAdam 1982, 73–77).

These demographic shifts were not merely a result of "push and pull" phenomena, although clearly the prospect of moving from the situation of agricultural peonage/sharecropping to that of waged-worker (whether in a factory or in some employment linked to the northern industrial economy) was a prospect devoutly to be wished. Hence the "pull" of the North. As for the "push," it derived not only from periodic downturns in the demand for cotton (or sugar, or tobacco, or turpentine), but had its origins in the repressive systems of peonage developed after Reconstruction was abandoned in 1877. With peonage, of course, went Jim Crow, disenfranchisement, significant racial terrorism, and grinding poverty.

But beyond the important structural factors of "push/pull," migration to and within the United States was shaped by a wide range of other pressures. Indeed, the migration patterns of the early twentieth century were quite "classical." Already in the late 1910s we see, for example, extensive recruitment of migrants, both by potential employers and by civil rights organizations like the Urban League; establishment of migratory circuits through which families and community organizations could invest in "pioneers" who would make initial northward forays, establish contacts and toeholds, and inform later migrants as to routes, destinations, potential employment opportunities, and sources of support.[10] The period saw the widespread creation and expansion of "receiving" areas: neighborhoods in which blacks already lived and continuity with sending communities down home was extensive. Here was the origin of the modern ghetto, the "up South" of Chicago, Philadelphia, Cleveland, and elsewhere.[11]

During the World War I epoch roughly half a million black people left the South (U.S. Bureau of the Census 1998; Marks 1989; Griffin 1995). In the South, more than a quarter-million moved from rural to urban settings. The modern urban ghetto was in large measure founded during this period, not only by the massive arrivals of southern blacks but also by the concerted efforts of urban white power brokers. These sought to restrict black boundaries of residence, to take advantage of the significant demand for housing blacks represented, and (very important), to foment and profit from white hostility to black neighbors (Kusmer 1976; Ballard 1987; Massey and Denton 1993). The early American sociological studies of urban development patterns, urban racial/ ethnic patterns, and migration (notably the Chicago studies), all emerged or consolidated during this period.[12]

"Up South"

Immediately after World War I, a wave of urban race riots, white rampages, and pogroms took shape in black neighborhoods throughout the country, demonstrating that the new black immigrants had not reached any "promised land" yet. In assaulting their black neighbors, the rioters of the "red summer" of 1919 harked back to the extensive antebellum tradition of racist mob violence, to the riots of the Civil War years, and to the targeting of (considerably smaller) black communities during the early Jim Crow period (Rhomberg 1997; Rudwick 1964; Tuttle 1997).

So widespread racial confrontation already existed in the United States during the interwar period. The great majority of black people still resided in the South, where Jim Crow continued unabated and peonage ("sharecropping") remained the chief form of survival. The southern peasantry was not exclusively black by any means, but the ubiquity of Jim Crow racial "etiquette" continuously reinforced the near-total disempowerment of the blacks, thus shoring up status differences between them and the equally impoverished white "croppers" with whom they shared a landlord. Enforced by lynching and night-riding mobs of hooded white terrorists (the KKK), southern racial "etiquette" required blacks to remove their hats in the presence of whites, to step off the sidewalk (where one existed) into the muddy street at the passage of a white, and to wait in such shops as would serve blacks until all whites had been served, no matter who had arrived first. A thousand other rules of this type were in place, most of them subject to the wildest interpretative variations imaginable. The institutionalized manifestations of Jim Crow are well-known: separate schools (where there were schools for blacks at all), separate transportation, separate accommodation in respect to food service or lodging, separate everything. These systems all had the sanction and force of law; to violate them was to break the law and subject oneself to the tender mercies of the police, courts, and jails of the South—that is, if one was lucky enough to avoid the retribution of informal enforcers active in the KKK (McMillen 1989; Litwack 1980).

How, then, can the interwar decades be described as a "confrontation"? Because the first wave of migration northward had occurred, there was a substantial presence of blacks in the industrial cities of the North and Midwest (and to some extent in the urban South). In the North these folk had the vote. They had waged work, often dirty and degraded, but infinitely preferable to the peonage of the cottonfields, the tobacco farms, or the sugar-beet or turpentine-producing facilities of the rural South. They had city churches, fraternal societies, and women's organizations; they had newspapers of their own and artistic/cultural facilities. And they had the beginnings of political organizations. Indeed, by the 1920s there were significant political and cultural stirrings in the urban black North: the Universal Negro Improvement Association under Marcus Garvey mobilized tens of thousands of U.S. blacks and had a range of diasporic links to the black Caribbean and elsewhere (Hill and Bair 1987; James 1998). The Harlem Renaissance saw a flowering of music, literature, and art that greatly exceeded previous possibilities. In film, in popular music, in theater, the "New Negroes" began to assert themselves.

Immigrant communities with roots outside the United States also developed substantially in the interwar years. There is no space here for a detailed treatment of the many distinct Asian and Latino communities that had evolved to significant size and complexity by the interwar period. I offer only a very small number of examples. The Southwest's rise to predominance in U.S. agriculture had begun by this time, made possible largely by immigrant Mexican and Asian labor. In Texas, Arizona, California, and elsewhere, extensive use was made of Mexican labor in agriculture and mining. Filipino, Japanese, and Chinese participation was significant in California (and Pacific Northwest) agriculture and fishing, among other occupations, and led to various early organizing efforts, as well as some historic strikes (Almaguer 1994; Friday 1995). Mainland Puerto Rican populations jumped during the World War I era, paralleling increased black flows to the Northeast and Chicago regions, in particular.

All these developments brought with them significant political conflicts. Although the overt racial terror of the South was not equaled elsewhere in the country, repression and violence were hardly absent from the racial scene in the North, Midwest, and West. In the Depression years, for example, when California began to receive vast inflows of the "dust-bowl refugees" from Oklahoma, Arkansas, and elsewhere (Steinbeck 1939), state and federal governments established a program of mass deportations of Mexicanos. Organized along racial lines and paying no heed to formal citizenship status, special Southern Pacific railroad trains removed many thousands of Mexicans not only across the border, but deep into the southwestern states of Jalisco and Michoacán.[13]

The first wave of internal migration reshaped the role of black folk in U.S. politics (and U.S. economic life and cultural life) more dramatically than any event since Reconstruction. Having transported themselves to the relatively more tolerant North and Midwest, blacks began to vote in much greater numbers than in the Jim Crow South. Having learned from the experiences of discrimination in the World War I armed forces and the riots of 1919, having educated themselves through greater access to public schooling and unprecedented participation in the arts and the emerging mass media, blacks in the North adopted a far more nationalist, far more diasporic, and far more race-conscious politics than they had ever achieved before, adhering in great numbers to the Garvey movement (Hill and Bair 1987; Clarke 1974).[14] Having gained a foothold (or toehold) in industrial labor, blacks began to organize from this base as well, mobilizing where possible along trade union lines (particularly under the leadership of A. Philip Randolph), confronting the racism of the generally exclusionary AFL unions, and gravitating toward the political left, notably to the Communist Party after 1928.[15]

Fighting World War II

The proximate origins of the civil rights movement lie in the social upheaval brought about by U.S. participation in World War II. There was, first of all, direct involvement in the fighting on the part of millions of soldiers and sailors of every racial classification. Drawn from their homes in provincial settings (or nascent ghettos and barrios) into a European or Pacific maelstrom, fighting men and women "of color" were in many cases rudely awakened: their insularity, their residual political torpor were unceremoniously stripped away. Many experienced North American racial injustice anew, or in new ways: the armed forces were, after all, segregated, with all the attendant degradation that racist practices imposed on men and women who were risking their lives for the country that was mistreating them. In some cases, for example, for Mexican and Japanese American soldiers, the very question of citizenship and "loyalty" was tied to military service as a matter of national policy. Military service thus overlapped with horrific collective and personal experiences: Japanese American soldiers of the highly decorated 442nd Infantry Battalion, for example, fought and died in the bloody Italian battles of Anzio and Monte Cassino while their families languished in U.S. internment camps. A number of Mexican American soldiers had experienced deportation in the 1930s. Blacks fought *within* the armed services for the rights taken for granted by whites: promotion and command opportunities based on merit; assignment to combat rather than restriction to menial service such as kitchen, laundry, or dockwork; and the opportunity to take on special assignments or become combat airmen.[16] While they struggled to fight for freedom, they had to contend with white mobs

and the threat of lynching, especially in the southern surroundings of many
military bases (Peery 1995; Killens 1963; Denby 1978 [1952]).[17]

Although the armed services remained segregated, sustained pressure by
black political influentials (notably A. Philip Randolph) and their white allies
(notably Eleanor Roosevelt) forced the Roosevelt administration to desegre-
gate war industries in 1941.[18] That Randolph could threaten a march on Washington—the key factor in moving Roosevelt to break with decades of deference
to Dixiecrats—was testimony to the growing political leverage of blacks, to an
influence that resulted from decades of demographic change. Obviously based
in the North (in the South few blacks could even vote), the threat of a march
was but one of numerous indicators that blacks were beginning to exercise
some political power, that they were beginning to enter the sphere of democracy. Truman's desegregation of the armed forces by executive order in 1947
was a significant step forward in the process initiated by Randolph (and long
sought by the NAACP and other civil rights groups). It reflected not only the
momentum created by earlier demands and protests, but also the northward
movement of black voters during and after the war, and importantly, the great
achievements of blacks in the armed forces.

Thus before and during World War II, a great deal of politicization and
"conscientization" had occurred, particularly in the black community but also
in other communities of color and among progressive whites. These changes
would perhaps appear minimal later, in the heat of the massive mobilizations
involved in the civil rights struggle. But in reality the groundwork for an unparalleled movement upsurge was being laid. What's past is prologue.

EMERGENCE OF THE CIVIL RIGHTS VISION

Beginning in the war years and accelerating after 1945, U.S. racial politics
underwent a striking metamorphosis.[19] This was the transformation of the U.S.
black population from its thorough subjugation and general relegation to rural
peonage in the pre–World War II period to its emergence after the war's end
as a largely mobilized and urbanized national community with egalitarian and
democratic commitments. Usually dated from the *Brown* decision of 1954 and
the Montgomery events of 1955 that marked the appearance on the scene of
Dr. King (then all of 26 years of age), the movement's birth struggles can be
located earlier.

Early Battles and Setbacks

Already in 1944 Gunnar Myrdal had issued a call for racial democratization
with the publication of his massive study *An American Dilemma* (1944).[20] This
book would become the blueprint for state-based racial reform in the postwar

era, strongly influencing debates about segregation and the run-up to the *Brown* decision, for example.

But already well before *Brown* and Montgomery, several groups of black activists and their allies had challenged U.S. racism at the United Nations, utilizing a series of petitions and manifestos that resembled abolitionist activities of a century earlier. The United Nations established a Commission on Human Rights in early 1946, soon after its founding. That commission undertook to make recommendations to the General Assembly regarding a variety of issues, including civil liberties, free speech, women's rights and status, and discrimination based on race, sex, language, or religion (Dudziak 1988, at footnote 194). In response, no less than three petitions against U.S. racism were rapidly filed. The National Negro Congress (NNC) filed "The First Petition to the United Nations from the Afro American People" in June 1946 (Aptheker 1971). The NAACP filed an extensive statement with the UN Commission, written by W. E. B. Du Bois, Milton Konvitz, Rayford Logan, and Earl Dickerson, entitled *An Appeal to the World: A Statement on the Denial of Human Rights in the Case of Citizens of Negro Descent in the United States of America and An Appeal to the United Nations for Redress* (Horne 1986; Horne 1994; Plummer 1996). In 1951, the Civil Rights Congress (CRC), responding to the General Assembly's passage in 1948 of the UN Convention on the Prevention and Punishment of the Crime of Genocide, presented a statement to the UN entitled *We Charge Genocide: The Historic Petition to the United Nations for Relief from a Crime of the United States Government Against The Negro People* (Civil Rights Congress 1970). The NNC petitition and the CRC petition were both produced by organizations with close ties to the Communist Party (CP). The NAACP petition and the *We Charge Genocide*/CRC petition both bore the signature of Du Bois, who was close to the CP but did not formally join until 1961.[21]

These developments served to remind both the world and Washington that U.S. racism was not only a domestic matter, but that it had international implications as well. By launching these petitions, radical tendencies within the movement sought to reinterpret the meaning of race and racism in the United States, to transform the country's racial politics by linking the issue to the revulsion at fascism (*We Charge Genocide*), to the anti-colonialism burgeoning in Africa and Asia, and to the emerging notion of human rights. They explicitly cited the connection between the denial of human and political rights to blacks in the United States—which they treated as a negation of democracy—and the growing worldwide demand for national liberation and decolonization. They linked discrimination and racism to the dawning of the Cold War: Du Bois et al. questioned the U.S. Cold War rhetoric, with its professions of adherence to democratic values and personal freedom, by documenting numerous instances of attacks on blacks, racial bigotry, and the like.

In contrast to the incrementalist and legalistic strategies through which mainstream civil rights organizations (including the NAACP) had sought to reform de jure discrimination, the petitions and appeals were challenges to white supremacy from the left. But this left-based challenge was not destined to triumph.

At roughly the same moment as the petitions were presented, conflict over U.S. racial politics came to a head in the majority party, the Democrats. From the "compromise" of 1876 through the years of the New Deal, indeed until 1948, the Democrats had accommodated the racist politics of their southern adherents, who in return had delivered the votes of the "Solid South," election year after election year, into the Party's columns.[22] It hardly needs adding that these southern votes were almost entirely white, since black enfranchisement in the South had been effectively scuttled in the late nineteenth century. This one-party racial empire, however, had come to coexist ever-more inconveniently with a reform-oriented and nearly social democratic wing that represented the Party's industrial working class base outside the South. So strange had the coalition become that in the Roosevelt years many blacks who could vote (that is, blacks living outside Dixie) abandoned their traditional home in the Republican Party to support the same national leadership that denied the vote (and virtually all rights and powers) to their southern brethren (Weiss 1983; Sitkoff 1978).[23] So volatile a situation could not continue indefinitely.

By 1946 the battle for control over the Democratic Party was already in full swing, with organized labor, the corporate liberal elite, and the Dixiecrats occupying the main divergent positions.[24] "Operation Dixie," an industrial organizing drive in the South, was soundly defeated in 1946. The loss of this effort to unionize the southern states (along the same imperfect but largely integrationist pattern that the industrial union confederation—the CIO—had developed in the North) was a massive setback for the cause of racial justice in the postwar United States. And more generally as well: it was a blow to democratic and egalitarian aspirations overall. Southern unionization would have meant more than increased wages in the underdeveloped South (and elsewhere). It might have signified a national turn toward policies of full employment and socialized health care, and the beginning of the end for Jim Crow. It would have vastly strengthened the Party's social democratic wing.

To bring about the defeat of Operation Dixie a coalition of center-right forces was assembled within the Democratic Party: anchored in the seemingly eternal power base of the southern congressional and senatorial delegation, it drew on the AFL unions, which were much more committed to racial exclusion than the CIO organizations.[25] Business interests, even northern and racially moderate ones, joined the resistance because they perceived resurgent unionism as a major political and economic threat. The use of anti-communist scare tactics, which would rapidly become a high national drama, yielded good results in this intra-Party battle. An important full employment measure was also killed off in 1946; Republicans and Dixiecrats gained seats in that off-year's elections; racial moderates in the unions and the Party came under attack as communist sympathizers; and probably of greatest importance, the threat of a multiracial unionized South that the Operation Dixie campaign represented was dead by 1947.

Soon liberal Democrats were taking up the anti-communist banner as well (Schlesinger 1946). The price exacted by the triumphant reactionary coalition within the Democratic Party—the political price one had to pay, that is, to avoid being attacked as soft on communism—was opposition to racial integration, or at least adherence to "moderation" on racial issues. The consequences of the unholy alliance between race-baiting and red-baiting would prove disastrous for both the causes of labor and of racial democracy: both the Taft–Hartley Act of 1948 and the decades-long delay of racial reform can be linked quite directly to the racial crisis of the Democratic Party in the late 1940s.

Although reactionary racial forces were gaining ground by the next presidential election, racial tensions still exploded at the 1948 Democratic Party convention. Two breakaway factions emerged: a "States Rights" group split off to run the South Carolina segregationist Strom Thurmond as its candidate, largely in opposition to Truman's (lukewarm) support for moderate civil rights initiatives.[26] Meanwhile, a loosely defined social democratic faction, strongly committed to civil rights, split off to run Henry Wallace, Truman's predecessor as vice president, on the "Progressive Party" ticket. Like the good and bad angels that sit on the cartoon hero's opposite shoulders and whisper contradictory messages in his ears, the two breakaway factions tugged antagonistically at the soul of the Democratic Party. But as long as the South remained "solid"— solidly segregationist, that is—there was no real contest. The massive defeat of Wallace signaled the go-ahead for full-scale red- and race-baiting, while Thurmond's capture of two southern states, although far from a complete triumph, suggested that the South would remain "solid" for years to come.

The 1948 battle for the soul of the Democrats was a tug-of-war that would thenceforth involve the nation: not only Democrats but also Republicans, not only in the South but also in the North. It was more than a battle over the future of the Party. It would eventually be fought out not only in established political arenas, but in the muddy streets of the Mississippi Delta and the concrete canyons of the northern ghettos.

At the heart of the turmoil were two contradictory tendencies, two opposing power blocs. The defenders of the racial status quo (led by southern white elites seeking to preserve their access to exploitable labor and the privileged political position of the underdeveloped and conservative South) at first lined up fairly solidly behind the barricades of *herrenvolk*[27] democracy. Especially in the acrimonious early days of the Cold War, they unquestioningly equated integration with communism, blithely using racial coding as a handy-dandy guide for red-baiting. If whites had black friends, or even were seen in the company of blacks who did not clearly evince their subordinate status, this was taken as prima facie evidence of red, or at least (as the phraseology went) "pink" sympathies. Similarly, "uppity" blacks who "forgot their place" or criticized U.S. racism (especially abroad) could be assumed to have been at least "duped by the reds" (Kutler 1982).

The group aligned with the Henry Wallace campaign was composed of old New Dealers, who were portrayed not only as "soft on communism" but also as "race-mixers" opposed to segregation. Indeed, there were socialists and communists of various tendencies in this group, but most were probably social democrats and laborites, closer to Harold Laski than either Stalin or Trotsky. Under the onslaught of the witch hunters, though, this tendency was rapidly evicted tout court from most positions of power. Those to the left of the diehard segregationists who remained in the Party were refigured as racial "moderates," who went no farther than to endorse the abolition of Jim Crow. Largely based in the North, these were "liberal" Cold Warriors who were able to establish their credentials by acquiescence, if not outright adherence, to the purges of J. Edgar Hoover, Joseph McCarthy, et al. The relatively few blacks who had established themselves in New Deal or left Democratic circles now found themselves marginalized, unless they embraced the new red-baiting ethos, not only in the United States but also on the international scene.[28]

Thus from the late 1940s on, a liberal anti-racism, or a moderate collusion with the "solid South," was established as the most progressive position available within the political mainstream. Because moderates were urban northerners with voting blacks in their districts, and because the key black political organizations close to the New Deal legacy (notably the NAACP) had submitted to Cold War orthodoxy (Williams 1998), a kind of racial centrism gained prominence, in both the Democratic and the Republican Parties. By the mid-1950s, as the NAACP and other civil rights organizations made some gains—largely by legal means rather than popular mobilization—as the furor of the red-baiting years died down, and as the State Department and CIA learned that explicit, state-sanctioned discrimination played very badly in the emerging Third World and even in Europe (Dudziak 1988; von Eschen 1997), this centrism slowly and incompletely became the new national common sense.

Mass Mobilization

In 1954 and 1955, the *Brown* decision and the Montgomery bus boycott announced the beginnings of a new stage of struggle for racial democratization, placing new pressures on racial "moderates." The story of the emergence of a new phase of civil rights activism, one characterized by mass mobilization, by sit-ins, by freedom rides, and most centrally by the involvement of "local people" in the South (Dittmer 1995; Payne 1995) who marched by the thousands (and were arrested, beaten, and murdered as well) is a familiar one (Waskow

1966; Branch 1988; McAdam 1982; Morris 1984; Carson 1981; Blauner, 1972; Bloom 1987). This mobilization represented the first opportunity to propose a radical democratic political agenda since the end of World War II and the reassertion of the racist right in the McCarthy period.

The challenge the movement posed to the "moderates," to the centrist politics of Cold War liberalism, was a substantial one. The racial moderates were now in a difficult position. They had to respond to the largely unprecedented welling-up of black popular mobilization. They were being called upon to oppose the racial dictatorship of the South, to abandon their long-standing political allies. They were being summoned, moreover, by a movement that had growing white support and mainstream political allies in both the national parties. The Democrats were particularly under the gun: they had to bridge the gap that yawned between the two main components of their constituency: the "solid South" and northern liberal voters (including of course the black vote). There were some attempts to define the problem as a peculiarly southern one, but it soon became clear that similar commitments to white supremacy survived "up South," that is, in the northern cities (Sugrue 1995).

So the moderates slowly came face-to-face with the depths of their racial crisis: they had to devise a reform agenda that would not threaten the national institutions or social structures that had been dependent, from time immemorial (or at least since 1877) on the submission of blacks. Among the deep-seated vulnerabilities that the resurgent black movement threatened to heighten were such relationships as:

- the regional economic imbalance that maintained a low-wage, non-unionized labor pool in the South (Franklin 1991);
- the system of employment discrimination that held all wages down through threats of black wage competition (if anti-racist employment policies were to be enacted and enforced), and through threats of immigrant wage competition (if anti-racist immigration policies were to be enacted and enforced) (Reich 1981);
- the entrenched racism of the U.S. welfare state, whose blatant biases had remained essentially unchallenged all the way from the New Deal[29] through the rise and fall of the "war on poverty"[30] in the 1960s;
- the disproportionate electoral power of the South, which was guaranteed to the Democratic Party through systematic black disenfranchisement (Carmines and Stimson 1989; Keyssar 2000);
- the widespread subsidization of white wealth, particularly holdings in real property, that flowed to the white working and middle classes through systematic residential discrimination;[31]
- and the system of racially hegemonic beliefs in the superiority and normalization of white identity, which gave a semblance of coherence to a wide range of nationalistic ideas and attitudes in the United States: that

the country was a "land of opportunity," with "liberty and justice for all," the linchpin of the "free world," committed to the "free enterprise system," and so on (Kinder and Sanders 1996; Bobo, Kluegel, and Smith 1996; Winant 1997a; Lipsitz 1998b).

These were simply some of the main issues that a nationally oriented black/anti-racist movement might have called into political question, if it had developed the organizational resources and the means of disseminating its views and arguments widely. Of course these prospects were not framed in so clear-cut a fashion over the 1950s and 1960s, as the modern civil rights movement was born. But as the witch-hunting died down, these threats that the movement posed to the taken-for-grantedness of white supremacy increasingly became the subjects of public debate (King 1994 [1963]).

THE LIMITS OF RACIAL REFORM

The enactment of civil rights legislation from 1964 to 1968 marked the apex of the movement's success. This was the culmination of a long-term struggle to extend democracy across the color-line, a struggle that had lasted for centuries, had taken place in all branches and levels of government, and had pervaded civil society, the military, and the psychic structure of every American. Once fairly launched around the turn of the twentieth century,[32] the civil rights movement had needed decades to achieve such minimal reforms as federal guarantees of the right to vote, civil sanctions against employment discrimination, and the outlawing of discrimination in public institutions.

But even as the movement attained its greatest successes—the enactment of its demands for laws prohibiting discrimination—the civil rights reforms seemed inadequate to many. The reform legislation was weak, but its interpretation by the judiciary and its enforcement by the executive were particulalrly ineffective (Kairys 1993). I discuss the limits of civil rights reform measures at greater length below.

If 1964–68 was the high tide of legislation, it was also the peak period of black rioting, a virtually unprecedented phenomenon in the United States.[33] Black "urban uprisings" were widely seen as an expression of dissatisfaction with the accomplishments of the movement and with the civil rights reforms in general. That these "race riots" were analyzed as manifestations of the continuing "powerlessness" felt by black people within "normal" politics, that they were, in fact, seen as political events at all, says a great deal about the general perception, black and white, that U.S. democracy continued to have significant racial limits.[34]

Much the same could be said about "black power." This concept—signifying a resurgence of black nationalism—appeared in 1965[35] as a radical rejection and reproach of the mainstream civil rights movement. Yet its followers' initial demands were not so distinct from the ethnic pluralism that moderate scholars and politicians were just then proposing as the essence of the movement's agenda.[36] So if black mobilization was finally issuing in black ethnic politics, as Irish, Italian, and even Jewish mobilization had previously done, why were so many people so uptight about "black power"? Why wasn't it simply a democratic achievement, a fulfillment of the civil rights vision, the incorporative democratizing outcome of reform, the "cultural pluralism" so admired in Little Italy, South Boston, or Poletown?[37]

In these and many other ways the civil rights vision was demonstrating its divisions even while it was being implemented. Movement activists and sympathizers, restive ghetto dwellers, and insurgents were mobilizing for its extension toward real social democratic redistribution.[38] They were working to extend the movement agenda, especially toward recognition of the links between U.S. racism and interventionism in the Third World.

In respect to both these social democratic and anti-interventionist aspirations, the role played by Dr. King is revealing. Although regularly cast as the leader of the moderate movement, King is better understood as a radical pragmatist who continually attempted to synthesize more sweeping movement goals of social transformation with practical political possibilities (Branch 1988; Branch 1998). Although he was the target of much criticism from both movement militants and racist reactionaries, King was certainly emblematic of a wide radicalization. The later years of the civil rights struggle witnessed a number of attempts on his part to transform the movement from a largely antiracist, domestically focused initiative to a broader egalitarian current with international as well as U.S.-based objectives. His organization of the "poor people's campaign," his backing for welfare rights organizing, his support for various strikes (including the March–April 1968 Memphis strike where Dr. King met his end), and of course, his explicit advocacy of anti-war and anti-imperialist as well as black nationalist (Cone 1991) positions, all illustrate these deeper commitments. As the most prominent civil rights leader, King's appeals to poor whites and his denunciations of the war were particularly pivotal; his development was emblematic of an emerging left potential in the United States, one whose roots were deeply planted in the black movement.[39]

But a consolidated radical vision could never materialize. The movement shift toward a radical democratic position was only partial and was beset by contradictions. As die-hard resistance to democratic reforms eroded, as the movement agenda came to be accepted in the suitably moderate form—of equal opportunity legislation and the withdrawal of support for official policies of segregation—the more radical movement critique of the *embeddedness* of racial dynamics throughout U.S. society was cast aside. This was a fundamental contribution of the movement: its recognition that race was a pillar of the country's social structure, that race pervaded both public and personal life from top to bottom. Of course, fully to confront the deeply implanted racism that descended like a great river from the most remote interior sources of U.S. history and culture was a virtually impossible task. Yet the black movement made perhaps the most sustained and widespread effort to do so during the 1960s.

In a certain way, indeed, the die-hard segregationists who argued that agreeing to integration and civil rights reform was acceding to revolutionary ("communist," etc.) change in the United States, were more in touch with the deeper implications of the movement challenge than were the moderate reformers, whether located inside the state apparatuses or inside the movement itself.[40] For they knew or at least sensed the deeper implications of the movement challenge. Perhaps they recoiled in horror, not principally because their interests, their sense of entitlement and privilege, was being threatened, but rather because they knew that their reactionary nationalism, their civil religion, was under attack.

Faced with these realities, the unity of the civil rights movement eroded rapidly after the mid-1960s. Its mainstream liberal supporters—and most of its white adherents—congratulated themselves on the victory of the enactment of civil rights reforms. But many movement activists, and much of its black membership, wondered how much change civil rights could bring, absent significant redistribution of income and major efforts to eradicate poverty. They wanted not only rights, but also the power and resources to achieve dramatic social change; they demanded not simply abstract and often unrealizable opportunities, but concrete results.

While moderates sought to downplay the significance of racial identity, movement radicals tried to reemphasize it. The debate over identity focused in crucial ways on the racial commitments of whites, what George Lipsitz has called "the possessive investment in whiteness" (Lipsitz 1998c; Winant 1998): would whites be able to move beyond their own racism, their own dependence, often unconscious, on the privileges conferred by white skin in the United States? Was American democracy, in the familiar dichotomy articulated by Martin and Malcolm respectively, a "dream" or a "nightmare"?

These divisions between moderates and radicals over matters not only of policy but also of identity were the inheritance of centuries-long conflicts in the U.S. social structure. They reflected the deep social chasm among the races, the U.S. version of apartheid. They flowed from the long tradition denying political rights to blacks, native peoples, and racialized immigrants, the undead legacy of *herrenvolk* democracy. And they revealed the depth to which racial categories had become institutionalized over the centuries.[41] Simultaneously, they epitomized the unraveling of these structures, the impossibility of sustaining a racial dictatorship, and the potential for an even more serious explosion of racially based movement opposition if serious reforms were not undertaken. Such ferocious fissures, rooted in the framework of U.S. society and history, could hardly be fully resolved by the movement; in some part, indeed, they were mirrored within it. They would continue to sunder, not only the black movement, but all racially based movements in the post–civil rights period. They would continue to divide racial identities—*all* identities, including those of whites—from the 1970s on (Winant 1994b).

Thus the moderates; what about the *radical* potentialities of the movement? These were evident in its contagiousness beyond the boundaries of blackness. Movement sensibilities, moderate or radical, spread to other insurgencies and other peoples, "infecting" them with a democratic fever. The movement re-ignited feminism and anti-imperialism, political/cultural themes that had lain dormant in the United States for decades.[42] It stimulated a range of non-black racial mobilizations: red, brown, and yellow. It also called whiteness into question in radical new ways, helped make sexual orientation a political issue for (almost) the first time,[43] and pushed existing popular political currents—notably the labor movement and the small but real socialist left—toward more radical democratic stances.

By forcing a massive national confrontation over the politics of race, the movement expanded the possibilities of democratic participation. In some ways (although certainly not completely or revolutionarily) the black movement and its allies reorganized American politics.[44] That the movement focused attention on what has come to be called, with some degree of depre-cation, "identity politics" and the "politics of difference" is not accidental. To invoke these themes, as well as to consider the "personal" and the encrusted political significance of language itself (what is now labeled, again in dispar-agement, "political correctness") was a hallmark of this new politics. For good reasons: awareness of these issues was the product of an *expanded and deepened grasp of the centrality of race in the construction of U.S. society and culture.* To make explicit the taken-for-grantedness of racial hierarchy, of "white supremacy" (think of that phrase not as some kind of cant, but as a description of a normal set of assumptions about social hierarchy and order) was to call all racial assumptions into question, not only at the macro-level of legislation, social pol-icy, and jurisprudence, but also at the micro-level of subjective experience. Thus anti-racist politics, especially in the United States but in various forms around the world as well, was the foundation of the "new" social movements of the postwar period.

But the racial reforms won by the civil rights movement were not limited only by the failure to address the deeper logic of race in U.S. history and culture. They were limited as well by their confinement to a largely symbolic effectiveness, by the hindrances placed between their apparent intent and their practical imple-mentation. A significant distance remained between the formal acknowledg-ment by Congress or the Supreme Court of black *rights* to equal justice, educa-tion, housing, or employment, and the actual *achievement* of those rights.

The elimination of Jim Crow *did not really occur*. Scandalously, this basic demand was not realized. Except in small-scale and largely symbolic gestures, segregation and discrimination, prejudice and privilege, and white supremacy in general, lived on. Employment discrimination (Kirschenman and Neckerman 1991; Burstein 1998; Hill 1993; Feagin and Sykes 1994), educational discrimination (Orfield, Eaton, and Jones 1997), environmental discrimination (Bullard 1997), discriminatory immigration, taxation, health, welfare, and transportation policies[45] (to name but the main dimensions of this issue) all continue in the present, at times amelioriated as a consequence of civil rights reform, but by no means uprooted or fundamentally altered from their pre–civil rights era configurations. The most egregious case of discrimination, that of *residential segregation*, was barely affected by civil rights reforms (Massey and Denton 1993).[46] Throughout the land, the same officials, the same offices, the same practices, that had faithfully enforced and regulated segregation during the pre–civil rights era, now were redefined, "regrooved." Legislators, administrators, and social policies that had formerly enforced housing discrimination or segregation in éducation, in employment or health care, now presented themselves as egalitarian and nondiscriminatory, having undergone little more than a superficial rhetorical adjustment, a sort of ideological facelift.

Even where reforms took place, they generally did not entail major shifts in social policy or personnel. Adjusted in certain ways, education, health care, and employment could still proceed in a racially stratified fashion. As if *Plessy v. Ferguson* had never been repealed, as if civil rights reforms had been almost entirely toothless measures, as if the mere appearance of racial democracy were all that the movement challenges of the postwar period had really required by way of a state reform policy response, segregation continued to flourish quite nicely in the post–civil rights era. Sure, it had been palliated, especially where access to rights and privileges (for example, an Ivy League education, a suburban home, an occasional seat on a corporate board) on the part of the crucial black bourgeoisie was concerned (Lena Williams 1991; Patricia J. Williams 1991; Graham 1995; Feagin and Sykes 1994). But for most black folk, for most "colored" people, inequality and segregation still ruled.

So the movement was torn. To recognize the profound tenacity and resilience of the long-established system of racial exclusionism and discrimination could easily lead to political "realism": from such a perspective moderate allies were indispensable. For those more in tune with the Democratic Party's continuing dependence on political centrism, on Cold War liberalism/anti-communism, on the imperative of maintaining white electoral support, moderate democratic reforms looked pretty good.

For those more committed to the movement's ideals, however, the idea of cooperating with the "moderates," of compromising with white supremacy, was anathema. What did racial "moderation" offer in answer to the ideals of these radical activists and intellectuals, who had already shed so much blood and spilled so much ink in the cause of justice and equality? A few symbolic gestures, some pious phraseology from self-righteous white lips? For movement adherents who by the later 1960s had become fully aware of the links between white supremacy and poverty/inequality, between white supremacy and imperialism, between white supremacy and gender inequality, the standard civil rights agenda of desegregation seemed ever-more inadequate. As the anti-war and women's movements—both to a significant extent offspring of civil rights—gained power and the practical difficulties of achieving even the moderate version of civil rights reform became clearer, the split within the movement only deepened (Carson 1981).

Worse yet for the radicals with the opportunity and courage to see it, neither alternative—placating the moderates or seeking to fulfill the vision of truly ending discrimination—was enough. Just as the possibilities for making limited gains in alliance with the racial moderates seemed pathetically inadequate, so too did the achievement of "civil rights" (in the sense of the elimination of segregation laws, the attainment of the franchise, etc.). Few could grasp the system of trenches that surrounded and fortified white supremacy,[47] the system that allowed civil rights reforms but at the same time preserved the large-scale social structure of racial hierarchy in the United States.

Without deprecating the movement that brought about this "great transformation,"[48] one must still note the partiality of the civil rights movement agenda. Like all other movements, it was shaped by its adversaries, oriented by what it sought to overthrow. The horizon of desegregation, of Jim Crow, like that of slavery a century earlier, marked a political boundary for much of the movement. Few could see beyond the "dream" of a desegregated world,[49] either to the endemic obstacles that desegregation presented, or to the inherent limits of the integrationist vision.

A STRATEGY OF INCORPORATION

Confronted by mass mobilization, the racial right also began to reveal its racial cleavages. The strategic alliance between the "solid South" and the northern moderates—rooted in the New Deal and reaffirmed in the early postwar years—started to come apart in the 1960s after the enactment of civil rights reforms. Party alignments were stretched, broken, and realigned. As racial mobilization deepened through the decade, race also became the cutting edge of the U.S. political system, shaping voting behavior, national elections, and party orientations. Ultimately, as Johnson and Nixon both realized, the situation threatened the Democratic Party's hold on power. The movement's mainstream opponents were divided as to how best to respond to its (re)appearance. As the spectacle provided by intransigent white supremacist opposition grew ever-more violent and desperate, "conservative" Republicans strategized about capturing the Democratic "solid South" and converting it into a long-term Republican base. Moderate Democrats were joined by moderate Republicans in advocating tempered support for civil rights reforms. And right-wing populism reemerged after decades of dormancy in the form of the (George) Wallace presidential campaigns, which effectively appealed to white working-class racism throughout the country (Edsall and Edsall 1992; Carmines and Stinson 1989; Phillips 1970; Carter 1999; Lesher 1995).

North–South schisms provided but one source of uncertain racial politics among the ruling elites of both parties. The exigencies of international politics and foreign policy offered another. Here the United States sought to present itself as the cornerstone of the "free world," an idea that clashed ironically with the lack of freedom for blacks. Especially in the South, where black campaigns for the franchise and minimal due process, for access to and inclusion in public institutions, gained worldwide attention, anti-black racism proved very damaging to U.S. international interests (Dudziak 1988; Ann Seidman 1994).

Yet the bedrock of conservatism in the United States was very much southern (and remains so even today). Numerous mainstream political crises that occurred over racial issues in the early postwar years serve as reminders of this: from the Dixiecrat schism at the Democratic National Convention in 1948 to the repudiation of the Mississippi Freedom Democratic Party at the Democratic National Convention in 1964, there was more than a little continuity. The Goldwater forces' rejection of civil rights legislation that same year, and the consequent shifting over of the "solid South" from the Democratic to the Republican column (famously noted by Lyndon Johnson and theorized at the time by Kevin Phillips), all attest to the continuing racial cleavages and disputes that fractured the white establishment, the ruling elite, in the postwar period (Phillips 1970; Edsall and Edsall 1992, 37). Even as racial "moderation" took center stage and a recognition of the need for racial reform gained strength, the adherents of such policies would not concede that substantive racial reform was needed to achieve lasting democratization. As we shall see, their refusal to support measures of "positive" discrimination (that is, affirmative action), and their quite early adoption of a "color-blind" racial rhetoric (Gordon 1964; Steinberg 1995) embodied long-standing continuities in U.S. racial policy.

In the aftermath of the civil rights reforms the forces of racial reaction also had to regroup. They could no longer sustain an implacable resistance to black demands for basic social rights, for such a posture risked their marginalization at the far right of the political spectrum. On the other hand, although white supremacy had certainly been shaken, it had not been destroyed. The cultural framework that supported it—the racial subjectivities, representations, and cognitive capacities of the U.S. populace—had not been comprehensively transformed. So the racial right, like its movement antagonists, was divided.

The nascent *new right* recognized that white supremacy was not dead, but only wounded. It therefore attempted to tap into repressed but still strong currents of racism in order to counter the black movement's egalitarian thrust. Born in the campaigns of George Wallace and Richard Nixon's 1968 "southern strategy," the new right developed a new subtextual approach to politics, which involved "coding" white resentments of blacks, and later of other minorities, women, and gays. The origins of the new right lie in the die-hard resistance to the black movement of the 1950s and 1960s already discussed. With the Wallace presidential campaign of 1968, this resistance crystallized as a national, electorally oriented, reactionary social movement. Wallace's right-wing populism recognized the deep threat that substantive racial equality posed to fundamental ideas about the kind of society and the kind of nation-state the United States was supposed to be. In effect, Wallace and his minions understood the same thing that black radicals and their allies had understood about the United States in the 1960s, although of course they were on opposite sides of the conflict. Through whatever optics they employed—anti-communism, racism, southern chauvinism, states' rights doctrines going back to Calhoun, agrarian populism, nativism, America First isolationism—the Wallace-ites and their numerous progeny grasped a deep truth: that white supremacy was not an excrescence on the basically egalitarian and democratic "American creed," but a fundamental component of U.S. society. To destroy it meant reinventing the country, the social order, the government.

Indeed, for the United States to come to terms in the mid-twentieth century with its own history of conquest and enslavement would have involved a deep national reckoning. Such an understanding would have severely threatened the foundations of the nation-state. The consequences of this agonizing self-appraisal would have included massive economic redistribution and the kind of atonement for white supremacy that was later to be associated with demands for compensatory programs such as "affirmative action"—or more properly, reparations. Thus the risk posed by the black movement—material, political, and psychic—to the key institutions of the *Pax Americana*, not to mention the majority of the U.S. population, the white majority, was profound.

Another approach was developed by the *neo-conservatives*, who in earlier, Democratic incarnations had been racial moderates: northern, white, and liberal supporters of civil rights. Disaffected by its post-1965 nationalist and class-based radicalisms but unwilling to engage in coded or subtextual race-baiting a la the right, these folks took up centrist positions on the right of the Democratic and left of the Republican Parties. Marked by their white ethnicity, their experience as the children of immigrants, and in particular by their youthful leftism and their struggles against anti-semitism (many key neo-conservatives were Jews), neo-conservative thinkers and politicians had made visceral commitments to what they saw as the core political culture of the United States: pluralism, consensus, gradualism, and centrism. They subscribed to an ethnicity-based model of race, derived quite consciously from the "immigrant analogy" (Omi and Winant 1994; Blauner 1972, 51–81). Their opposition to outright state-supported discrimination, which had temporarily allied them with the pre-1965 civil rights movement, thus had very different sources than that of their former movement allies. The idea of white supremacy as an abiding presence in American life was anathema to the neo-conservatives, for it called into question their idealized view of U.S. political culture.

Neo-conservatives abhorred the arguments of black militants—as typified in Malcolm's "What is looked upon as an American dream for white people has long been an American nightmare for black people" (Cone 1991, 89). In a striking way, the neo-conservatives reproduced the fearful and compensatory allegiance to whiteness exhibited in the late-nineteenth-century United States. Just as many whites in the nineteenth century had opposed slavery but resisted a comprehensive reorganization of their privileged status vis-à-vis emancipated blacks, so too the neo-conservatives opposed overt discrimination, but resisted an in-depth confrontation with the enduring benefits that race conferred on whites. Thus they sought to confine the egalitarian upsurge, to reinterpret movement ideas more narrowly and individualistically, and to channel them in more conservative directions. Their views aligned them with the white ethnics whose integration into mainstream American society resulted in conservative politics and a sense of "optional" ethnicity (Waters 1990). In practice neo-conservatism amounted to a denial of the significance of race in American life. This contrasted rather sharply with the new right's openness to racial coding and race-baiting.

Thus the racial reaction too was beset by divisions, in this case between the new right and neo-conservatives. These conflicts were probably not as deep as those confronting the civil rights movement and its post–1965 successors, but they were nevertheless real. Should the legacy of racial dictatorship and white supremacy, of *herrenvolk* democracy, be exploited or suppressed? Should the state uphold the civil rights legacy or undermine it? Should whites be mobilized *qua* whites—in defense of their racial privilege—or should the erosion of that privilege be anticipated or even encouraged? Such questions sharply problematized white identities in the post–civil rights period, and created serious difficulties for non-whites as well.[50]

NOTES ON THE CONTINUING SIGNIFICANCE OF RACE

The racial sea change wrought by the movement was incomplete; it was immediately challenged by backlash and a resurgent racial right; and the movement was itself split between moderates and radicals. In the early postwar years die-hard segregationism was able to fend off democratic challengers by linking race-baiting to red-baiting. But faced with a massive anti-racist movement of enormous determination, the "solid South" finally fissured in the 1960s. Certainly the crucial element in that democratic mobilization was the entry into the struggle of "local people,"[51] often at tremendous personal risk. But the movement could not have succeeded if the contradictions and backwardness of the old system of racial domination had not been demonstrated by major structural and cultural transformations after World War II.

The U.S. racial reforms were the outcomes of both national and transnational social transformations; they were overdetermined, the consequences of a piling up of numerous sociopolitical developments and demands. Among other things, they resulted from the massive requirements for black (and brown, and yellow) labor during and after the war, and the great migrations spurred by that necessity; from the recruitment, training, deployment, and eventual demobilization of many thousands of racial "minority" soldiers; and from the great tasks of social reorganization that these events posed in U.S. political and cultural life. The reforms were also the consequences of major ideological shifts: invigorated worldwide U.S. commitments to democratic rhetoric—required first by anti-fascist and then by anti-communist struggles—had to be demonstrated at home as well. These national (or nationalist) democratic commitments were incompatible with the system of racial dictatorship that had operated almost unimpeded in the South since the end of Reconstruction in 1877, and that had institutionalized a more benign but still oppressive form of white supremacy on a national scale. It was ironic that the very same equation that the Dixiecrats had employed successfully in the late 1940s to defeat civil rights—the ideological linkage between racial democracy and communism—returned in the 1960s in inverted form to challenge white supremacy itself. For as Martin and Malcolm and the activists of SNCC all argued, it was unsupportable to claim that the United States was "fighting for freedom" in Vietnam and elsewhere when the rights of U.S. citizens were systematically denied at home.

The partial victory of the civil rights movement was achieved by a synthesis of mass mobilization on the one hand, and a tactical alliance with U.S. national interests on the other. This alliance was brokered by racial "moderates," political centrists largely affiliated with the Democratic Party, who clearly perceived the need to ameliorate racial conflict and modernize racial dictatorship, but who also understood and feared the radical potential of the black movement. There was a price to be paid for civil rights reform: it could take place only in a suitably deradicalized fashion, only if its key provisions were articulated (legislatively, juridically) in terms compatible with the core values of U.S. politics and culture: individualism, equality, competition, opportunity, the accessibility of "the American dream," and the like.

This price was to be paid by the movement's radicals: leftwing nationalists, revolutionaries, and socialists (black, brown, red, yellow, and white), who were required to forego their vision of major social transformation or to face marginalization, repression, or death if they would not. The radical vision was an alternative "dream," Dr. King's dream, let us call it, a dream in which racial justice played the central part. To be "free at last" meant more than symbolic reforms and palliation of the worst excesses of white supremacy. It meant substantive social reorganization that would be manifested in egalitarian economic and political consequences. It meant something like social democracy, human rights, social citizenship in the Marshallian sense,[52] for blacks and other "minorities." But it was precisely here that the moderate custodians of racial reform drew their boundary line, both in practical terms and in theoretical ones (Steinberg 1995; Singh 1998). To strike down officially sanctioned racial inequality was permissible; to create racial equality through positive state action was not. The danger of redistribution—of acceding to demands to make substantive redress for the unjustified expropriation and restriction of black economic and political resources, both historically and in the present—was to be avoided at all costs.

Civil rights reform thus became the political agenda of the political center, which moved "from domination to hegemony" (Winant 1994b). The key component of modern political rule, of hegemony as theorized by Gramsci most profoundly, is the capacity to *incorporate opposition.* By adopting many of the movement's demands, by developing a comprehensive and coherent program of racial democracy that hewed to a centrist political logic and reinforced key dimensions of U.S. nationalist ideology, racial moderates were able to define a new racial "common sense." Thus they divided the movement, reasserted a certain stability, and defused a great deal of political opposition. This was accomplished not all at once, but over a prolonged period from about the mid-1960s to the mid-1980s. This partial reconfiguration of the U.S. racial order, based on real concessions and leaving major issues unresolved—such as the endurance of significant patterns of inequality and discrimination—has proved generally effective in reducing the political challenge posed by anti-racist movements in the United States. Certainly it has been more successful than the intransigent strategy of the die-hards would have been.

Yet the fundamental problems of racial injustice and inequality, of white supremacy, of course, remain: moderated perhaps, but hardly resolved. Therefore the meaning of race in the United States, and the ongoing significance of race for North American identities, also remains. Indeed the "American dilemma" may be more problematic than ever as the twenty-first century commences. For achieving this moderate agenda has required that the civil rights vision be drawn and quartered, beginning in the late 1960s and with ever-greater success in the following two decades. The tugging and hauling, the

escalating contestation over the meaning of race, has resulted in ever-more disrupted and contradictory notions of racial identity. The significance of race
(declining or increasing?), the interpretation of racial equality (color-blind or
color-conscious?), the institutionalization of racial justice (reverse discrimination or affirmative action?), and the very categories—black, white, Latino/
Hispanic, Asian American, and Native American—employed to classify racial
groups were all called into question as they emerged from the civil rights "victory" of the mid-1960s.

Not by any stretch of the imagination can this situation justify the claim that
racial injustice has largely been surpassed in a post–civil rights era. Yet such
views are not only common, but in many respects have become the new
national common sense in respect to race, acquiring not only elite and academic spokespeople, but also widespread mass adherence, especially among
whites. As a result, the already limited racial reform policies (affirmative
action) and the relatively powerless state agencies charged with enforcing civil
rights laws, such as the Equal Employment Opportunity Commission (EEOC),
developed in the 1960s, have undergone several decades of severe attack.
Forceful arguments have been made that the demands of the civil rights movement have largely been met, and that the United States has entered a post-
racial stage of its history. Advocates of such positions—usually classified as
"neo-conservative" (but sometimes also found on the left)—have ceaselessly
instructed racially defined minorities to "pull themselves up by their own boot-
straps," and in callous distortion of Martin Luther King Jr.'s message, have
exhorted them to accept the "content of their character" (rather than "the
color of their skin") as the basic social value of the country (Steele 1990; Thernstrom and Thernstrom 1997).

After the dust had settled from the titanic confrontation between the movement's radical propensities and the establishment's tremendous capacity for
reform, a great deal remained unresolved. Although the U.S. racial scenario
during the postwar decades is stalemated at the beginning of a new century, its
ambiguous and contradictory condition results from decades-long attempts
simultaneously to ameliorate race rebellion and to placate the *ancien regime
raciale*. The unending reiteration of these opposite gestures, these contradictory practices, itself testifies to the unresolved dilemmas and continuing significance of race in the United States.

To assess the present-day U.S. racial situation, the state of this complex set
of political (and sociocultural) compromises at the turn of the twenty-first century, is to examine the grounds for both residual complacency and potential
insurgence. It is to reaffirm the permanent importance of the questions that
the civil rights movement and its allies raised about the limitations of U.S.
democracy. Although the light of that movement illuminated a great deal as it
blazed across the postwar skies, by about 1970 the heavens were darkening

once again. The movement was once more marginalized, reduced to insisting once more on a radical democratic refusal of the racial common sense, as Du Bois and his allies had done a century earlier. To the extent that radical democratic approaches can reject the attempt to institute a post–civil rights, post-racial consensus, they serve to carry forward and update the legacy of the civil rights movement and its allies. In the concluding chapter of this volume I develop some arguments for this radical democratic approach, insisting that racial injustice remains not only a U.S. problem but also a worldwide one. Thus I hope to draw attention once more, a century after its first formulation, to a theme that can never be suppressed: the problem of the century (now the twenty-first century!) is still the problem of the color-line.

Eight

SOUTH AFRICA: WHEN THE SYSTEM HAS FALLEN

by Howard Winant and Gay Seidman

TWO PHOTOGRAPHS FRAME South Africa's image in the late twentieth century. In the first, taken in Soweto in 1976, a young woman holds the body of 13-year-old Hector Petersen, a black South African boy shot by police when he joined students demanding equal education—the kind of education denied to South Africa's black majority by the government policies collectively termed apartheid. In the second, taken eighteen years later, Nelson Mandela is sworn in as South Africa's first democratically elected president, promising to bring reconciliation and reconstruction to a country long divided by white supremacism.

In one decade South Africa has moved from pariah to exemplar. From its former position as the world's archetype of racial conflict and violence, the country has made the leap into democracy. Today, with a new (1996) constitution and a racially inclusive electoral process, South Africa seeks to be a racially inclusive society as well. This shift away from centuries of slavery and racial injustice is so dramatic that it echoes the decision by seventeenth-century European cartographers to name the continent's southern tip the "Cape of Good Hope," in place of the earlier, more meteorologically correct "Cape of Storms." Indeed, it holds out promises that extend beyond the country's borders to encompass the entire world: if racial justice and inclusion can be achieved (or even approximated) in South Africa, cannot other countries, especially those in the world's South, do likewise?

Real life, of course, is considerably more complicated than photographs can reveal. Although the destruction of official apartheid is still cause for celebration, and although significant steps have been taken toward a democratic opening in South Africa, in important ways the journey toward inclusion and justice is still very much underway. The legacy of apartheid, like a cure-resistant disease, lives on in the social structures, political institutions, and cultural attitudes of many who experienced it. The legacy also continues in peculiar and contradictory forms on the transnational level: it finds certain elective affinities with the new rules of the post–Cold War, post-colonial, post-industrial world market.

Racially speaking, during the last half of the twentieth century South Africa faced a transformation more complex, more deep-seated, than could ever be captured in just two photographs. Since Europeans first settled at the Cape in 1652, South Africa has been emblematic of (and deeply implicated in) the construction of racial modernity. Until the end of the twentieth century, South Africa's white population steadily reinforced the institutions of its racial order, subjecting the black majority of South Africans to forced labor, land dispossession, and political disenfranchisement as white supremacism was fortified.

In the post–World War II era, as the pressures for decolonization swept across the world's South, South Africa's white minority dug in its heels. Hector Petersen's death, like those of so many others, reflected the intransigence of a government willing to use enormous force to protect white supremacy. For a long time it was thought inconceivable that South Africa could become an inclusive, democratic society at all. For many years it was believed that white recalcitrance could only be dislodged by revolution, with all the blood and suffering that such conflict would involve.

That a less violent transition could take place—although hardly an entirely peaceful one—surprised and inspired the world. Nelson Mandela's 1994 election brought a tidal wave of new hope. Released from twenty-seven years of imprisonment only a few years before his triumph in South Africa's first democratic election, Mandela assumed office not only with a strong mandate, but with his egalitarian and multiracial commitments intact, and with all his magnanimity and political astuteness on full display. The fact that Nelson Mandela was now the country's president seemed nothing short of a miracle. His election was not his alone, of course, but that of his party, the African National Congress. That the ANC could nonviolently attain power after eighty-two years of struggle for democracy was also a great source of promise.

But as noted, after the formal end of apartheid, after the coming of democracy, the real work was just beginning. The new government faced enormous problems. Creating democracy is not only the work of regime transition, however violent or tranquil. It is also, and far more deeply, the work of *social organization*. It is a long process under the best of circumstances. In South Africa, where racial rule had been in place for centuries, where comprehensive disempowerment of the non-white population had for so long been the primary organizational principle of both politics and civic life, where until the 1990s the "highest stage of white supremacy" (Cell 1982) had been in relatively continuous operation, the social and political *re*organization necessary to undo the legacy of apartheid would prove to be an onerous task indeed.

This chapter summarizes and analyzes the rise and fall of apartheid in the post–World War II break period. It explores the social forces that undermined the old social order and that are working to construct a new, more egalitarian society. It considers the combination of national and transnational dynamics involved in both the downfall of apartheid and the reconstruction of a democratic South Africa. In particular the chapter asks, how is post-apartheid South Africa managing the range of issues bequeathed to it by the ancien regime it succeeded? How is the ANC government, with its long-standing commitment to non-racialism, handling the plethora of racial issues confronting the country as the new millennium dawns?

As black South Africans move into new positions of power and property, they not only have to reinvent the South African social structure; they also have to reinvent their political orientation. The vast majority of the country's people have now attained a new level of power and influence: as citizens, enfranchised and in a real sense liberated, they are no longer fighting for basic democracy. But on the other hand, the old order constantly reasserts itself: racial inequality remains; racial difference remains; racial attitudes remain. The long-term significance of race—in South Africa as elsewhere—is still in doubt.

So many problems of social change are posed by the South African transition that it looks more like a revolutionary transformation than a "simple" transition to democracy. Indeed, the destruction of apartheid had many revolutionary aspects: in the kind of oppositional effort and depth of organization that it required, in the degree of repression that had to be endured and transcended by those who desired democracy, and in the vast societal metamorphosis that it promised, many of the lineaments of revolution are visible. Yet the South African passage to democracy was *not* a full-scale revolution. Amazingly, it was accomplished relatively peacefully, despite the tremendous social upheaval and widespread violence that accompanied it.

The tremendous achievement of creating formal democracy, of establishing the principle of "one-person, one vote" in a society that for centuries had disenfranchised the majority of its population, was itself cause for rejoicing. But of course this was but the beginning of the South African transition. The real work remained to be done in 1994; it is underway now.

This chapter proceeds as follows. After this introduction there is a brief review of the *background conditions to apartheid.* Formalized in 1948, the apartheid system was significantly affected by the post–World War II racial break. But it was also the outcome of a long period of racist evolution that occurred under both British colonialism and the independent Union (see Chapter Five, above). In many ways the official establishment of the apartheid regime after the elections of 1948 was but the recognition that white supremacy was now *explicit and systematic* state policy.

After the 1948 election, the Nationalist Party set about *instituting apartheid*—the title of the next section of the chapter—as a means of overcoming this contradictory situation of *herrenvolk* democracy. The white rulers were responding to the increasing opposition that colonial and racist regimes had begun to encounter all over the world. Through an extensive program of legislation and regulation, they sought to overcome the inconsistencies between the informal practices of white supremacy that had persisted and deepened since colonial rule and the rising demands for the extension of democratic rights to all, which was the South African version of the worldwide racial break that succeeded World War II.

The following section discusses the functioning of the apartheid system at its height. The *highest stage of white supremacy* was never as rational and organized as it sought to be. The creation of apartheid involved both the South African state and civil society in an overt attempt to rationalize and reorganize racial rule. Far from accomplishing this end, of course, apartheid only exacerbated long-standing social and political contradictions of race. In the postwar South African system, the state committed itself to consistent partisanship on behalf of a small minority of the population. The burden this placed on any claim to legitimacy was unsupportable: in fact, the formal declaration of apartheid in 1948 was little more than an official recognition that racial dictatorship already existed. Beyond the *formal* limits of rational rule imposed by white supremacy, there were *substantive* limits: the widespread absence of legitimacy generated by apartheid necessarily bred confusion as well as opposition.

But of course apartheid could hardly have been purged of its irrationalities. The next section of the chapter considers the *contradictions of racial capitalism* that emerged over the post–World War II years. As the country developed and industrialized under the repressive regime of apartheid, the centrality of the industrial sector, with its increasing demand for labor, placed pressure on the system of racial rule. Labor migration patterns came into continual tension with the system of racial exclusion: these tensions were gendered as well as class- and race-based. Pretoria's attempts to manage these contradications by means of repressive modifications of the system of indirect rule—derived from the colonial past—exacerbated not just racial but also ethnic/cultural tensions. And as domestic political opposition increased, so too did international pressures.

The following section, entitled *building the movement*, traces the development of the anti-apartheid movement in the post–World War II break years. The democratic movement evolved during this prolonged period: it progressed from an early protest orientation based in the black elite, to a later quasi-revolutionary stage based in formidable mass-based insurgency. A younger, more militant generation of black leaders—that of Mandela, Tambo, and Sisulu—learned to use new tactics that would mobilize South Africans throughout the country. Gradually, black South Africans adopted strategies and tactics that reflected changes in their society: strikes, urban demonstrations, and boycotts. More urban and politically sophisticated, tempered by the experience of the war, thoroughly in touch with the anti-racist and anti-colonialist spirit then sweeping the world, and compelled in many ways by the repressiveness and intransigence of Pretoria itself, they moved steadily toward greater militance.

This section of the chapter reviews the black movement's step-by-step acquisition of the wherewithal to confront the apartheid regime. The resources required were formidable: not only a mass base and a workable program had to be created, but substantial linkages to global, post–World War II, anti-racist and anti-colonialist trends had to be built. Much of this work had to be done in clandestinity, in exile, and even in captivity. Tremendous internal divisions had to be overcome, and sophisticated and brutal means of repression had to be transcended. By the 1980s, the movement could draw upon and lead a huge groundswell of domestic opposition; this was clear in the destruction of apartheid. Although the apartheid regime attempted some reforms, movement activists successfully persuaded their followers that these were only superficial: perhaps blacks and whites would be allowed to sit together on park benches, but blacks would still be denied any real voice in politics or any share of the country's wealth.

The movement also built its international capabilities: it could both disrupt Pretoria's economic stability and effectively discredit the regime's last remaining semblance of political legitimacy. Without these resources and skills in place, it is doubtful whether even the overwhelming majority grouped in the ANC-led opposition could have succeeded in toppling white supremacy.

In the next section of this chapter attention turns to *post-apartheid conditions.* The inexorable clash between the national and international operations of capitalism vis-à-vis South Africa—a conflict heightened in numerous ways by anti-racist social movements, again both local and global—translated in democratic South Africa into another sort of tension. After 1994 the question of social transformation within the country has come into conflict with the transnational economy's demands for capitalist discipline—often termed "neoliberalism." In many respects the ongoing democratization of South Africa means the country's reintegration into the transnational world: the post–Cold War, neo-liberal world of massive economic (as well as cultural) interaction. Yet the new government's work of social reorganization demands public commitment to the progressive redistribution of resources, precisely the policies that transnational capital most condemns (and opposes, through such instrumentalies as the IMF and world financial markets). As the twenty-first century dawns, South Africa is perhaps the archetypal democratizing, post-authoritarian case among the nations of the world's South. On a variety of developmental terrains—economic, political, cultural, and even legal—the problems South Africa confronts in trying to undo the legacy of apartheid have the broadest possible implications for the entire world.

One of the most central dimensions of the country's confrontation with these challenges of social reorganization is how South African racial dynamics have been transformed, and continue to be revinvented, as the transition to democracy progresses. These concerns shape the concluding section of this chapter, which is entitled *Racial Conditions in Twenty-First Century South Africa.* In what ways will the racial patterns created not only under apartheid, but in the centuries-long run-up to apartheid, survive under a democratic and inclusionist system? In what ways can they be broken down and transcended? What sorts of policies, and indeed what new possibilities for lived experience, can be crafted in the new South Africa?

BACKGROUND CONDITIONS TO APARTHEID

Understanding the dynamics of apartheid and its transformation requires first recognizing the similarities and close ties between the construction of South Africa's racial order and the racial order that marked the modern world: apartheid was explicitly built on institutions that came out of South Africa's colonial experience, and South Africa's colonial experience was both defined by and constitutive of a global racial modernity. South Africa's history of conquest and slavery, racialization and resistance, is deeply implicated in the character of twentieth-century global society, just as South Africa's gold was implicated in the construction of a global financial order. From Saartjie Baartman, the South African woman whose naked body was put on display in nineteenth-century Paris as part of the effort to find a "scientific" basis for defining racial difference (Dubow 1995, 23; Gilman 1985, 76–108); to Cecil Rhodes, colonial governor and mining magnate who helped define British imperial power while constructing the migrant labor system that would undergird South African apartheid; South African individuals loom large in the construction of racial modernity—much as South African transformation at the turn of the twenty-first century looms large in the construction of a new world racial system today.

South African historiography, like that of most postcolonial societies, is marked by debates: over how to understand colonial invasion and conquest, and how to interpret relations between indigenous peoples and settlers of European descent. The facts themselves are relatively stark: from 1652, when Dutch merchants first sought to establish a supply-stop on Africa's southern tip, white settlement in the region involved many of the patterns of what would later be called apartheid: exploitation of local people and resources, political exclusion, and racial domination. In the mid-twentieth century, when the architects of apartheid sought to construct a more stable version of white minority rule, they could build on four centuries of experimentation with techniques of protecting white settlers' control over non-whites: over their movements, their labor, their families, and their political activities.

The history of white settlement in South Africa parallels the history of European imperialism more broadly. Beginning with mercantile interests seeking to promote long-distance sea-trade—first Dutch and then British—by the early nineteenth century colonial administrations at the Cape had come to view the southern African region as a site for potential settler expansion. In the mid-nineteenth century, imperial visions expanded still further, to encompass the mineral and agricultural wealth that colonies like South Africa might provide for a Europe in the throes of industrial transformation (see Chapter Five, above).

Many have argued that South Africa's twentieth-century system of racial classification—with its four main categories: white, Asian, coloured, and African—is linked to the legacy of strict Calvinism.[1] Others have attributed it to the resolution of the Anglo-Boer War, when British and Afrikaner politicians left the decision of how to define citizenship to each province (Marx 1998). Yet each of these arguments, which in essence blame South Africa's institutional-ized racial categorization on Afrikaans-speaking settlers, rather than on the British colonial government, ignores the close link between South Africa's min-eral discoveries in the last part of the nineteenth century and the tightening of already existing racial institutions.

A more persuasive historical argument about the origins of South African racial categories would emphasize the relationship among racial identity, labor exploitation, and the world economy. As South Africa was drawn into British imperialism's economic net, individuals increasingly found their economic chances closely linked to their racial category. For whites, especially those with property and education, racial policies translated into political rights that directly enhanced their interests. The state cleared land of original tenants, controlled the movements of people of color, and brought new workers from India or from elsewhere in the region to serve on farms and mines. White supremacist patterns of power and culture granted a special status to European settlers and European immigrants.

Non-whites remained strictly subjugated. Their subordinate status, though, differed by racial category. Indians, mainly brought as indentured laborers for Natal's sugar estates, were systematically distinguished from Africans. African men were employed as farm workers or as unskilled workers in the mines. African women were generally allowed to work in subsistence agriculture, or were drawn into domestic work for white households.

Importantly—and marking the dynamic character of the South African racial formation process—it is only in the late nineteenth century in South Africa that the distinct coloured category emerges. This social stratum is often defined as mixed-race, but in reality includes a range of groups: descendants of Muslim Malay slaves exported to Cape Town, descendants of the Cape's indigenous Khoisan peoples, and hybridized groups that resulted from white-black miscegenation.[2] The particularities of these people—their cultures, his-tories, and roles in South African society—demanded that they be distin-guished from the other racial categories. In response to white demands for special protections of Europeans—including efforts at urban segregation and attempts to reserve skilled jobs for workers defined as "white"—people who could claim a unique coloured identity asserted their difference from Africans, seeking to distinguish themselves politically, socially, and economically from the indigenous population.

Always the main thrust for institutionalized racial categorization came from whites: white employers and farmers, white politicians, and white workers. Each group used its political power to enforce protections for white supremacy in a particular arena. From the late nineteenth century, mining companies used racial controls to keep African laborers from fleeing the dangerous and difficult work of underground mining. Building on legislation developed one hundred years earlier at the Cape, the government required African men in the mining areas to carry passes. This allowed police to stop and challenge these men, and to prevent their return to farming in rural communities. White farmers used racial restrictions on African land ownership—particularly the 1913 Native Land Act, which set aside only about 13 percent of the land area for African farming—to translate the status of African peasant farmers into labor tenants on white-owned land, or to evict African farming communities to make way for commercial agriculture. And white workers steadily supported the "color bar" that systematically stratified the South African working class.

White property owners were not the only ones who defined their economic interests in racialized terms, or who used white supremacist policies to promote those interests. White workers, both British and Afrikaans-speaking, also did so. They rejected the possibility of unity between white and non-white workers. Unable to view Africans as true members of an industrial working class, white unions generally rejected black members, organizing a massive strike in 1922—the so-called Rand Rebellion—under the infamous slogan, "Workers of the World, Unite, and Fight for a White South Africa." Responsive to a virtually all-white electorate, the South African government acceded to white workers' demands: from 1932, the "civilized labor" policy ensured that better-paid, skilled jobs would be reserved for whites. Only unions with whites-only memberships were entitled to bargain with employers. In addition to their political disenfranchisement, black workers were barred from the better jobs and excluded from recognized unions. By the 1930s, the land areas set aside for African farming were overcrowded and showing signs of erosion. As Africans responded by moving to seek work in cities, new "influx control laws" were put in place, requiring them to get permits to live in white-designated areas. The obvious effort was to prevent the build-up of a black urban population.

Thus by the beginning of World War II, many of the institutions that would later be brought together under the apartheid policies of postwar South Africa were already in place. It is worth noting, however, that these orientations occasioned little international outrage during the first half of the twentieth century. They were holdovers from colonial rule, and from the era of "self-rule" of the early decades of the twentieth century. Such policies were still common in colonial settings around the world; they were hardly unique to South Africa in an era when colonial powers assumed that capitalism and colonialism required a racial state and entrenched racial division. Settlers and metropolitan rulers—that is, whites—routinely employed racial understandings in politics. Racialized disenfranchisement, land dispossession, restriction of indigenous populations to reservations, even racial exclusion by trade unions, were largely taken for granted by whites, if not by colonized peoples and their descendants.

INSTITUTING APARTHEID

South Africa began to look different in the era after World War II. As Harold MacMillan remarked, "the winds of change" were sweeping across Africa as the European powers were moving to grant their colonies self-rule, then independence.[3] But in South Africa, the white minority slammed the door on racial reforms or racial democratization, reasserting control by intensifying exclusion in every possible way. Returning World War II veterans[4] and militant young student leaders like Nelson Mandela began to insist that the democratic norms described in the Atlantic Charter should also apply to them.[5] Before the war the African National Congress had been relatively elitist and accommodationist. Now its leaders began to demand fuller democracy in South Africa, and sought to mobilize broad popular support among the increasingly urban and proletarianized black majority. Moreover, the effects of the war on South African society gave black South Africans new instrumentalities for disturbing white control. There was now a substantial urban black population, whose demonstrations and marches were visible and disruptive to ordinary whites' lives. Black workers, drawn into industrial work, began to organize independent unions and to demand higher wages and political rights.

Strikes and demonstrations, along with increased international scrutiny, provoked debate in the white population about South Africa's future. This debate involved a new political force: the explicitly segregationist Nationalist Party. Vehicle of a mobilized Afrikaans nationalist movement, the "Nats" insisted that South Africa's future lay in separate development rather than in a united future. The party was deeply committed to a system in which whites and blacks would live in their own spheres, the system that came to be known as apartheid. Although Afrikaans nationalism had always involved struggles over ethnicity among whites, at its center was a strong emphasis on white supremacy and racial control.

In 1948, a close election among an almost exclusively white electorate installed a new government, committed to a policy of entrenched white supremacism. The Nationalist Party, which would continue to govern South

Africa until 1994, came to power on a platform that embraced segregation and exclusion, and sought consciously to immunize white supremacism against any change, any threat, of majority rule. The framework of apartheid, elaborated over the next decade or so, is dramatically visible in a series of laws passed during the Nationalist Party's first years in power.

Three laws constructed rigid racial categories: the 1949 Prohibition of Mixed Marriages Act, which banned marriages between people of different racial categories; the 1950 Immorality Act, which made sex across the color-line illegal; and the 1950 Population Registration Act, which gave officials the power to classify all South Africans by race. Several other laws created the framework for strict urban segregation: the 1950 Group Areas Act designated urban areas by race, while the 1951 Prevention of Illegal Squatters Act, the misleadingly named 1952 Native Abolition of Passes Act, the 1954 Natives Urban Areas Act, and the 1957 Native Laws Amendment Act, together required that blacks carry permits with them at all times, and allowed officials forcibly to remove blacks from white-designated areas if they did not have explicit permission to be there. A series of other laws created the basis for the segregation of social life, from the Reservation of Separate Amenities Act (1953), which enforced social segregation in all public amenities from parks and libraries to buses and restaurants; to a series of laws that required segregation even in private schools, and created different curricula for children of different races. The evolving apartheid system sought to guarantee, as then Minister of Native Affairs (and later prime minister) Hendrik Verwoerd put it, that African children would not be shown "the green pastures of European society in which they are not allowed to graze." Instead it would make sure that "Natives will be taught from childhood to realize that equality with Europeans is not for them."[6] All these new measures were shored up by a series of draconian security laws, beginning with the 1950 Suppression of Communism Act, which allowed the government to ban political meetings and demonstrations and to define political opponents as communists—and then jail them without trial or place them under house arrest. Building on and extending existing institutions, apartheid reinforced white supremacy and tried to undermine any possibility of resistance.

THE HIGHEST STAGE OF WHITE SUPREMACY

For decades, South Africa's unique status rested on the extreme character of apartheid: the system of racial hierarchy and exclusion constructed following the Nationalist Party's election victory in 1948. To an unparalleled degree, South Africa demonstrated the persistence of racial inequality despite industrialization. South Africa tended to disprove the liberal vision of race: that industrialization would ameliorate inequality. It undercut the lingering tendency among modernization theorists to treat racial oppression as atavistic or vestigial.[7] At a time when decolonization movements were spreading and civil rights movements were challenging racial discrimination in the United States, South Africa was moving toward intensified segregation and complete disenfranchisement of its African majority—to the point that it denied its African inhabitants not only the right to vote, but even the right to call themselves South African.[8]

But apartheid went beyond exclusionary politics, urban segregation, or unequal public facilities. Long before the Nationalist Party took power in 1948, the British colonial government had created "native reserves" that set aside 13 percent of South Africa's land area for the roughly 75 percent of the population classified as African. After 1948, these reserves became "homelands" for black South Africans: blacks could work in white-designated areas, but they could never hope for citizenship in a larger South Africa. Instead, they were officially assigned to one of the African areas that were one day to be set adrift as "independent" countries. Blacks were required to carry passes to show they had permission to live, work, or travel in white-designated areas, and faced prison terms if they were caught without passes. Apartheid's policy of "separate development" treated rural Africans as temporary sojourners, who would leave their families behind while they came to work in the mines, farms, and factories, but return to their "homelands" at the end of their working lives. This circulatory migrant labor system was apartheid's cornerstone: black South Africans were denied citizenship in the land of their birth, but would continue to provide cheap labor to white-ruled South Africa. By the 1960s, the "homelands" policy had become the "separate development" policy: beginning under Verwoerd in the 1960s, successive Nationalist governments sought to convert the homelands into "bantustans" or quasi-separate nations.[9]

For most of the apartheid era, comparisons between South Africa and other countries emphasized the unique characteristics of South African segregation: it was "the highest stage of white supremacy," a carefully constructed scaffolding designed to protect white domination of the black majority far into the future (Cell 1982). Not surprisingly, most comparisons sought to explain why South Africa was different, offering reasons for South Africa's peculiarly virulent form of racial control. Before World War II, before the break, South Africa had not seemed so different from other European colonies, where white domination was unquestioned and white settler control over native populations was ubiquitous (Cooper 1996). But when decolonization began to take off after World War II, South Africa seemed to take a divergent path. Why, when the decolonization movements were sweeping across Africa in the 1940s, did South Africa turn toward new racial restrictions, rather than moving toward integration? From a similar starting point—a relatively similar racial order, in which white minorities controlled black majorities through political exclusion, through strict segregation, and through racialized controls at the workplace—South Africa moved in a different direction.

Of course, any attempt to rationalize racial rule is necessarily contradictory. The apartheid system went beyond naturalizing the social categories of race; that is something all racial systems tend to do. But by demarcating racial boundaries in social life to an unprecedented extent,[10] South Africa attempted to *freeze* racial categories both in institutional practices and in everyday life. Politically, the postwar South African state sought to "legitimate the illegitimate" (Greenberg 1987) by committing itself to consistent partisanship on behalf of a small minority of the population. This vitiated any claim to democracy: the formal declaration of apartheid in 1948 was in effect an official announcement that racial dictatorship was the law of the land. Beyond the *formal* limits of rational rule imposed by white supremacy, there were *substantive* limits: the widespread absence of legitimacy generated by apartheid necessarily bred inconsistency, frustration, and bewilderment as well as opposition.[11]

In many political analyses, South African exceptionalism was generally traced to dynamics in the white population, primarily in the relationship among mine-owners, white state officials, and white workers. Many studies attributed South Africa's odd trajectory to the character of the state. While some analysts argued that apartheid emerged out of the dynamics of Afrikaans nationalism and an unusually autonomous state bureaucracy (Marx 1998; O'Meara 1983; Posel 1991), most comparative analysts link racial concerns more explicitly to economic ones. Whites were protecting racial privilege, but they were also reinforcing a system that provided cheap black labor to white-owned mines and farms (Evans 1997). White supremacy involved not only racial discrimination, but, just as importantly, a specifically racial class system, where racial identities marked class status. Conscious state policies recreated the racial character of South African capitalism: policies to uplift poor whites or to limit black farmers' opportunities consistently reinforced racial inequality (Bundy 1979; Van Onselen 1982).

This perspective highlighted the racial character of the South African state: its minoritarian and repressive character built upon, and flowed fairly directly from, its colonial origins. The apartheid state, of course, permitted citizenship only to whites. But it was also an authoritarian, interventionist, capitalist state. Racial ideology served as its ideological glue; it permitted a hybrid form of rule often characterized as *herrenvolk* democracy (Van den Berghe 1967), but just as reasonably described as racial dictatorship. The relationships between different fractions of capital and the state, between white workers and the state, between white farmers and white industrialists, all helped explain the rigid character of South African minority rule. Institutions that were common to many colonial situations—racial hierarchies, native reserves, vagrancy laws, and the like—developed into the apartheid system, as different segments of the white population promoted sectoral interests under the umbrella of white domination. Thus the South African system of racial stratification—or more properly, the country's ongoing racial formation process—must be understood as an organizing dimension, not only an effect, of the South African political economy.

To be sure, many of apartheid's peculiarities—especially the combination of a migrant labor system, the pass law system, and the job reservation system, which blocked black mobility into even semi-skilled jobs—were state policies designed to allay white farmers' and mine-owners' concerns that manufacturers would pay higher wages, drawing black workers to cities and raising the cost of labor throughout South Africa. In the United States, southern industries ultimately ameliorated their Jim Crow practices under movement pressure during the 1960s (Greenberg 1980, 209–242; Kelley 1994, 77–100). South African manufacturers, in contrast, appeared unable to persuade other whites to abandon racial controls over workers, and were forced to learn to live with the high turnover, skills shortages, and instability that came with strict apartheid.

In significant ways apartheid South Africa was not just a white capitalist state but also a white workers' state. Just as capital benefited from the superexploitation of black workers made possible by apartheid, so too white workers sought to preserve a privileged position in the labor market by blocking black workers from attaining skilled or semi-skilled positions considered "reserved" for whites. Researchers disagree on explanations for white workers' racialized vision, sometimes emphasizing the way a racially exclusionary state reinforced racially divided labor markets (Bonacich 1981; Frederickson 1981; Greenberg 1980), sometimes emphasizing the way upper-class white politicians could manipulate working class racial attitudes (Cell 1982; Simons and Simons 1983). But clearly through most of this century, white workers generally allied with their employers and white politicians, rather than seeking to build a class-based coalition with the Africans who were increasingly joining the wage labor force.

So the social structure of apartheid was cumulatively reworked through the elaboration of a stream of new racial policies. Nevertheless, apartheid gradually became unworkable. There was growing movement pressure for democracy and inclusion, most primarily. New pressures came from growing demands within the country for democracy and freedom, above all. But they also stemmed from the increasing contradictions of racial rule. Both domestically and globally, South African white supremacy was challenged by the mounting racial insurgency of the post–World War II years.

CONTRADICTIONS OF RACIAL CAPITALISM

Although it built on existing institutions, apartheid also introduced a new intensity of repressive regulation: over the next decades, racial rule redefined South Africa's landscape in every way—socially, economically, and politically.[12]

As noted, apartheid froze racial categories: by the early 1950s, racial classification determined where individuals could live; where they could attend school and what they could study; whom they could marry; what jobs they could hold; and of course their political rights. While about three hundred individuals a year were able to get their categories legally changed—a fact that underlines the social character of racial categories[13]—most South Africans experienced racial categories as fundamental dividing lines: opportunities of every sort were shaped by the number on one's identity document. For whites, apartheid promised free and compulsory education; state-subsidized housing and social services; privileged access to jobs and property. But apartheid's distinctions also further reinforced racial divisions among blacks, separating Indians and coloureds from Africans in townships and schools, offering them different job possibilities, placing them under a distinct legal regime.

Apartheid also further heightened differences among Africans, depending on their location within South Africa. For Africans, apartheid involved not only political exclusion, but also a reinforced migratory labor system and a new set of political institutions in the rural bantustans; the divisions between those who had urban residence rights and those who were assigned to rural villages were strengthened, as were divisions between those who were willing to work in the bantustan administrations and those who rejected apartheid institutions. In town, in addition to producing segregated and inferior housing, apartheid enforced inferior education and limited opportunities for jobs or training for Africans. South Africans had perhaps only one reality in common: regardless of race, they all faced the real threat of severe repression if they pursued democratic or anti-racist goals.

Apartheid's institutions not only created and enforced radical differences in the experiences of different racial groups; they also constantly created new tensions and strains for South Africans who were trying to live within the interstices of apartheid. In particular, industrialization and urbanization—the results of the economic growth strategy pursued by the apartheid government—changed the South African landscape, bringing black workers and their families together and creating new venues where they could organize, mobilize, and protest. These folk repeatedly found themselves in contradictory situations, as they tried to figure out how to survive within the confines of an irrational set of laws and rules. At the same time, the increased dependence of South African society on international capital and markets also meant increased vulnerability to international pressures (see below). Here some of the principal tensions and contradictions of South African development are considered.

Industrialism

In many ways, economic growth through the 1960s was the glue that held South Africa's white minority together. Facing international condemnation following the Sharpeville massacre and the banning of opposition political parties in 1961, South Africa became increasingly isolated. It left the British Commonwealth and lost its vote in the United Nations. But the country's nominal diplomatic isolation was greatly ameliorated by the persistent support from the British and the American governments in international debates. South Africa remained central to the capitalist world, proving an attractive site for international investors through the mid-1970s, especially where gold and diamonds were concerned. Immediately after the Sharpeville massacre, international capital fled South Africa, reducing its foreign exchange reserves to such an extent that the country faced economic collapse. But within a few months, international banks had put together a large loan, helping South Africa through the crisis. By 1969, South Africa offered investors cheap and controlled labor, a sound infrastructure, and skilled white personnel to serve in managerial positions; it had become a favored site for international investors, garnering about 90 percent of direct foreign investment in manufacturing for the whole of the African continent. As a writer in *Fortune* magazine said in 1972, in a comment that was probably meant only slightly ironically,

> The Republic of South Africa has always been regarded by foreign investors as a gold mine, one of those rare and refreshing places where profits are great and problems small. Capital is not threatened by political instability or nationalization. Labor is cheap, the market booming, the currency hard and convertible. Such are the market's attractions that 292 American corporations and subsidiaries have established subsidiaries or affiliates there. Their combined direct investment is close to $900 million, and their returns on that investment have been romping home at something like 19 percent a year, after taxes. (Blashill 1972, 49)

With growth rates in manufacturing averaging about 9.1 percent per year between 1950 and 1974, South Africa's economy shifted from the largely agrarian and mining emphases of the immediate postwar period, to an increasingly urban and industrial profile. By 1970, service and manufacturing workers made up 51 percent of the workforce.

By the early 1970s, these shifts had begun to produce new tensions in South African society, both from the point of view of white employers and from that of Africans and their families. For employers, rapid growth seemed to make some aspects of apartheid problematic. Manufacturers complained that job reservation was blocking further expansion: especially since whites were moving steadily into civil service positions created to help administer apartheid, there were no longer enough skilled white workers to staff expanding industries. While many employers simply hired blacks in lower-skilled job categories, asking them to do more skilled work than they were paid for, there were still serious shortages of skilled workers.

The system of unequal education exacerbated this situation. Further, some industrialists complained that the migrant labor system made their workforce unstable. Although industrialists could renew the contracts of migrant workers annually, and many "migrant" workers stayed at the same factory for decades, the separation between family and home created by apartheid's assumption of circulatory migration always introduced an element of instability in the lives of workers, and thus destabilized their workplaces as well.[14] White farmers and mining companies tended to try to preserve the migrant system and the influx control laws, which generally kept black wages low, by channeling black workers to mines and farms rather than allowing them to seek work in cities. But manufacturers often expressed concern about the inflexibility of apartheid's rules, even when they supported apartheid's goal of protecting white supremacy.[15]

At the same time as capitalist development went forward in the industrial sector, poverty in rural areas was becoming more severe: mechanization on white-owned farms, combined with forced removals of African sharecroppers and peasants from white-designated areas, led to serious overcrowding on the already eroded bantustans. Increasingly in the early 1970s, people found their way to the edges of rapidly growing cities, legally or not. By the mid-1970s, social scientists estimated that even including a three-month stay in prison for breaking pass laws, African workers from some bantustans could earn about seven times as much in a year by moving illegally to work in industry as they could by staying behind.[16] As city governments turned a blind eye to the problem, squatter settlements grew up on the edges of townships. Black people had learned to operate within the interstices of the apartheid system.

Migration Patterns

The migrant labor system in post–World War II South Africa had evolved over almost a century. This system was regional, not just national: it recruited workers from virtually all of southern Africa as well as from within the country. In combination with highly restrictive land-use and social policies (in education, health, housing, policing, and so on), the labor system both restricted and organized the lives of African families in comprehensive ways. Migrant labor, particularly in the mines but in other industrial settings as well, confronted superexploitative labor conditions and limited pay-scales. The millions of households contributing workers (black men by and large) to the system were relegated to subsistence farming under highly constrained conditions as their only means of life-support. As Arrighi (1973), Wolpe (1972), and in a more general sense Wallerstein (1979a) argued, this system constituted a regressive redistribution of income to the extent that it released both capital and the state from the obligations of paying a living wage or maintaining even minimal social policies oriented to the needs of workers. From a Marxist point of view, the comprehensive enforcement of racialized divisions in the supply of labor—as seen clearly in South African labor policies—operated chiefly to increase rates of exploitation (Miles 1993).

What, then, were the contradictions involved in this racially organized system of acquiring and exploiting migrant labor? While the superexploitation/subsistence account certainly grasps some important elements of the apartheid system's operation in the post–World War II period, it misses others. Notably it neglects the political dimensions of the system: the conflicts and oppositional agency it generated. Once this account is expanded to emphasize the active role that migrants themselves played in shaping the labor process, once the tremendous demographic shifts set in motion by the demand for black labor are recognized, and once the gendered character of post–World War II migration within (and into) South Africa is noted, a more nuanced picture emerges of many of the sources of the resistance movements, the democratic movements, that would eventually threaten the apartheid system.

Even at the height of the apartheid regime's "success" in organizing the migratory system, mining firms and other employers were forced to respond to workers' demands. Seeking to protect their families from the ravages and wholesale neglect created by the labor migration system, workers sought to maintain a rural foothold as they moved into waged labor (James 1992; Moodie and Ndatshe 1994). In a parallel process, black South African women developed strategic responses to the constraints imposed by a gendered migration system. Under apartheid, African men were hired to work for cash, while African women were expected to remain in rural areas, engaged in subsistence agriculture unless they found jobs as domestic workers in white households. But already well before the 1948 onset of formal apartheid, African women were devising ways to subvert the spatial and labor restrictions that sought to relegate them and their families to the national periphery. In the post–World War II period they regularly moved to urban areas, legally or illegally, undermining the strict household division envisaged by apartheid's planners, and constantly redefining their locations and opportunities in the interstices of the urban economy (Cock 1989; Ramphele 1993; Seidman 1993).[17]

Indirect Rule and Cultural Tensions

British colonial authorities had been notorious for their use of indirect rule as a strategy for controlling the colonial hinterlands. After the Boer War these procedures were consolidated throughout South Africa and then bequeathed to the Union. The racialized colonial state granted citizenship to whites in urban areas, but placed rural Africans under the control of strong rural chiefs, who used claims of ethnicity and tradition to legitimate domination (Mamdani 1996; Laitin 1986).

As apartheid attempted to channel rural Africans through ethnically defined political institutions (the bantustans), these newly constructed identities—usually complex syntheses of originary myths and "invented traditions" serving the purposes of rule—took on a new importance in individuals' lives.

A similar pattern was visible in apartheid's attempts to reinforce ethnic divisions among blacks. In much of Africa, colonial administrations assumed that ethnic (often called "tribal", or "customary") identities were fundamental to Africans' worldviews. Indeed, traditional bonds are still frequently used to explain political dynamics in post-colonial societies. In South Africa, however, ethnicity among Africans was politicized from above: apartheid planners explicitly sought to link African ethnic identities to specific homelands in an attempt to legitimate "separate development." These processes set the pattern for conflicts between rural-based migrant workers and township residents that played out intensely in the anti-apartheid struggles of the postwar period— notably in conflicts between the ANC and the Inkatha Freedom Party—and that still operate in democratic South Africa (Mare 1993). Rejecting this process, black South Africans asserted their own *national* identity, insisting that ethnic identities had been broken down through industrialization and urbanization, as well as delegitimated through white efforts to manipulate and separate blacks. South Africa's township culture was a celebrated mix of elements long before "globalization" became a buzzword in cultural studies (Coplan 1994), and urban anti-apartheid activists often rejected ethnic labels as irrelevant (Greenstein 1995).

The cultural contradictions that suffused the apartheid regime demand further study by racial theorists. Although it is often seen—and obviously, correctly seen in some respects—as the paradigmatic case of racial stereotyping, racial formation in the apartheid system was in fact a very complex process, involving intense struggles between rulers and ruled over the meaning of race. The same tension that exists between race and ethnicity[18] elsewhere in the post-break world also operated in South Africa. As apartheid's framework channeled rural Africans through ethnically defined political institutions, these newly constructed identities—however artificial or invented—took on a new importance in individuals' lives: many were forced to become "citizens" of bantustans that they had never even seen. Bantustan authorities became the source of work permits and drivers' licenses, as well as providers of education for rural black children (Mare 1993; Hill 1964). Similar problems arose in the economy as labor markets were divided along ethnic lines and migration chains were established between industrial or mining centers and rural settings. As these social structures were deepened they also became subjects for political conflict: rural South African life became dependent on miners' remittances; unionization and community organization efforts opposed the system, but miners also interpreted their experiences at work through an ethnic lens (Guy and Motlatsi 1988; Moodie 1994).

National and Transnational Politics

The most important set of contradictions confronting the apartheid regime was of course political. Without question the efforts of black activists to mobilize a national resistance to white supremacy were the central features of democratic mobilization in the post-break period. The development of democratic opposition in post–World War II South Africa is discussed below. Here two other important dimensions of the immense project of challenging and ultimately abolishing apartheid will simply be mentioned: the significance of the ANC's commitment to multiracial participation and non-racialism as a political goal; and the transnational dimension of anti-apartheid activism.

A persistent tension existed in the movement between the insistence of the ANC, the key anti-apartheid movement organization, that the movement be multiracial and that its objective be a non-racialist South Africa, on the one hand; and the appeal of pan-Africanist, black consciousness rhetoric, as issued by more maximalist groups in the movement, on the other hand (Marx 1992; Gerhart 1978; Frederikse 1990; Fredrickson 1997b). These differences were significant but not practical impediments in the struggle against apartheid. Indeed, at the level of day-to-day politics, the conflict between the inclusive ANC and the ethnically particularistic Inkatha was probably more divisive, particularly after the late 1970s, when Inkatha's leaders became increasingly involved in government-supported efforts to demobilize ANC support. The strife between the ANC and the collaborationist Inkatha would continue into the post-apartheid period.

Notably, both the militant labor movement and most of the new urban groups that comprised the ANC's two main, mass-based constituencies, generally rejected racial identity as a basis for mobilization. Although they mobilized black industrial workers and black adherents in racially segregated townships, activists generally used non-racial principles in defining social movement constituencies. Obviously, racial discrimination and exclusion have been key issues, but during decades of anti-apartheid campaigning the ANC and allied groups—oriented by the non-racialism of the Freedom Charter, the organization's basic programmatic document—framed their issues in other terms: as students, workers, township residents, women.

A second and unique dimension of the South African anti-apartheid movement, and one that also embodied the contradictions of racial capitalism, was the transnational effectiveness of anti-apartheid mobilization. Opposition to apartheid appeared only gradually on the global economic and political terrains. It can be attributed in significant measure to the increasing global legitimacy acquired by anti-racist and anti-colonial movements in the aftermath of the break, particularly in the U.S. context.

Then there was the end of the Cold War: this certainly had a major dampening effect on the resilience of U.S. (and British, and French, and West

German . . .) support for apartheid. The apartheid regime was no longer seen as an ally (perhaps tainted but still valuable) in the "twilight struggle" against communism. And the effectiveness at the international level of the ANC and allied black South African activists, many of them exiles, came as a surprise to the authorities in Pretoria. Linked to a burgeoning domestic opposition and increasingly capable of threatening the economic viability of the apartheid regime, transnational anti-racist activism played an important role in bringing an end to South African racial dictatorship. The overall trajectory of this opposition, both domestic and transnational, is the focus of the chapter's next section.

BUILDING THE MOVEMENT

South Africa's black majority resisted the post-1948 regime of formal apartheid, beginning by organizing a series of campaigns against the new legislation through the 1950s. There were countless *local* struggles against the daily effects of apartheid, such as the Alexandra bus boycotts between 1940 and 1945, and again in 1957, in which crowds of Africans foreshadowed the Montgomery bus boycott. Another site of struggle was local refusals to comply with new liquor legislation: by making it illegal for them to brew or sell home-made beer, these laws removed one of the main avenues through which urban African women could earn an independent living. A very important form of black opposition in the 1950s involved efforts to prevent the forced removal of black residential areas located in the centers of many towns. The government steadily pushed black workers out to the newly constructed townships on the edge of white cities. Black resistance to these efforts often literally involved efforts to prevent bulldozers from crushing black houses, as in the famous case of Sophiatown, a racially mixed Johannesburg neighborhood famous for its bars and jazz, which was destroyed and replaced by white working class housing; the area was renamed "Triomf" ("Triumph").[19]

At the *national* level, campaigns against the new apartheid system occurred regularly through the 1950s. In 1952, the African National Congress—now led by a group of young, energetic activists more oriented toward building a popular mass movement—launched the Defiance Campaign, in which volunteers were to embark on civil disobedience in defiance of apartheid restrictions.

Black volunteers would ask for service at "whites-only" post-office counters and other segregated public facilities; white volunteers were to seek help at "blacks-only" counters. In the months preceeding the campaign, the ANC had seven thousand members; overwhelming enthusiasm for the campaign meant that within months, the ANC's membership swelled to about one hundred thousand, and after six months, some eight thousand volunteers had been arrested. As the campaign grew, its organizers began to think seriously in terms of crowding the jails and clogging the judicial system to such an extent it would break down. In response, seeking to discourage the campaign, judges and courts began to impose three-year sentences on volunteers, making it impossible for organizers to ask for such sacrifices.[20]

In 1955, the ANC began a national campaign to develop a general political program, a statement summarizing the democratic ideals of the majority population of South Africa. The organization sent out volunteers across black townships to talk to black South Africans about their aspirations; the results of this "movement research" were distilled into a single declaration. The document that resulted—the 1955 Freedom Charter—is a proclamation of world-historical significance, a ringing endorsement of non-racial democracy. The charter declares:

> We, the People of South Africa, declare for all our country and the world to know: that South Africa belongs to all who live in it, black and white, and that no government can justly claim authority unless it is based on the will of all the people; that our people have been robbed of their birthright to land, liberty and peace by a form of government founded on injustice and inequality; that our country will never be prosperous or free until all our people live in brotherhood, enjoying equal rights and opportunities; that only a democratic state, based on the will of all the people, can secure to all their birthright without distinction of color, race, sex or belief; And therefore, we, the people of South Africa, black and white together, equals, countrymen and brothers adopt this Freedom Charter; And we pledge ourselves to strive together, sparing neither strength nor courage, until the democratic changes here set out have been won. (ANC 1955)

The charter also reflected the movement's understanding that a truly universal democracy in South Africa would also have to deal with the economic inequalities created by colonialism and apartheid.

At roughly the same time (1956), women across South Africa organized a campaign against the pass system, under the famous slogan "You have struck a woman, you have struck a rock; you have unleashed a boulder, you will be crushed." Denied permission to hold a demonstration, the organizers asked thousands of women to come individually, each walking up to the prime minister's office to deliver a letter protesting the pass laws.

But none of these campaigns prevailed in the face of the government's commitment to reinforcing white supremacy. By 1961, the government's use of extreme repression produced a massacre at Sharpeville, near Johannesburg, when sixty-nine unarmed protestors trying to burn their passes outside a township police station were shot as they fled from riot police. In the tense days that followed, the government outlawed the African National Congress and all other political parties that called for one-person, one-vote. Despite international condemnation, the government rejected any effort to reform apartheid. Both the African National Congress and the separatist Pan-Africanist Congress decided that in the context of such severe repression, they would have to abandon their previous commitments to nonviolent political action. In the wake of Sharpeville, faced with a government willing to use armed violence against unarmed and peaceful protestors, the possibility of making progress toward democratic reforms by peaceful means was obviously nil. Under these circumstances the only alternative was to mount an armed struggle against the state. With most resistance leaders in prison and in exile through the 1960s, it would take years—as well as new structural shifts in South African society—for these organizations to be able to pursue new strategies of resistance.

Sharpeville is generally understood as marking a turning point in the antiapartheid movement. Yet it is also interesting that Sharpeville and the other repressive measures taken by the apartheid regime in the 1960s came at a moment when, in the world beyond South Africa's borders, anti-racist and anti-colonialist gains were at their apogee. This fact was hardly lost on the leadership of the South African government, which during the 1960s was busily elaborating yet more comprehensive plans for racial separatism and repressive rule under Prime Minister Hendrik Verwoerd.

By the late 1980s, the political capacity of the black majority and its allies had vastly increased, so that while the democratic, non-racial opposition could not yet overthrow the government, it was able to produce such a stalemate that the government had little choice but to release political prisoners, unban political parties, and begin to negotiate a transition to majority rule.

Uprisings of the 1970s and 1980s

Two separate popular uprisings in the early 1970s shaped the heightened opposition that marked apartheid's final years. First, a national strike wave in 1973, starting in Durban, demonstrated the new ability of black workers to disrupt production, particularly in factories, but even in some mines (Gay Seidman 1994, 172–174). While many employers responded brutally to strike efforts, others negotiated with their workers, revealing their dependence on a stable workforce and giving workers new hope that union organizing might not lead inevitably to imprisonment. Through the 1970s, a new labor movement, linked to the ANC and dedicated to organizing all South African workers on a non-racial basis, spread through South Africa's factories, despite the best efforts of the security police to prevent its emergence. By 1979, employers were demanding that the government allow them to recognize and negotiate with their employees' organizations: the new labor movement's ability to disrupt production made it a force no one could ignore.

In 1976, a second uprising demonstrated a different opportunity, and a different way in which industrialization and urbanization created new political possibilities for the African majority. In the early 1970s, employer complaints about labor shortages, and about the ways in which a badly educated population undermined productivity, led the government to agree to expand high school openings for African students. But even as it expanded schools for Africans, the government decided to impose Afrikaans as the language of instruction, rather than letting students choose between English and Afrikaans. African students rejected this ploy as an effort to impose the language of the oppressor, which would also have the practical consequence of forcing Africans to learn in a language that would not allow the international freedom granted by fluency in English.[21]

On June 16, 1976, students in Soweto, the enormous township outside Johannesburg, began to march toward the city, planning to demonstrate against the new education rules. Police fired on the demonstrators, killing several of them. Many more students were killed in the mayhem that followed. Over the next weeks, student protests around the country were severely repressed; black parents who tried to mediate between students and police found themselves detained without trial. Blaming much of the student unrest on the black consciousness movement, the government banned most black consciousness organizations and detained many activists. In 1977, police caught Steve Biko at a roadblock, detained him, beat him savagely, and allowed him to die of his injuries in the back of a police van. When activists around the country mobilized in horror at the news, the government outlawed most student and black consciousness groups, detaining hundreds of activists without trial and forcing hundreds more into exile.[22]

Despite the repression that crushed the 1976 student movement, in retrospect one can see that the uprisings of the 1970s marked the beginning of the end for apartheid. The internal tensions between apartheid and the effects of the government's industrialization program created many new openings for organization and resistance, while the decolonization of neighboring Mozambique, Angola, and, later, Zimbabwe meant that South Africa's borders were no longer protected from guerrilla incursion by a buffer of colonial states. After the uprisings of the mid-1970s South Africa never returned to the quiescence of the 1960s. In township after township, activists developed new political strategies, often maintaining clandestine connections to the illegal political parties while finding new opportunities for organizing against the daily mechanisms of apartheid. Activists organized around national issues such as the 1980 campaign to publicize the ANC's Freedom Charter; this was a legal way to publish and discuss the movement's democratic aspirations. Another key event of this time was the 1981 Free Mandela campaign.

Around more local issues as well—from support for striking local workers to campaigns for better urban services in specific townships—new strategies of mobilization took hold. In 1983, hundreds of small local groups—community associations, student groups, trade unions, and even soccer clubs—formed the United Democratic Front, a coalition with strong ideological and clandestine activist links to the exiled African National Congress. Parallel organizations with links to the black consciousness movement were formed in the same period, mobilizing community support for township-based protests against apartheid.

It is not possible to condense the dynamics of the rolling uprising of the 1980s into a single chapter: the complicated details of resistance in South Africa in this period defy quick summary. Each group had its own structural issues. Unions, naturally, were more likely to focus on workplace concerns and to target employers. Community groups were more likely to focus on political targets: black administrators working with the bantustan system, or with the "advisory" urban councils. Furthermore, each locality had its own political dynamics: these were often affected as much by individual activists' personalities and ideological choices as by the particular issues that dominated local community concerns.

Ideological debates raged. Some of these questions were organizational and strategic. Should community groups restrict their demands to legal questions, or should they risk repression by raising questions about long-term political goals? Should labor unions be shopfloor-based, or should they build strong links to workers' communities? Should they focus on employers, or should they target state policies that interfered with workers' lives both inside and outside the factory? What kinds of links should anti-apartheid groups have to banned organizations—particularly, by the 1980s, to the exiled leadership of the African National Congress? By then the ANC had established a strong clandestine network inside the country, and was funneling resources, including money, information, and activists, to legal anti-apartheid groups through the 1980s.

Clandestinity was important. From the early 1960s on, the ANC had been forced to turn toward armed resistance and underground activity. Throughout the decades that followed, anti-apartheid activists necessarily denied any links with banned organizations. Accounts of the later years of the struggle against apartheid, especially of the uprising of the 1980s, generally understate the importance of these clandestine connections.

For all movement groups, there were difficult debates revolving around the racial character of the anti-apartheid struggle. Should anti-apartheid organizations adopt a non-racial approach to organization, allowing anti-apartheid and liberal whites to join? Or should black activists exclude white sympathizers, to ensure that anti-apartheid activism would be controlled by blacks, and to assert the importance of black leadership in opposition to apartheid's racial domination? These questions of racial composition revolved not only around whites, but also around questions of commonalities among people classified as "Indian" or "coloured" as well as "African." Given the segregated character of apartheid, community groups would almost automatically be segregated, and it required specific efforts by activists to avoid persistent divisions between the different "non-white" groups, each of whose experiences were shaped by apartheid racial distinctions. Groups working in the non-racial tradition of the African National Congress generally accepted anti-apartheid sympathizers of all races, although de facto segregation often prevailed in specific community groups, or even in specific student or worker groups, based on apartheid geography. Groups close to the Pan-Africanist Congress line, or groups building on the black consciousness tradition, however, tended to view white sympathizers with more suspicion, although they popularized the strategy of bringing people divided as "Africans," "Indians," or "coloured" under a common rubric, "black," to overcome invidious distinctions.[23]

The divisions imposed by apartheid laws persisted in daily life, separating "African" from "coloured" communities geographically and socially; but activists tried hard to build links across those divisions, insisting that although the details differed from group to group, all South Africans of color suffered under apartheid's white supremacism. Energetic debates about the role of race in the anti-apartheid movement persisted, of course: should whites who were committed to the anti-apartheid struggle be permitted to join the leadership of anti-apartheid groups, or did white leadership in anti-apartheid organizations reinforce the psychological sense of inferiority imposed by a racist society? Should organizations that were based in racially segregated townships—and thus, effectively segregated—be criticized for sustaining racial divisions? Could groups organized around different logics—for example, trade unions organized on a class basis rather than a racial one, with a membership structure and a clear system of accountability—work in tandem with groups organized around issues of race and identity, with an activist structure that had no clear membership or accountability?[24]

These internal debates in the anti-apartheid movement, however, did not obscure a more fundamental set of tensions and debates among apartheid's supporters. Through the early 1980s, a rolling series of community protests against apartheid's racial exclusion underscored the essential tension of apartheid's goals: white South Africa depended on black labor, yet faced constant disruption by the same black workers and their families on whom economic growth—and political stability—would depend.

Further substantiating this general thesis of this book, the international context had changed dramatically: by the late 1970s, international pressure was mounting, and middle-class white South Africans were beginning to recognize that the "winds of change" that had seemed so far away in 1948, were now blowing down their necks. Since the 1961 Sharpeville massacre, representatives from newly independent countries, who had themselves only recently emerged from racialized colonial rule, had called on the United Nation's General Assembly to impose international sanctions against South Africa, although Britain and the United States just as regularly used their UN Security Council vetoes to block these efforts. But from the early 1970s, international initiatives began to take on new force—in part because exiled South Africans proved increasingly adept at mobilizing international opinion against the regime.

Some governments took unilateral moves against South Africa. Eastern European countries provided support to the African National Congress's guerrillas, and other countries took additional steps. Most important, the Organization of Petroleum Exporting Countries (OPEC) countries banned the direct sale of oil to South Africa in 1973, forcing South Africa to buy more expensive oil on the international open market. Western governments generally resisted efforts to impose sanctions, often arguing, as Henry Kissinger did in the early 1970s, that although the stable white regime in South Africa was of course racist and oppressive, it was familiar, and could be more depended on to protect Western interests, both in terms of South Africa's mineral reserves and its strategic control of the Cape sea routes, than any as-yet-untried black South African government (National Security Council Interdepartmental Group for Africa 1969).

By the mid-1970s, when first the 1973 strike wave and later the 1976 student uprising provoked new international interest and concern over apartheid, even Western governments began to take gradual steps to show their disapproval. This included accepting a 1977 United Nations ban on arms sales to South Africa, which forced the white minority regime to develop its own arms industry as part of its effort to protect white supremacy.

Since governments were slow to act, anti-apartheid activists turned to less formal kinds of pressure, frequently finding innovative ways to put pressure on white South Africa. The general approach was to try to isolate white South Africa from the community of nations. Especially in the context of the post-colonial and officially anti-racist world—the world of the break—international norms began to challenge the racial assumptions of the colonial era. In the new climate, grassroots campaigns often received a great deal of popular support, from civil rights groups, human rights organizations, and labor unions around the world. From the early 1960s on, anti-apartheid activists learned to attack South Africa from every angle, often mobilizing opposition to apartheid in arenas previously untouched by politics.

An important example was the approach developed by Dennis Brutus, a South African poet and exiled former political prisoner. Beginning in the mid-1960s he worked with anti-apartheid activists around the world to mount a remarkably effective international campaign blocking South African participation in international sports, arguing that South African teams should be banned from international competitions because the country practiced racial discrimination in training athletes, choosing teams, and hosting competitions (Brutus et al. 1971). Brutus pointed out that white South Africans, with a culture that glorified male athletes, would be especially sensitive to a sports ban. Certainly, through the twenty-five years the campaign persisted, white (male) South Africans expressed annoyance with their teams' exclusion from international rugby and cricket competitions at least as frequently as they did over debates in the UN General Assembly.[25]

Similarly, anti-apartheid campaigners around the world began in the mid-1960s to argue that the Western countries' economic links to South Africa effectively supported apartheid, and when Western governments were reluctant to adopt sanctions, activists began to focus on more grassroots targets. Sometimes, multinational investments were directly linked to the enforcement of apartheid pass laws; in 1971, workers at American and Canadian Polaroid plants demanded that their company withdraw from South Africa, when it was revealed that film and cameras made by the firm were used to produce the hated passes that South African blacks were required to carry.

By the early 1970s, however, these campaigns had become more diffuse. Students at American universities, and later, citizens in a range of municipalities and states, demanded that their institutions and governments sell all shares in transnational companies doing business in South Africa. Arguing that these companies profited from the cheap labor system embodied in apartheid, and that such firms supported the regime by providing strategic materials and paying taxes, these activists developed arguments about socially responsible investing that would later serve as the basis for a much broader set of concerns about global capitalism (Massie 1997).

Reform Initiatives—Too Little, Too Late

Facing a mounting uprising at home and growing international pressure abroad, the government began in the late 1970s to tinker with the apartheid framework, hoping that its reforms would incorporate enough of a black middle class to split the opposition. Legal and constitutional reforms through the early 1980s were aimed at creating a privileged non-white core, while excluding the black majority. Policies were designed to offer new channels of incorporation—gradually of course—to Africans living in white-designated cities. Perhaps the first indication of real change was a somewhat symbolic one: the "Mixed Marriages Act" was repealed in 1985, allowing people of different races to live together and even to marry.[26] But other reforms changed the face of South Africa much faster than reformers expected. In a legal recognition of a de facto reality, many more Africans were awarded permanent urban residence rights from 1979 on; not only could these urban residents keep their families with them in townships, but they were now permitted to own their own houses in townships (rather than simply renting them from the government),[27] to organize unions, and to elect representatives to township councils.

Such reforms also had political aspects. From the mid-1970s, the government began to force bantustan administrations to accept a nominal (and subordinate) independence from South Africa. Although most of the independent bantustans continued to receive funding from Pretoria, and although their economies depended on sending migrant black workers to white-designated South Africa, the government's strategy was obvious. In seeking permanently to exclude most rural black South Africans from claiming rights to full citizenship, it hoped to grant enough legal status to the bantustans to reduce international pressure, and to bring the small black elite that benefited from bantustan administrative posts into a coalition with the white-dominated regime.

In an even clearer strategy of divide-and-rule, the government implemented a new constitution in 1984, which offered South Africans classified as "Indian" and "coloured" the right to vote for separate houses of parliament—although the fact that white parliamentary representatives retained an effective veto over any decisions made by non-white representatives made it easy for activists to discredit the so-called reforms.

Anti-apartheid agitation expanded through the 1980s, as township activists persuaded more and more South Africans, mainly black, to resist government attempts to reassert control through demonstrations, boycotts, and strikes. As the resistance grew in strength during the latter half of the decade, there were increasingly bold attempts to challenge the regime's repression more directly: through organized efforts to prevent police patrols in the black townships, for example, by throwing stones and digging trenches. The strategy was to make the townships "ungovernable." In response, the government imposed increasingly draconian controls over anti-apartheid groups, preventing meetings, and detaining activists without charges, placing them under house arrest or in prison. The government imposed a state of emergency in 1985, and then renewed it repeatedly through the late 1980s, granting itself sweeping powers to detain individuals and prohibit previously legal activities.[28]

Such legal maneuvers were but the backdrop to brute force: government troops literally occupied black townships with tanks and guns, in some cases even surrounding townships with barbed wire to prevent protestors from disrupting white sections of town. Ten years later, testimony before the post-apartheid Truth and Reconciliation Commission confirmed an even darker side: throughout the apartheid era, but especially in the late 1980s and early 1990s, the police regularly engaged in kidnappings, torture, and assassination, while they continued to supply black vigilante groups with weapons as a way to stir up what the press called "black-on-black violence" in the townships, impeding community organization. And, of course, South Africa's armed forces continued to occupy the neighboring country, Namibia, and supported rebel movements in all the independent African states of the region, as a way to destabilize their post-colonial governments and block them from giving aid to South African guerrillas.

Nevertheless, anti-apartheid activists—often receiving aid from exiled South Africans as well as from international church groups and other transnational organizations committed to ending apartheid—persistently found new tactics to challenge apartheid, new spaces to organize. From the blank spaces that began to appear in newspapers when journalists protested against censorship, to the wildcat strikes that erupted constantly,[29] to the large political funerals that marked the deaths of activists, the anti-apartheid movement proved adept at finding new ways to express opposition to the regime, and to disrupt the smooth functioning of an urbanized industrial society. South Africa veered between resistance and repression, reform and opposition, seesawing back and forth as different fractions of the regime dominated policy and as anti-apartheid activists found new ways to mobilize opposition.

By 1989, the fractures in the ruling Nationalist Party were obvious. Although then-President P. W. Botha and his colleagues were clearly committed to maintaining white supremacy, the costs were mounting for white South Africa. International banks were refusing to roll over loan repayments. International bodies from the Commonwealth and the United Nations to the European Union were imposing severe sanctions on South African products. Individual governments, including the United States and Britain, had already instituted economic sanctions and were contemplating more serious ones. Faced with ongoing shareholder objections to South African investments, transnational corporations were beginning to withdraw, selling off their subsidiaries to local managers. Even those that remained in South Africa were minimizing their presence, refusing to reinvest in new machinery or equipment, failing to expand production.

In late 1989 Botha was forced to step down because of ill health. His successor, F. W. de Klerk, moved quickly. In his first address to parliament, on February 2, 1990, de Klerk announced he was about to do the unthinkable: he would release Nelson Mandela and all political prisoners and unban the African National Congress, the Communist Party, and all other political parties. South Africa would begin to move toward normalization.

Regime Transition

The four years of transition, from 1990 to the first full elections in 1994, seemed endless. The government engaged in lengthy and frequently stalemated rounds of negotiation with the ANC and other political parties, while constant

street battles between ANC supporters and other groups—both white supremacist militias and black paramilitary groups, often trained and armed by the
army and police—created an even higher death toll in those four years than
had been exacted during the state of emergency. At first, the government
appeared to believe it could limit the democratic transition, using various
methods to control policy. Suggestions included devices ranging from a racially
divided voters' roll, where white representatives would hold a veto, to a system
in which political voice would be linked to property, where (obviously) white
South Africans would continue to hold the lion's share of power. Clinging to
the hope that the government was so strong that it could resist demands for
full political change and for economic redistribution, de Klerk and his allies
thought they were negotiating from a position of strength, and that anti-
apartheid forces would be weak and divided during the transition.

But most South Africans soon recognized that this view was mistaken. When
Nelson Mandela walked out of Pollsmoor Prison, receiving a hero's welcome
from a generation of activists who had never known him, it became clear that
the government had underestimated the basis of support for the national liberation movement. As ANC leaders returned from prison and exile, they joined
activists from the internal opposition movement in demanding that the government allow full elections for a Constituent constitution.[30]

The fact of negotiations toward a democratic transition posed new challenges for the opposition movement. Just as white politicians were forced to
accept the inevitability of one-person, one-vote on a non-racial basis, anti-
apartheid activists had to understand that a democratic government would
have to protect property rights. At least at the beginning, it would have to
accept the existing economic inequalities growing out of centuries of racial
oppression. It would have to leave most white civil servants in place, even
though they had spent their careers defending white supremacy. Such compromises did not come easily. For four years, as the negotiations dragged on,
both sides readjusted their visions. By mid-decade, white supremacists realized
they could not expect to protect racial privilege in the new order, while anti-
apartheid activists understood that the transition would be more gradual than
they had hoped.

But even with those compromises, the importance of the transition in
South Africa cannot be underestimated. When the elections were finally held,
in April 1994, they produced the expected landslide for the ANC, which
received 62.65 percent of the vote. Its nearest competitor, the National Party,
received less than one-third of that total: 20.39 percent. The Inkatha Freedom
Party, with its base in Kwazulu-Natal, its complicated policy of ethnicism, and
its history of collaboration with the apartheid regime, managed 10.54 percent.
Other minor parties obtained very small percentages of the total of 19,533,498
votes cast (Jackson 1998, 11).[31]

As Nelson Mandela was inaugurated as the country's first democratically elected president, the entire world watched in awe. The South African air force—symbol of the old regime—dipped its wings to Mandela in a multicolored fly-over, marking the end of an old form of racial oppression, and offering at least the hope of that a different kind of social order might be constructed.

POST-APARTHEID CONDITIONS

Although it did not experience full-scale revolution, South Africa began a massive transition with its achievement of democracy in 1994. In many ways the country is exemplary: confronted by vast social problems, and burdened with a vast legacy of racial inequality and oppression, the ANC government has kept its "hands on the wheel," so to speak. The country has not relinquished the commitments to political inclusion that guided the ANC through many decades of opposition; but it has also not succumbed to radical temptations for instant redistribution and restructuring.

In some respects the arduous battles of the ANC's journey to power are its greatest resource. The resolute commitment to liberation from white supremacism that it nurtured among the masses of South Africans has served in turn to regulate it in power: the ANC cannot turn its back upon the black trade unions or the community groups in the townships and provinces. These millions of newly enfranchised citizens not only elected and reelected the ANC, but also expect great reforms from their party: housing, jobs, education, services, land. The acquisition of formal citizenship, of *racial freedom*, has created a certain political space, a cultural space, in which these masses are allowing the government to deliver on its more substantively difficult, more economic reform commitments. Despite the conflicts, the high levels of crime, the dire predictions of failure, they have not lost hope in democracy or in the ANC. So far, they have been patient.

Opposite to the masses the ANC has pledged to serve are the local and global capitalist interests who have a significant stake in the South African economy. These elites are also among the government's constituency. Some South African firms were among the most effective advocates for a transition to democracy, for the unbanning of the ANC and the release of Mandela, for the elimination of apartheid. At the international level as well, capital's belated but real abandonment of the white supremacist regime was an important factor in its downfall. That abandonment was conditioned by many factors, both international and domestic. Internationally these included the end of the Cold War, heightening protest against apartheid,[32] and the growing threat of international isolation and pariah status. Domestically, major South African business leaders came to realize that white supremacy was no longer tenable; they began to negotiate with the ANC, suggesting that if the organization would drop its socialist rhetoric, business would drop its support for white supremacism.

In the post-apartheid situation, capital has made clear that it will not support the socialist program that the ANC had long avowed. It has pushed for privatization and for restraint on redistributive policies. It has advocated acquiescence to the *neo-liberal orthodoxy* preached by lending agencies and financial markets throughout the world's North. It has sought to recruit a black elite into its corporate boardrooms.

Capital has also sought ways to compensate for the declining importance of gold—long South Africa's key resource—on the world market. Indeed, South Africa was for a long time a sort of monoculture, exporting and relying primarily on this precious metal. But in the last two decades the world demand for gold has changed significantly, chiefly because of shifts in financial markets. The growth prospects for South African capital, the conditions of workers in the mining sector, and the development strategy of the entire national economy have been set back by the deteriorating position of gold. So, as gold becomes more vulnerable to price fluctuations, South African firms hope to diversify exports, moving away from dependence on a single commodity to find new market niches for manufactured and agricultural products.

For many reasons, then, the South African government cannot repudiate capitalism, domestic or multinational. To do so would be both to depart from economic logic and responsibility, and to incur the wrath and discipline of global financial markets. The national crackup that would ensue would not mean "merely" the end of the masses' hopes for a better life; it would mean the destruction of a multiracial society, the occasion for white flight, and the descent of the black majority into a regime of scarcity and autarky. Where would the "miracle" be then?[33]

By 1999, the year Mandela stepped down from the presidency—to be replaced by his former deputy, Thabo Mbeki—the tensions inherent in the different projects of the ANC had become clear. At the political level, South Africa was remarkably democratic: the political aspirations of the black majority had clearly shaped the new constitution, and that sense of victory, of the assertion of citizenship and dignity, continues to mark South Africans' vision of the government. In addition, the government was responding to South Africans' demands for expanded social services: for the first time, social services including schools and hospitals were open to all South Africans, regardless of race, and poor South Africans could be sure that their children would have new opportunities, and new possibilities, in their future. Affirmative action in university admissions as well as in hiring for the civil service offered the possibility of new careers. Within only five years of the first democratic election, South Africa's elite and middle class was increasingly integrated, as skilled and educated black South Africans took their places next to their white counterparts.

Whites still owned much of the country's wealth, but there were visibly more black civil servants, business leaders, and politicians in top positions; private schools and the better public schools now welcomed black students as well as white, creating a sense that in the not-too-distant future, South Africa's elite will be fully integrated—although for the foreseeable future, given the legacies of economic and social inequalities, whites are likely to remain demographically overrepresented among the better-off part of the population.[34]

But at the level of economic policy, the ANC's increasingly trickle-down approach sometimes ran into conflict with its promises of reconstruction and inclusion. Trade unions, most of whose members are black, had long supported the ANC, but union leaders expressed real concerns about government economic policy, which seemed to favor tax breaks for business over subsidies for the poor. For poor black families, lacking the wherewithal to move into the formerly all-white suburbs, promises of better schooling and housing rang somewhat hollow: they remained in the all-black townships, or found themselves living in shacks in squatter settlements that expanded on the edges of all South Africa's cities. In its first five years, the ANC government built about one hundred thousand new houses, mainly for poorer black families; but the waiting lists for subsidized housing were so long that applicants knew they might have to wait years. The ANC government had an energetic water supply program, but in 1999, about half of South Africans still had no indoor plumbing. Moreover, given the levels of poverty in black communities, government water officials worried that a market-oriented water system could create a truly contradictory situation: poor South Africans would be unable to pay the bills for the water and electricity now flowing into their communities.

Debates over economic policy were mirrored, or perhaps exacerbated, by public debates over how best to deal with the racism and authoritarianism that still run through South African society. Under new laws that prohibit speech that incites racial hatred, a drunk white man in a bar who calls out racist insults can be punished; but few episodes are as clear or as easy as that. Indeed, the sites where race issues can be problematic are manifold. For example, there has been little programmatic effort as yet to retrain teachers and school staff to deal with racially mixed classrooms. And what about the police? How can they learn to work with black citizens to prevent and solve crimes, rather than treating citizens as enemies? What about the media? In early 2000, a public discussion began on how the media inadvertently helped perpetuate old racial stereotypes; yet there was as much outcry over the accusation that racism sometimes shaped white reporters' visions, as there was over the persistent white ownership of South Africa's newspapers and television stations. In these and many other policy arenas, debates are ongoing and innovations are being contemplated.

Thus at the start of the twenty-first century the South African transition away from apartheid was well underway, although obviously not free of difficulties. Led by an articulate and self-conscious group of reformers and blessed by an unusual degree of international legitimacy, the country appeared to offer new ways to think about both the consolidation of democracy and strategies for development at the turn of the century. Conversely, South African intellectuals and politicians were beginning to look beyond South Africa's borders for new insights into some of the most thorny issues of South African social relations, including race and racial politics.

Not only the government and political leaders, but social scientists too must avoid making facile judgments about fundamental economic policy questions. Whereas before the 1994 election, before the transfer of power to the ANC, students of the "democratic transition" in South Africa tended to suggest that anti-apartheid activists should avoid provoking a white backlash (Van Zyl Slabbert 1992; Adam and Moodley 1993), some of these same writers are now urging more concerted efforts at redistribution and criticizing the ANC for moving *too far* to the right (Adam, Van Zyl Slabbert, and Moodley 1998). Whereas progressive students of the Congress of South African Trade Unions (COSATU) and black trade unionism had earlier assumed that union demands for redistribution would receive sympathetic attention from the new state (Adler and Webster 1995), these same authors now recognize that the state's role has proved far more ambiguous. By 1999 Webster and Adler were arguing that South Africa was experiencing a "stalemate" between capital and labor. Only a "class compromise," they suggested, would allow the government to devise a new development strategy to balance growth with redistribution (Webster and Adler 1999).

At the same time redistribution could not proceed as fast as important "left" ANC constituencies wished. Two successive development plans—the Reconstruction and Development Program (RDP) and the Growth, Employment, and Redistribution Program (GEAR)—have failed to deliver, sparking some protest. Both Mandela and Mbeki upbraided these programs' critics on the ANC's left:

> GEAR, as I have said before, is the fundamental policy of the ANC. We will not change it because of your pressure. If you feel you cannot get your way, then go out and shout like opposition parties. Prepare to face the full implications of that line. (Nelson Mandela, quoted in Webster and Adler 1999, 369)

If the country has so far been able to maneuver successfully among the most varied potential pitfalls, if the credibility of the ANC remains intact despite inability to deliver the economic goods either to transnational capital or to the black masses,[35] this can best be attributed to the striking creativity with which the organization has tackled the enormous tasks of the transition. Moving from racial dictatorship to racial democracy requires the most serious encounters with both the grim experiences of the past and the possibilities of future transformations in institutions and political culture.

Consider, for example, the way South Africa—a post-authoritarian regime par excellence—has dealt with the legacies of human rights violations and repression. In many cases of democratization—for example, in Latin America—the abuses of former dictatorial regimes have been addressed only glancingly; authoritarian figures have been granted amnesty and permitted complete integration into the new democratic order, for example (Weschler 1990). South Africa, by contrast, took a firmer stance, offering amnesty only to those who fully disclosed their participation in gross violations of human rights, and threatening prosecutions of those who did not cooperate. Acting on a proposal by Bishop Desmond Tutu, the ANC government set up a Truth and Reconciliation Commission (TRC) to investigate the abuses of the apartheid regime.[36] The commission drew on examples from around the world, but its planners sought to avoid some of the pitfalls of similar efforts elsewhere. In particular, they wanted to avoid the powerlessness that prevented many such commissions from exploring the participation of still-powerful figures in acts of repression and violence (Asmal, Asmal, and Roberts 1997; Schaper-Hughes 1998). Steering a careful course between forgetting the past and provoking further social conflict, the TRC has changed the debate about how to deal with the painful memories of the authoritarian past. Although the process is hardly complete, the South African TRC has already become a subject of much discussion among activists and social scientists around the world.

This kind of institutional innovation is not limited to the truth and reconciliation process. The thoroughgoing reform of the South African state provides other examples of similar innovation, as South African policy-makers build on examples from around the world, but add their own adaptations. Specific innovations—ranging from the successful integration of two previously opposed armed forces, to the creation of a Gender Commission that will examine the implications for gender equity of every new law—have made South Africa's democratic transition unusually far-reaching.

Still the transition is very much in progress, with more accomplished in the formal than substantive sense. Having to manage the trade-off between the neo-liberal program and the pent-up demands of the country's poor still confronts the ANC government with a series of difficult choices. As Mandela had to do before him, Thabo Mbeki must walk the tightrope between these two contradictory agendas. Notably, that tightrope is also a racial one: to accede systematically to the demands of capital would be to fall back into the status quo ante of apartheid. Yet to concede too much to the black masses who furnish the ANC base would be to plunge the country into economic chaos.

To be sure, black South Africans still experience enormous unmet needs.

They face staggering rates of unemployment, inadequate housing, education, and health care. Crimes of poverty (robberies, assaults, carjackings, etc.) have reached dreadful levels. Perhaps the most serious social threat to the South African people is the burgeoning rate of HIV. Since the late 1980s South Africa has been confronted with this new and terrifying challenge.

Like many governments in Africa, the South African government was slow to realize the depth of the epidemic, or to create new public health programs that would slow its spread. President Mbeki in particular has proved reluctant to shift resources into fighting the disease. To the outrage of AIDS activists who point out that his stance works to undermine public awareness and education about HIV, Mbeki has repeatedly said that he views AIDS as a disease linked to poverty, has lent credibility to a marginal group of "dissenters" from scientific consensus on the causes of HIV (Jeter 2000), and has argued that the South African medical system is not capable of paying for or delivering the expensive drugs that are used to treat the disease in the developed world. But AIDS activists argue that even if international drug companies have priced those drugs out of the reach of most South Africans, the government should still take the steps that international experts consider critical for dealing with an epidemic of this magnitude. They argue too that fundamental issues of gender and sexuality—many of them both deeply rooted in traditional culture and exacerbated by modern media—must also be addressed.

By 2000 South Africa had still not established an effective AIDS testing or counseling program. It had not carried out public education efforts that would persuade people in the townships and rural areas to change their sexual behavior. It had not even initiated public health policies to prevent mother-to-infant transmission during labor. Meanwhile, according to a recent report by the UN HIV/AIDS program, a terrifying 20 percent of South African adults are HIV-positive. The rate of increase of infection is also frightening: 50 percent over a two-year period (UNAIDS 2000; Altman 2000). Obviously HIV is a lot more than an economic problem, despite Mbeki's denial of the epidemiological and socio-cultural dimensions of the calamitous epidemic. But he is not entirely wrong: the disease *is* an economic issue, a poverty issue, a problem of development.

Mindful of the need to deliver on their constituents' hopes to a greater extent than has yet proved possible, and aware of the converse but in some sense equivalent fears of capital (and many whites as well) that the ANC's thus-far disciplined approach to macro-economic policy might be abandoned, sophisticated progressives and technocrats have been developing a pragmatic alternative. Based on the principle of class compromise, it could as well be seen as a racial compromise: it would involve measured redistribution and the deepening of social security programs on the one hand, and a measure of economic streamlining and labor discipline on the other. The state's role would be to enforce the compromise, disciplining both labor and capital while acting in a neo-Keynesian fashion to invest in the country's infrastructure. It would thus foster both growth and inclusion (Webster and Adler 1999).[37]

This is a demanding set of arrangements, to be sure; but would it be a greater miracle than the establishment of democracy in 1994?

RACIAL CONDITIONS IN TWENTY-FIRST CENTURY SOUTH AFRICA

What does the complicated and prolonged transition to democracy reveal about racial conditions in South Africa? Long before its formalization in 1948, and fiercely indeed thereafter, apartheid was among the most extreme versions of anti-black racism ever to consolidate a state and organize a society. Its paranoid and minoritarian character marked it very deeply. Less planned than accreted over time, it was a synthesis of various historical influences: a rapacious and world-bestriding British colonialism on the one hand; and a fierce Boer withdrawal from modernity on the other. As a program, as a system of rule enacted in a series of measures after 1948, apartheid was almost an afterthought, a last-minute effort to tidy up and reorganize a system of racial hierarchy about to lose touch with the world that had spawned it.

For all its power and determination, however, the sustained drive to fortify and defend apartheid was no match for the commitment of the movement that would eventually overthrow it. At its starting-point in the early years of this century,[38] the movement that would ultimately destroy white supremacy was little more than a handful of members of the native (and Indian) elite: a few lawyers, teachers, and clerics. At its triumphant overthrow of the apartheid regime, the liberation movement included millions of supporters and drew upon a global network of organizational and allied resources.

In its steadfast commitment to democracy, in its stunning if still partial successes, and in the heroism of its activists and indeed of its mass constituency, the black liberation movement holds up a mirror, even a beacon, to the rest of the world. Notably for the dark world, the poor world, the southern world, the South African victory over white supremacism represents a possibility of freedom more galvanizing, more attractive, more exciting than mere inclusion in "McWorld" could ever be (Barber 1995).

The South African experience illuminates important questions of political and cultural practice that can have great meaning elsewhere. And yes, the transition to democracy in South Africa, the end of white supremacy there, also sheds light on scholarly questions as well, notably questions about the meaning of race in the modern world.

The ANC dedicated itself to a non-racialist vision of society in its basic programmatic document, the Freedom Charter. It still adheres to that vision, although in practice it manages racial divisions everywhere: how could it not, a mere handful of years after the toppling of apartheid? Certainly the non-racialist vision has proved very effective strategically, both in providing an ideal and goal for anti-apartheid mobilization before 1994, and in guiding the kinds of compromises that governance and development have required since 1994. Nor is non-racialism a mere ploy; in some ways this vision *still* constitutes an important ideal: if it does not mean the disappearance of racial differences, at least it points to their diminution. The Freedom Charter's vision dates from the heyday of apartheid, when racial identity was central to human identity; perhaps in the twenty-first century it can point the way to a society in which race will not immediately equate with rank, with hierarchy, with inequality.

Yet the vision of non-racialism cannot be counted upon to guide political processes and policy formation activities as the ANC attempts to steer the country in the direction of development and redistribution. In a situation where glaring racial inequalities characterize everyday life, effective state action cannot remain glued to this ideal. Yes, before 1994 it was an effective pole for the mobilization of opposition; yes, even today it remains valuable as a signpost pointing toward greater equality; but today and for the foreseeable future the non-racialism concept also serves *in practical terms* to deny the extent of the problem of racial injustice.

It must also be remembered that apartheid was opposed, not only by the non-racialist vision of the ANC, but also by those who upheld another vision: that of black consciousness. The activists and thinkers of the Pan-Africanist Congress (PAC) and the black consciousness movement were hardly an insignificant group, especially when they are seen as linked—and linked they were, just as the ANC was—to global progressive tendencies. Pan-African thought, Negritude, diasporic connections, significantly shaped the political opposition of the PAC and black consciousness. These groups were an important, if still minoritarian, current in the liberation movement. For the majority tendency, the ANC, there were also significant ideological linkages and influences: communism and socialism. As if locally reflecting twentieth-century conditions that obtained throughout the world, these two currents, although often opposed, were also allied in important ways. They played parallel roles in the liberation movement that freed, and still is freeing, South Africa.

The movement's attention was largely directed toward the elimination of white supremacism, toward the achievment of equality, of one-person, one-vote. In other words the movement was in large part "egalitarian" rather than "differentialist."[39] But of course anti-apartheid activism required constant racial awareness, in both its organizational and experiential dimensions. For example, the ANC was careful to maintain black leadership at its highest levels until very late in the struggle against apartheid.[40]

Still, the dualities of racial identity, the peculiar decenteredness of racial politics, and flexibility of the very meaning of race have not received much attention in South Africa. This may be a legacy of non-racialism, of official egal-itarianism. Perhaps only now, with the democratic transition properly and irre-versibly underway, can scholars and activists begin to problematize questions about racial formation processes in South Africa.

It is ironic that although racial difference has been such a central determi-nant of the South African social system, discussions about race have generally been relegated to points of lesser interest on political and even intellectual agendas. Why did this happen in a situation where the complexities of racial identities and racial politics were played out every day, where both institutions and individuals confronted the tension between rigid legal racial categories and the more fluid reality of human lives?

For many anti-apartheid activists, opposition to apartheid meant rejection of racialism: the all-encompassing racial optic that defined South African soci-ety from top to bottom. For the ANC, non-racialism was equivalent to univer-salism and democracy; it was an essential element in the resistance to apartheid's racial dictatorship. Other currents in the South African resistance—notably the PAC and later the black consciousness movement—were oriented more posi-tively toward racialism, as noted, largely because of their identification with pan-Africanism as a world movement.[41] But their positions, although important, were minority currents within the black liberation movement.

For progressive social scientists, the refusal to examine the dynamics of race reflected a conscious decision to avoid any link to the "scientific racism" so ram-pant in South African science.[42] Although some of South Africa's most inter-nationally renowned scholars demonstrated that racial categories cannot be physically defined (Tobias 1972), conservative white South African scientists were often deeply complicit in the reification of racial difference. Their efforts sometimes reached absurd extremes that resembled Nazi "racial science": for example, when mining industry researchers experimented with different racial abilities to withstand heat, as if melanin somehow altered the fundamental functioning of the human body (Dubow 1995; Adam 1995). To many South African social scientists who rejected these perversions of scientific inquiry, racial identities hardly seemed problematic at all: racial categories were so explicitly built into the legal and social framework that they seemed almost bio-logical (van den Berghe 1978).[43]

But even in South Africa, racial identities are fluid; racial politics are not set in stone, and racial dynamics merit more specific attention than they have often received. South African racial politics have not been static, but we have little sense of how and why they have changed. Changing over time, racial visions—among white nationalists, black consciousness activists, and non-racialists—have always been rooted in specific social movements, specific expe-riences, and specific conjunctures of South African history. The dynamics of this experiential dimension of race—in South Africa as elsewhere—remain a fruitful site for further investigation (Greenstein 1993).

In comparison to other countries, especially the United States, relatively little work has been done in South Africa on the micro-level dimensions of racial
formation. Social science generally lacks detailed knowledge of how South
Africans experienced, responded to, or for that matter challenged apartheid's
rigid racial categories in their daily lives. Yet over the nearly fifty years that these
categories carried legal implications, thousands of individuals were reclassi-
fied, either at their own behest or by official decree.[44] As elsewhere, in South
Africa too there are complicated sagas of hidden relationships across color-
lines, of corrupt officials and bribery, of "passing" and exposure.[45] These patterns underscore the social construction of race, both in terms of delineating
categories and in terms of assigning social meaning to those categories. Relatively few social scientists have thus far explored what this seamy underside of
apartheid's neat schema meant for individuals, or how South Africans con-
ceptualized or responded to the dilemmas posed by this complex and often
"messy" reality. What we know about how people "passed" in more privileged
categories, or sometimes rejected the possibility of "passing," largely depends
upon anecdotal or fictionalized sources. How did individuals deal with the contradictions created by classification: the situation of "poor whites," for example, or the "honorary white" status granted to those of Japanese descent?[46]

When considered not as an experiential, micro-level process but as a collective, macro-level one, racial formation in South Africa also poses important
dilemmas and research agendas. Activists have long proclaimed unity among
the non-white majority, especially since the black consciousness movement
emerged in the 1970s; but such claims sometimes obscure real racial tensions
within the "black" population, especially after the 1994 events. Incorporated
on very different terms into South African society, people classified as African,
Indian, or coloured often express deep racial antagonism against other groups.

Under apartheid, few anti-racist scholars were willing even to acknowledge
such sentiments, fearing to reinforce divisions. But since 1994, an explosion of
new claims based largely on racial identities—claims to "real" indigeneity, to
protected minority status, to restitution—has underscored the persistence of
these lines of racial (and ethnic) demarcation. Accepting the rhetoric of non-
racialism, or the democratic fiction that all citizens are individuals with equal
status, could create an explosive tinderbox for South Africa. Conversely, understanding the underlying dynamics of how racialized group identities are
constructed and maintained may be crucial to dealing with the divisive legacies
of apartheid.

These issues are not simply matters of historic interest. Without a better
sense of the dynamics of race in South Africa—the lived dynamics, that is, not
simply the legal categories described so often in discussions of apartheid—
uncertainty remains about how best to conceptualize potential changes in the
future. As yet there is no comprehensive assessment of how racial patterns are

changing in the post-apartheid era, or how reformers might seek to influence them. In less than ten years, for example, a black elite has emerged in South Africa, staffing the top levels of the civil service and taking seats in corporate boardrooms; but we know little about the character of their interactions with white subordinates, or the extent to which racial hierarchies really change (Adam 1997; Bond 2000). How will white civil servants work with new black politicians? How will white South African mining managers respond to the new political context, as they restructure production processes in the context of democratization and downsizing? What are the reactions—in workplaces, state institutions, the South African Defense Forces (SADF), and a host of other settings—to emerging patterns of blacks having authority over whites?

As yet, the extent and effectiveness of the national commitment to equality policies, as embodied in the democratic constitution, is also uncertain. While a significant commitment to implementing affirmative action policies has been made through the democratic constitution, the racial hierarchies surviving from the apartheid regime are very difficult to dismantle.[47] The introduction of affirmative action policies in democratic South Africa is advancing, although of course it remains a contentious issue (Ramphele 1995; Govender 1997, 1624–1628). Such other crucial policy shifts as school desegregation also require more research: how do teachers raised under apartheid—and often deeply implicated in the racial thinking so prevalent in South African societies—deal with problems of integration, when students come from different backgrounds and different cultures, as well as speaking different languages? To what extent, and how, can universities challenge the racial hierarchies of skills and accreditation that have so long marked even the most liberal white institutions, when faculty remain committed to retaining "standards" developed under apartheid?

These kinds of questions cry out for a new generation of comparative studies: the focus must now shift from comparing patterns of racism to comparing patterns of anti-racism. South Africa is hardly the first country to experience decolonization. Nor is it the first to attempt redress for racial dispossession and discrimination in the context of consolidating a new democracy. Other experiences, occurring all over the world as part of the post–World War II break, also confronted these patterns and social structures. The accomplishments and missteps of the United States, as well as those of the post-colonial countries of Africa and elsewhere, may well suggest new perspectives, new approaches to the challenges posed by apartheid's multiple legacies. But this formula runs in the other direction as well: South Africa's experience will also inform other efforts to increase and deepen racial justice all around the world.

Nine

BRAZIL: BACK TO THE FUTURE

THIS CHAPTER EXAMINES recent racial dynamics in Brazil. To consider Brazil and South Africa in sequential chapters has a certain dialectical or perhaps ironic logic. On first viewing, South Africa's racial obstinacy appears to be the very antipode of Brazil's *cordialidade* ("complaisance"), its relatively nonconflictual racial dynamics. Apartheid, South Africa's rigid system of racial classification, seems the polar opposite of Brazil's wildly miscegenated logic of racial identification. And South Africa's ultimate transition from racial dictatorship to democracy, from apartheid to political inclusion, seems to contrast rather sharply with the Brazilian ideal, enunciated at least from the 1930s on, of *racial democracy*. Indeed, South Africa only acknowledged the inevitability of the post–World War II racial break at the latest possible moment, while Brazil *anticipated* the worldwide break.

So it seems. But on deeper examination these apparent antinomies turn out to be convergent as well as opposite, for they are dialectically related. For even these two countries, seemingly so different in terms of their specific racial formations, share some fundamental features of the post–World War II global racial dynamic. At the macro-social or social structural level, both national societies have been marked by continuing and seemingly endemic patterns of racial inequality and injustice, and by racially based limitations on political and human rights. At the micro-social or experiential level, socialization and social reproduction processes in both countries are deeply structured by symbols of racial hierarchy: racially oriented systems of identity-creation and the demarcation of difference are ubiquitous in both societies. Despite the significant variations between the two countries' patterns of racial formation, even though they are seemingly most opposite, there is still a transcendent unity between them. Racial dynamics in both countries have been cast into crisis by the post–World War II break.

Brazil offers a distinctive illustration of these points. In that country from the 1930s on, leading voices both political and intellectual pledged their allegiance to a model of racial democracy. But informal mechanisms of racial exclusion and stratification have remained strong. Recognition of the rights and claims of the roughly 47 percent of the Brazilian population that is of

African descent has been very slow in coming.[1] Although the numbers have improved somewhat in recent decades, it is still true today that only a handful of prominent Brazilian politicians, business leaders, religious leaders, and recognized intellectuals are black. Where elite strata are concerned, only in sports and in entertainment is there a substantial black presence. Poverty, endemic in Brazil, is pandemic among blacks (Silva 1992). As of 1987, black literacy rates were half those of whites. Whites were 4.5 times more likely to have completed high school than blacks (Hasenbalg and Silva 1992, 82).[2] And notably, only since 1985 have literacy requirements been removed from the rules granting access to the ballot. Only since 1985, then, has democracy—in the limited but vital form of enfranchisement—even extended to most Afro-Brazilians. Only since then has there been anything even resembling racial democracy.[3]

Still, by proclaiming itself a racial democracy, Brazil was able to defuse much of the racial mobilization that other societies encountered during the postwar years, even though it did not institute the major social reforms that would have been required to move toward greater democracy or equality in practice. The country's success in giving the appearance, at least, that racism was not a major factor, that discrimination did not exist, was significant enough to lead UNESCO to sponsor an important series of social scientific studies on Brazilian racial themes in the early postwar years.

From the appearance of the UNESCO studies in the 1950s and 1960s the image of Brazil as a racial democracy has been attacked as a myth, as little more than a mask covering the face of widespread racial inequality, injustice, and prejudice (Andrews 1996; Andrews 1991, 225–231; Hanchard 1994; Azevedo 1975; Costa 1985b). Yet the myth endures: it has a powerful base in Brazilian national culture, and has been endlessly rearticulated, not only by leading intellectuals like Gilberto Freyre, but also in the extensive popular culture of the country: from the literature of the *cordel* (Moura 1976) to the *sambas de enredo* (Guillermoprieto 1990) and *telenovelas*.[4] Perhaps most important, the myth finds daily expression in the quotidian: Brazilian talk is permeated with racial discourse. The familiar corporeal dimensions of race—phenotype, in the form of skin color, hair texture, legs, nose, lips, butt, and so on—are subjects of ongoing discussion,[5] particularly where women's bodies are concerned (Burdick 1998; Goldstein 1999).

In this chapter I dispense with the term *myth* in dealing with the racial democracy theme, which necessarily plays a central part in the discussions that follow. I prefer to consider racial democracy as an *ideology*, by which I mean a representation of the complex relationship that exists between race and politics in Brazil.[6]

The Brazilian racial order, then, with its tenacious color continuum, with its "microsocial imbrication," experiences a certain immunization against racial politics, or at least against macro-level, institutional, state-centered racial politics. On the one hand, the country is still understood by much of its populace to be a racial democracy. On the other hand, race is still taken to be a commonsense, personal, physical matter, an experiential rather than social structural phenomenon. Thus do Brazilian racial formation processes dilute political demands where race is concerned.

Historically, the country has undergone repeated inoculations against racially based social movements. To acknowledge this (partial) racial exceptionalism is to recognize the (partial) validity of the central points made by Freyre from the 1930s on. Yes, of course, the Brazilian racial formation process is the outcome of a profound gestation. It derives from the unique form taken by Portuguese colonialism and from an extremely intense encounter with African slavery. It reflects a profound religiosity. It accepts, but also complexly regulates and evaluates, the widespread *miscigenaçaõ* that is central to Brazilian norms of sexuality, child-rearing, nurturance, and reproduction. Add to this the absence in Brazil of a traumatic transition from slavery to emancipation, the roughly even demographic balance between black and non-black populations (depending upon how one defines "black"), the experience with authoritarian populism under Vargas, and the existence of a long (1964–85) military dictatorship that made *all* social movement activity very perilous and difficult to sustain; and you get a sense of why Brazil is a particularly challenging test case for the thesis of the post–World War II racial break.

Yet Brazil meets that test, I think. For the reasons I have just listed ("immunization," etc.), the Brazilian racial system could encounter the impediments and challenges posed by the break only slowly. Unlike the other national/regional case studies presented here, the country was not hugely mobilized by World War II, and had only experienced limited racial conflict before the war. Here is another Brazilian parallel with South Africa: despite their formal citizenship status and their country's proclamation that it was free of racism, Brazilian blacks had surprisingly little access to the political system. This was true not because there was formal segregation or apartheid as in South Africa, but because their country underwent several prolonged periods of dictatorship. Even when there was some kind of democracy (from 1946–64, notably), blacks (as well as many impoverished Brazilians of all racial categories) were effectively disenfranchised by literacy requirements.

RACIAL POLITICS AND RACIAL THEORY IN BRAZIL

Although my primary interest in this chapter, as elsewhere in Part II of the book, is developments after 1945, after World War II, here I pick up the story of Brazilian racial formation in the 1930s. This was a pivotal period for both *racial politics* and *racial theory* in Brazil. I outline Brazilian racial formation by focusing in parallel on the development of these two aspects of twentieth-century Brazil. Where appropriate, I establish links between local and global processes as well.

During the 1930s the stage was set—again both practically and theoretically—for the Brazilian version of the post–World War II racial break. In the 1930s a series of significant economic, political, and demographic shifts were initiated under the extended rule of the populist president (and sometime dictator) Getúlio Vargas. The economic growth occasioned by the import-substitution industrialization begun in the 1930s meant an increasing demand for industrial labor in the cities, particularly in the Southeast, but also in other major urban centers throughout the country. Combined with the "push" factors associated with rural poverty (particularly in the arid Northeast), industrial "pull" worked to generate massive population movements: Brazil shared with the rest of Latin America and the global South a burgeoning urbanization. The appearance of *favelas* (shantytowns) in all the major cities (and their mushrooming in the postwar decades) was a clear indication of this, as was the general trend toward urbanization of what had previously been a largely rural black population.

Urbanized and proletarianized (or relegated to the urban informal economy), the Brazilian *povo* (the people, the masses) slowly became more politically aware, less fatalistic. Vargas's rise to power played a major role in this process as well. Beginning in the 1940s and gathering force through the self-examination occasioned by the UNESCO studies in the 1950s and 1960s, even Brazil—the supposed racial democracy—began to encounter itself as a racially conflictual society.

The final overthrow of the nationalist and populist Second Republic or New Republic occurred at a moment (1964) that roughly coincided with the apogee of worldwide anti-racist mobilization. Subsequent resistance to the prolonged military regime and efforts to restore democracy necessarily involved Afro-Brazilians, not *qua* blacks but as citizens with democratic aspirations. This experience of a dictatorship, which finally began to unravel only in the *abertura* at the end of the 1970s, constituted an important course of political education. During this sequence of events racial activists and theorists acquired a greater awareness of the global context in which even huge Brazil (often described as *um mundo inteiro*—a world in itself) was located. Many of the key ideological conflicts of the dictatorship era turned out to have racial dimensions: the Cold War, communism and anti-communism, nationalism, North–South conflicts, "dependency," and the historical legacy of colonialism were some of these. Activists were led by all this, and by the increasing influence of North American and African events,[7] to reassert the importance of anti-racist mobilization at home.

Although it has not developed a mass-based black movement, contemporary Brazil has seen the emergence of its most committed, most organized, and most permanent anti-racist *sensibility* to date. To employ the term *sensibility* is already to distinguish Brazilian anti-racist activities and awareness from other uses of the term *movement*.[8] The North American reference-points of the civil rights struggle; the South African mobilizations under the banners of the African National Congress, the United Democratic Front, or for that matter the Azanian People's Organization; the European term *new social movements*, which includes anti-racist groups like *SOS-Racisme* in France: none of these applies in Brazil, although there are numerous Brazilian groups and organizations that would identify themselves as part of the *movimento Afro-Brasileiro*. What I mean by a growing sensibility is a developing consciousness of race and racism, a contradictory awareness that both embraces and repudiates racial politics and racial identities, that both encompasses anti-racist movements and undermines them. This sensibility of and about race and racism will constitute a major theme in this chapter.

This chapter proceeds as follows. In the next section I consider *background conditions* to the postwar racial break in Brazil. Two principal legacies framed the break: the political incorporation of the multiracial Brazilian *povo* at the hands of Getúlio Vargas and the *Frente Negra Brasileira* (FNB); and the rearticulation of the meaning of race, at the hands of Gilberto Freyre, from the *branqueamento* or whitening model to that of racial democracy.

In the following section of the chapter I discuss *the rediscovery of race during the Second Republic*. Here as well there are two principal themes. The first is the significant upsurge of black political and cultural activity that took place at the end of the Vargas dictatorship. This development was linked to and informed by the worldwide acceleration of anti-colonialist and anti-racist activity that was taking shape at the time. The second theme is the efflorescence of social scientific investigation of race, both empirical and theoretical, that occurred in Brazil during the 1950s and early 1960s at the instigation of UNESCO. This work would have lasting effects, on both Brazilian and global racial dynamics. It would be tragically cut short—along with the nascent anti-racist and egalitarian social movements of the period—by the military coup of 1964 and the onset of dictatorship.

Not until the last phase of the dictatorship—the *abertura* ("opening") of 1979–85—would a *movement resurgence* take place in Brazil. Organizationally committed to independent black politics and theoretically more in tune with the global dimensions of race, black activism and racial theory would undergo another sharp upsurge and subsequent containment in the late 1970s and early 1980s. The innovations and limitations of this new movement upsurge, as well as the strengths and weaknesses of the racial theory that informed it, are surveyed in this section of the chapter. The section ends with a brief discussion of the *decline of the movement* in the transition to the (post–1985) Third Republic.

In the next section of the chapter I offer the outlines of a theory of *Brazilian racial formation*. In an effort to contribute to the burgeoning theoretical discussion on race in Brazil, I argue the necessity of an approach based on a linking of macro- and micro-social vantage points. I question the effectiveness of analyses that do not give sufficient weight to the experiential dimension of racial formation. This line of argument goes by various names: society-centered (as opposed to state-centered) accounts, the "politics of identity," subaltern studies, and so on. Once again attempting to depict the interrelationship between these Brazilian points and global racial developments under the sign of the break, I invoke some cherished authorities: Du Bois, Fanon, and Gramsci.

In this chapter's final section I discuss *racial formation in Brazil's Third Republic* (1985–present). I argue that, far from being contained by means traditional or new, an anti-racist sensibility is more evident in Brazil in the twenty-first century than ever before. I explore the sources of this tendency, relying largely on recent testimonial and ethnographic literature.

BACKGROUND CONDITIONS: THE 1930S

For Brazil the year 1945 marks not so much the end of World War II,[9] as the downfall of populist dictator Getúlio Vargas and the resumption of the Second Republic. Vargas had been in power for fifteen years, since the "Revolution of 1930"; he had established his corporatist *Estado Novo* (New State) by a further seizure of power in 1937.[10] Although the *Estado Novo* had repressed all political parties—including the *Frente Negra Brasileira*, which had registered as a party only in 1936—Vargas retained a tremendous base among the *povo*, both white and black.[11]

Vargas was an important modernizing force in Brazilian development. He greatly advanced the industrialization of the Brazilian economy. He introduced the growing urbanized masses (the *povo*) into political life (although not in a democratic way); his regime was repressive but not brutal. Still, as a populist, he also manipulated the *povo* and fostered a species of chauvinistic Brazilian nationalism. His overall relationship to the masses was charismatic and thus reflected the contradictions characterisic of populism (Laclau 1977a). It resonated with popular (especially black) mistrust of the republic, which from its inception had been perceived as the creature of the planter elites. Vargas's political stance interacted in a complex fashion with Freyre's reinterpretation of Brazilian national identity.

In its appeal to the *povo*, *Varguismo* was also necessarily and implicitly racial. To anachronize a political term employed by one of Vargas's many political heirs, *Varguismo's* populist nationalism was *moreno* ("brown").[12] The emergence of the *Frente Negra Brasileira*, Brazil's most significant black political organization, during Vargas's regime is not accidental. As was Vargas himself, the FNB was nationalistic, anti-immigrant, and *trabalhista* ("workerist"); like Vargas it was divided between socialist and fascist sympathies. Indeed, the FNB was greatly attracted to *Integralismo*, the Brazilian fascist movement. Relatively uninvolved with international issues (pan-Africanism and anti-colonial solidarity would not arrive in Brazil until the break period), the FNB was integrationist and inclusionist in its demands. Still, despite its ideological complexities, during its brief life-span the FNB first raised the possibility of an independent black politics in Brazil. It was suppressed along with all independent political parties when the *Estado Novo* was proclaimed in 1937, but it left a significant political legacy.

Vargas's populist rule garnered significant black support, even after the FNB was suppressed. Already in 1934 a new constitution (promulgated democratically but strongly influenced by Vargas) had decreed:

> There will be no privileges, nor distinctions because of birth, sex, race, personal profession or profession of parents, social class, wealth, religion, or political ideas. (*Constituições Brasileiras* 1978)[13]

Vargas's nationalism and populism endeared him to the poor, to blacks, to *favelados*. Even in the 1980s Caldeira's respondents recalled him affectionately:

> Getúlio was a president idolized by the people, and as long as he was alive the people were always with him, and he wasn't about to give up the presidency. . . . He was president for 19 years and they [his enemies] wanted to get him out, but they couldn't. They had no way to do it, the only way was to kill him. (Caldeira 1984, 280)[14]

The principal reasons for Vargas's popular support undoubtedly included his overthrow of the planter elite, which had provided the country's political class during the First Republic: "[T]he Vargas Revolution of 1930 kindled in Blacks a sense of liberation from social control by the once-dominant rural oligarchs" (Mitchell 1985, 111). Vargas's laborism and commitment to industrial development, his nationalizations (principally of steel and petroleum), and his institution of a minimum wage and social security program, also deeply resonated with the *povo*. Black support came largely from these same sources. Under Vargas Afro-Brazilians entered the industrial working class in large numbers.[15] Obtaining work in the factories of São Paulo (and elsewhere as well) in turn opened up a real avenue of mobility for those black workers fortunate enough to take advantage of it: trade unionism.[16] The appearance and growth of the FNB during the early years of the Vargas regime reflected black activists' perception of a strong coincidence of interests with the regime, at least in such practical matters as employment policy and social programs.[17] The flourishing black press of the period regularly endorsed the populism, nationalism, anti-immigration, and industrial policies promoted by the government.[18] Finally, Vargas legitimized (although also regulating) Afro-Brazilian religious and cultural traditions: notably *candomblé, samba,* and *capoeira,* which had been stigmatized and relegated to semi-clandestinity under the monarchy and First Republic (Browning 1995; Guillermoprieto 1990; Wafer 1991).

Yet Vargas also inherited the whitening ideal from his predecessors. This led to a series of significant dilemmas, for under Vargas's populist, developmentalist, and nationalist regime overt commitments to racial hierarchy and *branqueamento* could not be maintained. The transition from a rurally based to an urban model of capitalist development; the recruitment of the *povo,* and particularly the working class, as the regime's popular base; the restriction of immigration and the implementation under the *Estado Novo* of a *dirigiste* economic model; all these demanded a more sophisticated modernizing doctrine. A new account was needed of Brazilian identity: something more particular and inclusive, and especially something that could legitimate and justify Brazil's aspirations as an emerging nation-state and potential great power.

Gilberto Freyre, an anthropologist from the Brazilian northeast, was to become the source of that alternative account. In contrast to the subservient and paranoid racial doctrines that had characterized debates on national character during the Monarchy and First Republic, in sharp opposition to the whitening ideal with its inferiorization of all non-Europeans (and especially Africans and indigenous Americans) that had continued through the First Republic,[19] Freyre's *luso-tropicalismo* (roughly, "Portuguese-style tropical culture") justified and celebrated Brazilian identity as a coherent and enlightened synthesis of the three principal inheritances of the Brazilian nation.[20] Freyre offered a rich genealogy of contemporary Brazil, one whose modernity and openness—and whose apparent tolerance—contrasted sharply with the white supremacism of the abolitionist era and the early First Republic, with their hunger for European immigration and European ways, and their fear of *morenizaçao* ("browning") at the hands of the *libertos.* In an unending series of writings, some historical and others ethnographic, through a determined intervention in the public discourse, as an organizer of the first conference on Afro-Brazilian themes (in 1935), and by astute mobilization of both scholarly and popular audiences, Freyre was able to rearticulate Brazilian understandings of the meaning of both "nation" and "race" quite comprehensively.

Freyre's historical anthropology exercised an enormous influence over Brazilian national culture, as well as reshaping images of the country in the exterior (Needell 1995). Beginning with his 1933 work *Casa Grande e Senzala*—translated as *The Masters and the Slaves* (1986 [1933]) but literally meaning "the big house and the the slave quarters"—Freyre revisioned and rationalized the account of Brazilian national origins. He abandoned in part the previously taken-for-granted superiority of whiteness and the principles of racial hierarchy, substituting for these a new racial nationalism that vindicated and glorified miscegenation and hybridization. The Brazilian "new man (sic) of the tropics," according to Freyre, combined in his blood, his heredity, his very essence the racial qualities of the European, the African, and the Native American. Far from seeing the Brazilian *povo* as composed of "mongrels" or *devolués* (as the elites of the long immigration era [1872–1927] had characterized them), Freyre proposed a new, comparative-historical, and thoroughly modern alternative view: *luso-tropicalismo*, which he contrasted favorably with the inflexibility of the color-line in the United States.[21] His innovation was itself contradictory, though: on the one hand, he recognized the crucial black and native influences and presences in Brazilian society; on the other hand, he encouraged assimilation and thus denied both black difference and inequality.

In some respects Freyre's intellectual project was a revolutionary one. It demolished many racial axioms that had gone unquestioned for decades, even centuries: the racial hierarchy stressed by Gobineau and his successors, as well as the seemingly more scientific logic of eugenics, were repudiated. Furthermore, in his historical account of Brazilian social development, Freyre celebrated the hybridization and miscegenation that many earlier authorities had regarded with unrestrained horror.[22] For Freyre, quite to the contrary, interracial sex had bred the *novo homem* ("new man") of Brazil. Out of the proximity between the "big house" (*casa grande*) and the slave quarter (*senzala*) had come familiarity: "A widely practiced miscegenation tended . . . to modify the enormous social distance that otherwise would have been preserved between big house and slave hut" (Freyre 1986 [1933], xxix; see also Hanchard 1994, 52). Thus not only was Brazilian slavery more benign in Freyre's view than parallel slave systems elsewhere (notably in the U.S. South), but the racial pattern that emerged from it was much less conflictual, much more socially unified than the segregation policies taken for granted by the big bully to the north. Such a system would have been incomprehensible to the white supremacists of the United States, whose racial theories of the color-line and the one-drop rule could have no meaning in Brazil. Indeed, Brazil was an exception to the world racial order; as a racial democracy it could serve as an example to others.[23]

Yet for all its modernizing effects, for all its elective affinities with the populism, developmentalism, and nationalism of the *Estado Novo*, the overall effect of Freyre's work was to rationalize and justify the Brazilian racial order. There was a formidable contradiction in his racial outlook. On the one hand, he recognized and legitimated the permanence and depth of the Afro-Brazilian and (indigenous) presence and contributions to Brazilian national culture and social structure. In this way he challenged the blind white supremacy that had preceded him. But on the other hand, he also celebrated Brazil's racially inclusive capabilities, its hybridity (and sexuality).[24] This tended to defuse racial conflict far more effectively than the *branqueamento* project could ever do; Brazil was depicted as capable of a racial assimilation unimaginable elsewhere, particularly in the 1930s world of Jim Crow and Scottsboro, not to mention Hitler. Freyre's work thus had the consequence of denying both black difference and black inequality.

THE REDISCOVERY OF RACE

Vargas's departure in 1945 coincided with the end of World War II and the assertion of new emancipatory and egalitarian demands by "the wretched of the earth." The aspirations of former (and soon-to-be former) colonial peoples, notably African peoples—democratic, egalitarian, and anti-racist—lay at the heart of these new initiatives. In Brazil these themes resonated among veterans of the FNB and of the urban, trade-union oriented, and populist legacy of the *Estado Novo*. The hiatus imposed by Vargas's 1937 suppression of the *Frente Negra Brasileira* had not been debilitating overall, in part because blacks made progress under the *Estado Novo*, and in part because the FNB had become tangled up in *Integralismo* before its demise.

Consciously linking the black movement in Brazil to the African liberationist tradition, an important group of activists led by Abdias do Nascimento began to organize under the banner of *quilombismo* (a Brazilian version of pan-Africanism), mainly focusing their energies on Afro-Brazilian cultural activities, and explicitly seeking to locate Brazil in the pan-Africanist vision that was reaching its apogee in this period.[25] Thus in the period after 1945 black arts groups, publications, manifestos, and fledgling urban organizations reasserted themselves. Some of the main groups were the *Teatro Experimental do Negro*, the *Associação José do Patrocínio*, the *Congresso Nacional do Negro*, and the *Congresso Nacional das Mulheres Negras*. A national black *constituinte* (constitutional convention) was organized by activists in São Paulo to develop "a platform of demands to be presented to the upcoming Constituent Assembly, which would write the new constitution for the Second Republic" (Andrews 1991, 182). Black newspapers flourished. Black social and political clubs, trade union groups, and cultural organizations appeared in the cities, notably (but not only) in São Paulo and Rio. Many of these organizations owed their existence to the pioneering work of Abdias do Nascimento, the leading pan-Africanist and black nationalist in modern Brazilian history. Nascimento's political orientation also had a strand of *Varguismo* in it; in more recent years he has been associated in Rio de Janeiro with the PDT (Democratic Workers Party) of Leonel Brizola, a successor (through Goulart) of Vargas.

As these pan-Africanist and egalitarian activities went forward, academics and intellectuals also were led to a "rediscovery of race" by the UNESCO studies of the 1950s and 1960s. These research projects were originally inspired by the Freyrian model of racial democracy: they were initially designed to explore and document Brazil's supposed transcendence of racial prejudice and discrimination. That they "failed" at this task was of course fortuitous both for students of race and for Brazilian racial politics. In the 1950s and 1960s UNESCO initiated in Brazil one of the most significant research projects on racial dynamics ever undertaken. Seen as a whole these studies[26] stand as a powerful antithesis to the work of Freyre, which both gave them their initial impetus and their chief target of criticism.

Deriving its momentum from worldwide horror at the Holocaust and Nazi racism, and influenced by the Brazilian racial democracy paradigm as formulated by Freyre, UNESCO turned its gaze on racial dynamics in Brazil. The preliminary hypothesis flowed directly from Freyre's thesis: that the country offered a model of racial harmony other countries might emulate (Maio 1997).

These hopes would of course be dashed. But the UNESCO studies accomplished much more than simply challenging the ideology of racial democracy. They uncovered a great deal of suppressed history about Brazilian racial dynamics; they documented the complex system of cultural representations through which race was diffused into every aspect of Brazilian society; and they began the study of racial stratification in Brazil on the first systematic—if belated—basis. Dividing their labors among rural and urban social sectors, as well as examining regional differences in racial conditions, the UNESCO researchers and theorists provided the most systematic analysis of Brazilian racial dynamics ever undertaken.[27]

But the UNESCO analyses were themselves flawed. Largely proceeding from neo-Marxist premises, they tended toward *class reductionism* (Omi and Winant 1994). Arguing that racism was a "survival" from Brazil's centuries of slavery, they also suggested that a full-fledged class struggle would largely do away with the "problem" of race. In this regard these researchers were appropriate successors to Freyre, although the authors' left orientation and repression under the military regime (see below) contrasted sharply with the now-elderly Freyre's conservatism and outright support for the dictatorship (Carvalho 2000).

The leading voice among the UNESCO researchers was that of Florestan Fernandes, whose work, carried out fifty years ago, arguably remains the most comprehensive sociology of race relations in Brazil (Fernandes 1978). Fernandes was an "exceptionalist" like Freyre, but his Marxist viewpoint led him to stress the centrality of race in Brazil's development, not as a virtue but as a fault. For him race remained a "dilemma," whose "resolution" would clear the way for socialism, signifying at last the sociopolitical maturity of the nation. In other words, Fernandes still understood race as a *problem*, rather than a *condition* (Winant 1994a). It was not something to be celebrated a la Freyre, but something to be overcome, a holdover from the colonial and pre-capitalist past.

Fernandes at least recognized the continuing presence and significance of race; other UNESCO researchers tended to dismiss or minimize it. While the *Paulista* Fernandes' basic optimism was tempered by the question of whether the full modernization of class society could be achieved, the *Bahiano* anthropologist Thales de Azevedo saw evidence that this process was already far advanced: according to him, class conflict was *replacing* racial conflict in Bahia (Azevedo 1966, 30–43).[28] Marvin Harris, who worked closely with Azevedo, suggested that the Brazilian system of racial identification *necessarily* subordinated race to class.[29] Comparing Brazilian and U.S. racial dynamics, Harris echoed Freyre in arguing that the absence of a "descent rule" by which racial identity could be inherited, and the flexibility of racial meanings, led to a situation in which "[R]acial identity is a mild and wavering thing in Brazil, while in the United States it is for millions of people a passport to hell" (Harris 1964, 64). Another important North American scholar of Brazil, Charles Wagley, also took this position (Wagley 1969; Wagley 1972).

Perhaps the most striking limitation of the UNESCO studies was their nearly exclusive focus on racial inequality. This is not to deny the importance of the economic dimensions of race. However, the preoccupation with inequality to the near total exclusion of any other aspect of race is a logical feature of approaches that treat racial dynamics as manifestations of more fundamental class relationships. These analyses tend to see racial categories as relatively rigid and unchanging. The idea that racial meanings are themselves subject to conflict, susceptible to political rearticulation, a la cultural movements like Negritude or black power, does not arise in this literature.[30]

Besides contributing to the refounding of Brazilian social science, the UNESCO studies also intersected with the profound left-wing upsurge that overtook Brazil during the latter years of the Second Republic (1946–64); some of the principal UNESCO researchers—Fernandes, Cardoso, and Ianni—ran afoul of the military authorities who seized power in 1964 and put an end to the Second Republic.

During much of the dictatorship both progressive racial theorizing and anti-racist political action were prohibited. Many key figures were exiled or worse. Yet at the same time the exterior world was convulsed by racial struggle: in the United States civil rights and black power movements were grabbing world headlines; in South Africa the Sharpeville and Rivonia events heralded a new stage in the anti-apartheid struggle; in Africa and elsewhere the sun had finally set on the British and French Empires while the Portuguese colonies—deeply tied to Brazil by language, history, and culture—were embarking on armed struggles. Third World revolution, socialism and communism, and the northern "new lefts" also exercised their influences. As Brazilian exiles looked around the world's political convulsions, as they listened to Caetano Veloso and Gilberto Gil (themselves exiled to England), as they grappled with the works of UNESCO researchers Fernandes and Cardoso, they developed once again an important legacy for future practice and theory.

Largely in consequence of the UNESCO-sponsored work that began to appear in the 1950s, Brazilian universities—and particularly social scientists—became increasingly conscious of the problematic of race.[31] New forms of cultural and student activism emerged as well, stimulated in part by the worldwide movement upsurge of the 1960s. The Second Republic was generally a period of heightened popular movements; notably under the presidency of João Goulart (1961–64), a resurgent left, both urban and rural, pressed for social and land reform. During this period the educator and social theorist Paulo Freire developed his revolutionary literacy and political education campaigns in the *sertoes* and *favelas*. Rural mobilization for land reform and urban strike activity reached new heights. Left-wing parties, some invoking the heritage of Getúlio, others social democratic or communist, attained greater visibility in the *favelas* and on university campuses. The heightened conflicts of this period set the stage for the military's seizure of power in 1964 (Dreifuss 1981).

Brazilian military rule pioneered postwar Latin American methods of repression: the disappearances, systematic tortures, and draconian clampdowns on all forms of opposition and public expression that would become the continental political norms for twenty-five years (Archdiocese of São Paulo 1986; Weschler 1990). The military also decreed an end to all racially based organization and indeed all anti-racist expression, proclaiming such actitivies not only anti-Brazilian, anti-nationalist, and subversive, but even accusing activists and academics studying race of being "racist" themselves. The Brazilian census was purged of questions about racial identity during the dictatorship (Nobles 2000, 110–119; Andrews 1996). The Department of Sociology at Brazil's leading university, the Universidade de São Paulo, was closed. Its leading figures—Florestan Fernandes, Fernando Henrique Cardoso (future president of Brazil), and Octavio Ianni—who had been prominent UNESCO researchers, were arrested and then exiled. Nascimento too went into exile, teaching in an ethnic studies department in the United States.

During the Second Republic critical awareness of Brazilian racial dynamics developed considerably, in part as a resurgence of an important domestic heritage, but in great measure as a result of the influences felt in Brazil from the worldwide racial break that coincided in time with the Second Republic's lifespan. The impact of anti-colonialism and pan-Africanism on the resurgent Afro-Brazilian movement was large, but the movement itself remained small. The effects of the comprehensive UNESCO-initiated studies of Brazilian racial dynamics were extremely significant. These projects had the double effect of seriously challenging the ideology of racial democracy for the first time, and of comprehensively recasting Brazil as a crucial national setting in the unfolding world racial drama. They also reinvented Brazilian social science and reinserted it in the global intellectual community.

Despite their successes exposing racial inequalities in Brazil and calling into question the ideology of racial democracy, the UNESCO approaches encountered difficulties when they had to explain transformations in racial dynamics after slavery, and particularly the persistence of racial inequality in a developing capitalist society. Their tendency to see the continuity of racial inequality as a manifestation of supposedly more fundamental class antagonisms (their "reductionism") resulted in an inability to see race as a theoretically flexible, as opposed to an a priori, category.

The military coup of 1964 not only put a stop to the popular mobilization that was occurring under the Second Republic, including its anti-racist and pan-Africanist components; it also impeded both anti-racist mobilization and critical social scientific studies of race. Some of the practitioners of these arts were driven into exile, where they could at least continue their work, albeit under less congenial circumstances.[32] They were the lucky ones; those who were not able to flee the country were reduced to the silence of inactivity, or to that of the grave. Large-scale anti-racist mobilization would not resume within Brazil until the last years of the dictatorship, the *abertura* period.[33]

BLACK MOVEMENT RESURGENCE

Beginning in the mid-1970s, a new black movement emerged in Brazil. Organizationally committed to independent black politics and theoretically more in tune with the global dimensions of race, black activism and racial theory would undergo another sharp upsurge and subsequent containment during the last phase of the military dictatorship, the period of *abertura* (1979–85). For the first time in forty years, a black political organization with credible national aspirations appeared on the scene: the *Movimento Negro Unificado* (MNU). The MNU combined the egalitarianism and inclusionism of the FNB with a strong *black consciousness* orientation traceable both to the early years of the Second Republic and to a much-increased awareness of the international dimensions of black politics.

This group profoundly embodied not only the legacy of past black struggles, of the FNB and the UNESCO researchers' repudiation of the Freyrian vision of racial democracy; it also incorporated a plenitude of global influences, derived from the vast range of diasporic African political struggles. Marxist, pan-Africanist, feminist, Negritude, and *quilombista* orientations, to name but the main currents, coexisted (always somewhat uneasily) in the MNU.[34] The experience of prolonged military dictatorship and of widespread involvement in democratic and oppositional movements of all kinds—at the workplace, in schools and universities, in women's groups, in religious and cultural organizations, and so on—also played an important part in preparing Afro-Brazilians for a new black movement initiative. Even before the appearance of the MNU, a host of other black groups were set up, mainly adopting the protective coloration of research institutes or community self-help organizations to avoid attracting the still-uptight military regime's attention.[35]

The MNU was initially named the *Movimento Negro Unificado Contra Discriminação Racial* ("United Black Movement Against Racial Discrimination"). Although the very use of the term *discriminação* signified a shift from domestic racial parlance (which would have employed the term *preconceito*—"prejudice"), questions soon arose about the focus on discrimination, which was of course viewed as important but perhaps too narrow; the limitations of the FNB in the 1930s were perceived as including both its integralism and its integrationism (Gonzales 1985; Andrews 1991, 322, n. 32).

The MNU aimed to incorporate a wide range of independent black organizations under its umbrella. Maria Ercilia do Nascimento offers an imposing list of groups that took part in the organization's initial *Ato Público* ("public appearance") on July 7, 1978, which I repeat here to indicate the range of founding entities:

Centro de Cultura e Arte Negra (CECAN), São Paulo ("Center for Black Culture and Art");
Instituto de Pesquisas da Cultura Negra (IPCN), Rio de Janeiro ("Institute for Research on Black Culture");
Centro de Estudos Brasil-Africa ("Center for Brazilian-African Studies");
Renascença Clube, Rio de Janeiro, ("Renaissance Club:");
Nucleo Socialista ("Socialist Nucleus");
Olorum Babá-Min (a *Candomblé* society);
Sociedade de Intercambio Brasil-Africa (SINBA), Rio de Janeiro ("Society for Brazilian-African Exchange");
Grupo de Atletas Negros, São Paulo ("Black Athletes' Group");
Afro-Latino-America;
Instituto Brasileiro de Estudos Africanistas (IBEA), São Paulo ("Brazilian Institute for African Studies");
Juventude Judaica ("Jewish Youth Group");
Convergencia Socialista ("Socialist Convergence");
Grupo Decisão ("Decision Group");
Associacão Cristã de Beneficencia (ACBB), São Paulo ("Christian Association for Charity");
Escola de Samba Quilombo, Rio de Janeiro ("*Quilombo* Samba School").[36]

What is striking about this group of organizations, which were only the preliminary signatories and participants in the MNU's founding, is its tremendous variety. Artistic, cultural, and religious groups (inluding Catholic, Candomblé, and Jewish-identified ones), pan-Africanists, socialists, athletic and social clubs are represented. International connections as well as local and national ones are highlighted. Yet the signatory groups are also, obviously, small organizations, some consisting only of a few people. The MNU was founded as a vanguard, not a mass organization. It was initially regionally restricted as well (to Rio and São Paulo), although it would later come to include groups from other states as well (Gonzales 1985). Such was the rebirth of Afro-Brazilian activism.

Racial theory had also advanced substantially by the time of the *abertura*. As exiles returned and younger activists and students became involved, a new variety of theory emerged, one that built on yet also rejected even the UNESCO studies. Comparatively oriented and informed as much by U.S. and African influences as by the legacy of Freyre and Fernandes, this body of work emphasized neither the incorporative aspects of Brazilian models of race (a la Freyre), nor the need to transcend racial divisions in order to foment a Brazilian socialism (a la Fernandes). Instead, it focused attention on the resilience of Brazilian racism. I have labeled this the "structuralist" school of Brazilian racial studies (Winant 1992).[37]

Already in the first years of military rule, new work on race in Brazil showed the influence of the international movement upsurge of the break period, notably the U.S. civil rights movement. In a book both drawing upon and criticizing the UNESCO studies, historian Carl Degler suggested various ways in which racial inequality could *persist* while still remaining subordinated to class conflicts. Degler's rich comparative analysis of Brazil and the United States concluded that because Brazil distinguished mulattos from blacks, and afforded them greater social mobility—which he labeled the "mulatto escape hatch"— racial polarization had been avoided there. Pointing to the same flexibility of racial categories that Harris had documented, Degler made extensive claims for the escape hatch in Brazilian racial history. If there was an escape hatch, he argued, then the U.S. pattern of growing racial solidarity would not occur; thus at least for some blacks (that is, mulattos) questions of class would automatically take precedence over those of race. Other blacks, recognizing that mobility was available to the lighter-skinned, would seek this possibility, if not for themselves then for their children. Because the escape hatch already provided this opportunity for the lighter-skinned blacks, Degler claimed, the task was to extend it to blacks in general.

Degler's book suffered from a lack of empirical evidence for the escape hatch hypothesis, however. Later work on Brazilian racial stratification refutes the claim that significant differences in mobility or life chances exist between blacks and mulattos (Silva 1985). Besides tending to revert to archaic views of whitening as the preferred solution to Brazil's racial problems, this analysis also saw economic mobility (and thus, integration in class society) as the key question in Brazilian racial dynamics.

In the same year (1971) political scientist Amaury de Souza made a similar argument that had less recourse to historical data and instead focused on whitening as a sort of rational-choice model, in which blacks had to weigh the costs of individual mobility against those of racial solidarity; consequently, a type of "prisoner's dilemma" confronted any effort to organize black political opposition (de Souza, 1971; see also Bastide, 1965).[38]

Two influential texts of the 1970s were Dzidzienyo (1971) and Hasenbalg (1979). Both sought to explain racism's resilience in Brazil. Hasenbalg drew attention to the country's "smooth preservation of racial inequalities," and pointed to the "delicate mixture of ideological controls and social cooptation [that] was the most successful means of obtaining the acquiescence of Brazilian blacks" (Hasenbalg 1979, 260). Dzidzienyo characterized the Brazilian racial system as achieving "*without tension* the same results as do overtly racist societies" (1971, 14).

Profoundly affected by postwar international developments and written with a full awareness of the repressive military dictatorship still operating in Brazil, these and other similar works argued the necessity of recreating an independent Brazilian black movement. Dzidzienyo, a Ghanaian, was deeply influenced by the African anti-colonial struggle, by the pan-Africanist legacy that had passed through Nkrumah and the struggle against Portuguese colonialism then proceeding in Guinea-Bissau, Angola, and Mozambique. He resonated as well with the Brazilian pan-Africanism represented by Abdias do Nascimento's *quilombismo*. Hasenbalg, an Argentinian, framed his study of Brazilian racism as a systematic comparison with the United States. His neo-Marxism built on Fernandes' work, but questioned its class reductionism.

Such analyses as Dzidzienyo's and Hasenbalg's, and a host of other work by activists and scholars (Santos 1984; Moura 1983), helped galvanize a new generation of black activism. These studies, along with the continuing pan-Africanist currents linked to Abdias do Nascimento (1979), were considerably less "exceptionalist" about Brazilian racial dynamics than previous schools of thought—notably the racial democracy viewpoint associated with Freyre, but also the UNESCO studies—had been. Of course, the structuralists of the 1970s and 1980s recognized the particularities of the Brazilian racial system, but they did not hesitate to invoke comparative models, to acknowledge diasporic political influences, or to propose a more politically radical challenge to the system than had been available before.

But for all the theoretical innovation that occurred in the 1970s and 1980s, significant problems remained. Degler's presumptive mulatto upward mobility did not exist. The analyses proposed by Dzidzienyo and Hasenbalg tended to relegate the masses of blacks to problematic passivity in their attribution to elites of the capacity to preserve the Brazilian racial order "smoothly," "without tension." Where was the *povo* in this equation?

It is true, as Hanchard (1994) notes, that the black organizations and individuals active in the MNU were necessarily "elite" as well; they were relatively privileged, better educated, already politically and culturally "tuned in." In terms of its composition, the MNU probably corresponded rather closely to the counter- or insurgent elites that were brought into existence by anti-racist and anti-colonialist movements all over the world in the aftermath of the World War II break, and that wound up leading nationalist revolutionary movements as well as becoming neo-colonial power-brokers in much of the Third World.[39]

But the structuralist writers tended to assume that there was virtually no awareness or opposition to racial injustice and inequality among the *povo*, the subaltern. Here they tended to give too much credit to the ideology of racial democracy, which despite its continuity encountered more micro-level awareness and antagonism than they recognized. For all their merits, these works did not yet grasp the residual agency of the racially subaltern.[40] Furthermore, the structuralist analyses of the 1970s and 1980s tended to downplay the conflicts evident in racial discourse and cultural action, especially within the black community, and indeed among the infinite varieties of black identity. With a view that Brazilian racial discourse still effectively served to mask inequality, it was harder to see that the cultural dynamics of race—the racial politics of identity—were also conflictual, contested terrain.

Movement Decline?

After its initial success in calling into being an organization of organizations, a "united front" or umbrella group of Afro-Brazilian activism, organizational problems became more and more evident within the MNU. Among these were the limited resources available, which Hanchard (1994, 128) sees as a central issue in the MNU's decline. This was certainly important, but the uneasy coexistence within the group of numerous political and cultural projects, directed at a wide range of different constituencies, ultimately proved a more significant limitation. The organization continued to operate well into the Third Republic. Indeed, it never exactly died: its name is still invoked periodically by activists whose primary affiliation is to another group, usually local, that was a component of the MNU.

Yet its decay requires explanation. How could an entity that included so much analytical capacity, movement experience, and internal variety not consolidate for the long haul as an effective tribune for the many millions of Afro-Brazilians who were its potential constituents?

Much of the excitement unleashed by the MNU's formation was a product of its boldness in appearing when it did: the MNU presented itself as a voice of opposition in a still-repressive political climate. It was a harbinger, both for blacks and for democrats of all identities, of the end of the dictatorship. As the *abertura* continued and then was succeeded by the Third Republic (1985), the component groups of the MNU deepened their work in many different ways.

They acquired alternate allegiances and alliances. Different political parties (chiefly of the left) sought to co-opt their constituencies and enlist their support. State agencies at all levels (from the federal to the municipal) began to establish black departments of various kinds.[41] Interest in black cultural production rose: increased freedom of expression meant more opportunities to publish, exhibit, and perform. Religious modes of expression and incorporation also increased, as did opportunities to create international connections, affiliating with (or obtaining support from) a variety of NGOs.

As a result, the centrifugal pressures within the united front of the MNU increased dramatically, simply for organizational reasons. It became much harder to view the MNU as the primary locus of black political allegiance, especially because there were so many divergent directions within it. And as the dictatorship finally passed into the historical dustbin, anti-racist mobilization lost some of its urgency, as did other forms of democratic activism.

Maria Ercilia do Nascimento's account of the MNU's decline focuses on ideological conflicts within the group. She highlights three main centrifugal dynamics: differentiation by racial status;[42] racial particularism versus broader-based anti-capitalism;[43] and divisions over the priorities of black movement politics itself (Nascimento 1989; Andrews 1991; Hanchard 1994).[44]

But do these issues indicate a failure of the MNU to develop as a viable black political organization or party? Such a view misses the extent to which the Brazilian black movement did in fact "take off" as the dictatorship came to an end and the Third Republic was born. The activities of the MNU and its constituent groups gave rise to ongoing efforts at black mobilization, activities that have sustained a wide variety of political and cultural engagement over two decades. These projects have registered some significant effects on state institutions and political parties. For example, anti-racist provisions were adopted in the 1988 constitution and after (Guimarães 1998), a few black candidates were elected to major political offices (notably to the federal senate and mayorship of São Paulo),[45] and black caucuses were set up in major political parties (notably in the *Partido de Trabalhadores*, the Workers' Party). Perhaps most significant, the black political upsurge represented by the MNU advanced the process of racial *conscientização* that continues today on a relatively widespread basis.

To be sure, the MNU and its adherent groups and supporters were not able to mount a major challenge to the powerful ideology of racial democracy, although they certainly denounced it more effectively than ever before. They did not galvanize a mass movement equivalent to the civil rights/black power upsurge in the United States or the ANC in South Africa. Yet as I have tried to show, these movements too achieved only partial successes, bringing about reforms and advancing the cause of racial justice, but also revealing the continuity, tenacity, and resilience of white supremacy.

Racial equality has *not* made appreciable advances in Brazil. Once more, Brazilian racial dynamics are not what they seem. In defiance of the common impression that Brazil is so much more "integrated" than the United States, that in contrast to the United States problems of inequality are "really about class, not race," recent quantitative research has documented that racial segregation is not only substantial but actually on the increase in Brazil (again, in contrast to the United States), and that racial inequality is actually considerably more acute in Brazil than in the United States (Telles 1992; Telles 1994; Andrews 1992).

APPLYING RACIAL FORMATION THEORY IN BRAZIL

Much has been made of the continuity of racial inequality and racist cultural attitudes in Brazil, and of the inability of any organized black movement permanently and comprehensively to occupy the national political stage in debates over race (Hasenbalg 1992). Certainly there is some truth to these pessimistic assessments: no coordinated national movement has come into being since the decline of the MNU.

There is a persistent tendency to attribute the supposed absence of race from the political sphere not only to the influence of the ideology of racial democracy, but to the absence of formal (that is, legal) state-enforced segregation. Anthony W. Marx is the most recent social scientist to claim that the relative absence of black movement activity in Brazil results from the lack of "explicit rules of segregation and categories of exclusion." According to Marx, by avoiding what he calls "race-making" the Brazilian state has sharply constrained "racial identity formation and potential conflict" (Marx 1998, 262). This familiar analysis is valuable in many respects, but seems to me to rely too heavily on a state-centered vision of racial politics.[46] While explaining quite effectively what the ideology of racial democracy (Marx too calls it a "myth": see 1998, 164–177) accomplishes for racial rule, such analyses have little to say about how it operates among the racially ruled, the subaltern. If it is a myth, why are they "fooled" by it? If it is not a myth, how does racial democracy "deliver" for Afro-Brazilians in civil society, in an everyday life characterized by substantial inequality and anti-black prejudice?

In my view it is impossible to avoid "race-making," aka racial formation, in a racialized society. In my own work too I have emphasized the centrality of the state, and I have struggled to see racial formation processes as a complex and uneven interaction between state and civil society. However, to analyze race in Brazil—and more generally as well—we need an adequate theoretical toolbox: only concepts of race-making that afford to human subjects their awareness and agency can hope to undertake the task.

In this chapter I have used the term racial *sensibility* to denote the vital political dimensions of this popular agency. I emphasize that this attention to the micro-level in no way diminishes the importance of "normal" politics; it simply seeks to augment it and complement it by recognizing the centrality, in both state and civil society, of what is sometimes called "identity politics," what I have associated in this work with the concept of subalternity. By invoking this (post-) Gramscian term and focusing on the racial sensibility of the Brazilian *povo* I hope to suggest why racial formation is still a very live issue in Brazil today, and why the anti-racist movement has not been defeated or contained, even if it cannot bestride the political stage. I make use of of such theorists as W. E. B. Du Bois and Frantz Fanon as well as Gramsci, all in the effort to highlight how contentious and contradictory racial sensibility is.

There is a good deal of evidence that an anti-racist sensibility persists and is even increasing in Brazil today: there has been a great proliferation of anti-racist and black consciousness groups and organizations throughout the country.[47] At the level of state racial policy too there are many new developments, prompted in some measure by black activism, and even by the presidency of Fernando Henrique Cardoso, an internationally known sociologist, former student of Florestan Fernandes, and recognized expert on racial matters in Brazil. Cardoso's extensive writings and public statements on themes of racial equality and racial justice far outshadow those of his predecessors (Cardoso 1996). Affirmative action policies are being implemented, although so far only very partially and not without significant debate (Guimarães 1999; Kachani 1996).

Yet in many respects the issues raised by the worldwide racial break in its Brazilian manifestations remain unresolved. It is obvious that Brazilian racism will continue to be challenged, yet as numerous scholars have suggested, such a project will require new strategies (Hanchard 1994; Burdick 1998; Winant 1994a; Twine 1997; Guimarães 1999; Santos 1993). The growth of organized and explicitly political groups—of integrationist and egalitarian orientation for the most part—will undoubtedly continue. Several political parties, notably the PT (Workers Party), have given new attention to racial matters and even formed black caucuses, a development that would have been anathematized just a few years earlier (Coordenação Nacional de Entidades Negras/PT 1998; Gomes dos Santos 1992).

Groups that Hanchard (1994) has described as "culturalist" will also remain significant: these overlap not only with political organizations but also with educational, and "identitarian" (in the sense of "self-help" or "support" groups: for women,[48] youth, residents of particular communities, etc.). Recent work by Burdick reclaims (and complexifies) religious terrain as a site for Afro-Brazilian anti-racist mobilization (Burdick 1998; see also Bastide 1978 [1960]; Brandão 1980). State agencies at various levels of the federal system, universities with their research institutes and student activisms, and professional organizations of various types all have real ties to the projects of anti-racism and Afro-Brazilian social and community development.

Such an inventory is necessarily partial; what it begins to describe is not so much a movement as what Gramsci would call a "hegemonic bloc" (or in this case, to be more accurate, a "counter-hegemonic bloc"). While providing vital foci to such a bloc, no array of collective entities, however complete, could fully contain the racial formation project that Afro-Brazilians are undertaking as the new millennium commences. What must be added is the element of critical race consciousness, what I have here called racial sensibility. This is heterodox, not regularly available for organization, and subject to vibrant contrarieties: for it both expresses the experiences and needs arising from the variegated experience of Afro-Brazilian life, and is often infused with the commonsense racial ideology of mainstream Brazilian culture, which still tends to minimize racial differences and downplay racism. It is in these struggles, in these racial dualisms and heterodoxies as well as in the efforts of more traditional movement organizations, that Brazilian racial formation is taking place.

THE THIRD REPUBLIC

The movement's central efforts during the whole period after World War II—after the fall of Vargas, after the resumption of the Second Republic, through the long military dictatorship, and up to the present as well—have been directed at challenging the ideology of racial democracy, the Freyrian account that racism does not exist in Brazil, as a consequence of the country's profoundly miscegenated heritage and development. The Freyrian position is of course more than a theory; it is itself a *praxis*. It is a national racial formation project in its own right, a formidable one, that the black movement and its allies have had difficulty countering.

In many ways the movement's task, and its theory's task as well, is not to debunk the idea of racial democracy, but to reinvent it, to rearticulate it. It is to work out the answers—in *praxis*, once more, in theory combined with action—to these questions: What would a racially inclusive and egalitarian society look like in Brazil? In what concepts and practices would racial justice consist? How could an alternative vision of racial democracy—one untainted by the conservative apologetics and racial laissez-faire of Freyre—be lived out or worked toward? To these questions answers must be posed not only at the *macro-level* of collective action aimed at transforming state policies and social structures. Significant as those concerns are, they do not penetrate to the *micro-level* of what has been called identity politics, experiential politics. The racial formation approach suggests that only in the interaction and linkage of these two dimensions of race can racial democracy be reinvented and radicalized.

I have already noted that most of the anti-racist movement activity occurring since 1945 originated among middle-class blacks (Hanchard 1994; Andrews 1991). Both the emergence of a subaltern or insurgent elite in Brazilian racial politics and the problem of mobilizing potential movement constituencies among the *povo* or masses are strikingly similar to patterns emerging in world-wide anti-colonial politics during the post–World War II period. In Brazil as elsewhere, black leaders and anti-racists have tended to emerge from more privileged strata, from the middle classes. Certainly there are important exceptions—leaders who arose from the urban *favelas* and rural *sertoes*. But political success often involves education, access to international circuits of ideas and funding, and familiarity with social movement models developed elsewhere. In Brazil too the subalternity dynamic applies. Beyond all these Brazilian particularities regarding miscegenation, hybridity, and putative racial democracy, the question of mass mobilization among the subaltern is also a classic Fanonian problem: that of overcoming the introjection of the dominant white/colonial values, of recognizing the "fact of blackness" (Winant 1994d). I return to Fanon in a moment.

As some of the key theorists of subaltern studies have demonstrated (Chakrabarty 1988; Chatterjee 1988), mass involvement in radical politics occurs only rarely, and is usually related to desperate experiences: the sense that there is not much left to lose. Failing that, anti-colonial and anti-racist movements have generally lacked large-scale mass participation. Their organization successes have generally involved the usual suspects: students, those with some history of militancy, unionists, and so on. Even in the U.S. South, as Robin D. G. Kelley argues, much black mobilization took the form of acting out the hidden transcripts of the subaltern (Kelley 1994; see also Piven and Cloward 1977; Dittmer 1995).[49]

"Brazil is different." Of course, but not *that* different. If any single factor distinguishes its racial conditions from those of the other cases examined in this book, it is surely the ideology of racial democracy. But as will be seen below, "ordinary" Afro-Brazilians are acting out their hidden transcripts in opposition to this ideology as well.

In order to explain racial formation processes in the Third Republic, I wish to emphasize two key points. First, *movements have indirect influence*. This is true of both the aggregate experience of domestic anti-racism in Brazil, and of the increasing influence of global racial movements on Brazil. Second, not just elites, but the masses too, "ordinary people," engage in the production of racial meanings and actions: *everybody has a racial praxis*. This is likely to be contradictory, almost inevitably so, but it is a form of agency; it has sociopolitical consequences; it is something theorists cannot ignore.

The Indirect Influence of Movements

If the black consciousness movement of the MNU failed to ignite a massive political upsurge grounded in the Brazilian *povo*, did it fail utterly and absolutely?

Clearly not. I have already argued that the MNU and its component organizations both expressed and stimulated a growing black consciousness orientation, particularly in the 1980s when the Third Republic was being constructed. There were many indications of growing racial awareness at the official level: the creation of government agencies such as the *Fundação Cultural Palmares* at the national level, the *Conselho de Participação e Desinvolvimento da Comunidade Negra* in São Paulo and the *Secretaria pela Promoção e Defesa Afro-Brasileiro* in Rio, the passage of a series of laws against *discriminação ou preconceito de raça, por religião, etnia, ou procedencia nacional* ("discrimination or prejudice based upon race, religion, ethnicity, or national origin"),[50] and the formation of black caucuses in several political parties. Increased attention to racial matters in the popular media—notably in *telenovelas* (the Brazilian passion), newspaper and magazine articles, and popular music—also seems to be a movement legacy.[51]

Another crucial setting of indirect movement influence is that of religious institutions. I have been greatly impressed by Burdick's (1998) account of growing racial awareness in the Catholic and pentecostal churches. Although I would not presume to evaluate his ethnographic data, it is notable that the evidence he cites: of the burgeoning cult of the slave martyr Anastácia, of the "inculturated" mass,[52] and particularly of the racial theodicy woven into urban pentecostalism, all reflects the influence of black consciousness movements, both from within Brazil and from abroad.[53]

Mass Racial Praxis

That the Brazilian *povo* is racialized, that the subaltern must function *dia-a-dia* in a hierarchized racial system, is not news. Nor is it surprising that "ordinary people" have absorbed the dominant Brazilian ideology of racial democracy. Yet a significant literature of recent (Third Republic) vintage, both of the movement *testimonio* genre (Ivanir dos Santos 1999; Thereza Santos 1999), and in the more familiar form of ethnographic research, suggests that the experience of racial ambivalence and contradiction is spreading among subaltern blacks (Sheriff 1997). A great deal of the ambivalence that has been documented is that of black women (Burdick 1998; Goldstein 1999). But as Ivanir dos Santos, the son of a *favela* prostitute, demonstrates, men are not immune from racial ambivalence either (see also Burdick 1998, 135). It centers on the intersection of racial and sexual identity, which in itself is also nothing new: this theme harks back not only to Freyre but to abolition-era discourse about whitening.[54]

What *is* new is the critical recognition among "ordinary people," among the *povo*, of the existence of racism itself. Consciousness about the operation of racism at the micro-level in black people's (and notably black women's) desire *de se branquear* ("to whiten themselves") is far more manifest than in the past. Until recently these impulses were viewed as normal and natural; they still are to a large extent. But there is increasing evidence that on the micro-level, the experiential level, a kind of proto-black consciousness is emerging about these issues: a "black is beautiful" tendency in embryo, let us call it. The Afro-Brazilian women whom these anthropologists have observed are by no means free of the old system of stereotypes: about the liabilities of *pele escura* (dark skin), *cabelo crespo* (nappy hair), *nariz chato* ("annoying," in other words flat, nose), and the like. Yet they also have developed a critical awareness of the racism those views internalize.

In Burdick's research (1998) much of this new consciousness comes from religious sources: not the New World African religions of *Candomblé* and *Umbanda,* but from pentecostalism and renovationist currents in Catholicism; he offers pages of *testimonios* of black *cariocas*—largely but not entirely women—affirming the greater self-respect and satisfaction they now feel with their racial identity as a result of becoming a *crente* (believer). Although Burdick stresses the explicit rejection by most of his black *crentes* and Anastácia devotees of any political interest in Brazilian racial dynamics (and the reciprocal mistrust of Christianity on the part of some black movement militants), the thrust of his research documents the upsurge of religiously based racial awareness under the Third Republic:

> Has pentecostal "everyday" black ethnicity ever become translated into "non-everyday" politicized ethnicity? . . . The short answer to this question is "yes." We identified a surprising number of efforts on the part of black pentecostals to make the defense of black ethnic identity and the fight against racism ongoing project of their churches. (145)

Sheriff's (1997) research documents a similar amplification of racial attitudes among blacks in a Rio favela. As with Burdick's findings, many respondents repeat the old shibboleths of Brazilian racial democracy, but at numerous moments they express the wish for real equality, true racial democracy.

In both studies some respondents claim to have had contact with black movement activists. Many of those interviewed reject any type of political or collective response to Brazilian racism, although a few are more positive about movement activities. Still, even when rejecting political action, many blacks interviewed or observed by these researchers indicate an understanding of the pervasiveness of racial hierarchy.[55] They are often divided between their deeply inculcated beliefs in and quotidian participation in whitening efforts on the one hand, and their incipient critique of the self-denigration of this set of beliefs on the other.

Thus the ordinary Afro-Brazilian of low means—the worker, the *favelado/a,*

the *empregada, criada,* or *babá*[56]—finds herself caught between two racial strategies in her efforts to improve her life. The first alternative is the traditional
whitening strategy. This does not appear to be about racism at all. It offers a
familiar everyday routine: hair-straightening, the search for a partner who is
clarinho ("light-skinned"), or perhaps a *coroa* (an older, well-off, and usually
white man who will take her as a mistress; see Goldstein 1999). It may involve
a wholesale denial of the importance of racial identity in one's life-world
(Twine 1997), which implies a Fanonian intrapsychic violence and repression
(see below).

The second alternative very likely has religious rather than overtly political
roots, at least for the majority of blacks. It does involve a measure of black consciousness, however. Here the search is for self-acceptance as a *preta* or *negra,*
probably because "that's the way God made me," but just possibly because only
by "assumindo a nossa côr" ("accepting our color") can there be any hope of
moving toward racial equality.[57]

These dynamics bring to the fore both Fanon's and Du Bois' insights.
Fanon's passionate call to colonized blacks to dispense with their rulers' racial
logic, to confront and overcome their self-hatred, was made in the service of
national liberation, of revolution. But even looked at more narrowly, from the
standpoint of cultural analysis or within the radical black psychoanalysis that
was Fanon's particular vantage-point, his demand that blacks cease to introject
the racial values and norms of their oppressors may be seen as a direct challenge to the ideology of racial democracy, a repudiation of the political psychology of Freyre.[58]

Du Bois' concept of racial dualism captures the chronic but usually low-
intensity crisis in which Brazilian racial politics operates today. A crisis, as Gramsci famously noted, is a situation in which "the old is dying but the new cannot
be born." Here the old synthesis, the ideology of racial democracy, has come
under very serious challenge yet still retains a substantial resilience. I have
argued that Brazilian processes of racial formation are more intertwined with
global ones today than ever before. Perhaps it is worthwhile, then, to analogize
the double consciousness Du Bois (1989 [1903]) detected in the United States
a century ago to that which now operates in Brazil. At the turn of the twentieth century the dominant racial ideology in the United States was the quietism
of Booker T. Washington. The state was disinclined to enforce the egalitarian
provisions of the U.S. Constitution, as the contemporary Brazilian state is now
unwilling to enforce its new anti-discrimination laws.[59] And considerable deference and forbearance on the part of blacks was demanded as the price to be
paid for even grudging toleration in subordinate status, a situation similar to
present-day racial conditions in Brazil. In the United States at that time, only
a rudimentary anti-racist movement could operate; furthermore, the recognition of black solidarity and pride was largely religiously grounded. Both these

conditions now apply, mutatis mutandis, in Brazil. Yet from this century-old U.S. situation slowly arose a significant challenge to racial inequality, built on past experiences, of both emancipation and dictatorship. This situation of racial dualism in the turn-of-the-twentieth-century United States may well resemble that of present-day Brazilian racial formation processes.[60]

Fanon Versus Freyre

Perhaps even more than in the northern societies such as the United States, where the state attempted to enforce the white-black distinction (however ineffectually), perhaps even more than in the colonial societies that Fanon most centrally addresses, where the white-black distinction was articulated in national terms (however unsuccessfully), in Brazil there was and is the most extensive development of *racial ambivalence*. This ambivalence lurks as a subversive racial presence: within the body politic, within everybody, and indeed within every body. Its presence, its partial and often denied awareness of race, can be repressed and negated, incorporated and celebrated, or—as is very often the case—simultaneously romanticized and detested. But at the level of politics the articulation of this universalized and half-hidden racial awareness, it is feared, would unleash widespread disorder and imperil progress, thus challenging the two basic ideological pillars of the nation.

Contrast this analysis—imported from "without," from the globalized and historicized racial conflict that provides Fanon's logic—to the analysis of Freyre, who works from "within" and seeks fervently to preserve the particularities of Brazilian racial logic. Seen in this light Freyre seems a "loyal" twin brother to the "rebellious" Fanon. For Freyre too recognized the omnipresence of an ambivalent racial "otherness," but rationalized and thereby repressed it as the "new man of the tropics," a new racial synthesis, what Hanchard would call "racial exceptionalism" (Hanchard 1994). But whereas Freyre's approach demanded the repression of racial difference in the service of *ordem e progresso,* Fanon is willing to confront the ambivalence of "otherness," and to disrupt the society in order to achieve justice.

Drawing on Fanon's work, we can see in the struggles of Afro-Brazilians not only an effort to gain admission, to be recognized as individuals with equal rights, but also an effort to partake in the general social movement to create democracy from below, to achieve not only formal representation but participation. To go beyond the present understandings both academic and practical, to advance in a deeper way toward racial justice in Brazil, would involve calling into question not only the ambivalences of black identity, but also those of white identity.[61] It is notable how little the developing field of whiteness studies (or of critical race studies for that matter) has as yet been applied to the Brazilian situation.

From this perspective our understanding of Brazilian racial politics could take a very different shape. Rather than appearing at long last among the previously quiescent black masses, and thus fulfilling what more and more seems an elusive, almost utopian hope, mobilization might appear as a series of options for identification, in which blacks could recognize themselves—at least partially—in various organizational and ideological forms. Whites too—at least some whites—could be expected to make some new recognitions around hybridity. The 1994 acknowledgment by President Fernando Henrique Cardoso that he too has *um pé na cozinha* ("a foot in the kitchen," that is, some black blood),[62] can be treated not as an admission of white hybridity, but as an invitation to whites to contemplate alternatives to the ideology of racial democracy. This challenge to racial inequality—admittedly overly optimistic for now, but not necessarily forever—could be transformed into a challenge to the general inequality which in Brazil is so extreme. It could point to the redistribution of resources so long overdue in a country where, after all, half the population is arguably non-white. It is perhaps ironic that the former socialist and long-time student of race Cardoso now coquettishly invites a return to his old radicalism by admitting he is black.[63]

Racial Dualism

The public articulation and exploration of racial dualism would itself be a major advance. Many black people undoubtedly still succeed in denying the significance of their racial identity. They are "avoiders," as Twine (1997) documents at length. Their ability not only to deny, but to *avoid* their own racial identity is aided by the tremendous depth of the ideology of racial democracy. What good is an ideology, after all, if it cannot effectively identify its adherent's identity, if it cannot (in Althusser's terminology) "interpellate" its bearer (Althusser 1971, 170–177)?

A smaller number of Afro-Brazilians manage to arrive at a position of black militance—perhaps via a "nationalist" or pan-Africanist politics like *quilombismo*, perhaps via some variety of communism or socialism that maintains an active critique of racism. As noted, these are likely to be relatively privileged blacks, whose education or social status perhaps has led them to a more explicitly politicized identity. These are the insurgent counter-elite, to evoke subalternity theory's designation. They have a vital role to play, both in movement-building and because the influence of movements may extend far beyond the numbers movement groups actually are able to organize. But still and all, insurgent counter-elites are tremendously subject to the pitfalls of vanguardism, as occurred in the MNU, for example.

If most Afro-Brazilians are not black militants, most are not avoiders either.[64] They are caught in the middle. Upholding the ideology of racial democracy, they must still be on their guard against the racial slights so common in Brazilian society: being followed in a store, habitually deferring to whites, being expected to laugh at jokes with denigrating racial content.[65] Furthermore, the continuity of *preconceito de marca* ("skin-color prejudice") imposes the necessity of "rating" people by appearance: dark or light, *preto* or *mestiço*, straight hair or "brillo"? Thus black identity is not only burdensome in Brazil, but the hierarchization of color, the color continuum (Harris 1964) undermines Afro-Brazilian solidarity to a greater extent than it does in the United States or other societies with relatively clear-cut color-lines.[66]

The experiences and orientations of these Afro-Brazilians who are "caught in the middle" best illustrate the applicability of the concept of racial dualism to Brazil. To be sure, the situation of double consciousness may persist for a long time: the discomfort it implies, and the tacit rewards one is offered for going along with it may be preferable to the pain involved in confronting it.[67] Yet, as I have noted, the evidence indicates that the rearticulation of the meaning of race is in fact underway at the micro-level, the experiential level, as well as making some progress in the political system. To be sure, this process is in an uncertain and preliminary stage, with no clear outcome yet visible. The very fact that it is mediated by sexuality and religion, rather than by political movements (at least in a direct sense) indicates the continuing salience of the racial democracy ideology, which in its dominant Freyrian form also emphasized these themes. It is inevitably painful to acknowledge the incompleteness, the fissuring, involved in dualistic racial identity. It hurts to own up to the existence of what Du Bois famously called "two souls, two thoughts, two unreconciled strivings; two warring ideals in one dark body" (Du Bois 1989 [1903], 5). But for Afro-Brazilians to be able to mobilize, both in respect to the singularities of racially framed experiences, and simultaneously around the commonalities of inequality and deprivation they experience as citizens of Brazil, a deeper recognition of the depth of racial ambivalence and the conflicted nature of Brazilian racial identities will be essential.

Ten

EUROPE: THE PHANTOM MENACE

FROM SEPTEMBER 1996 to March 1997, the French parliament debated a bill that would have required ordinary French citizens to report the movements of foreign nationals into or out of their homes. The bill contained a seemingly small modification of existing visa regulations, but its potential effects were large: it threatened to turn the citizenry into extensions of the national immigration control apparatus, violating principles of civil liberties. To some opponents, the proposed measure was redolent of policies employed in Nazi-occupied France to root out and deport Jews. To others, it was a transparent ploy of conservative Premier Alain Juppé to co-opt the issue of immigration from the fascist National Front (NF), notably at a time when domestic unemployment was dangerously high—about 13 percent (Simons 1997).

Report all foreigners? What is racist about that? If I were to bring a group of my North American students to France, perhaps on an educational tour, would the law have required our hosts to report us?

Well, no, because we are citizens of a northern, industrial country. While Japanese, North Americans, and citizens of the EU countries would not have been affected (or rather, while those hosting them would not have been), French hotel-keepers, and ordinary French householders who opened their homes to visitors from the world's South, broadly speaking, would have been required under the proposed law to file regular and official reports on the movements of their foreign guests.

Perhaps that *is* racist then. After all, those the law favored were largely white, weren't they, and those it would have more closely controlled were largely black and Arab.

Well, yes *and* no. A fairly large proportion of French citizens are themselves black and Arab. Some former French colonies, such as the Caribbean islands of Guadeloupe and Martinique, are themselves *departements* of France, whose residents are as formally French as Bretonnais (not that the Bretons don't retain a certain anti-Parisian nationalism), Savoyards, or Provençals. But certainly, it is the large cohorts of Maghrebines and sub-Saharan Africans, as well as Palestinians, Iraqis, Lebanese—the list goes on and on, and implicitly links those already in the country with those who merely aspire to immigrate—who alarmed the government.

Nor was the proposed measure unchallenged. Diverse groups of opponents emerged, including associations led by prominent French artists and academics, others composed of lawyers and judges, and so on. Members of several groups demanded to be arrested for violating the law, and other forms of civil disobedience also got underway.

In this relatively minor French controversy, selected from a vast number of parallel incidents,[1] we can begin to discern many of the troubling racial issues the Western European nations face as the region moves toward greater integration and self-definition. Why is the immigration and presence of certain, but not all, foreigners an issue in France, as it is in many other northern countries? How have citizenship policies (and restrictions on citizenship) developed in these countries, and how are they affected by regional integration? How has the European (not just French) history of imperial rule in North and Central Africa, as well as the Middle East, and in Asia and Latin America, influenced Europe's present racial demography? It what ways has it drawn into the EU countries many of whose origins may be traced back to these regions? In what ways has it fomented the current "native"—French, Dutch, British, even Italian and German—hostility to these racialized minorities? How has the regional economy been affected by immigration? To what extent has the postwar dependence of various European nations on low-waged immigrant labor—the *gastarbeiter* ("guest worker") programs of the 1950s and 1960s, for example—come into conflict with these countries' continuing nationalist commitments? To what extent is the failure to integrate immigrants, the reluctance (at best) to facilitate a racially pluralist political culture, merely symptomatic of European recalcitrance in the face of regional integration tout court?

This is an enormous list of questions. And there are more yet.

The resurgence of the problematic of race in Western Europe is certainly a great signifier. But of what? Of the range and depth of political conflicts to come? Of the ironic termination of half a millennium of imperial adventure? Of the desolate and genocidal internal breakdown in the mid-twentieth century? Of a well-advanced but still difficult pluralization at the twentieth century's end? Of the reappearance of fascism which, like some vampire, has escaped its postwar coffin to prowl Europe again? Of the "end of the nation-state" in the era of globalization?

There are even greater depths in this set of problems: consider the political implications of the multiracialization of Europe. Does the racially inflected fin-de-siècle pattern of social stratification signal the exhaustion of the social democratic vision, the Marshallian concept of social citizenship (Marshall 1964; Bulmer and Rees 1996), in the face of demands for inclusion judged to be unmanageable? How about the matter of human rights? The EU countries have in general presented themselves as supporters of human rights principles: they have founded numerous commissions for refugee rights, for example, and have maintained liberal political asylum policies, at least until recently.[2] Geography and history have placed Europe in the forefront of these issues: plagued by ongoing atrocities in the Balkans, challenged by the long-term consequences of the demise of the Soviet Union and German reunification, and still conscious of the horrors enacted on their soil by the Nazis (and their local collaborators), Europeans have had little choice but to uphold these standards. Until now, that is. Does the deepening of racial division in Western Europe, accompanied by the rise of right-wing (indeed neo-fascist) agitation against immigrants, signal an increasing obsolescence of European human rights commitments?

Consider too the problematization of the nation-state. Created in large measure by practices of conquest/exclusion and imperial expansionism begun in Europe half a millennium ago (see Chapter Three, above), the nation-state is perceived as quite threatened today. The permanent settlement of millions of relative newcomers—both citizens and denizens (Hammar 1990) of non-European origin—greatly deepens perceptions of the nation-state's fragility, especially on the political right. But from other positions too, from those located at the center of the political spectrum, and even from some found on the left, there is anxiety and mistrust about immigration and citizenship issues.

That is the "official" political crisis, the crisis of the state, of parties, and of administrative and legislative institutions of all types (among them the French National Assembly, as noted above). But there is also a crisis of European civil society. Faced with widespread racial heterogeneity—the seeming permanence of Muslim enclaves, if not "ghettos," the presence of substantial numbers of "newcomers,"[3] the upsurge of multiculturalism—many Europeans will acknowledge, and far more perhaps experience unconsciously, a certain everyday confusion, a quotidian incapacity to make pragmatic sense out of the plethora of "others" now on the scene. This cultural puzzlement is far from universal. But to the extent that it exists it is obviously fertile ground for nativist mobilization, some of which has been quite successful.[4]

What part does race play in all this? Debates on immigration and citizenship, both academic and political, are generally cautious about invoking the "R" word. Preferred locutions tend to rely on the terminology of nationality and ethnicity/culture; where necessary to signify themes of stratification and inequality, class language may be invoked. In many European settings, as in Brazil, to focus attention on race is to risk being labeled "racist."[5]

All this is entirely to be expected in a Europe wrestling with the significance of national identity in an intense and unprecedented way, a Europe habituated over centuries to thinking of itself as the headquarters of enlightenment, a Europe accustomed to socialism—at least as an established opposition—and thus preoccupied as well with themes of class. Yet as this chapter's opening example illustrates, a racial subtext is indeed present in the prolonged reorganization of European (and especially EU) identities and politics. The 1997 French National Assembly debate demonstrated that French (and more generally, European) concerns were not so much about the formulation of *comprehensive policies* of inclusion or exclusion, but rather about who the *specific subjects* of inclusion or exclusion should be. Not all outsiders preoccupy the European "native" or "nativist." Should we be surprised that it is those from the world's South—post-colonials, blacks, Muslims[6]—who occasion these anxieties?

Of course, many equivalent examples or racialized misgivings could be cited: incidents and instances of German, Italian, English, or Dutch provenance have been documented and analyzed in great number.[7] What is important here is not the dawn of racial awareness in Western Europe, where the application of racial categories to human identities around the world may be said to have originated (or at least to have been elaborately theorized for the first time), and where racial classification has been practiced in various forms for half a millennium. No, what is notable is the *internalization* of these differences *within* Europe, the collapse of the previous distinctions of "Europe and its others," of "mother-countries" and colonial "children," of "world-historical" peoples and "historyless" peoples, of "settlers" and "wogs." This is the transformed element in post-colonial Europe, in the contemporary EU: this is what has problematized race anew.

Of course a racially heterogeneous Europe is not unprecedented. Neither ancient Europe, medieval Europe, nor imperial Europe were ever exclusively white.[8] But the contemporary volume of post-colonial immigrants, denizens, and citizens has combined with the claims of these "others" to social rights of various kinds, and has catalyzed as well the updated reaction to this pluralization and these claims, in the form of neo-fascism. These factors, working together, have ushered into Western Europe a new type of racial dynamics, a new heterogeneity, yes, but also a *new racism*. In this situation rights are in contention: rights of citizenship, to be sure, but also rights of social citizenship, with attendant claims on the welfare state. Such rights may be termed *egalitarian*. Then there are "cultural rights," which bring into play questions of religion, language, tradition, diasporic/divided loyalties, and various degrees of pluralism, hybridization, or even exclusion and separatism. Such rights may be termed *differential*.[9]

This combination of quantitative and qualitative sociopolitical transformations is what has racialized contemporary Europe. It is this shift, very much a product of the post–World War II break, that I propose to highlight here.

This chapter considers the evolution of contemporary European racial dynamics, focusing on the post–World War II period. In order to set the stage properly, I begin with an overview of *the waning of empire*, a backward glance at the uneven breakdown of racial dominion during the late imperial period. Imperial rule was racial rule, although patterns of power of course varied tremendously. Such questions as how much an empire relied upon colonial settlement, how much it employed traditional (pre-colonial) structures of power, how much economic mobility it would tolerate among subject peoples, and indeed how willing it was to grant those colonial subjects rights at all (not only in the colonies, but also in the metropoles), were all infused with racial meaning. These issues would recur in the post-colonial epoch, echoing the old established strains of the national and Eurocentric racial music in a strangely familiar, yet also dissonant and even shocking, way.

After that overture, the chapter arrives at *postwar patterns of immigration*. Centuries of colonial deployment of millions of settlers (of all classes) throughout far-flung dominions, combined with the socialization of millions of colonial subjects to be "junior partners" (or collaborators) in colonial rule, could hardly fail to have important consequences once the project of imperial dismantlement—or "national liberation"—had begun to advance in the years after World War II. From this complex dynamic came the return of settlers—*pieds noirs*, let us call them, but not only French; there were British, Dutch, and Portuguese returnees as well. Here in a section on *the return of settlers and the immigration of post-colonials* to the mother-countries and to Europe more generally, I discuss the aftermath of decolonization as a problematic of repatriation.

The most pressing issue in postwar Europe was of course not decolonization but the problem of reconstruction: millions had died all across Europe and the Continent lay in ruins. Just to clear the rubble and rebuild, much less to restart peacetime economic activity, would require enormous quantities of labor. So the resettlement of displaced persons, the return of settlers, and the recruitment of immigrant colonials all coincided to a significant degree with the unprecedented labor demand of the first postwar, "boom" decades. The next section of this chapter addresses this *problem of labor demand*, focusing on postwar patterns of immigration to what would be the three central EU countries, the United Kingdom, France, and Germany.

Then, in the early 1970s, came the "morning after," the end of the party. Recession and the oil crisis meant that the gates of immigration would tighten if not close; the entryway had already been narrowing for some time. Over the 1970s restrictive measures were enacted everywhere; over the 1980s and 1990s, as movement toward the unification of Europe gathered steam, a regime of exclusion largely removed the early postwar welcome mat. Yet barring the door was an illusion by then: the pluralization of Western Europe had become a fact on the ground.

So in the next section I address the question of *citizenship and national identity*. Today the (relatively) new heterogeneity of the EU population confronts the still-strong imperative to maintain the political, cultural, and economic unity of the "nation" against the perceived onslaught of "others." All this is occurring in parallel with the well-advanced initiative of regional integration under the mantle of the European Union. Integration is something of an economic imperative, but it is also anti-national. It erodes national identities and boundaries, and demands a higher level of regional policy coordination, particularly in respect to immigration and citizenship.

Conflicts over the *integration* of Europe elide with anxiety and confusion about the *integrity* of Europe. Inexorably, these problems express themselves in battles not only about regional identity—although that remains a crucial issue—but rather in struggles over national identity, which is itself a confluence of cultural, political, and economic themes. European nationalism today is necessarily defensive and reactionary: its hostility to the presence of racialized "others" is fueled above all by *ressentiment*, but also evinces the political opportunism that an atmosphere of high unemployment can be expected to facilitate. At present nationalists are split between intransigent, far right/neo-fascist parties and sects, and more sophisticated advocates of what Taguieff (2001 [1988]) has called "racial differentialism." A good deal of literature has addressed both currents, pointing out the substantial overlaps and also the contradictions between these tendencies. These are themes I examine in the next section, where I first look at *neo-fascism*, then at the so-called *new racism*, and then at the influence these pernicious tendencies have had on mainstream politics—their achievement of *convergence on the European right*. My principal aim here is not to summarize or critique the large bodies of work that already exist on these subjects, but to consider the political challenges posed by the now-permanent racial heterogeneity of the European Union, both to the forces of racial reaction and to anti-racist movements.

Thus we arrive at the conflict-ridden present: Western Europe has become restrictive but is already pluralized; nationalism is on the rise but so is regionalism; and much of the pressure these unresolved tensions generate is vented against the ethnocultural minorities, the "others." They are inexorably racialized. They are not-yet-Europeans, who may have achieved some measure of permanence, who are sometimes citizens but more often denizens, but who lack full acceptance, full political and social rights. They are "outside a boundary" in millennial Europe. And they are differentiated from within as well as from without: by their multiple communities, by conflicts over gender, religion, assimilation, and numerous other issues.

Amidst all this complexity, racially identified minorities continue to find themselves under attack. Sometimes physical, permanently political, and often chillingly immediate and personal, attack takes many forms, of which the chief variants are discrimination and exclusion. Under such circumstances, social movement activity is inevitable, indeed vital. Thus in the next section of this chapter I consider *dilemmas of anti-racist mobilization* in Europe. As restrictive and exclusionary pressures grew in the EU countries, movements of various types developed to oppose these tendencies and to defend racialized minority communities. The groundwork for these efforts had been laid earlier, of course: often in anti-colonial politics, as well as through organizations of ethnic/disaporic provenance and solidarity. The resurgence of neo-fascism—a phenomenon that had never been completely rooted out—also sparked a great deal of movement-building and solidarity-oriented activity. At present, a leading European NGO that seeks to coordinate anti-racist and human rights groups lists more than 1,500 organizations that define themselves as specializing in anti-racist organization and education Europe-wide (United for Intercultural Action 2000).

Yet it is difficult to establish the parameters of anti-racist activity, in part because the meaning of race itself is undergoing such tumultuous change in the post–World War II period, in the aftermath of the break. Explicitly anti-racist activity is only part of the story. How about social service provision to racialized minorities, or political agitation for better housing or health care? How about community development, where the community might be Surinamese, Moroccan, or Dominican? How about feminist mobilization, for example, against putatively traditional male "prerogatives" that may include violence, child abuse, or female genital mutilation? My argument here is that since the racial dimension of European institutions and identities is so profound, so fundamental to the history and social structure of Europe, efforts to achieve a broader equality and a more full-fledged democracy that goes "all the way down," so to speak, of necessity must incorporate a significant anti-racist component. In many ways, human rights-oriented, gender-conscious, anti-fascist, and pro-democracy mobilization is itself profoundly anti-racist.

The chapter concludes with some potentially subversive, and possibly utopian, thoughts on the *emancipatory possibilities of European racial formation.*

THE WANING OF EMPIRE

As I have already argued in Part I, the devolution of imperial rule was a protracted process, a series of events that went on for centuries. In this chapter the central concern is the legacy of imperial rule for the "heartland," the mother-countries. Not just the "headquarters" either, the Elysees or Whitehalls. Not all the members of the present-day EU, after all, were imperial metropoles in the earlier decades of the century. Some, like Britain and France on a grand scale, and the Netherlands, Belgium, and Portugal to a more limited degree, did seek to preserve their empires even after World War II. Others, like the Scandinavian countries and Spain, had long since abandoned their early imperial projects. Others still, notably Germany and Italy, had entered the process very late, had been able to grab their few colonies only at the very dusk of the imperialist era, and had then lost even these few colonies after World War I. These countries attempted to revive a version of imperialism during their fascist periods.[10]

As occurred elsewhere in the world, Europe experienced the worldwide racial break as a consequence of World War II. Here I deal with this rupture largely as the exhaustion of the old system of racial rule. The economic and political advantages of imperialism had already been diminishing for some time when the Depression and then the outbreak of war itself began to alter the significance of race profoundly. Awareness slowly dawned during the war, as the entire "free world" was exhorted to save itself from the brutality and irrationality of fascism and authoritarianism, that a postwar return to the old ways of imperial rule might be difficult to arrange. And then there were the horrors of the death camps, the fulfillment par excellence of the racist vision. So between the achievement of popular mobilization for self-emancipation at its periphery, and the enactment of racial genocide in its heartland, Europe at long last arrived at the limits of the racial logic that had powered its rise over five centuries to the apex of "civilization."

Europe had been the center of the old racial system, of course, the *capo di tutti capi* in the global racial hierarchy. The breakdown of this structure was a complex and prolonged process: heralded in the anti-colonial upsurges of the nineteenth century, prefigured by the self-determination rhetoric shared by Wilsonianism and Leninism, and then finally accomplished in the mid-twentieth century after the trauma of fascism and two world wars.

By the onset of World War II the old world racial logic had largely run its course, although this was by no means obvious in imperial control-rooms. Those advantages of colonial exploitation that remained had largely slipped away during the Great Depression of the 1930s, when metropolitan attention was preoccupied by the crisis at home.[11] As interest in colonial (or neo-colonial) matters waned in London, Paris, and even Washington, strategies for political autonomy and economic development started to emerge in the colonies themselves. With the war's eruption, the imperial backwaters of Asia and Africa became major battle zones, important areas for military recruitment, and rear areas free from Axis rule.

The exhaustion of the old order was also conspicuous in the Holocaust. This genocide was the culmination or perhaps *Götterdämmerung* of the racism that had persisted in Europe since premodern times, most notably in the form of anti-semitism, but also in the general (or "common") sense of the racial hierarchization of the world. The Nazi assault on the Jews has been analyzed, notably by Bauman (1989), as a singular intersection of the premodern and the modern: it put the technically advanced and bureaucratic state in the service of a primordial form of hatred that had prefigured and anticipated modern racism, but predated the rise of capitalism and seaborne empire, the appearance of the modern nation-state, and the Enlightenment.[12] While the Holocaust would hardly be the last instance of systematic, state-organized genocide, it would prove to be the last time such all-encompassing violence could be exercised in the face of the virtual obliviousness—or willful ignorance—of the rest of the world. In this sense the Holocaust, for all its engineering, planning, and technical execution, was still a premodern event.[13]

The darkling tendrils of imperial twilight were already evident at Potsdam and Yalta in the hopelessly atavistic Churchillian vision of the war's goals: not just the defeat of the Axis but the restoration of the glory of empire. Although these objectives were shared in significant measure by Roosevelt and (junior partner) De Gaulle, the return to colonial sway was never a serious option. The mere fact that the Allies had conscripted heavily in the colonies, that they had militarized hundreds of thousands of British and French (and even Dutch) colonials in opposition to the Axis powers, was almost sufficient in its own right to scupper any and all attempts to reinvent the old *imperia*, whether British, French, Dutch, or Portuguese. There was more than a little irony in the spectacle of World War II English recruitment in Accra, Lagos, or Mombasa; or of Free French appeals for recruits in Dakar, Lomé, or Djibouti, all of them centering on stirring exhortations by Churchill and De Gaulle to join the fight for freedom, to struggle against dictatorial and brutal German occupation, not only in North Africa or Asia, but in Europe itself. The very success of these efforts would transition seamlessly into postwar battles for emancipation from the imperial system. As in the United States, where this continuity was perceived more in terms of democratization than in terms of national independence, the mobilization of the racially subordinated would have enormous political consequences.

In any case the post–World War II assault on colonialism that began so comprehensively in the 1940s—in India, in the Dutch, French, and British East Indies—and that soon flared in Africa as well, meant a serious reorientation of Europe's geopolitical and cultural position in the world. The two great colonial powers—Britain and France—did not go quietly into that good night.[14] The French in particular maintained an intransigent posture for decades—in Southeast Asia, where they were finally ground to pieces at Dien Bien Phu; and in North Africa, where their downfall was only accepted after cataclysmic political battles had been fought at home.

There is no need to revisit this familiar history here, but I must at least note the intersection of these colonial vespers with the revving up of the Cold War. That the West irrevocably associated the colonial demand for national liberation with communism was not illogical, for communists had been the backbone of much of the anti-Axis resistance that shaped nationalist aspirations on various imperial frontiers. But this association was not inevitable either. The Indian

Congress, the Algerian Front de Liberation Nationale (FLN), and Sukarno in Indonesia, all had their own specific political agendas. They were not under the sway of Stalin, and generally saw the defeat of the Axis as a moment of "opening" in the world political system. Even those who *were* communists, like Ho Chi Minh and Mao, were independent and often opposed Stalin's efforts at control. This perception was entirely invisible in London, Paris, or Washington for that matter.

POSTWAR PATTERNS OF IMMIGRATION

The Return of Settlers and the Immigration of Post-Colonials

In the early phases of imperial rule European settlement and emigration had been vital components of conquest and domination. During their imperial salad days, many of the mother-countries shipped great numbers of their citizens abroad as colonial settlers. These emigré groups provided the new planters, administrators, and colonial elites in the far-flung British, French, and Dutch and Portuguese outposts.[15] Of course, many emigrants from the metropoles were of the "lower social orders" as well: indentured, conscripted, kidnapped, or transported perhaps, or simply fleeing poverty or persecution at home. Many were occupying soldiers who "went native" (Stoler 1991). Others emigrated to *avoid* conscription for colonial or metropolitan warfare.

Such were the settlers whose provenance was metropolitan. But settlers came from other European countries too: notably Italy, Greece, the Slavic and Russian regions, and Ireland.[16] These sending countries were too poor or disunited to export colonial adminstrators and planters; instead they disgorged millions of impoverished peasants to equip Europe's periphery with their white (or almost white) yeomen farmers and their nascent working classes.[17]

Still another class of settlers were more involuntary arrivals: they were first and foremost slaves, and then later—after abolition—peons. These were the only "settlers" to arrive in the colonies from non-European regions.[18] It is notable that both slaves and peons were sometimes transported from one colony to another. Many African slaves, for example, were "seasoned" in the Caribbean before being resold to the North American mainland. South Asian and East Asian peons were recruited from regions where extensive colonization was not feasible. I am thinking here of the transportation, largely in the nineteenth century, of South Asians to Africa and the Americas, and of the "settlement" during roughly the same period of East Asian immigrants— Filipinos, Chinese, and Japanese—again largely to the Americas. These vast population movements were certainly not free of coercive elements: for as I have already noted, colonial powers sought mass labor for plantation agriculture, for mining, for deforestation, and for railroad building, especially once slavery had been abolished. Under such circumstances, and where positive incentives to relocate were not generally forthcoming, migration more often took the form of forced (and managed) expulsion than voluntary departure. And then too, colonial powers, especially the British, had long-standing commitments to policies of *divide et impera* in their colonies, policies that sometimes required the diversification of local populations.[19]

Settlement, then, was a highly stratified phenomenon. It varied tremendously over time, and was complexly linked to the economic and political viability of the colonial project. Beyond that, settler-ruled society was the source of endless sociocultural signification and of endlessly variably racial formation projects. Some examples: the genocidal Belgian adventures in the Congo (Hochschild 1998); the "European city" versus "the Casbah"; the sexualized orientalist fascination with purdah, the harem, the veil (Lowe 1991; McClintock et al. 1997); the complexities of the "white man's burden," and the latter-day romances (of Hollywood, for example) with the adventures and relationships of supposed "primitives," faithful natives, heroic white sahibs, and so on, in the imperial periphery (Nixon 1994).

The eventual return of these settlers in the postwar years, then, tended to fuel a residual but real continuity of colonial racial dynamics, now transplanted back to the mother-country. Post-colonial France in particular, but also Britain and Holland, had to absorb many disillusioned and expropriated whites, people who considered themselves thoroughly French or British or Dutch, as well as many who had miscegenated, who had "gone native," who were "*metis*" or "*Indos*" or "coloreds" of one kind or another. And then there was another teeming category for absorption: former colonial subjects, who sought labor, education, and mobility of various kinds, and were prepared to brave the hostility and resentment of their former masters in pursuit of these objectives. For these post-colonial subjects too, now relocated (or recruited, or in exile) in the metropole, there was a parallel spectrum of attitudes: as with immigrant groups worldwide, some saw themselves more as sojourners than permanent residents, some were refugees, some were economic migrants. As new generations came on the scene, issues of assimilation and assimilability arose. Cultural orientations, both young and old, varied from traditionalism and nationalism to conformism and assimilationism.

The Problem of Labor Demand

In the early postwar period, a new set of repercussions made itself felt in Europe: the problem of *labor demand*. The Continent lay in ruins; tens of millions of Europeans had lost their lives; the victorious Allies had fallen out and were soon skirmishing in Greece and elsewhere. The task of reconstruction was immense, and with financing courtesy of the new hegemonic power—the United States, through the Marshall Plan—there was no excuse for delay.

Yet labor was not easily found. The battered Europeans turned to Latin

Europe, the Maghreb, and their colonial outposts. British and French recruiters scoured the Caribbean: Jamaicans and Barbadians, Martinicans and even Haitians were lured to London and Paris to staff the London Transport and the Paris Metro, to rebuild and reopen the factories of Coventry and Lille (Paul 1997, 64–89; Weil 1995). The West German and Dutch governments also recruited labor on a large scale, particularly from Turkey. *Gastarbeiter* in Germany made significant contributions to national reconstruction. Active recruitment brought a lot of immigrants, but these numbers were exceeded by unorganized immigration. Millions flowed north, spurred by the "pull" of labor demand and the "push" of limited economic opportunities (as well as political ferment) in the colonies and the newly independent states.

Thus arose a new racial regime within Western Europe: at its center were the issues of pluralized identity and citizenship, but a whole range of other questions accompanied the arrival and establishment of these millions of immigrants: national identities (religious, political, linguistic, etc.); regional power balances (the proper role of the West and its culture, the claims of the North on world resources); and the general contours of globalization were all called into question. It was difficult to obtain labor, it turned out, except in the form of people, and in the postwar political world, these people wanted rights. Many of them wanted to stay on, or to send for their families. Millions more needed refuge as their settler status crumbled, or as their identification with the old imperial powers—a posture that had been carefully cultivated for generations by colonial administrations—now turned into a terrible (perhaps life-threatening) political liability. Now they found themselves in new and unfamiliar political categories: *Beurs* and *Harkis* in France, *Indos* and *spijtoptanten* in the Netherlands,[20] repatriates and Afro-Caribbeans (and "Pakis") in the United Kingdom, and in many countries, *gastarbeiter* of various designations.

Although postwar patterns of migration within and into Western Europe were complex (and difficult to measure),[21] and although many hundreds of thousands were post-colonial repatriates and refugees of various types, the foundational dynamic in the pluralization of these societies was labor migration. Here I offer a brief overview of immigration patterns in selected countries.

Migration to Britain

Early postwar experiments were made by the British with "voluntary workers" (DPs, desperate Italians and Slavs, etc.), who were used principally for employment in unskilled construction and agriculture. Around 200,000 European immigrants had entered Britain by 1951 (Kay and Miles 1992), not counting Irish immigrants who totaled about 350,000.[22] "New Commonwealth" immigration to Britain had topped half a million by the end of the 1950s, when the first recessions in the postwar economic boom period began to slow labor demand. By 1981, when the last vestiges of residual citizenship rights for post-colonial immigrants were removed,[23] roughly 1.5 million had immigrated, of whom about half were Afro-Caribbean. Although immigration rates slowed with the reduction in labor demand and with the enactment of restrictive policies (both under Labor and Conservative governments, from the 1960s to the 1980s), the flow of immigrants continued as families sought reunification and established migration chains between Britain and its various sending regions continued to operate.[24] By 1995, the foreign resident (non-citizen) population in the United Kingdom totaled a bit more than 2 million people, or 3.4 percent of the national population. Looking at racially identifiable minorities by origin (that is, including both citizens and non-citizens), there were about 5 million non-white people in the United Kingdom. Of these, about half were themselves or were descended from South Asian immigrants; about 20 percent had Afro-Caribbean origins, and something less than 100,000 were from West Africa (OECD 1997, 29; Small 1994, 61–63).

Although quite a small percentage of the British population (about 9 percent), in the aggregate this was a minority sufficiently large to rekindle old imperial and nationalist embers that had not cooled so entirely over the postwar years. As immigration restriction reached its peak in the United Kingdom during the early 1980s, it coincided with the Falklands/Malvinas war and Margaret Thatcher's romantic invocation of imperialist tropes, many of them blatantly racial:

> When we started out there were the waverers and the fainthearts, the people who thought that Britain could no longer seize the initiative for herself . . . that Britain was no longer the nation that had built an empire and ruled a quarter of the world. Well they were wrong. The lesson of the Falklands is that this nation still has those sterling qualities which shine through our history. (Quoted in Miles 1993, 74–75)[25]

Migration to France

French recruitment of "guestworkers" began soon after the war. The *Office Nationale d'Immigration* was set up in 1946 as a recruitment and job placement agency. Immigration was viewed as an aspect of labor policy and a "rotational" orientation was dominant. It was assumed, in other words, that immigrant labor was only temporarily resident. This was based in part on the strong assimilationist/integrationist orientation of French political culture—expressed in very clear ways in *jus soli* naturalization policies (Brubaker 1992)—and in part on the power of the French trade unions, which sought to minimize wage competition (Hollifield 1994, 150). Much of the earlier postwar immigration to France was stimulated by labor demand, and drew primarily on southern European sending areas (initially Italian, then Portuguese[26] and Spanish).

From the 1950s on, though, the Maghreb, particularly Algeria, became a major sending area, and the African colonies/post-colonies also developed into sources of labor. Large numbers of North Africans could immigrate as citizens (although they would still have to become legalized residents) until Algeria obtained its independence in 1962. This also applied to some Caribbean immigrants, but not to residents of those colonies (like Mali, most of Senegal, and Chad—aka French West Africa) that had not been incorporated as supposed provinces (*departements*) of the motherland. More parallel to Germany (*pace* Brubaker) than Britain, France experienced rapid and fairly uninterrupted economic growth—and hence increasing labor demand—from the end of the war to the oil shocks of the early 1970s.

But because France underwent the most prolonged and painful decolonization process of any of the old imperial powers, by the 1960s labor demand had ceased to be the primary motivation for immigration. The "pull" of French economic growth was replaced by the "push" generated by the disruption and upheaval of anti-colonial war and independence. Tunisia and Morocco ended their semi-colonial status as French protectorates in the 1950s. The prolonged and bitter war over Algeria that brought down the Fourth Republic and returned De Gaulle to power, also fostered mass immigration. As Hollifield notes:

> In effect the process of decolonization—which created a special category of protected immigrants who were quasi-citizens of France—together with high economic growth rates made a mockery of French control policies in the 1960s. The legacy of decolonization has continued to play havoc (well into the 1990s) with attempts by French governments to control immigration, because individuals in various African countries who were born during French rule still have the legal right to ask for "reintegration" into the French nation. (1994, 153–154)

By the end of the 1960s, there were 600,000 Algerians, 140,000 Moroccans, and 90,000 Tunisians in France. There were about 250,000 Caribbeans, and perhaps 50,000 French West Africans as well (Castles and Miller 1998, 74; Hollifield 1994, 151; Feldblum 1999, 22).[27] The presence of such substantial minorities was more than sufficent to set in motion a series of transnational migration chains in which linkages between sending and receiving areas enabled a continuous migratory flow. By 1995, the Muslim population of France—largely composed of Maghrebine immigrants and their descendants, plus a substantial number of Turks and West Africans—was 1,953,000, or 3.4 percent of France's population.[28]

This was more than enough "others" to spark a significant upsurge in heterophobia, Islamophobia, and racism. France is a country with relatively liberal naturalization policies, so there was no prospect that integrating this small number of post-colonials or their descendants would somehow overwhelm French society and culture, substituting pita for baguettes. Yet such objections, such doubts about the very possibility (or the desirability) of integrating such "others" into the French "way of life," were precisely what made the motors of racism turn in France (Feldblum 1999; Wieviorka 1993; Weil 1995; Brubaker 1992; Balibar and Wallerstein 1991).

Migration to Germany

By the 1950s civilian rule had been restored in West Germany. The central task of reconstruction was being addressed, but the comprehensive ruination of the country was still an ever-present reminder of the work that remained to be done. And beyond clearing the rubble, there lay the task of revivifying the country's economy. Where were the workers needed for such enormous assignments to be found? There were no German colonies from which former subjects could be recruited. The only early postwar source of immigration to pulverized West Germany was ethnic Germans (*vertriebene*) who had been expelled from territories in the East that associated their presence, not incorrectly, with the Nazi years.[29]

By the late 1950s, after the most pressing rebuilding and reconstruction had been completed, the government recognized the country's persistent labor shortages by beginning to recruit foreign workers, establishing a National Labor Office (the *Bundesanstalt für Arbeit*) for this purpose. This state agency was empowered to foment immigration from southern, mostly Mediterranean countries, and negotiated the arrangements under which this activity would be carried out with the appropriate governments: principally Italy, Greece, Morocco, and most important, Turkey. Turks immigrated in particularly large numbers, especially during the 1960s period of rapid German (and world) economic growth, a developmental stage that was only ended by the oil shocks and recession of the early 1970s.[30]

Because these workers were defined as temporary, as sojourners, because their much-needed labor contribution was the factor that drove the Bonn government to admit and indeed to seek them, and because they could not be naturalized under German citizenship laws, they acquired the name *gastarbeiter* ("guest worker"). Although there was some return back to the sending countries, it quickly became clear that these "guests" had moved in. They would stay on, have children and grandchildren, and come to constitute a new German "other." As families were reunited or new ones started, businesses established, mosques built, and Turkish districts created, these migrants ceased to be newcomers and became denizens (Gitmez and Wilpert 1987; Hammar 1990; Soysal 1994), a permanent presence in German life. Yet all the while their citizenship rights were denied, under the principles of *jus sanguinis*. Since they were unable to naturalize, the most crucial validation of their permanent presence, of their acceptance in Germany—recognition by the state of their equality, of their economic, political, and social rights (to use the Marshallian formulation)—was also denied them. Under these conditions a deep racial antagonism formed easily.

CITIZENSHIP AND NATIONAL IDENTITY

So, in these three national pillars of the EU, and in the rest of Western Europe as well, pressing dilemmas of cultural identity and national integrity were raised in the postwar years. The most serious of these were issues of citizenship policies and civil/political/social rights.[31] These themes were intimately tied to issues of democracy and human rights, to the deepening of regional integration, and to the consolidation of Europe's role in the emerging global economic system. In many respects the established form of the European nation-state was overtaken, indeed bypassed, in the post–World War II period, the period of the break.

The nation-state developed (as I have argued in Part I) not only from the rise of capitalism and the overthrow of absolutism that began with the North American and French Revolutions, but also as a racial phenomenon: modern nations, especially European ones, were created in the tumultuous processes that founded empires, organized the conquest of the non-European world, and created the system of Atlantic slavery as the first global enterprise. Nation-states were contentious but also interdependent collective actors, jealous of their sovereignty vis-à-vis other nations, and increasingly vulnerable to demands for domestic legitimation.[32] Only in this situation could the modern concept of citizenship even arise. Before the nineteenth century, conditions of "mechanical solidarity" largely obtained: passports did not exist, travel was limited to military and colonial expedition, commercial activity, coerced migration, and elite adventure. Under such circumstances citizenship was a nebulous matter, more ethnocultural than national-political, and certainly not bureaucratically rationalized.

But as empires developed and colonies grew, as the wholesale transport of millions of laborers, slaves and peons, famine victims, and soldiers became routine, citizenship became subject to state management. In no sense was it ever possible to ensure the ethnic or racial homogeneity of nations, but regulation of populations was now feasible, and citizenship became the principal instrumentality for allocating rights and duties in what was now civil society. What resulted was the progressive expansion of the franchise, the development of regular systems of taxation, the elaboration of systems of conscription for military service, and the distribution of various economic benefits offered by the state to its "loyal" and "law-abiding" subjects. These were the "positive" features of citizenship; they centered on *inclusion, obligation,* and *privilege.* They depended on the existence of "negative" features of citizenship: *exclusion, oppression,* and *disadvantage.* Not only non-citizens, but less-favored members of society found themselves on the negative side of the citizenship ledger: women, non-property-holders, slaves and their descendants (even after emancipation), the colonized and the conquered.

But by the mid-twentieth century these "modern" concepts of citizenship too were in trouble: the boundaries between the privileged and the disadvantaged came under attack and began to blur. The post–World War II crisis of citizenship arose in part from the massive immigrations that threatened the positive concept of citizenship as membership, as privilege (Brubaker 1992; Walzer 1983). But the roots of the crisis went far deeper than that. First, as I have shown, this influx of immigrants with which states (especially European ones) had to cope was a human tide of their own making. Many of the EU countries, and all the "advanced" ones, actively recruited immigrants in the postwar years from southern Europe and from the world's South. Second, the breakdown of colonial rule was also a breakdown of systems of citizenship, at least citizenship conceived as "membership" (Brubaker 1992). As they relinquished their empires, Britain, France, the Netherlands, even Germany[33] and Portugal were compelled to accept massive numbers of immigrants whose varying provenance and ethnic/racial identity was trumped by the fact that they had been "loyal subjects" who could claim membership, in other words, citizenship, in the ex-colonial mother country. A third factor in the postwar crisis of citizenship was the discrediting of racial discrimination itself after the break. Before World War II in many countries around the world—the United States is an excellent example here—there was a world of difference between one's possession of citizenship rights de jure and one's ability to exercise those rights de facto. Voting, access to social services such as education or health benefits, even the ability to find adequate housing or employment, were often greatly impeded by discrimination. In such a situation, what does "membership" mean? "Second-class" citizenship for racialized minorities, in other words, was a built-in feature of many national societies long before there were large populations of denizens who occupied the limbo between legal residence (which they possessed) and citizenship (which they were denied).[34] So the fundamental reason for the overcoming and bypassing of the modern system of citizenship was the breakdown of the system of racial subordination on which it rested.

Right behind these issues of citizenship stood questions of national identity. Migration, regional integration, and globalization all erode the particularity of the nation, generating internal and regional conflict and potentially impeding the nation's ability to operate in an increasingly interdependent economic environment. In many EU countries (Spain, Britain, Belgium, Italy), national unity is under constant pressure from separatist or ethnic tensions. Most of the EU countries were themselves brought into being at the dawn of the modern age by ferocious ethnonational and racial conflicts. Although we hardly expect these nations to break up in the new millennium, during the postwar decades they have developed far more heterogeneous populations. Their newfound ethnic pluralism raises questions about the cultural unity of "the nation"—French, German, British, and so on—as Margaret Thatcher (among many others) noted.[35] European national identities that had previously been sustained by the existence of an intense division between the national *volk* and the colonial (or Jewish) "others" have now been put in question by the presence of substantial populations of internal "others." These groups may be described in ethnic terms, in terms of cultural difference: religious, linguistic, or lifestyle. But they are inevitably racialized.

Citizenship and inclusion are issues not only of politics and culture, but also of development. Just as earlier (from the late 1940s to the 1960s) the Western European national economies required the immigration of "others," particularly to satisfy labor needs, so now (and from the mid-1970s on, in fact), their development has required the restriction, if not the outright exclusion of "others," now redefined as "undesirables." Citizenship, then, is not only a problem of rights but also of distribution. Immigration would never have emerged as a social or political problem if it hadn't signified a desire on the part of the world's "have-nots" to share in Europe's wealth, to live among the "haves," to partake of the social rights that Marshall argued were the most advanced stage in the evolution of citizenship (Marshall 1964; Bulmer and Rees 1996). In the post–World War II years migration to Europe was stereotypically a journey undertaken by the descendants of those who had for centuries provided Europe with labor and wealth. Now they appeared at the doorsteps of their old imperial masters, not only proffering new kinds of service, but demanding entry, inclusion, and equality.

In response, their old masters became far less welcoming. Not only did they move to restrict immigration, but also to coordinate immigration policy. This is a crucial dimension of regional integration, for in a more unified Europe where borders are greatly reduced in importance, where movement and residence are relatively unrestricted, porous borders in one country mean leakage into the entire region. Thus in a series of agreements stretching from 1985 forward—Schengen, Dublin, and Amsterdam—the developing EU has sought to adopt a uniform immigration policy. It has struggled to resolve Europe's eternal double standard of citizenship policy: the *jus soli* versus *jus sanguinis* antinomy.[36] And it has even begun to move toward a resolution of the dilemma of denizenship: the presence of millions of permanent residents who lack citizenship rights.[37]

During the 1990s the rate of migration into Western Europe from the world's South seemed to stabilize or even slow. The more restrictive immigration policies worked out as part of the process of European integration—notably the Schengen agreements of 1985—certainly played a significant part in this. But the changing political economic context in which migration takes place was also crucial. Unemployment has remained high in Western Europe. Although the EU is a long way past the boom years of the 1950s and 1960s, a long way beyond active labor recuitment, especially of unskilled labor, immigration does not simply stop. Receiving-country families still seek to be reunited with those who remain behind. Sending-country families, communities, and organizations still designate particular persons to migrate as a way of improving their situations back home.[38] Repatriation of remittances by immigrants to their sending countries is one of the most significant means by which resources are redistributed from the world's rich North to its poor South. Skilled workers, if not unskilled ones, are still in demand. Despite efforts to restrict their admission, there is a constant flow of refugees (Zolberg et al. 1989) from the South and East to the North and West.[39] Migrant populations—and the denizen communities that have come into being over the postwar decades—are stratified by class: many migrants come with sufficient capital and connections to facilitate their entry. On a world scale (as far as can be ascertained) more than half of all migrants are women; family reunification may drag these women across the globe, but so may low-waged and stigmatized labor markets: the demand for servants, for sex workers, or for "nimble fingers" in the needle trades or electronics (Phizacklea 1983; Phizacklea 1990).

In short, the structural dimensions of migration have not been significantly altered: neither regional integration, nor the fall of the Berlin Wall and the collapse of the Soviet bloc, nor the economic slowdown in Europe have been sufficient, either independently or in the aggregate, to transform the fundamental factors that in the postwar decades have generated immigration from the "less developed" countries (southern or eastern) to Europe. The dynamics of global economic inequality; the absence of democratic rights, women's rights, and human rights; and the presence of transnational networks of every type—communal/ethnic connections, political NGOs, and familial ties—constitute the ensemble of ingredients that impels continuing migration, however much the amplitude of these human waves may wax and wane. As a result of the longevity and profundity of these patterns, and after their consolidation in the earlier postwar decades, communities of non-Europeans are now well established throughout the EU. For all these reasons, Western Europe is not now, and can never be, a racially homogeneous society, a "white" territory.[40]

Latter-day European concerns with the "integrity of the nation"—both on the policy level and on the (nationalist) political level—are not only efforts to preserve cultural patterns and verities. Nor are they merely attempts to sustain established systems of political inclusion/exclusion, involving the allocation of rights and benefits, the democratic tradition of the West, and so on. They are also struggles to insulate already present white ("native") populations, to protect those at the top of the world class-system, the possessors of the best life-chances, let us say, from the demands of the lower orders. Northern, not merely Western, interests (not only identities) are at stake here.

After the break, after decolonization, after the Cold War, after the Treaty of Rome and the Maastricht agreements, European nationalism had to be reframed.[41] In the EU countries the disruptive character of the period gave rise to major nationalist impulses and political movements, even though there was no real threat to the state and national borders, which remained permanent (with the obvious exception of German reunification). Two significant nationalist tendencies arose, both driven in significant measure by opposition to the racial pluralization of Europe. These were *neo-fascism* and *new racism*. Both currents sought to build on older nationalist traditions, on political and cultural orientations that significantly antedated the break and World War II. Both neo-fascism and new racism appealed to the glory days of imperialism; both responded to fears of job competition and residual cultural chauvinism. Each echoed its antecedents: the earlier fascisms and mainstream conservative politics of the interwar period. Yet both tendencies also sought to reinvent these traditions (Hobsbawn and Ranger 1983; Anderson 1991) in light of the globalizing and regionalizing shifts that Europe was undergoing in the postwar period. In this reinvention, race would prove to be the crucial element.

NEO-FASCISM

Neo-fascism emerged in Western Europe from the embers of World War II. Many adherents of Italian and German fascism, both in those countries and elsewhere on the Continent, went underground in the early years after World War II, when trials and summary executions of collaborators were occurring, and when the Allies were conducting denazification programs.[42] Yet fascism never died. It never lacked adherents, even though in the early postwar decades it was politically marginalized. It would resurface again in a wide range of ideas and political practices, modified in various ways to fit the post–World War II situation.

Fascism was never consistent, not to mention coherent, either in its earlier incarnations or in its contemporary forms. Although racism is a central weapon in its arsenal, not all fascisms are equally racist. At the ideological center of fascism, if there is one, is nationalism. All fascisms insist upon the fundamental unity of the nation, the possibility (chimerical or utopian from any rational viewpoint) of overcoming conflicts and differences in the transcendent unity of the national. From here the racial connection is very familiar: the racialized outsider is unassimilable and therefore an enemy. Often in league with the Jew (who, being without a nation, is always an outsider), the racial "other" is a parasite upon the national body, a despoiler of sacred national and cultural traditions. The nation is in danger of being swamped by these outsiders. The key institutions of society have already been subverted; only through a massive appeal to the true, hardworking folk "who built this country" (white, French, English, Christian, American, etc.), only by return to the "traditional" values, can its grandeur be restored. In its aspirations to hegemony fascism too must construct its subjects: they are the productive members of society, the patriots, the "true" Germans, Frenchmen, and the like. They have been betrayed by the "others," the parasites, who don't share in the national culture, who don't believe in hard work, who don't belong in the fatherland.

Fascism's subjects are gendered and sexed as well. Its relegation of women to the realms of *kinder, kirche, küche* is well-known (Durham 1998; de Grazia 1991). Its contradictory stance on homosexuality—its rampant official homophobia underlain by a deep homoeroticism—was already evident during the interwar years (Mosse 1985, 153–180; Theweleit 1987). In its contemporary neo-fascist form, its key ideologists have been keen to associate their organizations with anti-abortion campaigns and with the demonizing of gays, particularly gay men. The French *Front Nationale*, for example, has stoked fears of AIDS, linking it in classical fashion to xenophobic and nationalist themes (Fysh and Wolfreys 1998, 55; Smith 1994).[43]

In class terms, fascism's potential constituencies are displaced and unemployed workers and downwardly mobile members of the middle classes, "natives" whose vulnerabilities are most highlighted by modern (or for that matter postmodern) social transformations and displacements.[44] Thus the postwar racial break that is this book's central theme may be seen as a natural stimulus for neo-fascist mobilization, grist for the fascist mill. In response to the increased social heterogeneity of post–World War II Europe, to the growing presence of darker faces, of Muslims (also consummate outsiders, a revivified threat from ancient times), of non-native languages and cultural styles, this constituency has proved to be available for *radically conservative mobilization*.[45] Appeals based on the putative rending of the national community, the threat to national traditions posed by racial pluralization, have been the most basic of neo-fascist political themes.[46] Ideological narratives based upon them can take various forms: they can be coded subtextually for elections, or grunted while carrying out beatings or lynchings, defacing synagogues or mosques, attacking immigrant workers' hostels, or bashing gays. What is crucial is the reliance on a politics of resentment, fear, and exclusion, the ability to link race and class (and often gender as well), and the hunger for an authoritarian solution to uncertainty and vulnerability.

Fascism was never entirely discredited ideologically. It continued to operate on the extreme right in many countries, effectively linking up with the West as the Cold War rapidly polarized the world. In post–World War II Europe anti-communism meant the curtailment of anti-Nazi activities and even the recruitment of "ex"-Nazis by U.S. and British intelligence (this also occurred in the Soviet Union). CIA anti-communist activity in Italy and Greece involved collaboration with Italian "ex-"fascists as well. Thus higher-up survivors were permitted to organize, to go into exile (via the famous Odessa network and "ratline"), and to enter the service of repressive regimes throughout the world (particularly in Latin America, but also in South Africa, the Middle East, and elsewhere).[47] Meanwhile, at the popular level, millions who had been swept up by the fascist "expressive totality" (Benjamin 1973, 241, 251) now resumed "normal" life. Would it be logical to assume that fascism had made no lasting imprint upon them, or at least upon many thousands of them?

In the voluminous literature on historical fascism, perhaps no debate is so revealing and rich, and certainly none is as profound, as the one over the role of race in "classical" fascism.[48] The centrality of racism in Nazism, of course, is not in question, but it is notable that even Hitler and Goebbels, as well as other lesser Nazis, focused their anti-semitic venom on the Jews' lack of nationality and supposed parasitism. They linked this "homeless" and "rootless" quality to a deep biologism, of course, but it was the Jews' inherent exteriority to the national whole that counted most. It is not necessary here to pursue the dynamics of Nazi racism any deeper;[49] it is enough to note that, whether in the German or Italian (or other) versions, fascist ideology sacralizes a national community, which it strives to unify (across class lines as well) by differentiating it from "others" who cannot be integrated by virtue of some putatively indissoluble difference.

Postwar neo-fascism largely adopted this axiom, only modifying it as necessary to oppose the particular racial pluralisms that had developed in Western Europe by the mid-1960s. While anti-semitism remained a preoccupation—as evinced by anti-Jewish diatribes, attacks on Jewish cemeteries at Carpentras (Ferrarotti 1994) and elsewhere, and strenuous efforts at Holocaust denial (Vidal-Naquet 1992)—the principal targets of neo-fascist hostility shifted. Although anti-semitism remained important, Jews were no longer the main problem: it was now the immigrants, the Turks, the Algerians, the Muslims, and the blacks who represented the unassimilable "other."

Violence against immigrants carried forward as well. For example, in Mölln (Germany), in the New Cross fire (Britain), and in the destruction of a mosque in Amersfoort (the Netherlands), arson attacks were made against immigrants. Numerous beatings and killings, riots and rampages on the part of neo-fascist gangs, skinheads, and football hooligans have been documented. Such assaults tested the resolve of the various European states to protect racially identifiable minorities, and laid the groundwork for extreme right political recruitment, including recruitment among police and armed forces (Witte 1996). However, they also produced anti-racist protest and counter-movements (Désir 1985;

European Youth Centre 1995), and thus led the traditional right-wing parties (and even some neo-fascists) to distance themselves from violence, even if they condoned or encouraged it clandestinely.[50]

Neo-fascist parties have made considerable headway in the EU countries since their founding (or resuscitation), generally in the 1960s. The *Front Nationale* (France), the *Freiheitliche Partei Österreich* (Austria), and the *Vlaams Blok* (Belgium) have perhaps been the most successful to date (measured by votes), but in nearly every country there have been significant neo-fascist interventions. These parties have uniformly enunciated an anti-immigrant, xenophobic program, whose resemblance to 1930s fascist discourse is sometimes uncanny: for example, "Three million unemployed, that's three million immigrants too many!" was a familiar *Front Nationale* slogan of 1995 (Gourevitch 1997, 110; Fysh and Wolfreys 1998; Feldblum 1999).

Are there any differences between these millennial fascists and their great-grandparents of the 1920s through the 1940s? On what grounds can I refer to the present crew as *neo*-fascists? I suggest that there are three main differences, which, while far from total, require a demarcation between the two fascist generations. First, the nationalism of the neo-fascists, while still quite central, is undergoing a significant although uneven modification: in parallel with the regionalization of Western Europe, it is also becoming less country-specific, becoming a Euronationalism. Second, the neo-fascist parties are developing on a diverse political right, with which they are largely symbiotic: they overlap and assist, as well as compete with, traditional right-wing political formations. Third, and very much in line with the latter point, the racism of the neo-fascist parties, while sometimes virulent and explicit, is more often "differentialist" (Taguieff 2001 [1988]) and implicit.[51] This claim, often no more than a disguise useful to mask intense hatreds, programs for mass expulsions, revocation of citizenship, and the like, is what permits the uneasy but real confluence with the mainstream right. It is an important point of convergence with the new racism discussed below.

Euronationalism may sound like a contradiction in terms, but it reflects a recognition that in many respects European integration is not only a done deal, but also a strategic step in a world where economic and political power have definitively passed out of European hands. The global predominance of the United States, as evidenced in the widening transatlantic gaps in unemployment and growth rates that appeared in the 1990s, is the main indicator of this situation (Sivanandan 1990, 153–160; Small 1994, 93). First in the Gulf War and then in the Balkan crises, Europe was seemingly incapable of acting in a definitive political/military fashion. This underlined perceptions on the extreme right of European debility,[52] especially since the former Yugoslavia was itself European territory and home to a sizable Muslim population.

Extensive interaction among European neo-fascists—their quasi-unification as a tacit "international"—also fuels this Euronational orientation, as do threats of swamping, not only by postcolonial immigration but by "hordes" (a new "Yellow Peril"?) from the East.[53] Finally, early lessons from some of the "founding fathers" of fascism, notably the English fascist Oswald Mosley, the German "National Bolshevists" Otto and Gregor Strasser, and the Italian fascist Julius Evola, among others, taught that only a united Europe could aspire to the status of a world power.[54]

The diversity of the political right means that competition and collaboration among neo-fascists and mainstream right-wing parties becomes a standard feature of national and regional politics. Restrictive immigration policies, proposed by the Gaullist French Interior Minister Charles Pasqua in 1993 in order to co-opt the anti-immigrant thrust of the *Front Nationale*, were merely one example of this.[55] Efforts by the Conservative Party in the United Kingdom to co-opt the anti-immigrant thrust of the National Front and the racist rhetoric of Enoch Powell in the run-up to the 1979 elections that brought Margaret Thatcher to office also qualify here; Thatcher first employed her swamping trope in this campaign. Right-wing think tanks in various countries—notably the *Groupement de Recherche et d'Etudes pour la Civilisation Européene* (GRECE) and *Clube de L'Horloge* (Clock Club) in France (Taguieff 2001 [1988]),[56] as well as the Social Affairs Unit and Centre for Policy Studies in Britain (Ansell 1997, 145)—played important roles in developing these tactics. The National Front returned the favor of Tory co-optation of "their" racial issues by attempting to infiltrate the Conservative Party once it was in power (Harris 1994, 34–35). This was relatively unsuccessful, though, since the Conservatives had outflanked the NF: Thatcher had made anti-immigrant themes her own through the new racism to a significant extent.

THE NEW RACISM IN BRITAIN AND FRANCE

The new racism reflected the changed circumstances that accompanied the worldwide racial break associated with the defeat of fascism in World War II and the destruction of what remained of European colonialism. It was also an adaptation on the part of the mainstream right to the growing anti-immigrant agitation by neo-fascist parties.

The new racism should be seen as a worldwide racial project developed on the right after the full effects of the postwar racial break had made themselves felt in the 1960s. For mainstream conservative parties and intellectuals the new racism was an effort to reconceptualize the political meaning of race in order to be able to distance themselves from what was now a rather discredited white supremacism.[57] The old racism had retained a commitment to biologism and notions of superiority/inferiority. The new racism broke with that viewpoint: it rejected (at least officially) concepts of "natural" inequality, and instead stressed "cultural" differences. These were ostensibly non-hierarchized, but generally congruent with national borders, and with supposedly homogeneous national cultures.

The new racism had the effect of *displacing* the hostile, competitive, and anxiety-ridden themes which figured race as "otherness," but which had been stigmatized in the post–World War II period—and especially in the 1960s. These tropes could hardly be eliminated or uprooted, for they signified the most fundamental social structures, both global and local: the North-South divide, the international division of labor, the ongoing legacies of colonialism, to name but a few. Yet they could hardly be reaffirmed either. Any explicitly racist discourse, or officially racist policy (in other words, any state activity that explicitly sanctioned racial discrimination), would have been immediately discredited.[58] In short, concepts of racial difference had to be reinterpreted or rearticulated in at least ostensibly non-racial ways.

Britain

The first EU country to experiment with the new racism was Britain. Why was Britain first? To offer only the briefest of lists: after the post–World War II break, race was a more explicit and well-defined phenomenon in that country than elsewhere in Western Europe. Only Britain (with the exception of the neutral countries Sweden and Switzerland) had avoided fascist defeat and occupation in World War II; hence there was less bad odor, so to speak, in Britain than elsewhere in Europe about the use of racial labels or engagement in racial politics. The centuries-long commitment to Irish rule with its strong ethnonational (or quasi-racist) character was important: Ireland was a link to the British colonial past. Arguably Ireland had provided a template for racial rule around the world (Allen 1994). The role of Powellism was important too: Enoch Powell's 1960s fire-and-brimstone oratory about "race-mixing" shook Britain up in the 1960s and placed racial issues on the political agenda far more explicitly than ever before, or at least since 1945.

Powell won for the Tories a certain amount of working-class support; that is, he cut into Labour's base.[59] In general the left was in serious disarray throughout the recessionary 1970s; Labour was divided politically and strategically bereft, not only on immigration and race, but even on its traditional "bread and butter" issues such as trade union rights and welfare issues. As I have argued, immigration restrictions had been developing since the virtual completion of decolonization (with serious controls already in place in 1962). When in 1972 the Labour goverment accepted a large number of East Indian refugees from Idi Amin's Uganda, this fueled the fires of Powellism and added significantly to the National Front's popularity as well. Thatcher's rise to power followed; as noted, in her early campaigns she was especially eager to play the race card (Layton-Henry 1992).

Thatcher's evolving new racist rhetoric largely (although not totally) eschewed explicit race-baiting, focusing instead on nationalist and culturalist themes. The overall thrust was a reinforced concept of Englishness, of the uniqueness of the English character, of English political virtues (Barker 1981; Ansell 1997; Small 1994). This was a political discourse that groped toward a "positive" and "implicit" rhetoric of race, a discussion of "us" rather than "them." But of course, by defining Englishness in a framework redolent of the old imperial glories, by elevating the supposed national virtues to a high altar, Thatcher tacitly denigrated the "others" who, she implied, did not share these qualities. Nor was her commitment to accentuate the positive all that pure. Consider, for example, her Powellism in a speech given at the height of her campaign in 1978:

> We are a British nation with British characteristics. Every nation can take some minorities, and in many ways they add to the richness and variety of this country. But the moment a minority threatens to become a big one, people get frightened. (Solomos 1989, 130)[60]

This in a country with a relatively small proportion of racially identified minorities, it should be remembered (something like 7.5 percent, by the most generous estimate, in 1978). But the political demand for anti-immigration policy had been well cultivated by the National Front and within the Conservative Party by the late 1970s. With an active neo-fascist movement and a pronounced racial right in her own party, Thatcher put the new racism to good use.

Labour Party responses to British racial politics were mixed. The rise of the National Front did not merit more than pro forma condemnation from the Party, although militants (largely from the Party's left) were involved in numerous street-level confrontations with neo-fascists. Not only did the Party fail to develop a serious anti-racist position, but as the new racism took hold on the right, both the established leadership and traditional bases of the Party demonstrated that they wanted nothing to do with race. In particular, the unions saw racial issues as potentially very divisive. But because the Party appealed to racially identified minority voters, some response was needed. This turned out to be the half-hearted attempt to create "black sections," which despite its limitations was able to elect a small number of black MPs.[61] Although a full assessment of the interaction between the new racism and the British social democratic left is beyond the present work's scope, Labour's uncertainty, confusion, and consequent unwillingness to mobilize undoubtedly conceded territory to the right beginning in the 1970s, while at the same time opening the Party to Conservative attacks on the theme of "reverse racism."[62]

France

Once shown to be successful in the United Kingdom, the new racism crossed the English Channel easily.[63] On the Continent and particularly in France it developed farther, elaborating a more ideologically worked-out form: that of racial *differentialism*. Pierre-André Taguieff (2001 [1988];1990) introduced this term in order to distinguish between varieties of racism emphasizing one or the other of the two fundamental aspects of racial/racist concepts: (in)equality and difference. In its British versions (Powellism and then Thatcherism) the new racism had moved some distance away from the purer forms of racial hierarchization that had been central to European forms of imperial rule, especially British ones. Yet the chief British innovation in terms of the racist doctrine employed was to shift the discourse away from negative race-baiting, and toward positive claims about the British nation and culture. But only in part. The subtextual coding of racist animosity, so evident in the United States, for example, was readily recognizable, especially in Powell's earlier and more transitional formulations. In Taguieff's terms, this was still "inegalitarian" racism, at least in part.

In the French case there was also overlap, but the balance between the two terms was quite distinct from British usages. Differentialism occupied quite a bit more of the stage; this permitted a considerably greater openness to neofascism, among its various important consequences.

The doctrine of differentialism was adapted by the *Front Nationale* in the 1980s, permitting that party to evolve from a rather disorganized concatenation of die-hard colonialists (e.g., *Algérie française* types, *pieds noirs*), neo-fascists, Poujadists, and anti-semites into a formidable political force located on the ultra-right.[64] Racial differentialism was also at the core of a quite detailed reformulation of right-wing ideology, produced under the auspices of such think-tanks as the GRECE and the *Club de L'Horloge*. This position explicitly advocated what I have called Euronationalism and consciously saw itself as appropriating and applying the analyses of Italian Marxist Antonio Gramsci to the needs of the right. By the mid-1980s the *Front Nationale* had become somewhat Euronationalist as well (Fysh and Wolfreys 1998, 112–114).[65]

As a new racist political current, although it began from the same cultural and national moorings as the English version, French racial differentialism went much further. Developed first as a reaction to the upheavals of 1968, it attacked *universalism* as a doctrine of the left.[66] It presented itself as the true *anti*-racism, which must oppose universalism as a kind of political *métissage*. According to this view, "[T]rue racism is the attempt to impose a unique and general model as the best, which implies the elimination of differences" (Taguieff 1990; cited from Bulmer and Solomos 1999, 207). The French racial right could designate its positions as "the authentic anti-racism" (ibid.), for at least in its ideal-typical differentialist form it did not rely on a conception of racial hierarchy at all. From this standpoint different cultures could be seen as inherently "equal," incomparable and incompatible—"apples and oranges"—and therefore resistant to any schema of hierarchy or uneven development.[67] Of course, the explicitly anti-immigrant rhetoric of the *Front Nationale*—"When we come in, they [the immigrants] go out," said one of their most familar slogans—leaves little doubt about the implicit racial hierarchy Le Pen et al. had in mind. The *Front Nationale*, Le Pen wrote in 1989, is a "bio-political movement, a reaction of health against the threat of death contained in decadence, the subversion of invasion from the outside" (cited in Betz 1994, 129).

To argue *from the extreme right* that there is a "right to be different" is to give a valuable object lesson in racial formation. At first glance such a proposition seems libertarian, unobjectionable, pluralistic, and democratic. Such positions can seemingly be detached as well, not only from chauvinist and supremacist views, but also from the "us versus them" version of the new racism. An early innovation in the new racism, as I have noted, was to focus attention away from the supposed defects of the "other," concentrating instead upon the positive qualities of the native national constituency whose support is sought. Differentialism, a later, more formidable version of the new racism, can imagine the equality of "us and them," or more properly, the irrelevance of racial hierarchy of any type. The key point is the "fundamentalism of difference" (Taguieff 2001 [1988]).

Yet, as becomes obvious upon reflection, the "right to be different" can mean the propriety, even the duty, to preserve one's culture, one's nation, even one's region of the globe, from the pernicious assaults of "others" who seek to (choose your verb carefully here) dilute, dissolve, derail, or even deracinate it. The paranoid style is of course much in evidence in Le Pen's pronouncements.[68]

So the same viewpoint that sees cultural difference, rather than (in)equality, as the fundamental dimension of race, that sounds so democratic, can be compatible with fascism. From the purely differentialist viewpoint, there can be no acceptance of even a moderate *métissage*, a little absorption of (let us say, non-European or non-white) immigrants. Thatcher's allowance, quoted above, that "Every nation can take some minorities, and in many ways they add to the richness and variety of this country," would not flow readily from Le Pen's lips. So despite its ostensible departure from supremacist/inegalitarian forms of racism, differentialism is actually far more amenable to fascist forms of racism. While it claims to repudiate racial hierarchy and discriminatory forms of racism, it finds a new rationale for even more brutal forms, such as mass deportations. Taguieff equates differentialism with genocide, in contrast with milder "inegalitarianism":

The logic of inegalitarian racism is illustrated by domination and exploitation of the imperialist type, which are legitimated by a paternalistic project of "inferior peoples"—and their educability is thereby suggested. Whereas the logic of differentialist racism, centered on the imperative of preserving proper identity and governed by the phobia of mixture (*métissage* and so on), is developed either as a politics and ethic of *apartheid* or as a racio-eugenic program of exterminating the irretrievable "waste" of humanity (less the "inferior" or "not as capable" than the "parasites" and other "harmful" figures of an animalized and demonized infrahumanity). It is hardly difficult to judge which of these two logics is the worst. (Ibid., 408–409).

Thus differentialism allows its adherents to have it two ways: they can claim adherence to democratic norms and even present themselves as the "true anti-racists," but at the same time scapegoat to their heart's content and threaten to carry out ethnic cleansing. Differentialism has become essential to the neo-fascism, not only of the *Front Nationale*, but of the many other groups and parties that have sought to locate themselves within "normal" political sphere: the German *Republikaner*, the Austrian *Freiheitliche Partei Österreichs* (FPÖ), the Belgian *Vlaams Blok*, and others. Nor does the influence of differentialism stop there: as in the British case (and the German case, and throughout the EU in various forms), both the established French right and to a lesser but real extent the established French left absorbed and recapitulated the new racism of neo-fascism. I have already noted the efforts of Gaullist Interior Minister Charles Pasqua to introduce restrictive immigration policies in 1993, and of the *Union pour la Democratie Française* (UDF) Premier Alain Juppé to increase surveillance on *étrangers* in 1996–97; these are but two small examples of what has been a widespread effort to redefine and restrict French citizenship, an effort that was stimulated by the extreme right, but gained adherents in wider circles.

The baiting of immigrants, for example, took place not only on the mainstream right, but even on the left. In one notorious instance, Socialist Edith Cresson, who was briefly Premier in 1991–92, threatened mass deportations of immigrants, although she was never able to carry out so repressive a policy (Feldblum 1999, 57–76; Fysh and Wolfreys 1997, 170–201). The *Parti Communiste Français* (PCF) also distinguished itself that year in the so-called bulldozer incident, when a Communist mayor attacked and wrecked a hostel scheduled to be used by immigrants from Mali (ibid., 159). Both the French right and the French left, then, made political use of racism; undoubtedly, though, the right converged considerably more than the left with the *Front Nationale*. On balance, the left—particularly the Socialists, the politically viable left—largely sought to co-opt the anti-racism movement, notably *SOS-Racisme*, far more than they indulged in open race-baiting. This left convergence with the anti-racist movement, although obviously preferable to the right's convergence with the *Front Nationale*, also shares the new racism perspective (see below).

At the same time as a broad consensus for restriction tendentially gained ground, a substantial anti-racist mobilization limited the political viability of any but incremental increases in restriction and discriminatory policies. The particular forms of French nationalism—the French "idiom of nationhood," which Brubaker (1992, 162–163) instructively compares to its German counterpart—are uniquely assimilationist and deeply committed to the principles of *jus soli*. As a result, both the mainstream political discourses on race—right and left—run into problems: the right because it must accommodate itself to the French version of the "melting pot" ideal of assimilation (Noiriel 1996) while its heart inclines toward adoption of a *jus sanguinis* system; the left because it wants to admit and accept racially defined minorites only if they agree to shed their "otherness" entirely and proclaim their full French identity.[69] This has not prevented either repeated conservative party efforts, both on the part of the *Rassemblement pour la Republique* (RPR), and by the UDF, to institute reactionary racial policies grounded in the new racism, or Socialist initiatives (apparently quite successful) to co-opt and manipulate anti-racist movements like *SOS-Racisme* for electoral gain.[70]

CONVERGENCE ON THE EUROPEAN RIGHT

The rearticulation of racism in Europe over the years since the post–World War II break has had the effect of "making racism respectable." It has been very extensively analyzed (Barker 1981; Ansell 1997; Miles 1993; Gilroy 1991; Wieviorka 1995; Balibar and Wallerstein 1991; Hockenos 1993; Martiniello 1995). It is obviously replete with contradictions and variations, both regional and intranational, that cannot be reviewed here. What is important is to recognize that the combination of neo-fascism and the new racism has created a right-wing convergence within the European political system.

Sometimes explicit and sometimes tacit, the convergence between the traditional right/conservative parties and neo-fascism has permitted the reappearance of the radical right after decades in the political wilderness; it has reinforced and modernized traditional conservatism, giving it an authoritarian populist base,[71] and it has challenged more fundamentally than ever before the principles of social citizenship, the welfare state, and social democracy. Throughout Europe there has been at least a partial rappprochement between neo-fascists and the traditional right, as differentialism has moved toward becoming the official right-wing racial ideology. In some countries this convergence has taken shape under the discipline of the traditional right-wing parties, which have moved decisively to co-opt the race issue, thus forestalling the access of a neo-fascist/ultra-right party to the political mainstream. Britain is the most prominent example here.

Elsewhere divisions in the established right, abetted by talented maneuvering, have allowed neo-fascist parties to gain a serious electoral foothold. Here the French case is paradigmatic: efforts by the established right to co-opt the *Front Nationale* were ineffective, in part because the mainstream right is split between the UDF (itself composed of conflicting factions) and the Gaullist RPR, and in part because Le Pen preached the homilies of racial differentialism far more fervently than Chirac, Pasqua, Balladur, Juppé, or the rest of the right-wing cast could ever hope to do.

A third, intermediate scenario involves a neo-fascist party's efforts to "moderate" its own appeal, in other words to co-opt the mainstream conservatives. The crucial elements here are embrace of "free market/free trade" positions, in other words, abandonment of the *dirigiste* economic orientations characteristic of "classical" fascism in favor of something closer to Reaganism/Thatcherism. This has been the strategy employed by Jörg Haider and the Austrian FPÖ,[72] by the Scandinavian Progress parties (*Fremskridtspartiet*/Denmark and *Fremskrittspartiet*/Norway), and by the Lega Nord in Italy.[73]

The common theme across the entire spectrum of the recrudescent European right—traditional and extreme, mainstream and neo-fascist—is the centrality of anti-immigrant positions. Racism, notably differentialist racism, is decisive for the right's political appeal. The convergence of the various currents of the right is based on this ideological cement, as Gramsci might have called it.[74] It is a racism greatly influenced by the legacy of the break, a racism quite unlike the variety employed during the Hitler and Mussolini eras. Yet it does some of the same "work" in these millennial times that the old racism did in the interwar period: the political "work" of creating exclusive sociopolitical communities out of more inclusive ones, of building organization and power at the expense of "others" who must be rejected, expelled, or even eliminated. Without this common factor, this articulating principle of racial difference, it is hard to imagine how a powerful European right could have developed from the late 1970s to the present day.

DILEMMAS OF ANTI-RACIST MOBILIZATION

On the left there has been ambivalence rather than consolidation in respect to the new racism. While social democratic parties have generally recognized the dangers of neo-fascism and denounced their conservative rivals' coziness with it, they have not been immune to the blandishments of the new racism either. The reasons for this are not difficult to discern: a defensiveness in the face of right-wing resurgence, a more than residual nationalism, a nervousness about unemployment and wage competition, grief and bewilderment at the losses of the welfare state, of social citizenship (and especially unwillingness in this situation to try to extend social citizenship to *étrangers, ausländer,* immigrants). The new racism has certainly not made the same inroads on the left that it has on the right, but its effects there have hardly been negligible.

The racism that reared up in post-colonial Western Europe was not really new. It was a revamped and refurbished successor to the fascism and colonialism that had been discredited and wounded after World War II, that had been defeated in the drive for decolonization, but that had never been destroyed completely. Now "mainstreamed" through the good offices of the traditional right, and also by the indifference or tacit cooperation of the left, this new racism proved a formidable antagonist.

Radical democrats, anti-fascists, and particularly the European minority communities who found themselves under attack, especially after 1980 or so, faced a tremendous challenge in opposing the new racism. The challenge arose from the contradictions and unresolved qualities of the post–World War II break. On the one hand, a decidedly reactionary politics had swept over Europe (and the West): these changes were both initiated by an upsurge of racism and provided reinforcement for racism's development. On the other hand, the arrival and settling-in of millions of racialized "others" throughout Western Europe; the crucial contributions these groups had made to the reconstruction of the European economy after the war; the positive association between their presence and the defeat of fascism (as well as the end of colonial wars); and the cosmopolitanism and cultural "opening" stimulated by their presence (in music and film, for example) meant that a permanent anti-racist constituency also existed.[75] Linked to the various left parties and progressive organizations that operated throughout Europe (the new left, human rights and solidarity groups, the women's movement), deeply embedded in the universities and the arts, anti-racism came to operate as a social movement, amorphous and unconsolidated in many ways, but not without influence.

Both the new racism and anti-racism dug deep roots in the politically polarizing context of postwar Europe. The racial pluralization of Western Europe, as I have illustrated here, was an important dimension of this polarization. Over the postwar decades, race became a thoroughly embedded, deeply structural phenomenon. Although it was frequently not acknowledged as such—for it was often seen in ethnic (that is, cultural) terms or in terms of national minorities[76]—race was still evident everywhere:

- In the deepening racial stratification of the division of labor, with attendant practices of wage and employment discrimination (Wallraff 1988; Tristan 1987; Lutz 1993; Essed 1993; Model 1991).[77]
- In the contradictory demands for state racial policies at all levels from the

local to the supranational, demands that expressed both reactionary, discriminatory interests and anti-racist (pluralist, human rights-oriented)
ones.[78]

- In ethnonational conflicts both of a majority/minority orientation and
  of an inter-minority sort, for example, over the scope of the term *black* or
  among different national/ethnic minorities (Turks versus Kurds, *Harkis*
  versus *Beurs*, Anglo-Pakistanis versus Anglo-Indians);[79] and over gender/
  sex issues of various types.[80]

- In national and EU level cultural transformations wrought by racial pluralization (Wieviorka 1995, 102–123; Hall 1996a); for example, linguistic
  transformations and conflicts, conflicts between religious practices and
  state policy,[81] and the notable racial diversification and syncretization of
  popular and artistic media, such as film and pop music (Gilroy 1990).

Thus racial pluralization created opportunities both for the resurgence of
fascism and the growth of the political right, and for the expansion of democracy and the creation of a new anti-racist culture of inclusion. At the broadest
level of generality, the racial break in Western Europe brought into being an
enormous repoliticization of race.

The political right took great advantage of the new situation. For the political left, however, my assessment (and a significant literature as well) suggests
that the break brought confusion and narrow successes at best. In the space
available here I cannot review the full range of left responses to the whole
post–World War II break period. Instead, I focus on the existing limitations and
future prospects of efforts to mobilize against racism and in defense of racial
heterogeneity in contemporary Western Europe. My main objective is to show
how the new racism poses significant challenges to anti-racist movements, and
how those challenges in turn offer fertile ground for the expansion of democracy in the next century.

The new racism enjoys several advantages over anti-racism. It can be expressed in recognizable and ostensibly positive terms: the nation, traditional
cultural themes, even the family and patriarchy. It benefits from mainstream
patriotic ideology, which depicts the various European nations as having
achieved the ideals of democracy. The revolutionary French heritage is a particularly strong example: the Jacobin legacy, the strong commitment to *laicité*,
the Declaration of the Rights of Man and Citizen, and so on. There are equiv-
alents everywhere: Thatcher's statement that "The British character has done
so much for democracy," for example. Even in Germany, where the legacy of
democracy is weak, there are powerful tropes of revulsion against fascism and
shame about the Holocaust. These gloss over the unresolved political and
social status of Turkish and other minorities, depicting Germany as already an
inclusive democracy.[82]

So throughout Western Europe, the new racism can present itself as anti-racist. When charged with racism or even fascism, its spokespeople can invoke national democratic ideals. They can count on being recognized by a majority of the population, the "natives," as playing familiar political tunes, even if these same people may not consider themselves to be oriented to the political right. This brings to mind Zizek's explanation of the "spectral" nature of ideology, the suggestion that ideological systems work by a getting the subject to "fill in the blanks."[83]

The new racism, then, does important ideological "work" on the right. It presents itself as both conservative and democratic, articulating popular fears—which have been cultivated for centuries—in an organized and intelligible way in respect to national culture (French, English, Dutch, etc.) as well as linking these fears with supposed Western values. Unquestionably this is at least partly disingenuous: the extreme right certainly has no serious commitment to democracy, and there is no shortage of "shock troops"—skinheads, avowed Nazis, terrorists of various sorts—to act out its deep authoritarianism. Yet in Western Europe today, with power still (thankfully) beyond its grasp, the right employs democratic means for the most part.

Well, what about the left? No less than the right, the European left has wrestled with racial politics over the past few decades. No less than the right, the left has been divided by racial issues. Is it proper even to associate the left with the anti-racist movement?

By and large, the answer is yes. Throughout the EU countries, an enormous number of political and cultural initiatives, local, national, and international in scope, have come into being, particularly over the 1980s and 1990s, as minority groups sought to defend their rights and as organizations concerned with human rights and multiculturalism attempted to mobilize in solidarity. Sometimes defined as anti-racist, sometimes as ethnonational, sometimes as youth-oriented, sometimes as feminist or gay, these groups have varied tremendously in their degree of political combativeness, their level of coordination, even their self-consciousness.

The anti-racist movement can best be understood by the use of a multi-dimensional categorization, for it includes organizations and groups of every ethnonational provenance and every location: from the most local to the most global. The movement should be seen as largely based in civil society, not as an adjunct of political parties or of state or EU agencies. Yet the parties and states, as well as the European Parliament and its commissions and apparatuses, have all taken an abiding interest in racial politics and policy as well.

Here I can offer only a general conception and critique of EU anti-racist politics. My approach stresses, above all, the centrality of the distinction between *racial self-definition* and *anti-racist solidarity*. Self-definition can be understood as *collective activity proceeding from within communities identified as racial or ethnonational entities.* It involves complex and sometime contradictory dynamics of *rearticulation, independence,* and *recognition of internal conflict.*

Within the EU countries minority communities obviously vary enormously in their racial self-definitions, their sociopolitical situations, their links to the "old country," and their diasporic, religious, linguistic, or other forms of cultural unity and disunity. Political mobilization, when it occurs within or among these communities, also varies tremendously. There is no necessary link between the experience of discrimination and hostility on the part of "native" populations on the one hand, and minority demands for extension of citizenship rights, democratic guarantees, and anti-racist reforms on the other. While minority mobilization in support of inclusionist, pluralist, democratic, and human rights-based claims has certainly occurred, conservative and anti-democratic positions also exist among racially identified minority groups.[84]

The collective activity of minority community-based groups is at its most effective in anti-racist mobilization that fulfills the interrelated conditions of *rearticulation* and *autonomy.* Rearticulation takes place when groups are able to reframe racist identifications—derogatory and discriminatory concepts and practices—as terms of resistance and mobilization. The most notable example of this is the deployment of the term *Beur* in France as a "defiant assertion of 'Arabness' in the face of the pejorative charge with which it is frequently invested" (Fysh and Wolfreys 1998, 157),[85] and the organization of numerous *Beur*—that is, explicitly Arab—youth groups. *Autonomy* means the independent capacity for action, the ability to maintain an active, growing base, the ability freely to assess the political situation, to formulate strategy, and to avoid subordination, not only to opponents, but even to allies.

Recognition of internal differences is a difficult but crucial dimension of anti-racist political mobilization. The assumption that a particular ethnonational minority (Pakistanis in Britain, Turks in Germany, Malians in France, etc.) constitutes an undivided "community" is obviously problematic. Of the many internal differences that shape every group—for example, generational or religious distinctions and disagreements—perhaps the most important are those of *gender.* Throughout the EU countries, racially indentified minority women have organized *qua* women as well as along ethnic lines, often coming into conflict with the sexism and authoritarianism of their husbands, fathers, and brothers. This set of conflicts will be familiar to students of contemporary social movements around the world: it can be risky to raise the questions of equality and democracy within a group already beleaguered by inequality and lack of democracy proceeding from the larger society. It requires courage and political conviction. The women who do so will likely be charged with lack of solidarity, with abandonment of their national cultures (an ironic echo of the new racism's charges against racialized "others"), with abdication of their feminine roles. They may be subject to retribution, even violence. Yet without entering into complex theoretical discussion of this problem of the intersections of the anti-racist and feminist movements, it is still necessary to assert that unless the effort is made to create equality and democracy within a minority community, it will be difficult to obtain these necessities in the larger society. The importance of minority women's involvement in the anti-racist movement has not been properly recognized to date (but see Connolly and Patel 1997; Anthias and Yuval-Davis 1992; Campani 1998).

What, then, of *solidarity*? A great deal of experience from around the world, especially the difficult lessons learned in the post–World War II break, teaches that minority-based democratic movement organizations that fail to define their own political orientations or build their own constituencies, or that fall into tutelary positions vis-à-vis more established parties or groups, lose their political viability. They may expect to be tokenized, or worse, completely dissipated. They may become subject to what Spivak has called the "epistemic violence" of being confined within the category of the "other," a situation that in many ways reproduces the old racism of the colonial era (Spivak 1987).

Anti-racist solidarity is achieved only when basic conditions for self-definition, self-activity, and community organization have been met. Yet such solidarity is politically indispensable under conditions of permanent minoritarian status. It may be defined as the *conscious coordination of anti-racist commitment and action across ethnonational and racial boundaries*. Put another way, effectiveness in anti-racist mobilization depends on the ability to make allies. What is living and useful about the rather debased construct of multiculturalism, what is politically meaningful about it, can be identified with this concept of solidarity. Solidarity-based organizations can be distinguished from minority-based ones, at least ideal-typically (indeed, this whole discussion is necessarily ideal-typical),[86] because they are not organized along particular ethnonational or racially oriented community lines. They are in this sense relatively more open to variegated membership. They are oriented to issues of political citizenship (defense of *sans papieres*, for example) or social citizenship (such as opposition to various forms of discrimination). Solidarity organizations may operate locally or focus on a particular issue: for example, there are numerous groups attempting to combat racist football hooliganism: one such is "Football Unites, Racism Divides."

The foregoing has already hinted at the limitations of the anti-racist movement (or more properly, movements) in the face of the new racism. Unity among the many ethnonational communities identified as racialized minorities is difficult to achieve; if the term *diversity* retains any meaning, it at least indicates the enormous variety of Europe's internal "others." Furthermore, within given communities there are class, generational, religious, and a variety of other cultural differences and conflicts. Thus, if any synthesis of perspectives and actions of racialized minorities is to be achieved, it will likely take a defensive form: the very term *anti-racism* already indicates this. In other words, what can bring these communities together, what can build political unity among them—and even within them—is not their positive qualities, not who they are; rather, it is their negative qualities, who they are not. They are not white, not "native," often not citizens; they do not have the proper papers; they do not have equal access to employment, the welfare state, the political arena.

Solidarity groups, no matter how well-intentioned, exhibit this defensiveness, and indeed often exacerbate it. Consider the slogan *"Touche pas à mon pote"* ("Don't touch my friend"—the French *SOS-Racisme* motto of the 1980s). Although certainly valuable as a statement of support for racialized minorities, it is limited to symbolic opposition. *SOS-Racisme* could not propose anything programmatic, and wound up as an electoral arm of the *Parti Socialiste.*

Anti-racist mobilization, by virtue of its defensive orientation, tends toward *victimology:* the portrayal of the immigrant, the denizen (or even the racial minority citizen), the Muslim, the African, Asian, Maghrebine, Palestinian, or Jew—it is a long list—as the victim of racism. The dangers of dividing society into two great groups, victimizers and victims (aka whites and non-whites), are great. Such a conception *reduces race to racism.* It obliterates the importance of race in organizing and reproducing both global and national social structures, in shaping both historical and contemporary patterns of culture. It looks narrowly at the conflicts of the present, although—as I have shown in Part I of this book—race has been a constitutive dimension of the entire modern era.

Further still, racial victimology cannot see the positive dimensions of racially identified minority status: the commonality and creativity, the vitality of racial identity. Racial signification, racial belonging, and particularity cannot be understood merely as products of racism! Certainly that dimension is present; but like any other form of social differentiation—religion, say, or gender; indeed, like cultural and national identities—racial distinction has been created from *within* as well as without. It is, as Du Bois stressed, dualistic (Winant 1997b). But it is far more than mere victim status, far more than a passive response to relative powerlessness. Finally, victimological understandings of racism have the perverse effect of *normalizing* whiteness,[87] and thereby ratifying the outsider status of all those defined as non-natives. Thus anti-racism, despite what may be the intentions of its adherents—to oppose injustice and "epistemic violence"—often colludes with it.

Another important dimension of anti-racist movements has been their relationships with the state: the state at all levels, from the local to the supranational. In recent decades, after the post–World War II break, state agencies have taken on more contradictory racial roles. Under the old racism the state was the instrumentality of discrimination and exclusion; under the new racism, it has become the means for opposing racism as well, *at the same time as its old role remains in place.* In the institutional apparatus of the EU, for instance, there are commissions of inquiry, anti-discrimination, and even affirmative action policies, and ongoing anti-racist cultural fora and media. At the same time there is Schengen, with its attempts to coordinate restrictive immigration policies on a regional level, its efforts to narrow and straighten the gateways of entry into a still gleaming, still Marshallian, still largely white Europe. Similar conflictual imperatives operate at other levels of the state: the national, provincial, and local. So while some official recognition that racism persists is obviously valuable, that acknowledgment is hardly unalloyed. Worse, it has the perverse effect of removing anti-racist social agency from the realm of civil society, from the control of racially identified minority subjects, and vesting that agency in the state itself.[88] Thus, state racial policies at all levels also operate on the victimological terrain at best—when they are not creating more victims, that is.

The new racist political forces, considered as a historic bloc (Gramsci), do not have these problems of disunity, victimology, or loss of agency. The dominant culture, the national and Euronational *mythos*, facilitate their convergence on the right—on the reactionary, authoritarian, and culturally traditional terrain of politics. Where differences exist among distinct tendencies on the right, these tend to be ideological rather than ethnonational or cultural. Thus a sophisticated new racism tends to unify and articulate discord on the right, bridging considerable political chasms. For example, there are important disagreements on the European right between those who support the "free market" and oppose the welfare state on the one hand, and those who take a more authoritarian and *dirigiste* position in economic policy matters on the other. With some exceptions, this division equates with the Reaganite/Thatcherite tendency among traditional conservative parties in the former case, and to the neo-fascist formations in the latter.[89] The new racism often serves as the ideological glue that holds these divergent rightist tendencies together.[90]

EMANCIPATORY POSSIBILITIES OF EUROPEAN RACIAL FORMATION

What is there about race, what materials does race provide, that could serve anti-racist movements as an equivalent ideological glue? If the divisions on the right do not yawn so widely as those on the left, perhaps they can be better exploited than they have been up to now by the anti-racist left. While it would be presumptuous to make political suggestions from across the Atlantic, some very general analytical points can be presented here. These may be of use in efforts to advance the anti-racist movement, which suffers not so much from lack of adherents as from lack of theoretical clarity and strategic direction.

First of all, the new racism position remains unconsolidated. In many respects the new racism retains extreme irrationalities and is replete with historical amnesia. It neglects or denies a millennial history of population movements, race-mixing, and the like.[91] But while such counter-arguments are important, they are not decisive. The degree of political momentum that can be mobilized in favor of or against this racialized nationalism of the right will be most crucial in the long run.

While massive numbers of people in some (although not all) of the EU countries have joined marches and engaged in protest against resurgent racism and neo-fascist violence, few opportunities have been created for programmatic, organized, "routine" anti-racist politics. Based on the analysis offered here, it is understandable why this should be so: to a significant extent the racial politics of the traditional right have converged with those of neo-fascism, and even the left has flirted with overt racism and immigrant-baiting. Where the left has resisted racist appeals, it has done so by incorporating and co-opting anti-racism movements like *SOS-Racisme* into "politics as usual." So established political forces do not yet have the tools to carry out the job of anti-racist mobilization.

Meanwhile, racially identified minorities must confront the high degree of racial chauvinism which the northern "democratic" national cultures still contain. It is certainly understandable why a second-generation Pakistani or Afro-Caribbean in England, a French Arab or Beninois, or a German of Turkish descent, might have a difficult time embracing what is still in many ways a *herrenvolk*-based national identity: the "white man's country," the white man's continent, the white man's world. For these *Beurs*, these "others," it is difficult to espouse, let us say, multiculturalism, from within a former colonial center.

From the standpoint of racialized "others" and those in solidarity with them, consciousness of the world-historical nature of white supremacy is not merely a relic of the postwar anti-colonial struggles, although it is that in part. Rather it is a well-established and probably permanent feature of the globalized racial system.

This is an era of ever-greater global integration, a period when Western Europe in particular is moving rapidly toward a post-national political structure. Under such circumstances right-wing insistence upon the mystical and irrational integrity of various national cultures and identities is more absurd than ever. As I have argued in Part I of this book, there was never a moment in the modern era, the era of the nation-state, when nations were ethnically pure. Today the claims of traditional nationalism seem terribly outmoded. In the new millennium, after the century of the Holocaust, of decolonization, of apartheid and "ethnic cleansing," is it not reasonable to expect the majorities of the EU countries to recognize the inevitability, the profound truths, the tremendous values, of heterogeneity?

Political organizations and prominent public figures must rise to this challenge; to some extent they already are shouldering this task, in Europe as elsewhere.[92] In the near future these lines of confrontation may seem quite antiquated. No longer capable of sustaining itself as a "fortress," a racially pluralized Europe may develop into a racial crossroads of sorts, where citizenship is regional and where large numbers of people no longer see themselves as "minorities" but as members of diasporic communities: Afro-Europeans, Arab-Europeans, Indo-Europeans.

Still, if the ascent of the right is to be effectively countered, the progressive reformulation of national identities remains a crucial task, something that no amount of regional or diasporic organization can replace. Beyond combating the new racism, the political project of European anti-racism may develop into something quite unprecedented: it may be able to create a new type of citizenship that is simultaneously national, regional, and diasporic. It might be a great gift to the EU, and to Europe as a whole, to recognize the transnational scope of identity and politics in the twenty-first century.

Interestingly, W. E. B. Du Bois made a lot of these points, regarding race at least, one hundred years ago. In "The Conservation of Races" (1995 [1897]) he argued that full democratic rights and an end to discrimination of all sorts were compatible with pluralism and indeed nationalism. Du Bois' point about the inherently divided and conflictual character of both individual and national identities must be deeply understood and taken to heart. That message remains important for any attempt to reverse and rearticulate the global rise of the right. It remains crucial for any attempt to understand the burgeoning racialized heterogeneity that characterizes contemporary European society.

We cannot achieve solidarity with others by repressing our differences. But we might be able to do so by exploring our differences as both individual and collective experience.

Eleven

CONCLUSION: MILLENNIUM ARRIVES?

WHAT IS THE GLOBAL racial situation as the third millennium dawns? Will the color-line be as centrally "the problem of the twenty-first century" as it was the problem of the twentieth? One hundred years after Du Bois made his famous statement, how true does it remain?

The present moment is unique in the history of race. Not only in the United States but around the world, a centuries-old pattern of white supremacy has been more fiercely contested, more thoroughly challenged, *in living lifetimes*, than has ever occurred before. As a result, for the first time in modern history, there is widespread support for what had until recently been a "dream," Dr. King's dream, let us say, of racial equality.

Yet white supremacy is hardly dead. It has proven itself capable of absorbing and adapting much of the dream, repackaging itself as "color-blind," pluralist, and meritocratic. Paradoxically, in this reformed version racial inequality can live on, still battening on all sorts of stereotypes and fears, still resorting to exclusionism and scapegoating when politically necessary, still invoking the supposed superiority of "mainstream" (aka white) values. Defenders of the racial status quo largely ceased advocating white supremacy several decades ago. Since then they have cheerfully maintained that equality has *already* been achieved. It is rather ironic that this new, officially *post-racial* politics may be more effective in containing the challenges posed by movements for racial justice over the post–World War II epoch than any intransigent, overtly racist backlash could possibly have been.

This book reinterprets the new world racial system in an age of globalization, an era that has generally dispensed with the explicit racial hierarchies of the past: colonialism, labor reserves, segregation and apartheid, and candid avowals of racial hierarchy. Although the old system has been formally demolished, it manages to live on informally, vampire-like, as the organizing principle of the worldwide social structure it was crucial in creating.

The concept of race has given rise to the fundamental social structures we take for granted, just as our ancestors did. Economy, society, politics, culture, and identity have been racially shaped categories, racially defined relationships, for centuries. Their racial contents have become so embedded in our worldview that they have acquired a certain transparency, a taken-for-granted quality.

Yet for all its ubiquity and seeming obviousness, race is very much an *invented* concept, both the product and in important ways the producer of the modern world. The genealogy of capitalism from plunder to mercantilism to industrialism; the gestation of modern labor relations and patterns of stratification; the development of modern systems of political power, legitimate authority, and even democracy; and indeed the framing of modern notions of social identity itself, would all be inconceivable without race. The race-concept operates not only as an idea but as a practical necessity: it is both discursive and coercive (to use Foucauldian terms);[1] it is definitive for both domination and resistance.

The race-concept has always been flexible and fungible too. Racial ideas and practices—racial *praxis*, so to speak—emerged over time as a kind of world-historical *bricolage*, accretively and experimentally. Race is not "natural" but sociohistorical. It was only gradually invented. It only slowly and unevenly complexified as a key property of modernity itself. At its origins were ancient tropes of human distinctiveness. But over a *longue duree* that we can date (somewhat arbitrarily) from the appearance of Portuguese caravels off the West African coast in 1441—that is, from the beginnings of European seaborne empire—race has exhibited a remarkable elective affinity with the exigencies of exploitation and rule. It is not the same today as it was last year, much less five centuries ago; it is not the same in London as it is in Sri Lanka, Rondônia, Dakar, or Detroit; yet it has a certain unity. It can be ideal-typified like any other fundamental social category or human distinction: class, gender, nationality, or ethnicity, for example. It is no more likely to be superseded or transcended than these other fundamental signs of social variability.

So what's new? How is the race-concept different now, at the start of the new millennium, from what it was in the time of Henry the Navigator and Columbus? What is so significant about the period since World War II, the recent decades I have characterized as a transitional era, a unique period in which a racial break took place?

As the twenty-first century dawns, the world racial situation is quite distinct from its antecedents, from the old world racial system of more-or-less explicit white supremacy. Sure, there were early parallels, rehearsals, and prefigurations of the racial break that occurred around the end of World War II. But the world was racially organized in a quite different way during the imperial epoch that ended with World War II, than it was—and is—in the post-break period.

After World War II the meaning and politics of race were more comprehensively challenged than ever before in modern history. Although overshadowed by the wars—cold and hot—and the rivalries of the postwar decades, the postwar racial break was a momentous world-historical event, a political shift whose full importance has still not been recognized.

The break was not a sudden occurrence, but a decades-long process. It was not a uniform event but a confluence of nationally and regionally specific confrontations within the old world racial system: that of colonialism and empire, white supremacy, and northern, metropolitan rule. The conflicts between the old forms of rule and their challengers—democrats, nationalists, socialists, and radicals of various types—were not absolute or unprecedented. But they added up. They converged in a ruptural unity. They consummated a long history of resistance. They called into question the previously uncontroversial domination of the world's rural and less "developed" South by its metropolitan and industrial North.

After World War II, decolonization spread throughout that South, sometimes achieving its emancipatory aims by peaceful or at least largely political means, and sometimes requiring prolonged warfare to dislodge the occupying power. In related processes, desegregation and racial pluralization took place in the world's North. The migration of previously impoverished ex-colonials and former peasants landed millions of dark faces in the world's metropoles; and these newly urbanized groups mobilized and pressed for their political and social rights, contesting the entrenched customs and institutionalized patterns of white supremacy and racism in numerous countries.

In much of the world racially based movements took political center-stage. Their demands for inclusion and autonomy, in turn, induced serious crises in national political systems. As regimes steeped in discriminatory or exclusionist traditions were pressured to innovate and reform, a new world racial system began to emerge. The national/regional cases examined here are some of the main examples of this transition, but they are hardly the only ones.

The confrontation between movements for racial justice and decolonization on the one hand, and white supremacist nation-states and imperial powers on the other, created and consolidated new models of politics and new cultural norms. These patterns of movement-building, of incorporative state reform policies, and of cultural/identity politics, have exercised great influence across the entire globe.

The break changed everything, then. Or did it? Certainly these movements achieved some great gains and brought about important reforms in state racial policy. But as the twenty-first century dawns, the world as a whole, and various national societies as well, are far from overcoming the tenacious legacies of colonial rule, apartheid, and segregation. The world still experiences continuing confusion, anxiety, and contention over race.

Although the break contained many revolutionary aspects, it could not be consolidated as a revolutionary upsurge, such as had occurred in the aftermath of the bourgeois revolutions and the death of absolutism. Although the reforms implemented by various states in response to racial challenges contained many democratizing aspects, they could not be established as a new "mode of rule," such as occurred with earlier democratic upsurges (Markoff

1996). The post–World War II racial break therefore contains important lessons about the contemporary role of politics, about post-colonial and post-industrial conflict and change, and about the interaction of state and society in what may turn out to be a post-revolutionary age.

In the following section of this concluding essay, entitled "The Racial *Longue Duree*," I interpret the historical sociology of race as a process of cumulative and circular development (Myrdal), a set of contradictory and overdetermined factors (Althusser) that was fundamental to the rise of the modern world. Although I make some summary comments on this immense historical journey, I do not recapitulate the account given in Part I of this book. Rather, I concentrate on the fundamental social fact of the racialization of the world. The creation and development of racial meaning, racial conflict, racial oppression, and racial identity were—and remain—central components of the modern world system.

The next section is entitled "Reaching the Breaking Point." Here I reflect upon the gestation of the post–World War II racial break; I outline its origins and discuss why it occurred when it did. I emphasize the significance of earlier moments of crisis and resistance, the exhaustion of the old world racial system, the tendential coalescence and rise of opposition, and the ultimate incorporation and thus diffusion of movement demands in a new system of racial hegemony.

The following section, "Reawakenings," summarizes and compares the national/regional cases—the United States, South Africa, Brazil, and the European Union—examined in Part II of this book. Each case-study country or region brought its own particularities to the break period; each had its own profound gestation in the developing system of modernity, the old world racial system. Each was representative of distinct tendencies in modernity's construction; each had, and still retains, a particular racial scenario, a unique racial formation.

Within each national or regional society and in the transnational context, racial conflict challenged these countries/regions' sociopolitical structures and cultural logics. In each case, and as part of a larger global process, there was a response that combined reform and incorporation. Despite crucial sociopolitical transformations that occurred in each country as part of the post–World War II break, enormous racial dilemmas and contradictions persist in each case study country/region. The political mobilizations, state-based reforms, and shifts in systems of racial signification and identity that occurred in the postwar process of global racial formation were surely decisive. Yet worldwide racial conflict and contradiction persist—and can be expected to continue—in the twenty-first century. Since this is the case, the claim that white supremacy and racial injustice have now been relegated to the past must be challenged forcefully.

For the truth is that, despite the bad odor racism has acquired, despite the significant curtailment that democratic reforms have imposed on racial hierarchies and practices, despite the discrediting of most (if not all) racist belief-systems and theories, despite all that: racism survives. It has largely been transformed *from a system of domination to a system of hegemony.* This is the key point emphasized in the next section of this chapter. Racism still distributes advantages and privileges effectively (at least from the standpoint of the privileged); it still pervades the exercise of political power; it still shapes ideas about history, society, community, and identity. But because it has made significant democratic concessions to the racially identified "others" it formerly sought systematically to exclude and degrade, because it has greatly increased its ability to incorporate opposition, racism can now operate as a taken-for-granted, almost unconscious common sense. It no longer needs nearly so much explicit state enforcement as it did before the break. Although some degree of state-based racial repression (for example, in policing and imprisonment) will probably always be necessary, today states *undermine* racism by advocating or enforcing explicitly white supremacist policies.

Thus over the entire course of modern history, in each of the contemporary case studies, and in the world as a whole, the conflictual character of race that Du Bois theorized as double consciousness or racial dualism continues to operate. That is the agenda-setting framework for the new millennium, the twenty-first century.

The final section of this chapter is entitled "Of Our Political Strivings." Drawing once more on the Duboisian vision, this is an assessment of the world racial situation as the twenty-first century dawns. Here I draw up a political balance-sheet on the half century of racial struggle since World War II. I note the accomplishments of the anti-colonialist and anti-racist movements that carried out the vital emancipatory struggles of the twentieth century. I also recognize the successes—not entire but nevertheless significant—of the state-based reform initiatives that incorporated but also blunted those movement initiatives. I seek to outline the political opportunities and pitfalls that attend the stalemated legacy of the post–World War II racial break.

Race is still important. In the new millennium race can still shape radical alternatives to the global system. What might such alternatives be? Since the momentum of the anti-racist and anti-colonialist movements that followed World War II has largely been defused, to what new insurgencies can we look for efforts to advance the cause of racial democracy and racial equality? Can increased racial equality and augmented racial democracy remain practical political objectives in an era of racial hegemony that claims to be color-blind and multicultural? In answering these questions, I suggest, we may yet be guided by some key concepts first formulated by Du Bois: notably his idea of double consciousness (or racial dualism) and his analysis of the "veil."

THE RACIAL *LONGUE DUREE*

The modern world system, as Wallerstein has comprehensively argued, was a disaggregated empire. Although it shared many attributes with its imperial predecessors, on the whole it was historically unique. Its comprehensiveness alone distinguished it from earlier empires, from Rome or the various Chinese imperial dynasties, from the Mongols or the Aztecs. From its headquarters in Europe it encircled the globe; no other historical empire had achieved globality. But more unique still was the modern imperial system's lack of unity. It was not held together by a central monolithic ruler, but rather by the developing system of capitalism. This global network of power and wealth had no single center, no Rome or Athens, no Teotihuacan. It was a group of imperial regimes that fought among themselves as well as cooperating. It was unified by the common identity that all shared: their Europeanness, which confronted all the world's "others": the actual or at least potential subjects of imperial rule.

The modern world system was financed not by tribute, as early empires had been, but by exploitation. At first its economy operated largely through plunder and despoliation: this admittedly resembled its ravenous antecedents more closely than the more sophisticated economic organization that developed later. But after an initial period of predation had tapped out the principal mines and soils, after not only the resources but also the bodies of the accessible native inhabitants had been destroyed, infected, or exhausted, a new system of exploitation came into being: the trading, mercantilist form of capitalism. This was an intermediate stage between the coercion of early conquest and the market-driven industrialism yet to come: mercantilism was a combination of market- and state-based regulation of trade.

Mercantilism and early industrialism both relied on slavery. Slaves themselves, as well as their produce, were the key commodities in trade. Slave labor was employed in many proto-industrial settings (notably in sugar mills), as well as in plantation agriculture. Beyond that, the commodities produced by slave labor were central to metropolitan manufacture. So even the more sophisticated economic system of industrial capitalism could hardly dispense with coercion, the chattelization of the "others."

Slavery eventually became obsolete, but not until it had been deployed in the modern world system for a quarter of a millennium; nor was it ever definitively and comprehensively surpassed. By the mid-nineteenth century or so slavery was no longer an efficient means for the acquisition and exploitation of mass labor. After industrialism—and popular resistance—had reached a certain stage, slavery had to be replaced with other forms of labor extraction, by socially instituted economies (Polanyi) that were once more intermediate entities: the "half slave and half free" forms of peonage, segregation, labor reserves, and colonial subalternity. Still, slavery remained as a "spectre" even after its abolition was largely complete, signifying the limits of "free" labor under capitalism, the constant threat (and in many places, the everyday reality) of peonage, and the permanent truncation of a democracy that did not extend to the realm of the economic.

As a political system, as a form of rule, the modern world system evolved from absolutism toward inclusion. But only slowly, slowly, as those in power encountered opponents and rivals who were becoming more formidable. As monarchs and aristocrats confronted the limits of absolutism in the developing modern world system—beginning more or less with the English revolutions—they developed greater needs, needs that only their subjects could fulfill. In successive stages they turned to their militaries, their bourgeoisies, their colonizers and settlers, their workers, and even to their peasantries for support, organizing new political systems in the process. The origins of democracy lie here: by slowly incorporating the voices of political subjects, political domination acquired the legitimacy that was required to operate the levers of power in the modern world. But this mode of rule, however inclusive of subjects or absorptive of opponents, could hardly do away with coercing the "others."

Very large numbers of people, excluded before these innovations, were still excluded after them: natives, colonial subjects, peasants, slaves, and peons (and of course, women everywhere) could have no voice in the shaping of affairs. Their subalternity—their combined privation, subjugation, and difference—relegated them to voicelessness and oppression. It limited their capacity for mobilization either for purposes of exploitation or of resistance: they were relatively inaccessible to elites, whether ruling or insurgent. Although it generally ratified the power and privilege of elites, the cloud of subalternity also had a silver lining: it limited the exercise of hegemony over the great masses of the "wretched of the earth." Neither their colonial and racist rulers of yore, nor their newer nationalist and/or socialist ones who came to power after the post–World War II racial break, could count on the mass support, the "consent" of the subaltern, which hegemony demands. The only alternative form of rule available, even to these new elites, was domination.

As a cultural system, as a framework of understanding, signification, and representation, the modern world system sanctified the modes of knowledge and belief extant in Europe at the time of its inception. This is no surprise: various Christianities accompanied various imperial flags; Catholics and Protestants both blessed and justified the seizure of land, resources, and persons on the part of Spain, Portugal, England, Holland, and France. Travel writers, poets, historians, novelists, and philosophers soon followed. For most of these exegetical authorities, "their" natives, "their" slaves, were pagans, heathens, gentiles. The subjects of empire, it was endlessly repeated, would not respond to reason, but only to force. They were sensual and emotional, lazy and childlike. Their "masters" claimed to come by their authority—sacred and profane—legitimately, by way of their superior qualities, and particularly through the superiority of their religion. The inferiority of their subjects was hardly ever in doubt: natives and slaves could in some cases be converted, but could never attain true spiritual parity with their masters and teachers. Slaves or colonial subjects might write spellbinding accounts of their adventures (like Olaudah Equiano/Gustavus Vassa) or even poetry (like Phyllis Wheatley or Jupiter Hammon); they might attain rhetorical levels at least equal to their masters (like Frederick Douglass), yet at the level of common sense, at the everyday level where ideology does its most essential work, they would still remain "other." As Enlightenment doctrine spread, native and enslaved subjects would be fitted into alternative explanatory and representational schemata: they might be "noble savages" or "missing links"; they might demonstrate "surprising potential for civilization," but they would always play Caliban to European Prospero (Mannoni 1964).

Why did such cultural racism persist in the face of the assaults against it? How could racism survive the age of revolution—with its democratic aspirations and commitments to equality and natural rights? To be sure, the immense achievements and commitments to resistance on the part of the subjugated themselves strongly argued against the canonical logic of racial hierarchy. But this was hardly sufficient even to dent the edifice of white supremacist ideology. There was an immense amount of self-interest involved in preserving racist ideology, for one thing: colonial powers both metropolitan and creole, settlers and workers who enjoyed racial privileges, and even aspirant natives (as well as mixed-race folk) who had come to identify with their rulers, all had staked their lives and fortunes (if not necessarily their sacred honor) on the established racial order. Beyond this there was the unconscious acceptance, the taken-for-grantedness of racial stratification and subjugation,[2] whose logic was repeatedly reinforced and improved upon by what seemed to be the latest scientific and even humanistic wisdom. The rise of eugenics is a prominent example of this capacity to innovate within and rework existing racist tropologies.

The capacity of white supremacy to survive at a cultural level, though, should be seen as more than a matter of self-interest and preservation of privilege, more even than a matter of unconscious, quotidian acceptance. It must also be understood as a relationship, a *theft of identity* from the subjugated on the part of their "superiors." By relegating most of the world's population to the inferior status of lesser and indeed "other" beings, by using them to represent identities antithetical to those of the putatively superior and "civilized" West, Enlightenment culture in all its scientific, political, and humanistic forms—beginning in early modernity and continuing today—performed spectacular acts of symbolic violence. Consistent with other modes of exploitation that racism made feasible, the use it made of the "other" to produce the "self," the appropriation of racial difference in the service of inequality, must be seen as a fundamental source for the persistence of racism into the period of late modernity, indeed up to and including the present. Not only the denigration of the "other," but the elevation of whiteness, was produced and preserved through this process.

These were some of the organizational features of the phenomenon of race; I have presented them here very schematically, seeking only to distill and summarize them from the more detailed overview offered in Part I of this book. These elements were not unprecedented in early modern Europe. Their precursors may be found in the Crusades, the *reconquista*, and the Inquisition.[3] Yet it is only with the rise of world-bestriding European empire, only with the beginning congelation of the modern world system, that the planet experienced full-scale racialization. And this phenomenon—in part taxonomical, in part coercive, in part discursive, in part religious, in part mercantile—once loosed on the world, was self-sustaining.

Thus, at a certain historical moment, racial classification became an indispensable indicator of social location, of life chances, of power. Once organized, it organizes. Racial categories were not intrinsic or natural. Rather, they were *useful* for the work of conquest and enslavement (as well as for the work of resistance) because they provided a handy-dandy index of power relations, one that traversed various practical and theoretical spheres (religion, science, poetry, business), and one that was recognized throughout the world system, transcending national and imperial differences.[4]

From this vantage-point it is easier to understand why resistance to racial oppression, as well as conflicts over the meaning of race, have a recursive quality over the course of the modern age. Abolitionist struggles, for example, recapitulated early attempts on the part of African monarchs to prohibit slave-trading (Thornton 1998; Davidson, Buah, and Ajayi 1977), and anticipated twentieth-century civil rights and anti-colonial campaigns. This circularity, though, is not mere repetition. It is aggregative (in Myrdal's terms, cumulative) because the experience of past cycles is built upon and reworked. For example, enslaved Kongolese still very much in contact with legacies of resistance to slave-kidnapping in the sixteenth century, proved to be crucial fighters in the Haitian revolution at the turn of the nineteenth century (Thornton 1993), one of the most crucial events in the century of abolitionism. The Haitian revolution in turn played an important role in pan-Africanist ideology and radical black movement activity of the twentieth century. To cite just one more example: Jefferson's musings on black inferiority in *Notes on the State of Virginia* (1781) received a scientific imprimatur from the likes of Galton and Pearson in the turn-of-the-twentieth-century eugenics era, and then found more recent echoes in the biologistic racism of *The Bell Curve* (1994).

The process of racial formation ramified, and indeed globalized, during the age of empire, making the modern world system possible, and indeed becoming a world racial system itself. Racial identities acquired the obviousness, the taken-for-grantedness, that is still so much in evidence today. The global hierarchy of "Europe and its others" became a racial *fact*—a "collective representation" in

Durkheim's (1995 [1912]) sense—as it became an economic, political, and cultural one.

Yet racial formation was far more than a system of domination, far more than a mere reduction of most of the world's peoples to the designations of "backwardness," "fit only for service," and so on. From the early days of exploration and conquest "the fact of blackness" (Fanon)—and "otherness" in general: Jewish, Arab, "native," Asian identities as well—was contested terrain. And since all this was relational, the "fact of whiteness" was problematized as well. Resistance among the subjugated, as well as moral and religious revulsion among the dominant, cast the system into repeated crises. Contact and intermingling among rulers and ruled—miscegenation and hybridization—created a series of ambiguous and contradictory racial identities. Interest in the absolute forms of exploitation associated with slavery and conquest waned over time, as more sophisticated and less contentious techniques of relative exploitation were worked out.

Nor was innovation ever merely ameliorative either. As the technological and organizational capabilities of racial domination increased over the centuries, its political repertoire also developed. Tendencies toward moderation in racial rule coexisted with efforts to increase its thoroughness and brutality. Thus not only racial reformism, but racial genocide too thrived and "improved" throughout the modern age (Bauman 1989).

These tendencies crystallized as the age of empire gave way to the age of revolution, as absolutism was called into question as much by anti-racist resistance (although the term *racism* of course did not exist yet) as by doctrines of natural rights, creole opposition to metropolitan rule, and developing capitalism's chafing at mercantilist restrictions on trade. In the aftermath of the North American, Haitian, and French revolutions; in the Latin American anti-colonial upsurge of the nineteenth century; through the transformation of African exports from human chattel to primary goods; with the large-scale appearance of industrial capitalism came *abolitionism.*

Abolitionism was the first transnational social movement (Keck and Sikkink 1998). It was a complex and uneven synthesis among highly divergent forces: it encompassed revolutionary slaves and enlightened capitalists, pragmatic politicians and religiously inflamed crusaders, creole nationalists and imperial modernizers. It required a full century to carry out its task, and at its demise (at the turn of the twentieth century) still left some manifestations of slavery intact. Yet the movement's accomplishments were enormous.

Here again a shift in racial rule cannot be labeled as either cause or effect. For all the differences internal to the movement, abolitionism was an outcome—an *effect*—of the obsolescence of the slavery system. Without entering into the debates about whether slavery was still profitable in the nineteenth century[5]—and particularly after the U.S. Civil War—I have argued that as a result of industrial development and because of the rise of democratic politics, widespread population movement, burgeoning mass culture, and insurgency among the enslaved themselves, abolition's triumph was inevitable at mid-century. The U.S. Civil War was a key turning-point in the abolitionist struggle, both because it marked the incompatibility of slavery with large-scale industrialization, and because of the key role played by enslaved black people in the Union's victory. By withdrawing their labor, abandoning the plantations where they had been confined, and joining the Union armies as fighters and workers, black people took important, indeed quasi-revolutionary, action in support of their own emancipation and that of Africans everywhere (Du Bois 1977 [1935]).

Yet abolition was also a *cause* of modernization and democratization. Without the destruction of the slave system, especially in the United States but elsewhere as well, neither capitalism nor popular sovereignty—however incomplete that remained—could have advanced very far. In the aftermath of abolition came extension of the suffrage to propertyless males in the metropoles, the upsurge of trade unionism and socialism, the vast migratory waves of the late nineteenth century, and the rise of the modern systems of social stratification and rationalized administration described by Weber. New forms of social science—the eugenics phenomenon—sought to justify racial stratification on modern technical grounds.

Of course abolition did not eliminate racial subjugation. But it modernized and reformed it; it heightened the contradictions within the world racial system. Certainly the demands of "free" workers were still held in check to a significant extent by the threat of competition from ex-slaves and colonized peoples; and the latter groups could hardly be characterized as "free" either, even after abolition: rather, they were resubjugated in the status I have designated *peonage*. Yet the experience of participation in the abolitionist movement bestowed an unprecedented degree of political voice (Hirschmann) on the racially subjugated and colonized. Previously they had been entirely relegated to the sphere of political "war of maneuver": to flight, subversion, or subcultural resistance, and often to mere resignation. The most advanced form of "war of maneuver"—armed struggle—was only occasionally possible, although many attempts were made at revolt. But with abolitionism and after emancipation, a measure of political standing became accessible, although of course only to a few and in only in certain settings. This transition toward political "war of position" would develop, beginning in the later nineteenth century and increasing dramatically in the twentieth, into full-scale anti-colonialism, nationalism, socialism, and cultural insurgency on a wide series of fronts.

REACHING THE BREAKING POINT

Beginning with World War II and continuing in the period after it, opposition to racial stratification and racial exclusion once again became major political conflicts. Civil rights and anti-racist movements, as well as nationalist and indigenous ones, fiercely contested the racial limitations on democracy. These movements challenged the conditions under which racialized labor was available for exploitation in the former colonies as well as in the metropoles. They rendered old forms of political exclusion problematic, and revealed a panoply of mainstream cultural icons—artistic, linguistic, scientific, even philosophical—to be deeply conflictual. They drew on the experience of millions who had undergone military mobilization followed by an embittering return to a segregated or colonized homeland.

Such movements recognized anew their international character, as massive postwar labor demand sparked international migration from the world's South to its North, from areas of peasant agriculture to industrial areas. They understood themselves as humanistic and emancipatory. Anti-racists appealed to the horror felt around the world at the depravity of the Nazi genocide of the European Jews. Anti-racists strove as well to take advantage of the anti-fascist legacy responsible for the founding of the United Nations; they linked fascism not only with racism but with conquest and with colonial rule. They reacted to intensifying Cold War competition, which made a worldwide issue out of "freedom," both by demanding their own freedom and by questioning the freedom of "internal colonies"—in the United States and elsewhere. These enormous transformations manifested themselves in a vast demand to complete the work begun a century before with slavery's abolition. They sparked a worldwide break with the tradition of white supremacy.

The idea of a post–World War II racial break is obviously somewhat problematic. As I have stressed at various points in the book, the break had numerous precedents and rehearsals, the foremost of which was the abolitionist movement. The crisis confronted by the old world racial system in the aftermath of World War II was also prefigured, notably by World War I and its aftermath. The failure of Du Bois and his pan-Africanist allies' attempts to influence the Versailles conference in an anti-colonial direction was paralleled by similar efforts—only slightly more successful—to appeal to the United Nations after the end of World War II.[6] Here once again, the cumulative and circular paradigm prevails. And just as interventions at Versailles and at the UN in New York are recapitulative, so too post–World War II anti-colonial struggles had been anticipated by those of the nineteenth century (Domínguez 1980).

What qualifies the post–World War II period as a racial break, then? The answer is not only that there was an immense *quantity* of challenges posed to any possibility of restoring the old world racial system after the war, but also that these contentious issues had a new *quality*, an affinity. They resembled and overlapped with each other to an unprecedented degree. The legacy of the war itself made this so: the war had engulfed the world as no other conflict had done; it had thrown together combatants from every corner of the globe, mobilized every possible resource, and framed its aims—not incorrectly—as an apocalyptic struggle against barbarism.[7]

In theorizing the break I have made use of Althusser's concept of over-determination, which I have linked not to the Freudian origins from which Althusser derived it, but rather to the fundamental insights of pragmatism. The key point I want to make is that the intensity and comprehensiveness of the war's mobilization swept up untold millions of participants—both combatants and those on the various "home fronts"—into a thoroughgoing reinterpretive project whose effects were *dislocating, resituating, and symbolic.* Forced to dispense with old habits, faced with the necessity of understanding one's relationships and actions anew, plunged into a maelstrom of unnerving fears and tremulous hopes, entire peoples—or at least significant portions of many groups—were required to rethink their lives and aspirations. Many underwent experiences of politicization or *conscientização* (Freire (1993 [1970]—"consciousness-raising") although the specific political content of the consciousness being raised varied. For most the experience of the war was hardly uplifting: it was tedium, deprivation, and bewilderment, or worse. But for the generation that fought the war, it was the galvanizing event of a lifetime, indeed of world history. At a collective, experiential level, it was a shock to the world system that could leave very little untouched.

Since it brought so many separate issues—economic, political, and cultural—into its zone of conflict, since it disrupted and reoriented both entire societies and individuals, the war may be seen as a *world-scale democratizing event.* Add to this the cumulative and circular causation model of Myrdal, which suggests that key issues, crucial conflicts and agendas of development were highlighted and renewed by the war's upheaval. From this analysis I argue that the post–World War II racial break was an overdetermined event of *global racial formation,* brought about by a unique combination of historical circumstances and social structures that reached a ruptural level, a degree of social change, rarely attained in a single historical moment.

The war touched off a whole series of transformations, which I have discussed in detail in the contemporary comparative section of this book (Part II), and to which I turn in a moment. Yet it is important here to note that the break, for all its tumultuousness, for all its seemingly revolutionary character, was no more a complete undoing of the past than it was an unprecedented event. For all its redistributive, democratizing, and empowering effects, for all the vast demographic transformations it engendered, and for all the reform of state policies and institutions that it ultimately brought about, the break was only a *partial* challenge to the old world racial order. Why was it limited in such a way?

I have attempted to answer that question in the case study accounts of racial conflict in key post–World War II national settings. This concluding essay now turns to those countries/regions.

REAWAKENINGS

At the war's end, the *United States* was forced to confront its global predominance, which had been newly consolidated during and after World War II, but
also newly problematized. Hegemonic and imperious, the United States was
also a society profoundly divided by race.

The emergence of the civil rights movement in the post–World War II years
revitalized the democratic agenda at the height of the Cold War and after the
blight of McCarthyism. Yet the movement, for all its promise, was itself deeply
divided: between moderates and radicals, and over the dynamics of racism
itself. Although it accomplished the goals of the moderates, the movement
failed to confront the embeddedness of race in the social and psychic structures of American life. Both moderates and radicals played a role in this failure. Moderates accepted the limited concession of integrationist reforms as
an adequate institutional response to movement demands. Radicals rejected
these concessions, but gave their faith to revolutionary programs—both
nationalist and socialist—that were inappropriate to the U.S. context and
never had a chance of realization. These combined with riots (or "uprisings")—spontaneous outbursts of mass anger, looting, and disruption—to fuel
state racial policies of repression. The result was that the movement's relatively
manageable demands were incorporated within the status quo, while its radical demands for social justice and black power—with their disruptive, participatory, and redistributive content—were systematically rejected.

Since no comprehensive structural reforms were achieved and no serious
economic redistribution or extension of democracy took place, the net effect
of all the movement's heroic labors was largely—although not totally—symbolic. Thus at the millennium's turn, even after undergoing limited racial
reforms, the country still labored under the formidable legacy of the white
supremacy that had been crucial to its foundation. Neglect and repression
remained the preferred means to contain (and maintain) the country's ghettos
and barrios. In a greed-driven frenzy the post-industrial elite rushed to export
and cheapen labor, to undermine public services and education, and to subdue
the consequences of these tendencies—rebellion, disorder, and crime—via
the police and prison apparatuses. In this atmosphere the U.S. elite allowed
inequalities of all sorts (not just racial ones) to fester, all the while reassuring
itself that the bad old days of white supremacy had now been surmounted. So
racial stratification, racial exclusion and disempowerment, and white supremacist culture survived—in repressed and denied form, to be sure—but as formidable social structures and cultural demarcations nevertheless.

Although formally decolonized in 1931–32, *South Africa* still carried out
colonialism's last stand. The country resisted until the 1990s the inevitable
undoing of a racial regime that had endured, mutatis mutandis, since the sev-

enteenth century, and that had come to symbolize all the injustice of northern rule and white supremacy.

But even after abolishing the apartheid system and instituting the democratic principle of one person, one vote, South Africa still confronted a daunting set of problems: ferocious inequalities and pressing demands for redistribution of resources topped the list of policy priorities. Intensive disciplinary pressures, originating both among the world's neo-liberal financial powers and among local white elites, severely constrained the ANC government's ability to undo the systematic white privilege left behind by apartheid. A significant underground economy, a pattern of migration that is difficult to organize and control, and a serious problem of crime are also among the continuing problems left over from the apartheid era. And confronted by the mounting AIDS crisis, even the exemplary ANC government seems paralyzed, at least as this is written. South Africa has changed dramatically since apartheid's fall; compared to conditions there only a couple of decades ago, the present situation seems almost miraculous. Yet the legacy of apartheid lives on as well—in the form of grinding poverty and racial tension—under the reluctant supervision of those who had been and still remain its most committed opponents.

Brazil had sought for decades to portray itself as the exemplar of a miscegenated, post-racial society, developing an ideology of racial democracy through a succession of modernizing political regimes, many of which were hardly democratic themselves. Although that ideology did blunt the edges of white supremacy and racial stratification, it could hardly efface the underlying structural logic of race, which had penetrated Brazilian society every bit as thoroughly as it did other nations around the world. After the country finally returned to civilian rule in 1985, it experienced an upsurge of social movements, some of which were racially oriented. Although popular belief in racial democracy remained widespread, many Brazilians now recognized the presence of racial injustice in their country. Severe inequality and segregation continued to plague the economy; the political system; access to education, health care, and housing; and the "justice" system. Popular attitudes about race were enormously contradictory, indeed quite generally riven, between a new anti-racism and the old racial democracy position. Religious institutions, the popular media, and even the government all contributed to the erosion of racial quietism too, so race-consciousness in Brazil slowly increased.

Thus as the country slowly came face to face with its deep dependence on racial inequality and injustice, the shallowness of its newfound democratic commitments was revealed. The lines between crime and *ordem e progresso* (the national motto) became increasingly blurred. Off-duty police murdered homeless (black) children nightly in the streets, hiring themselves out to local businesses to "keep Rio clean." Drug gangs took over the administration of poor (black) neighborhoods, bribing or fighting off the hopelessly outclassed and corrupt police in order to run the *favelas* themselves. Rural gun-thugs teamed with police and military units to drive impoverished (black) peasants from land on which they were squatting. Although the racial dividing-lines were not as manifest in Brazil as they were in the United States or elsewhere, although there were white street kids, white landless peasants, and white *favelados* as well as blacks, the country's glaring racial stratification grew steadily harder to ignore. Who could doubt that the days of the ideology of racial democracy were numbered?

The *European Union*, the old imperial heartland, experienced a virtual transfiguration in the post–World War II years. Not only did much of the region lie in ruins at first, but whole populations had been wiped out and displaced. Europe had to be rebuilt from the ground up: for this tremendous resources (provided in large measure by the United States) and immense amounts of labor (provided to a significant extent by non-European workers) were necessary. As it recruited the workers needed to clear away the rubble and jump-start the economy, Europe was simultaneously required to divest itself of its colonies. Later, as former immigrant workers and ex-colonials transformed themselves into citizens and denizens, the various European nation-states slowly advanced toward integration and regionalism. These ineluctable tendencies—economic reconstruction, decolonization, demographic pluralization, and unification— all forced the region, sometimes kicking and screaming, into the era of multiraciality. But a host of pressing problems remained: citizenship was often unavailable or at least hard to obtain; immigration was difficult to control; and both colonialism and fascism had bequeathed dangerous and anti-democratic legacies that continued to thrive.

Western Europe's struggle with race at times came to resemble a mass neurosis, a Freudian "return of the repressed." In a situation where the permanent (and indeed increasing) presence of millions of ex-colonials could not be denied or undone, many long-standing European national and regional self-images—the superiority of Western values; the glories of the Enlightenment; the virtues of pluralism, tolerance, and human rights; and the superiority of the welfare state—were cast into doubt. The ironic if not disgraceful spectacle of European social democracy being thrown to the winds in order to avoid sharing resources with the descendants of former colonial subjects would no doubt have fortified Hegel's belief in the "cunning of history." The resurgence and even relegitimation of fascism—at least in its streamlined form of far-right racial differentialism and resurgent interest in the "fortress Europe" ideology—would no doubt have tickled the fancies of Oswald Mosley, Julius Evola, and Pierre Poujade. At the same time, a host of pluralist, multiculturalist, and anti-racist mobilizations made their voices heard, sometimes in confused and contradictory ways, but nevertheless in clear advocacy of human rights and democratic incorporation of the millions of ex-colonials now securely encamped in the

European metropoles. In short, although often disguised as cultural tension, political directionlessness, economic pressure, national identity crisis, or the birth-pangs of federalism, racial conflict continued to loom as a significant issue in Europe as the new millennium dawned.

Across the cases, and across the planet, the issues raised by the break remain unresolved. In a variety of forms, the racial hierarchy that built the modern world perseveres even as the postmodern world seeks to ameliorate it. How could it be otherwise? The old system of racial rule was comprehensive and integral to every institution, every economy, every state, every culture, every identity. Would it not be naive to expect that a few political transitions, or even the experience of world war, decolonization, movement upsurge, and democratic reform, would be sufficient to dispense with it? No, this beast will not so easily slink back into its cave.

RACISM: FROM DOMINATION TO HEGEMONY

At the turn of the twenty-first century the world has largely dispensed with the overt racial hierarchies that existed before the post–World War II racial break: colonialism, racially demarcated labor reserves, explicit policies of segregation and apartheid, and candid avowals of racial superiority and inferiority all appear today as hopeless atavisms, relics of a benighted past. International organizations like the UN have for decades made opposition to racism a central priority. And the globalized "culture industry"—from Hollywood to Bollywood, from Disney to Globo to Benneton—has produced a continuing stream of anti-racist messages: legitimating interracial romance and friendship, stigmatizing prejudice and discrimination, and fostering the hybridization of cultures and styles.

Yet as all this anti-racist policy-making, multiculturalism, and hybridization proceeds, the vast gaps between North and South, haves and have-nots, whites and "others," also persist. Pick any relevant sociological indicator—life expectancy, infant mortality, literacy, access to health care, income level—and apply it in virtually any setting, global, regional, or local, and the results will be the same: the worldwide correlation of wealth and well-being with white skin and European descent, and of poverty and immiseration with dark skin and "otherness." Sure, there are exceptions: there are plenty of exploited white workers, plenty of white welfare mothers both urban and rural, plenty of poor whites throughout the world's North; and there are a smattering of wealth-holders "of color" around the world too. But these are outliers in the planetary correlation of darkness and poverty.

In analyzing patterns of inequality, of stratification, it is impossible fully to distinguish the effects of race and class. These factors interact both locally and globally; they have shaped each other over historical time and continue to do so in the present. For instance, is the black worker at General Motors' plant in Ohio, or at Volkswagen's plant in the ABC region of São Paulo for that matter, so much worse off than the white worker beside him (or her) on the assembly line? Not so much. The real local discrepancies are between those who have fairly reliable, even unionized jobs, and those relegated to poverty and the informal economy.[8] And then there are the global discrepancies: auto workers' wages in the ABC, heartland of the highly developed Brazilian manufacturing economy, home base of the *Confederação Unificado dos Trabalhadores* (CUT—the militant Brazilian trade union confederation), and site of some of the most desirable jobs in the national economy, average about 10 percent of U.S. wages for the same work.[9]

Nor do we have to look at stratification to recognize the continuing significance of race. When we turn to the world political system, to the social structure of domination and subjugation, to the allocation of voice and voicelessness, the point is confirmed again. A worldwide political class exercises power from corporate boardrooms and government ministries alike: how multiracial, how committed to racial equality, is this select group? Of course at the commencement of the twenty-first century, after the end of colonialism and the conclusion of the Cold War, political rule can claim to be democratic almost everywhere. But democracy now means little more than that the citizenry "periodically enjoys the right to withold their acclaim," as Jürgen Habermas remarked (Habermas 1997; see also Habermas 1996).[10]

In such a system the racial gradations of power and powerlessness can sometimes be confusing, but long-standing patterns of racial hierarchy still hold. Do citizens of the core nations of the metropolitan North, do the whites of the world, exercise much political power? No, they do not. How much "freedom" (in the sense of the relative absence of coercion, the availability of personal autonomy) do they possess relative to the racialized "others" both in the northern metropoles and "down home" in the world's South? There are two answers. First, in a given local/national setting—in Los Angeles or Frankfurt, Fortaleza or Durban—whites experience a sense of belonging, a sense of entitlement, that blacks, immigrants, racialized "others," rarely if ever enjoy. Second, on a global level, however disfranchised, however yoked to a low-skilled and inadequately paid job, however resentful of those in command, however manipulable by racists both "old" and "new," the ordinary *schmo* in the world's North—in the still largely white bastions of Europe and North America and ("honorary white") Japan—disposes of a greater basket of life chances, greater freedom, than most of his or her southern brothers and sisters could even imagine.[11]

Culturally too the old system rules. Whence cometh the ideals, the near universal representations, the recognizable icons and idols: where do Michael Jordan and Michael Jackson and Michael Mouse live? In Hollywood, of course (or perhaps in Orlando)! Whose names adorn the canonical bookshelves, whose artworks hang in the museums, whose films does the world stand in line to see? Yes, here again there are exceptions: there is the vast treasurehouse of black music that rules the audio world from Bensonhurst to Bahia,[12] even if it is harnessed to the profit-making imperatives of global media conglomerates; there is not only Hollywood but also Bollywood; there is Chris Ofili, who scandalized New York Mayor Giuliani with his painting *Black Madonna.* But "McWorld" (Barber 1995) is still a largely northern place.

To make sense of these developments and dilemmas, we must rethink the concept of racism. Just as the meaning of race has proved to be malleable and fungible, changing dramatically in the years since World War II, for example, so too the meaning of *racism* has changed over time. The attitudes, practices, and institutions of the epochs of colonialism, segregation, or apartheid may not have been entirely eliminated, but neither do they operate today in the same ways as they did half a century ago. Employing a similar logic, it is reasonable to question whether concepts of racism that were developed in the early postwar period, when the limitations of both nationalist revolution and moderate programs of reform had not yet been encountered, could possibly remain adequate to explain racial dynamics and conflicts in the twenty-first century.

Today racism operates in societies and institutions that explicitly condemn prejudice and discrimination. In the era that succeeded the post–World War II racial break, the conflicts between anti-racist movements and reform-oriented regimes resulted in a new pattern of racial rule, one that makes concessions without surrendering fundamental power. Put somewhat differently: after half a millennium in which global power and capitalist development had been based on racial domination, opposition to the coercive rule required by this old world racial system simply became too strong. Faced with increasingly assertive demands for democracy and national liberation—demands that sometimes reached revolutionary levels of mobilization and involved prolonged armed conflict—the world racial system underwent a transition *from domination to hegemony.* Segregation and colonialism—at least in their explicit, state-enforced forms—were abandoned as the principal instrumentalities of racial rule.

But having conceded this much, northern rule, metropolitan rule, capitalist rule, found its stability largely restored. The new world racial system could maintain much of the stratification and inequality, much of the differential access to political power and voice, much of the preexisting cultural logic of collective representation and racial hierarchy, without recourse to comprehensive coercion or racial dictatorship. Since the political energy and support available to its movement adversaries was limited, a new era of world racial equilibrium could be proclaimed. Opposition was now effectively reduced: since the moderates had been effectively satisfied by reforms, only radical groups remained restive; they could be contained by a combination of marginalization and repression.

In the age of racial hegemony, then, what forms does racism take? To the extent that the transition from domination to hegemony has been accomplished, it is racism's reinforced structural role, its "cleaned-up," "streamlined," and "mainstream" manifestations, that allow it to survive and indeed go largely politically unchallenged at the dawn of the twenty-first century.[13]

Today racism must be identified by its consequences. Racism has been largely— although not entirely, to be sure—detached from its perpetrators. In its most advanced forms, indeed, it has no perpetrators; it is a nearly invisible, taken-for-granted, commonsense (Gramsci) feature of everyday life and global social structure.[14]

Under these conditions—racial hegemony—racism may be defined as *the routinized outcome of practices that create or reproduce hierarchical social structures based on essentialized racial categories.*[15] This definition seeks a comprehensiveness that may not be fully attainable. It leaves enough room to contain the old, instrumental, forms of racism—such as prejudice and discrimination, racial code words, and the like—but focuses attention on new, structural forms that can operate more or less automatically. It incorporates the analyses that critiqued the European new racism (Barker 1981; Taguieff 2001 [1988]; Miles 1993; Wieviorka 1995; Ansell 1997; Gilroy 1999), but seeks to place that important work in a global framework.

There can be no timeless and absolute standard for what constitutes racism, because social structures undergo reform (and reaction) and discourses are always subject to rearticulation. The concept of racism should not be invested with any permanent content. Instead racism should be seen as a property of certain—but by no means all—political projects that link the *representation* and *organization* of race, that engage in the "work" of racial formation. Such an approach focuses on the "work" essentialism does for domination, and the "need" domination displays to essentialize the subordinated.[16] It allows comparison of different national/regional cases of racial formation, such as those I have presented here. All these countries/regions are in transition from racial domination to racial hegemony. The case study settings both overlap and diverge: each has a unique location and genealogy, yet all partake in the world racial system; all were reshaped during the post–World War II racial break.

OF OUR POLITICAL STRIVINGS

The tremendous accomplishments of the anti-racist and anti-colonial movements that succeeded World War II have now been incorporated. In the decades after the war it seemed at times that these movements might not only found independent post-colonial states, but that they might reorganize global society, even demolish capitalism. At the start of the twenty-first century, however, the outlook is far less promising. At the local/national level many formerly powerful anti-racist movements have lost their adherents and some their political moorings. Some are reduced to defending the limited racial reforms won in earlier moments, for example, affirmative action policies, against the specious claims of public institutions that they are now color-blind, meritocratic, post-racial. Other movements and activists put their energies into multicultural projects, which (again defensively) advocate pluralism and tend to reduce racism to a strictly cultural phenomenon. At the global level the still-impoverished nations of the former Third World, even the formerly revolutionary and still officially communist ones, seek direct private investment and curry favors from the gnomes of London, Zurich, and the IMF.

In earlier times and places—say, during the later 1960s in the United States—it seemed that the "Third World within" might finally achieve the power and claim the wealth so long denied it: redistribution of resources, community control, massive rebuilding of the inner cities, black power (and red power, brown power, yellow power) would accomplish in a "second reconstruction" what had been denied and betrayed one hundred years earlier. But today, at the turn of the twenty-first century, the ghettos, barrios, and reservations are still neglected, still occupied by trigger-happy police, still immiserated; and no serious political movement is in sight.

The vast social movements that democratized the old world racial system, that did away with official policies of racial exclusion, disfranchisement, segregation, and degradation, have now lost a great deal of their support. Formerly they could lead whole peoples in the direction of emancipation; now they struggle to define their purpose. The disruption of the old world racial system during and after the post–World War II racial break has given rise to a "new world racial system" characterized not by racial domination, but instead by racial hegemony. This new system can maintain white supremacy better than the old one could. This system of racial hegemony can present itself as color-blind and multicultural, not to mention meritocratic, egalitarian, and differentialist, all the while restricting immigration, exporting industry (and pollution) to the low-waged South, and doing away with the welfare state in the North.

So while some racial mobility has been achieved, fierce racial inequalities persist: globally they mirror the North-South patterns that colonial rule developed and the *Pax Americana* has continued. In local settings, racial inequalities also continue to operate: by and large the descendants of slaves, indigenous and occupied peoples, refugees, and migrants continue to be subjugated to the descendants of landholders and slavemasters, occupiers and European settlers.

While some political power has passed from colonialists' and segregationists' hands into darker hands, both the global political system and its local variants have survived and prospered in the transition to a new world racial system.

Contemporary political systems of rule—both global and local—descend rather directly from the old world racial system. How independent are the rulers of southern nation-states, even relatively developed ones like South Africa and Brazil, from the discipline of world financial markets and institutions like the IMF? How effective is political representation—black, immigrant, indigenous—even in settings where those formerly excluded on racial grounds can now vote?

Culturally too the transition to hegemony has been contradictory. Well before the post–World War II break the world's "others" were crucial sources of signification: artistic, musical, philosophical, religious, and scholarly insights and techniques were deeply rooted outside the West, even though the "big heads" of Europe laid claim to sole possession of advanced knowledge in all these areas. Already adept at reworking these cultural riches, in the period after the break the metropolitan "culture industries" moved to take possession them, to commodify and purvey them on a global scale. But although ready, willing, and able to market reggae, soka, or samba, say, anywhere in the world, the metropolitan powers still claimed to possess the superior cultures, to live in the home of reason and the center-stage of history (Sen 2000b; Davidson 1992). They still required the *difference* of the world's "others," whose cultures they purported now to value far more than in the past, in order to define their own identities.[17]

So what's left after all this conflict and accommodation? Is the picture so bleak that the legacy of half a millennium of resistance to racial rule must now be abandoned? After the tremendous upsurge of the break, after the partial but real triumphs of recent decades, has the worldwide movement for racial equality and justice, for emancipation and self-determination, finally been defeated, not by force and repression, but by co-optation and incorporation? How should racial hegemony be confronted politically, or even politically understood?

The definitive answer to this question cannot be given on paper. Only in political action, in organization and mobilization, will present-day racial dilemmas and contradictions be resolved. Researchers and writers, even those who identify with movements for social justice, are ultimately led by those movements. They cannot, and I cannot, presume to offer political prescriptions.

Yet it is clear that despite recent setbacks, fertile ground remains for new anti-racist initiatives. However successfully the new world racial order was able to incorporate the anti-racist and anti-colonial demands asserted during the break, it was not able fully to transform the inequalities and injustices that generated those demands. It could defuse and blunt the basis of racial opposition, but it could hardly eliminate it. Under no circumstances could the system move "beyond race," despite its claims to post-raciality, color-blindness, multiculturalism, and so on.

So what's left? The fundamental elements of resistance to racial injustice and inequality that remain intact, that have been largely untouched by the incorporative initiatives of the new world racial system, may form building-blocks for the new anti-racist movements. Both in the case study countries/regions and more generally, counter-hegemonic movements may emerge as significant challenges to the world racial system.

There are three fundamental reasons, three ineluctable social facts, that suggest that the struggle against white supremacy will continue around the world: first, *global racial inequality and injustice remain*; second, *race-consciousness endures*; and third, *racial politics is pervasive*. In what follows I present the arguments for these three claims, necessarily in a brief and schematic way. I then conclude with some notes on the Duboisian legacy.

Global Racial Inequality and Injustice Remain

Indeed, they are more visible now, in the age of the Internet and globalized media, than ever before. Where there is injustice and oppression, there is resistance. A powerful argument can be made that opposition to injustice is the main form that political opposition takes in the modern world (Moore 1978).

In all the national/regional case studies examined here, racial stratification remains a significant issue: that unemployment levels are higher and income levels lower for those with dark faces across the world is hardly news. The complex phenomenon known as globalization is itself a major mechanism of resource redistribution—but mainly in a regressive direction.

In the world's North globalization tends toward deindustrialization. The work that can be exported consists of the less skilled factory jobs that are held by immigrants and the working poor—who are disproportionately people "of color." Much of the low-waged work that remains in the metropolitan countries is located in sweatshops, in agriculture, in the service sector, and in the informal economy. Assaults on the welfare state—both on the spending and revenue side—also have regressively redistributive consequences. Many of these developments—competition for jobs, association of immigrants and non-whites with crime, objections to the welfare state and calls for tax reduction—are framed racially.

In the world's South globalization takes the form of neo-liberal economic discipline. The ability to extract primary resources at low cost, unburdened by government regulation, labor organization, or environmental restrictions, is the primary force driving globalization here. Often the importation of factory work doesn't mean serious industrial development or foreign direct investment: more likely it involves an ongoing search for easy acquisition of resources and for cheap and submissive labor. Such policies combine with the austerity and compulsory debt-service enforced upon the South by the International Monetary Fund to maintain much of the population of the South—not only those in countries decolonized only after World War II but even the great majority in an industrially developed country like Brazil—in a state of impoverishment (Greider 1997).

This is an outline—very schematically summarized here—of current world patterns of economic inequality and injustice. Although often seen in terms of global *social* stratification, in terms of environmental destruction, and in terms of gender inequalities (sweatshops and *maquilas*, for example, tend to exploit women at high levels), these injustices are rarely characterized as *racial*. Yet is it not clear that they flow fairly continuously from patterns established in the now-departed colonial epoch?

A movement against the depredations of globalization has begun to appear, drawing on a range of supporters: chiefly environmentalists, trade unions, and religious groups (as well as assorted radical groups committed to direct action). In demonstrations against the World Trade Organization (WTO) in Seattle in 1999, and against the IMF and World Bank in Washington, DC in 2000, this coalition first attracted major attention. Protests in Geneva, Paris, Bangkok, and Prague have also taken place. Real questions have been raised as to how much support the anti-WTO (or anti-globalization) movement can count on from the world's South, where impoverishment is severe enough to make even employment in a sweatshop or *maquila* seem desirable, and where even relatively progressive governments sympathetic to trade unionism—such as the ANC government in South Africa—are subject to immense pressure from the world's financial power-centers.[18] As of yet this movement has exhibited relatively little racial awareness. It remains to be seen if this initiative will acquire the depth and organizational strength needed to operate on a global scale, but it is already achieving limited results (somewhere between substantive and symbolic) in respect to its demands for debt relief.

Race-Consciousness Endures

One of the most important accomplishments of the worldwide racial mobilizations that confronted colonialism and white supremacy during and after World War II was their reinterpretation (or if one prefers this term, their rearticulation) of the meaning of race and the significance of racial identity. Building upon the immense labors of their ancestors and predecessors, these movements systematically fostered awareness and pride among the world's subjugated and subaltern peoples. To be sure, the creation and nurturing of race-consciousness is a highly uneven and contradictory process. It combines potentially emancipatory elements, such as rejection of stereotypes and "internalized racism," with potentially chauvinistic and even fascist ones (Gilroy 1996). Although in many cases it was the work of revolutionary nationalism to awaken and enunciate concepts of pride, solidarity, and cultural awareness among the racially subordinated, these projects were themselves undertaken by insurgent elites, as we have learned from subalternity theory (see Chapter Five, above). They did not preclude, and in some cases actively fostered, new forms of subordination and voicelessness among black, native, or colonized peoples. They could not avoid, and in some cases actively participated in, the degradation of race-consciousness into a commodified and depoliticized form (dashikis, kente cloth, blaxploitation films, etc.).

Yet with all these limitations there has been an indisputably enormous increase in racial awareness throughout the world as a consequence of the upheavals of the break and its aftermath. This awareness is open to further articulation, and by no means inherently emancipatory. There can be no permanent formulas here.[19] Yet the vastly augmented presence of race-consciousness in the world, although contradictory and flexible, still works as a sort of transnational inoculation against post-racialism in all its forms: notably the color-blind viewpoint in the United States and the racial differentialism evident in Europe.

This expanded awareness also acts as a reminder to those on the left who have remained committed to an outmoded notion of anti-racism as integration pure and simple—for example, some in the South African ANC who remain die-hard adherents to the vision of non-racialism articulated in the 1955 Freedom Charter—that the old world racial system is definitively dead, and that a new vision of racial justice and equality must be developed. The fact that race-consciousness has expanded so much in the aftermath of the break also has consequences in Brazil, where it works to erode the tenacious ideology of racial democracy. The old charge that to criticize or even to acknowledge the presence of racism was ipso facto to perpetuate it, is less tenable today, due to the growing debates and discussions about race in the political sphere, in popular media, in religious venues, and in everyday life.

Racial Politics is Pervasive

Despite the decline of anti-racist movements in the new world racial order, a significant legacy of the break and its aftermath remains relatively intact. It is the pervasiveness of racial politics, the recognition that racial hierarchies and systems of signification permeate social institutions from the most comprehensive and global to the most small-scale and experiential. A notable and intriguing feature of race is its ubiquity, its presence in both the "smallest" and the "largest" features of social relationships, institutions, and identities. Much of the impetus behind the "politicization of the social," the reconceptualization of politics that has occurred in recent decades, was derived from anti-racist social movements. The democratizing challenge posed after World War II to "normal" systems of domination and power, "accepted" divisions of labor, and "rational-legal" means of legitimation, all had inescapable racial dimensions. Racially based movements, then (and the "second wave" feminism that followed and was inspired by them), problematized the public-private distinction basic to preexisting political cultures. After World War II, the range of political issues that existed, and the number and sorts of political actors afforded any voice, was greatly expanded beyond the political norms of the years before the break.[20]

These transformations were also reflected in political theory and political sociology, where older approaches to democratic theory, social movements, and the state were challenged, for example, by "political process" models (McAdam 1982; Morris and Mueller 1992). Recognition of the pervasiveness of politics also appears in the revival of interest in pragmatist sociology, in symbolic interactionism, in "constitution" theories of society (Joas 1996; Giddens 1984), and in the belated revival of interest in the work of W. E. B. Du Bois (West 1989; Lewis 1993, Winant 1997b).[21]

Mention of Du Bois brings me to the final points I want to make. Du Bois's astonishing career stretched from the eventide of the U.S. Civil War to the aftermath of the postwar racial break. He lived to see the sun set on the great colonial empires whose ravages he had opposed for seventy years, and to greet the dawn of the modern civil rights movement in the United States, for which he had laid so much groundwork. In a less well-known speech, given at a conference in 1960, Du Bois (then 92 years of age) contemplated the consequences of these victories, and of the new political situation that black people would find themselves in their aftermath:

[W]hat we must now ask ourselves is when we become equal American citizens what will be our aims and ideals and what we will have to do with selecting these aims and ideals. Are we to assume that we will simply adopt the ideals of Americans and become what they are or want to be and that we will have in this process no ideals of our own?

That would mean that we would cease to be Negroes as such and become white in action if not completely in color. We would take on the culture of white Americans doing as they do and thinking as they think.

Manifestly this would not be satisfactory. Physically it would mean that we would be integrated with Americans losing first of all, the physical evidence of color and hair and racial type. We would lose our memory of Negro history and of those racial peculiarities which have long been associated with the Negro. We would cease to acknowledge any greater tie with Africa than with England or Germany. We would not try to develop Negro music and Art and Literature as distinctive and different, but allow them to be further degraded as is the case now. We would always, if possible, marry lighter-hued people so as to have children who are not identified with the Negro race, and thus solve our racial problem in America by committing race suicide. (Du Bois 1973 [1960], 149–150)

Du Bois confronted this tendency, not very different from the color-blind position of the present day, with the same radical democratic alternative he had been proposing over the course of the entire century. He recognized at its dawning the outlines of the new world racial system that would not be fully realized for many decades. He identified very early the limits of the moderate civil rights vision: the United States could not undo its deep commitment to white supremacy, at least not without a fundamental social upheaval. Blacks would be asked to absorb the costs of their inclusion, not whites. The price black people would be asked to pay in return for full inclusion was self-negation: the repudiation of their particularity and the unlearning of their history. Determined to maintain both the demand for full equality and the integrity of black identity, Du Bois *refused to choose* between the two terms of "American" and "Negro."

Du Bois ends his talk with a series of revolutionary commitments: the world, he says, is "going socialist." Black people should support a socialist transition in the United States as the only route to full equality; they should also dedicate their resources to self-determination and autonomous development for their own community. Du Bois also reiterates his long-standing commitments to pan-Africanism and the well-being (again, within the socialist framework), of the formerly colonized peoples of the South.

What can we take from this talk today? As I have noted, the injunction against race "suicide" remains convincing. The socialist alternative that Du Bois embraced (and about which he was perhaps willfully naive) is dead: the Stalinist and Maoist systems were certainly no democratic alternative for blacks in the United States or the "wretched of the earth" in general. Without repudiating the ideals of socialism—of cooperation, egalitarianism, and democratic self-rule—we probably have to reject Du Bois' complacency about the "actually existing forms" that socialism took at this time.[22]

Yet at the same time the contours of the Duboisian political formula of racial dualism—what he calls "the possibility of black folk and their cultural patterns existing in America without discrimination and on terms of equality" (150)—seems, if extrapolated to a global level, a good starting-point for revisioning a political program for the next century or so. This vision remains strong. It continues as a radical pole of attraction. It is a "North Star" that shines yet.

To return to the Duboisian dictum with which I began this chapter: at the start of the twenty-first century the world as a whole, and various national societies as well, are far from overcoming the tenacious legacies of colonial rule, apartheid, and segregation. All still experience continuing confusion, anxiety, and contention about race. Yet the legacies of epochal struggles for freedom, democracy, and human rights persist as well.

Despite the enormous vicissitudes that demarcate and distinguish national conditions, historical developments, roles in the international market, political tendencies, and cultural norms, racial differences still operate as they did in centuries past: as a way of restricting the political influence, not just of racially subordinated groups, but of all those at the bottom end of the system of social stratification. In the contemporary era, racial beliefs and practices have become far more contradictory and complex. The old world racial order has not disappeared, but it has been seriously disrupted and changed. The legacy of democratic, racially oriented movements,[23] and anti-colonialist initiatives throughout the world's South, remains a force to be reckoned with. But the incorporative (or if one prefers this term, hegemonic) effects of decades of reform-oriented state racial policies have had a profound result as well: they have removed much of the motivation for sustained, anti-racist mobilization.

In this unresolved situation, it is unlikely that attempts to address worldwide dilemmas of race and racism by ignoring or transcending these themes, for example, by adopting so-called color-blind or differentialist policies, will have much effect. In the past the centrality of race deeply determined the economic, political, and cultural configuration of the modern world. Although recent decades have seen an efflorescence of movements for racial equality and justice, the legacies of centuries of racial oppression have not been overcome. Nor is a vision of racial justice fully worked out. Certainly the idea that such justice has already been largely achieved—as seen in the color-blind paradigm in the United States, the non-racialist rhetoric of the South African Freedom Charter, the Brazilian rhetoric of racial democracy, or the emerging racial differentialism of the European Union—remains problematic.

Will race ever be transcended? Will the world ever "get beyond" race? Probably not. But the entire planet still has a chance of overcoming the stratification, the hierarchy, the taken-for-granted injustice and inhumanity that so often accompanies the race-concept. Like religion or language, race can be accepted as part of the spectrum of the human condition, while it is simultaneously and categorically resisted as a means of stratifying national or global societies. Nothing is more essential in the effort to strengthen our commitments to democracy and social justice, and indeed to global survival and prosperity, as we enter a new millennium.

Notes

CHAPTER ONE. INTRODUCTION

1. Here is what I mean by "race": *a concept that signifies and symbolizes sociopolitical conflicts and interests in reference to different types of human bodies.* Although the concept of race appeals to biologically based human characteristics (so-called phenotypes), selection of these particular human features for purposes of racial signification is always and necessarily a social and historical process. There is no biological basis for distinguishing human groups along the lines of "race," and the sociohistorical categories employed to differentiate among these groups reveal themselves, upon serious examination, to be imprecise if not completely arbitrary (Omi and Winant 1994).

2. There were certainly other "others," notably Asians. These peoples, though, tended (with some exceptions) to come later under the sword of European subjugation, and to be relatively less deracinated by that process, although they were hardly immune to it.

3. Some examples of this sort of argument may be found in Winant 1994a, 37–68; Winant 1997b.

4. What is *racism?* Although this term only appeared in the twentieth century, the ideas and practices it denotes arose with the dawn of the modern era (Bulmer and Solomos 1999; Goldberg 1993). As a world-historical phenomenon, racism is so large and so diverse that no definition can encompass all its varieties. A minimally adequate concept must take into account the social and historical constructedness of race itself (see note 1, above). It must also recognize the linkage among racial concepts, actions, and social structures. This begins to indicate some of the problems involved; an enormous literature has arisen to address such themes (see Goldberg 1990; Taguieff 2001 [1988]). With this in mind racism can be provisionally defined as inhering in one or more of the following: *(1) signifying practice that essentializes or naturalizes human identities based on racial categories or concepts; (2) social action that produces unjust allocation of socially valued resources, based on such significations; (3) social structure that reproduces such allocations.* See also Chapter Eleven, below.

5. The activities of the United Nations in respect to global issues of racism and racial discrimination illustrate some of the ways global racial politics have shifted in the post–World War II era. As this book goes to press, the General Assembly is preparing an important world conference on racism, which will be convened in South Africa in August 2001.

But the UN's efforts to comprehend and combat race and racism stretch from its founding. Already in the 1940s U.S. activists and intellectuals brought several petitions and denunciations to various United Nations fora (see Chapter Seven, below). UNESCO has conducted numerous conferences and published various studies on such themes as race and colonialism, the African slave trade, and so on (UNESCO 1981; UNESCO 1979a; UNESCO 1979b; Montagu 1952). UNESCO also sponsored an important series of studies on race and racism in South Africa (e.g., Cohen 1986) and Brazil (see Chapter Nine, below). On the UN as an arena for LDC and southern politics at the global level, see Krasner 1985.

Then in the early 1960s, as newly independent and post-colonial countries began to exercise influence at the United Nations—particularly in the General Assembly, where their votes came to dominate—the UN was pressured to take action against racism and racial discrimination. The formulation in 1965 of the International Convention Against All Forms of Racial Discrimination was a result, not only of these countries' demands, but also of the rising tide of opposition to South African apartheid, especially in the aftermath of the

Sharpeville (1960) massacre. It also expressed a continuing international affinity with the U.S. civil rights movement, whose leader Martin Luther King Jr. had just been awarded the Nobel Peace Prize, and which was then at the height of its confrontation with the North American version of apartheid. The 1965 Resolution's "preambular paragraphs," notes the British racial theorist Michael Banton, "present racial discrimination as caused by racist doctrines and colonialism" (Banton 1999, 608).

6. The United States was a latecomer to the field of international deliberations on racial matters. In fact, it refused for thirty years to sign the UN convention just discussed, the one that called for the elimination of all forms of racism.

7. See Hanchard 1992. Nancy Leys Stepan notes the ambiguity of early-twentieth-century Latin American commitments to *mestizaje* as a response to racism (Stepan 1991). For Vasconcelos especially, there was a significant eugenicist dimension involved, which grew in importance as he moved rightward politically. Freyre signed a 1935 manifesto against racism. In his early days Freyre criticized both North American racism (he had observed it while studying under Franz Boas at Columbia University) and the Brazilian ideal of whitening (*branqueamento*). Later in life (especially during the years of dictatorship: 1964–85) Freyre inveighed against any black Brazilian identification with the U.S. or South African black movements. See Carvalho 2000.

8.

"And until the ignoble and unhappy regimes
That hold our brothers (sic) in Angola, in Mozambique,
South Africa sub-human bondage
Have been toppled, utterly destroyed
Well, everywhere is war, we say war."
(Marley 1976, following Selassie 1963)

Note the extent to which these views continue to apply, as much in "post-colonial" Angola, still riven by civil war; as in southern Africa.

9. See Mamdani 1996; Adam et al. 1997a. Mamdani and Adam have engaged in spirited debate over the continuing significance of South African racial issues. See Mamdani 1997; Adam 1997.

10. This can also be applied to women, gays, the aged, and youth. In other words, the complex of issues we designate as "human rights" calls into question the supposed realization of democracy in the West, centrally in respect to race, but also in terms of other (non-racial) aspects of identity.

11. The term *Jubilee* refers to the biblical injunctions against transferring debts, slave status, or accumulated property in land across generations. At the time of the biblical "Jubilee" (roughly once every fifty years), debts were to be cancelled, slaves emancipated, and land returned to its original cultivators. The website of the Jubilee 2000 movement to cancel the external debt of the poor nations can be found at http://www.j2000usa.org.

12. Thus the question of who is indebted to whom is itself a major political issue.

13. If the "40 acres and a mule" program had been carried out during the Reconstruction period in the United States (instead of being scuttled by order of President Andrew Johnson in 1868), the process of "making whole" the injustices of slavery would not only have been greatly facilitated in North America, but also on a world-historical scale. In truncated fashion this argument is proposed by Du Bois in *Black Reconstruction* (1977 [1935]), but of course cannot be fully worked out.

CHAPTER TWO. THE HISTORICAL SOCIOLOGY OF RACE

1. This argument is presented in greater depth in Omi and Winant 1994.

2. There is a wide range of methodological limits to most social scientific approaches to race, limits that cannot be addressed in depth here. Schematically speaking, most social scientific approaches to race are *nomothetic* in terms of methodology: that is, they follow scientific norms assumed to operate universalistically. Thus they propose to investigate a clear cause-effect relationship between two or more sets of variables, some of which are known

(dependent) and others of research interest (independent). The need for precise specification of each variable's dimensions, and for strict separation between cause and effect variables, is basic to such techniques.

But if race is as constitutive of social order as I suggest it is, then assigning it to one or the other side of this equation is problematic. On the one hand, to treat racial phenomena as dependent variables—the effects of other, putatively more fundamental or "objective" social structures or relationships (such as social class, cultural identity, or nationality)—is prone to reductionism, as I have shown elsewhere (Omi and Winant 1994). On the other hand, to consider racial dynamics as independent variables—studying, say, the effects of race on family dynamics or employment patterns—tends to ignore the tremendous variability of the race-concept, which operates both as a social structure and a dimension of lived identity/experience. The flexible and malleable character of race, which has evolved over an immense historical span, cannot be captured if it is merely treated as a fixed category. See Wallerstein 1991, 242–244.

3. No early empire could attain truly global scope. None could exist without a central administrative nucleus, a politico-military authority that extended and disciplined the imperial domain, directing the empire's accumulative flow toward the center by various means (tributary, coercive, etc.), and accepting no rivalry within the boundaries of the system.

4. Of course this is undertaken in light of many influences, among them "world-system" analysis and the pragmatic, progressive social science of Myrdal, as well as such other currents as Foucauldian post-structuralism and Gramscian theory.

5. For example, the magisterial work of Braudel 1975. See especially Braudel's treatment of slavery in vol. III.

6. In his story "In the Penal Colony" Franz Kafka depicts an infernal machine of punishment, designed to execute insubordinate natives in a prison colony located on an unnamed tropical island. The form of capital punishment is brutal and prolonged: tortuously, slowly, the rule which the condemned has violated (in the story, this rule is "HONOR THY SUPERIORS!") is written with needles on the condemned's body, embellished and elaborated until at last, bleeding from the very words it has defied, covered with the mark of its own shame, the body dies and is discarded (Kafka 1961).

7. Let this overly general assertion be qualified: early modern European relations with littoral African states and kingdoms, and indeed with native Americans (first in the Caribbean and then more widely), were not immediately and uniformly those of conquerors and subjects. There were wide variations in the early experiences of transcontinental contact. African fighters repelled European raids and efforts at pillage. In the fifteenth century, for example, there were naval battles between Portuguese vessels and large war canoes off the Senegambian and Kongolese coasts (Thornton 1998, 37–40). There were wars among Portuguese, Angolan, and Kongolese forces—often involving shifting patterns of alliance—as late as the end of the sixteenth century. Such experiences led to trading rather than raiding relationships (or complex combinations of the two), which often endured for long periods (Miller 1988, 551–552). In the early plantation experiments on the Atlantic islands, in early African slavery in the Americas (Rout 1976; Davidson 1961), and in the centuries-long process of subjugation of American native peoples, similar interweavings of depredation and coexistence can be discovered. Overall, of course, tendencies toward outright conquest and hierarchization, and the abundant testimonies of racialization, do predominate. But these patterns too are more circular and cumulative than abrupt, immediate, or unproblematic for the particular European power involved.

8. Such distinctions must always be seen as schematic, for several reasons: early imperial missions of raiding or trading were staffed at all ranks by a variable and itinerant lot of seamen, soldiers, and freebooters of all types, many of whom were mercenaries, not "citizens." (Columbus himself is the most ready example.) Later imperial trading and shipping bred a seafaring working class whose national and indeed racial particularities tended to be homogenized by its conditions of labor (Rediker 1987).

9. Many of the slave revolts that took place throughout the hemisphere were organized along ethnic/linguistic lines (Thornton 1998).

10. For debates on Williams' thesis, see Solow and Engerman 1987; Wood 1997; Drescher 1999.

11. Voluminous literatures exist on virtually every imaginable aspect of slavery. In Chapter Three I discuss slavery at greater length, although writing on the topic is so extensive that I cannot claim to address it thoroughly.

12. See also Engerman and Genovese 1975; Fogel and Engerman 1974; Fogel 1989; Williams 1994 [1944].

13. By "peonage" I mean coerced forms of labor that do not extend to chattel status. Serfdom, bound labor, and *corvée* could be mentioned here. Some forms of landless peasant labor, for example, tenant farming and sharecropping, also qualify. Where arrangements of superexploitation short of chattel slavery exist, it is worthwhile to classify them as peonage, even though they may involve some wages or in-kind exchanges of value.

14. For U.S. defenses of the moral superiority of slavery as against waged forms of labor exploitation, see Wish 1960; see also Genovese 1992b; and Fredrickson 1971 on these points.

15. In those areas where feudalism was slow to decay or left behind significant social residues, for example, in Russia and Junker-dominated Prussia, peonage remained the prevalent method of extracting labor (Kolchin 1987). In other areas peonage operated through traditional systems of peasant-based agriculture. Still elsewhere, for example, in the Caribbean and East Africa, indentured labor was imported by colonial powers (through recruitment of South Asian labor in these cases) as an alternative or competitive strategy to slavery-based or traditional peasant-based systems of exploitation. The regulatory aspects of these developments, and their underlying racial logics, are quite apparent. Although not racialized everywhere (Russia, for example, retained its interest in the Jewish "other" whose racial difference was not deeply significant there), in most of the imperial world Europeans ruled non-European "others." Thus racial distinctions came largely although variably to coincide with political-economic and cultural ones.

16. But what is "excessive"? Slave labor almost always takes place under the shadow of brutality.

17. This was especially the case after: (1) the effects of contagious diseases began to be felt throughout the Americas; (2) the depredations of early slave-labor mining schemes, particularly under the Spanish, laid waste many indigenous populations; and (3) the inadequacy of the supply of indentured servants (largely white) to the developing plantation agriculture system was recognized, particularly in the North American colonies (Klein 1986; Tannenbaum 1992 [1947]).

18. Already in Weber's treatment of slavery—focused on the classical period, particularly Rome (Max Weber 1976)—there is the argument that high demand for slave labor and its products are crucial to its profitability, for in times of slack the maintenance of slaves can become a drain on their owners; slaves cannot be laid off like wage laborers. In respect to Weber and race more generally, see Weber 1978, 385–387; Manasse 1947; Rex 1980; Guillaumin and Poliakov 1974; Guillaumin 1995.

Whether the maintenance of slaves is a fixed cost, whether their mistreatment is involved in this determination, remains an open question. Owners of course had varying interests in maintaining the well-being of their slave "capital." When new "supplies" (i.e., replacements) were readily available, slavocratic regimes were more draconian (Schwartz 1985; Toplin 1972; Berlin 1998). See Chapter Three, below.

19. Although once more, between peonage and southern waged labor there may be distinction without difference.

20. In *Don Quixote* and *The Tempest*, to pick two prominent works.

21. Notably las Casas, who argued for the Indians' humanity and suggested their innate suitability for conversion, did not hesitate to recommend the substitution of African for Native American enslavement.

22. Consider, among many possible examples, Verdi's *Aida* (1871). Another high art object worth mentioning is the painting by Joseph M. W. Turner, *The Slaveship* (1840), which is a clear denunciation of the slave trade. The painting is probably based on a 1783 incident in which the masters of the slave ship *Zong,* lost at sea and despairing of their voyage's prof-

its, decided to throw their living cargo into the ocean, the better to offset their losses with the ship's insurers (see Thomas 1997, 489–490). It hangs in the Museum of Fine Arts, Boston.

23. "Threatened by the absolutism of the king, the nobility had reverted to the argument of an ancient race in order to claim freedom and equality—for themselves alone. The revolutionary bourgeoisie took up the challenge, rejected the Germanic myth, and replaced it with a Gallic one (still traceble in the popular adventures of [the French comic book series *Asterix and Obelisk*). Historian Guizot, for instance, would picture the French Revolution as a veritable war between two peoples" (Rooy 1990).

24. Gobineau 1984 [1853–55]; Biddiss 1970; Todorov 1993; Rooy 1990. Both John Lukács and George M. Fredrickson analyze the extensive correspondence between Gobineau and Tocqueville, who were friends; see Lukács 1974; Fredrickson 1997a. As many of these writers make clear, Gobineau's racism is rather more anti-democratic and counter-egalitarian than full-fledged white supremacy. Unlike his proto-Nazi successor Houston Stewart Chamberlain, he is not particularly anti-semitic. His hostility to Africans is explicit, but less color-oriented than Europeanist. Gobineau's antagonism is to what he sees as race-mixing: thus Finns and Magyars (European descendants of Mongol invasions) are also perceived as threatening. Gobineau, let it be noted, was a French diplomat (ambassador to Brazil as well as elsewhere), an early Orientalist who wrote on ancient Greek and Persian texts, and a historian of Norwegian piracy in France. He also published fiction and poetry.

25. The 1914 breakdown of the Second International indicated the endurance of this ambivalence into the twentieth century.

26. Of course, this is not to characterize Marxism in toto by such positions. Marx's comments on the barbarity of slave-trading ("the turning of Africa into a warren for the commercial hunting of black skins"), and on the brutalities of Asian and Latin American conquest as well, have often been noted.

A noteworthy exception to the Marxian founding fathers' somewhat sanguine attitude toward imperialism may be found in Luxemburg's *The Accumulation of Capital* (1951 [1923]), which sees the world's hinterlands as a permanently necessary source of regressive subsidization for capitalism, notably in their coerced use as an under- (or un-) valued source of exploitable labor. Wallerstein (1979a) shares some of this optic.

27. The Duboisian dictum is in *The Souls of Black Folk* (1989 [1903], 1). It should be remembered that Du Bois located the color-line, not only in the United States, but as a global phenomenon. His analysis of racism focused not only on the aftermath of African enslavement in the United States, but also on the unraveling of European empires, and on the fate of "the darker nations of the world—Asia and Africa, South and Central America, the West Indies and the islands of the South Seas" (Du Bois 1995 [1915], 645).

CHAPTER THREE. LEARNING TO CATCH HELL

1. Many discursive conventions have been applied to the racial body, each bearing its own theoretical presuppositions. For present purposes, it is enough to evoke some of the terms in which "somatic normativity" has been expressed.

2. With small exceptions, neither the classical nor the contemporary literatures on the transition from "pre-capitalist economic formations" to capitalism have much to say about race. In *Capital I* (1967) Marx refers in passing to the racial dynamics of "primitive accumulation," equating early conquest, pillage, and African slavery with the dispossession of European (notably English) peasantries. To mention only a few works: the otherwise magnificent books of E. P. Thompson on enclosure (1975); of Paul M. Sweezy et al. on the breakdown of the feudal order and the rise of the bourgeoisie (1976); of Robert Brenner on the onset of mercantilism in England (1993); of Barrington Moore on the "making of the modern world" (1966); of Karl Polanyi on the role of the state in constructing—and later destroying—the system and ideology of the capitalist "free market" (1980 [1944]); and of Theda Skocpol on the revolutionary crisis of the ancien régime (1979), are all quite circumspect—to put it generously—about racial matters. This list could go on, and certainly is not intended to diminish these books' valuable qualities. But despite their many merits, these accounts also suffer

from their racial blinkers: Moore's chapter on the U.S. Civil War inadequately reinvents Du Bois's account in *Black Reconstruction* (Du Bois 1977 [1935]), which is not cited and which Moore presumably did not consult. Skocpol does not make use of James's *The Black Jacobins* 1989 [1938] and does not discuss the Haitian revolution in her section on France. Karl Polanyi, who worked on slavery in West Africa after writing *The Great Transformation*, does not discuss the significance of the slave trade for the rise of capitalism in England. Albert O. Hirschman's important reflection of the rise of capitalist market rationality (1977) takes little interest in the centrality and persistence of slavery in rising capitalism.

3. I neglect here the important question of the European price inflation brought about by the massive infusion of precious metals in the sixteenth and seventeenth centuries. For some discussions of this topic, see Goldstone 1984; Braudel 1972, vol. I, 462–542; Wallerstein 1974, 66–131.

4. Indeed, the immediate precedent for the Atlantic slave trade—sugar slavery in the Mediterranean—began as an insular project (under Italian control, in Cyprus and Crete) precisely because defeat in the Crusades had forced the Europeans to withdraw from the Middle East.

5. And final tentative peace, after the Treaty of Westphalia in 1648.

6. For material on the founding of Spain and the origins of its empire, see Ladero Quesada et al. 1998; O'Gorman 1961; Clendinnen 1989; Abu-Lughod 1989.

7. Economies instituted by states (Polanyi 1980 [1944]); "entrepreneurship" outside state purview; forms of state "licensing" ("captaincies," encomienda, mixed companies of various sorts).

8. For an extensive example of this argument, see Allen 1994.

9. Freyre 1986 [1933]; for a parallel account on this point, see Buarque de Holanda 1973.

10. It is worth remembering not only the vast intellectual contributions proceeding from the Islamic world in the Middle Ages, but also the role of Arab scholarship in preserving the classical European heritage from destruction. Thus not only in their original works in mathematics and astronomy, in history and philosophy (for example, Ibn Khaldun [1332–1406]); not only in their cultural policies (generally tolerant and pluralistic toward Jews and Christians who did not seek to subvert or convert Muslim regimes); but also through their preservation of much Greek philosophy and literature, medieval Arabs helped found modern Europe. No Moors, no Augustine, for instance. Maybe no Aristotle either.

11. According to Kiernan, by the mid-1500s fully one-tenth of Lisbon's population consisted of slaves (Kiernan 1969, 10).

12. African gold production was substantial before the onset of colonialism, as it was in the twentieth century: "In the later Middle Ages, Africa accounted for something like two thirds of world gold production, and it was the largest source of supply from the eleventh to the seventeenth centuries" (Appiah 1998, 69). Reader (1999) stresses that Africans—particularly Ghana—largely produced gold for export, first to the Arab world and then to Europe, and that they valued practical metals like copper more than "precious" ones.

13. Critical perspectives on this point are widely available. See Mudimbe 1994; Davidson 1992.

14. The "triangular trade" widely noted in the literature on North American and Caribbean slavery was but one instance of such circuits. See Findlay 1990. Klein (1986, 145–146) disputes the relevance of this term to the economics of slavery in Latin America (and particularly in Brazil), but the balance of the evidence is against him. For views contrary to his, see the passages from Solow 1991 and Fogel 1989 quoted below.

15. Brazil's Minas Gerais gold boom came later, after the turn of the eighteenth century, when the preeminence of *nordestino* sugar had long been ceded to the Caribbean. The principal miners in and around Ouro Preto were enslaved blacks (as the name of that beautiful town perhaps suggests). See Miller 1988; Moura 1988.

16. Las Casas 1992; Clendinnen 1989. Brutal Portuguese treatment of slaves, as well as slave-hunting by the so-called *bandeirantes* in the Brazilian *sertão*, earned denunciation too, notably by Father Antonio Vieira (Cohen 1998; Blackburn 1997). Africans of various statuses

sometimes participated in the supposedly heroic expeditions of the *bandeirantes*; this was the case elsewhere in Latin America as well (see Davidson 1961; Rout 1976).

17. Initially Brazil's unexplored territory was allocated by the Portuguese Crown to favored nobles as "captaincies." The sugar-cultivation area of the northeast became known as the *Reconcavo* as the plantation system developed.

18. So, basing herself on Charles Boxer's "scorecard," Barbara L. Solow says that in the seventeenth century "Holland played Portugal in Africa and tied, Holland played Portugal in Asia and won, [and] Holland played Portugal in Brazil and lost" (Solow 1991, 67).

19. Of course, there were considerable risks associated with the slave-owning enterprise, particularly financial risks. But during the "takeoff" period for British slavery in the eighteenth century, these risks were notably lessened.

20. Debates about the timing and varieties of this transition remain important. James's (1989 [1938]) insistence that the Caribbean sugar-mill (or we might say, the Brazilian *engenho* or Cuban *ingenio*) was the earliest site of capitalist industrial production, considerably antedating Manchester's "dark satanic mills," remains convincing.

21. In *Capitalism and Slavery* (1994 [1944]), Eric Williams famously accounts for racism itself (notably Britsh racism) as an outcome of the exploitative relationships of slavery. Although I disagree with the economic determinism of this position, Williams's thesis nevertheless retains great importance in respect to its detailed exposition of the dependence of developing capitalism on slavery. See Solow and Engerman 1987; Drescher 1999.

22. There are grand debates on this point as well. Certainly slaveholders were more concerned with their human property's well-being at some times and places than at others. For the present, it is enough to point out that it was the slaveholders' concern (or lack of it), their "regime" so to speak, rather than the autonomy of their chattels, that ultimately mattered.

23. Of course, this should not be taken to mean that there were no disputes about the meaning of race or about the boundaries and sources of racial difference. These concepts are inevitably, inexorably, contentious, and fungible. See Omi and Winant 1994; Winant 1994a.

24. There were notable exceptions, especially in the Caribbean and Central America, where the U.S. "big stick" took a racial form. See Helg 1990.

CHAPTER FOUR. THE EMPIRE STRIKES BACK

1. Writing in 1917, Du Bois linked racial slavery not only to the origins of modernity, but to class struggle:

> When we speak of modern African slavery we think of modern slavery as a survival of ancient slavery. But it was not. The cleft between the two was absolute. Modern slavery was the beginning of the modern labor problem, and must be looked at and interpreted from that point of view unless we would lose ourselves in an altogether false analogy. Modern world commerce, modern imperialism, the modern factory system and the modern labor problem began with the African slave trade. The first modern method of securing labor on a wide commercial scale and primarily for profit was inaugurated in the middle of the 15th century and in the commerce between Africa and America. Through the slave trade Africa lost at least 100,000,000 human beings, with all the attendant misery and economic and social disorganization. The survivors of this wholesale rape became a great international laboring force in America on which the modern capitalistic movement has been built, and out of which modern labor problems have arisen. (Du Bois 1995, 653)

2. See also Cooper and Stoler 1997.

3. Many types of slavery continued in the world's periphery into the twentieth century. In the clove plantations of Zanzibar it continued until World War I. Slave labor in cocoa production was maintained by the Portuguese Empire in Guinea-Bissau—linked in this case to British chocolate manufacturers like Cadbury—until at least 1920. (See the essays on latter-day African slavery in Klein 1993.) Heritable bonded labor status persists in both India and Pakistan, and racial slavery continues in Mauretania and Sudan (Bales 1999; Cotton 1998; Finnegan 2000). Sexual slavery—of women and girls for prostitution and domestic service—exists throughout the world (Sakhrobanek, Boonpakdi, and Janthakeero 1997).

4. Discussion here draws upon Finley 1960; Meillassoux 1991; Miers and Kopytoff 1977; Lovejoy 1983; Miller 1988; Lasker 1972; and Garcia 1944.

5. Lewis (1970) suggests that although there was intermittent anti-black prejudice in Islam, such attitudes did not generate any racialized orientation to slavery. Islam operated in the Atlantic slave complex both to facilitate and to oppose African enslavement. Arabs from the North had been the most established slave-trading partners before the advent of the Europeans, and thus established something of a precedent for the trade. In the wake of efforts to curtail the Atlantic trade from the early nineteenth century on, the trans-Sahara and Indian Ocean trades revived, largely under Arab auspices. On the other hand, Islamic voices from the Qu'ran forward, and Muslim opponents of slavery both in Africa and in the Americas, drew on religious sources to justify resistance. See Drake 1990; Toledano 1998. See also Chapter Five, below.

6. Slaves were also exported as a means of sending captured opponents—religious, military, political—into exile. "Panyarring," the enslavement of those who could not repay their debts, was also widespread.

7. A continuing flow of newly enslaved Africans reached the Americas, pouring steadily out of Africa right up to the moment of emancipation. Although subject to a certain ebbing, notably in the nineteenth century—brought about by the various revolutionary upsurges in the Americas, by the lackluster but official British and American prohibitions on the slave trade after 1808, and by the U.S. Civil War—the demand for slave labor continued unabated for centuries, and indeed increased fairly steadily. Thus enslaved Africans in the Americas generally had at least some sources of information—perhaps unreliable and intermittent, but by no means nonexistent—about their countries of origin, as well as a continually renewed sense of Africanity (Hausa, Mayombe, Bakongo, Duala, etc.). This fact tends to obviate the debate over the extent of African "cultural survivals." See the articles by Herskovits and Frazier in van den Berghe 1978. The continuing interchange between Africa and America *under conditions of slavery* is just beginning to receive the mainstream attention it deserves.

8. For example, Thornton revises James's claim that the Haitian revolution was largely the outcome of the spread of French revolutionary ideals to the colony. He does this by documenting the presence of Kongolese military and political culture in revolutionary Haiti (Thornton 1991; Thornton 1993).

9. "The language . . . employed to describe the slaves as they passed through the city was liberally studded with terms . . . derived from livestock handling: the infants were *crias*, 'young' animals; the adults were 'head' (*cabeças*); they lived in *quintais* ("pens"), sometimes literally amidst the swine kept also in these 'yards'; and the principal eighteenth century compilation of commercial law and practice bluntly headed its chapter regarding provision for cargoes at sea as 'Marine Insurance for Slaves and Beasts'" (Miller 1988, 394). Compare Gilroy 1993, 215, n. 75 on North American terminology for slaves and Nazi terms for Jews.

10. Miller also offers a detailed account of the economy of slave "production" with a focus on Angola (and much material on Brazil as well). He estimates survival rates of slaves taken from the Angolan interior, propelled through the journey to Luanda or Benguela, undergoing the middle passage, and finally reaching "placement" (that is, sale) in Brazil, as 25 to 40 percent.

11. The appearance and growth of resistance to conquest and enslavement is theoretically intelligible as a cumulative and circular process, to return once more to Myrdal's pragmatic interpretation (see Chapter Two, above). Such an approach might invoke that contemporary sociological form of pragmatism, symbolic interactionism, applying it to the accretive ("cumulative") process though which small acts of resistance built toward greater ones, and to the imperative of (re)interpretation that enslaved and subjugated people had constantly ("circularly") to reenact in their refusal of "social death" (Patterson 1982). As far as I know there has been no attempt explicitly to apply symbolic interactionism (Blumer 1969; Blumer 1958; Blumer and Duster 1980) to the sociology of slavery, although there are hints of such an approach in the latter article. Obviously I cannot pursue this line of analysis here, but similar pragmatic themes recur throughout this book.

12. "And what about acquiescence?" a friend asked. Certainly there was plenty of it: demoralization, resignation, self-loathing, and collaboration. Slavery and conquest, like other forms of domination and exploitation, could not have survived, let alone prospered, if they had not been able to secure the cooperation of their subjects with more than the lash. This chapter emphasizes resistance because of the central role it played in overcoming slavery, challenging imperialism, and dynamizing democracy.

Such an approach must necessarily avoid enormous controversies and forego engagement with huge bibliographies. Just as I do not enter here into the vast debate about the organization, profitability, or ideology of the various systems of slavery and conquest, so too I do not attempt to sort out the many theories of the identities of these systems' subjects. Some of these accounts have emphasized resistance (e.g., Stampp 1956; Helg 1995). Some have stressed deracination and acquiescence (e.g., Elkins 1976; Tannenbaum 1992 [1947]). Still others have highlighted the varieties of paternalism that characterized slavocratic and imperial regimes (Genovese 1974; Freyre 1986 [1933]). There are many other dimensions to the literature as well, for example, debates about the role of cultural factors in sparking resistance. In the Americas until recently, there was controversy about African "survivals" and cultural domination (e.g., the Herskovits–Frazier debate, excerpted in van den Berghe 1978), and about religious syncretism (Bastide 1978 [1960]; Stuckey 1987). Subsequently, as the influence of African historical studies increased, these concerns were superseded by a diasporic focus (Kilson and Rotberg 1976; Lemelle and Kelley 1994; Thompson 1987; Okpewho, Davies, and Mazrui 1999; Walters 1995).

13. Slave revolts were often betrayed, for example, and some whites did ally with enslaved blacks, especially as abolitionism advanced. Racial solidarity was not so monolithic that it could overcome interethnic conflict among the enslaved (Thornton 1998) or entirely obviate moral or religious objections to slavery among the whites.

14. Here I cannot explore the complex relationships that developed in the Americas between Africans and indigenous peoples. Certainly these varied tremendously, running from alliance and amalgamation to enmity. At some moments and in some places, "miscegnated" and interbred peoples developed as a result of prolonged contact between maroons and Indians. In other times and situations, Africans and native peoples fought each other, raided each other (Africans were among the Brazilian *bandeirantes*, for example), or even enslaved each other. But the predominant picture was less internecine struggle and more alliance against the whites (Forbes 1993).

15. See the discussion of the Haitian revolution in this chapter, below.

16. A few citations must inadequately substitute for the range of material out there: Di Leonardo 1991; McClintock et al. 1997; and Stoler 1995 offer important overviews on the intersections of race and gender in colonialism. Hodes 1997 uncovers a substantial amount of black male-white female union under North American slavery and in its aftermath. There is a large literature on "miscegenation": Rogers 1967–72; Williamson 1980; Gutierrez 1991; Allen 1986; Mörner 1967; Freyre 1986 [1933]; Freyre 1959..

17. For interesting treatments, see Hine 1979; Brown 1996; Hodes 1997; Rawick 1972a. See Chapter Five for further discussion of miscegenation and hybridity issues. For African materials, see Bay 1998; Robertson and Klein 1983. For Brazilian cases, see Borges 1992; for Southeast Asian instances, see Stoler 1997.

18. I do not mean to deny the presence of syncretic religious practices, such as those studied by the estimable Roger Bastide (1978 [1960]). Rather, in suggesting that religious adherence among the racially subordinated transcended the merely adaptive, that it informed resistance practices on all experiential levels from the micro- to the macro-political, I am embracing a newer and more radical anti-racist and anti-colonialist sociology of religion (Fields 1985; Bontemps 1992).

19. I am no military historian, and so may be unaware of appropriate literatures. But with all the study of anti-colonial struggle, including military struggle, throughout the modern world from Africa (Knight 1995); from Latin America (Domínguez 1980); to Indonesia (Reid 1974); to the Great Plains (Greene 1994); has there been any comparative social scientific work (historical, sociological, etc.) on military resistance to conquest and enslavement?

20. Of these the most famous is Frederick Douglass's battle in the barnyard with Covey, the "slave breaker." See Douglass 1987; McFeely 1991.

21. Slave narratives are more available in the United States than elsewhere, due in large part to the interviews conducted in the 1930s under a project supported by the Works Progress Administration. See Rawick 1972b; Lester 1978; Mellon 1988. Research on the experience of slavery proceeds apace nearly everywhere in the Americas. See, for example, Cope 1994; Russell-Wood 1982.

Looking at the North American mainland and the British Caribbean, Michael Mullin distinguishes three periods of resistance. The first phase of the early eighteenth century followed the consolidation of the slavocratic order and coincided with a great increase of slave-trading; spontaneous and violent outbreaks, often marked by African customs and practices, characterize this period. A second phase, from the 1760s to the early 1800s, coincides with large-scale upheavals in the plantation system (brought on by the Seven Years' War/"French and Indian War," North American Revolution, and Haitian revolution); in this phase, according to Mullin, a more cautious subversion and sabotage, based in the plantations, predominates. The third phase was characterized by large, organized rebellions, led by acculturated (sometimes free) blacks, who were reacting to the more onerous and repressive regimes imposed by planters as fears of slave uprisings grew (Mullin 1993).

22. Besides his work on Surinam, Price (1996) offers the definitive collection of materials on *marronage*. On Jamaica, see also Campbell 1988.

23. An early republican rebellion—the *Inconfidencia* revolt (1789)—centered in the gold-mining town of Ouro Preto and led by merchants and intellectuals, also intersected with slave resistance and *quilombismo* (Chiavenato 1989; Mendes 1986). Slaves provided most of the mine labor, of course, and a number of *quilombos* were established in the region. The largest Minas *quilombo*, known as Ambrósio, was destroyed in 1746, at the height of the mining boom. Its population may have been as high as ten thousand at this time (Moura 1988, 225).

24. In contemporary Brazil a government agency, the *Fundação Cultural Palmares*, has been created to evaluate land claims made by the descendants of *quilombo* residents. See Chapter Nine, below.

25. On the Palmares *quilombo* and its leader/king, Zumbi, see Alves Filho 1988; Carneiro 1966; Freitas 1984; Moura 1972; Kent 1965.

26. See the amazing book by Kevin Mulroy (1993), upon which this paragraph draws.

27. And on behalf of slaveowners who were vexed by frequent losses of their human property via the "railroad."

28. Palmares was organized along clan lines and self-sufficient in agricultural production, although also engaged in raiding the colonial outposts (Portuguese and Dutch plantations) in the vicinity.

29. There is disagreement on the population of Palmares, but most researchers accept a figure of at least twenty thousand at the *quilombo*'s height. See Klein 1986, 200.

30. But for some efforts in this direction, see Genovese 1992a; Aptheker 1983; James 1985 [1938]; Craton 1982c; Klein 1986, 189–215; Segal 1995, 89–157.

31. The following section relies upon Davis 1975; Davis 1966.

32. Article I, Sect. 2 concerns the determination of representation in Congress and the assessment of taxes. Apportionment of representatives is to be based on a certain number of "free persons, including those bound to service for a term of years [that is, indentured servants or prisoners], and excluding Indians not taxed, [and] three fifths of other persons." The latter phrase is the notorious "three-fifths compromise" which included slaves for apportionment purposes at three-fifths the value of a "free person."

Article I, Sect. 9 concerns the soonest time at which Congress might lawfully regulate the slave trade (although as noted, the word *slave* is not mentioned). Regarding this clause, see also Article V, which prohibits its early amendment.

Article IV, Sect. 2 is the first fugitive slave provision of the new nation: it establishes the obligation to return to their masters those "held to service or labor in one state, under the laws thereof, [and] escaping into another." Although it implicitly concerns both slaves and convicts, its central object was to lessen the prospect of slaves escaping to the free states.

33. For example, in one famous 1783 case, *Quock Walker v. Nathaniel Jennison*, the court ruled that the 1780 Massachusetts Bill of Rights had de facto abolished slavery in that state (Cover 1975, 42–49). It should be noted that this decision occurred only a few years after Lord Mansfield rendered his epoch-making ruling in the English *Somerset* case.

34. Northern states in general were more likely to do this, but even Virginia manumitted black veterans in 1782 (Smith 1997, 104).

35. Other slave uprisings that exceed the ordinary definition of the term *revolt* and approach the status of "revolutions" occurred in Barbados in 1816 (Craton 1982a); in Demerara (British Guyana) in 1823 (Viotti da Costa 1994); and in Jamaica in 1830–31 (Reckford 1968; Craton 1982b; see also Holt 1992). All these events were profoundly influenced by the Haitian struggles of a few decades earlier.

36. The Haitian events can hardly be given full treatment here. Valuable accounts include: James 1989 [1938]; Fick 1990; Trouillot 1995; Nicholls 1996; Dupuy 1989; and Knight 2000. Scott (1986) provides an important review of the effects of the revolution on slave resistance and abolitionism throughout the Atlantic system.

37. Trouillot compares the world's unwillingness to accept the realities of Haiti with its denial of the Nazi Holocaust. That is acceptable, given the scale and lasting effects of the Haitian upheaval. An even greater parallel might invoke the epochal shifts brought about by other major revolutions like the Russian and French examples (the latter in large measure of a piece with the Haitian events). While the present account focuses on the overdetermined *causes* of the revolution, it is impossible to ignore its *effects*, which are Trouillot's main concern. These included repeated failed interventions against the uprising, massive fear among slaveholders and capitalists, and geopolitical realignments, among others.

38. The British alone lost more than sixty thousand soldiers in Haiti, the French about the same number. Dessalines ordered the summary execution of all remaining whites in 1805, possibly at the instigation of the British (James 1989 [1935], 307–308). The 1800 "war of the knives" between blacks and mulattoes prefigured (albeit in smaller scale) recent Rwandan events. Revolutionary brutality, it should be remembered, flowed fairly directly from the atrocity-laden French slavocracy that preceded it.

39. The Convention abolished slavery on February 4, 1794, although Napoleon was to revive it in 1802. Definitive abolition throughout the French Empire whould not occur until 1848.

40. James (1989 [1935]), who understands the linkages between Haiti and Paris very well (including how the upheavals in Haiti radicalized those in Paris), is perhaps not aware of the African connection to the Haitian struggle. As noted, a significant group of Toussaint's fighters were veterans of intense civil wars in the Congo, where they had gained experience in guerrilla warfare before being captured and sold into slavery on Saint Domingue. See Thornton 1991; Thornton 1993.

41. This entire analysis has borrowed heavily from the essay "Contradiction and Overdetermination" in Althusser 1969. Although Althusser's analysis focuses on the Russian revolution, it has more general applications. It is notable how many of the acclaimed accounts of the French Revolution manage to ignore Haiti almost entirely (for example, Skocpol 1979). A recent neo-Marxist analysis that grants Haitian events a measure of the importance they deserve is Stinchcombe 1995.

42. This role is improperly assigned to the North American Revolution, for the United States largely recoiled in horror from the Haitian events, refusing even to recognize the country for decades. The United States did benefit from the fact that the revolution terminated French dreams of American empire, though; the Louisiana purchase of 1803 was a direct result of French defeat in Haiti.

43. Still, Bolivar chose to embrace the cause and to identify himself with the Haitian struggle, launching some of his campaigns from there. For his campaigns as for others throughout the continent, slave emancipation and independence proved inseparable. Indeed, the 1811–21 fighting in what would become Venezuela bore some resemblance to the Haitian conflicts (see below). See also Nicholls 1996, 46–47.

44. Independence only came to Venezuela in 1830 after brutal warfare and the breakup of Bolivar's dream of a *Gran Colombia*. Full emancipation did not happen until the 1860s.

45. In Brazil the peculiar gradualism of the transition to independence did not facilitate the mass recruitment of black soldiers that revolutions brought about elsewhere. The bloody *Guerra do Paraguai* of the 1860s did mobilize and then manumit many enslaved blacks, however (Russell-Wood 1975). In Cuba the resilience of Spanish rule was probably the main factor in delaying abolition, despite plenty of black insurgency and *marronage* (Scott 1986; Helg 1990). Another exceptional case is Argentina, which mobilized its blacks in the 1810–23 period, during which, led by San Martin, they took part in anti-colonial wars not only in Argentina but in Chile, Ecuador, and Peru. Later much of the Afro-Argentine population left the country under duress, crossing the Plata to Uruguay (Andrews 1980).

46. These two Catholic leaders, as is well known, chiefly opposed enslavement of indigenous peoples. They approved the substitution of African enslavement for that of Native Americans, although late in his life las Casas came to criticize that as well.

47. In 1688, the the first public anti-slavery protest, mounted by Quakers, took place in the Germantown section of Philadelphia. In 1758, the Philadelphia Quaker Meeting voted to exclude any member who bought or sold slaves.

48. See Hoetink 1971; see also Tannenbaum 1992 [1947].

49. Curtin 1969 has for a long time been a principal source. More recent work has tended to revise Curtin's numbers upwards somewhat: see Rawley 1981; Inikori et al., 1986; Lovejoy 1989.

50. This is the feature of southern pro-slavery discourse, for example, that of George Fitzhugh, that has attracted avowed leftists like Eugene D. Genovese. See Genovese 1992b; Genovese 1996. For a digest of contemporary southern writings defending slavery and criticizing the "heartless" wage slavery of the North, see Wish 1960.

51. The number of blacks in Britain at this time was still very low. Nor were there early-nineteenth-century race-baiters to threaten British workers with low-waged black competition (that neo-fascist phenomenon was still a century in the future).

52. I dislike the term *American exceptionalism* with its implication of a European template for political development. The argument made here, in necessarily brief form, is that the uniqueness of U.S. politics flows from the centrality of race in national development and democratic genealogy.

53. On Brown's complex legacy, see Oates 1984; Du Bois's biographical essay (1997 [1909]) meditates profoundly on the question of white anti-racism; as does Russell Banks's recent novel on Brown, *Cloudsplitter* (1998).

54. The January 16, 1865 Special Field Order 15 of General William T. Sherman allocated land to emancipated blacks in areas under Union military occupation:

> The islands from Charleston, south, the abandoned rice fields along the rivers for thirty miles back from the sea, and the country bordering the St. Johns River, Florida, are reserved and set apart for the settlement of the negroes now made free by the acts of war and the proclamation of the President of the United States.

Further, Sherman ordered that tillable land be made available to former slaves:

> [E]ach family shall have a plot of not more than (40) forty acres of tillable ground, and when it borders on some water channel, with not more than 800 feet water front, in the possession of which land the military authorities will afford them protection, until such time as they can protect themselves, or until Congress shall regulate their title. The Quartermaster may, on the requisition of the Inspector of Settlements and Plantations, place at the disposal of the Inspector, one or more of the captured steamers, to ply between the settlements and one or more of the commercial points heretofore named in orders, to afford the settlers the opportunity to supply their necessary wants, and to sell the products of their land and labor. (Berlin et al. 1990, 338–340).

Thus the origins of the "40 acres." Of the mule there was nothing in this order, although Sherman later arranged to loan mules to the settlers. A later attempt by Radical Republicans to regularize and generalize this scheme throughout the occupied Confederacy was enacted in Congress but vetoed by Andrew Jackson. See also Foner 1988, 70–71; Oubre 1978.

55. These themes are pursued further in the next chapter.

56. Classical political economy has an anti-slavery tradition going back to Montesquieu.

Adam Smith criticized slavery on purely capitalist grounds in 1776, arguing that the cost of slave upkeep was generally greater than "free" labor wage costs. However, he qualified these positions in respect to sugar and tobacco cultivation, which he said were "exceptional" cases! See Smith 1994 [1776], 80.

57. The U.S. Civil War is rarely seen as an international crisis of modernity and capitalist development, much less as an instance of nineteenth-century imperialism. On British interventionism, see Jones 1992.

58. The slave trade was ended in 1807, and the institution of slavery was abolished in 1833. See Temperly 1972; Anstey 1975; Thomas 1997.

59. Disraeli was to make the best case for this position, echoing Adam Smith, ironically, almost a century after *The Wealth of Nations* had appeared. See Polanyi 1980 [1944], 212.

60. The bloody *Guerra do Paraguai* (1865–70), in which many blacks fought, did have some similar effects: it resulted in thousands of manumissions. See Russell-Wood 1975.

61. A member of the royal Bragança dynasty, Pedro II assumed the throne when his father, the Portuguese emperor who had been exiled in Rio, was able to return to Lisbon in 1831. Recognizing that Brazilians would reject reunion with Portugal, Pedro I abdicated in favor of his son (then only 6 years of age), thus creating an independent Brazil.

62. By 1888, probably two-thirds of all blacks in Brazil, or (very speculatively) at least 6 million people, were free. See Graham 1999; Toplin 1972.

63. Most famous among this mixed-race *classe meia* was probably Joaquim Maria Machado de Assis (1839–1908), the modernist writer of *Dom Casmurro*, among other works.

64. *O lei do ventre livre* (the law of the free womb) was passed in 1871, but was in fact a cynical and symbolic measure. Children could still be held to service until they turned 21, but only those born after the law's passage. Older slaves were not freed by the law.

65. Skidmore 1993 [1974] locates the whitening dynamic at the center of Brazilian national formation. Particularly in the late nineteenth century, Brazilian politics (largely elite politics, of course) were thoroughly enmeshed with racial issues. Skidmore's account approximates what in other work I have called a racial formation approach. Yet because it is an explicitly intellectual and political history, little attention is afforded to the thorny question of popular agency, especially that of Afro-Brazilians, in the development of Brazilian racial politics. On "racial formation," see Omi and Winant 1994; Winant 1994a.

66. Much to the chagrin of Afro-Brazilians, who remembered the abolitionist sympathies of the last Braganças, and mistrusted the elites and army officers who had founded the republic (through a "cordial" coup d'etat). Blacks no doubt recognized the republicans as partisans of the whitening project. See Viotti da Costa 1985; Scott 1988.

CHAPTER FIVE. NINETEENTH-CENTURY NIGHTMARES, TWENTIETH-CENTURY DREAMS

1. To be sure the social fact of working-class multiracialism had long predated abolition, especially in more mercantile and transnational sectors of the economy (Rediker 1987); but after abolition it continued to deepen and proliferate, in both the hinterlands and the metropoles.

2. "Barrès was one of the first thinkers in Europe to employ the term 'national socialism'" (Sternhell 1994, 11; see also idem 1972).

3. On the complexities of Wagner's anti-semitism and his essay "Das Judentum in der Musik," see Weiner 1995.

4. The contradictory elements of the gestation of modern racial theory in Europe are typified by Lombroso's work. Committed to a biologistic theory of criminality, Lombroso was also a Jew and a moderate socialist.

5. For a detailed synthesis of these intellectual currents and their political/cultural consequences, see Mosse 1978.

6. Eric Hobsbawm has written of the "long nineteenth century," which he dates from the French Revolution to the onset of World War I. The "racial nineteenth century" could be similarly demarcated: beginning with the Haitian revolution, passing through the era of

abolition and the U.S. Civil War, and terminating with the meeting of Kitchener and Marchand at Fashoda in 1898. Or it could be dated from the publication in 1807 of Hegel's *The Phenomenology of Mind*, with its famous critique of slavery, to Du Bois's *The Souls of Black Folk*, where the "problem" has shifted from its nineteenth-century form of slavery, to its twentieth-century one: the color-line.

7. They concerned the ethics of slavery, for example, and the qualifications for citizenship. See Finley 1960; Hannaford 1996.

8. To be sure, there were occasional exceptions, for example, las Casas's or Vieira's defenses of the Indians in Spanish and Portuguese America (see Chapter Three, above). Yet these too were limited to revision of the taken-for-granted paradigm, not fundamental questioning of it.

9. Although the institution of slavery confronted numerous assaults throughout the nineteenth century, it was never destroyed. It persisted, and continues still, at the margins of the capitalist system. Thousands are still enslaved in Africa (Cotton 1998; Bales 1999; Finnegan 2000), and various forms of non-chattelized slavery (bound labor, wageless work, etc.) may be found all around the world.

10. West African depopulation has also been related to the pronounced preference for male captives in the Atlantic slave trade (Thornton 1983).

11. The Portuguese slave trade from Mozambique to Brazil, for example, developed only in the late eighteenth century. There are not many studies of the Atlantic slave trade from Mozambique. I have learned what I could from Newitt (1995); Isaacman (1972) deals mainly with the slavery-based plantation system within Mozambique; Hill (1996 [1844]) is a brief period-based account of the Mozambique slave trade.

12. Ralph A. Austen estimates at approximately 300,000 the numbers of East Africans exported to Ottoman imperial as well as South Asian destinations during the nineteenth century. Ethiopians and Sudanese sent from Djibouti, Massawa, and other Red Sea/Gulf of Aden embarkation points totaled almost 500,000. African slaves sent to Egypt (both by water routes from East Africa and the Horn, and by West-to-East trans-Sahara land routes) totaled 362,000. Slaves reaching the Maghreb (not including Morocco) by South-to-North trans-Sahara land routes totaled 350,000. Morocco received some 300,000 slaves from sub-Saharan Africa during this period as well (Austen 1998; Austen 1992). There are certainly debates about these numbers, but even if they are eventually revised downward, they remain startling. Note that these figures do not include the flow of slaves into the Ottoman Empire from the north: the "white" slaves of the Caucasus and Balkan regions.

13. On the rule of Mehmet Ali/Muhammad Ali and his grandson/successor Ismail, see Lewis 1987, 23–25. Toledano (1998) stresses the Ottoman preference for female to male slaves; the relatively limited presence of concubinage and harem slavery as elite, and hence not widespread, practices; the presence of numerous "white" slaves (Georgian, Circassian) whose status was higher than that of darker, African slaves; the relative benignity of slavery under Islam; and the reform of imperial slavery in the mid-nineteenth century.

14. "The last big trans-Saharan slave caravan arrived in Libya in 1929" (Finnegan 2000, 53). Slavery was abolished by Saudi Arabia in 1962 and by Libya in 1969.

15. "Tippu Tip had supplied porters to Stanley, who had known enough not to ask too many questions about why they were sometimes in chains" (Hoschchild 1998, 130). This was in 1892. Already in 1887 Tippu Tip had agreed to serve as governor of the eastern section of the Congo; this was but one of his many deals with King Leopold II (ibid.).

16. These debates are in many ways continuous with the well-known controversy between Walter Rodney and J. D. Fage in the 1960s over the dynamics of the Atlantic slave trade. See Rodney 1966; Fage 1969. Thanks to Professor Tukufu Zuberi for bringing me up to speed on this literature. Cooper 1993a provides an extensive summary of this and related material.

17. Even in the early part of the nineteenth century the abolition of the trade had "rendered illegal as much as nine-tenths of European trade with the coast of West Africa. A huge economic vacuum was thus created and the British hoped it might be filled by the encouragement of the cultivation of exportable commodities" (A. Adu Boahen, quoted in Wallerstein 1976, 35).

18. It may seem paradoxical that as slavery receded in importance—not only as a means

of acquiring and disciplining labor, but also as the primary commodity in trade—race *continued and indeed expanded* as an organizing principle of economic life. But closer examination rather quickly suggests why this occurred: the requirement for cheap and coercible labor certainly played a part, but the dynamics of stratification, the political conflicts that resulted from the partial successes of abolitionism, and the culturally entrenched *habitus* of racial identification itself—which had endured for centuries by this time—also contributed in crucial ways to the resilience of the race-concept in the aftermath of slavery. I have more to say about these matters below; here I focus on economic issues.

19. Similar arguments have been put forward by neo-Marxist writers such as Thompson (1967) and Gutman (1976b) in respect to developing labor systems in metropolitan countries.

20. As well as those independent states—notably in the Americas—that maintained a significant extractive or plantation-based sector of their economies.

21. At the turn of the twentieth century, large peasantries persisted in many metropolitan countries. Migration was extensive, and in the aftermath of abolition, both geographical and status mobility for peasants (say, from Eastern Europe), and even for ex-slaves (say, from the Caribbean) was often possible. Thus no clear territorial or caste-like boundary is intended here. Yet on a world scale, uneven development may be seen to have corresponded, however generally and imperfectly, to the color-line. This is what is meant, I think, by Du Bois's comment.

22. An important new literature reinterpreting colonial dynamics—and challenging anthropological and historical paradigms of the colonized "other"—has surged in the past few years. Some highlights among numerous works: Coquery-Vidrovitch et al. 1988; Cooper and Stoler 1997; Cooper et al. 1993b; Torgovnick 1990; Clifford and Marcus 1986.

23. A 1828 decree largely abolished slavery and theoretically did away with "apprenticeship" among the Khoikhoi, the principal enslaved indigenous group. The latter practice, little more than slavery by another name, nevertheless continued throughout the century.

24. A considerable amount of indentured servitude (notably of Chinese) also existed, and the Boers also employed various early versions of "intermediate" forms of labor coercion, for example, "apprenticeship." In large measure these were euphemisms for slavery. Another notable distinction of the Boers—more comparable to the U.S. case than to other zones of Africa—is their early settlement as an "independent" white colonial group. See Fredrickson 1981, on whom the following section relies.

25. The same waves washed over the Americas and Australia, notably. Among many sources, see Higham 1994 [1955]; Lesser 1999.

26. Especially after a major confrontation between white workers and the state over this issue in 1922. On the gestation of the color bar, the "poor white problem," and the strike of 1922, see Fredrickson 1981, 229–233.

27. Convict labor, for example, had been employed extensively in the diamond mines for decades. "At various times between 1873 and 1887, the Kimberley jails housed as many as 67,000 prisoners. The De Beers Mining Company, soon the dominant force in the mining industry, built a convict-station for 3000 to 4000 convict miners" (Greenberg 1980, 153). Since imprisonment for vagrancy and pass law violation was widespread, thousands of convict workers could be made available by the state to the mining sector of capital on a regular basis.

28. The "Cape Coloured" category came into being in the nineteenth century as a miscegenated, largely urbanized racial group to whom the colonial regime was willing to concede some autonomy. "Coloureds" could thereafter largely escape the superexploited economic niche that I have labeled *peonage*, since they were not consigned to agricultural or extractive labor. Despite their relative advantages, of course, they remained subordinated to whites; in general, they strove to distinguish themselves from the fully inferiorized natives. See Fredrickson 1981, 131–135; Carstens 1966; James et al. 1996.

29. This account varies somewhat from the comparative work of Anthony Marx (1998), from which I have nevertheless benefited in various ways. Marx's study locates racial formation within the "nation-building" approach long associated with such analysts as Eisenstadt and Rokkan 1973; Bendix 1977; and Steinmo 1992; see also Fredrickson 1999. Fredrickson's

criticism of Marx stresses the "society-centered" (as opposed to Marx's "state-centered") dimensions of racial politics and racial formation. Fredrickson's argument that class dynamics must be given more weight in studying racial formation than Marx does, overlaps in some ways with the position I am taking here regarding the "socially instituted economy." Although I have relied considerably on Fredrickson's work I would go farther still in arguing for the multileveled importance of racial dynamics in structuring *both* states and societies in the modern epoch: economically, politically, and culturally. This is the position I have associated with Myrdal's formulation about circular and cumulative causation (see Chapters One and Two, above).

30. Moore (1966) argues that the mid-nineteenth century United States faced an epochal choice. One option was adoption of a gradualist and reform-oriented democracy: an English-type model of development, based on the generalization of industrialism and abolition of the peasantry. The other possibility was to accept an authoritarian, ethnonational, Prussian-German model: rule by a hegemonic class alliance composed of plantocrats and industrialists, who would not care a fig about democracy, much less racial or even ethnic inclusion. (The German instance of this was the famous "marriage of iron and rye." See Moore 1966, 130.)

Moore's view is probably too Eurocentrist; although primarily concerned with the meaning of the Civil War, he is more interested in slavery than race; his essay on the United States was seemingly written without the benefit of Du Bois' *Black Reconstruction*. Yet despite these flaws, Moore reasonably concludes that the "Compromise of 1877" (Du Bois' "counter-revolution") resolved the developmentalist conflict through the victory of the industrial North. But not without paying a price. The "compromise" preserved the Southern hinterland as a backward agricultural neo-colony. Since the defeated planters were beholden economically to the national banks for credit, and to Washington for connections to national politics, they could be conceded a significant measure of local authority within the boundaries of the former Confederacy. Thus the economic development of the United States toward industrialism and urbanism, and the broad political contours of *herrenvolk* democracy, were not only achieved at the expense of blacks, but depended upon the abandonment of blacks to peonage and powerlessness in the South. For generally parallel views, an indispensable source is C. Vann Woodward. See Woodward 1974; Woodward 1966; Woodward 1951; see also Holt 1982.

31. These two concepts were not significantly different during the nineteenth century, when any group (Jews, Irish, Slavs, etc.) could seemingly qualify as a "race." Only in the mid-twentieth century did a viable (if still ideal-typical) distinction between race and ethnicity develop. See Omi and Winant 1994.

32. Du Bois terms the "Compromise of 1877" by which Hayes entered the White House a "counter-revolution." This was the termination of Reconstruction and the relegitimation of racial exclusion and white supremacy colloquially known as "Jim Crow." Among the many scholars working in the Duboisian tradition here, see especially Foner 1988; Jaynes 1986; Wood 1968; Gillette 1979; Franklin 1994.

33. Black troops had been recalled earlier; those that remained were restricted in various ways: their efforts to protect freedpeople's communities from white riots and assaults by local (white) police were often deemed impolitic by their commanders, both on the spot and in Washington. For an 1866 example, see Rosen 1999.

34. Although the 1877 strike, as noted, was spontaneous in most respects, the National Labor Union (NLU), the most prominent labor organization of the time, had rejected or tabled several appeals by black leaders for recognition of black workers on a free and equal basis. Thus, says Du Bois,

> [T]he labor leaders went into the labor wars of 1877 having disarmed themselves of universal suffrage. And thus in 1876, when Northern industry withdrew military support in the South and refused to support longer the dictatorship of labor, they did this without any opposition or intelligent comprehension of what was happening on the part of the Northern white worker. (1977 [1935], 359)

The fledgling Knights of Labor, which had been founded in Philadelphia in 1869, would in subsequent decades advocate a more multiracial industrial unionism, as would the anarcho-syndicalist IWW. But these organizations played no significant part in the 1877 events. See Voss 1993; Weir 1996.

35. A particularly poignant instance of the practice of trade unionist racial exclusionism was the 1903 strike by sugar-beet workers (largely Mexican and Japanese) in Oxnard, California. The strikers' appeals to the Gompers-led American Federation of Labor for recognition and support were met by the Federation's refusal to recognize a union that included Asian workers. To their credit, the Mexican members of the Oxnard union (the Japanese-Mexican Labor Association—JMLA), whose affiliation the AFL did *not* reject, refused to abandon their co-workers:

> In the past we have counselled, fought, and lived on very short rations with our Japanese brothers, and toiled with them in the fields, and they have been uniformly kind and considerate. We would be false to them and to ourselves and to the cause of unionism if we accepted privileges for ourselves which are not accorded to them. (J. M. Lizarras, secretary of the Mexican branch of the JMLA, in Almaguer 1994, 202)

36. On these events, see Skidmore 1993 [1974], 79–83; Topik 1996.

37. These debates about the effects of race on national development, as might be expected, also dealt heavily with issues of eugenics and miscegenation (Skidmore 1993 [1974]). I touch on these themes in a later section of this chapter.

38. The inhabitants of Canudos were largely impoverished blacks and *mestiços* from the arid backlands, who fit more in the category of primitive rebel than criminal. The fierce Catholic fundamentalism of their leader Antonio Conselheiro also partook of a kind of primitive communism, a rejection of the republic, and an effort to establish the kingdom of heaven on earth. The community and its repression is the subject of the Brazilian classic *Os Sertoes* by Euclides da Cunha (translated as *Rebellion in the Backlands,* Cunha 1995 [1902]) and also renovelized by Mario Vargas Llosa as *The War of the End of the World* (1984). See also Levine 1992.

39. A practiced historian of Bahia reports, though, that the drumming fell silent during Lent, in the well-established (and much debated) pattern of Brazilian syncretism (Borges 1993, 50). See also Wimberly 1988; Oliveira 1998; Borges 1992.

40. European workers in Brazil at the time, particularly Italians, also showed a preference (obviously distasteful to their bosses) for anarcho-syndicalism.

41. At this time Japan was engaged in intensive efforts to modernize its economy. Hard-hit by the world economic crisis of the 1890s and unable to continue its support for emigration to the United States in the wake of that country's Asian exclusion acts, Japan encouraged emigration to South America.

42. Emigration was also a major factor. Tens of thousands of Afro-Caribbeans worked in Panama on the construction of the Canal, for example. Twenty thousand black Barbadians alone worked on the Canal, as did substantial numbers of Jamaicans and other Caribbeans (Segal 1995, 165, 178). These groups would respond very positively to Garveyism, especially in its early, trade-unionist forms (see below).

The flow of migrants to the United States and the United Kingdom was also greatly increased in the early decades of the twentieth century (James 1998). These migration patterns both overlapped and conflicted in large measure with the ebb and flow of northward migration and urbanization on the part of Afro-American former slaves and their descendants.

43. The founding statements of sociological theory were above all concerned to explain the emergence of modernity in Europe. While Marx, Weber, and Durkheim were highly cognizant of the dynamics of empire, the problems of inequality, and the questions we would now group under the rubric of "development," their social theories revolved around the "specter haunting Europe": a specter, if not of communism, at least of class struggle and social upheaval.

On the other hand, Marx, Weber, Durkheim, et al. could hardly escape some reckoning with the problem of the "other," however she or he was defined: as plundered and exploited laborer, as "primitive" or "uncivilized," or as "traditional" and mechanically solidaristic. Although this reckoning was not at the top of their explanatory priorities, these great thinkers were not immune from the racial stereotyping endemic to their times.

I have already mentioned the ambivalences of Marx and Engels toward colonialism: although critical of its depredations and implacably opposed to slavery, they also saw its "modernizing" characteristics as ultimately beneficial for the hinterlands. See Chapter Two, above.

Weber's treatment of the concept of *ethnie* under the rubric of "status" (a relational category based on "honor") presages a social constructionist approach to race. While in Weber's voluminous output there is no intensive consideration of the modern imperial phenomenon, there are numerous instances of European chauvinism (especially during the World War I years, when Weber was somewhat afflicted with German nationalism—see Weber 1994, 131; Weber 1995, 255). In fairness, Weber also recognizes racism, notably anti-black racism in the United States. See his remarks on U.S. racial attitudes in Weber 1958, 405–46. Weber's sensitivity to U.S. racial matters may be attributed, at least in part, to the orientation provided him by Du Bois. See Lewis 1993, 225, 277.

Durkheim too ranks the world Eurocentrically, distinguishing rather absolutely between "primitive" and "civilized" peoples based on the limited ethnology available to him; he also muses somewhat racialistically: racial categories are employed as "social types" in *Suicide*, for example. See Fenton et al. 1984. For a spirited defense of Durkheim's philosophical anthropology, see Fields's "Introduction" to Durkheim 1995 [1912].

My thanks to Professor Peter Baehr for helping me clarify some of these matters.

44. Well before this the philosophical foundations of Enlightenment racism had been laid. As I have already noted, the great thinkers of the Enlightenment—Hume, Diderot, Kant, Hegel, et al.—were given to displays of ignorance, condescension, and wild stereotyping on racial matters. These (largely eighteenth century) statements appear quite embarrassing today. See Eze 1997; Count 1950.

45. Gobineau's friend Tocqueville is also an early racial theorist of sorts. But race does not assume in Tocqueville's work the primacy it receives in Gobineau. Tocqueville, although pessimistic about racial matters and committed to the French *mission civilizatrice* in Algeria, is not the reactionary conservative that Gobineau is. In his study of the United States, for example, he notes clearly the injustice and rancor produced by the slave system. See Lukács 1974; Biddiss 1970; Fredrickson 1997a; Todorov 1993.

46. This is not the place to do intellectual history, but Gobineau's hostility to the legacy of the French Revolution is quite striking. Mosse notes that for Gobineau,

> [B]lacks also fitted into the scheme of contemporary politics. Gobineau gave them the characteristics by now [1850] traditional in racial thought: little intelligence, but overde-veloped senses which endowed them with a crude and terrifying power. The blacks were a mob on the loose, the masses that Gobineau envisaged (sic) in action during the French Revolution and in his own lifetime, eternal *sans culottes* who had collaborated with the middle classes to destroy the aristocratic France for which he yearned. (Mosse 1978, 53)

The conflict between a *volkish* romantic reaction and a modernizing politics that would generate both the liberal and radical/socialist visions of democracy may still be seen in the famous pronouncement of Goebbels upon the Nazi accession to power (1933) that "today the year 1789 is erased from history." This claim about the racial origins of fascism, should be read against the contrary views of Sternhell (1994), who stresses the variability of racism within fascism, and prefers to locate fascism's origins in Sorel.

47. Darwin in turn owed something to Malthus. Chase (1977) understands "scientific racism" as proceeding from the publication in 1798 of Malthus's *Essay on the Principle of Population*. As his title indicates, Chase considers these Malthusian origins as class-, not race-based. He distinguishes between "scientific" and "gut" racisms:

> Created in England, the birthplace of the Industrial Revolution, the original 'enemies list' of scientific racism consisted solely of people who were as white, as Protestant, and infinitely more Anglo-Saxon than the members of the Hanoverian Succession who then, as now, occupied the throne of England. To be sure, many of the early proponents of scientific racism were also social anti-Semites, anti-Catholics, and white supremacists. It is even true . . . that in due time the old-fashioned American gut racists were able to make tragically effective use of the high-toned literature and lexicon of scientific racism in such

non-economic efforts as the forging of the 1924 barriers against further Italian, Jewish, and other non-Nordic immigration to the United States.

Still, according to Chase's interpretation, scientific racism "remains color-blind and free of all racial, religious, and cultural biases. It is not concerned with people but, simply, with what is known as the maximization of profits and the minimization of taxes on these profits" (Chase 1977, 3–4). Desite the many merits of Chase's exhaustive research, I retain my doubts about this claim, given the vast assortment of Negrophobic, anti-semitic, and nativist statements that were put on the record by Galton, Pearson, Fisher, Keith, and other leading eugenicists.

48. One uses this term with some caution, but in many respects it is an accurate description of eugenics, which had both elite leadership (intellectual/scientific and political) and a significant mass following, particularly among the white middle classes in the metropoles, but also among whites in colonial settings (and soon enough in newly independent countries like Brazil).

49. The Webbs in England, as well as Harold Laski, are among the many examples that could be cited here. Laski as a youth was a protégé of Galton, who referred to him as "my wonderful boy-Jew." Laski also studied under Karl Pearson in London (Chase 1977, 644). In the United States, Oliver Wendell Holmes' famous opinion in the *Buck v. Bell* case, upholding the government's right to sterilize a "feeble-minded" person against her or his will, placed him firmly in the eugenics camp. Feminists like Victoria Hoodhull and Margaret Sanger also flirted with eugenics. See Woodhull 1891; Gordon 1990, 120; Sanger 1923, 81–82.

50. Notably in the severely restrictive 1924 U.S. Immigration Act, but also in numerous other actions and policies around the world. See Higham 1994 [1955]; Smith 1997, 446–448.

51. It must be noted, however, that eugenics survived Nazism, although the term itself acquired a bad odor and was largely suppressed. For example, in 1973 the American Eugenics Society took a new name: Society for the Study of Social Biology. It renamed its journal as well: *Eugenics Quarterly* became *Social Biology*. Controversies over the book *The Bell Curve*, the Pioneer Foundation, and the Human Genome Project, among others, all illustrate the persistence of eugenic themes into the twenty-first century (Duster 1990; Kevles and Hood 1992; Smith and Sapp 1997).

52. I am indebted to Professor Tukufu Zuberi of the University of Pennsylvania for acquainting me with the wider implications of the racial genealogy of inferential statistics.

53. The few critical salvos that were mounted issued from the pens of blacks and Jews. Already in 1879 the black activist and scholar Martin R. Delaney attacked the early physical anthropology of Africa for its racial bias, with a book entitled *Principia of Ethnology: The Origins of Race and Color. . . .* Du Bois' 1897 essay "The Conservation of Races" attempted a "transvaluation" of the racial hierarchy implicit in eugenics. See note 77, below. Other early black critics of the eugenics paradigm included Kelly Miller, professor of mathematics at Howard University, who demonstrated the statistical shortcomings of some of the key eugenics texts of the turn of the twentieth century. Franz Boas, founder of the field of cultural anthropology, was perhaps the most effective critic of physical anthropology's compromised relationship to eugenics; Boas's writings and scholarly activism contributed significantly to the first unraveling of the eugenic fabric in the 1920s. In this note I have drawn heavily on Stepan and Gilman 1993.

54. Subversion and covert resistance were practiced as well, but such "infrapolitics" did not hold out much hope of regime change. See Scott 1990.

55. I have already noted the many variations that characterized post-slavery political regimes. In Haiti or the United States, where armed conflict had ended slavery, a period of experimentation with the political empowerment of emancipated former slaves dawned quickly, and was rapidly extinguished. In other national and regional settings, where colonialism and even slavery died much more slowly, political action (in the sense of "voice," or "entrism") on the part of the racially subordinated was not even on the horizon until the mid-twentieth century.

56. A good example here is the activities of the British in turn-of-the-century Latin America, notably in Brazil and Argentina. See Platt 1973.

57. Of course there were immense variations in nineteenth-century patterns of colonial rule. To offer but a few examples: as the century wore on, although Disraeli and other "modern" colonialists had questioned the logic of aggressive imperialism, other powers—the Germans and Italians and even little Belgium—made their last-minute plays for empire. In 1898, the United States consolidated its position as an imperial power, reappropriating Spanish possessions in the Caribbean and East Asia. As abolitionism became official ideology and supposedly more "enlightened" and "humane" principles of rule were advanced, plunder and genocide got underway again too: under the auspices of Cecil Rhodes, King Leopold II in the Congo, and General von Trotha in southwest Africa, among others. As colonial ministries in London and Paris squabbled among themselves—reformers versus expansionists, English partisans of "masterly inactivity" versus advocates of the "Forward School" (see Gilmour 2000)—the final bloody scramble for African turf was staged in the Sudan (see Lewis 1987), and the three-way Boer War, replete with atrocities, settled the future of South Africa.

58. An arresting phrase: if the earth has ends, does it also have beginnings?

59. In earlier work, Omi and I made a similar argument for the United States:

> Slaves who escaped, forming communities in woods and swamps; Indians who made war on the United States in defense of their peoples and lands; Chinese and Filipinos who drew together in Chinatowns and Manilatowns in order to gain some measure of collective control over their existence—these are some examples of the movement of racial opposition *outward*, away from political engagement with the hegemonic racial state.
>
> These same slaves, Indians, Asians (and many others), banned from the political system and relegated to what was supposed to be a permanently inferior sociocultural status, were forced *inward* upon themselves as individuals, families, and communities. Tremendous cultural resources were nurtured among such communities; enormous labors were required to survive and develop elements of an autonomy and opposition under such conditions. These circumstances can best be understood as combining with the violent clashes and necessity of resistance (to white-led race riots, military assaults, etc.) which characterized these periods, to constitute a racial *war of maneuver*. (Omi and Winant 1994, 80–81)

60. For biographical material on Rebouças, see Spitzer 1989.

61. See Goodman 1998. There were also black movements of this type; see Moses 1998; Stuckey 1987.

62. Omi and I, once again in previous work focused on the United States, put the argument this way:

> A strategy of war of position can only be predicated on political struggle—on the existence of diverse institutional and cultural terrains upon which oppositional political projects can be mounted, and upon which the racial state can be confronted. (Omi and Winant 1994, 81; emphasis removed)

63. This contrast is necessarily ideal-typical. Some degree of domination remains even in the most inclusive democracies. The crucial point here, though, is the transition from exclusion to inclusion. More extensive discussion of the Gramscian theory underlying this account may be found in Buci-Glucksmann 1979. I apply the domination/hegemony distinction to U.S. racial politics in Winant 1994c; Hanchard 1994 employs it in discussion of Brazilian racial politics. See also Hall 1996b.

64. This claim is not as contradictory as it may seem. The "crystallization" to which I refer is the final process of "carving up the world," especially Africa, that had taken place on paper in Berlin and Brussels and had become colonialist practice after Fashoda. Late entries into the imperial racket—principally, Germany, Italy, and the United States—had grabbed what they could by the turn of the century. Meanwhile the old colonial powers were cutting back their commitments to the "great game," seeking ways of maximizing their returns and minimizing their costs, experimenting with ideas of native tutelage that at least implied greater autonomy at the edge of empire, and even considering abandoning the "white man's burden" in favor of more indirect forms of rule.

65. Its occurrence was contemporary with Du Bois's study of the 7th Ward of Philadelphia.

66. I am construing "subaltern studies" as a radical democratic theoretical orientation that has attained a broader and more diverse currency since its South Asian-focused founders laid its groundwork in the 1970s and 1980s. Although the Indian context received primary attention, later concepts of "subalternity" have circled the globe, extended beyond strictly post-colonial settings, and addressed all the central axes of emancipatory thought and practice. Although hardly without internal conflicts and debates, the subaltern studies school has performed a vital service in reorienting a great deal of insurgent theory (and to some extent, practice) in this radical democratic direction. Its implications for global racial studies cannot be overstated.

67. Elsewhere I have argued that the post–World War II racial reforms, as well as broader social and political shifts in U.S. racial dynamics, force us to extend the concept's meaning to other racially defined groups (Winant 1997b).

68. This is the familiar concept—also pioneered in Du Bois (1977 [1935])—that however poor and downtrodden a white might feel himself to be, he (the concept does seem slightly male) could always take comfort in the fact that "at least I'm not black."

69. This applies particularly to "race-mixing" between black/native men and white/European women. In a short review of the immense historical sweep of race-mixing in the United States, Gary B. Nash shows how unstable and threatening the color-line has always been in that country, both theoretically and practically. Theoretically the color-line, hypodescent customs, the one-drop rule, and the like never made good sense; the idea that people can only belong to one race was particularly absurd. Practically, sex and hybridization, as well as marriage and love, concubinage and rape, "passing," the erotism of trangressing racial boundaries, and the seeming self-interest of whitening one's offspring were necessarily built into a racially hierarchical social order (Nash 1999). Seen in comparative light, this set of recognitions evokes many already extensive literatures, notably those of the "two variants of race relations" in the Americas (Hoetink 1971), and the rich psychohistorical and feminist accounts now available on the "intersectionality" of race and sex (Williamson 1980; Williamson 1986; Bederman 1995; Stoler 1991; Goldstein 1999; Gates 1990).

70. "Hypodescent" is Marvin Harris's term for the one-drop rule of racial classification: "This descent rule requires Americans to believe that anyone who is known to have had a Negro ancestor is a Negro" (Harris 1964, 56).

71. The number of lynching victims can only be approximated. An assiduous inventory of cases reported between 1882 and 1951 counted 4,730 persons lynched (Guzman 1952, 275–279), but then, as now, it is unlikely that all cases came to light. What is a lynching, after all? Extralegal execution takes place constantly, in many suspicious circumstances ranging from accident to willful murder. Law enforcement officials are hardly immune from charges of lynching as well.

Perhaps more revealing of the prevalence and normalization of lynching in the United States is the recently curated exhibition of lynching photographs and postcards, also published in book form as *Without Sanctuary: Lynching Photography in America* (Allen et al. 2000). Not so much the existence of these photographs, but their very ordinariness, makes a devastating comment on the practice of racial terrorism in the United States. Many of these images are reproductions of souvenir photographs themselves sold at the scene of the lynching, as if the events were no more than family outings or trips to the amusement park.

72. Space does not permit a parallel discussion of South African white racial dualism here, but I have already proposed a similar argument in respect to this: national consolidation in the wake of the Boer War was achieved through policies of white supremacy (well before the formal elaboration of apartheid in 1948). The tentative unity of Afrikaners and English-speakers could be accomplished only if the emancipatory consequences—for blacks—of abolition and the modernization of British colonial rule were forestalled. See Chapter Eight, below.

73. There were African victories too. See Redmayne 1968; Ranger 1967; Klein 1968; Cartey and Kilson 1970.

74. Washington's influence on Marcus Garvey is well-known. His impact on the career of John L. Dube, first president of the South African Native National Congress (which became the African National Congress [ANC] in 1923) is discussed in Fredrickson 1995, 119–120. See also Marable 1976. Although by no means accommodationist, the ANC pursued a

reform-oriented anti-apartheid strategy until the 1960s, when the Sharpeville massacre catalyzed its shift to armed struggle. See Chapter Eight, below.

I have not been able to find much evidence of Washington's impact on Brazil.

75. Black activist, historian, preacher, and journalist George Washington Williams played a central role in exposing and denouncing the Congo atrocities; see Franklin 1985. Future Chicago School sociologist Robert Ezra Park wrote denunciatory reports for Washington; see Lyman 1994, 85–98.

76. Trinidadian Henry Sylvester Williams was one of the 1900 conference's main organizers, along with Du Bois. Another prominent participant was Anna Julia Cooper, who in 1906 would be dismissed from her post as principal of the M Street School in Washington, D.C. at the instigation of Booker T. Washington, who considered her too close to Du Bois' views. See Lemert and Bhan 1998.

77. This essay has sometimes been badly read in recent debates. In my view, Appiah's (1992) treatment misses Du Bois' political claims, preferring to critique the essay's commitments to a "race-concept" Appiah finds flawed and unscientific.

78. My thanks to Professor Lucius Outlaw for making me aware of this connection.

79. The two policies were in fact related: access to the ballot was limited to those who could demonstrate their ability to read. *Analfabetização* (illiteracy) was depicted as an instance of "Negro deficit," evidence of backwardness, a failure to adjust to emancipated status, and general unsuitability for democracy. Before 1945 the franchise was witheld by various property-based restrictions as well as literacy requirements. After 1945, literacy requirements alone were used to (dis)qualify voters. See Andrews 1991, 144–145. A substantial eugenicist element was also at work here. See Fernandes 1978, vol. 1, 100–101; especially Fernandes's notes on Oliveira Vianna.

80. "Mass-based unrest continued into the 1910s with the naval mutiny of 1910 in Rio, the Contestado Rebellion in Santa Catarina (1912–1916), the general strike of 1917, the anarchist uprising of 1918, and continued strike activity in 1919 and 1920. . . . Black people formed part of this rising tide of organization and ferment" (Andrews 1991, 144).

81. On the other hand, Fernandes' magisterial work also depicts the rise of the Brazilian black movement in the 1920s and 1930s as a *Segunda Abolicão*, a "second Abolition." He is arguing that Brazilian racial conditions were so unfavorable that heroic efforts were required simply to assert basic black rights. The absolute lack of resources available to blacks, plus the determined state policy aimed at their marginalization and abandonment in the name of *branqueamento*, were the proximate causes of their anomie. See Fernandes 1978, vol 2.

82. These terms locate racial solidarity as the central feature of black nationalism, eschewing concepts focusing on territoriality or statehood. In adopting the assertion that "The concept of racial solidarity is essential to all forms of black nationalism" (Bracey, Meier, and Rudwick 1970, xxvi), I recognize the problematic character of the concept, which must embrace profound historical, religious, local/regional, and ideological differences. For sophisticated treatments of the multidimensionality of concepts of black nationalism and pan-Africanism, see Stuckey 1987; Drake 1987–90; Glaude 2000.

83. At least in the Duboisian account of it, with its "general strike" and racially based working class fractions, with its radicals and reactionaries, and with its undoing in 1876 and after (Du Bois 1977 [1935]).

84. There were battles in Africa as well: Togo, Cameroon, and Tanganyika (Tanzania) saw fighting. In East Africa the campaign occupied the whole four years of the war; the last German troops to surrender were holdouts in Tanganyika. The war also affected South Africa, where Afrikaner support for Germany posed problems for the British. Hertzog and the Nationalists sought to leave the British Commonwealth and perhaps even enter the war on the German side, but under the leadership of Smuts and Botha the newly formed Union took the Entente side and seized the German colony of South-West Africa (Namibia). Smuts and Botha (both Afrikaners, both former generals in the Boer War, as was Hertzog) wound up signing the Versailles Treaty. Hertzog's subsequent (1924) electoral victory consolidated Nationalist/Afrikaner political power and intensified anti-British/anti-Anglophone ethnic antagonisms.

85. Racial propaganda was of course used on both sides. A 1918 German propaganda leaflet directed at black U.S. troops in France reads as follows:

TO THE COLORED SOLDIERS OF THE UNITED STATES ARMY

Hello, boys, what are you doing over here? Fighting the Germans? Why? Have they ever done you any harm? Of course some white folks and the lying English-American papers told you that the Germans ought to be wiped out for the sake of humanity and Democracy. What is Democracy? Personal freedom; all citizens enjoying the same rights socially and before the law. Do you enjoy the same rights as the white people do in America, the land of freedom and Democracy, or are you not rather treated over there as second class citizens? Can you get into a restaurant where white people dine? Can you get a seat in a theatre where white people sit? Can you get a seat or a berth in a railroad car, or can you even ride in the South in the same street car with the white people? And how about the law? Is lynching and the most horrible crimes connected therewith, a lawful proceeding in a Democratic country? Now all this is entirely different in Germany, where they do like colored people; where they treat them as gentlemen and as white men, and quite a number of colored people have fine positions in business in Berlin and other German cities. Why, then, fight the Germans only for the benefit of the Wall Street robbers, and to protect the millions that they have loaned to the English, French, and Italians? You have been made the tool of the egotistic and rapacious rich in America, and there is nothing in the whole game for you but broken bones, horrible wounds, spoiled health, or death. No satisfaction whatever will you get out of this unjust war. You have never seen Germany, so you are fools if you allow people to make you hate us. Come over and see for yourself. Let those do the fighting who make the profit out of this war. Don't allow them to use you as cannon fodder. To carry a gun in this service is not an honor but a shame. Throw it away and come over to the German lines. You will find friends who will help you. (Hunton and Johnson 1920, 26–39, 53–54)

86. Because these patterns are discussed at length in Part II of this book, I will not dwell on them here. For more detailed treatments, see Henri 1975; Marks 1989; Stovall 1996; Du Bois 1995 [1919]; Rathbone 1978; Michel 1982.

87. Large firms recruited industrial labor in the South, as did the Urban League and various other black organizations. See Marks 1989; Du Bois 1993 [1920].

88. In the May 1919 *Crisis*, just returned from France, Du Bois wrote the editorial "Returning Soldiers," which his biographer David Levering Lewis says "would go a long way toward redeeming the perceived imprudence of 'Close Ranks,'" his earlier editorial calling on blacks to support the U.S. war effort:

"We are returning from war! *The Crisis* and tens of thousand of blackmen (sic) were drafted into a great struggle. For bleeding France and what she means and has meant to us and humanity and against the threat of German race arrogance. . . .

"This is the country to which we Soldiers of democracy return. This is the fatherland for which we fought! But it is not *our* fatherland. It was right for us to fight again. The faults of our country are our faults. Under similar circumstances we would fight again. But by the God of heaven, we are cowards and jackasses if now that the war is over, we do not marshall every ounce of our brain and brawn to fight a sterner, longer, more unbending battle against the forces of hell in our own land.

"We return.
"We return from fighting.
"We return fighting.

"Make way for Democracy! We saved it in France, and by the Great Jehovah, we will save it in the United States of America, or know the reason why." (Lewis 1993, 578)

On Du Bois and the " red summer," see Lewis 1993, 579–580.

89. For a more detailed treatment of the ABB and its leader Cyril Briggs, see James 1998, 155–184. It must be noted, although there is no space to develop this theme here, that "black-

red" relationships in the United States, the Americas in general, and Africa as well were subject to tremendous variation and frequent conflict. Briggs was expelled from the Communist Party in 1942 for excessive "Negro nationalism." George Padmore, Richard Wright, Claude McKay, and many other illustrious black leaders, scholars, and artists fell out with the Party in the decades following the Comintern's adoption (in 1922) of a resolution on the "Negro National Question" that McKay had helped write. C. L. R. James, ever the Marxist theoretician, preferred the Trotskyist movement and was a left-wing dissident even there. Du Bois criticized the Communist Party (CPUSA) at various times, notably at the height of his "left" period, provoked by differences over the Scottsboro case (see Du Bois 1995 [1931]; Du Bois 1991 [1940], 298–299). Yet he never repudiated the Party and never denounced the brutality of Stalin; see his obituary for the Soviet dictator (Du Bois 1995 [1953]). He joined the Party only in 1961, at the age of 93, more in protest at his treatment by the red-baiting United States than in solidarity with the Party. Horne (1986) offers a fine treatment Du Bois' relationship with communism during the later years of his long life. For discussion of some of the complex relations between the black and communist movements, see Robinson 1983.

90. Fredrickson analyzes in some depth the Industrial and Commercial Workers Union (ICU) of South Africa, a group that at its height claimed a quarter-million members and upheld Garvey-like positions. Another important group of the same general type was the *Frente Negra Brasileira* (Brazilian Black Front), although it was founded later (1931). In its brief lifetime—it was suppressed by Vargas in 1937—the FNB experienced numerous political problems: it underwent a significant left-right schism, with one wing attracted to *Integralismo*, the Brazilian fascist movement, and the other to socialism. It also adopted strongly nativist positions that alienated it from the left, and was divided by issues of class. Historical questions persist about the degree of mass support the FNB was able to attract: it claimed a membership as high as two hundred thousand (see Moura 1983), but the actual figures were undoubtedly lower (Andrews 1991, 149; Mitchell 1977, 161). However many members it could attract, the FNB was still an important effort on the part of Afro-Brazilians to assert a black, egalitarian position in mainstream politics. See Chapter Nine, below; see also Fernandes 1978, vol. 2; Andrews 1991, 146–156; Pinto 1993.

91. Fredrickson and Moses both see Garvey's messianism as continuous with, if not deriving from, the Ethiopian currents of Henry McNeal Turner and Edward Wilmot Blyden. Fredrickson also notes Garvey's use of social Darwinism, which clashed with the redemptive message of Ethiopianism: "Ethiopia shall stretch our her arms" (Fredrickson 1995, 156). Du Bois had Ethiopianist residues in his thought too; see Moses 1978, 156–169.

92. Garvey's antagonism toward "mulattoes" was very public; it derived from the Jamaican experience of profound, almost caste-like distinctions between blacks and browns. Of course, the value of light skin had some resonance on the North American mainland as well, but the system of hypodescent, of the virtually unbreachable color-line, was something Garvey never quite comprehended.

93. There is an analogy here to a contemporary organization, the Nation of Islam, led by Louis Farrakhan. Garvey's anti-semitism is another point of convergence between the UNIA and the NOI.

94. "All the things that Hitler was to do so well later Garvey was doing in 1920 and 1921. He organized storm troopers who marched, uniformed, in his parades, and kept order and gave colour to his meetings" (James 1985 [1938], 53; see also Gilroy 1996, 79).

Garvey also made the well-known statement, "We were the first Fascists. We had disciplined men, women, and children in training for the liberation of Africa. The black masses saw that in this extreme nationalism lay their only hope and readily supported it. Mussolini copied fascism from me but the Negro reactionaries sabotaged it" (Gilroy 1976, 80; Hill and Bair 1987; Moses 1978, 295).

CHAPTER SIX. NOTES ON THE POSTWAR BREAK

1. Beyond this, the undoing and removal of racial categorization and racial identification after centuries of their existence would have been problematic on an altogether differ-

ent level. These categories and identities, however unjust and irrational they had been upon their initial institutionalization, had become over half a millennium profoundly established terms of collective self-recognition and organization among the racially subordinated themselves. The challenge facing efforts to create racial democracy, equality, and justice, it turns out, is not to eliminate racial distinctions, but to reinvent them as non-hierarchical concepts and social locations. See Chapter Eleven, below.

2. The Leninist and Wilsonian models of self-determination clashed profoundly in the interwar years, notably after the founding of the Third International (or Comintern), which explicitly sought to foment anti-colonial revolution. These conflicts anticipated the Cold War competition that would sweep the Third World in the post–World War II years. Comparison between these two phases of the colonialism/anti-colonialism (or North/South, or white/non-white) struggles would make an interesting study in comparative historical sociology, but is largely beyond the scope of the present work. Nor do I wish to suggest that these two general "models" of self-determination were at all coherent or internally uniform. Churchill's and Roosevelt's continuing commitments to colonial restoration, even after World War II, are well-known; more apt successors to the tradition of Versailles could scarcely be imagined. Stalin's readiness to play fast and loose with the "national question" is equally obvious. Lenin and Wilson, the twentieth-century progenitors of the doctrine of self-determination, were hardly averse to subordinating this principle to their conceptions of Soviet or U.S. self-interest.

3. See Chapter Four, above.

4. See Wallerstein 1991, on which this methodological account draws heavily. The journal edited by Wallerstein, *Review*, devoted a special issue to the theme of "Nomothetic vs. Idiographic Disciplines: A False Dilemma?" in 1997 (*Review* 20, nos. 3–4 [Summer/Fall 1997]). This debate has its origins in the German *methodenstreit* that occurred a century earlier.

5. See Chapters Two and Three, above.

6. See Chapter Eleven, below.

CHAPTER SEVEN. UNITED STATES

1. Seen in historical context, movement figures maintained a high degree of unity, despite the many differences and debates they steadily experienced. For a few sources among many, see Carson 1981; Zinn 1965; Morris 1984; Bloom 1987; Van Deburg 1992; Bloom and Breines 1995.

2. The most prominent example of this kind of anticipatory thought was undoubtedly Myrdal's *An American Dilemma* (1962 [1944]), but a great deal of thought was given to this topic in the black press as well.

3. And at the expense of Asian immigrants (especially in the West) and Mexicans in the Southwest. See Saxton 1971; Almaguer 1994; Montejano 1987; Perlman 1950.

4. As early as the California gold rush, the presence of Chinese immigrants had been a source of vital labor, as well as a spark of racial tension (Almaguer 1994; Takaki 1993; Wong and Chan 1998). By the later decades of the nineteenth century, anti-Chinese agitation had reached significant levels in the West, where it served as a racist linchpin of working-class and even "socialist" organization (Sandmeyer and Daniels 1991; Saxton 1971).

The recruitment of Asian women took a variety of different forms, depending on the period in which it occurred and the demand that it was designed to fulfill. See Matthaei and Amott 1990; Glenn 1986, on Japanese American women's experiences; Ling 1998, on Chinese American women's experiences. For contemporary connections, see Espiritu 1997; Stier 1998.

5. In the United States it was (and is) an unavoidable fate to be racialized, but that doesn't mean racialization happens overnight. See Omi and Winant 1994.

6. In this respect the great waves of late-nineteenth-century Atlantic immigrants shared a racialization experience with the Irish, who had preceded them by half a century or more. After their arrival in great numbers half a century earlier, the Irish were subjected to quasi-racist discrimination and prejudice. They overcame this to a significant extent as the decades

passed, notably by acquiring public employment in the cities, in the police and fire departments; by determinedly operating their franchise in a "machine" politics model; and by insisting on their whiteness vis-à-vis blacks. Obviously, these alternatives were not available to blacks or other racially defined minorities, but they could be emulated to varying degrees by later-arriving European immigrants. See Miller 1985. Roediger (1991) and Ignatiev (1995) explore Irish-black dynamics in the nineteenth century, stressing the depth of Irish anti-black racism. Rolston (1999) highlights the splits in nineteenth-century Irish-American racial orientations caused by these incentives to identify with white supremacy, on the one hand, and the depth of commitments to anti-colonialism on the other.

7. Blauner's (1972) distinction between voluntary and involuntary immigration was posed as a refutation of ethnicity-based theories of race that equated the experience of U.S. blacks with that of European immigrants. To be sure, more recent work on immigration would question this dichotomy, preferring to view the decision to migrate as a continuum: a complex mixture of responses to both coercive conditions and the perception of opportunities. Still, enslavement and conquest clearly represented motivations for "migration" that were quite different from, say, impoverishment (or even famine or pogroms). Thus Blauner's account retains some schematic or ideal-typical validity. See Omi and Winant 1994.

8. The Italian American, Polish, Jewish (as well as other "white ethnic") experiences may be usefully compared with the earlier Irish one. See, among a large literature, Lieberson 1980; Thomas and Znaniecki 1984 [1923]; Glazer and Moynihan 1970 [1963]; Steinberg 1981; Roediger 1991; Saxton 1990; Richards 1998.

9. By no means were black workers welcomed with open arms into factory labor. Many plants refused to hire them. In others, segregated "internal labor markets" prevailed, relegating them to the dirtiest and most dangerous jobs, and foreclosing promotion and seniority. In the Gompers era and after, the American Federation of Labor was segregationist, refusing to organize black workers at worst, sometimes agreeing grudgingly to "colored unions" (a recipe for division and defeat) at best. In return for these favors, black workers sometimes served as strikebreakers. Within the mainstream labor movement, only the United Mine Workers sought to organize across labor lines. Before the transformative migrations of World War I, the Knights of Labor and the IWW had demonstrated some of the possibilities of trans-racial unionism as well, but the mainstream labor movement would not break with its explicitly discriminatory policies until the dawn of the CIO era in the late 1930s and the massive northward migrations of World War II. There is a vast literature on this complex set of themes. Among many sources, see Mink 1986; Reid 1930; Gutman 1976b; Lipsitz 1994; Spero and Harris 1968 [1931]; Dubofsky 1969; Voss 1993; Cox 1970 [1948]. In perhaps the most sophisticated class-based (or neo-Marxist) account of U.S. racial history to be offered in recent years, Michael Goldfield argues that the "divide and conquer" principle evident since the earliest days of North American colonialism and slavery, continues mutatis mutandis to fortify capitalist class power in the United States (Goldfield 1997).

10. These patterns have now been amply theorized in the literature (Massey and Duran 1987; Grasmuck and Pessar 1991; Portes and Walton 1981). They would be repeated a fortiori in the 1940s, when a far more comprehensive social mobilization on behalf of war-making would occur.

11. Of course, substantial black presence in the urban North predated the World War I migrations, as Du Bois documents in *The Philadelphia Negro* 1998 [1899]. But the full-blown residential segregation associated with the term *ghetto* dates from the later migrations.

12, Park 1950; Park, Burgess, and McKenzie 1967; Wirth 1964; Thomas and Znaniecki 1984 [1923], among others. For a good overview, see Bulmer 1984. The later work of Drake and Cayton was firmly rooted in these approaches, and also contains extensive comments on black migratory patterns (Drake and Cayton 1993 [1945]). It must be stressed that this black migration was occurring in a context that included extensive European immigration, as well as the roughly parallel flow of poor southern whites—often fleeing similar patterns of debt peonage, and of course toting their racial attitudes as well—to the very same cities.

13. To be sure, Mexicans were not immigrants at all when considered as a community, but a variegated group of descendants of a now independent former colony, who had been

conqured and then granted citizenship rights as part of the Treaty of Guadalupe-Hidalgo (1848). See Almaguer 1994; Barrera 1979; Montejano 1987; Pitt 1970.

14. African-American internationalism burgeoned during the 1920s and 1930s. With notable exceptions, U.S. scholarship has not recognized the extent of black awareness of, and involvement in, the international scene. But concern for African issues was always present, and took many different forms over the centuries. To make only a few rudimentary comments: from the African Zionism of Edward Blyden to the various Christian uplift and missionary orientations of Alexander Crummell and the AME efforts in late-nineteenth-century South Africa, U.S. blacks sought to ameliorate colonialist depredations in Africa (Stuckey 1987; Glaude 2000; Fredrickson 1995). Deriving from numerous sources and blending with religious, civic, and political trends that were deeply embedded in the U.S. black community (and the diaspora as well), Duboisian pan-Africanism not only preceded Garveyism by decades, but continued through the post–World War II period of decolonization. With the assistance of Robert E. Park, Booker T. Washington investigated and denounced the Congolese genocide of King Leopold of Belgium (Lyman 1994). During the 1930s U.S. blacks sought to support Ethiopia against Mussolini's ravages (Kelley 1994). Nor was African-American internationalism strictly Africa-oriented: especially as a result of their solidarity with the UNIA and socialist and communist movements, African-Americans involved themselves ever more deeply in events in the Caribbean, the western hemipshere, and even Europe and Asia. During the Spanish civil war blacks joined and supported the Lincoln Brigade (Kelley 1994; Horne 1986). They even flirted with solidarity for Japan, a burgeoning "colored" imperial power (Lipsitz 1998a). On this wide range of issues, see Plummer 1996; von Eschen 1997; selections from James 1992; and numerous writings of Du Bois (Lewis 1995).

15. Pressured by the Comintern to compete more effectively with the Garvey movement, the CPUSA made organizing blacks and combating racism (both in the society as a whole and within its own ranks) a priority from the late 1920s on. Somewhat out of touch with U.S. racial realities, Moscow developed its analysis of the "Negro problem" in light of communist understandings of the "national question" in Europe. Still, despite its questionable theories, the CP undoubtedly did much to mobilize and support black folk during the Depression years and after. For good treatments of some of these issues, see Davis 1967; Naison 1985; Horne 1986; Denby 1978 [1952]; Robinson 1983; Buhle 1987.

16. The story of the U.S. Army Air Corps 332nd Fighter Group, the "Tuskegee airmen," has recently received renewed attention. This group of black combat pilots distinguished itself after laboriously winning the Army Air Force's approval for their training and deployment. See Scott and Womack 1998.

17. "In April 1944 Corp. Rupert Timmingham wrote *Yank* magazine. 'Here is a question that each Negro soldier is asking,' he began. 'What is the Negro soldier fighting for? On whose team are we playing?' He recounted the difficulties he and eight other black soldiers had while traveling through the South—'where Old Jim Crow rules'—for a new assignment. 'We could not purchase a cup of coffee,' Timmingham noted. Finally the lunchroom manager at a Texas railroad depot said the black GIs could go around back to the kitchen for a sandwich and coffee. As they did, 'about two dozen German prisoners of war, with two American guards, came to the station. They entered the lunchroom, sat at the tables, had their meals served, talked, smoked, in fact had quite a swell time. I stood on the outside looking on, and I could not help but ask myself why they are treated better than we are? Why are we pushed around like cattle? If we are fighting for the same thing, if we are to die for our country, then why does the Government allow such things to go on? Some of the boys are saying that you will not print this letter. I'm saying that you will.'

"In ETO [European Theater of Operations] many black soldiers were assigned to prisoner duty. It is the universal testimony of the German POWs interviewed for this book that they got better treatment from black than white guards, to the point that the POWs had a saying, 'The best American is a black American'" (Ambrose 1997, 345–346). I am indebted to Gabriel Winant for drawing my attention to this passage.

18. "President Roosevelt's Executive Order 9981 [corrected number—HW] mandated fair hiring in defense industries, but it took concerted direct-action strikes and mass demonstrations

by minority workers and their supporters to secure even a modicum of what Roosevelt's executive order promised" (Lipsitz 1998c, 38; see also Mershon and Schlossman 1998).

19. There are numerous accounts of the transition from exclusion to insurgency. One of the best is McAdam 1982, which places the development of the movement at its center and accounts for its emergence using a "political process model." In previous, somewhat similar work (Omi and Winant 1994), I have emphasized the shift away from a restrictive and exclusionary political framework whose fundamental logic was coercive, to one of incorporation and tendentially greater inclusion (Winant 1994c). Such accounts address the expansion of political opportunities and black agency during this period, as well as the shifting cultural articulation (or "framing") of emergent black subjectivity, but tend to neglect the international context of wartime and postwar anti-racist mobilization.

20. Myrdal's (1944) study was initiated and supported by a powerful wing of the U.S. corporate-liberal elite, led by Frederick R. Keppel of the Carnegie Corporation. Keppel had rejected the idea of hiring a black social scientist like E. Franklin Frazier or W. E. B. Du Bois, instead seeking a credible (and unarguably white) "outsider" who could advance the cause of racial reform in a sufficiently moderate tone of voice. Myrdal's emphasis on democratization was suitably balanced, from this point of view, by his insistence on black assimilation. On the gestation of the Myrdal book, see Southern 1987; Jackson 1990; Stanfield 1985.

21. Du Bois, "Application for Membership . . . ," in Lewis 1995. Du Bois was 92 at the time. It should be noted that although the NAACP filed its "Appeal to the People of the World," in the red-baiting and race-baiting late 1940s, the organization was at pains to distance itself from communism and socialism, as well as from prominent black leftists like Du Bois (one of its founders) and Paul Robeson. Indeed, a willingness to repudiate these figures before various inquisitorial committees was often the price prominent blacks had to pay to avoid blacklisting (Horne 1994; Williams 1998).

22. The "solid South" also functioned as a formidable check on the New Deal agenda in Congress, obviously. See Katznelson, Geiger, and Kryder 1993; Brown 1999a.

23. Despite this shift, a substantial current of black Republicanism persisted. Black adherence to the Party was the product of a variety of factors: loyalty to the Radical Republican legacy, repugnance for the Dixiecrats, and the influence of Republican liberalism from Willkie to Rockefeller, among others. See Ashmore 1994; Brooke 1966.

24. The following section draws on Lichtenstein 1989; Kelley 1993; Lipsitz 1994; Singh 1998. See also Painter 1979.

25. There was plenty of anti-communism in the CIO as well, though. In fact, the link between race-baiting and red-baiting was probably the key element in the defeat of Operation Dixie:

> CIO leaders sought to deflect southern xenophobia by excluding Communists and other radicals from participation in Operation Dixie. Thus resources of the Communist-led trade unions and of Popular Front institutions like the Southern Conference for Human Welfare and the Highlander Folk School were shunted aside. Of course, CIO anti-communism was not alone responsible for the defeat of Operation Dixie; the decisive battles in the key textile mill towns were over by the end of 1946, before this very issue became all-consuming. But the labor movement's internal conflict may well have turned a tactical defeat into a disorganized rout. For example, two of the most dynamic unions in the postwar South, the Mine, Mill, and Smelter Workers and the Food and Tobacco Workers, were heavily black organizations hospitable to the Communists. By 1949 locals of these unions were being systematically raided by anti-Communist CIO unions. The crisis came to a head in Alabama when [Philip] Murray's own Steelworkers broke the Mine, Mill local that represented militant black iron miners around Birmingham. Recruiting their cadre from elements close to the KKK, USW locals in northern Alabama blended anticommunism with overt racism to raid the Mine, Mill union and destroy one of the black community's most progressive institutions. The legacy of this fratricidal conflict extended well into the 1960s when Birmingham became synonymous with brutal white resistance to the civil rights movement. (Lichtenstein 1989, 137)

26. Truman's most significant action on behalf of civil rights was his 1947 Executive Order 9981 desegregating the armed forces (Mershon and Schlossman 1998). This had a particularly strong effect in the South, where militarism was strong and military installations were disproportionately concentrated. Truman also formed a civil rights commission whose report "To Fulfill These Rights," noted that U.S. racism had negative global effects.

27. That is, exclusive democracy, where full participative rights are denied to all who are not white, male, and of a higher socioeconomic status.

28. The NAACP, National Negro Congress, National Council of Negro Veterans, Southern Negro Youth Congress, and numerous other black or black-led organizations were thrown into severe internal crises by the racial reaction of the late 1940s. All contained at least some leading left members, and some had grown close enough to the CP to earn the label of "Communist Front" by 1948 or so. The Council on African Affairs, an anti-colonialist and anti-apartheid group that had included Du Bois, Robeson, Adam Clayton Powell Jr., and Mary McCleod Bethune on its board, split apart in 1948 when key staffer Max Yergan announced that the organization had grown too close to the "reds." See Plummer 1996, 191; Anthony 1994. Yergan's long career as a key black left activist took a sharp right turn after 1948.

29. The New Deal's protections for workers—for example, minimum wage, Social Security, and the right to unionization—excluded domestic and agricultural workers. These provisions were crafted carefully in order to placate southern interests. See Brown 1999a.

30. Many of the programs set in motion by the Economic Opportunity Act of 1964 (the "war on poverty") emphasized remediation of the "cultural disadvantage" supposedly associated with racial difference (Quadagno 1994).

31. See Oliver and Shapiro 1995. This system was definitively anchored in de facto national racial policy, as embodied in the Federal Housing Authority, the tax laws, the transportation system, and the education system, among others. See also Conley 1999; Massey and Denton 1993; Lipsitz 1998c.

32. Any starting-point cited will necessarily be somewhat arbitrary, since race was constitutive of North American society from the first contact with Europeans. That racial struggles took place from the very beginning is indisputable. But "civil rights" is a different matter, involving the extension of democracy and the curtailment or elimination of racial dictatorship.

To date the emergence of a civil rights "movement" to the early twentieth century is thus not illogical. At this moment Du Bois proposed his critique of Booker T. Washington's accommodationist policies, policies that specifically renounced political participation. The Niagara movement and especially the NAACP represented the first large-scale black efforts to operate politically, that is, as democratic social movements advancing the cause of black participation in U.S. democracy.

As Derrick Bell comments:

> To think of the civil rights struggle of African Americans as having lasted for only a century is misleading. The truth is that African Americans have sought racial justice in this country for not one century but for more than three. By even the most conservative estimates, 300 years is a long time, particularly when for two-thirds of that time, the resistance to racial justice is met in a nation that boasts its provision of 'freedom and justice for all.' At some point, even the most noninquisitive must wonder whether there isn't a hidden connection that secures liberty and justice for whites on the subordinate status of blacks. (Bell 1993, 73)

33. Before the mid-1960s, the term *race riot* had referred to *white* assaults on black communities, to rampages and pogroms that at times (for example, in 1919) took on national proportions. The idea that blacks might "riot" (or "rebel," or stage "uprisings"), that they might assault white-owned property, white police and firefighters, or whites in general—even if all this activity were pretty much confined within the black "ghetto"—would have been almost inconceivable, or at least quite shocking, before World War II.

34. See Piven and Cloward 1977 on the uses of "disruption"; Lipsky 1969 on protest as a political resource; see also McAdam 1982.

35. Although Richard Wright had used the phrase as a book title in 1954 (Wright 1954).

36. Glazer and Moynihan made this their central argument:

One looked at the demands of the civil rights movement in 1963—equality in the vote, equality in the courts, equality in representation in public life, equality in accommodations—saw that they existed more or less in New York City [!], and concluded that the political course of the Northern Negro would be quite different from that of the Southern Negro. He [sic] would become part of the game of accommodation politcs—he already was—in which posts and benefits were distributed to groups on the basis of struggle, of course, but also on the basis of votes, money, and political talent, and one concluded that in this game the Negro would not do so badly. (Glazer and Moynihan 1970 [1963], x)

37. In fact, by 1969, when the Democrat Moynihan had aleady gone to work for Nixon, the president was able to rearticulate the once-radical vision of "black power" as a form of "black capitalism," thereby propitiating the racial moderates (black and white) within the Republican Party; throwing some meat to the scrapping dogs in the Democratic kennel; and nicely offsetting the racist subtext of the "southern strategy" that had got him elected in the first place. Moynihan's 1969 memo to his boss urging a racial policy of "benign neglect" should also be remembered.

38. To say nothing about dreams of revolution and idealization of national liberation movements conducting (and sometimes winning) anti-colonial armed struggles throughout the world. Consider Malcolm X:

The white man knows what a revolution is. He knows that the black revolution is worldwide in scope and nature. The black revolution is sweeping Asia, sweeping Africa. It's raising its head in Latin America. The Cuban revolution, that's a revolution. They overturned the system. Revolution is in Asia. Revolution is in Africa. And the white man is screaming because he sees revolution in Latin America. How do you think he'll react to you when you learn what a real revolution is? (Malcolm X 1990 [1963])

39. Now that his heroic status is enshrined, neo-conservatives and new rightists endeavor to claim him as their own, basing their distortions on a few sentences from the "I Have A Dream" speech. Let King's later years be remembered for his internationalism, his democratic socialism, his support for what is now called "affirmative action," and his organization of the "poor people's campaign," as well as the final days in Memphis (Garrow 1988; Branch 1988; Branch 1998; Carson 1998).

40. See the discussion of the origins of the "new right" below.

41. The very concept of "institutional racism" had its origins in the mid-1960s, and expressed a deep dissatisfaction with the limits of traditional concepts of racism that were based on prejudice and discrimination models. Among the wide literature on the concept, see Knowles and Prewitt 1969; Carmichael (Ture) and Hamilton 1992; Miles 1989; Winant 1998.

42. Another important arena of mobilization at this moment was connection between racism and sexism. This was a product of the civil rights movement. Notably, the idea that "the personal is political," although properly associated with the women's movement, has its origins in the black movement. Women civil rights workers had to fight to participate in decision-making and leadership. Furthermore, the movement's efforts to challenge personal racism led to an overall increased level of awareness about oppressive attitudes and behaviors. This then translated into women's liberation and planted the seeds for the feminist reawakening of the late 1960s, so-called second-wave feminism by 1969. See Evans 1979; Carson 1981; King 1987.

43. Magnus Hirschfeld, who is considered the founder of the gay rights movement, was also a student of racism, and perhaps the first to use the term. His principal concern here, appropriately enough for a Jewish homosexual in Nazi Germany, is anti-semitism. See Hirschfeld 1938.

44. Here again is the shift from "war of maneuver" to "war of position": that is, toward a political framework in which democratic rights are already somewhat present and inclusion

is already the norm (see note 19, above). The situation of "racial hegemony" can be usefully contrasted with that of "racial domination." See Omi and Winant 1994; Winant 1994c.

45. On immigration politics and policy, see Perea 1997; Portes 1995: Grasmuck and Pessar 1991; Waldinger 1995; Hu-Dehart 1999. On discrimination in taxation policy, see Oliver and Shapiro 1995; Schiller 1995. On health politics and policy, see Semmes 1996; Byrd and Clayton 2000. On welfare, see Quadagno 1994; Brown 1999b; Delgado 1997; on race and transportation, see Labor/Community Strategy Center, *A New Vision of Urban Transportation: The Bus Riders Union's Mass Transit Campaign,* available from the Labor/Community Strategy Center, 3780 Wilshire Blvd., Suite 1200, Los Angeles, CA 90010, USA. The Labor/Community Strategy Center is a multiracial anti-corporate "think-tank/act-tank" dedicated to ending discrimination in the system of transportation.

46. For a small sample of the available literature, see also Yinger 1997; Kirp et al. 1996; Haar 1996; Huttman 1991.

47. "The same thing happens in the art of politics as happens in military art: war of movement increasingly becomes war of position, and it can be said that a State will win a war in so far as it prepares for it minutely and technically in peacetime. The massive structures of the modern democracies, both as State organisations, and as complexes of associations in civil society, constitute for the art of politics as it were the 'trenches' and the permanent fortifications of the front in the war of position: they render merely 'partial' the element of movement which before used to be 'the whole' of war, etc." (Gramsci 1971, 503).

48. In earlier work (1994) Omi and I use this phrase, of course lifted from Polanyi, to characterize the interaction of movement pressure and state reform that was the political "paradigm shift" of the civil rights era.

49. To be sure, some radicals and visionaries did indeed question the civil rights program from a variety of perspectives. Nationalists and communists, most prominently, doubted whether integration could ever be achieved, not to speak of whether it was even desirable. See Van Deburg 1992; numerous selections in Roediger 1998. These perspectives were rooted in deep traditions in the black community, as well as other radical traditions. They understood not only the obstacles to integration, but also the problematic nature of integrationism in a white supremacist context. Not only that: radical objections to integration recognized, as the "mainstream" civil rights movement did not, how fundamental the challenge of racial inclusion would be to the distribution of resources and the system of political rule in the United States.

50. For more on black conservatism, see Boston 1988.

51. See Dittmer 1995, for a detailed account of mass participation in the Mississippi freedom movement. Mass participation in civil rights movement was not always forthcoming: it was subject to threats of violence and ostracism, among other deterrents. A substantial literature on "political processes" of movement building has examined the civil rights movement in detail. See McAdam 1982; Morris 1984; McAdam et al. 1996.

52. See Marshall 1964; Bulmer and Rees 1996. Invoking Marshall in the U.S. context must be done with some caution. But without endorsing his overall perspective, it is still useful to think about "racially conscious social citizenship" as the proximate goal of the civil rights movement.

CHAPTER EIGHT. SOUTH AFRICA

1. See Moodie 1975. In a more recent book, however, Moodie's approach to the genealogy of racism in South Africa is closer to the one presented here (Moodie and Ndatshe 1994).

2. Some of these groups developed their own cultures, and sometimes their own languages, on the borders of the expanding Cape Colony during the nineteenth century. See Fredrickson 1981.

3. This was the phrase used by Harold MacMillan, then British prime minster, in a speech to the South African parliament in 1960.

4. By the end of 1940, the South African Defence Force had 137,000 men in uniform. Altogether, during 1940–45, over 335,000 South Africans served in the Defence Force, of

whom over one-third were black or "coloured." As in World War I, black South Africans were forbidden to carry firearms. Instead they were made servants, laborers, and watchmen in a body that became known as the South African Native Military Corps (Parsons 1993, 267–268). See also Sampson 1999, 31.

5. "The Atlantic Charter from the African's Point of View," a document adopted unanimously by the Annual Conference of the African National Congress at Bloemfontein in December 1943 argues, among other things, that

> The soldiers of all races, Europeans, Americans, Asiatic, and Africans, have won their claim and the claims of their peoples to the four freedoms by having taken part in this war which can be converted into a war for human freedom if the settlement at the Peace Table is based on human justice, fair play, and equality of opportunity for all races, colors, and classes. (Reprinted in Ebrahim 1998, 396–414; see also Sampson 1999, 45–57)

6. Hendrik Verwoerd, then minister of native affairs and later prime minister, during the parliamentary debate over the Bantu Education Act of 1953; quoted in Troup 1976, 22.

7. See Hartz 1964; Hunter 1965. Another version of this "vision" may be found in the work of the UNESCO theorists in Brazil. See Chapter Nine, below.

8. Some of the material in this section appeared in a different form in Seidman 1999.

9. Every black was to be stripped of South African citizenship and assigned citizenship in such a bantustan; black presence in South Africa proper was to be restricted to authorized workers whose status would be temporary, and the bantustans themselves would be wholly submissive "nations"—internal colonies that were formally no longer "internal." This policy was substantially implemented, but also was subject to tremendous structural contradictions, notably around labor issues. It also engendered enormous opposition, both inside and outside the country. See Hill 1964.

10. There are of course some comparative similarities here: notably Nazi Germany (Bauman 1989; Mosse 1978; Burleigh and Wippermann 1991; Adam 1995). U.S. comparisons also merit consideration in this context; see in particular Fredrickson 1981; Fredrickson 1995; Fredrickson 1997d. Greenstein 1993 makes an interesting comparison between South Africa and Israel.

11. Space limitations here require that emphasis be placed largely on the partiality (or racial partisanship) embodied in apartheid during the post–World War II period, but a valuable literature exists on the psychological dimensions of apartheid. See Lambley 1980; Welsh 1981; Bloom 1998.

12. Portions of this section appeared in earlier form in Seidman 1999.

13. These figures rose during the final years of apartheid. In 1984, for example, 795 race reclassifications took place, and in 1985, the figure was 1,167. See South African Institute of Race Relations 1985, 3–4.

14. African workers and their families felt the effects of these tensions severely in their daily lives. As industrialization proceeded, African workers moved to the country's industrial centers, seeking jobs in new factories and living in single-sex migrant hostels built by the government for the expanding workforce. Large dormitories built to house these migrants still stand on the edge of every industrial site in South Africa, silent witnesses to the efforts of apartheid's architects' efforts to house this new, "temporary" population.

15. Greenberg emphasizes these sectoral differences among whites, particularly among distinct sectors of South African capital (1980, 176–208). See also Greenberg 1987.

16. See Saul and Gelb 1986, 149. "Staying behind" meant farming in the unproductive soil of the bantustan, or seeking work as a farm laborer on its edges.

17. This material is drawn from Seidman 1999.

18. The socially constructed character of race always operates at the unclearly defined and tension-filled interface between the phenotypical and the cultural. Racial categorization is necessarily attached to the body: no matter how nuanced it may appear, then, it still involves a certain "lumping," a degree of stereotypification. The meaning of this process of racialization varies: it some settings and circumstances, it can serve to subjugate; in others it can work to resist subjugation. See Omi and Winant 1994; Winant 1994a.

19. A good critique of apartheid's urban policies is Goldberg 1993, 185–205.

20. The chief organizer of the Defiance Campaigns was Mandela, who was designated "volunteer-in-chief." See Fredrickson 1997c; Sampson 1999, 67–76.

21. On the 1976 uprising in Soweto, as well as its broader consequences, see Hirson 1979.

22. Arnold 1978 collects Biko's views on black consciousness and South African movement politics. See also Pityana et al. 1991.

23. See Fredrickson 1997b and Pogrund 1991 on Robert Sobukwe's evolving positions on these issues; see also Pityana et al. 1991 on these issues in the black consciousness framework.

24. On these general questions, see Gay Seidman 1994, 227–234.

25. President Mandela won tremendous white applause simply by appearing at the 1995 rugby World Cup match wearing the jersey of the Springbok team; the South African rugby team had formerly been banned from international competition because it had been all-white in the apartheid era.

26. This was symbolic because the social and geographic segregation created by apartheid continued, but real in the sense that it removed one of the legal pillars of apartheid's framework.

27. Through the early 1980s, black South Africans began to move into central cities illegally, renting apartments in downtown Johannesburg that had been vacated by whites moving out to tree-lined suburbs. By the mid-1980s, cities like Johannesburg and Cape Town were gradually forced officially to acknowledge the creation of "grey" areas of housing, where those who could afford to do so could rent houses and apartments no matter what their racial identification cards said—even while police continued to enforce segregationist laws. As more and more people of color brought their families to urban townships from impoverished rural areas, as they joined unions at workplaces or community organizations in their urban townships, or as they moved into the city centers—forced by government-induced housing shortages in black townships to take the risk of police harassment—apartheid's rigid social structures and racial boundaries became increasingly out of step with a more complicated reality. See Wilson and Ramphele 1989.

28. On general patterns of insurgency in the 1980s, see Marx 1992, Davis 1987, Murray 1987.

29. Workers engaging in these strikes developed some creative new tactics: for example, they would deny they had any leaders in order to prevent arrests and other forms of government harassment. See Seidman 1994.

30. For detailed accounts of the transition process, see Waldmeir 1997, Sparks 1995.

31. The 1994 election is analyzed most thoroughly in Johnson and Schlemmer 1996.

32. As seen, for example, in the divestment movement and the waves of demonstrations and arrests—often of prominent persons—at the South African embassy in Washington.

33. As early as 1992, Nelson Mandela announced in a surprise press conference at the Johannesburg airport that all South Africans, white and black, had to recognize the danger that persistent political instability posed for the national economy. Warning South Africans of all political persuasions that they could not afford continued stalemate in the negotiations about how to run elections, he stated that he would ask the ANC to abandon its insistence on redistribution of property as a basic tenet of the new government. Mandela pointed to the economic disasters that had occurred in Mozambique and Angola when skilled white businessmen and artisans fled after independence came in the mid-1970s. He said that the new government would have to promise to protect private property as a way to sustain and restore business confidence—confidence that was required to ensure continued investment, and thus, continued job creation (Waldmeir 1997, 256).

34. A "moderate" initiative to defend some of these privileges is under development in the form of the Democratic Alliance (DA), an opposition party formed in early 2000 as a coalition between the old Democratic Party of Helen Suzman—for many years a white parliamentary critic of apartheid—and the more accommodationist wing of the Nationalist Party. The latter has now effectively split between the die-hard Freedom Front, led by former general Constand Viljoen, which taps into ongoing white *ressentiment* and is demanding an Afrikaner "homeland"; and the DA. Led by Tony Leon, the Democratic Alliance also caters

to white fears but uses a lower-key subtextual approach: it works through "code words." The DA has attracted considerable support among coloured and Indian voters as well. In the December 5, 2000 local elections it won 22.5 percent of the national vote, and maintained control of one province, the Western Cape.

> Before the election, I went to a local DA meeting, where Tony Leon was the star speaker. "I'm not just here to scare you," announced Leon to his almost completely white audience. He then proceeded to do little else. You could have been forgiven for leaving the meeting with the impression that our government was intent on driving the persecuted, hard-working whites, if not into the sea, certainly out of their homes. (Rostron 2000)

35. On these matters more generally, see Klug 2000.

36. It also sought information about ANC abuses (of suspected collaborators, for example), although these were obviously of a different scale than those of the white supremacist government.

37. The future direction of South African development policy is a matter of complex debate. Clearly thoroughgoing class-based (and implicitly, race-based) compromise will be necessary to achieve any inclusive form of development. A very wide range of issues have been raised in this context: taxation systems, fiscal and monetary policy, levels of indebtedness, and export-development strategies are but some of the main issues on the table.

38. This leaves unmentioned the earlier resistance and global connections that date back to the first contacts between native peoples and Europeans at the dawn of the modern age; but see Part I of this book.

39. These terms derive from Taguieff 2001 [1988]; they receive a fuller treatment in Chapter Ten, below.

40. An interesting related question, which cannot be explored here, is the role of white involvement in the anti-apartheid resistance. Movement organizations have dealt in different ways with the contradictions of white involvement. Sympathetic whites provided important resources and support for black resistance; indeed some died under torture by the apartheid police (Dr. Neil Aggett, for example) or were casualties of state-sponsored terrorism (Ruth First and Albie Sachs, for example). But the presence of whites can also problematize issues of leadership and autonomy (Simons and Simons 1983; Lazerson 1994; Sachs 1990).

The U.S. version of this dilemma was discussed by Malcolm X:

> I mean nothing against any sincere whites when I say that as members of black organizations, generally whites' very presence subtly renders the black organization automatically less effective. Even the best white members will slow down the Negroes' discovery of what they need to do, and particularly of what they can do—for themselves, working by themselves, among their own kind, in their own communities. (Malcolm X with Alex Haley 1965, 376).

41. Such figures as Robert Sobukwe and Steve Biko were by no means "black racists," however. Although their movements at times adopted "maximalist" pan-Africanist positions, their fundamental orientations were those of anti-colonialism and self-determination. On Sobukwe, see Pogrund 1991; Fredrickson 1997b. On Biko, see Arnold 1978; Pityana et al. 1991.

42. Portions of the following section appeared in earlier form in Seidman 1999.

43. Sociobiological approaches to race are still common throughout the modern world although hardly as prevalent as they were a century ago. See Chapter Five, above.

44. See note 13, above. On the question of racial classification and reclassification under apartheid, see Lelyveld 1985, 85–93; Posel 1999. For U.S. analogies, see Domínguez 1994; Davis 1991.

45. See Lelyveld 1985 for numerous tales of this type; Watson 1970 gives various accounts of "passing" among the coloured population.

46. A valuable social scientific literature now seeks to dissect colonial racial categories in terms of their concerns over sexuality, class, and control (Stoler 1995); such work is only beginning in respect to South Africa. See McClintock 1995.

47. The 1996 constitution contains a provision enabling affirmative action programs in

democractic South Africa: "Equality includes the full and equal enjoyment of all rights and free-doms. To promote the achievement of equality, legislative and other measures designed to pro-tect or advance persons, or categories of persons, disadvantaged by unfair discrimination may be taken." *Constitution of the Republic of South Africa, 1996.* Chapter 2, Section 9, No. 2.

On January 26, 2000, the South African parliament passed the Promotion of Equality and Prevention of Unfair Discrimination bill, which President Mbeki signed into law on Feb-ruary 4. This bill complements the bill of rights provisions in the 1996 constitution, banning discrimination based on race, gender, sex, pregnancy, marital status, ethnic or social origin, color, sexual orientation, age, disability, religion, conscience, belief, culture, language, and birth. It sets up "equality courts" to adjudicate charges of discrimination. Although at this writing it is too early to evaluate the effectiveness of this measure, it obviously reflects a con-tinuing ANC anti-racist commitment. The egalitarian orientation of this legislation is also consistent with the long-standing ANC policy of non-racialism.

CHAPTER NINE. BRAZIL

1. According to the 1991 census, Brazil is 52 percent white, 42 percent brown (*pardo*), 5 percent black, 0.4 percent yellow (i.e., of Asian descent), and 0.2 indigenous (IBGE 1991, 162–164). Needless to say, there are significant questions about the census categories employed, the thoroughness of the census, and the means by which persons were assigned to particular classifications—by their own lights or by the racial perceptions of census enu-merators. Therefore the accuracy and meaningfulness of the census numbers are themselves subject to question. See Nobles 2000; Wood 1991.

2. These statistics include both the *preto* and *pardo* categories under the category "black." They are too old to be fully reliable; they are based on the National Household Survey—the *Pesquisa Nacional por Amostra de Domicílio* (PNAD) 1982 data. For generally corroborative data, see Andrews 1992; Datafolha 1995.

3. And besides all that, how much democracy has Brazil really enjoyed? The First Repub-lic lasted until 1930. The 1930–37 period was complex, dominated by Getúlio Vargas, whose *Estado Novo*—a dictatorship—began in 1937. The Second Republic was restored in 1946 and continued until 1964, to be followed by more than two decades of military dictatorship. The present (Third) republic has existed only since 1985. So democracy itself, not to mention *racial* democracy, is far from consolidated in Brazil. These topics receive more extensive treatment below,

4. A *cordel* is a string on which kiosks and newsstands traditionally displayed popular booklets and storybooks for sale. This cheap reading matter played a significant part in dis-seminating popular culture, and still flourishes in the age of mass media. *Sambas de enredo* are current sambas, often composed for carnival competitions. *Telenovelas* are serialized televi-sion dramas, vastly popular in Brazil and often widely exported as well. They resemble soap operas, but are usually both more literary and more dramatic. They do not run on forever like U.S. soaps, but have a more concentrated and focused trajectory and pacing. They are passionately watched and discussed throughout the country.

5. In an important early article, Nogueira labeled this type of discourse *preconceito de marca* ("prejudice of appearance") and distinguished it from *preconceito de origem* ("prejudice of origin"), which he equated with the U.S. hypodescent or one-drop rule (Nogueira 1985 [1954]). He thus posed an early challenge to the framework of the UNESCO research, which was just getting off the ground at that point.

6. This ideology, like any, must "work": that is, it must link the concepts of race and racial identity to the key sociopolitical structures of Brazil; it must situate racial subjects more or less effectively. Or else what is its point? At the same time, because it is a representation, a distillation of a complex, historically variable, and contradictory set of social relationships, the ideology of racial democracy may be expected to contain inaccuracies and inconsisten-cies, and to represent some subject-positions and interests better than others. That is the work that ideologies do. But if it becomes too obviously inaccurate, if it travesties its mater-ial, if it fails to situate Brazilian subjects adequately, it will lose its effectiveness.

7. Many on the Brazilian left spent significant periods in exile, often in Europe and the United States, especially during the first decade of the dictatorship.

8. Brazilians traditionally have problems with race-consciousness in any form, including positive or anti-racist racial awareness. A common charge one faces if one tries to discuss racial matters, or even if one denounces a racist act, is that simply acknowledging race is itself racist.

9. Brazil participated in the war only to a very limited extent. It sent a contingent of troops to fight with the Allies in the Italian campaign. Interestingly, the commander of the Brazil Expeditionary Force, as it was called, was Humberto Castelo Branco, the general who in 1964 would lead the coup against President João Goulart. Castelo Branco had retained close ties with the United States since World War II days; U.S. warships were deployed in Guanabara Bay in 1964 as a signal of support for the coup. See Dreifuss 1981.

10. The "revolution" was really a coup d'etat that overthrew Julio Prestes, the last president under the First Republic; Prestes had defeated Vargas in the presidential election of that year. Vargas consolidated his power and achieved some legitimacy by convoking a Constituent Assembly that promulgated a new constitution in 1934; among other things, the 1934 document ratified his presidency. Yet faced with continuing opposition and unrest, Vargas abolished what remained of democracy in 1937 with his proclamation of the *Estado Novo.* Forced from power in 1945, he was able to win election to the presidency under the Second Republic in 1950. However, he clashed with the military in 1954. Threatened with removal, Vargas committed suicide in August 1954.

11. On the FNB, see Fernandes 1978, vol. 2; Bastide and Fernandes 1971; Moura 1988; Andrews 1991; Mitchell 1977. See also Chapter Five, above.

12. Leonel Brizola, governor of Rio de Janeiro state in the 1970s and 1980s, was a political descendant of Vargas and nephew of the last democratically elected president of the Second Republic, João Goulart. Brizola had presidential ambitions himself and adopted the slogan *socialismo moreno* (brown socialism) in the 1980s.

13. Despite this provision, though, the 1934 constitution was a racially mixed bag, marked by significant eugenicist influences that had survived largely unmodified from the early Republican debates over *branqueamento.* Promulgated just before the impact of Freyre's *Casa-Grande e Senzala,* the 1934 constitution was in some ways the last stand of the official whitening doctrine (Stepan 1991, 162–169; Mitchell 1999, 124).

Although not qualifying as a fully fascist regime, the *Estado Novo* exhibited some of those characteristics: its state-centeredness or *dirigisme,* authoritarian populism, repressiveness, and anti-democratic commitments. There were notable anti-semitic tendencies in the Vargas regime as well (Lesser 1995; Levine 1970; Carneiro 1988). *Varguismo* was also influenced by the Integralist movement led by Plinio Salgado (as was the FNB), and of course by the rise of fascism in Europe. However, Vargas did not hesitate to put down an abortive integralist uprising in 1938, and Brazil joined the Allied cause in World War II.

14. As this quote indicates, Vargas's suicide is still seen as suspicious by many.

15. Vargas's nationalism was also strongly nativist, another point on which his interests converged with those of blacks. His restriction of immigration itself constituted an important benefit for Afro-Brazilians, who had been hurt by job competition with immigrants.

16. Although Vargas strictly limited trade union independence during the *Estado Novo* period, he also favored trade unions as part of the corporatist/populist setup of his regime:

> As Afro-Brazilians entered industrial employment, they automatically became part of the state-regulated labor movement created in the 1930s under Getúlio Vargas and maintained in place under the Second Republic. Although no figures are available on union membership by race, the frequent mention of union activities in the black press and the regularity with which black social and cultural organizations used union halls and facilities for their activities suggest that black workers, and even black organizations, received an unexpectedly (in light of Afro-Brazilians' previous experience with official Brazilian institutions) warm welcome in the union movement. This suggestion is further confirmed by the fact that by the mid-1950s individual Afro-Brazilians were starting to show up in positions of union leadership, a trend which became pronounced in the 1960s and 1970s. (Andrews 1991, 186–187; see also French 1992; Seidman 1994).

Although I cannot expand on this point here, the accessibility and support provided by trade unions (meeting places, official recognition, and so on) suggests that, like religious institutions, clubs, and cultural/performance spaces, unions offered some of the early possibilities of resource mobilization necessary to reconstitute the black movement after the destruction of the FNB in 1937. For U.S. parallels, see Morris 1984.

17. The 1936 decision of the FNB to register as a political party was undoubtedly driven by an overly-optimistic sense of what could be accomplished by an explicitly black party. The "extreme right-wing chauvinism" visible in the group (there were left voices as well) also indicates disorientation. Its suppression scarcely a year after this, although of course a product of Vargas's dictatorial commitments, may have saved the FNB from eventual self-destruction. See Andrews 1991, 150–156; Fernandes 1978; Mitchell 1977.

18. On the black press, see Bastide 1973, 131–145; Moura 1988, 204–217.

19. Notably under the influence of Raimundo Nina Rodrigues (1945) and Francisco José Oliveira Vianna (1934).

20. The image of Brazil as a synthesis of three races has a whole literature of its own, much of it a reflection, whether sympathetic or critical, of the Freyrian argument. See Haberly 1983; da Matta 1984.

21. Freyre had been a student of Franz Boas at Columbia University in New York during the 1920s.

22. Although this was the general pattern, there were some significant exceptions: most notably Euclides da Cunha (1995 [1902]). For a contemporary symposium on this general theme, see Ribeiro et al. 1996.

23. Mitchell provocatively surveys right-wing intellectual Miguel Reale's reading of Freyre to illustrate how theoretically sophisticated Freyre's perspective is. Reale reads Freyre as a Hegelian dialectician, whose contradictory moments or terms are racial. The *casa grande* and the *senzala* can clearly be linked quite directly to the master-slave dialectic in Hegel. However,

> In Reale's reading of Freyre, the dialectical relationships in society are not necessarily resolved into a new synthesis, but nevertheless are preserved and kept in place through the functioning of social institutions. Social institutions therefore become the essential cement that allow (sic) for the inherent antagonisms of a society to play themselves out in some sort of a permanent and stable way. (Mitchell 1999, 127)

24. Freyre's theories of sex and gender are an early instance of race/gender/class "intersectionality," although hardly a progressive one. He locates the hybrid female—the *mulata*—at the crossroads of Brazilian national gestation. His sexual romanticization of the *mulata* parallels that of his fellow *nordestino*, Jorge Amado, author of *Gabriela, Clavo y Canela* and *Dona Flor e Seus Dois Maridos*. But miscegenation (and rape—of which Freyre is quite aware) are not the only "intersections" Freyre highlights. He rhapsodizes at length about the Brazilian use of slave nurse-maids, for example. See Freyre 1986 [1933], 349; see also Burdick 1998, 48. The child of a Pernambucana planter family, himself born in a *casa grande* in the era of abolition, Freyre was supposedly suckled by a black wet-nurse himself. See Needell 1995.

25. Nascimento was greatly influenced in his early years by the FNB and was linked, like many other activist Afro-Brazilians of the period, to *Integralismo*. His subsequent odyssey placed him firmly in the pan-Africanist tradition, and also led him leftward to an "African socialism." See Nascimento 1985; Hanchard 1994, 181, n. 11.

26. Some of the main works produced under UNESCO sponsorship were Fernandes 1978; Bastide and Fernandes 1971; Azevedo 1955; Harris 1964, Wagley 1972; Cardoso and Ianni 1960.

27. Parts of the following section appeared in different form in Winant 1992.

28. Azevedo presents the process of transition as a shift from racially identified status or prestige groups to classes. Formerly, whites were identified as a superior status group and blacks, conversely, as an inferior group. Race served as an indicator of status, but the deeper, more "objective" category of class is a matter of economics, not of color or prestige. Thus race becomes less salient as class formation proceeds. See Azevedo 1966, 34; see also Guimarães 1999, 129–146.

29. These arguments led Eugene Genovese to defend the conservative Gilberto Freyre (as well as Frank Tannenbaum and others) from the explicitly radical and "materialist" attack of Harris. Genovese perceived in Freyre a far more complex and "totalizing" view of the meaning of race in Brazil than he found in Harris (Genovese 1971, 41–43).

30. The optic of the UNESCO studies was markedly domestic; this was a logical outcome of their guiding premise: to reveal the secret of the absence of racism in Brazil. Even their general debunking of that premise did not turn these researchers' gaze in a comparative direction. This is somewhat surprising in light not only of the general sophistication and knowledgeability of these writers, but also because of the substantial involvement in these projects of non-Brazilian scholars. Bastide, for example, was contemporary with Fanon; Harris and Wagley ignore Du Bois. In an anthology he edited, van den Berghe excerpts the famous debate between Melville Herskovits and E. Franklin Frazier on diasporic issues (which touches on Brazil), but this debate concerns the presence or absence of African cultural survivals in the Americas, not racism per se (van den Berghe 1978). A partial exception is Harris 1964, who contrasts the hypodescent (one-drop rule/color-line) system of racial classification in the United States to the color continuum of Brazil. This distinction echoes Freyre in two ways: it emphasizes racial hybridity in the Brazilian context; and it draws on the same regional (*nordestino*) research focus that informed Freyre's work. It also intersects with the work of many others, notably Hoetink 1971.

31. Maio 1997 argues that the UNESCO studies provided the foundational impetus for the creation of modern social science (notably sociology and anthropology) in the Brazilian academy. Here lie some of the intellectual origins of the current president of the Republic, sociologist Fernando Henrique Cardoso.

32. Although exile was not conducive to political or empirical work on Brazilian racial dynamics, it did provide important international connections, in terms of both movement activity and intellectual influence. These connections were bidirectional: Brazilian exiles not only learned about the range of anti-racist movements, for example, but brought Brazilian issues to the attention of the world.

33. While the repressiveness of the military regime, especially from 1968 to 1974, certainly curtailed opposition, smaller-scale anti-racist activity did not entirely disappear. Consciousness of race, and of the links between anti-racism and democracy, was maintained in many spheres: in community and culturally oriented groups, in religious settings, in schools and workplaces, and in clandestine activity. Indeed, while activists ran the risk of arrest, torture, and death at the hands of the military, they were also sustained by racial solidarity and race-consciousness. See Hanchard 1994, 77–78.

34. Testimonies of MNU activists, as well as the considerable research literature on the organization, clearly illustrate these participants' familiarity with the international dimensions of the black movement. Frequent references are made, not only to pan-Africanist themes but to specific national and international movements and authorities: Negritude, the U.S. civil rights and black power movements, the ANC and black consciousness movement in South Africa, Martin Luther King Jr., Malcolm X, Nelson Mandela, and Steve Biko. See Nascimento 1989.

35. Some of the limited mobilization that existed before the emergence of the MNU also took the form of cultural politics, typified most centrally by the "black soul" movement. On "black soul," see Rodrigues da Silva 1980; Hanchard 1994, 110–119; Nascimento 1989, 90–100.

36. This list was drawn from Nascimento 1989, 88.

37. Dzidzienyo 1971 and Hasenbalg 1979 were some of the key scholarly works that played this role. Skidmore's important book (1993 [1974]), as well as his early article comparing the United States and Brazil (Skidmore 1972), were also vital sources of insight for Afro-Brazilian intellectuals—many of them active in the MNU. See also Dzidzienyo 1985; de Souza 1971; Silva 1985; Degler 1986 [1971]. My somewhat awkward use of the "structuralist" label is not intended to refer to the French social theory of that name, but instead to recognize these authors' insistence on the profoundly imbricated social structural qualities of racism in Brazil. Portions of my 1992 text are utilized here, although in modified form.

38. In other words, blacks have to choose between trying to improve racial conditions by collective action (organization, political mobilization, *conscientização*, etc.), which necessarily involves assuming and defending a black identity; or following the strategy of *auto-embranquecimento* ("self-whitening"), which necessarily involves denying or mitigating blackness: straightening the hair, marrying "light," and so on. This analysis has turned out to have real staying power in light of recent ethnographic research; see the discussion of "Racial Formation in the Third Republic," below.

39. That many in the MNU became embroiled in ultra-left politics and vanguardism is hinted at in Nascimento 1989 and Gonzales 1985.

40. I definitely do not mean to reproach these particular writers for their neglect of the subalternity theme. During the 1970s such approaches were just being worked out in the South Asian context, and the first major work incorporating these views to appear in the United States—James Scott's *Weapons of the Weak*—was still a decade in the future.

41. At first these were chiefly tokenistic ones (advisory councils, channels for grievances, etc.). After 1985, however, and especially with the election of Cardoso, the pace of racially oriented state activity picked up somewhat. The human rights commitments of the government were expanded; the *Fundação Cultural Palmares* was set up to resolve black restitution and land-claims issues dating back to the extensive archipelago of *quilombos* that had existed during the era of slavery. Investigation and adjudication of charges of discrimination made under the new constitution and further anti-racist legislation became a reality (Guimarães 1998). In short, limited but real racial reforms were undertaken under the Third Republic.

42. "Divided by class and segments of classes, fractured by miscegenation which established a scale that runs from the 'darker' to the 'lighter' in color, blacks and mestiços [in the MNU] didn't easily achieve consensus and unity" (Nascimento 1989, 126).

43. "During the 1970s it seemed for a while that the MNU, at least in its initial stages, was the only force capable of strengthening the black struggle for a movement with a comprehensive view, in which racism could be seen and denounced as an essential component of capitalist exploitation. . . .

"The movement tried, and in a certain sense succeeded in framing proposals, all the while being menaced by the deep divergences among its members, by isolation, and by the impact of its acceptance of Negritude." (Nascimento 1989, 126)

44. The MNU found it "difficult to move across the various realms of multiraciality." In particular, the construction of a black identity was difficult, for there was division over how much the movement's emphasis should be placed on negritude, and how much on civil and citizenship rights (Nascimento 1989, 127).

45. A valuable overview of black electoral activity at the federal level is available in Johnson 1998.

46. I also criticize Marx's model along these lines in Chapter Five, above.

47. Not only black groups, but also indigenous rights groups, have increased their presence in the Third Republic. Led by what Jonathan Warren has labeled "non-traditional" Indians, these groups exhibit an unprecedented degree of savvy, organizational ability, and international connectedness.

I regret the absence of attention given in this chapter to Brazilian indigenous issues and movements, as well as "other others": Japanese Brazilians, Jews and Arabs, and various other racial-ethnic communities. Space simply does not permit me to give these groups and issues the consideration they deserve. Warren 1998 and Lesser (1999) provide the reader with some valuable "take-off points" for further study. On Jews in Brazil, see Lesser 1995. On Japanese in Brazil, see Reichl 1988; Tsuchida 1978; Saito and Maeyama 1973.

48. For discussions of Afro-Brazilian women's issues—stratification, mobilization, consciousness, and so on—see, amidst a vast literature: Damasceno 1999; Bairros 1991; Lovell 1994; Goldani 1991; Gilliam and Gilliam 1995; Carneiro and Santos 1985; Simpson 1993.

49. The concept of hidden transcript refers to the ways in which subjugated and impoverished people challenge the system of domination in everyday, ostensibly apolitical ways: by dragging their feet, pretending not to understand orders, "shuckin and jivin," "liberating" necessary goods and services they consider that they are owed, and in innumerable other

ways. Mostly the subaltern are not in a position to "fight the power" overtly and openly, although obviously there are exceptions: outrage and spontaneous eruptions of anger can spark mass action even when conditions are far from desperate. But this is rare.

50. Guimarães 1998, 27. Guimarães studied the treatment of complaints lodged by blacks about acts of discrimination and expressions of prejudice. He reviewed charges (brought under the new anti-discrimination laws enacted in the Third Republic) that were made at local police delegations in São Paulo. He also examined mainstream newspaper reporting on prejudice and discrimination cases. He found that complaints and media awareness of racism both increased markedly in the 1990s, but old-style patterns of dismissal and denial were maintained as well.

51. See the first epigraph of this book (Veloso 1994) for one of a multitude of examples.

52. A Catholic mass modified in "Afrocentric" ways, to include drumming, dancing, and numerous influences from New World African religious traditions like *candomblé*. In many respects the inculturated mass can be understood as an effort within the Church to practice syncretism "in reverse" in order to appeal to Afro-Brazilians.

53. Many of the pentecostal churches studied by Burdick have their roots in U.S. black pentecostalism. This connection parallels the missionary work carried out in late-nineteenth- and early-twentieth-century South Africa by the North American AME church. See Fredrickson 1995, 80–92; see also Comaroff and Comaroff 1991; Ranger 1986.

54. For example, Twine's (1997) ethnography, set in a rural town in Rio de Janeiro state, documents a systematic unwillingness (or inability) on the part of Afro-Brazilian respondents to acknowledge racism. It is hard not to respond to this account by inferring a (Fanonian type of) repression on the part of these respondents. Racism is something they *do not want* to know about; that they *cannot let themselves understand.*

55. Burdick in particular emphasizes the chasm that still divides experiential, micro-level critical awareness of racism from explicitly political, movement-oriented, macro-level awareness.

56. Black women's traditional work roles as family servants: *empregada* (maid); *criada* (young girl-babysitter); *babá* (older woman-babysitter).

57. Here we see the continuing relevance of De Souza's analysis (1971). See note 38 above.

58. For an early Brazilian statement about these issues, posed from a standpoint similar to Fanon's, see Santos Souza 1983.

59. This refers to the *Cão* law of 1989, which outlawed racial discrimination and racist violence.

60. Material in this section appeared in preliminary form in Winant 1994d.

61. What would a repudiation of the ideology of racial democracy mean for whites? What reassurances does the claim that Brazil lacks the racial hierarchy—present elsewhere in the world—offer to whites? Possibly it is this factor, the insecurity of white identity, that underlies those defenses of the ideology of racial democracy that are still mounted quite frequently (Fry 1991; Fry 1995).

62. See Reichmann 1999, citing the *Folha de São Paulo*, May 31, 1994.

63. "Oh no!" some of my Brazilian friends exclaim, "You don't understand! He didn't say that he was black, just that he was *a little bit* black!" But that is precisely the point about racial ambivalence that I am trying to make.

64. Recent research by the Datafolha group, the first systematic inquiry into racial attitudes in Brazil, indicates that around 90 percent of Brazilians believe that whites are prejudiced against blacks; significantly, whites accept the truth of this statement at almost the same high rates as blacks and mixed-race (*pardos*) Brazilians do. The survey employed the same racial categories as the 1991 Brazilian census. See Datafolha 1995; Turra and Venturi 1995; Telles 1999.

65. For example, the following joke (adapted from Goldstein 1999):

Q: What does a black pregnant woman have in common with a car being repaired?
A. They are both waiting for a monkey (*macaco*).

66. As I have noted throughout this book, the distinction between the color-line and color continuum, between the "two modes of racial consciousness" (Hoetink 1971) has

always been ideal-typical. There are hierarchies of color everywhere in a thoroughly racialized world. Light skin correlates to greater mobility in the United States as well as in Latin America (Davis 1991); the Anglophone Caribbean has its "brownings" (James 1998); and South Africa its "coloureds." Conversely, the distinction "white-other" manages to retain importance even in Brazil. None of these qualifications, however, negates the fundamental point: racism endures.

67. But even those in my other categories, the "militants" and the "avoiders," are subject to dualism: for the "militants" cannot utterly purge themselves of the values acquired through socialization under the sign of racial democracy, and the "avoiders" are reminded in a thousand ways that they are black. They are the subjects of a familiar *dito* ("saying") repeated to me once by a taxi-driver: "*Se voce se esquecer de que voce é preto, um branco lembrarálo.*" (If you forget that you are black, a white will remind you.)

CHAPTER TEN. EUROPE: THE PHANTOM MENACE

1. Many other incidents are not so minor. Expulsions and deportations of immigrants, for example, as well as mobilizations of resistance to such practices, have become common. Perhaps the most famous incident of such confrontations took place at the Church of Saint-Bernard in Paris. After a prolonged campaign for sanctuary on the part of three hundred undocumented Africans (the *sans-papiers*), and notwithstanding the presence of a large number of human rights and solidarity-oriented demonstrators, French security forces broke down the church doors in the early morning of August 23, 1996, and forcibly evicted the protesters. The West Africans were deported soon afterward. The strategy of church occupations continued, however. As of mid-1998, at least seven church occupations had occurred, along with other protests. Deportations of *sans-papieres*, begun under the Juppé government, continued under the Socialist Premier Jospin. See Cisse 1998.

2. Refugee rights may be a relic of the past in the fin-de-siècle EU, though. Probably the last vestige of "openness to the South" was the German asylum law, which was ostensibly a political, not an economic, measure (an increasingly nonexistent distinction anyway). This policy allowed for the large-scale influx of both economic migrants and political refugees from Central Europe and the Balkans, until it was repealed in 1993 with broad support across the political spectrum from right to left. The Schengen agreement of 1985 attempted to regulate restrictive asylum policies as part of a coordinated effort to regularize immigration to the EU (for more on Schengen, see below). In the aftermath of these developments, those refugees allowed to immigrate at all are generally treated as temporary residents, for example, in the case of Kosovars who fled the "ethnic cleansing" and NATO bombings of 1999.

3. Perceptions of "difference" are less affected by a substantial dilution of the "native" populations of the EU countries, as is sometimes asserted by right-wingers, than by other factors. Chief among these would presumably be the pre–World War II pattern of racial homogeneity at home: when the colonial "others" were largely—although of course not totally—kept outside the mother-country's borders, the congruence of national and racial frontiers was easier to perceive and "normalize." A second factor of importance in shaping new uncertainties about racial heterogeneity is undoubtedly the rate of immigration. In the postwar period the numbers of "newcomers" increased considerably, especially in the 1950s and 1960s, but at a relatively steady pace across the decades. "Newcomer" fertility rates, too, significantly exceed their "native" European counterparts. For more extensive treatment of these issues, see below.

4. In comparison with the United States, the Western European societies certainly lack as extensive an experience of pluralization and *domestic*, racialized, cultural hierarchy. This can be traced to the large-scale (although not total) absence of racial slavery on their soil; to the absence (again, not entirely total, but almost) of a history of conquest and deracination of the indigenous populations; and to the foundational role of immigration in the construction of the nation. All these patterns, of course, deeply characterize North American history, for good and ill. Nor is the United States free of a substantial nativist history of its own.

5. In some measure as a response to the political and neo-fascist right, anti-racist organizations and projects have spread across Europe as well. Official organizations and commissions

at the state and regional levels have been created to monitor racial "problems." Non-governmental and humanitarian groups, as well as explicitly political ones, have sprung into action, lobbying and providing services, as well as agitating and demonstrating. Immigrant and minority groups have also proliferated, organized along a variety of axes: by national origin, by religious orientation, youth groups, and so on. See below.

6. These categories of immigrants—and more deeply of "others"—were the fixations of the restrictive immigration laws enacted in 1993, the so-called Pasqua laws.

7. From a vast literature, see such works as Basch et al. 1994; Freeman 1979; Linke 1999; and Joly 1998.

8. It is of course anachronistic even to suggest that whiteness existed in premodern Europe.

9. This distinction draws on the work of Taguieff (2001 [1988]). These matters are discussed more fully below.

10. Perhaps it is too large a stretch to label the Nazi drive for *lebensraum* and extraterritorial domination as "imperialism." Perhaps too the atavistic dreams of Mussolini for a new Roman empire don't quite qualify. Stalin too could be labeled "imperialist." Still, pending a serious study of the links—romantic, predatory, genocidal—between the rise of "classical" European imperialism from the sixteenth to the eighteenth centuries and the brief but brutal totalitarian revival of many of these practices in the twentieth century, this use of the term will have to serve.

As Bauman notes:

> Stalin's and Hitler's victims were not killed in order to capture and colonize the territory they occupied. Often they were killed in a dull, mechanical fashion with no human emotions—hatred included—to enliven it. They were killed because they did not fit, for one reason or another, the scheme of a perfect society. Their killing was not the work of destruction, but creation. They were eliminated, so that an objectively better human world—more efficient, more moral, more beautiful—could be established. A Communist world. Or a racially pure, Aryan world. In both cases, a harmonious world, conflict-free, docile in the hands of their (sic) rulers, orderly, controlled. People tainted with ineradicable blight of their past or origin could not be fitted into such [an] unblemished and shining world. Like weeds, their nature could not be changed. They could not be improved or re-educated. They had to be eliminated. (Bauman 1989, 92–93; see also Arendt 1968; Gilman and Katz 1991)

Maybe the best application of the designation would be to Japan's (another latecomer) "Greater East Asia Co-prosperity Sphere," a more traditional effort to project naval and economic power regionally.

11. This echoes Frank's famous argument about the "development of underdevelopment" in Latin America. Frank's early work on historical capitalism in Latin America—for example on the "primitive accumulation" thesis, the "Indian problem," and the "internal colonialism" analysis—can be read as a neo-Marxist analysis of the role of race in the region's economic history. See Frank 1966; Frank 1969; Hall 1980.

12. See Chapter Three, above. Mosse 1978 and Poliakov 1977 offer valuable discussions on the provenance and genealogy of anti-semitism.

13. This is not to say the world now takes sufficient notice of such events, obviously. But it is no longer an option to feign ignorance of them either. Case in point: the United States blocked efforts in the UN Security Council to intervene against the 1994 genocide in Rwanda. The benefit of knowing that genocide is happening—as opposed to not knowing—remains dubious if nothing is done to prevent it or check it. But it is still better to know than not to know.

14. The Dutch recognized fairly quickly that their East Indian dominion was unsupportable, but they still had to be kicked out of Indonesia by serious armed struggle (Reid 1974). The Portuguese made a very belated exit from Africa in the 1970s, but only when their futile efforts at suppression of insurgency had so alienated their own troops that they provoked revolution (or at least the overthrow of fascism a la Salazar/Caetano) at home.

15. Elsewhere, for example, in Eastern Europe, large ethnonational subpopulations—notably German *aussiedler* or *volksdeutscher*—were left over from previous expansionist or imperial projects. This was a different class of "settler" whose previous colonial status had not generally been racialized, and who had also not retained formal citizenship in the mother-country. But there are also qualifiers to these assertions: when the Nazi armies appeared in the East, the status of local *volksdeutscher* obviously increased in a virtually colonial pattern. And when these same people sought (or were forced to) return to Germany in the post–World War II period, they were able to claim German citizenship under *jus sanguinis* laws, principles that held over from the fascist period.

There is another somewhat parallel case of emigrant return in the postwar period: this is the so-called *pieds noirs* in France. These French colonials returned after the Algerian defeat. Their citizenship was never in question and did not depend on "blood," however.

16. These countries may be characterized, following Wallerstein, as "semi-peripheral."

17. Ireland is a particularly advanced case of this impoverished outflow, for it alone among the entire contemporary EU was itself a colony.

18. Various dimensions of slavery and coercive migration, as well as resistance on the part of these groups of "settlers," are explored in Part I, above.

19. Sometimes such policies meant playing off local traditional rulers and ethnic groups against each other, as in Nigeria, for example (Laitin 1986). Elsewhere it meant creation of middleman minorities distinguished by race, as in East Africa (Cooper 1987; see also Mamdani 1996). Still elsewhere as in the Caribbean, such policies depended upon another round of mass labor importation, a post-slavery "peon trade," so to speak, in furtherance of the imperial objective of *divide et impera* vis-à-vis the exploited (Rodney 1981).

20. *Spijtoptanten* was the name attached to "Indos"—those of mixed Dutch-Indonesian origins—who elected to remain Indonesian citizens upon independence, but subsequently changed their minds and immigrated to Holland. An effective summary of the history of immigration to the Netherlands, which includes good material on postwar Dutch repatriation and "guest worker"/labor migration patterns, is Lucassen and Penninx 1997. On earlier Indo-European *métissage*, see Stoler 1991; Stoler 1997.

21. Measurement problems arise principally as consequences of differences in categorization. Citizenship status, for example, greatly affects how migrants are categorized. In France, because their sending areas were already *départements* and they were already citizens, immigrants from Guadeloupe, Martinique, or colonial Algeria were merely moving within the country, as if a North American were merely moving from Honolulu to Los Angeles. Further, naturalization was regularized under principles of territoriality (*jus soli*); in fact, France for a time had a policy of *double jus soli* for post-colonial immigrants (Feldblum 1999), and dual citizenship in general is far from a dead issue in Europe. In Germany, by contrast, citizenship was until recently an ethnonational matter (*jus sanguinis*), non-Germans could not obtain it and would remain separately classified on national grounds ("Turks," etc.), even to the third generation. Non-territorial ethnic Germans (*aussiedler*), however, were unproblematically naturalized upon arrival. East Germans (*übersiedler*) became citizens en masse with unification. On top of all that, postwar preoccupations with human rights made for broad legal provision where refugee questions and political asylum were concerned. In Britain, Irish immigration was unhindered and conferred quasi-citizenship status (notably the franchise, in many but not all cases); citizens of Commonweath countries could immigrate easily until the sun finally set on the British Empire in the 1960s, although covert racial criteria were employed to distinguish among them.

These matters are discussed more broadly below. The point here is that although plentiful statistics exist, it isn't always clear "who is considered what." Citizen and immigrant may be the same person or family, refugee and *gastarbeiter* may coincide (a perennial problem everywhere, but particularly in Europe), and denizens who are denied citizenship rights (and forced to maintain their connections to a sending country they may never have seen) may acquire permanent, tacit recognition and residency rights (Hammar 1990; Soysal 1994; Joppke 1998; Favell 1998). Finally, data collection is far from perfect, much immigration is never reported, and numerous ambiguous cases exist.

22. Ireland has been a perpetual sending area for British migrants, and remains so even today. In the postwar period the Irish had full political rights, including the franchise, but also experienced significant discriminination. Where they white? Were they post-colonials? See Rolston 1999.

23. Immigration restriction for Commonwealth arrivals was quite explicitly targeted toward non-whites, although the "Commonwealth" classification made this a coded, implicit matter, thus foreshadowing the new racism (see below). Already in 1952, anxieties were being expressed in Parliament about non-white immigration; with the passage of the 1962 Commonweath Immigrants Act this became more open with the emergence of a tacit "white Britain policy" (Castles and Kosack 1985; Sivanandan 1982). A continuing series of restrictive measures culminated under Thatcher in the 1981 British Nationality Act, which effectively cut off any remaining claims on the part of Commonwealth residents to immigration rights (Solomos 1989; Small 1994; Layton-Henry 1992).

24. There is a large literature on migration chains and the complex transnational social structures that sustain contemporary migration processes. These greatly exceed merely economic or political "push/pull" dynamics (which of course still retain their importance as well), involving household and family structures, specialized recruiting of many types, worldwide communications media and systems of remittance, diverse political and cultural organizations, and the maintenance of a variety of migration facilities and resources at the grassroots level in both sending and receiving regions. See Massey et al. 1998; Portes 1995; Cornelius, Martin, and Hollifield 1994; Soysal 1994; Castles and Miller 1998.

25. Mrs. Thatcher's famous 1978 remark on the swamping of Britain by relatively minuscule group of immigrants is well-known, but bears repeating:

> [T]he British character has done so much for democracy, for law, and done so much throughout the world, that if there is a fear that it might be swamped, people are going to react and be more hostile to those coming in. (Quoted in Miles 1993, 76; see also Barker 1981; Ansell 1997; Small 1994, Gilroy 1991)

These comments were made well before the Falkland/Malvinas war. They were delivered in the context of an upsurge in the popularity of the neo-fascist and explicitly racist British National Front, and have been interpreted as a maneuver to draw votes from this quarter (Hill 1988).

26. Young Portuguese men, for example, went to France in large numbers to avoid being drafted for the African colonial wars being fought by dictators Salazar and Caetano in the 1960s and early 1970s.

27. But note that there are uncertainties and discrepancies in these numbers. See note 21 above.

28. This is the number of immigrants from Islamic states according to 1990 information from the OECD (SOPEMI 1990), extrapolated to 1995 by Jonathan Fox for the Minorities At Risk Research Group at the University of Maryland (derived from the MAR Dataset available at http://www.bsos.umd.edu/cidcm/mar/list.html). The creators of this dataset also note:

> The 1990 estimate includes 619,900 from Algeria, 584,700 from Morocco, 207,500 from Tunisia and 201,500 from Turkey. This figure also includes an additional 300,000 illegal immigrants from these states although some estimate that there may be as many as 1,000,000 such illegal immigrants. It does not include naturalized French citizens of North African origin of whom it is estimated there are more than 200,000. Country population from UN population estimates.

As I have already pointed out, there are inherent reliability issues in some of these data (see note 21, above). See also Gurr et al. 1993.

29. These *vertriebene* had resided in Eastern European areas annexed to the Third Reich before and during the war. Other ethnic Germans, the *aussiedler*, also were vested in the postwar period with reentry rights and citizenship via German *jus sanguinis* citizenship policies (policies dating back to 1913 that remained in force, through everything, until the 1990s).

Aussiedler were not necessarily *vertriebene*, although in many cases there was overlap between the two categories. The distinction between them, though, recognizes that many ethnic Germans were not expelled in the aftermath of the war, but voluntarily left when they could for the more prosperous BRD (Brubaker 1992; Wilpert 1993). In some respects the *aussiedler* more resemble the Dutch *spijtoptanten* more than they do any coerced or refugee group of migrants.

30. In 1973 the Bundestag enacted the so-called *Ausländerstopp* in an effort to close off the flow of Turkish immigration, but this law, like restrictions attempted elsewhere, only had limited success. By the time of its passage, there were about 2.6 million foreign workers in the BRD, most of them of Turkish origin, and an overall *Ausländer* population of more than 4 million (Castles et al. 1984). By 1995 this number had increased to about 7.175 million, or 8.8 percent of the population; note, however, that this figure refers to the reunited Germany (OECD 1997, 29).

31. As will already be clear, an enormous literature has developed that addresses these problems in terms of citizenship. See, among many sources, Brubaker 1992; Caplan and Feffer 1996; Joppke 1998; Favell 1998; Martiniello 1995; Roche and van Berkel 1997; Balibar and Wallerstein 1991.

32. Stinchcombe's observation about the legitimacy of political rule is interesting here. The state's authority depends not only on its acceptance by those of whom it rules (legitimation "from below") but also and perhaps more crucially on its acceptance by *other states*: "It has often been observed that the stability of power depends on legitimacy, and that power created by naked force is, in the long run, precarious. . . . [T]he person *over whom power is exercised* is usually not as important as *other power holders*" (Stinchcombe 1968, 150; see also Tilly 1985).

33. I refer here to the Nazi "empire," perhaps a bit of a stretch. But the influx of *vertriebene* into postwar West Germany certainly was an outcome of the destruction of the Third Reich.

34. In the foregoing discussion, necessarily brief, I find myself more in agreement with Soysal's (1994) characterization of contemporary Europe as shaped by "post-national" membership, and more critical not only of Brubaker's position, but of Joppke's (1998) argument against this view. The central issue, in my view, is not some abstract "globalization," nor the supposed superiority of the political culture of the West (neither of which, of course, can be dismissed in any absolute way), but the breakdown of the preexisting global racial regime in the aftermath of World War II.

35. And as the resurgence of separatist impulses in northern Italy, Scotland, and Belgium, as well as the familiar case of Spain, also remind us.

36. Brubaker's (1992) work on the tensions between the German and French citizenship models, and on the importance of exclusivism in guaranteeing an effective citizenship policy, now seems to have been overtaken by events in respect to the former matter (as the Germans move toward abandoning their ethnonational, *jus sanguinis* approach), but as current as ever in respect to the latter issue. For important discussions, see Joppke 1998; Favell 1998.

37. Here large problems remain, especially in Germany. The Schröder (SPD-Green) government, under pressure in this area both from the Schengen signatories—Belgium, France, Germany, Greece, Italy, Luxembourg, the Netherlands, Portugal, and Spain (and since 1996, even Austria)—and from its domestic political base, which had brought to bear substantial mobilization for liberalization of citizenship laws, proposed a dual nationality reform that would have allowed denizens (notably Turks) to naturalize as Germans while still retaining citizenship in their countries of origin. But this plan encounted serious opposition from the right in elections of early 1999, and was therefore reworked. At this writing a new plan is under discussion, the so-called option model. This would extend citizenship only to children of denizens who were born in Germany, provided that they choose German citizenship—no possibility of dual passports—at the age of 18 or 23. In this concession Schröder is actually adopting a *Freie Demokratische Partei* (FDP) proposal. By abandoning dual citizenship, this measure would leave actual immigrants (i.e., those born outside Germany) in the limbo of denizenship; this is an obvious concession to the *jus sanguinis* principle. See Cohen 1999.

38. In this process, a family or village will select an appropriate emigrant, often a young man, judged to be skilled, trustworthy, and likely to find employment in the receiving country; they will then invest in this person's journey, expecting to be reimbursed or subsidized in return once the emigrant is established. Once settled in the receiving country, the initial migrant can facilitate the settlement of subsequent immigrants, send for additional family members, and dispatch regular remittances back home. This sequence of events is a cursory description of the migration chains discussed above. See Massey 1998; Grasmuck and Pessar 1991; Portes 1995.

39. Indeed fears of swamping by immigrants from southern sending nations have been reinforced by fears of immigrant flows from the East.

40. European whiteness is itself a socially constructed phenomenon, as I have argued in Part I, above. Its development in parallel with the rise of colonialism and slavery was always contested from within as well as from without. Many Europeans were never considered fully white: Muslims, Jews, Irish, Mediterraneans of various provenance, Slavs, even Finns. And some Africans, Americans, and Asians have been permanent residents in Europe since its rise to hegemony. With all these qualifications duly noted, though, the racialization of Europe as the land of the "whites" had become an established stereotype by the late seventeenth century, and still remains one today (Bonnett 1998). And not for no reason: the white coding still works quite well to distinguish the "haves" from the "have-nots," the dominant from the subordinate, the "developed" from the "less-developed." Racism lives.

41. In the East, as borders were redrawn and ferocious ethnonational (often quasi-racial) warfare broke out, massive suffering and the creation of refugees by the millions ensued. In this situation (which is outside the scope of the present study) nationalism took on a particular statist meaning: as Brubaker has argued, it was states that acted to constitute (or reframe) nations, not nationalist social movements that created states (Brubaker 1996). Efforts to generalize this model to a comprehensive (or even all-European) theory of nation-building and nationalism are surely oversimplified, however.

42. The Spanish and Portuguese versions of fascism retained state power until the mid-1970s. Latin American fascisms, greatly influenced by Franco in particular, but also hospitable to Nazism, held power fairly steadily during the post–World War II period in various countries. I assert these continuities without claiming that the many varieties of fascist rule were all alike; obviously fascism has taken many forms. I merely wish to underline the resilience of the phenomenon.

43. See Smith 1994 for an extensive treatment of homophobia in the British new right.

44. For some detailed analyses of the sociopolitical bases of the contemporary extreme right, see Kitschelt 1997 and Betz 1994. Compare Brustein 1998; Fritzsche 1998 on the inter-war period.

45. Such a formulation avoids characterizing neo-fascism as a "revolutionary" movement. It can certainly be claimed that the fascisms of the 1920s and 1930s had a revolutionary character:

> Fascism's politically revolutionary effect—the imposition of an authoritarian regime as an illiberal solution to crises—reveals its socially conservative and counter-revolutionary essence. For this reason we can describe fascism as the culmination of the *conservative revolutionary* tradition. (Neocleous 1997, 57; emphasis original)

But the postwar neo-fascist movements and parties have thus far not shown much revolutionary potential. For analyses of the political limitations of the extreme right in contemporary Europe, see Kitschelt 1997; Betz 1994.

46. This claim draws on Anderson's (1991) conception of the nation as an "imagined community." For a social-psychological account of some of the same phenomena, see Billig 1995.

47. See Ryan 1984; Bower 1984; Simpson 1988; Anderson and Anderson 1986.

48. Obviously I cannot enter this territory in the present work. It suffices to note that early French and Italian fascists were not uniformly anti-semitic or racist. Italian racial laws were not promulgated until 1938, although anti-black racism was consolidated earlier as a

feature of Mussolini's African imperialism. See Sternhell 1994, 4–5; Mason 1981. For a contrary view that necessarily focuses on Nazism, see Mosse 1985.

49. For some useful examples of the enormous literature on this question, however, see Burleigh and Wippermann 1991; Goldhagen 1996; Browning 1991.

50. There was nothing new about this either; Hitler did the same thing. For example, he "soft-pedaled or left altogether unmentioned his anti-semitism when speaking to men of big business, having recognized its unpopularity in those circles" (Henry Ashby Turner, *German Big Business and the Rise of Hitler*, cited in Neocleous 1997, 103–104).

51. Perhaps consciously echoing Mussolini, perhaps not, Le Pen famously put matters this way: "I love my daughters more than my nieces, my nieces more than my cousins, my cousins more than my neighbors" (Gourevitch 1997, 84).

In Mussolini's version, the formulation is as follows: "Before I love the French, the English, the Hottentots, I love Italians. That is to say I love those of my own race, those that speak my language, that share my customs, that share with me the same history" (Gregor 1969, 246–247; see also Neocleous 1997, 35–36).

52. Le Pen and the National Front opposed French involvement in the Gulf War as French subservience to U.S. and Israeli interests. With varying degrees of energy, European neo-fascists also opposed the 1990s NATO military commitments in respect to Bosnia and Kosovo, especially the bombing of Serbia.

53. Immanuel Wallerstein anticipated some of these anxieties in an early article (Wallerstein 1979b).

54. On Mosley's Euronationalism, see Skidelsky 1975. On the range of adherents to this position, see Harris 1994, 28–31.

55. Before the infamous Pasqua laws were introduced, the Socialist Party under Mitterand also played the game of supporting Le Pen. It loosened requirements for gaining assembly seats, on the presumption that the *Front Nationale* would siphon support away from the mainstream right, and flirted with immigration restriction as well (Fysh and Wolfreys 1998, 170–203).

56. *Groupement de Recherche et d'Etudes pour la Civilisation Européene*, led by Alain de Benoist; the *Club de l'Horloge*, led by Yvan Blot, grew out of the GRECE and was originally in the orbit of the mainstream right. Linked to Charles Pasqua, it broke with the Gaullist RPR in 1989 and allied with the *Front Nationale*. See Fysh and Wolfreys 1998, 103–104.

57. Here I consider the new racism in its Western European manifestations only. On "racial projects," see Omi and Winant 1994; Winant 1994a.

58. This is not to suggest that racist discourse must be explicit in order to qualify as racist, or that discrimination is the sole means in which racism can operate as social policy. Indeed if the new racism achieved anything, it demonstrated precisely how flexible and fungible racism can be. See Winant 1998.

59. Although space does not permit sufficient treatment here, the importance of Powell in shifting the terms of British racial discourse—and thus in exemplary fashion, Western European racial discourse—cannot be overstated. Powell occupied a transitional position between the old and the new racism. While systematically constructing a populist narrative of racial fear, replete with subconscious and subtextual elements (the familiar themes of black crime, sexual predation, dirt, etc.), Powell was continually working motifs of national and cultural difference into his discourse as well. In his claims to be representing black constituents as well as whites, to be "defending" British values from alien "onslaughts," he carved out the terrain that Thatcher would exploit a few years later. His racially based challenge to the Tory leadership, for which he was dismissed from the shadow cabinet in 1968, also demonstrated the political potential of racial appeals in British politics: his censure by Heath prompted large demonstrations in his support, and showed how vulnerable Labour constituencies were to racist appeals. From the extensive literature, see Hall et al. 1978; Lawrence 1982; Smith 1994; Hiro 1991; Sivanandan 1982.

60. Many other examples could be cited. By the way, who are the "minorities" and who the "people" (the ones who "get frightened," etc.)? White minorities (religious ones, for example)

were presumably not who Thatcher had in mind. Nor, it appears, did the "minorities" to whom she was referring qualify as "people" who presumably might also "get frightened."

61. An important debate on the British left in this period concerned the parameters of "blackness." Was it primarily African and Afro-Caribbean in character, or was it more comprehensive, including South Asians, for example? This set of issues is quite multidimensional in respect to racial theory, encompassing questions of white supremacism and the nature of whiteness, ethnic versus racial concepts of social identity, and the political dynamics of racial formation, to name only some main themes. In retrospect these uncertainties and disagreements can be seen as reflections of the defensive character of anti-racism in the post–World War II context of the break, and in the face of the new racism on the right. See Sivanandan 1982.

62. For a general assessment, see Jeffers 1993. In the 1983 elections Thatcher and Co. apparently felt that they had reaped all the gains they could expect from their earlier new racist maneuvers. They now sought to recoup their moderate racial image by attacking Labour on racial grounds. A Conservative poster from that campaign showed a black man in a business suit with the slogan, "Labour says he's black. Tories say he's British" (reproduced in Gilroy 1991, 58). See Husbands 1988.

63. This is of course a mere metaphor. The racial right was as well-established on the Continent as in the United Kingdom, and as I have argued above, could drawn on a wide range of prefigurations, both organizational and ideational. The uniqueness of the British example for the rest of Western Europe was the successful "mainstream" political articulation of racist themes pioneered by the Conservatives.

64. This is not to suggest that confusions and contradictions have been overcome. Take religious issues, for example. Le Pen, a non-practicing Catholic, has had to accommodate the fundamentalist Catholic current very prevalent on the French right. The latter group appears overly moderate in the eyes of the followers of the excommunicated Cardinal Marcel Lèfebvre, opponent of Vatican II, who also form a tendency in the *Front Nationale*. Then there is paganism (!): in the 1990s the leader of the GRECE, Alain de Benoist, was advocating a *volkisch* cult of the Nordic gods, sometimes referred to as Indo-Europeanism—very much in the *blut und boden* style of Nazism but deeply at odds with Catholicism, orthodox or heretical. See Fysh and Wolfreys 1997, 99, 120–122.

65. Le Pen was a deputy in the European Parliament in Strasbourg and chaired its Commission of the Right. He sought with considerable success to establish the FN as the leading right-wing party, and to cement alliances with other compatible forces. Ideologically in numerous ways the FN was Eurocentric. It did not oppose the assimilation of Portuguese migrants, for example, in the same way it did Maghrebines. But it refused to endorse the Maastricht agreements, which it denounced as subordinating France (and Europe) to unfair global competition.

66. The GRECE intellectuals worked much of this position out in the 1970s: "All races are superior. All have their proper genius. . . . One may therefore say that each race is superior to the others in carrying out the achievements that belong to it" (Alain de Benoist, cited in Taguieff 2001 [1988], 423). Taguieff comments that "This is a reformulation of racism in a nominalist (that is, antiuniversalist) problematic." Note too the echoes of Herder.

67. Incidentally, this reasoning rearticulates the humanistic and progressive cultural anthropology of the Boasian tradition, notably (for the GRECE group are French, after all) of the work of Claude Levi-Strauss. See Policar 1990; Taguieff 2001 [1988], 297–300.

68. "What do I have to do to not be racist?" Le Pen asked Philip Gourevitch. "Marry a black woman . . . ? With AIDS, if possible?" (Gourevitch 1997, 114).

69. Here I endorse the "political process" approach that Feldblum employs to account for recent French racial politics: "Stripped down, the convergence on integration exposed the already increasing commonalities in rhetorical logic and themes between Right and Left, even if their intentions were dissimilar and political immigration agendas divergent" (Feldblum 1999, 116; see also McAdam 1982; McAdam et al., 1996).

70. Even the *grandes philosophes* of the French academic left are torn by these issues: for example, Pierre Chaunu and Alain Touraine both served on a *Commission de Sages* on nationality issues in 1987, leading Chaunu to worry that "France was losing itself through exten-

sion" (Feldblum 1999, 175) and Touraine to argue that "The left has abandoned the idea of a multicultural France, which was dangerous" (ibid., 123). Compare Bourdieu's criticism of the mainstream parties (Bourdieu 1998, 15–18).

71. The work of Stuart Hall (1988; Hall and Jacques 1990; Hall et al. 1978) has been crucial in theorizing this concept. See also Betz 1994; Laclau 1977a; Balibar 1991.

72. Haider has also made (unconvincing) gestures at distancing himself from the stigma of Nazism, which he condemned in 1993 as "the most atrocious criminal regime" (Betz 1994, 124). In 1999 parliamentary elections the FPÖ took second place. The controversial entry of the party into the Austrian government occurred after this chapter had already been prepared; I can devote no more than this note to that development.

73. This admittedly cursory sketch draws heavily on Kitschelt, who argues that "the successful New Right does not combine authoritarianism, nationalism, and corporatist economic visions, but authoritarianism, ethnic particularism, and market liberalism. . . . Both in intellectual appeal as well as in electoral coalition, the successful contemporary extreme Right is different from the historical extreme Right, as represented by German national socialism or Italian fascism" (Kitschelt 1997, 277).

74. "The problem is that of preserving the ideological unity of the entire social bloc *which that ideology serves to cement and unify*" (Gramsci 1971, 328; my emphasis).

75. None of these factors was unmixed or without contradictions: perceptions that immigration heightened competition in labor markets, that it undermined traditional forms of authority, and that it eroded cultural cohesion, were of course also present. These were to become touchstones for the new racism.

76. As I have argued above, the absence of an *internal* racial history in Europe, the relegation of racial issues to *external* features of the national life—especially colonialism and imperialism—were largely responsible for the difficulties encountered in "processing" racialized identities and racism. Both as a "normal" dimension of every social life, and as a political variable, race retained a certain unfamiliarity. There were, of course, major exceptions to this pattern: the experience of Jews culminating in the Holocaust, above all. And as I have already stressed, there never was a moment when people "of color" were not present in Europe. Arguably the roots of differentialist racism are to be found here, in the artificial racial uniformity that formed a "spectral" (Zizek) racial ideology in Europe.

77. See Leisink and Coenen 1993. Günter Wallraff's undercover reporting, which involved posing as a Turk and working under extremely dangerous and degrading circumstances, effectively demonstrated the extent of employment discrimination in Germany. Wallraff also reveals the depth of anti-Muslim and anti-Turkish bigotry. Anne Tristan's undercover reporting focused more on political dynamics; she became a secretary in the Marseilles offices of the *Front Nationale*. From this experience she was able to document the role of racism in the inner workings of the Party. These are two heroic journalists.

78. Among the many examples that may be cited here are the battles between the Greater London Council (GLC) and Margaret Thatcher, which led in part to her abolition of the GLC (Gilroy 1991, 136–148); struggles over welfare policies (Leisink 1997; Liebfried and Pierson 1995; Banton 1985); and the European Union's developing coordination of citizenship and migration policies. See the EU website on citizenship, http://europa.eu.int/citizens/, for a good introduction to this information.

79. See Hall 1996a; Modood and Werbner 1997; Sivanandan 1982; Rath 1993.

80. Notably female genital mutilation, purdah, arranged marriage, and so on. See Toubia 1995; Dorkenoo and Elworthy 1992; Mayer 1999.

81. For example, the 1989 *hijab/foulard* ("headscarf") affair in France, which pitted orthodox Islamic strictures against women exposing their hair against the state-based laicism that descended from the Revolution. See Feldblum 1997, 129–145; Fysh and Wolfreys 1998, 174–178. On "Islamophobia" in general, see Halliday 1999.

82. After attacks on Turkish hostels in 1993 hundreds of thousands of Germans participated in night marches and vigils against racism, the so-called *lichterketten* ("lighted candle") marches. At least in the former West Germany there has been a relatively strong inoculation against resurgent fascism in the political system: hence the weakness of the German *Repub-*

likaner stands in striking contrast to the strength of the *Front Nationale* in France. See Betz 1994; Kitschelt 1997; Wilpert 1993. In the newly incorporated East this claim would not apply.

83. "Let us examine anti-Semitism. It is not enough to say that we must liberate ourselves of so-called 'anti-Semitic prejudices' and learn to see Jews as they really are—in this way we will certainly remain victims of these so-called prejudices. We must confront ourselves with how the ideological figure of the 'Jew' is invested with our unconscious desire, with how we have constructed this figure to escape a certain deadlock of our desire.

"Let us suppose for example that an objective look would confirm—why not?—that Jews really do financially exploit the rest of population, that they do sometimes seduce our young daughters, that some of them do not wash regularly. Is it not clear that this has nothing to do with the real roots of our anti-Semitism . . . ?

"Let us ask ourselves a simple question: In the Germany of the late 1930s, what would be the result of such a non-ideological, objective approach? Probably something like: 'The Nazis are condemning the Jews too hastily, without proper argument, so let us take a cool, sober look and see if they are really guilty or not; let us see if there is some truth in the accusations against them.' Is it really necessary to add that such an approach would merely confirm our so-called 'unconscious prejudices' with additional rationalizations? The proper answer to anti-Semitism is therefore not 'Jews are not really like that' but 'the anti-Semitic idea of Jew has nothing to do with Jews; the ideological figure of a Jew is a way to stitch up the inconsistency of our own ideological system'" (Zizek 1994, 326; see also Smith 1994, 38).

84. The response to the Iranian *fatwa* against Salman Rushdie, in the wake of the latter's publication of *The Satanic Verses*, is the best-known example of this conservative and anti-democratic trend. In the interests of full disclosure, I must note that I dedicated an earlier book to Rushdie at the height of his ordeal.

85. The term *Beur* is itself a reworking of the French slang term for Arab. Its orgin is the word *Arabe* said backwards: "Ebara," which then transforms into "*eBeur*" and "*Beur.*" The process will be familiar to North American readers:

> [*Beur*] . . . indicates something slightly different from our parents' identity but at the same time the affimation of an Arab origin. More exactly, it expresses the emergence of a new aspect of French identity: the existence of *French* Arabs. Up until then, France had known only Arabs *in France.* (Said Bouamama, cited in Fysh and Wolfreys 1998, 157; emphasis original).

86. Because in reality the "boundaries" upon which the theoretical distinctions proposed here are not all that firm and recognizable. Individual and group identities, cultural constructs, and political orientations, inter alia, are all subject to contestation and uncertainty. See Winant and Omi 1994; Winant 1994a. On ethnocultural "boundaries," see Barth 1969.

87. White identities are racial identities. As a growing body of analytical work suggests, the tendency to "normalize" whiteness—to consider whites as non-racialized—was a central feature of colonialism, of white supremacy, of modernity. Thus the racialization of whiteness is a crucial recent development in the global racial formation process. In its own way it represents a break with the largely unquestioned white supremacy of the past; thus it is linked to the post–World War II break that is the subject of this book. Recognizing this, though, merely opens the way to conflict and contestation over the meaning of whiteness. Thus the "right to be different" espoused by the *Front Nationale* may be seen as a racial formation project: a new racist or differentialist effort to defend whiteness by linking it to French nationality and culture. Anti-racist movements too must develop a new view of whiteness which avoids "normalizing" it. Indeed, "everyday people" must also revise their view of whiteness. European work on this topic is still in its early stages. See Phoenix 1998; C. Hall 1992, Ware 1992. In the United States, "whiteness studies" are developing apace. See Roediger 1991; Frankenberg 1997; Winant 1997a; Fine et al. 1997.

88. This is obviously a complicated issue that cannot be drawn out fully in this space. For similar arguments in the U.S. context, see Crenshaw et al. 1995; Brown 1995. In the European context, see Gilroy 1999.

89. As I have noted this characterization is necessarily ideal-typical. Groups and parties of the FPÖ (Austria) type, for instance, whose neo-fascist provenance is not in doubt, curry respectability by adherence to orthodox free marketism. Meanwhile, traditional conservatives, like the post-Thatcher Tories, continue to balk at the Euro and the free market, preferring their own macro-economic apparatus: the City of London.

90. The Gramscian glue once again. See note 74, above.

91. Yet the new racism still creates confusion among progressive anti-racist thinkers. An unfortunate example here is the admirable Pierre-André Taguieff, on whose work *La Force du Préjuge* I have drawn quite extensively in this chapter, and whose ability to theorize the new racism in its differentialist variant goes a long way toward explaining its effectivity on the French right (and beyond). In more recent work (1995), he has taken the anti-racist movement to task for not reasserting the capacity of French society to assimilate and integrate the racialized "others," for asserting from the left, in other words, the same "right to be different" that he criticizes the *Front Nationale* for claiming. This is an understandable position, but problematic (in my view) because it refuses to challenge a whole series of obsolescing verities: the French national *mythos*, the class reductionism of the left, the theme of racial identity as illusory. Taguieff should be commended for his firm opposition to the FN, but fraternally criticized for expecting minorities to convince French "nativists" (of both right and left) that they really can be French, that they would indeed even *want* to assimilate so wholly into French society. Is the national culture so complete, so fully realized, that its adaptation to the new (and permanent) racial heterogeneity of French society is inconceivable? Cannot Taguieff find ways of defending racial pluralism in France? Can he not support the *Beur* (and African, and Caribbean, and Asian, etc.) communities and organizations more on their own terms? Can he not help the *Parti Socialiste* and the solidarity movements find the courage to assert the "*droit a la différence*" from the left (Vishniac 1991)?

Yet, having said this, I fear that I presume too much. I do not wish to single out Taguieff, whom I greatly admire. Other important thinkers on the French left, for example, Alain Touraine, have taken very similar positions. National political culture is extremely difficult to challenge.

92. Scholars and artists like Pierre Bourdieu, Paul Gilroy, Günter Grass, Nadine Gordimer, Stuart Hall, Toni Morrison, Hélène Cixous, and Cornel West come to mind here. This is a distinguished list, to be sure, but necessarily a somewhat arbitrary one.

CHAPTER ELEVEN. MILLENNIUM ARRIVES?

1. For discussion of Foucault's approach to race, see Stoler 1995.

2. Edward Said has effectively noted the working of this process in literary forms. See his 1993 discussion of the taken-for-grantedness of Caribbean plantation slavery in Austen's *Mansfield Park*. Many other examples could be cited, of course.

3. The doctrine of *limpieza de sangre*, for example, definitively established the Inquisition's anti-semitism as racial rather than ethnic: by designating Jewish identity as essential and corporeal, impervious to religious conversion, the Church located Jewishness not as a religious doctrine or cultural orientation, but as an intrinsic and ineffable difference.

4. Consider the famous *Amistad* events, for example. Here a group of enslaved Africans revolting against an illegal (by British and U.S. law) Spanish slaver and trying to repatriate themselves to West Africa were impounded and imprisoned in Connecticut, a "free state." These Africans were processed under a complex and competing set of laws and rules: maritime, fugitive slave, piracy, abolitionist, North American state and federal, Spanish, and so on. Yet the one fact that was never in doubt was the race of the persons involved. The *Amistad* case illustrates—among many other things—the unifying effects that use of racial categories achieved at the international level, despite the fact that systems of racial classification always vary from country to country.

As an aside, I do not wish to imply that racial classifications *in fact* efface ethnic, national, class, or political distinctions. In many cases racial solidarity has not functioned smoothly, either for the uses of subjugation or for those of resistance; intra-racial conflict is very common throughout the modern era. I merely argue that racial categorization corresponded crudely to power dynamics in early modern colonial and slavery-based societies. This correspondence "had legs"; it accreted and ramified throughout the world system, complete with its ability to organize both racial oppression and racial resistance.

5. For all the value of these debates, they are also marked by a severe economic reductionism. Among the many voices I have cited, see particularly Williams 1994 [1944]; Fogel 1989; Solow and Engerman 1987; and Drescher 1999.

6. Du Bois—by then an octogenarian—was again involved in these initiatives. See Du Bois, Konvitz, Logan, and Dickerson 1947.

7. This was not entirely unprecedented, but tended to greater truth value than had obtained during World War I, notwithstanding the presence of the Stalinist regime among the ranks of the "freedom fighters," the racist character of much of the Pacific war, and obviously, the colonialist commitments of the Allies.

8. This is not to deny that discrimination persists in the internal labor markets of manufacturing firms and in trade unions as well. Nor is it to assert that black and white workers receive the same treatment from the police, in the housing market, at their children's schools, and so on.

9. On the international dynamics of the automobile industry, see Maynard 1998. On the ABC and CUT, see French 1992.

10. In the German elections that Habermas was analyzing, a major theme voiced by the Christian Democrats of Helmut Kohl was so-called *ausländerkriminalität*: the charge that it was (largely racialized) immigrants and non-German denizens who were responsible for crime.

11. The tendency to view indices of well-being as measures of class—as quantifiable Weberian life chances—itself must be looked at critically. In an important intervention in this area, Amartya Sen has argued that the dominant optic in the field of ("welfare" and "development") economics systematically neglects the qualitative dimensions of human well-being, which he links to the attainment of *freedom* and the achievement of *capability*. See Sen 2000a.

12. Indeed, Bahia is not only the birthplace of Caetano Veloso (whose fierce critique of global racism serves as this book's epigraph), but the home of Olodum, a musical/political organization that has dedicated itself to black political education on a national scale. See their website at http://www.e-net.com.br/olodum/.

13. Certainly prejudice and discrimination are still very much present, even if they are no longer overtly advocated. In particular spheres—for example, among many police forces and prison guards (see Parenti 1999), in many corporate boardrooms, in certain "smoke-filled" political campaign headquarters—explicitly racist discourse is still the norm.

14. For a more detailed discussion focused on the United States, see Winant 1998. This approach has much in common with the theoretical current known as *critical race theory*. A valuable collection of writings from that general perspective is Crenshaw et al. 1995.

15. I am sorry to offer such a mouthful as a definition, but it seems to be unavoidable.

16. It is also important to distinguish racial awareness from racial essentialism. Attribution of merits or faults, allocation of values or resources, and/or representations of individuals or groups on the basis of racial categories should not be considered racist in and of themselves. Such projects may in fact be quite benign. Of course, any of these projects may be considered racist, but only if they meet the criteria I have just outlined: in other words, a combination of essentialization and subordination must be present.

17. The foremost theorist of the rearticulations of racial difference is Pierre-André Taguieff 2000 [1988].

18. See Singh 1999; *Race and Class* 1998–99. Organizations that can provide information on these topics are Global Exchange (website: www.globalexchange.org); Focus on the Global South (website: www.focusweb.org); and Jubilee 2000 (website: www.j2000usa.org).

19. To attempt to answer these questions even in part is to plunge into the theoretical and practical endeavors of racial formation. For my own efforts in this area, see Omi and Winant 1994.

20. In non-U.S. settings, the "new social movement" phenomenon has not always been so clearly recognized as racially structured. This is particularly notable in Europe, where its study was prompted by the vicissitudes of the new left, the resurgence of feminism, the rise of green politics, and the upsurge of terrorism in the 1970s (Melucci 1989). But in the Third World the rethinking of political theory and political sociology in terms of issues of subjectivity and of "identity" often took on a racial dimension. Consider the legacy of Fanon, for example.

21. For the past few decades all three of these themes have been developed in a body of theoretical work that goes under the general heading of *racial formation theory*. As one of the founders of this approach, I must admit to the lack of consensus, as well as the overall incompleteness, of this theoretical current. Still, racial formation theory at least begins to provide the theoretical tools needed to make sense of the new world racial order described here. Indeed, this book is no more than an attempt to use such tools in a comparative historical framework.

To summarize the racial formation approach: (1) it views the meaning of race and the content of racial identities as unstable and politically contested; (2) it understands racial formation as the intersection/conflict of racial "projects" that combine representational/discursive elements with structural/institutional ones; (3) it sees these intersections as iterative sequences of interpretations ("articulations") of the meaning of race that are open to many types of agency, from the individual to the organizational, from the local to the global (Omi and Winant 1994).

22. Obviously I cannot engage this issue profoundly here. I simply note that the question of new forms of socialism remains theoretically open, and that emerging global conflicts over the inequalities in the global economic system (see above) retain links with the socialist tradition.

23. For example, the U.S. civil rights movement, anti-apartheid struggles, *SOS-Racisme* in France, the *Movimento Negro Unificado* in Brazil.

Bibliography

Abu-Lughod, Janet L. *Before European Hegemony: The World System A.D. 1250–1350.* New York: Oxford University Press, 1989.

Adam, Heribert, and Kogila Moodley. *The Opening of the Apartheid Mind: Options for the New South Africa.* Berkeley: University of California Press, 1993.

Adam, Heribert. "Anti-Semitism and Anti-Black Racism: Nazi Germany and Apartheid South Africa." Paper presented at the Kaplan Center of the University of Capetown, March 1995.

Adam, Heribert, Kogila Moodley, and Frederik van Zyl Slabbert. *Comrades in Business: Post-Liberation Politics in South Africa.* Cape Town: Tafelberg, 1998.

Adam, Heribert. "Empowerment . . . or Self-Enrichment?" *Electronic Mail and Guardian.* Johannesburg, South Africa. October 31, 1997.

Addams, Jane. *Twenty Years at Hull-House.* New York: Macmillan, 1938.

Adler, Glenn, and Edward Webster. "Challenging Transition Theory: The Labor Movement, Radical Reform and Transition to Democracy in South Africa." *Politics and Society* 23, no. 1 (March 1995).

Adorno, Rolena. "The Discursive Encounter of Spain and America: The Authority of Eye-witness Testimony in the Writing of History." *The William and Mary Quarterly* (April 1992).

African National Congress. *The Freedom Charter.* Adopted at the Congress of the People, Klip-town, June 26, 1955. New York: United Nations Centre Against Apartheid, 1979.

Alexander, Jeffrey, et al., eds. *The Micro-Macro Link.* Berkeley: University of California Press, 1987.

Allen, James, Hilton Als, John Lewis, and Leon F. Litwack, eds. *Without Sanctuary: Lynching Photography in America.* Santa Fe: Twin Palms, 2000.

Allen, Paula Gunn. *The Sacred Hoop: Recovering the Feminine in American Indian Traditions.* Boston: Beacon, 1986.

Allen, Robert. *Reluctant Reformers: Racism and Social Reform Movements in the United States.* Washington, DC: Howard University Press, 1974.

Allen, Theodore. *The Invention of the White Race.* New York: Verso, 1994.

Almaguer, Tomás. *Racial Faultlines: The Historical Origins of White Supremacy in California.* Berkeley: University of California Press, 1994.

Althusser, Louis. "Contradiction and Overdetermination." In *For Marx.* Translated by Ben Brewster. New York: Pantheon, 1969.

Althusser, Louis. "Ideology and Ideological State Apparatuses (Notes towards an Investigation)." In *Lenin and Philosophy and Other Essays.* Translated by Ben Brewster. New York: Monthly Review Press, 1971.

Altman, Lawrence K. "U.N. Warning AIDS Imperils Africa's Youth." *The New York Times,* June 28, 2000.

Alves Filho, Ivan. *Memorial dos Palmares: O Movimento Precursor da Libertação Negro no Brasil.* Rio de Janeiro: Xenon, 1988.

Ambrose, Stephen E. *Citizen Soldiers: The US Army from the Normandy Beaches to the Bulge to the Surrender of Germany.* New York: Simon and Schuster, 1997.

Anderson, Benedict. *Imagined Communities: Reflections on the Origin and Spread of Nationalism.* 2nd ed. New York: Verso, 1991.

Anderson, Elijah. "Introduction." In W. E. B. Du Bois. *The Philadelphia Negro: A Social Study.* Centennial Edition. Philadelphia: University of Pennsylvania Press, 1996.

Anderson, Margo, and Stephen Fienberg. *Who Counts?: The Politics of Census-Taking in Contemporary America.* New York: Russell Sage Foundation, 1999.

Anderson, Scott, and Jon Lee Anderson. *Inside the League: The Shocking Expose of How Terrorists, Nazis, and Latin American Death Squads Have Infiltrated the World Anti-Communist League.* New York: Dodd, Mead, 1986.

Andrews, George Reid. "Racial Inequality in Brazil and the United States: A Statistical Comparison." *Journal of Social History* 26 (1992).

Andrews, George Reid. "Brazilian Racial Democracy, 1900–1990: An American Counterpoint." *Journal of Contemporary History* 31, no. 3 (July 1996).

Andrews, George Reid. *Blacks and Whites in São Paulo, Brazil, 1888–1988.* Madison: University of Wisconsin Press, 1991.

Andrews, George Reid. *The Afro-Argentines of Buenos Aires, 1800–1900.* Madison: University of Wisconsin Press, 1980.

Ansell, Amy Elizabeth. *New Right, New Racism: Race and Reaction in the United States and Britain.* New York: New York University Press, 1997.

Anstey, Roger. *The Atlantic Slave Trade and British Abolition, 1760–1810.* Atlantic Highlands, NJ: Humanities Press, 1975.

Anthias, Floya, and Nira Yuval-Davis. *Racialised Boundaries: "Race," Gender, Colour, Class and the Anti-Racist Struggle.* London: Routledge, 1992.

Anthony, David. "Max Yergan and South Africa: A Transatlantic Interaction." In Sidney J. Lemelle and Robin D. G. Kelley, eds. *Imagining Home: Class, Culture, and Nationalism in the African Diaspora.* London; New York: Verso, 1994.

Appiah, Kwame Anthony. *In My Father's House: Africa in the Philosophy of Culture.* New York: Oxford University Press, 1992.

Appiah, Anthony Kwame. Review of John Reader, *Africa: Biography of a Continent.* In *The New York Review of Books.* December 17, 1998.

Aptheker, Herbert, ed. *Afro-American History: The Modern Era.* New York: International Publishers, 1971.

Aptheker, Herbert. *American Negro Slave Revolts.* 5th ed. New York: International Publishers, 1983.

Archdiocese of São Paulo. *Torture in Brazil: A Report [Brasil, Nunca Mais].* Translated by Jaime Wright. Edited by Joan Dassin. New York : Vintage, 1986.

Arendt, Hannah. *Antisemitism.* New York: Harcourt, Brace & World, 1968.

Arendt, Hannah. *The Origins of Totalitarianism.* New York: Harcourt Brace Jovanovich, 1973.

Aristotle. *Politics.* Translated by Harris Rackham. Cambridge, MA: Harvard University Press, 1959.

Arnold, Millard, ed. *Steve Biko: Black Consciousness in South Africa.* New York: Random House, 1978.

Arrighi, Giovanni. "Labour Supplies in Historical Perspective: A Study of the Proletarianization of the African Peasantry in Rhodesia." In idem and John Saul. *Essays on the Political Economy of Africa.* New York: Monthly Review Press, 1973.

Ashmore, Harry S. *Civil Rights and Wrongs: A Memoir of Race and Politics, 1944–1994.* New York: Pantheon, 1994.

Asmal, Kader, Louise Asmal, and Ronald Suresh Roberts. *Reconciliation Through Truth: A Reckoning of Apartheid's Criminal Governance.* 2nd ed. New York: St. Martin's, 1997.

Austen, Ralph A. "The 19th Century Islamic Slave Trade from East Africa (Swahili and Red Sea Coasts): A Tentative Census." In William Gervase Clarence-Smith, ed. *The Economics of the Indian Ocean Slave Trade in the Nineteenth Century.* Totowa, NJ: Frank Cass, 1989.

Austen, Ralph A. "The Mediterranean Islamic Slave Trade out of Africa: A Tentative Census." *Slavery and Abolition* 13, no. 1 (1992).

Axford, Barrie. *The Global System: Economics, Politics, Culture.* New York: St. Martin's, 1995.

Azevedo, Celia Maria Marinho de. *Onda Negra, Medo Branco: O Negro no Imaginário das Elites, Século XIX.* São Paulo: Paz e Terra, 1987.

Azevedo, Thales de. *As Elites de Côr: Um Estudo de Ascensão Social.* São Paulo: Nacional, 1955.

Azevedo, Thales de. *Cultura e Situação Racial no Brasil.* Rio de Janeiro: Civilização Brasileira, 1966.

Azevedo, Thales de. *Democracia Racial: Ideologia e Realidade.* Petrópolis: Vozes, 1975.

Baber, Zaheer. "Religion, 'Race' and Riots: The 'Racialization' of Communal Identity and Conflict in India." Paper presented at the Annual Meeting of the American Sociological Association. Chicago, August 1999.

Bairros, Luiza. "Mulher Negra: O Reforço da Subordinação." In Peggy A. Lovell, ed. *Desigualdade Racial no Brasil Contemporaneo.* Belo Horizonte: CEDEPLAR/UFMG, 1991.

Bakewell, Peter. *Silver Mining and Society in Colonial Mexico: Zacatecas, 1546–1700.* Cambridge, UK: Cambridge University Press, 1971.

Bakewell, Peter. *Miners of the Red Mountain: Indian Labor in Potosí, 1545–1650.* Albuquerque: University of New Mexico Press, 1984.

Bales, Kevin. *Disposable People: New Slavery in the Global Economy.* Berkeley: University of California Press, 1999.

Balibar, Etienne. "Is There a Neo-Racism?" In Etienne Balibar and Immanuel Wallerstein. *Race, Nation, Class: Ambiguous Identities.* New York: Verso, 1991.

Balibar, Etienne, and Immanuel Wallerstein. *Race, Nation, Class: Ambiguous Identities.* New York: Verso, 1991.

Ballard, Allen B. *One More Day's Journey: The Making of Black Philadelphia.* Philadelphia: Institute for the Study of Human Issues, 1987.

Banks, Russell. *Cloudsplitter.* New York: HarperCollins, 1998.

Banton, Michael, *The Idea of Race.* London: Tavistock, 1977.

Banton, Michael. "Racism Today: A Perspective from International Politics." *Ethnic and Racial Studies* 22, no. 3 (May 1999).

Banton, Michael. *Promoting Racial Harmony.* New York: Cambridge University Press, 1985.

Barber, Benjamin R. *Jihad vs. McWorld.* New York: Times, 1995.

Barkan, Elazar. *The Retreat of Scientific Racism: Changing Concepts of Race in Britain and the United States Between the World Wars.* Cambridge; New York: Cambridge University Press, 1992.

Barker, Martin. *The New Racism: Conservatives and the Ideology of the Tribe.* London: Junction, 1981.

Barnes, Sandra T., ed. *Africa's Ogun: Old World and New.* Bloomington: Indiana University Press, 1997.

Baron, Harold. "The Demand for Black Labor: Historical Notes on the Political Economy of Racism." *Radical America* 5, no. 2 (1971).

Baronov, David Mayer. *The Process of Working-Class Formation: The Abolition of Slavery in 19th-century Brazil in World-Historical Perspective.* Ph.D. dissertation, State University of New York at Binghamton, 1994.

Barrera, Mario. *Race and Class in the Southwest: A Theory of Racial Inequality.* Notre Dame: University of Notre Dame Press, 1979.

Barth, Frederik, ed. *Ethnic Groups and Boundaries: The Social Organization of Culture Difference.* Boston: Little, Brown, 1969.

Basch, Linda, Nina Glick Schiller, and Cristina Szanton Blanc. *Nations Unbound: Transnational Projects, Postcolonial Predicaments, and Deterritorialized Nation-States.* Langhorne, PA: Gordon and Breach, 1994.

Bastide, Roger. *The African Religions of Brazil: Toward a Sociology of the Interpenetration of Civilizations.* Translated by Helen Sebba. Baltimore: Johns Hopkins University Press, 1978 [1960].

Bastide, Roger. "A Imprensa Negra em São Paulo." In idem. *Estudos Afro-Brasileiros.* São Paulo: Perspectiva, 1973.

Bastide, Roger. "The Development of Race Relations in Brazil." In Guy Hunter, ed. *Industrialization and Race Relations: A Symposium.* New York: Oxford University Press, 1965.

Bastide, Roger, and Florestan Fernandes. *Brancos e Negros em São Paulo.* 3rd ed. São Paulo: Nacional, 1971.

Bauman, Zygmunt. *Modernity and the Holocaust.* Ithaca: Cornell University Press, 1989.

Bay, Edna G. *Wives of the Leopard: Gender, Politics, and Culture in the Kingdom of Dahomey.* Charlottesville: University of Virginia Press, 1998.

Bederman, Gail. *Manliness and Civilization: A Cultural History of Gender and Race in the United States, 1880–1917.* Chicago: University of Chicago Press, 1995.

Beiguelman, Paula. *A Crise do Escravismo e a Grande Imigração.* 2nd ed. São Paulo: Brasiliense, 1981.

Bell, Derrick. "Remembraces of Racism Past: Getting Beyond the Civil Rights Debate." In Herbert Hill and James E. Jones Jr., eds. *Race in America: The Struggle for Equality.* Madison: University of Wisconsin Press, 1993.

Bendix, Reinhard. *Nation-building and Citizenship: Studies of Our Changing Social Order.* 2nd ed. Berkeley: University of California Press, 1977.

Benjamin, Walter. *Illuminations.* Translated by Harry Zohn. New York: Schocken, 1973.

Berg, Barbara J. *The Remembered Gate: Origins of American Feminism: The Woman and the City, 1800–1860.* New York: Oxford University Press, 1978.

Berlin, Ira, Thavolia Glymph, Steven F. Miller, Joseph P. Reidy, Leslie S. Rowland, and Julie Saville, eds. *The Wartime Genesis of Free Labor: The Lower South.* New York: Cambridge University Press, 1990.

Berlin, Ira. *Many Thousands Gone: The First Two Centuries of Slavery in North America.* Cambridge, MA: Harvard University Press, 1998.

Berlin, Isaiah. *The Crooked Timber of Humanity: Chapters in the History of Ideas.* Edited by Henry Hardy. Princeton: Princeton University Press, 1990.

Betz, Hans-Georg. *Radical Right-Wing Populism in Western Europe.* New York: St. Martin's, 1994.

Beverley, John. *Subalternity and Representation: Arguments in Cultural Theory.* Durham: Duke University Press, 1999.

Bhabha, Homi K. *The Location of Culture.* New York: Routledge, 1994.

Biddiss, M. D. *Father of Racist Ideology: The Social and Political Thought of Count Gobineau.* London: Weidenfeld and Nicholson, 1970.

Billig, Michael. "Socio-Psychological Aspects of Nationalism: Imagining Ingroups, Others, and the World of Nations." In Keebet von Benda-Beckman and Maykel Verkuyten, eds. *Nationalism, Ethnicity, and Cultural Identity in Europe.* Utrecht: ERCOMER, 1995.

Bittker, Boris I. *The Case for Black Reparations.* New York: Random House, 1973.

Blackburn, Robin. *The Making of New World Slavery: From the Baroque to the Modern, 1492–1800.* London; New York: Verso, 1997.

Blashill, John. "Proper Role of U.S. Corporations in South Africa." *Fortune* (July 1972).

Blauner, Robert. *Racial Oppression in America.* New York: Harper and Row, 1972.

Blaut, J. M. *The Colonizer's Model of the World: Geographical Diffusionism and Eurocentric History.* New York: Guilford, 1993.

Bloom, Alexander, and Wini Breines, eds. *Takin' It to the Streets: A Sixties Reader.* New York: Oxford University Press, 1995.

Bloom, Jack M. *Class, Race and the Civil Rights Movement.* Bloomington: Indiana University Press, 1987.

Bloom, Leonard. *Identity and Ethnic Relations in Africa.* Aldershot, UK: Ashgate, 1998.

Blumer, Herbert, and Troy Duster. "Theories of Race and Social Action." In Marion O'Callaghan, ed. *Sociological Theories: Race and Colonialism.* Paris: UNESCO, 1980.

Blumer, Herbert. "Race Prejudice as a Sense of Group Position." *Pacific Sociological Review* 1, no. 1 (Spring 1958).

Blumer, Herbert. *Symbolic Interactionism: Perspective and Method.* Englewood Cliffs, NJ: Prentice-Hall, 1969.

Boas, Franz. "Race Problems in America." In George W. Stocking, ed. *The Shaping of American Anthropology, 1888–1911: A Franz Boas Reader.* Chicago: University of Chicago Press, 1974.

Boas, Franz. "The Problem of the American Negro" (1921). In idem. *Race and Democratic Society.* New York: Augustin, 1945.

Bobo, Lawrence, James R. Kluegel, and Ryan A. Smith, "Laissez-Faire Racism: The Crystallization of a 'Kinder, Gentler' Anti-black Ideology." Offprint: Russell Sage Foundation, June 1996.

Bolland, O. Nigel. "Colonization and Slavery in Central America." In Paul E. Lovejoy and Nicholas Rogers, eds. *Unfree Labour in the Development of the Atlantic World.* Ilford, Essex: Frank Cass, 1994.

Bonacich, Edna. "Capitalism and Race Relations in South Africa: A Split-Labor Market Analysis." *Political Power and Social Theory* 2 (1981).

Bond, Patrick. *Elite Transition: From Apartheid to Neoliberalism in South Africa.* London: Pluto, 2000.

Bonnett, Alastair. "Who Was White? The Disappearance of Non-European White Identities and the Formation of European Racial Whiteness." *Ethnic and Racial Studies* 21, no. 6 (November 1998).

Bontemps, Arna Wendell. *Black Thunder: Gabriel's Revolt, Virginia, 1800.* Boston: Beacon, 1992.

Borges, Dain. *The Family in Bahia, Brazil, 1870–1945.* Stanford: Stanford University Press, 1992.

Borges, Dain. "Salvador's 1890s: Paternalism and Its Discontents." *Luso-Brazilian Review* 30, no. 2 (1993).

Boston, Thomas. *Race, Class and Conservatism.* Boston: Allen & Unwin, 1988.

Bourdieu, Pierre. *Acts of Resistance: Against the Tyranny of the Market.* Translated by Richard Nice. New York: New Press, 1998.

Bower, Tom. *Klaus Barbie: The Butcher of Lyon.* New York: Pantheon, 1984.

Bracey, John H., Jr., August Meier, and Elliot Rudwick, eds. *Black Nationalism in America.* Indianapolis: Bobbs-Merrill, 1970.

Branch, Taylor. *Pillar of Fire: America in the King Years, 1964–65.* New York: Simon and Schuster, 1998.

Branch, Taylor. *Parting the Waters: America in the King Years, 1954–63.* New York: Simon and Schuster, 1988.

Brandão, Carlos. *Os Deuses do Povo.* Petrópolis: Vozes, 1980.

Braudel, Fernand. *The Mediterranean and the Mediterranean World in the Age of Philip II.* 2 vols. Translated by Siân Reynolds. New York: Harper & Row, 1972–73.

Braudel, Fernand. *Capitalism and Material Life, 1400–1800.* Translated by Miriam Kochan. New York: Harper Colophon, 1975.

Breen, T. H., and Stephen Innes. *"Myne Owne Ground": Race and Freedom on Virginia's Eastern Shore, 1640–1676.* New York: Oxford University Press, 1980.

Breman, Jan et al., eds. *Imperial Monkey Business: Racial Supremacy in Social Darwinist Theory and Practice.* Amsterdam: VU Press, 1990.

Brenner, Robert. *Merchants and Revolution: Commercial Change, Political Conflict, and London's Overseas Traders, 1550–1653.* Princeton: Princeton University Press, 1993.

Brooke, Edward William. *The Challenge of Change: Crisis in our Two-Party System.* Boston: Little, Brown, 1966.

Brooks, Roy L., ed. *When Sorry Isn't Enough: The Controversy over Apologies and Reparations for Human Injustice.* New York: New York University Press, 1999.

Brown, Kathleen M. *Good Wives, Nasty Wenches, and Anxious Patriarchs: Gender, Race, and Power in Colonial Virginia.* Chapel Hill: University of North Carolina Press, 1996.

Brown, Michael K. "The Policy Settlement of 1935." In idem. *Race, Money, and the American Welfare State.* Ithaca: Cornell University Press, 1999a.

Brown, Michael K. *Race, Money, and the American Welfare State.* Ithaca: Cornell University Press, 1999b.

Brown, Wendy. *States of Injury: Power and Freedom in Late Modernity.* Princeton: Princeton University Press, 1995.

Browning, Barbara. *Samba: Resistance in Motion.* Bloomington: Indiana University Press, 1995.

Browning, Christopher. *The Path to Genocide: Essays on Launching the Final Solution.* New York: Cambridge University Press, 1991.

Brubaker, Rogers. *Citizenship and Nationhood in France and Germany.* Cambridge, MA: Harvard University Press, 1992.

Brubaker, Rogers. *Nationalism Reframed: Nationhood and the National Question in the New Europe.* New York: Cambridge University Press, 1996.

Brundage, David Thomas. *The Making of Western Labor Radicalism: Denver's Organized Workers, 1878–1905.* Urbana: University of Illinois Press, 1994.

Brundage, W. Fitzhugh. *Lynching in the New South: Georgia and Virginia, 1880–1930.* Urbana: University of Illinois Press, 1993.

Brustein William. *The Logic of Evil: The Social Origins of the Nazi Party, 1925–1933.* New Haven: Yale University Press, 1998.

Brutus, Dennis, et al. "International Boycott of Apartheid Sport." Paper prepared for the United Nations Unit on Apartheid. United Nations Unit on Apartheid, Notes and Documents, no. 16/71, April 1971.

Buarque de Holanda, Sérgio. *Raízes do Brasil.* 7th ed. Rio de Janeiro: José Olympio, 1973.

Buci-Glucksmann, Christine. "State, Transition, and Passive Revolution." In Chantal Mouffe, ed. *Gramsci and Marxist Theory.* London: Routledge, 1979.

Buhle, Paul. *Marxism in the United States: Remapping the History of the American Left.* London: Verso, 1987.

Bullard, Robert D., ed. *Unequal Protection: Environmental Justice and Communities of Color.* San Francisco: Sierra Club, 1997.

Bulmer, Martin. *The Chicago School of Sociology: Institutionalization, Diversity, and the Rise of Sociological Research.* Chicago: University of Chicago Press, 1984.

Bulmer, Martin, and Anthony M. Rees, eds. *Citizenship Today: The Contemporary Relevance of T. H. Marshall.* Bristol, PA: UCL Press, 1996.

Bulmer, Martin, and John Solomos, eds. *Racism.* New York: Oxford University Press, 1999.

Bundy, Colin. *The Rise and Fall of the South African Peasantry.* Berkeley: University of California Press, 1979.

Burdick, John. *Blessed Anastácia: Women, Race and Popular Christianity in Brazil.* New York: Routledge, 1998.

Burleigh, Michael, and Wolfgang Wippermann. *The Racial State: Germany 1933–1945.* New York: Cambridge University Press, 1991.

Burstein, Paul. *Discrimination, Jobs and Politics: The Struggle for Equal Employment Opportunity in the United States Since the New Deal.* Chicago: University of Chicago Press, 1998.

Butler, Elizabeth Beardsley. *Women and the Trades, Pittsburgh, 1907–1908.* New York: Charities Publication Committee, 1909.

Byrd, W. Michael, and Linda A. Clayton. *An American Health Dilemma: A Medical History of African Americans and the Problem of Race.* New York: Routledge, 2000.

Caldeira, Teresa Pires do Rio. *A Política dos Outros: O Cotidiano dos Moradores da Periferia e o que Pensam do Poder e dos Poderosos.* São Paulo: Brasiliense, 1984.

Calhoun, Craig, ed. *Habermas and the Public Sphere.* Cambridge, MA: MIT Press, 1992.

Campani, Giovanni. "Present Trends in Women's Migration: The Emergence of Social Actors." In Danièle Joly, ed. *Scapegoats and Social Actors: The Exclusion and Integration of Minorities in Western and Eastern Europe.* New York: St. Martin's, 1998.

Campbell, Mavis Christine. *The Maroons of Jamaica, 1655–1796: A History of Resistance, Collaboration, and Betrayal.* Granby, MA: Bergin & Garvey, 1988.

Caplan, Richard, and John Feffer, eds. *Europe's New Nationalism: States and Minorities in Conflict.* New York: Oxford University Press, 1996.

Cardoso, Fernando Henrique. "Discurso do Presidente da República no Seminario Internacional "Multiculturalismo e Racismo: o Papel de Ação Afirmativa nos Estados Democráticos Contemporáneos." Palacio do Planalto, July 2, 1996.

Cardoso, Fernando Henrique, and Octávio Ianni. *Côr e Mobilidade Social em Florianopolis: Aspectos das Relações entre Negros e Brancos numa Comunidade do Brasil Meridional.* São Paulo: Nacional, 1960.

Carmichael, Stokely (Kwame Ture), and Charles V. Hamilton. *Black Power: The Politics of Liberation in America.* New York: Vintage, 1992.

Carmines, Edward G., and James A. Stimson. *Issue Evolution: Race and the Transformation of American Politics.* Princeton: Princeton University Press, 1989.

Carneiro, Edison. *O Quilombo dos Palmares.* 3rd ed. Rio de Janeiro: Civilizaçaõ Brasileira, 1966.

Carneiro, Maria Luiza Tucci. *O Anti-Semitismo no Era Vargas.* São Paulo: Brasiliense, 1988.

Carneiro, Sueli, and Thereza Santos. *Mulher Negra.* São Paulo: Nobel/Conselho Estadual da Condição Feminina, 1985.

Carroll, Patrick J. *Blacks in Colonial Veracruz: Race, Ethnicity, and Regional Development.* Austin: University of Texas Press, 1991.

Carson, Clayborne, ed. *The Autobiography of Martin Luther King, Jr.* New York: Warner, 1998.

Carson, Clayborne. *In Struggle: SNCC and the Black Awakening of the 1960s.* Cambridge, MA: Harvard University Press, 1981.

Carstens, W. Peter. *The Social Structure of a Cape Coloured Reserve, A Study of Racial Integration and Segregation in South Africa.* New York: Oxford University Press, 1966.

Carter, Dan T. *From George Wallace to Newt Gingrich: Race in the Conservative Counterrevolution, 1963–1994.* Baton Rouge: Louisiana State University Press, 1999.

Cartey, Wilfred, and Martin Kilson, eds. *The Africa Reader: Colonial Africa.* New York: Random House, 1970.

Carvalho, Mario Cesar. "Céu & Inferno de Gilberto Freyre." *Folha de Sao Páulo.* May 12, 2000.

Casas, Bartolomé de las. *The Devastation of the Indies: A Brief Account (Brevísima Relación de la Destrucción de las Indias).* Translated by Herna Briffault. Baltimore: Johns Hopkins University Press, 1992.

Castles, Stephen, and Godula Kosack. *Immigrant Workers and Class Structure in Western Europe.* New York: Oxford University Press, 1985.

Castles, Stephen, and Mark J. Miller. *The Age of Migration: International Population Movements in the Modern World.* Rev. ed. New York: Guilford, 1998.

Castles, Stephen, et al. *Here for Good: Western Europe's New Ethnic Minorities.* London: Pluto, 1984.

Cell, John W. *The Highest Stage of White Supremacy: The Origins of Segregation in South Africa and the American South.* New York: Cambridge University Press, 1982.

Centre for Contemporary Cultural Studies. *The Empire Strikes Back: Race in 70s Britain.* London: Hutchinson, 1982.

Cervantes de Saavedra, Miguel. *Don Quixote.* Ozell's revision of the translation of Peter Motteux. New York: Modern Library, 1930.

Chakrabarty, Dipesh. "Conditions for Knowledge of Working-Class Conditions." In Ranajit Guha and Gayatri Chakravorty Spivak, eds. *Selected Subaltern Studies.* New York: Oxford University Press, 1988.

Chan, Sucheng, ed. *Entry Denied: Exclusion and the Chinese Community in America, 1882–1943.* Philadelphia: Temple University Press, 1991.

Chase, Allan. *The Legacy of Malthus: The Social Costs of the New Scientific Racism.* New York: Knopf, 1977.

Chatterjee, Partha. "More on Modes of Power and the Peasantry." In Ranajit Guha and Gayatri Chakravorty Spivak, eds. *Selected Subaltern Studies.* New York: Oxford University Press, 1988.

Chaunu, Pierre. *European Expansion in the Later Middle Ages.* Translated by Kattarine Bertram. New York: Elsevier, 1979.

Chiavenato, Julio José. *As Várias Faces da Inconfidência Mineira.* São Paulo: Contexto, 1989.

Cisse, Madjiguene. *Sans-Papiers: A Woman Draws the First Lessons.* London: Crossroads, 1998.

Civil Rights Congress (U.S.). *We Charge Genocide: The Historic Petition to the United Nations for Relief from a Crime of the United States Government Against The Negro People.* Edited by William L. Patterson. New York: International Publishers, 1970.

Clarke, John Henrik, ed. *Marcus Garvey and the Vision of Africa.* New York: Random House, 1974.

Clendinnen, Inga. *Ambivalent Conquests: Maya and Spaniard in Yucatan, 1517–1570.* New York: Cambridge University Press, 1989.

Clifford, James. "Tell About Your Trip: Michel Leiris." In idem. *The Predicament of Culture: Twentieth-Century Ethnography, Literature, and Art.* Cambridge, MA: Harvard University Press, 1988.

Clifford, James, and George E. Marcus, eds. *Writing Culture: The Poetics and Politics of Ethnography.* Berkeley: University of California Press, 1986.

Cock, Jacklyn. *Maids and Madams: Domestic Workers under Apartheid.* Rev. ed. London: Women's Press, 1989.

Cohen, Roger. "Right-Wing March Showcases Germany's Disenchanted." *The New York Times,* February 28, 1999.

Cohen, Thomas M. *The Fire of Tongues: António Vieira and the Missionary Church in Brazil and Portugal.* Stanford: Stanford University Press, 1998.

Cohen, Robin. *Endgame in South Africa?* Paris: UNESCO, 1986.

Cole, Jeffrey A. *The Potosí Mita, 1573–1700: Compulsory Indian Labor in the Andes.* Stanford: Stanford University Press, 1985.

Collins, Randall. "Iterated Ritual Chains, Power and Property: The Micro-Macro Connection as an Empirically Based Theoretical Problem." In Jeffrey Alexander et al., eds. *The Micro-Macro Link.* Berkeley: University of California Press, 1987.

Colona, Fanny. "Educating Conformity in French Colonial Algeria." In Frederick Cooper and Ann Laura Stoler, eds. *Tensions of Empire: Colonial Cultures in a Bourgeois World.* Berkeley: University of California Press, 1997.

Comaroff, Jean, and John L. Comaroff. *Of Revelation and Revolution: Christianity, Colonialism, and Consciousness in South Africa.* Chicago: University of Chicago Press, 1991.

Cone, James H. *Martin and Malcolm in America: A Dream or a Nightmare.* Maryknoll, NY: Orbis, 1991.

Conley, Dalton. *Being Black, Living in the Red: Race, Wealth, and Social Policy in America.* Berkeley: University of California Press, 1999.

Connolly, Clara, and Pragna Patel. "Women Who Walk on Water: Working across 'Race' in Women Against Fundamentalism." in Lisa Lowe and David Lloyd, eds. *The Politics of Culture in the Shadow of Capital.* Durham: Duke University Press, 1997.

Constituções Brasileiras. São Paulo: Sugestões Literarias, 1978.

Constitution of the Republic of South Africa, 1996. As adopted on May 8, 1996, and amended on October 11, 1996, by the Constitutional Assembly. Website: http://www.polity.org.za/govdocs/constitution/saconst.html.

Cooper, Frederick. *On the African Waterfront: Urban Disorder and the Transformation of Work in Colonial Mombasa.* New Haven: Yale University Press, 1987.

Cooper, Frederick. "Africa and the World Economy." In Frederick Cooper et al., eds. *Confronting Historical Paradigms: Peasants, Labor, and the Capitalist World System in Africa and Latin America.* Madison: University of Wisconsin Press, 1993a.

Cooper, Frederick, et al., eds. *Confronting Historical Paradigms: Peasants, Labor, and the Capitalist World System in Africa and Latin America.* Madison: University of Wisconsin Press, 1993b.

Cooper, Frederick. "Conflict and Connection: Rethinking Colonial African History." *American Historical Review* 99 (December 1994).

Cooper, Frederick. *Decolonization and African Society: The Labor Question in French and British Africa.* New York: Cambridge University Press, 1996.

Cooper, Frederick, and Ann Laura Stoler, eds. *Tensions of Empire: Colonial Cultures in a Bourgeois World.* Berkeley: University of California Press, 1997.

Coordenação Nacional de Entidades Negras (CONEN). "O Partido dos Trabalhadores e a Questão Racial." Plenary Statement, Belo Horizonte, August 9, 1998. Available at website: www.pt.org.br/racismo/cartamg.htm.

Cope, Douglas. *The Limits of Racial Domination: Plebeian Society in Colonial Mexico City, 1660–1720.* Madison: University of Wisconsin Press, 1994.

Coplan, David B. *In the Time of Cannibals: The Word Music of South Africa's Basotho Migrants.* Chicago: University of Chicago Press, 1994.

Coquery-Vidrovitch, Catherine, et al., eds. *Pour une Histoire du Développement: États, Sociétés, Développement.* Paris: L'Harmattan, 1988.

Cornelius, Wayne A., Philip L. Martin, and James F. Hollifield, eds., *Controlling Immigration: A Global Perspective.* Stanford: Stanford Univesity Press, 1994.

Costa, Emília Viotti da. *Crowns of Glory, Tears of Blood: The Demerara Slave Rebellion of 1823.* New York: Oxford University Press, 1994.

Costa, Emília Viotti da. *Da Monarquia á República: Momentos Decisivos.* 3rd ed. São Paulo: Brasiliense, 1985a.

Costa, Emília Viotti da. "The Myth of Racial Democracy: A Legacy of the Empire." In idem, ed. *The Brazilian Empire: Myths and Histories.* Chicago: University of Chicago Press, 1985b.

Cotton, Samuel. *Silent Terror: A Journey into Contemporary African Slavery.* New York: Harlem River, 1998.

Count, Earl W., ed., *This Is Race: An Anthology Selected from the International Literature on the Races of Man.* New York: Henry Schuman, 1950.

Cover, Robert M. *Justice Accused: Antislavery and the Judicial Process.* New Haven: Yale University Press, 1975.

Cox, Oliver Cromwell. *Class, Caste, and Race: A Study in Social Dynamics.* New York: Monthly Review Press, 1970 [1948].

Craton, Michael. "Bussa's Rebellion: Barbados 1816." In idem, *Testing the Chains: Resistance to Slavery in the British West Indies.* Ithaca: Cornell University Press, 1982a.

Craton, Michael. "The Baptist War: The Jamaican Rebellion of 1831–31." In idem. *Testing the Chains: Resistance to Slavery in the British West Indies.* Ithaca: Cornell University Press, 1982b.

Craton, Michael. *Testing the Chains: Resistance to Slavery in the British West Indies.* Ithaca: Cornell University Press, 1982c.

Crenshaw, Kimberlé, et al., eds. *Critical Race Theory: The Key Writings That Formed the Movement.* New York: New Press, 1995.

Cunha, Euclides da. *Rebellion in the Backlands (Os Sertões).* Translated by Samuel Putnam. London: Picador, 1995 [1902].

Curtin, Philip D. *The Atlantic Slave Trade: A Census.* Madison: University of Wisconsin Press, 1969.

Curtin, Philip D. *Africa Remembered: Narratives by West Africans from the Era of the Slave Trade.* Madison: University of Wisconsin Press, 1967.

D'Anjou, Leo. *Social Movements and Cultural Change: The First Abolition Campaign Revisited.* New York: Aldine de Gruyter, 1996.

Da Matta, Roberto. *Relativizando.* 4th ed. Petrópolis: Vozes, 1984.

Damasceno, Caetana Maria. "Woman Workers of Rio: Laborious Reinterpretations of the Racial Condition." In Rebecca Reichmann, ed. *Race in Contemporary Brazil: From Indifference to Inequality.* University Park: Pennsylvania State University Press, 1999.

Darwin, Charles. *The Descent of Man, and Selection in Relation to Sex.* Princeton: Princeton University Press, 1981 [1871].

Darwin, Charles. *On the Origin of Species by Means of Natural Selection, or the Preservation of Favored Races in the Struggle for Life.* New York: New York University Press, 1988 [1859].

Datafolha. *300 Anos de Zumbi: Os Brasileiros e o Preconceito de Côr.* São Paulo: Datafolha, 1995.

Davidson, Basil. *Black Mother: The Years of the African Slave Trade.* Boston: Little, Brown, 1961.

Davidson, Basil, F. K. Buah, and J. F. Ade Ajayi. *A History of West Africa 1000–1800.* Rev. ed. London: Longmans, 1977.

Davidson, Basil. *The Black Man's Burden: Africa and the Curse of the Nation-State.* New York: Random House, 1992.

Davis, David Brion. *The Problem of Slavery in the Age of Revolution, 1770–1823.* Ithaca: Cornell University Press, 1975.

Davis, David Brion. *The Problem of Slavery in Western Culture.* Ithaca: Cornell University Press, 1966.

Davis, F. James. *Who Is Black? One Nation's Definition.* University Park: Pennsylvania State University Press, 1991.

Davis, Horace J. *Nationalism and Socialism: Marxist and Labor Theories of Nationalism to 1917.* New York: Monthly Review Press, 1967.

Davis, Stephen M. *Apartheid's Rebels: Inside South Africa's Hidden War.* New Haven: Yale University Press, 1987.

Dawley, Alan. *Class and Community: The Industrial Revolution in Lynn.* Cambridge MA: Harvard University Press, 1976.

de Grazia, Victoria. *How Fascism Ruled Women: Italy, 1922–1945.* Berkeley: University of California Press, 1991.

de Souza, Amaury. "Raçae Política no Brasil Urbano." *Revista Administracão de Empresas,* 2, no. 4 (1971).

Degler, Carl. *Neither Black Nor White: Slavery and Race Relations in Brazil and the United States.* Madison: University of Wisconsin Press, 1986 [1971].

Delgado, Richard. *The Coming Race War? And Other Apocalyptic Tales of America After Affirmative Action and Welfare.* New York: New York University Press, 1997.

Denby, Charles (Matthew Ward). *Indignant Heart: A Black Worker's Journal.* Boston: South End, 1978 [1952].

Désir, Harlem. *Touche Pas à Mon Pote.* Paris: Grasset, 1985.

Di Leonardo, Michaela, ed. *Gender at the Crossroads of Knowledge: Feminist Anthropology in the Postmodern Era.* Berkeley: University of California Press, 1991.

Dikötter, Frank, ed. *The Construction of Racial Identities in China and Japan.* Honolulu: University of Hawai'i Press, 1997.

Diouf, Sylviane A. *Servants of Allah: African Muslims Enslaved in the Americas.* New York: New York University Press, 1998.

Dittmer, John. *Local People: The Struggle for Civil Rights in Mississippi.* Urbana: University of Illinois Press, 1995.

Domínguez, Jorge I. *Insurrection or Loyalty: The Breakdown of the Spanish American Empire.* Cambridge, MA: Harvard University Press, 1980.

Domínguez, Virginia R. *White by Definition: Social Classification in Creole Louisiana.* New Brunswick: Rutgers University Press, 1994.

Dorkenoo, Efua, and Scilla Elworthy. *Female Genital Mutilation: Proposals for Change.* London: Minority Rights Group, 1992.

Douglass, Frederick. *Narrative of the Life of Frederick Douglass, an American Slave, Written by Himself: Authoritative Text, Contexts, Criticism.* Edited by William L. Andrews and William S. McFeely. New York: Norton, 1987.

Drake, St. Clair. *Black Folk Here and There: An Essay in History and Anthropology.* 2 vols. Los Angeles: Center for Afro-American Studies, UCLA, 1987–90.

Drake, St. Clair, and Horace R. Cayton. *Black Metropolis: A Study of Negro Life in a Northern City.* Chicago: University of Chicago Press, 1993 [1945].

Dreifuss, René Armand. *A Conquista do Estado.* Petrópolis: Vozes, 1981.

Drescher, Seymour. "Cart Whip and Billy Roller: Anti-Slavery and Reform Symbolism in Industrializing Britain." *Journal of Social History* 15 (September 1981).

Drescher, Seymour. *Capitalism and Antislavery: British Mobilization in Comparative Perspective.* New York: Oxford University Press, 1987.

Drescher, Seymour. *From Slavery to Freedom: Comparative Studies in the Rise and Fall of Atlantic Slavery.* New York: New York University Press, 1999.

Drinnon, Richard. *Facing West: The Metaphysics of Indian Hating and Empire Building.* Minneapolis: University of Minnesota Press, 1980.

Du Bois, W. E. B. "The Conservation of Races" [1897]. In David Levering Lewis ed. *W. E. B. Du Bois: A Reader.* New York: Henry Holt, 1995.

Du Bois, W. E. B. *The Philadelphia Negro: A Social Study.* Philadelphia: University of Pennsylvania Press, 1998 [1899].

Du Bois, W. E. B. "Report of the Pan-African Conference, held on the 23rd, 24th, and 25th July, 1900, at Westminster Town Hall, Westminster, S.W. [London]." In David Levering Lewis, ed. *W. E. B. Du Bois: A Reader.* New York: Henry Holt, 1995.

Du Bois, W. E. B. *The Souls of Black Folk.* New York: Penguin, 1989 [1903].

Du Bois, W. E. B. "The Talented Tenth." In Booker T. Washington et al. *The Negro Problem: A Series of Articles by Representative American Negroes of To-Day.* Miami: Mnemosyne, 1969 [1903].

Du Bois, W. E. B. *John Brown: A Biography.* Armonk, NY: M. E. Sharpe, 1997 [1909].

Du Bois, W. E. B. "The African Roots of the War" [1915]. In David Levering Lewis, ed. *W. E. B. Du Bois: A Reader.* New York: Henry Holt, 1995.

Du Bois, W. E. B. "The Negro's Fatherland" [1917]. In David Levering Lewis, ed. *W. E. B. Du Bois: A Reader.* New York: Henry Holt, 1995.

Du Bois, W. E. B. "An Essay Toward a History of the Black Man in the Great War" [1919]. In David Levering Lewis, ed. *W. E. B. Du Bois: A Reader.* New York: Henry Holt, 1995.

Du Bois, W. E. B. "Brothers, Come North" [1920]. In David Levering Lewis, ed. *W. E. B. Du Bois: A Reader.* New York: Henry Holt, 1995.

Du Bois, W. E. B. *Africa, Its Geography, People, and Products; and Africa, Its Place in Modern History* [1930]. Millwood, NY: KTO, 1977.

Du Bois, W. E. B. "The Negro and Communism" [1931]. In David Levering Lewis, ed., *W. E. B. Du Bois: A Reader.* New York: Henry Holt, 1995.

Du Bois, W. E. B. *Black Reconstruction: An Essay Toward a History of the Part which Black Folk Played in the Attempt to Reconstruct Democracy in America, 1860–1880.* New York: Atheneum, 1977 [1935].

Du Bois, W. E. B. *Dusk of Dawn: An Essay Toward an Autobiography of a Race Concept.* New Brunswick, NJ: Transaction, 1991 [1940].

Du Bois, W. E. B., Milton Konvitz, Rayford Logan, and Earl Dickerson, for the National Association for the Advancement of Colored People. *An Appeal to the World: A Statement on the Denial of Human Rights in the Case of Citizens of Negro Descent in the United States of America and An Appeal to the United Nations for Redress.* N.p.: New York, 1947.

Du Bois, W. E. B. "The Talented Tenth: Memorial Address" [1948]. In David Levering Lewis, ed. *W. E. B. Du Bois: A Reader.* New York: Henry Holt, 1995.

Du Bois, W. E. B. "The Negro and Communism" [1931]. In David Levering Lewis, ed. *W. E. B. Du Bois: A Reader.* New York: Henry Holt, 1995.

Du Bois, W. E. B. "On Stalin" [1953]. In David Levering Lewis, ed.. *W. E. B. Du Bois: A Reader.* New York: Henry Holt, 1995.

Du Bois, W. E. B. "Whither Now and Why" [1960]. In idem. *The Education of Black People: Ten Critiques 1906–1960.* Edited by Herbert Aptheker. Amherst: University of Massachusetts Press, 1973.

Du Bois, W. E. B. "Application for Membership in the Communist Party of the United States of America" [1961]. In David Levering Lewis, ed. *W. E. B. Du Bois: A Reader.* New York: Henry Holt, 1995.

Dubofsky, Melvyn. *We Shall Be All.* New York: Quadrangle, 1969.

Dubow, Saul. *Scientific Racism in Modern South Africa.* New York: Cambridge University Press, 1995.

Dudziak, Mary L. "Desegregation as a Cold War Imperative." *Stanford Law Review* 41, no. 1 (November 1988).

Dupuy, Alex. *Haiti in the World Economy: Class, Race, and Underdevelopment Since 1700.* Boulder: Westview, 1989.

Durham, Martin. *Women and Fascism.* New York: Routledge, 1998.

Durkheim, Emile. *The Elementary Forms of Religious Life.* Translated by Karen E. Fields. New York: Free Press, 1995 [1912].

Duster, Troy. *Backdoor to Eugenics.* New York: Routledge, 1990.

Dzidzienyo, Anani. *The Position of Blacks in Brazilian Society.* London: Minority Rights Group, 1971.

Dzidzienyo, Anani. "The African Connection and the Afro-Brazilian Connection." In Pierre-Michel Fontaine, ed. *Race, Class, and Power in Brazil.* Los Angeles: CAAS/UCLA, 1985.

Ebrahim, Hassen. *The Soul of a Nation: Constitution-Making in South Africa.* Cape Town: Oxford University Press, 1998.

Edsall, Thomas Byrne, and Mary Edsall. *Chain Reaction: The Impact of Race, Rights, and Taxes on American Politics.* Rev. ed. New York: Norton, 1992.

Eisenberg, Peter L. *The Sugar Industry in Pernambuco: Modernization Without Change, 1840–1910.* Berkeley: University of California Press, 1974.

Eisenstadt, Shmuel Noah, and Stein Rokkan. *Building States and Nations.* Beverly Hills, CA: Sage, 1973.

Elkins, Stanley M. *Slavery: A Problem in American Institutional and Intellectual Life.* 3rd ed. Chicago: University of Chicago Press, 1976.

Elphick, Richard, and Hermann Giliomee, eds. *The Shaping of South African Society, 1652–1840.* 2nd ed. Middletown, CT: Wesleyan University Press, 1989.

Engels, Friedrich. *The Condition of the Working Class in England in 1844.* Translated and edited by W. O. Henderson and W. H. Chaloner. Oxford: Blackwell, 1958 [1845].

Engerman, Stanley L., and Eugene D. Genovese, eds. *Race and Slavery in the Western Hemisphere; Quantitative Studies.* Princeton: Princeton University Press, 1975.

Eschen, Penny von. *Race Against Empire: Black Americans and Anticolonialism, 1937–1957.* Ithaca: Cornell University Press, 1997.

Espiritu, Yen Le. *Asian American Women and Men: Labor, Laws and Love.* Thousand Oaks, CA: Sage, 1997.

Essed, Philomena. "The Politics of Marginal Inclusion: Racism in an Organisational Context." In John Solomos and John Wrench, eds. *Racism and Migration in Western Europe.* Providence, RI: Berg, 1993.

European Youth Centre. "All Different All Equal: Ideas, Tools and Resources for Intercultural Education" (Education Packet). Strasbourg: ECRI, 1995.

Evans, Ivan. *Bureaucracy and Race: Native Administration in South Africa.* Berkeley: University of California Press, 1997.

Evans, Sara. *Personal Politics: The Roots of Women's Liberation in the Civil Rights Movement and the New Left.* New York: Vintage, 1979.

Eze, Emmanuel Chukwudi. *Race and the Enlightenment: A Reader.* Cambridge, MA: Blackwell, 1997.

Fage, J. D. "Slaves and Society in Western Africa, 1445–1700." *Journal of African History* 10 (1969).

Farnsworth, Clyde H. "The Betrayed Maori Are Calling for a Reckoning." *New York Times,* March 20, 1997.

Favell, Adrian. *Philosophies of Integration: Immigration and the Idea of Citizenship in France and Britain.* New York: St. Martin's, 1998.

Feagin, Joe R., and Melvin P. Sykes. *Living With Racism: The Black Middle Class Experience.* Boston: Beacon, 1994.

Feldblum, Miriam. *Reconstructing Citizenship: The Politics of Nationality Reform and Immigration in Contemporary France.* Albany: State University of New York Press, 1999.

Fenton, Steve, et al. *Durkheim and Modern Sociology.* Cambridge, UK: Cambridge University Press, 1984.

Fernandes, Florestan. *A Revolução Burguesa no Brasil: Ensaio de Interpretação Sociológica.* 2nd ed. Rio de Janeiro: Zahar, 1976.

Fernandes, Florestan. *A Integração do Negro na Sociedade de Clases.* 2 vols. 3rd ed. São Paulo: Atica, 1978.

Ferrarroti, Franco. *The Temptation to Forget: Racism, Anti-Semitism, Neo-Nazism.* Westport, CT: Greenwood, 1994.

Fick, Carolyn. *The Making of Haiti: The Saint-Domingue Revolution from Below.* Knoxville: University of Tennessee Press, 1990.

Fields, Barbara Jeanne. *Slavery and Freedom on the Middle Ground: Maryland During the Nineteenth Century.* New Haven: Yale University Press, 1985.

Fields, Karen. *Revival and Rebellion in Colonial Central Africa.* Princeton: Princeton University Press, 1985.

Findlay, Ronald. "The 'Triangular Trade' and the Atlantic Economy of the Eighteenth Century: A Simple General-Equilibrium Model." *Essays in International Finance* 177. International Finance Section, Department of Economics, Princeton University, March 1990.

Fine, Michelle, et al., eds. *Off White: Readings on Race, Power, and Society* New York: Routledge, 1997.

Finley, Moses, ed. *Slavery in Classical Antiquity: Views and Controversies.* Cambridge, UK: W. Heffer, 1960.

Finley, Moses. *Politics in the Ancient World.* New York: Cambridge University Press, 1983.

Finnegan, William. "A Slave in New York." *The New Yorker,* January 24, 2000.

Fisher, Allan. *Slavery and Muslim Society in Africa.* London: Hurst, 1970.

Fogel, Robert William, and Stanley L. Engerman. *Time on the Cross: The Economics of American Negro Slavery.* Boston: Little, Brown, 1974.

Fogel, Robert William, *Without Consent or Contract: The Rise and Fall of American Slavery.* New York: Norton, 1989.

Foner, Eric. *Nothing but Freedom: Emancipation and its Legacy.* Baton Rouge: Louisiana State University Press, 1983.

Foner, Eric. *Reconstruction: America's Unfinished Revolution, 1863–1877.* New York: Harper & Row, 1988.

Foner, Philip. *History of Black Americans: From Africa to the Cotton Kingdom.* Westport, CT: Greenwood, 1975.

Forbes, Ella. *"But We Have No Country": The 1851 Christiana, Pennsylvania, Resistance.* Cherry Hill, NJ: Africana Homestead Legacy, 1998.

Forbes, Jack D. *Africans and Native Americans: The Language of Race and the Evolution of Red-Black Peoples.* 2nd ed. Urbana: University of Illinois Press, 1993.

Foucault, Michel. *The Order of Things: An Archaeology of the Human Sciences.* New York: Vintage, 1973.

Frank, Andre Gunder. *Capitalism and Underdevelopment in Latin America: Historical Studies of Chile and Brazil.* Rev. ed. New York: Monthly Review Press, 1969.

Frank, Andre Gunder. "The Development of Underdevelopment." *Monthly Review* 18, no. 4 (September 1966).

Frankenberg, Ruth, ed. *Displacing Whiteness: Essays in Social and Cultural Criticism.* Durham: Duke University Press, 1997.

Franklin, John Hope. *George Washington Williams: A Biography.* Chicago: University of Chicago Press, 1985.

Franklin, John Hope. *Reconstruction after the Civil War.* 2nd ed. Chicago: University of Chicago Press, 1994.

Franklin, Raymond S. *Shadows of Race and Class.* Minneapolis: University of Minnesota Press, 1991.

Fraser, Steve, and Gary Gerstle, eds. *The Rise and Fall of the New Deal Order, 1930–1980.* Princeton: Princeton University Press, 1989.

Frederikse, Julie. *The Unbreakable Thread: Non-Racialism in South Africa, 1975–1990.* Bloomington: Indiana University Press, 1990.

Fredrickson, George M. *The Black Image in the White Mind: The Debate on Afro-American Character and Destiny, 1817–1914.* New York: Harper & Row, 1971.

Fredrickson, George M. *White Supremacy: A Comparative Study of American and South African History.* New York: Oxford University Press, 1981.

Fredrickson, George M. *Black Liberation: A Comparative History of Black Ideologies in the United States and South Africa.* New York: Oxford University Press, 1995.

Fredrickson, George M. "Race and Empire in Liberal Thought: The Legacy of Tocqueville." In idem. *The Comparative Imagination: On the History of Racism, Nationalism, and Social Movements.* Berkeley: University of California Press, 1997a.

Fredrickson, George M. "Prophets of Black Liberation." In idem, *The Comparative Imagination: On the History of Racism, Nationalism, and Social Movements.* Berkeley: University of California Press, 1997b.

Fredrickson, George M. "Nonviolent Resistance to White Supremacy: The American Civil Rights Movement and the South African Defiance Campaigns." In idem, *The Comparative Imagination: On the History of Racism, Nationalism, and Social Movements.* Berkeley: University of California Press, 1997c.

Fredrickson, George M. *The Comparative Imagination: On the History of Racism, Nationalism, and Social Movements.* Berkeley: University of California Press, 1997d.

Fredrickson George M. "The Strange Death of Segregation." *New York Review of Books* 46, no. 10 (May 6, 1999).

Freeman, Gary P. *Immigrant Labor and Racial Conflict in Industrial Societies: The French and British Experience, 1945–1975.* Princeton: Princeton University Press, 1979.

Freire, Paulo. *Pedagogy of the Oppressed.* Translated by Myra Bergman Ramos. New York: Continuum, 1993 [1970].

Freitas, Décio. *Palmares; A Guerra dos Escravos.* 5th ed. Porto Alegre: Mercado Aberto, 1984.

French, John D. *The Brazilian Workers' ABC: Class Conflict and Alliances in Modern São Paulo.* Chapel Hill: University of North Carolina Press, 1992.

Freyre, Gilberto. *Ordem e Progresso: Processos de Desintegração das Sociedades Patriacal e Semipatriarcal no Brasil sob o Regime do Trabalho Livre: Aspectos de um Quase Méio Século de Transição do Trabalho Escravo para o Trabalho Livre: e da Monarquia para a República.* 2 vols. Rio de Janeiro: Jose Olympio, 1959.

Freyre, Gilberto. *The Masters and the Slaves: A Study in the Development of Brazilian Society.* Translated by Samuel Putnam. Berkeley: University of California Press, 1986 [1933].

Friday, Chris. *Organizing Asian American Labor: The Pacific Coast Canned-Salmon Industry, 1870–1942.* Philadelphia: Temple University Press, 1995.

Fritzsche, Peter. *Germans into Nazis.* Cambridge, MA: Harvard University Press, 1998.

Fry, Peter. "Politicamente Correto Num Lugar, Incorreto Noutro?" *Revista Estudos Afro-Asiaticos* 21 (December 1991).

Fry, Peter. "O Que a Cinderela Negra Tem a Dizer Sobre a 'Política Racial' no Brasil." *Revista USP* 28 (1995).

Fysh, Peter, and Jim Wolfreys. *The Politics of Racism in France.* New York: St. Martin's Press, 1998.

Galton, Francis. *Hereditary Genius: An Inquiry into its Laws and Consequences.* New York: St. Martin's, 1978 [1869].

Garcia, Carlos Bosch. *La Esclavitud Prehispánica entre los Aztecas.* Mexico, DF: Centro de Estudios Históricos, Colegio de Mexico, 1944.

Garretón M., Manuel A. *Hacia una Nueva Era Política: Estudio sobre las Democratizaciones.* México, DF: Fondo de Cultura Económica, 1995.

Garrow, David J. *Bearing the Cross: Martin Luther King Jr. and the Southern Christian Leadership Conference.* New York: Vintage, 1988.

Gates, Henry Louis, Jr., and Cornel West. *The Future of the Race.* New York: Knopf, 1996.

Gates, Henry Louis, Jr., ed. *Reading Black, Reading Feminist.* New York: Penguin, 1990.

Gellner, Ernest. *Nations and Nationalism.* New York: Oxford University Press, 1983.

Genovese, Eugene D. *In Red and Black: Marxian Explorations in Southern and Afro-American History.* New York: Pantheon, 1971.

Genovese, Eugene D. *Roll, Jordan, Roll: The World the Slaves Made.* New York: Pantheon, 1974.

Genovese, Eugene D. *From Rebellion to Revolution: Afro-American Slave Revolts in the Making of the Modern World.* Baton Rouge: Louisiana State University Press, 1992a.

Genovese, Eugene D. *The Slaveholders' Dilemma: Freedom and Progress in Southern Conservative Thought, 1820–1860.* Columbia: University of South Carolina Press, 1992b.

Genovese, Eugene D. *The Southern Tradition: The Achievement and Limitations of an American Conservatism.* Cambridge, MA: Harvard University Press, 1996.

Gerhart, Gail M. *Black Power in South Africa: The Evolution of an Ideology.* Berkeley: University of California Press, 1978.

Giddens, Anthony. *The Constitution of Society: Outline of the Theory of Structuration.* Berkeley: University of California Press, 1984.

Gillette, William. *Retreat from Reconstruction, 1869–1879.* Baton Rouge: Louisiana State University Press, 1979.

Gilliam, Angela, and Onik'a Gilliam. "Negociando a Subjetividade de Mulata no Brasil." *Estudos Feministas* 3, no. 2 (1995).

Gilman, Sander L. *Difference and Pathology: Stereotypes of Sexuality, Race, and Madness.* Ithaca: Cornell University Press, 1985.

Gilman, Sander L., and Steven T. Katz. *Anti-Semitism in Times of Crisis.* New York: New York University Press, 1991.

Gilmour, David. "The Empire's New Clothes." *The New York Review of Books,* February 24, 2000.

Gilroy, Paul. "One Nation Under a Groove: The Cultural Politics of 'Race' and Racism in Britain." In David Theo Goldberg, ed. *Anatomy of Racism.* Minneapolis: University of Minnesota Press, 1990.

Gilroy, Paul. *There Ain't No Black in the Union Jack: The Cultural Politics of Race and Nation.* Chicago: University of Chicago Press, 1991.

Gilroy, Paul. *The Black Atlantic: Modernity and Double Consciousness.* Cambridge, MA: Harvard University Press, 1993.

Gilroy, Paul. "Revolutionary Conservatism and the Tyrannies of Unanimism." *New Formations* 28 (Spring 1996).

Gilroy, Paul. "The End of Anti-Racism." In Martin Bulmer, and John Solomos, eds. *Racism.* New York: Oxford University Press, 1999.

Gitmez, Ali, and Czarina Wilpert. "A Micro-Society or an Ethnic Community? Social Organization and Ethnicity Among Turkish Immigrants in Berlin." In John Rex et al., eds. *Immigrant Associations in Europe.* Brookfield, VT: Gower, 1987.

Glaude, Eddie S. *Exodus! Religion, Race, and Nation in Early 19th Century Black America.* Chicago: University of Chicago Press, 2000.

Glazer, Nathan, and Daniel P. Moynihan. *Beyond the Melting Pot: The Negroes, Puerto Ricans, Jews, Italians, and Irish of New York City.* 2nd ed. Cambridge, MA: MIT Press, 1970 [1963].

Glenn, Evelyn Nakano. *Issei, Nisei, War Bride: Three Generations of Japanese American Women in Domestic Service.* Philadelphia: Temple University Press, 1986.

Gobineau, Comte Arthur de. *The Moral and Intellectual Diversity of Races* (*Essai sur l'inégalité des races humaines*). New York: Garland, 1984 [1853–55].

Goldani, Ana Maria. "Desigualdade Racial nas Trajetórias de Vida Familiar das Mulheres Brasileiras." In Peggy A. Lovell, ed. *Desigualdade Racial no Brasil Contemporaneo.* Belo Horizonte: CEDEPLAR/UFMG, 1991.

Goldberg, David Theo, ed. *Anatomy of Racism.* Minneapolis: University of Minnesota Press, 1990.

Goldberg, David Theo. *Racist Culture: Philosophy and the Politics of Meaning.* Cambridge, MA: Blackwell, 1993.

Goldfield, Michael. *The Color of Politics: Race and the Mainsprings of American Politics.* New York: New Press, 1997.

Goldhagen, Daniel Jonah. *Hitler's Willing Executioners: Ordinary Germans and the Holocaust.* Boston: Little, Brown, 1996.

Goldstein, Donna. " 'Interracial' Sex and Racial Democracy in Brazil: Twin Concepts?" *American Anthropologist* 101, no. 3 (1999).

Goldstone, Jack A. "Urbanization and Inflation: Lessons from the English Price Revolution of the Sixteenth and Seventeenth Centuries." *American Journal of Sociology* 89 (1984).

Gomes dos Santos, Revanilda. *Partidos Politicos e Eleitorado Negro.* Master's thesis, PUC-São Paulo, 1992.

Gonzales, Léila. "The Unified Black Movement: A New Stage in Black Political Mobilization." In Pierre-Michel Fontaine, ed. *Race, Class, and Power in Brazil.* Los Angeles: CAAS/UCLA, 1985.

Goodman, Paul. *Of One Blood: Abolitionism and the Origins of Racial Inequality.* Berkeley: University of California Press, 1998.

Gordon, Linda. *Woman's Body, Woman's Right: A Social History of Birth Control in America.* 2nd ed. New York: Penguin, 1990.

Gordon, Milton. *Assimilation in American Life: The Role of Race, Religion, and National Origins.* New York: Oxford University Press, 1964.

Goscinny and Uderzo. *Asterix and Obelix* (comic book series). Translated by Anthea Bell and Derk Hockridge. London: Hodder and Stoughton, various dates.

Gossett, Thomas F. *Race: The History of an Idea in America.* New York: Schocken, 1965.

Gould, Stephen Jay. *The Mismeasure of Man.* New York: Norton, 1981.

Gourevitch, Philip. "The Unthinkable: How Dangerous is Le Pen's National Front?" *The New Yorker,* April 28–May 5, 1997.

Govender, Karthigasen. Remarks at "Rethinking Equality in the Global Society" conference, held at Washington University School of Law. *Washington University Law Quarterly* 75 (November 1997).

Graham, Lawrence Otis. *Member of the Club: Reflections on Life in a Racially Polarized World.* New York: HarperCollins, 1995.

Graham, Richard, ed. *The Idea of Race in Latin America, 1870–1940.* Austin: University of Texas Press, 1990.

Graham, Richard. "Free African Brazilians and the State in Slavery Times." In Michael Hanchard, ed. *Racial Politics in Contemporary Brazil.* Durham: Duke University Press, 1999.

Gramsci, Antonio. *Selections from the Prison Notebooks.* Edited by Quinton Hoare and Geoffrey Nowell-Smith. New York: International Publishers, 1971.

Grant, Madison. *The Passing of the Great Race.* New York: Arno, 1970 [1916].

Grasmuck, Sherri, and Patricia R. Pessar. *Between Two Islands: Dominican International Migration.* Berkeley: University of California Press, 1991.

Greenberg, Stanley B. *Race and State in Capitalist Development: Comparative Perspectives.* New Haven: Yale University Press, 1980.

Greenberg, Stanley B. *Legitimating the Illegitimate: States, Markets and Resistance in South Africa.* Berkeley: University of California Press, 1987.

Greene, Jerome A., ed. *Lakota and Cheyenne: Indian Views of the Great Sioux War, 1876–1877.* Norman: University of Oklahoma Press, 1994.

Greene, Lorenzo J. "Mutiny on the Slave Ships," *Phylon* 5 (1944).

Greenstein, Ran. "Racial Formation: Towards a Comparative Study of Collective Identities in South Africa and the United States." *Social Dynamics* 19, no. 2 (1993).

Greenstein, Ran. *Genealogies of Conflict: Class, Identity, and State in Palestine/Israel and South Africa.* Hanover, NH: University Press of New England, 1995.

Greenwald, Maurine W., and Margo Anderson, eds. *Pittsburgh Surveyed: Social Science and Social Reform in the Early Twentieth Century.* Pittsburgh: University of Pittsburgh Press, 1996.

Gregor, A. James. *The Ideology of Fascism: The Rationale of Totalitarianism.* New York: Free Press, 1969.

Greider, William. *One World, Ready or Not: The Manic Logic of Global Capitalism.* New York: Touchstone, 1997.

Griffin, Farah Jasmine. *"Who Set You Flowin'?" The African-American Migration Narrative.* New York: Oxford University Press, 1995.

Guha, Ranajit. "Introduction." In idem, ed. *A Subaltern Studies Reader, 1986–1995.* Minneapolis: University of Minnesota Press, 1997.

Guha, Ranajit, and Gayatri Chakravorty Spivak, eds. *Selected Subaltern Studies.* New York: Oxford University Press, 1988.

Guillaumin, Colette, and Leon Poliakov. "Max Weber et les Théories Bioraciales du XXième Siècle." *Cahiers Internationaux de Sociologie* 41 (1974).

Guillaumin, Colette. "The Idea of Race." In idem. *Racism, Sexism, Power, and Ideology.* New York: Routledge, 1995.

Guillermoprieto, Alma. *Samba.* New York: Random House, 1990.

Guimarães, Antonio Sérgio Alfredo. *Preconceito e Discriminação: Queixas de Ofensas e Tratamento Desigual dos Negros no Brasil.* Salvador da Bahia: Novos Toques/UFBA, 1998.

Guimarães, Antonio Sérgio Alfredo. *Racismo e Anti-Racismo no Brasil.* São Paulo: Editora 34, 1999.

Gurr, Ted Robert, et al. *Minorities at Risk: A Global View of Ethnopolitical Conflicts.* Washington, DC: U.S. Institute of Peace Press, 1993.

Gutierrez, Ramón A. *When Jesus Came, the Corn Mothers Went Away: Marriage, Sexuality, and Power in New Mexico, 1500–1846.* Stanford: Stanford University Press, 1991.

Gutman, Herbert G. "The Negro and the United Mine Workers of America: The Career and Letters of Richard L. Davis and Something of their Meaning, 1890–1900." In idem. *Work, Culture, and Society in Industrializing America: Essays in American Working-Class and Social History*. New York: Knopf, 1976a.

Gutman, Herbert G. *Work, Culture, and Society in Industrializing America: Essays in American Working-Class and Social History*. New York: Knopf, 1976b.

Guy, Jeff, and Thabane Motlatsi. "Technology, Ethnicity and Ideology: Basotho Miners and Shaft-Sinking on the South African Gold Mines." *Journal of Southern African Studies* 14, no. 2 (1988).

Guzman, Jessie Parkhurst. *1952 Negro Yearbook: An Annual Encyclopedia of the Negro*. Tuskegee: Tuskegee Institute, 1952.

Haar, Charles M. *Suburbs under Siege: Race, Space, and Audacious Judges*. Princeton: Princeton University Press, 1996.

Haberly, David T. *Three Sad Races: Racial Identity and National Consciousness in Brazilian Literature*. New York: Cambridge University Press, 1983.

Habermas, Jürgen. *The Structural Transformation of the Public Sphere: An Inquiry into a Category of Bourgeois Society*. Translated by Thomas Burger and Frederick Lawrence. Cambridge, MA: MIT Press, 1989.

Habermas, Jürgen. *Between Facts and Norms: Contributions to a Discourse Theory of Law and Democracy*. Translated by William Rehg. Cambridge, MA: MIT Press, 1996.

Habermas, Jürgen. *A Berlin Republic: Writings on Germany*. Translated by Steven Rendall. Lincoln: University of Nebraska Press, 1997.

Hall, Catherine. *White, Male, and Middle-Class: Explorations in Feminism and History*. New York: Routledge, 1992.

Hall, Stuart, et al. *Policing the Crisis: Mugging, the State, and Law and Order*. New York: Holmes & Meier, 1978.

Hall, Stuart. "Race, Articulation, and Societies Structured in Dominance." In Marion O'Callaghan, ed. *Sociological Theories: Race and Colonialism*. Paris: UNESCO, 1980.

Hall, Stuart. *The Hard Road to Renewal: Thatcherism and the Crisis of the Left*. New York: Verso, 1988.

Hall, Stuart. "New Ethnicities." In David Morley and Kuan-Hsing Chen, eds. *Stuart Hall: Critical Dialogues in Cultural Studies*. New York: Routledge, 1996a.

Hall, Stuart. "Gramsci's Relevance for the Study of Race and Ethnicity." In David Morley and Kuan-Hsing Chen, eds. *Stuart Hall: Critical Dialogues in Cultural Studies*. New York: Routledge, 1996b.

Hall, Stuart, and Martin Jacques, eds. *New Times: The Changing Face of Politics in the 1990s*. New York: Verso, 1990.

Haller, Mark H. *Eugenics: Hereditarian Attitudes in American Thought*. New Brunswick: Rutgers University Press, 1963.

Halliday, Fred. " 'Islamophobia' Reconsidered." *Ethnic and Racial Studies*. 22, no. 5 (September 1999).

Hammar, Tomas. *Democracy and the Nation State: Aliens, Denizens, and Citizens in a World of International Migration*. Brookfield, VT: Gower, 1990.

Hanchard, Michael. "Taking Exception: Race and the Limits of Liberal Nationalism in Cuba, Mexico, and Brazil." Paper presented at the Latin American Studies Association Annual Meetings, Los Angeles, 1992.

Hanchard, Michael. *Orpheus and Power: The Movimento Negro of Rio de Janeiro and São Paulo, Brazil, 1945–1988*. Princeton: Princeton University Press, 1994.

Hanchard, Michael. "Afro-Modernity: Temporality, Politics, and the African Diaspora," *Public Culture* 11, no. 1 (Summer 1999).

Hannaford, Ivan. *Race: The History of an Idea in the West*. Washington, DC: Woodrow Wilson Center Press/Baltimore: Johns Hopkins University Press, 1996.

Harris, Geoffrey. *The Dark Side of Europe: The Extreme Right Today*. Rev. ed. Edinburgh: University of Edinburgh Press, 1994.

Harris, Marvin. *Patterns of Race in the Americas*. New York: Walker, 1964.

Hartz, Louis. *The Founding of New Societies: Studies in the History of the United States, Latin America, South Africa, Canada, and Australia*. New York: Harcourt, Brace and World, 1964.

Hasenbalg, Carlos A. "Negros e Mestiços: Vida, Cotidiano, e Movimento." In Nelson do Valle Silva and Carlos A. Hasenbalg. *Relações Raciais no Brasil Contemporâneo*. Rio de Janeiro: Rio Fundo/IUPERJ, 1992.

Hasenbalg, Carlos A. *Discriminação e Desigualdades Raciais no Brasil*. Rio de Janeiro: Graal, 1979.

Hasenbalg, Carlos, A., and Nelson do Valle Silva. "Raça e Oportundidades Educacionais no Brasil." In Nelson do Valle Silva and Carlos A. Hasenbalg, *Relações Raciais no Brasil Contemporâneo*. Rio de Janeiro: Rio Fundo/IUPERJ, 1992.

Hegel, G. W. F. *The Phenomenology of Mind*. Translated by J. B. Baillie. New York: Harper & Row, 1967 [1807].

Helg, Aline. "Race in Argentina and Cuba, 1880–1930: Theory, Policies, and Popular Reaction." In Richard Graham, ed. *The Idea of Race in Latin America, 1870–1940*. Austin: University of Texas Press, 1990.

Helg, Aline. *Our Rightful Share: The Afro-Cuban Struggle for Equality, 1886–1912*. Chapel Hill: University of North Carolina Press, 1995.

Henri, Florette. *Black Migration: Movement North, 1900–1920*. Garden City: Anchor/Doubleday, 1975.

Henry, Charles P. *Culture and African American Politics*. Bloomington: Indiana University Press, 1990.

Herrnstein, Richard, and Charles Murray. *The Bell Curve: Intelligence and Class Structure in American Life*. New York: Free Press, 1994.

Hero, Rodney E. *Faces of Inequality: Social Diversity in American Politics*. New York: Oxford University Press, 1998.

Herskovits, Melville J. *The New World Negro*. Bloomington: Indiana University Press, 1966.

Heuman, Gad. *The Killing Time: The Morant Bay Rebellion in Jamaica*. Knoxville: University of Tennessee Press, 1994.

Higham, John. *Strangers in the Land: Patterns of American Nativism, 1860–1925*. New Brunswick: Rutgers University Press, 1994 [1955].

Hill, Christopher R. *Bantustans: The Fragmentation of South Africa*. New York: Oxford University Press, 1964.

Hill, Herbert. "Black Workers, Organized Labor, and Title VII of the 1964 Civil Rights Act." In Herbert Hill and James E. Jones Jr., eds. *Race in America: The Struggle for Equality*. Madison: University of Wisconsin Press, 1993.

Hill, Pascoe Grenfell. *Fifty Days on Board a Slave-Vessel: In the Mozambique Channel, April and May, 1843*. N.P.: Black Classic, 1996 [1844].

Hill, Ray. *The Other Face of Terror: Inside Europe's Neo-Nazi Network*. London: Grafton, 1988.

Hill, Robert A., and Barbara Bair, eds. *Marcus Garvey: Life and Lessons, A Centennial Companion to the Marcus Garvey and Universal Negro Improvement Association Papers*. Berkeley: University of California Press, 1987.

Hine, Darlene Clark. "Female Slave Resistance: The Economics of Sex." *Western Journal of Black Studies* 3 (1979).

Hing, Bill Ong. *Making and Remaking Asian America through Immigration Policy, 1850–1990*. Stanford: Stanford University Press, 1993.

Hiro, Dilip. *Black British White British: A History of Race Relations in Britain*. 2nd ed. London: Grafton, 1991.

Hirsch, Arnold R., and Joseph Logsdon, eds. *Creole New Orleans: Race and Americanization*. Baton Rouge: Louisiana State University Press, 1992.

Hirschfeld, Magnus. *Racism*. Translated and edited by Eden and Cedar Paul. London: V. Gollancz, 1938.

Hirschman, Albert O. *The Passions and the Interests: Political Arguments for Capitalism Before its Triumph*. Princeton: Princeton University Press, 1977.

Hirschman, Albert O. *Exit, Voice, and Loyalty: Responses to Decline in Firms, Organizations, and States*. Cambridge, MA: Harvard University Press, 1970.

Hirson, Baruch. *Year of Fire, Year of Ash: The Soweto Revolt, Roots of a Revolution?* London: Zed, 1979.

Hobsbawm, Eric J. *The Age of Revolution, 1789–1848.* New York: New American Library, 1962.

Hobsbawm, Eric J., and Terence Ranger, eds. *The Invention of Tradition.* New York: Cambridge University Press, 1983.

Hobsbawm, Eric J. *The Age of Empire, 1875–1914.* New York: Pantheon, 1987.

Hochschild, Adam. *King Leopold's Ghost: A Story of Greed, Terror, and Heroism in Colonial Africa.* Boston: Houghton Mifflin, 1998.

Hockenos, Paul. *Free to Hate: The Rise of the Right in Post-Communist Eastern Europe.* New York: Routledge, 1993.

Hodes, Martha. *White Women, Black Men: Illicit Sex in the Nineteenth Century South.* New Haven: Yale University Press, 1997.

Hodes, Martha, ed. *Sex, Love, Race: Crossing Boundaries in North American History.* New York: New York University Press, 1999.

Hoetink, Harmannus. *Caribbean Race Relations: A Study of Two Variants.* New York: Oxford University Press, 1971.

Hofstadter, Richard. *Social Darwinism in American Thought.* New York: G. Braziller, 1959 [1955].

Hollifield, James F. "Immigration and Republicanism in France: The Hidden Consensus." In Wayne A. Cornelius, Philip L. Martin, and James F. Hollifield, eds., *Controlling Immigration: A Global Perspective.* Stanford: Stanford University Press, 1994.

Holloway, Thomas H. "The Coffee *Colono* of São Paulo: Migration and Mobility." In Kenneth Duncan and Ian Rutledge, eds. *Land and Labour in Latin America: Essays on the Development of Agrarian Capitalism in the Nineteenth and Twentieth Centuries.* New York: Cambridge University Press, 1977a.

Holloway, Thomas H. "Immigration and Abolition: The Transition from Slave to Free Labor in the São Paulo Coffee Zone." In Dauril Alden and Warren Dean, eds. *Essays Concerning the Socioeconomic History of Brazil and Portuguese India.* Gainesville: University Press of Florida, 1977b.

Holloway, Thomas H. *Immigrants on the Land: Coffee and Society in São Paulo, 1886–1934.* Chapel Hill: University of North Carolina Press, 1980.

Holt, Thomas C. "Marking: Race, Race-making, and the Writing of History." *American Historical Review* 100, no.1 (February 1995).

Holt, Thomas C. *The Problem of Freedom: Race, Labor, and Politics in Jamaica and Britain, 1832–1938.* Baltimore: Johns Hopkins University Press, 1992.

Holt, Thomas C. " 'An Empire Over the Mind': Emancipation, Race, and Ideology in The British West Indies and the American South." In J. Morgan Kousser and James M. McPherson, eds. *Region, Race, and Reconstruction: Essays in Honor of C. Vann Woodward.* New York: Oxford University Press, 1982.

Horne, Gerald. *Black and Red: W. E. B. Du Bois and the Afro-American Response to the Cold War, 1944–1963.* Albany: State University of New York Press, 1986.

Horne, Gerald. *Black Liberation, Red Scare: Ben Davis and the Communist Party.* Newark: University of Delaware Press, 1994.

Hroch, Miroslav. "From National Movement to the Fully-Formed Nation: The Nation-Building Process in Europe." *New Left Review* 198 (March–April 1993).

Hroch, Miroslav. *Social Preconditions of National Revival in Europe: A Comparative Analysis of the Social Composition of the Patriotic Groups Among the Smaller European Nations.* Cambridge: Cambridge University Press, 1985.

Hu-Dehart, Evelyn, ed. *Across the Pacific: Asian Americans and Globalization.* Philadelphia: Temple University Press, 1999.

Huber, Joan, ed. *Macro-Micro Linkages in Sociology.* Newbury Park, CA: Sage, 1991.

Hunt, Nancy Rose. " 'Le Bebe en Brousse,' European Women, African Birth Spacing, and Colonial Intervention in Breast Feeding in the Belgian Congo." In Frederick Cooper and Ann Laura Stoler, eds. *Tensions of Empire: Colonial Cultures in a Bourgeois World.* Berkeley: University of California Press, 1997.

Hunter, Guy, ed. *Industrialisation and Race Relations: A Symposium.* New York: Oxford University Press, 1965.

Huntington, Samuel P. "The Coming Clash of Civilizations; Or, the West Against the Rest." *New York Times.* June 6, 1993.

Hunton, Addie Mae, and Kathryn M. Johnson. *Two Colored Women with The American Expeditionary Forces.* Brooklyn: Brooklyn-Eagle, 1920.

Husbands, Christopher. "Extreme Right-Wing Politics in Great Britain." *West European Politics* 11, no. 2 (April 1988).

Huttman, Elizabeth D. *Urban Housing Segregation of Minorities in Western Europe and the United States.* Durham: Duke University Press, 1991.

Ianni, Ottavio. *As Metamorfoses do Escravo: Apogeu e Crise da Escravatura no Brasil Meriodional.* 2nd ed. São Paulo: Hucitec, 1988.

IBGE (Instituto Brasileiro de Geografia e Estatística). Censo Demográfico 1991: *Características Gerais da População e Instrução.* Rio de Janeiro: IBGE, 1991.

Ichioka, Yuji. *The Issei: The World of the First Generation Japanese Immigrants, 1885–1924.* New York: Free Press, 1988.

Ignatiev, Noel. *How the Irish Became White.* New York: Routledge, 1995.

Inikori, Joseph, et al. *The Chaining of a Continent.* Paris: UNESCO, 1986.

Isaacman, Allen F. *Mozambique: The Africanization of a European Institution; The Zambesi Prazos, 1750–1902.* Madison: University of Wisconsin Press, 1972.

Jackson, John. "The 1994 Election: An Analysis." In F. H. Toase and E. J. Yorke, eds. *The New South Africa: Prospects for Domestic and International Security.* New York: St. Martin's, 1998.

Jackson, Walter. *Gunnar Myrdal and America's Conscience.* Chapel Hill: University of North Carolina Press, 1990.

James, C. L. R. *A History of Negro Revolt.* 3rd ed. London: Race Today, 1985 [1938].

James, C. L. R. *The C. L. R. James Reader.* Edited by Anna Grimshaw. Lexington, MA: Blackwell, 1992.

James, C. L. R. *The Black Jacobins: Toussaint L'Ouverture and the San Domingo Revolution.* 2nd ed. New York: Vintage, 1989 [1938].

James, Wilmot, ed. *The State of Apartheid.* Boulder: Lynne Rienner, 1987.

James, Wilmot, et al., eds. *Now That We Are Free: Coloured Communities in a Democratic South Africa.* Boulder: Lynne Rienner, 1996.

James, Winston. *Holding Aloft the Banner of Ethiopia: Caribbean Radicalism in Early Twentieth-Century America.* New York: Verso, 1998.

Jaynes, Gerald David. *Branches Without Roots: Genesis of the Black Working Class in the American South, 1862–1882.* New York: Oxford University Press, 1986.

Jeffers, Syd. "Is Race Really the Sign of the Times or Is Postmodernism Only Skin Deep?: Black Sections and the Problem of Authority." In Malcolm Cross and Michael Keith, eds. *Racism, the City, and the State.* New York: Routledge, 1993.

Jencks, Christopher, and Paul E. Peterson, eds. *The Urban Underclass.* Washington, DC: Brookings Institution, 1991.

Jeter, Jon. "Mbeki vs. AIDS Experts." *The Washington Post,* May 16, 2000.

Joas, Hans. *Pragmatism and Social Theory.* Translated by Jeremy Gaines, Raymond Meyer, and Steven Minner. Chicago: University of Chicago Press, 1993.

Joas, Hans. *The Creativity of Action.* Translated by Jeremy Gaines and Paul Keast. Chicago: University of Chicago Press, 1996.

Johnson, Ollie A. "Racial Representation and Brazilian Politics: Black Members of the National Congress, 1983–1999." *Journal of Interamerican Studies and World Affairs* 40. no. 4 (1998).

Johnson, R. W., and Lawrence Schlemmer, eds. *Launching Democracy in South Africa: The First Open Election, April 1994.* New Haven: Yale University Press, 1996.

Johnson, Sterling. *Black Globalism: The International Politics of a Non-State Nation.* Aldershot, UK: Ashgate, 1998.

Joly, Danièle, ed. *Scapegoats and Social Actors: The Exclusion and Integration of Minorities in Western and Eastern Europe.* New York: St. Martin's, 1998.

Jones, Gareth Stedman. *Languages of Class.* New York: Cambridge University Press, 1984.

Jones, Greta. *Social Darwinism and English Thought: The Interaction Between Biological and Social Theory.* Atlantic Highlands, NJ: Humanities Press, 1980.

Jones, Howard. *Union in Peril: The Crisis over British Intervention in the Civil War.* Chapel Hill: University of North Carolina Press, 1992.

Joppke, Christian. "Immigration Challenges the Nation-State." In idem, ed. *Challenge to the Nation-State: Immigration in Western Europe and the United States.* New York: Oxford University Press, 1998.

Kachani, Morris. "Igualdade Desigual." *Veja* (May 22, 1996).

Kafka, Franz. *The Penal Colony and Other Stories.* Translated by Willa and Edwin Muir. New York: Schocken, 1961.

Kairys, David. *With Liberty and Justice for Some: A Critique of the Conservative Supreme Court.* New York: New Press, 1993.

Karcher, Carolyn. *The First Woman in the Republic: A Cultural Biography of Lydia Maria Child.* Durham: Duke University Press, 1994.

Katz, Michael B., and Thomas J. Sugrue, eds. *W. E. B. Du Bois, Race, and the City: The Philadelphia Negro and Its Legacy.* Philadelphia: University of Pennsylvania Press, 1998.

Katznelson, Ira, Kim Geiger, and Daniel Kryder. "Limiting Liberalism: The Southern Veto in Congress, 1933–1950." *Political Science Quarterly* 108, no. 2 (Summer 1993).

Kay, Diana, and Robert Miles. *Refugees or Migrant Workers? European Migrant Workers in Britain 1946–1951.* London: Routledge, 1992.

Keck, Margaret E., and Kathryn Sikkink. *Activists Beyond Borders: Advocacy Networks in International Politics.* Ithaca: Cornell University Press, 1998.

Keith, Arthur. *Nationality and Race from an Anthropologist's Point of View.* Oxford: Oxford University Press, 1919.

Kelley, Robin D. G. "The Black Poor and the Politics of Opposition in a New South City, 1929–1970." In Michael B. Katz, ed. *The "Underclass" Debate: Views from History.* Princeton: Princeton University Press, 1993.

Kelley, Robin D. G. *Race Rebels: Culture, Politics, and the Black Working Class.* New York: Free Press, 1994.

Kent, R. K. "Palmares: An African State in Brazil." *Journal of African History* 6, no. 2 (1965).

Kevles, Daniel J. *In the Name of Eugenics: Genetics and the Uses of Human Heredity.* New York: Knopf, 1985.

Kevles, Daniel J., and Leroy Hood, eds. *The Code of Codes: Scientific and Social Issues in the Human Genome Project.* Cambridge, MA: Harvard University Press, 1992.

Keyssar, Alexander. *The Right to Vote: The Contested History of Democracy in the United States.* New York: Basic, 2000.

Kiernan, Victor G. *The Lords of Human Kind: Black Man, Yellow Man, and White Man in an Age of Empire.* Boston: Little, Brown, 1969.

Killens, John Oliver. *And Then We Heard the Thunder.* New York: Knopf, 1963.

Kilson, Martin L., and Robert I. Rotberg, eds. *The African Diaspora: Interpretive Essays.* Cambridge, MA: Harvard University Press, 1976.

Kinder, Donald R., and Lynn M. Sanders. *Divided by Color: Racial Politics and Democratic Ideals.* Chicago: University of Chicago Press, 1996.

King, Wilma. *Stolen Childhood: Slave Youth in Nineteenth-Century America.* Bloomington: Indiana University Press, 1995.

King, Martin Luther, Jr. *Letter from the Birmingham Jail.* San Francisco: Harper, 1994 [1963].

King, Mary. *Freedom Song: A Personal Story of the 1960s Civil Rights Movement.* New York: Morrow, 1987.

Kirp, David, John P. Dwyer, and Larry A. Rosenthal. *Our Town: Race, Housing, and the Soul of Suburbia.* New Brunswick: Rutgers University Press, 1996.

Kirschenman, Joleen, and Kathryn M. Neckerman. " 'We'd Love to Hire Them, But . . .': The Meaning of Race for Employers." In Christopher Jencks and Paul E. Peterson, eds. *The Urban Underclass.* Washington, DC: Brookings Institution, 1991.

Kitschelt, Herbert. *The Radical Right in Western Europe: A Comparative Analysis.* Ann Arbor: University of Michigan Press, 1997.

Klein, Herbert S. *African Slavery in Latin America and the Caribbean.* New York: Oxford University Press, 1986.

Klein, Martin A. *Islam and Imperialism in Senegal: Sine-Saloum, 1847–1914.* Stanford: Stanford University Press, 1968.

Klein, Martin A., ed. *Breaking the Chains: Slavery, Bondage, and Emancipation in Modern Africa and Asia.* Madison: University of Wisconsin Press, 1993.

Klug, Heinz. *Constituting Democracy: Law, Globalism and Political Reconstruction in South Africa.* New York: Cambridge University Press, 2000.

Knight, Franklin W. "The Haitian Revolution." *The American Historical Review* 104, no. 1 (February, 2000).

Knight, Ian. *The Anatomy of the Zulu Army: From Shaka to Cetshwayo 1818–1879.* Mechanicsburg, PA: Stackpole, 1995.

Knowles, Louis L., and Kenneth Prewitt, eds. *Institutional Racism in America.* Englewood Cliffs, NJ: Prentice-Hall, 1969.

Kolchin, Peter. *Unfree Labor: American Slavery and Russian Serfdom.* Cambridge, MA: Harvard University Press, 1987.

Krasner, Stephen D. *Structural Conflict: The Third World Against Global Liberalism.* Berkeley: University of California Press, 1985.

Kühl, Stefan. *The Nazi Connection: Eugenics, American Racism, and German National Socialism.* New York: Oxford University Press, 1994.

Kusmer, Kenneth, *A Ghetto Takes Shape: Black Cleveland, 1870–1930.* Urbana: University of Illinois Press, 1976.

Kutler, Stanley I. *The American Inquisition: Justice and Injustice in the Cold War.* New York: Hill and Wang, 1982.

Labor/Community Strategy Center. *A New Vision of Urban Transportation: The Bus Riders Union's Mass Transit Campaign.* Available from the Labor/Community Strategy Center, 3780 Wilshire Blvd., Suite 1200, Los Angeles, CA 90010, USA.

Laclau, Ernesto. "Toward a Theory of Populism." In idem, *Politics and Ideology in Marxist Theory: Capitalism, Fascism, Populism.* London: Verso, 1977a.

Laclau, Ernesto. "Toward a Theory of Populism." In idem, *Politics and Ideology in Marxist Theory: Capitalism, Fascism, Populism.* London: Verso, 1977.

Laclau, Ernesto, and Chantal Mouffe. "Post-Marxism Without Apologies." In Ernesto Laclau. *New Reflections on The Revolution of Our Time.* London: Verso, 1990.

Ladero Quesada, Miguel Angel, et al., eds. *La Reconquista y el Proceso de Diferenciación Política, 1035–1217.* Madrid: Espasa-Calpe, 1998.

Ladurie, Emmanuel Le Roy, Jean-Noël Barrandon, Bruno Collin, Maria Guerra, and Cécile Morrisson. "Sur les traces de l'argent du Potosi." *Annales: Économies, Sociétés, Civilisations* 45, no. 2 (March–April 1990).

Laitin, David D. *Hegemony and Culture: Politics and Religious Change among the Yoruba.* Chicago: University of Chicago Press, 1986.

Lambley, Peter. *The Psychology of Apartheid.* Athens: University of Georgia Press, 1980.

Lapouge, Georges Vacher de. *L'Aryen: Son Rôle Social.* Paris: Fontemoing, 1899.

Lasker, Bruno. *Human Bondage in Southeast Asia.* Westport, CT: Greenwood, 1972.

Law, Robin. *The Oyo Empire c.1600–c.1836: A West African Imperialism in the Era of the Atlantic Slave Trade.* Oxford: Clarendon, 1977.

Lawrence, Errol. "Just Plain Common Sense: The 'Roots' of Racism." In Centre for Contemporary Cultural Studies. *The Empire Strikes Back: Race in 70s Britain.* London: Hutchinson, 1982.

Layton-Henry, Zig. *The Politics of Immigration: Immigration, "Race," and "Race" Relations in Postwar Britain.* Cambridge, MA: Blackwell, 1992.

Lazerson, Joshua N. *Against the Tide: Whites in the Struggle Against Apartheid.* Boulder: Westview, 1994.

Lechner, Norbert. *Los Patios Interiores de la Democracia: Subjetividad y Política.* Santiago, Chile: FLACSO, 1990.

Lee, Everett, Ann Ratner Miller, Carol P. Brainerd, and Richard A. Easterlin. *Population Redis-*

tribution and Economic Growth in the United States, 1870–1950. Vol. 1, *Methodological Considerations and Reference Tables.* Prepared under the direction of Simon Kuznets and Dorothy Swaine. Philadelphia: American Philosophical Society, 1957.

Leisink, Peter, and Harry Coenen. *Work and Citizenship in the New Europe.* Brookfield, VT: Edward Elgar, 1993.

Leisink, Peter. "Work and Citizenship in Europe." In Maurice Roche and Rik van Berkel, eds. *European Citizenship and Social Exclusion.* Brookfield, VT: Ashgate, 1997.

Lelyveld, Joseph. *Move Your Shadow: South Africa, Black and White.* New York: Penguin, 1985.

Lemelle, Sidney J., and Robin D. G. Kelley, eds. *Imagining Home: Class, Culture, and Nationalism in the African Diaspora.* London; New York: Verso, 1994.

Lemert, Charles, and Esme Bhan, eds. *The Voice of Anna Julia Cooper: Including* A Voice from the South *and Other Important Essays, Papers, and Letters.* Lanham, MD: Rowman & Littlefield, 1998.

Leon-Portilla, Miguel, ed. *The Broken Spears: The Aztec Account of the Conquest of Mexico.* Boston: Beacon, 1992.

Lesher, Stephan. *George Wallace: American Populist.* Reading, MA: Addison-Wesley, 1995.

Lesser, Jeffrey. *Welcoming the Undesirables: Brazil and the Jewish Question.* Berkeley: University of California Press, 1995.

Lesser, Jeffrey. *Negotiating National Identity: Immigrants, Minorities, and the Struggle for Ethnicity in Brazil.* Durham: Duke University Press, 1999.

Lester, Julius, ed. *To Be a Slave.* 2nd ed. New York: Dell, 1978.

Levi-Strauss, Claude. *The Savage Mind.* Chicago: University of Chicago Press, 1966.

Levine, Robert M. *The Vargas Regime: The Critical Years, 1934–48.* New York: Columbia University Press, 1970.

Levine, Robert M. *The Vale of Tears: Revisiting the Canudos Massacre in Northeastern Brazil, 1893–1897.* Berkeley: University of California Press, 1992.

Lewis, Bernard. *Race and Color in Islam.* New York: Harper, 1970.

Lewis, Bernard. *Race and Slavery in the Middle East: An Historical Enquiry.* New York: Oxford University Press, 1990.

Lewis, David Levering. *Race to Fashoda: European Colonialism and African Resistance in the Scramble for Africa.* New York: Henry Holt, 1987.

Lewis, David Levering. *W. E. B. Du Bois: Biography of a Race, 1868–1919.* New York: Henry Holt, 1993.

Lewis, David Levering, ed. *W. E. B. Du Bois: A Reader.* New York: Henry Holt, 1995.

Lichtenstein, Nelson. "From Corporatism to Collective Bargaining: Organized Labor and the Eclipse of Social Democracy in the Postwar Era." In Steve Fraser and Gary Gerstle, eds. *The Rise and Fall of the New Deal Order, 1930–1980.* Princeton: Princeton University Press, 1989.

Lieberson, Stanley. *A Piece of the Pie: Black and White Immigrants Since 1880.* Berkeley: University of California Press, 1980.

Liebfried, Stephan, and Paul Pierson. "The Dynamics of Social Policy Integration." In idem, eds. *European Social Policy: Between Fragmentation and Integration.* Washington, DC: Brookings Institution, 1995.

Light, Ivan, and Edna Bonacich. *Immigrant Entrepreneurs: Koreans in Los Angeles, 1965–1982.* Berkeley: University of California Press, 1988.

Ling, Huping. *Surviving on the Gold Mountain: A History of Chinese American Women and Their Lives.* Albany: State University of New York Press, 1998.

Linke, Uli. *Blood and Nation: The European Aesthetics of Race.* Philadelphia: University of Pennsylvania Press, 1999.

Lipietz, Alain. "Post-Fordism and Democracy." In Ash Amin, ed. *Post-Fordism: A Reader.* Cambridge, MA: Blackwell, 1994.

Lipsitz, George. *Rainbow at Midnight: Labor and Culture in the 1940s.* Urbana: University of Illinois Press, 1994.

Lipsitz, George. " 'Frantic to Join . . . the Japanese Army': Beyond the Black-White Binary."

In idem, *The Possessive Investment in Whitneess: How White People Profit from Identity Politics*. Philadelphia: Temple University Press, 1998a.

Lipsitz, George. "'Swing Low, Sweet Cadillac': Antiblack Racism and White Identity." In idem, *The Possessive Investment in Whitness: How White People Profit from Identity Politics*. Philadelphia: Temple University Press, 1998b.

Lipsitz, George. *The Possessive Investment in Whiteness: How White People Profit from Identity Politics*. Philadelphia: Temple University Press, 1998c.

Lipsky, Michael. *Protest in City Politics: Rent Strikes, Housing, and the Power of the Poor*. Chicago: Rand McNally, 1969.

Litwack, Leon F. *Been in the Storm So Long: The Aftermath of Slavery*. New York: Random House, 1980.

Lott, Eric. *Love and Theft: Blackface Minstrelsy and the American Working Class*. New York: Oxford University Press, 1993.

Lovejoy, Paul E. "Background to Rebellion: The Origins of Muslim Slaves in Bahia." In Paul E. Lovejoy and Nicholas Rogers, eds. *Unfree Labour in the Development of the Atlantic World*. Ilford, Essex: Frank Cass, 1994.

Lovejoy, Paul E. *Transformations in Slavery: A History of Slavery in Africa*. New York: Cambridge University Press, 1983.

Lovejoy, Paul E., and Nicholas Rogers, eds. *Unfree Labour in the Development of the Atlantic World*. Ilford, Essex: Frank Cass, 1994.

Lovejoy, Paul E."The Impact of the Slave Trade on Africa." *Journal of African History* 30 (1989).

Lovejoy, Paul E., and Jan S. Hogendorn. *Slow Death for Slavery: The Course of Abolition in Northern Nigeria, 1897–1936*. New York: Cambridge University Press, 1993.

Lovell, Peggy A. "Race, Gender, and Development in Brazil." *Latin American Research Review* 29 (1994).

Lowe, Lisa. *Critical Terrains: French and British Orientalisms*. Ithaca: Cornell University Press, 1991.

Lowe, Lisa, and David Lloyd, eds. *The Politics of Culture in the Shadow of Capital*. Durham: Duke University Press, 1997.

Lucassen, Jan, and Rinus Penninx. *Newcomers: Immigrants and their Descendants in the Netherlands, 1550–1995*. Translated by Michael Wintle. Amsterdam: Het Spinhuis, 1997.

Lukács, John, ed. *"The European Revolution" [Tocqueville] and Correspondence with Gobineau*. Westport, CT: Greenwood, 1974.

Luna, Luiz. *Coronel Dono do Mundo: Síntese Histórica do Coronelismo no Brasil*. Rio de Janeiro: Livraria Editora Cátedra, 1983.

Lutz, Helma. "Migrant Women, Racism, and the Dutch Labour Market." In John Solomos and John Wrench, eds. *Racism and Migration in Western Europe*. Providence, RI: Berg, 1993.

Luxemburg, Rosa. *The Accumulation of Capital*. Translated by Agnes Schwarzschild. New Haven: Yale University Press, 1951 [1923].

Lyman, Stanford M. "Robert E. Park's Congo Papers: A Gothic Perpective on Capitalism and Imperialism." In idem. *Color, Culture, Civilization: Race and Minority Issues in American Society*. Urbana: University of Illinois Press, 1994.

Lynch, John. *The Spanish-American Revolutions, 1808–1826*. New York: Norton, 1986.

MacLean, Nancy. *Behind the Mask of Chivalry: The Making of the Second Ku Klux Klan*. New York: Oxford University Press, 1994.

Maio, Marcos Chor. *A História do Projeto UNESCO: Estudos Raciais e Ciencias Sociais no Brasil*. Ph.D. dissertation: Instituto Universitario de Pesquisas do Rio de Janeiro (IUPERJ), 1997.

Malcolm X, with Alex Haley. *The Autobiography of Malcolm X*. New York: Random House, 1965.

Malcolm X. "Message to the Grass Roots." In George Breitman, ed. *Malcolm X Speaks*. New York: Grove Weidenfeld, 1990.

Malcolm X. Speech in New York City, May 1, 1962. In James H. Cone, *Martin and Malcolm in America: A Dream or a Nightmare*. Maryknoll, NY: Orbis, 1991.

Malone, Ann Patton. *Sweet Chariot: Slave Family and Household Structure in Nineteenth-Century Louisiana.* Chapel Hill: University of North Carolina Press, 1992.

Mamdani, Mahmood. *Citizen and Subject: Contemporary Africa and the Legacy of Late Colonialism.* Princeton: Princeton University Press, 1996.

Mamdani, Mahmood. "Now Who Will Bell the Fat Black Cat?" *Electronic Mail and Guardian.* Johannesburg, October 17–23, 1997.

Manasse, Ernst Moritz. "Max Weber on Race." *Social Research* 14 (1947).

Manning, Patrick. *Slavery, Colonialism, and Economic Growth in Dahomey, 1640–1960.* New York: Cambridge University Press, 1982.

Manning, Patrick. *Slavery and African Life.* New York: Cambridge University Press, 1990.

Manning, Patrick. *Francophone Sub-Saharan Africa, 1880–1995.* 2nd ed. New York: Cambridge University Press, 1998.

Mannoni, Octave. *Prospero and Caliban: The Psychology of Colonization.* 2nd ed. New York: Praeger, 1964.

Marable, Manning. *African Nationalist: The Life of John Langaliblele Dube.* Ph.D. dissertation, University of Maryland, 1976.

Marable, Manning. *W. E. B. Du Bois: Black Radical Democrat.* Boston: Twayne/G. K. Hall, 1986.

Marcuse, Herbert. *Reason and Revolution: Hegel and the Rise of Social Theory.* 2nd ed. Boston: Beacon, 1960 [1941].

Mare, Gerhard. *Ethnicity and Politics in South Africa.* London: Zed, 1993.

Markoff, John. *Waves of Democracy: Social Movements and Political Change.* Thousand Oaks, CA: Pine Forge/Sage, 1996.

Marks, Carole. *Farewell—We're Good and Gone: The Great Black Migration.* Bloomington: Indiana University Press, 1989.

Marks, Jonathan. *Human Biodiversity: Genes, Race, and History.* New York: Aldine de Gruyter, 1995.

Marks, Shula. *The Ambiguities of Dependence in South Africa: Class, Nationalism, and the State in Twentieth Century Natal.* Baltimore: Johns Hopkins University Press, 1986.

Marley, Bob, and the Wailers. "War." *Rastaman Vibration.* Island Records, 1976.

Marshall, T. H. *Class, Citizenship, and Social Development.* Garden City, NY: Doubleday, 1964.

Martí, José. *Our America: Writings on Latin America and the Struggle for Cuban Independence.* Translated by Elinor Randall, with additional translations by Juan de Onis and Roslyn Held Foner. Edited by Philip S. Foner. New York: Monthly Review Press, 1977.

Martiniello, Marco, ed. *Migration, Citizenship and Ethno-National Identities in the European Union.* Brookfield, VT: Ashgate, 1995.

Marx, Anthony W. *Making Race and Nation: A Comparison of the United States, South Africa, and Brazil.* New York: Cambridge University Press, 1998.

Marx, Anthony W. *Lessons of Struggle: South African Internal Opposition, 1960–1990.* New York: Oxford University Press, 1992.

Marx, Karl. *Capital.* Edited by Frederick Engels. New York: International Publishers, 1965–67.

Mason, Tim. "Open Questions on Fascism." In Raphael Samuel, ed. *People's History and Socialist Theory.* London: Routledge, 1981.

Massey, Douglas S., and Jorge Duran. *Return to Aztlán: The Social Process of International Migration from Western Mexico.* Berkeley: University of California Press, 1987.

Massey, Douglas S., and Nancy A. Denton. *American Apartheid.* Cambridge, MA: Harvard University Press, 1993.

Massey, Douglas S., et al. *Worlds in Motion: Understanding International Migration at the End of the Millennium.* New York: Oxford University Press, 1998.

Massie, Robert K. *Loosing the Bonds: The United States and South Africa in the Apartheid Years.* New York: Doubleday, 1997.

Matthaei, Julie, and Teresa Amott. *Race, Gender, Work: A Multicultural Economic History of Women in the United States.* Boston: South End, 1990.

Mayer, Ann Elizabeth, *Islam and Human Rights: Tradition and Politics.* 3rd ed. Boulder: Westview, 1999.

Maynard, Micheline. *The Global Manufacturing Vanguard: New Rules from the Industry Elite.* New York: Wiley, 1998.

Mazumdar, Pauline M. H. *Eugenics, Human Genetics, and Human Failings: The Eugenics Society, Its Sources and Its Critics in Britain.* New York: Routledge, 1992.

McAdam, Doug, et al., eds. *Comparative Perspectives on Social Movements: Political Opportunities, Mobilizing Structures, and Cultural Framings.* New York: Cambridge University Press, 1996.

McAdam, Doug. *Political Process and the Development of Black Insurgency, 1930–1970.* Chicago: University of Chicago Press, 1982.

McClintock, Anne. *Imperial Leather: Race, Gender, and Sexuality in the Colonial Conquest.* New York: Routledge, 1995.

McClintock, Anne, et al., eds. *Dangerous Liaisons: Gender, Nation, and Postcolonial Perspectives.* Minneapolis: University of Minnesota Press, 1997.

McFeely, William S. *Frederick Douglass.* New York: Norton, 1991.

McMillen, Neil R. *Dark Journey: Black Mississippians in the Age of Jim Crow.* Urbana: University of Illinois Press, 1989.

Mead, George Herbert. *Philosophy of the Act.* Chicago: University of Chicago Press, 1938.

Meillassoux, Claude. *The Anthropology of Slavery: The Womb of Iron and Gold.* Translated by Alide Dasnois. Chicago: University of Chicago Press, 1991.

Mellon, James, ed. *Bullwhip Days: The Slaves Remember.* New York: Weidenfeld & Nicolson, 1988.

Melucci, Alberto. *Nomads of the Present: Social Movements and Individual Needs in Contemporary Society.* Philadelphia: Temple University Press, 1989.

Mendes, Candido. *A Inconfidência Brasileira: A Nova Cidadania Interpela a Constituinte.* Rio de Janeiro: Forense-Universitária, 1986.

Mershon, Sherie, and Steven L. Schlossman. *Foxholes and Color Lines: Desegregating the U.S. Armed Forces.* Baltimore: Johns Hopkins University Press, 1998.

Michel, Marc. *L'Appel à l'Afrique: Contributions et Réactions à l'effort de Guerre en A.O.F. (1914–1919).* Paris: Publications de la Sorbonne, 1982.

Midgley, Clare. *Women Against Slavery: The British Campaign, 1780–1870.* London: Routledge, 1992.

Miers, Suzanne, and Igor Kopytoff, eds. *Slavery in Africa: Historical and Anthropological Perspectives.* Madison: University of Wisconsin Press, 1977.

Miles, Robert. *Racism.* London: Routledge, 1989.

Miles, Robert. *Racism after "Race Relations."* London: Routledge, 1993.

Mill, John Stuart. *Principles of Political Economy.* Edited by Jonathan Riley. New York: Oxford University Press, 1994 [1848].

Miller, Joseph C. *Way of Death: Merchant Capitalism and the Angolan Slave Trade, 1730–1830.* Madison: University of Wisconsin Press, 1988.

Miller, Kerby A. *Emigrants and Exiles: Ireland and the Irish Exodus to North America.* New York: Oxford University Press, 1985.

Mills, Kenneth. *Idolatry and Its Enemies: Colonial Andean Religion and Extirpation, 1640–1750.* Princeton: Princeton University Press, 1997.

Mink, Gwendolyn. *Old Labor and New Immigrants in American Political Development.* Ithaca: Cornell University Press, 1986.

Mintz, Max M. *Seeds of Empire: The American Revolutionary Conquest of the Iroquois.* New York: New York University Press, 1999.

Mintz, Sidney W. *Sweetness and Power: The Place of Sugar in Modern History.* New York: Viking, 1985.

Mitchell, Michael. *Racial Consciousness and the Political Attitudes and Behavior of Blacks in São Paulo, Brazil.* Ph.D. dissertation, Indiana University, 1977.

Mitchell, Michael. "Blacks and the Abertura Democrática." In Pierre-Michel Fontaine, ed. *Race, Class, and Power in Brazil.* Los Angeles: CAAS/UCLA, 1985.

Mitchell, Michael. "Miguel Reale and the Impact of Conservative Modernization on Brazilian Race Relations." In Michael Hanchard, ed. *Racial Politics in Contemporary Brazil.* Durham: Duke University Press, 1999.

Model, Suzanne. "Ethnic Inequality in England: An Analysis Based on the 1991 Census." *Ethnic and Racial Studies* 22, no. 6 (November 1999).

Modood Tariq, and Pnina Werbner, eds. *Debating Cultural Hybridity: Multi-Cultural Identities and the Politics of Anti-Racism.* London: Zed, 1997.

Montagu, Ashley. *Man's Most Dangerous Myth: The Fallacy of Race.* 6th ed. Walnut Creek, CA: AltaMira/Sage, 1997 [1942].

Montagu, Ashley. *Statement on Race: An Extended Discussion in Plain Language of the UNESCO Statement by Experts on Race Problems.* 2nd ed. New York: Schuman, 1952.

Montejano, David. *Anglos and Mexicans in the Making of Texas, 1836–1986.* Austin: University of Texas Press, 1987.

Moodie, T. Dunbar. *The Rise of Afrikanerdom: Power, Apartheid, and the Afrikaner Civil Religion.* Berkeley: University of California Press, 1975.

Moodie, T. Dunbar, and Vivienne Ndatshe, *Going for Gold: Men, Mines and Migration.* Berkeley: University of California Press, 1994.

Moore, Barrington, Jr. *Social Origins of Dictatorship and Democracy: Lord and Peasant in the Making of the Modern World.* Boston: Beacon, 1966.

Moore, Barrington, Jr. *Injustice: The Social Bases of Obedience and Revolt.* White Plains: M. E. Sharpe, 1978.

Moreno Fraginals, Manuel. *The Sugarmill: The Socioeconomic Complex of Sugar in Cuba, 1760–1860.* Translated by Cedric Belfrage. New York: Monthly Review Press, 1976.

Morgan, Edmund S. *Inventing the People: The Rise of Popular Sovereignty in England and America.* New York: Norton, 1988.

Morgan, Edmund S. *American Slavery, American Freedom: The Ordeal of Colonial Virginia.* 2nd ed. New York: Norton, 1995.

Mörner, Magnus. *Race Relations in the History of Latin America.* Boston: Little, Brown, 1967.

Morris, Aldon D. *The Origins of the Civil Rights Movement: Black Communities Organizing for Change.* New York: Free Press, 1984.

Morris, Aldon, and Carol McClurg Mueller, eds. *Frontiers in Social Movement Theory.* New Haven: Yale University Press, 1992.

Moses, Wilson Jeremiah. *The Golden Age of Black Nationalism, 1850–1925.* New York: Oxford University Press, 1978.

Moses, Wilson J., ed. *Classical Black Nationalism: From the American Revolution to Marcus Garvey.* New York: New York University Press, 1996.

Mosse, George L. *Toward the Final Solution: A History of European Racism.* New York: Howard Fertig, 1978.

Mosse, George L. *Nationalism and Sexuality: Middle-Class Morality and Sexual Norms in Modern Europe.* Madison: University of Wisconsin Press, 1985.

Moura, Clovis. *O Preconceito de Côr na Literatura de Cordel: Tentativa de Analise Sociológica.* São Paulo: Resenha Universitária, 1976.

Moura, Clovis. *Rebeliões da Senzala: Quilombos, Insurreiçoes, Guerrilhas.* Rio de Janeiro: Conquista, 1972.

Moura, Clovis. *Brasil: As Raizes do Protesto Negro.* São Paulo: Global, 1983.

Moura, Clovis. *As Injustiças de Clio: O Negro Na Historiografia Brasileira.* Belo Horizonte: Oficina de Livros, 1990.

Moura, Clovis. *Sociologia do Negro Brasileiro.* São Paulo: Atica, 1988.

Mudimbe, V. Y. *The Idea of Africa.* Bloomington: Indiana University Press, 1994.

Mullin, Michael. *Africa in America: Slave Acculturation and Resistance in the American South and the British Caribbean, 1736–1831.* Urbana: University of Illinois Press, 1993.

Mulroy, Kevin. *Freedom on the Border: The Seminole Maroons in Florida, the Indian Territory, Coahuila, and Texas.* College Station: Texas A & M University Press, 1993.

Murray, Martin. *South Africa: Time of Agony, Time of Destiny: The Upsurge of Popular Protest.* London: Verso, 1987.

Murray, Martin. *Revolution Deferred: The Painful Birth of Post-Apartheid South Africa.* London: Verso, 1994.

Myrdal, Gunnar. *An American Dilemma: The Negro Problem and Modern Democracy.* New York: Harper & Row, 1962 [1944].

Myrdal, Gunnar. *Economic Theory and Under-Developed Regions.* London: Duckworth, 1963.

Naison, Mark. *Communists in Harlem during the Depression.* New York: Grove, 1985.

Nascimento, Abdias do. "Quilombismo: The African-Brazilian Road to Socialism." In Molefi Kete Asante and Kariamu Welsh Asante, eds. *African Culture: The Rhythms of Unity.* Westport, CT: Greenwood, 1985.

Nascimento, Abdias do. *Mixture or Massacre? Essays in the Genocide of a Black People.* New York: Afrodiaspora, 1979.

Nascimento, Maria Ercilia do. *A Estrategia da Desigualdade: O Movimento Negro dos Anos 70.* Master's thesis: PUC-São Paulo, 1989.

Nash, Gary B. "The Hidden History of Mestizo America." In Martha Hodes, ed. *Sex, Love, Race: Crossing Boundaries in North American History.* New York: New York University Press, 1999.

National Security Council Interdepartmental Group for Africa. *Study in Response to National Security Study Memorandum 39: Southern Africa.* AF/NSC—IG 69. August 15, 1969.

Needell, Jeffrey D. "Identity, Race, Gender, and Modernity in the Origins of Gilberto Freyre's *Oeuvre.*" *American Historical Review* 100, no. 1 (February 1995).

Neocleous, Mark. *Fascism.* Minneapolis: University of Minnesota Press, 1997.

Netanyahu, Benzion. *The Origins of the Inquisition in Fifteenth Century Spain.* New York: Random House, 1995.

Newitt, Malyn. *A History of Mozambique.* Bloomington: Indiana University Press, 1995.

Ng, Franklin, ed. *Asian American Women and Gender.* New York: Garland, 1998.

Nicholls, David. *From Dessalines to Duvalier: Race, Colour, and National Independence in Haiti.* Rev. ed. New Brunswick: Rutgers University Press, 1996.

Nixon, Rob. *Homelands, Harlem, and Hollywood: South African Culture and the World Beyond.* New York: Routledge, 1994.

Nobles, Melissa. *Shades of Citizenship: Race and the Census in Modern Politics.* Stanford: Stanford University Press, 2000.

Nogueira, Oracy. "Preconceito Racial de Marca e Preconceito Racial de Origem: Sugestão de um Quadro de Referencia para a Interpretação do Materia Sobre Relações Raciais no Brasil." In idem. *Tanto Preto Como Branco: Estudos de Relações Raciais.* São Paulo: Queiroz, 1985 [1954].

Noiriel, Gérard. *The French Melting Pot: Immigration, Citizenship, and National Identity.* Translated by Geoffroy de Laforcade. Minneapolis: University of Minnesota Press, 1996.

Oates, Stephen B. *To Purge this Land with Blood: A Biography of John Brown.* 2nd ed. Amherst: University of Massachusetts Press, 1984.

O'Callaghan, Marion, ed. *Sociological Theories: Race and Colonialism.* Paris: UNESCO, 1980.

OECD. *Trends in International Migration: Annual Report 1996.* Paris: OECD, 1997.

O'Gorman, Edmundo. *The Invention of America: An Inquiry into the Historical Nature of the New World and the Meaning of its History.* Bloomington: Indiana University Press, 1961.

Okihiro, Gary Y. *Cane Fires: The Anti-Japanese Movement in Hawaii, 1865–1945.* Philadelphia: Temple University Press, 1991.

Okpewho, Isidore, Carole Boyce Davies, and Ali Mazrui, eds. *The African Diaspora: African Origins and New World Identities.* Bloomington: Indiana University Press, 1999.

Oliveira, Maria Ines Cortes de. *O Liberto: O Seu Mundo e os Outros; Salvador, 1790–1890.* Salvador: Corrupio, 1988.

Oliver, Melvin L., and Thomas M. Shapiro. *Black Wealth/White Wealth: A New Perspective on Racial Inequality.* New York: Routledge, 1995.

O'Meara, Dan. *Volkskapitalisme: Class, Capital, and Ideology in the Development of Afrikaner Nationalism, 1934–1948.* New York: Cambridge University Press, 1983.

Omi, Michael, and Howard Winant. *Racial Formation in the United States: From the 1960s to the 1990s.* Rev. ed. New York: Routledge, 1994.

Ong, Paul. "Chinese Labor in Early San Francisco: Racial Segmentation and Industrial Expansion." *Amerasia* 8, no. 1 (1981).

Orfield, Gary, Susan E. Eaton, and Elaine R. Jones. *Dismantling Desegregation: The Quiet Reversal of Brown v. Board of Education.* New York: New Press, 1997.

Oubre, Claude F. *Forty Acres and a Mule: The Freedmen's Bureau and Black Land Ownership*. Baton Rouge: Louisiana State University Press, 1978.

Painter, Nell Irvin. *The Narrative of Hosea Hudson: His Life as a Negro Communist in the South*. Cambridge, MA: Harvard University Press, 1979.

Palmer, R. R. *The Age of the Democratic Revolution: A Political History of Europe and America, 1760–1800*. Princeton: Princeton University Press, 1959.

Pang, Eul-Soo. *Bahia in the First Brazilian Republic: Politics of Coronelismo*. Gainesville: University Press of Florida, 1978.

Parenti, Christian. *Lockdown America: Police and Prisons in the Age of Crisis*. New York: Verso, 1999.

Park, Robert E. *Race and Culture*. Glencoe, IL.: Free Press, 1950.

Park, Robert E., Ernest W. Burgess, and Roderick D. McKenzie. *The City*. Chicago: University of Chicago Press, 1967.

Parsons, Neil. *A New History of Southern Africa*. 2nd ed. London: Macmillan, 1993.

Pasquino, Pasquale. *Sieyes et l'invention de la constitution en France*. Paris: O. Jacob, 1998.

Pateman, Carole. *The Sexual Contract*. Stanford: Stanford University Press, 1998.

Patterson, Orlando. "Slavery and Slave Revolts: A Sociohistorical Analysis of the First Maroon War, 1665–1740." *Social and Economic Studies* 19 (1970).

Patterson, Orlando. *Slavery and Social Death*. Cambridge, MA: Harvard University Press, 1982.

Patterson, Thomas C. *Inventing Western Civilization*. New York: Monthly Review Press, 1997.

Paul, Kathleen. *Whitewashing Britain: Race and Citizenship in the Postwar Era*. Ithaca: Cornell University Press, 1997.

Payne, Charles M. *I've Got the Light of Freedom: The Organizing Tradition and the Mississippi Freedom Struggle*. Berkeley: University of California Press, 1995.

Peery, Nelson. *Black Fire: The Making of an American Revolutionary*. New York: New Press, 1995.

Perea, Juan F., ed. *Immigrants Out!: The New Nativism and the Anti-Immigrant Impulse in the United States*. New York: New York University Press, 1997.

Perinbanayagam, R. S. *Signifying Acts: Structure and Meaning in Everyday Life*. Carbondale: Southern Illinois University Press, 1985.

Perlman, Selig. *The History of Trade Unionism in the United States*. New York: Augustus Kelley, 1950.

Phillips, Kevin. *The Emerging Republican Majority*. New York: Anchor, 1970.

Phizacklea, Annie, ed. *One Way Ticket: Migration and Female Labour*. London: Routledge and Kegan Paul, 1983.

Phizacklea, Annie. *Unpacking the Fashion Industry: Gender, Racism, and Class in Production*. New York: Routledge, 1990.

Phoenix, Ann. "Representing New Identities: 'Whiteness' as Contested Identity in Young People's Accounts." In Khalid Koser and Helma Lutz, eds. *The New Migration in Europe: Social Constructions and Social Realities*. New York: St. Martin's, 1998.

Pinto, Regina. *O Movimento Negro em São Paulo: Luta e Identidade*. Master's thesis, Universidade de São Paulo, 1993.

Pipes, Daniel. *Slave Soldiers and Islam*. New Haven: Yale University Press, 1981.

Pitt, Leonard. *The Decline of the Californios: A Social History of the Spanish-Speaking Californians, 1846–1890*. Berkeley: University of California Press, 1970.

Pityana, Barney, et al., eds. *Bounds of Possibility: The Legacy of Steve Biko & Black Consciousness*. London: Zed, 1991.

Piven, Frances Fox, and Richard A. Cloward. *Poor People's Movements: Why They Succeed, How They Fail*. New York: Vintage, 1977.

Platt, Anthony M. *The Child Savers: The Invention of Delinquency*. Chicago: University of Chicago Press, 1969.

Platt, D. C. M. *Latin America and British Trade, 1806–1914*. New York: Barnes & Noble, 1973.

Plummer, Brenda Gayle. *Rising Wind: Black Americans and U.S. Foreign Affairs, 1935–1960*. Chapel Hill: University of North Carolina Press, 1996.

Pogrund, Benjamin. *Sobukwe and Apartheid*. New Brunswick: Rutgers University Press, 1991.

Polanyi, Karl. *Dahomey and the Slave Trade: An Analysis of an Archaic Economy.* Seattle: University of Washington Press, 1966.

Polanyi, Karl. *The Great Transformation.* Boston: Beacon, 1980 [1944].

Polanyi, Karl. "The Economy as Instituted Process." In Karl Polanyi, Conrad M. Arensberg, and Harry W. Pearson, eds., *Trade and Market in the Early Empires: Economies in History and Theory.* New York: Free Press, 1957.

Poliakov, Léon. *The Aryan Myth: A History of Racist and Nationalist Ideas in Europe.* Translated by Edmund Howard. New York: New American Library, 1977.

Policar, Alain. "Racism and its Mirror Image." *Telos* 83 (Spring 1990).

Portes, Alejandro, and John Walton. *Labor, Class, and the International System.* New York: Academic, 1981.

Portes, Alejandro, ed. *The Economic Sociology of Immigration.* New York: Russell Sage Foundation, 1995.

Posel, Deborah. *The Making of Apartheid, 1948–1961: Conflict and Compromise.* New York: Oxford University Press, 1991.

Posel, Deborah. "The Epistemology and Politics of Racial Classification in Apartheid South Africa." Paper presented to the African Studies Association of Australia and the Pacific. Perth, Australia, 1999.

President's Initiative on Race Advisory Council (John Hope Franklin, Chair). *One America in the 21st Century: Forging a New Future.* Washington, DC: U.S. Government Printing Office, 1998.

Price, Richard. *Alabi's World.* Baltimore: Johns Hopkins University Press, 1990.

Price, Richard. *First-Time: The Historical Vision of an Afro-American People.* Baltimore: Johns Hopkins University Press, 1983.

Price, Richard. *Maroon Societies: Rebel Slave Communities in the Americas.* 3rd ed. Baltimore: Johns Hopkins University Press, 1996.

Quadagno, Jill S. *The Color of Welfare: How Racism Undermined the War on Poverty.* New York: Oxford University Press, 1994.

Race and Class 40, nos. 2–3 (October 1998/March 1999). Special Issue: "The Threat of Globalism."

Ramphele, Mamphela. *A Bed Called Home: Life in the Migrant Labour Hostels of Cape Town.* Athens: Ohio University Press, 1993.

Ramphele, Mamphela. *The Affirmative Action Book: Towards an Equity Environment.* Cape Town: IDASA Public Information Centre, 1995.

Ranger, Terence O. *Revolt in Southern Rhodesia, 1896–97: A Study in African Resistance.* Evanston: Northwestern University Press, 1967.

Ranger, Terence O. "Religious Movements and Politics in Sub-Saharan Africa." *African Studies Review* 29 (March 1986).

Rath, Jan. "The Ideological Representation of Migrant Workers in Europe: A Matter of Racialisation?" In John Solomos and John Wrench, eds. *Racism and Migration in Western Europe.* Providence, RI: Berg, 1993.

Rathbone, Richard. "World War I and Africa: Introduction." *Journal of African History* 19, no.1 (1978).

Rawick, George P. *From Sundown to Sunup: The Making of the Black Community.* Westport, CT: Greenwood, 1972a.

Rawick, George P., ed. *The American Slave: A Composite Autobiography.* Westport, CT: Greenwood, 1972b.

Rawley, James A. *The Transatlantic Slave Trade: A History.* New York: Norton, 1981.

Rawls, John. *Political Liberalism.* New York: Columbia University Press, 1993.

Reader, John. *Africa: A Biography of a Continent.* New York: Vintage, 1999.

Reckford, Mary. "The Jamaican Slave Rebellion of 1831." *Past and Present* 40 (1968).

Rediker, Marcus Buford. *Between the Devil and the Deep Blue Sea: Merchant Seamen, Pirates, and the Anglo-American Maritime World, 1700–1750.* Cambridge; New York: Cambridge University Press, 1987.

Redmayne, Alison. "Mkwawa and the Hehe Wars." *Journal of African History* 3 (1968).

Reich, Michael. *Racial Inequality: A Political-Economic Analysis.* Princeton: Princeton University Press, 1981.

Reichl, Christopher Albert. *Japanese Newcomers in Brazil: A Social Model of Migration.* Ph.D. dissertation, University of Iowa, 1988.

Reichmann, Rebecca, ed. *Race in Contemporary Brazil: From Indifference to Inequality.* University Park: Pennsylvania State University Press, 1999.

Reid, Anthony. *The Indonesian National Revolution, 1945–1950.* Westport, CT: Greenwood, 1974.

Reid, Ira De A. *Negro Membership in American Labor Unions.* New York: Negro University Press, 1930.

Reis, João José. *Slave Rebellion in Brazil: The Muslim Uprising of 1835 in Bahia.* Baltimore: Johns Hopkins University Press, 1993.

Review 20, nos. 3–4 (Summer/Fall 1997). Special Issue: "Nomothetic vs. Idiographic Disciplines: A False Dilemma?"

Rex, John. "The Theory of Race Relations—A Weberian Approach." In Marion O'Callaghan, ed. *Sociological Theories: Race and Colonialism.* Paris: UNESCO, 1980.

Rhomberg, Christopher. *Social Movements in a Fragmented Society: Ethnic, Class, and Racial Mobilization in Oakland, California, 1920–1970.* Ph.D. dissertation, University of California, Berkeley, 1997.

Ribeiro, Darcy, et al. *Mestiço é que é Bom!* Rio de Janeiro: Revan, 1996.

Richards, Anna Marie. *New Right Discourse on Race and Sexuality: Britain 1968–1990.* New York: Cambridge University Press, 1994.

Richards, David A. J. *Italian Americans: The Racializing of an Ethnic Identity.* New York: New York University Press, 1998.

Robertson, Claire C., and Martin A. Klein, eds. *Women and Slavery in Africa.* Madison: University of Wisconsin Press, 1983.

Robinson, Cedric J. *Black Marxism: The Making of the Black Radical Tradition.* London: Zed, 1983.

Robinson, Randall. *The Debt: What America Owes to Blacks.* New York: Dutton, 2000.

Roche, Maurice, and Rik van Berkel, eds. *European Citizenship and Social Exclusion.* Brookfield, VT: Ashgate, 1997.

Rodney, Walter. *How Europe Underdeveloped Africa.* Washington, DC: Howard University Press, 1981a.

Rodney, Walter. *A History of the Guyanese Working People, 1881–1905.* Baltimore: Johns Hopkins University Press, 1981b.

Rodney, Walter. "African Slavery and Other Forms of Social Oppression on the Upper Guinea Coast in the Context of the African Slave Trade." *Journal of African History* 7 (1966).

Rodrigues, Raimundo Nina. *Os Africanos no Brasil.* 3rd ed. São Paulo: Nacional, 1945.

Rodrigues da Silva, Carlos Benedito. "Black Soul: Aglutinaçao Espontanea ou Identidade Etnica: Uma Contribuição ao Estudo das Manifestações Culturais no Meio Negro." Paper presented at the Fourth Annual Meeting of the Associação Nacional de Posgraduação e Pesquisas em Ciencias Sociais (ANPOCS), 1980.

Roediger, David R. *The Wages of Whiteness: Race and the Making of the American Working Class.* New York: Verso, 1991.

Roediger, David, ed. *Black on White: Black Writers on What It Means to Be White.* New York: Schocken, 1998.

Rogers, Joel A. *Sex and Race: Negro-Caucasian Mixing in All Ages and All Lands.* 9th ed., 3 vols. New York: Helga M. Rogers, 1967–72.

Rogin, Michael Paul. *Fathers and Children: Andrew Jackson and the Subjugation of the American Indian.* New York: Knopf, 1975.

Rogin, Michael. *Blackface, White Noise: Jewish Immigrants in the Hollywood Melting Pot.* Berkeley: University of California Press, 1996.

Rolston, Bill. "Are the Irish Black?" *Race and Class* 40, nos. 5–6 (1999).

Rooy, Piet van. "Of Monkeys, Blacks, and Proles: Ernst Haeckel's Theory of Recapitulation."

In Jan Breman, et al., eds., *Imperial Monkey Business: Racial Supremacy in Social Darwinist Theory and Practice.* Amsterdam: VU Press, 1990.

Rosen, Hannah. " 'Not That Sort of Woman': Race, Gender, and Sexual Violence During the Memphis Riot of 1866." In Martha Hodes, ed. *Sex, Love, Race: Crossing Boundaries in North American History.* New York: New York University Press, 1999.

Rosenberg, Daniel. *New Orleans Dockworkers: Race, Labor, and Unionism, 1892–1923.* Albany: State University of New York Press, 1988.

Ross, Robert. "Emancipations and the Economy of the Cape Colony." In Michael Twaddle, ed. *The Wages of Slavery: From Chattel Slavery to Wage Labour in Africa, the Caribbean, and England.* Portland, OR: Frank Cass, 1993.

Rostron, Bryan. "They Cling On, By Their Fingernails." *New Statesman* (UK), December 18, 2000.

Rout, Leslie B., Jr. *The African Experience in Spanish America, 1502 to the Present Day.* New York: Cambridge University Press, 1976.

Rudwick, Elliot. *Race Riot at East St. Louis July 2, 1917.* Carbondale: Southern Illinois University Press, 1964.

Rueschemeyer, Dietrich, and Theda Skocpol, eds. *States, Social Knowledge, and the Origins of Modern Social Policies.* Princeton: Princeton University Press, 1996.

Russell-Wood, A. J. R. *The Black Man in Slavery and Freedom in Colonial Brazil.* New York: St. Martin's, 1982.

Russell-Wood, A. J. R. *The Portuguese Empire, 1415–1808: A World on the Move.* Baltimore: Johns Hopkins University Press, 1998.

Russell-Wood, A. J. R., ed. *From Colony to Nation: Essays in the Independence of Brazil.* Baltimore: Johns Hopkins University Press, 1975.

Ryan, Allan A. *Klaus Barbie and the United States Government.* Frederick, MD: University Press of America, 1984.

Sachs, Albie. *Running to Maputo.* New York: HarperCollins, 1990.

Sacks, Benjamin. *South Africa: An Imperial Dilemma; Non-Europeans and the British Nation, 1902–1914.* Albuquerque: University of New Mexico Press, 1967.

Said, Edward. *Culture and Imperialism.* New York: Knopf, 1993.

Saito, Hiroshi, and Takashi Maeyama. *Assimilação e Integração dos Japoneses no Brasil.* Petrópolis: Vozes, 1973.

Sakhrobanek, Siriphon, Nattaya Boonpakdi, and Chutima Janthakeero. *The Traffic in Women: Human Realities of the International Sex Trade.* London: Zed, 1997.

Sampson, Anthony. *Mandela: The Authorized Biography.* New York: Knopf, 1999.

Sandmeyer, Elmer Clarence, and Roger Daniels. *The Anti-Chinese Movement in California.* Urbana: University of Illinois Press, 1991.

Sanger, Margaret, *The Pivot of Civilization.* London: Jonathan Cape, 1923.

Santos, Ivanir dos. "Blacks and Political Power." In Michael Hanchard, ed. *Racial Politics in Contemporary Brazil.* Durham: Duke University Press, 1999.

Santos, Joel Rufino dos. *O Que é Racismo?* Sao Paulo: Brasiliense, 1984.

Santos, Joel Rufino dos. "A Luta Organizada Contra o Racismo." In *Atrás do Muro da Noite.* Brasilia: Fundaçao Cultural Palmares, 1993.

Santos, Thereza. "My Conscience, My Struggle." In Michael Hanchard, ed. *Racial Politics in Contemporary Brazil.* Durham: Duke University Press, 1999.

Santos Souza, Neusa. *Tornar-Se Negro.* Rio de Janeiro: Graal, 1983.

Saul, John S., and Stephen Gelb. *Crisis in South Africa.* 2nd ed. New York: Monthly Review Press, 1986.

Saville, John. *1848: The British State and the Chartist Movement.* New York: Cambridge University Press, 1987.

Saxton, Alexander. *The Rise and Fall of the White Republic: Class Politics and Mass Culture in Nineteenth-Century America.* New York: Verso, 1990.

Saxton, Alexander. *The Indispensable Enemy: Labor and the Anti-Chinese Movement in California.* Berkeley: University of California Press, 1971.

Scheper-Hughes, Nancy. "Undoing: Social Suffering and the Politics of Remorse in the New South Africa." *Social Justice* 25, no. 4 (Winter 1998).

Schiller, Bradley R. *The Economics of Poverty and Discrimination.* 6th ed. Englewood Cliffs, NJ: Prentice-Hall, 1995.

Schlesinger, Arthur M., Jr. "The Liberal Fifth Column in America." *Partisan Review* (Summer 1946).

Schwarcz, Lilia Moritz. *Retrato em Branco e Negro: Jornais, Escravos, e Cidadãos em São Paulo no Final do Século XIX.* São Paulo: Companhia das Letras, 1987.

Schwartz, Stuart B. *Sugar Plantations in the Formation of Brazilian Society: Bahia, 1550–1835.* Cambridge: Cambridge University Press, 1985.

Scott, James C. *Domination and the Arts of Resistance: Hidden Transcripts.* New Haven: Yale University Press, 1990.

Scott, Julius Sherrard, III. *The Common Wind: Currents of Afro-American Communications in the Era of the Haitian Revolution.* Ph.D. dissertation, Duke University, 1986.

Scott, Lawrence P., and William M. Womack. *Double V: The Civil Rights Struggle of the Tuskegee Airmen.* East Lansing: Michigan State University Press, 1998.

Scott, Rebecca J. *Slave Emancipation in Cuba: The Transition to Free Labor, 1860–1899.* Princeton: Princeton University Press, 1986.

Scott, Rebecca J., Seymour Drescher, Hebe Maria Mattos de Castro, George Reid Andrews, and Robert Levine. *The Abolition of Slavery and the Aftermath of Emancipation in Brazil.* Durham: Duke University Press, 1988.

Scott, Rebecca J. "Defining the Boundaries of Freedom in the World of Cane: Cuba, Brazil, and Louisiana After Emancipation." *American Historical Review* 99, no. 1 (February 1994).

Scott, Sir Walter. *Ivanhoe.* New York: Dodd, Mead, 1944.

Segal, Ronald. *The Black Diaspora.* New York: Farrar Straus and Giroux, 1995.

Seidman, Ann. "Apartheid and the U.S. South." In Sidney J. Lemelle and Robin D. G. Kelley, eds. *Imagining Home: Class, Culture, and Nationalism in the African Diaspora.* London; New York: Verso, 1994.

Seidman, Gay W. " 'No Freedom Without the Women': Mobilization and Gender in South Africa, 1970–1992." *Signs: Journal of Women in Culture and Society* 18, no. 2 (Winter 1993).

Seidman, Gay W. *Manufacturing Militance: Workers' Movements in Brazil and South Africa, 1970–1985.* Berkeley: University of California Press, 1994.

Seidman, Gay W. "Is South Africa Different? Sociological Comparisons and Theoretical Contributions from the Land of Apartheid." *Annual Review of Sociology* 25 (1999).

Selassie, Haile. Speech to the 18th Session of the United Nations General Assembly, October 4, 1963.

Semmes, Clovis E. *Racism, Health, and Post-Industrialism.* Westport, CT: Praeger, 1996.

Sen, Amartya. *Development as Freedom.* New York: Knopf, 2000a.

Sen, Amartya. "East and West: The Reach of Reason." *The New York Review of Books,* July 20, 2000b.

Shakespeare, William. *The Tempest.* Edited by Frank Kermode. Cambridge, MA: Harvard University Press, 1958.

Shapiro Gilbert, et al. *Revolutionary Demands: A Content Analysis of the Cahiers de Doleances of 1789.* Stanford: Stanford University Press, 1998.

Shaw, Carolyn Martin. *Colonial Inscriptions: Race, Sex, and Class in Kenya.* Minneapolis: University of Minnesota Press, 1995.

Sheriff, Robin E. *"Negro is a Nickname That Whites Gave to Blacks": Discourses on Color, Race, and Racism in Rio de Janeiro.* Ph.D. dissertation, City University of New York, 1997.

Shklar, Judith N. *American Citizenship: The Quest for Inclusion.* Cambridge, MA: Harvard University Press, 1991.

Silva, Nelson do Valle. "Updating the Cost of Not Being White in Brazil." In Pierre-Michel Fontaine, ed. *Race, Class, and Power in Brazil.* Los Angeles: CAAS/UCLA, 1985.

Silva, Nelson do Valle. "Côr e Pobreza no Centenário da Abolição." In idem and Carlos A. Hasenbalg. *Relações Raciais no Brasil Contemporâneo.* Rio de Janeiro: Rio Fundo/IUPERJ, 1992.

Simkins, Francis Butler. *Pitchfork Ben Tillman, South Carolinian*. Baton Rouge: Louisiana State University Press, 1944.

Simons, Marlise. "Report Foreign Guests? French Tempers Flare." *New York Times*, February 20, 1997.

Simons, Jack, and Ray Simons. *Class and Colour in South Africa, 1850–1950*. London: International Defence and Aid, 1983.

Simpson, Amelia. *Xuxa: The Mega-Marketing of Gender, Race, and Modernity*. Philadelphia: Temple University Press, 1993.

Simpson, Christopher. *Blowback: America's Recruitment of Nazis and Its Effects on the Cold War*. New York: Weidenfeld & Nicolson, 1988.

Singh, Kavaljit. *The Globalization of Finance: A Citizen's Guide*. London: Zed, 1999.

Singh, Nikhil Pal. "Culture/Wars: Recoding Empire in an Age of Democracy." *American Quarterly* 50, no. 3 (September 1998).

Sitkoff, Harvard. *A New Deal for Blacks: The Emergence of Civil Rights as a National Issue*. New York: Oxford University Press, 1978.

Sivanandan, A. *A Different Hunger: Writings on Black Resistance*. London: Pluto, 1982.

Sivanandan, A. *Communities of Resistance: Writings on Black Struggles for Socialism*. New York: Verso, 1990.

Skidelsky, Robert. *Oswald Mosley*. New York: Holt, Rinehart and Winston, 1975.

Skidmore, Thomas E. *Black into White: Race and Nationality in Brazilian Thought*. Durham: Duke University Press, 1993 [1974].

Skidmore, Thomas E. "Towards a Comparative Analysis of Race Relations in the United States and Brazil Since Abolition." *Journal of Latin American Studies* 4, no. 1 (1972).

Skocpol, Theda. *States and Social Revolutions: A Comparative Analysis of France, Russia, and China*. New York: Cambridge University Press, 1979.

Small, Stephen Augustus. *Racial Differentiation in the Slave Era: A Comparative Study of People of 'Mixed-Race' in Jamaica and Georgia*. Ph.D. dissertation, University of California, Berkeley, 1989.

Small, Stephen. *Racialized Barriers: The Black Experience in the United States and England in the 1980s*. New York: Routledge, 1994.

Smith, Adam. *An Inquiry into the Nature and Causes of the Wealth of Nations*. Edited by Edwin Cannan. New York: Modern Library, 1994 [1776].

Smith, Anna Marie. *New Right Discourse on Race and Sexuality: Britain 1968–1990*. New York: Cambridge University Press, 1994.

Smith, Anthony D. *The Ethnic Origins of Nations*. New York: Blackwell, 1987.

Smith, Rogers M. *Civic Ideals: Conflicting Visions of Citizenship in US History*. New Haven: Yale University Press, 1997.

Smith, Edward, and Walter Sapp, eds. *Plain Talk About the Human Genome Project: A Tuskegee University Conference on Its Promise and Perils . . . , and Matters of Race*. Tuskegee: Tuskegee University Press, 1997.

Snowden, Frank M. *Before Color Prejudice: The Ancient View of Blacks*. Cambridge, MA: Harvard University Press, 1983.

Sobredo, James D. *From American "Nationals" to the "Third Asiatic Invasion": Racial Transformation and the Filipino Exclusion Act, 1898–1934*. Ph.D. dissertation, University of California, Berkeley, 1998.

Solomos, John. *Race and Racism in Contemporary Britain*. London: Macmillan, 1989.

Solow, Barbara L. "Capitalism and Slavery in the Exceedingly Long Run," In idem, ed. *Slavery and the Rise of the Atlantic System*. New York: Cambridge University Press, 1991.

Solow, Barbara L., and Stanley L. Engerman, eds. *British Capitalism and Caribbean Slavery: The Legacy of Eric Williams*. New York: Cambridge University Press, 1987.

Solow, Barbara L., ed. *Slavery and the Rise of the Atlantic System*. New York: Cambridge University Press, 1991.

Sombart, Werner. *The Quintessence of Capitalism: A Study of the History and Psychology of the Modern Business Man*. Translated and edited by M. Epstein. New York: H. Fertig, 1967.

SOPEMI. *Trends in International Migration*. Paris: OECD, 1991.

South African Institute of Race Relations. *Race Relations Survey 1985.* Johannesburg: South African Institute of Race Relations, 1985.

Southern, David W. *Gunnar Myrdal and Black-White Relations: The Use and Abuse of An American Dilemma.* Baton Rouge: Louisiana State University Press, 1987.

Soysal, Yasemin Nuhoglu. *Limits of Citizenship: Migrants and Postnational Membership in Europe.* Chicago: University of Chicago Press, 1994.

Sparks, Allister Haddon. *Tomorrow is Another Country: The Inside Story of South Africa's Road to Change.* New York: Hill and Wang, 1995.

Spencer, Herbert. *The Evolution of Society: Selections from Herbert Spencer's Principles of Sociology.* Edited by Robert L. Carneiro. Chicago: University of Chicago Press, 1967.

Spero, Sterling D., and Abram L. Harris. *The Black Worker.* New York: Atheneum, 1968 [1931].

Spitzer, Leo. *Lives in Between: Assimilation and Marginality in Austria, Brazil, and West Africa, 1780–1945.* New York: Cambridge University Press, 1989.

Spivak, Gayatri Chakravorty. *In Other Worlds: Essays in Cultural Politics.* New York: Routledge, 1988.

Stampp, Kenneth M. *The Peculiar Institution: Slavery in the Ante-Bellum South.* New York: Knopf, 1956.

Stanfield, John H., II. *Philanthropy and Jim Crow in American Social Science.* Westport, CT: Greenwood, 1985.

Stanley, Amy Dru. *From Bondage to Contract: Wage Labor, Marriage, and the Market in the Age of Slave Emancipation.* New York: Cambridge University Press, 1998.

Stannard, David E. *American Holocaust: The Conquest of the New World.* New York: Oxford University Press, 1992.

Starobin, Robert S. *Industrial Slavery in the Old South.* New York: Oxford University Press, 1970.

Stavenhagen, Rodolfo, and Diego Iturralde, eds. *Entre la Ley y la Costumbre: El Derecho Consuetudinario Indígena en América Latina.* México, DF: Instituto Indigenista Interamericano, 1990.

Steele, Shelby. *The Content of Our Character 1990: A New Vision of Race in America.* New York: St. Martin's, 1990.

Steinbeck, John. *The Grapes of Wrath.* New York: Viking, 1939.

Steinberg, Stephen. *The Ethnic Myth: Race, Ethnicity, and Class in America.* New York: Atheneum, 1981.

Steinberg, Stephen. *Turning Back: The Retreat from Racial Justice in American Thought and Policy.* Boston, MA: Beacon, 1995.

Steinmo, Sven et al., eds. *Structuring Politics: Historical Institutionalism in Comparative Analysis.* New York: Cambridge University Press, 1992.

Stepan, Nancy Leys. *"The Hour of Eugenics": Race, Gender, and Nation in Latin America.* Ithaca: Cornell University Press, 1991.

Stepan, Nancy Leys, and Sander L. Gilman. "Appropriating the Idioms of Science: The Rejection of Scientific Racism." In Sandra Harding, ed. *The "Racial" Economy of Science: Toward a Democratic Future.* Bloomington: Indiana University Press, 1993.

Sternhell, Zeev. *The Birth of Fascist Ideology: From Cultural Rebellion to Political Revolution.* Translated by David Maisel. Princeton: Princeton University Press, 1994.

Sternhell, Zeev. *Maurice Barrès et le Nationalisme Français.* Paris: A. Colin, 1972.

Stier, Haya. "Immigrant Women Go to Work: Analysis of Immigrant Wives' Labor Supply for Six Asian Groups." In Franklin Ng, ed. *Asian American Women and Gender.* New York: Garland, 1998.

Stinchcombe, Arthur L. *Sugar Island Slavery in the Age of Enlightenment: The Political Economy of the Caribbean World.* Princeton: Princeton University Press, 1995.

Stinchcombe, Arthur L. *Constructing Social Theories.* New York: Harcourt, Brace and World, 1968.

Stoddard, Lothrop. *The Rising Tide of Color Against White World-Supremacy.* With an introduction by Madison Grant. New York: Scribner, 1920.

Stoler, Ann Laura. "Carnal Knowledge and Imperial Power: Gender, Race, and Morality in Colonial Asia." In Michaela di Leonardo, ed. *Gender at the Crossroads of Knowledge: Feminist Anthropology in a Postmodern Era.* Berkeley: University of California Press, 1991.

Stoler, Ann Laura. *Race and the Education of Desire: Foucault's History of Sexuality and the Colonial Order of Things*. Durham: Duke University Press, 1995.

Stoler, Ann Laura, "Sexual Affronts and Racial Frontiers: European and the Cultural Politics of Exclusion in Colonial Southeast Asia." In Ann Laura Stoler and Frederick Cooper, eds. *Tensions of Empire: Colonial Cultures in a Bourgeois World*. Berkeley: University of California Press, 1997.

Stovall, Tyler. *Paris Noir: African Americans in the City of Light*. Boston: Houghton Mifflin, 1996.

Stuckey, Sterling. *Slave Culture: Nationalist Theory and the Foundations of Black America*. New York: Oxford University Press, 1987.

Sugrue, Thomas J. *The Origins of the Urban Crisis: Race and Inequality in Postwar Detroit*. Princeton: Princeton University Press, 1995.

Sweezy, Paul M., et al. *The Transition from Feudalism to Capitalism*. Atlantic Highlands, NJ: Humanities Press, 1976.

Taguieff, Pierre-André. *The Force of Prejudice: On Racism and Its Doubles*. Translated by Hassan Melehy. Minneapolis: University of Minnesota Press, 2001; original French edition 1988.

Taguieff, Pierre-André. "The New Cultural Racism in France." *Telos* 83 (Spring 1990); also excerpted in Martin Bulmer and John Solomos, eds. *Racism*. London: Oxford University Press, 1999.

Taguieff, Pierre-André. *Les Fins de l'Anti-racisme: Essai*. Paris: Editions Michalon, 1995.

Takaki, Ronald. *A Different Mirror: A History of Multicultural America*. Boston: Little, Brown, 1993.

Tannenbaum, Frank. *Slave and Citizen: The Negro in the Americas*. Boston: Beacon, 1992 [1947].

Tarrow, Sidney. *Power in Movement: Social Movements, Collective Action, and Politics*. New York: Cambridge University Press, 1994.

Taussig, Michael T. *Shamanism, Colonialism, and the Wild Man: A Study in Terror and Healing*. Chicago: University of Chicago Press, 1986.

Taylor, Charles, et al. *Multiculturalism and "The Politics of Recognition."* Princeton: Princeton University Press, 1992.

Telles, Edward. "Segregation by Skin Color in Brazil." *American Sociological Review* 57 (1992).

Telles, Edward. "Industrialization and Racial Inequality in Employment: The Brazilian Example." *American Sociological Review* 59 (1994).

Telles, Edward. "Afro-Brazilian Identity, Mobilization, and Segregation." In Michael Hanchard, ed. *Racial Politics in Contemporary Brazil*. Durham: Duke University Press, 1999.

Temperly, Howard. *British Antislavery, 1833–1870*. London: Longman, 1972.

Thernstrom, Stephan, and Abigail Thernstrom. *America in Black and White: One Nation, Indivisible*. New York: Simon & Schuster, 1997.

Theweleit, Klaus. *Male Fantasies*. Vol. 1: *Women, Floods, Bodies, History*. Translated by Stephan Conway et al. Minneapolis: University of Minnesota Press, 1987.

Theweleit, Klaus. *Male Fantasies*. Vol. 2: *Male Bodies: Psychoanalyzing the White Terror*. Translated by Stephan Conway et al. Minneapolis: University of Minnesota Press, 1987.

Thomas, Hugh. *The Slave Trade: The Story of the Atlantic Slave Trade 1440–1870*. New York: Simon and Schuster, 1997.

Thomas, W. I., and Florian Znaniecki. *The Polish Peasant in Europe and America*. Edited by Eli Zaretsky. Urbana: University of Illinois Press, 1984 [1923].

Thompson, E. P. "Time, Work-Discipline, and Industrial Capitalism." *Past and Present* 38 (1967).

Thompson, E. P. *Whigs and Hunters: The Origin of the Black Act*. New York: Pantheon, 1975.

Thompson, Robert Farris. *Flash of the Spirit: African and Afro-American Art and Philosophy*. New York: Random House, 1983.

Thompson, Vincent Bakpetu. *The Making of the African Diaspora in the Americas, 1441–1900*. New York: Longman, 1987.

Thompson, Vincent Bakpetu. *Africa and Unity: The Evolution of Pan-Africanism*. Harlow, UK: Longmans, 1969.

Thornton, John. "Sexual Demography: The Impact of the Slave Trade on Family Structure." In Claire C. Robertson and Martin A. Klein, eds. *Women and Slavery in Africa*. Madison: University of Wisconsin Press, 1983.

Thornton, John. "African Soldiers in the Haitian Revolution." *Journal of Caribbean History* 25 (1991).

Thornton, John. " 'I Am the Subject of the King of Kongo': African Political Ideology and the Haitian Revolution." *Journal of World History* 4, no. 2 (1993).

Thornton, John. *Africa and Africans in the Making of the Atlantic World, 1400–1680.* 2nd ed. New York: Cambridge University Press, 1998.

Tilly, Charles, ed. *The Formation of National States in Western Europe.* Princeton: Princeton University Press, 1975.

Tilly, Charles. "War Making and State Making as Organized Crime." In Peter Evans et al., eds. *Bringing the State Back In.* New York: Cambridge University Press, 1985.

Tilly, Charles. *Coercion, Capital, and European States, 990–1992.* Cambridge, MA: Blackwell, 1990.

Tobias, Phillip V. *The Meaning of Race.* 2nd ed. Johannesburg: South African Institute of Race Relations, 1972.

Todorov, Tsvetan. *On Human Diversity: Nationalism, Racism, and Exoticism in French Thought.* Translated by Catherine Porter. Cambridge, MA: Harvard University Press, 1993.

Todorov, Tsvetan. *The Conquest of America: The Question of the Other.* Translated by Richard Howard. New York: Harper & Row, 1984.

Todorov, Tzvetan. *On Human Diversity: Nationalism, Racism, and Exoticism in French Thought.* Translated by Catherine Porter. Cambridge, MA: Harvard University Press, 1993.

Toledano, Ehud R. *Slavery and Abolition in the Ottoman Middle East.* Seattle: University of Washington Press, 1998.

Tolnay, Stewart Emory, and E. M. Beck. *A Festival of Violence: An Analysis of Southern Lynchings, 1882–1930.* Urbana: University of Illinois Press, 1995.

Topik, Steven C. *Trade and Gunboats: The United States and Brazil in the Age of Empire.* Stanford: Stanford University Press, 1996.

Toplin, Robert Brent. *The Abolition of Slavery in Brazil.* New York: Atheneum, 1972.

Torgovnick, Marianna. *Gone Primitive: Savage Intellects, Modern Lives.* Chicago: University of Chicago Press, 1990.

Toubia, Nahid. "Female Genital Mutilation." In Julie Peters and Andrea Wolper, eds. *Women's Right's, Human Rights.* New York: Routledge, 1995.

Tristan, Anne. *Au Front.* Paris: Gallimard, 1987.

Trouillot, Michel-Rolph. *Silencing the Past: Power and the Production of History.* Boston: Beacon, 1995.

Troup, Freda. *Forbidden Pastures: Education Under Apartheid.* London: International Defence and Aid Fund, 1976.

Tsuchida, Nobuya. *The Japanese in Brazil, 1908–1941.* Ph.D. dissertation, University of California, Los Angeles, 1978.

Turra, Cleusa, and Gutavo Venturi. *Racismo Cordial: A Mais Completa Analise sobre Preconceito de Côr no Brasil.* São Paulo: Atica, 1995.

Tuttle, William M., Jr. *Race Riot: Chicago in the Red Summer of 1919.* Urbana: University of Illinois Press, 1997.

Twine, France Winddance. *Racism in a Racial Democracy: The Maintenance of White Supremacy in Brazil.* New Brunswick, NJ: Rutgers University Press, 1997.

UNAIDS (Joint United Nations Program on HIV/AIDS). Report on the Global HIV/AIDS Epidemic. Geneva: UNAIDS, 2000. Available on the Internet at http://www.unaids.org/ epidemic_update/report/index.html.

UNESCO. *General Conference: Declaration on Race and Racial Prejudice Adopted by the General Conference of UNESCO at its Twentieth Session:* Paris, November 27, 1978. Paris: UNESCO, 1979a.

UNESCO. *La Trata Negrera del Siglo XV al XIX: Documentos de Trabajo e Informe de la Reunion de Expertos Organizada por la UNESCO en Puerto Principe, Haiti:* 31 de Enero al 4 de Febrero, 1978, Barcelona: Serbal, 1981.

UNESCO. *Round Table on Apartheid:* March 21, 1978, Paris. Paris: UNESCO, 1979b.

United for Intercultural Action, 2000. Website: http://www.united.non-profit.nl.

United States Bureau of the Census. *Historical Statistics of the United States.* Washington, DC: U.S. Government Printing Office, 1998.

Van Deburg, William L. *New Day in Babylon: The Black Power Movement and American Culture.* Chicago: University of Chicago Press, 1992.

Van den Berghe, Pierre L., ed. *Race and Racism: A Comparative Perspective.* 2nd ed. New York: Wiley, 1978.

Van den Berghe, Pierre L. *South Africa: A Study in Conflict.* Berkeley: University of California Press, 1967.

Van Onselen, Charles. *Studies in the Social and Economic History of Witwatersrand, 1886–1914.* 2 vols. New York: Longman, 1982.

Van Zyl Slabbert, Frederik. *The Quest for Democracy: South Africa in Transition.* New York: Penguin, 1992.

Vansina, Jan. *Kingdoms of the Savanna.* Madison: University of Wisconsin Press, 1966.

Vansina, Jan. *Paths in the Rainforests: Toward a History of Political Tradition in Equatorial Africa.* Madison: University of Wisconsin Press, 1990.

Vargas Llosa, Mario. *The War of the End of the World.* Translated by Helen R. Lane. New York: Farrar Straus Giroux, 1984.

Vasconcelos, José. *La Raza Cósmica: Misión de la Raza Iberoamericana.* Madrid, Spain: Ediciones Aguilar, 1966 [1924].

Veloso, Caetano, and Gilberto Gil. *Tropicália 2.* Elektra Nonesuch 79339–2, 1994.

Verdi, Giuseppe. *Aïda*; opera in four acts. Libretto by Antonio Ghislanzoni; English translation by Walter Ducloux. New York: G. Schirmer, 1963 [1871].

Vianna, Francisco José Oliveira. *Raça e Assimilação.* São Paulo: Nacional, 1934.

Vidal-Naquet, Pierre. *Assassins of Memory: Essays on the Denial of the Holocaust.* Translated by Jeffrey Mehlman. New York: Columbia University Press, 1992.

Vishniac, Judith. "French Socialists and the 'Droit à la Différence': A Changing Dynamic." *French Politics and Society* 9, no. 1 (Winter 1991).

Von Eschen, Penny M. *Race Against Empire: Black Americans and Anticolonialism, 1937–1957.* Ithaca: London: Cornell University Press, 1997.

Voss, Kim. *The Making of American Exceptionalism: The Knights of Labor and Class Formation in the 19th Century.* Ithaca: Cornell University Press, 1993.

Wafer Jim. *The Taste of Blood: Spirit Possession in Brazilian Candomblé.* Philadelphia: University of Pennsylvania Press, 1991.

Wagley, Charles. "From Caste to Class in Northern Brazil." In Melvin M. Tumin, ed. *Comparative Perspectives on Race Relations.* Boston: Little, Brown, 1969.

Wagley, Charles, ed. *Race and Class in Rural Brazil.* New York: Columbia University Press, 1972.

Waldinger, Roger. *Still the Promised City? African-Americans and New Immigrants in Post-Industrial New York.* Cambridge, MA: Harvard University Press, 1995.

Waldmeir, Patti. *Anatomy of a Miracle: The End of Apartheid and the Birth of the New South Africa.* New York: Norton, 1997.

Walker, David. *David Walker's Appeal to the Coloured Citizens of the World.* Edited by Peter P. Hinks. University Park: Pennsylvania State University Press, 2000 [1829].

Wallerstein, Immanuel. *Africa, the Politics of Independence: An Interpretation of Modern African History.* New York: Vintage, 1961.

Wallerstein, Immanuel M. *The Modern World-System.* 3 vols. New York and San Diego: Academic, 1974, 1980, 1989.

Wallerstein, Immanuel M. "The Three Stages of African Involvement with the World Economy." In Peter C. W. Gutkind and Immanuel Wallerstein, eds. *The Political Economy of Contemporary Africa.* Beverly Hills, CA: Sage, 1976.

Wallerstein, Immanuel M. "The Rise and Future Demise of the Capitalist World System." In idem, *The Capitalist World-Economy.* Cambridge, UK; New York: Cambridge University Press, 1979a.

Wallerstein, Immanuel M. "The Two Modes of Ethnic Consciousness: Soviet Central Asia in Transition." In idem, *The Capitalist World-Economy.* Cambridge, UK; New York: Cambridge University Press, 1979b.

Wallerstein, Immanuel M. "The Myrdal Legacy: Racism and Underdevelopment as Dilemmas." In idem, *Unthinking Social Science: The Limits of Nineteenth-Century Paradigms.* Cambridge, UK: Polity, 1991.

Wallerstein, Immanuel M. *Historical Capitalism.* New York: Verso, 1995.

Wallraff, Günter. *Lowest of the Low.* London: Methuen, 1988.

Walters, Ronald W. *Pan-Africanism in the African Diaspora: An Analysis of Modern Afrocentric Political Movements.* Detroit: Wayne State University Press, 1995.

Walters, Ronald. "White Racial Nationalism in the United States," *Without Prejudice* 1, no. 1 (Fall 1987).

Walvin, James. *Questioning Slavery.* New York: Routledge, 1986.

Walzer, Michael. *Spheres of Justice.* New York: Basic, 1983.

Ware, Vron. *Beyond the Pale: White Women, Racism and History.* London: Verso, 1992.

Warren, Jonathan W. "The State of Indian Exorcism: Violence and Racial Formation in Eastern Brazil." *Journal of Historical Sociology* 11, no. 4 (1998).

Washington, Mary Lynn. *White, Black, or Mulatto?* Ph.D. dissertation, Department of Sociology, Johns Hopkins University, 1997.

Waskow, Arthur I. *From Race Riot to Sit-in: 1919 and the 1960s: A Study in the Connections between Conflict and Violence.* Garden City, NY: Doubleday, 1966.

Waters, Mary. *Ethnic Options: Choosing Identities in America.* Berkeley: University of California Press, 1990.

Watson, Graham. *Passing for White: A Study of Racial Assimilation in a South African School.* London: Tavistock, 1970.

Weber, Eugen Joseph. *Peasants into Frenchmen: The Modernization of Rural France, 1870–1914.* Stanford: Stanford University Press, 1976.

Weber, Max. *From Max Weber: Essays in Sociology.* Edited and translated by Hans H. Gerth and C. Wright Mills. New York: Oxford University Press, 1958.

Weber, Max. *Economy and Society.* Berkeley: University of California Press, 1978.

Weber, Max. *The Agrarian Sociology of Ancient Civilizations.* Translated by R. I. Frank. London: New Left, 1976.

Weber, Max. *Weber: Political Writings* Edited and translated by Peter Lassman and Ronald Speirs. New York: Cambridge University Press, 1994.

Weber, Max. *The Russian Revolutions.* Edited and translated by Gordon C. Wells and Peter Baehr. Ithaca: Cornell University Press, 1995.

Webster, Edward, and Glenn Adler. "Toward a Class Compromise in South Africa's 'Double Transition': Bargained Liberalization and the Consolidation of Democracy." *Politics and Society* 27, no. 3 (September 1999).

Weil, Patrick. *La France et ses Étrangers: L'Aventure d'une Politique de L'Immigration de 1938 à Nos Jours.* Rev. ed. Paris: Gallimard, 1995.

Weiner, Marc A. *Richard Wagner and the Anti-Semitic Imagination.* Lincoln: University of Nebraska Press, 1995.

Weir, Robert E. *Beyond Labor's Veil: The Culture of the Knights of Labor.* University Park: Pennsylvania State University Press, 1996.

Weiss, Nancy J. *Farewell to the Party of Lincoln: Black Politics in the Age of FDR.* Princeton: Princeton University Press, 1983.

Welsh, David. "Constraints on, and Functions of, Research in Sociology and Psychology in Contemporary South Africa." In John Rex, ed. *Apartheid and Social Research.* Paris: UNESCO, 1981.

Weschler, Lawrence. *A Miracle, a Universe: Settling Accounts with Torturers.* New York: Pantheon, 1990.

West, Cornel. *The American Evasion of Philosophy: A Genealogy of Pragmatism.* Madison: University of Wisconsin Press, 1989.

Whitten, Norman E. *Black Frontiersmen: A South American Case.* Cambridge, MA: Schenkman, 1974.

Wieviorka, Michel. *The Arena of Racism.* Translated by Chris Turner. Thousand Oaks, CA: Sage, 1995.

Wieviorka, Michel. "Tendencies to Racism in Europe: Does France Represent a Unique Case, or is it Representative of a Trend?" In John Solomos and John Wrench, eds. *Racism and Migration in Western Europe.* Providence, RI: Berg, 1993.

Williams, Eric. *Capitalism and Slavery.* Chapel Hill: University of North Carolina Press, 1994 [1944].

Williams, George Washington. "A Report on the Congo-State and Country to the President of the Republic of the United States of America." In John Hope Franklin. *George Washington Williams: A Biography.* Chicago: University of Chicago Press, 1985 [1890].

Williams, Juan. *Thurgood Marshall: American Revolutionary.* New York: Times Books, 1998.

Williams, Lena. "When Blacks Shop, Bias often Accompanies Sale." *New York Times,* April 30, 1991.

Williams, Patricia J. *The Alchemy of Race and Rights.* Cambridge, MA: Harvard University Press, 1991.

Williamson, Joel. *New People: Miscegenation and Mulattoes in the United States.* New York: Free Press, 1980.

Williamson, Joel. *A Rage for Order: Black-White Relations in the American South Since Emancipation.* New York: Oxford University Press, 1986.

Wills, Gary. *Lincoln at Gettysburg: The Words That Remade America.* New York: Simon & Schuster, 1992.

Wilpert, Czarina. "The Ideological and Institutional Foundations of Racism in the Federal Republic of Germany." In John Solomos and John Wrench, eds. *Racism and Migration in Western Europe.* Providence, RI: Berg, 1993.

Wilson, Francis. "Farming 1866–1966." In Monica Wilson and Leonard Thompson, eds. *The Oxford History of South Africa.* Vol. 2. New York: Oxford University Press, 1969–71.

Wilson, Francis, and Mamphela Ramphele. *Uprooting Poverty: The South African Challenge.* New York: Norton, 1989.

Wimberly, Fayette Darcell. *The African Liberto and the Bahian Lower Class: Social Integration in Nineteenth-Century Bahia, Brazil, 1870–1900.* Ph.D. dissertation, University of California, Berkeley, 1988.

Winant, Howard. "Rethinking Race in Brazil." *Journal of Latin American Studies* 24, no. 1 (1992).

Winant, Howard. *Racial Conditions: Politics, Theory, Comparisons.* Minneapolis: University of Minnesota Press, 1994a.

Winant, Howard. "Dictatorship, Democracy, and Difference: The Historical Construction of Racial Identity." In idem, *Racial Conditions: Politics, Theory, Comparisons.* Minneapolis: University of Minnesota Press, 1994b.

Winant, Howard. "Where Culture Meets Structure: Race in the 1990s." In idem, *Racial Conditions: Politics, Theory, Comparisons.* Minneapolis: University of Minnesota Press, 1994c.

Winant, Howard. "The Fact of Blackness in Brazil." In idem, *Racial Conditions: Politics, Theory, Comparisons.* Minneapolis: University of Minnesota Press, 1994d.

Winant, Howard. "Behind Blue Eyes." In Michelle Fine et al., eds. *Off White: Readings on Race, Power, and Society* New York: Routledge, 1997a.

Winant, Howard. "Racial Dualism at Century's End." In Wahneema Lubiano, ed. *The House That Race Built: Black Americans, US Terrain.* New York: Pantheon, 1997b.

Winant, Howard. "Racism Today: Continuity and Change in the Post-Civil Rights Era." *Ethnic and Racial Studies* 21, no. 4 (July 1998).

Wirth, Louis. *On Cities and Social Life: Selected Papers.* Edited by Albert J. Reiss. Chicago: University of Chicago Press, 1964.

Wish, Harvey, ed. *Antebellum Writings of George Fitzhugh and Hinton Rowan Helper on Slavery.* New York: Capricorn, 1960.

Witte, Rob. *Racist Violence and the State: A Comparative Analysis of Britain, France, and the Netherlands.* New York: Longman, 1996.

Wolf, Eric R. *Europe and the People Without History.* Berkeley: University of California Press, 1982.

Wolpe, Harold. "Capitalism and Cheap Labour-Power in South Africa: From Segregation to Apartheid." *Economy and Society* 111 (1972).

Wong, Kevin Scott, and Sucheng Chan, eds. *Claiming America: Constructing Chinese American Identities During the Exclusion Era.* Philadelphia: Temple University Press, 1998.

Wood, Betty. *The Origins of American Slavery: Freedom and Bondage in the English Colonies.* New York: Hill and Wang, 1997.

Wood, Charles H., and José Alberto Magno de Carvalho. *The Demography of Inequality in Brazil.* New York: Cambridge University Press, 1988.

Wood, Charles H. "Categorias Censitárias e Clasificações Subjetivas de Raça no Brasil." Unpublished paper, 1991.

Wood, Forrest G. *Black Scare: The Racist Response to Emancipation and Reconstruction.* Berkeley: University of California Press, 1968.

Woodhull, Victoria C. "The Rapid Multiplication of the Unfit. . . ." Pamphlet. New York: N.P., 1891.

Woodward, C. Vann. *Origins of the New South, 1877–1913.* Baton Rouge: Louisiana State University Press, 1951.

Woodward, C. Vann. *Reunion and Reaction: The Compromise of 1877 and the End of Reconstruction.* Boston: Little, Brown, 1966.

Woodward, C. Vann. *The Strange Career of Jim Crow.* New York: Oxford University Press, 1974.

Wright, Richard. *Black Power: A Record of Reactions in a Land of Pathos.* New York: Harper, 1954.

Wright, Winthrop. *Café Con Leche: Race, Class, and National Image in Venezuela.* Austin: University of Texas Press, 1990.

Yellin, Jean Fagan, and John C. Van Horne, eds. *The Abolitionist Sisterhood: Women's Political Culture in Antebellum America.* Ithaca: Cornell University Press, 1994.

Yinger, John. *Closed Doors, Opportunities Lost: The Continuing Costs of Housing Discrimination.* New York: Russell Sage Foundation, 1997.

Young, Robert. *Colonial Desire: Hybridity in Theory, Culture, and Race.* New York: Routledge, 1995.

Zinn, Howard. *SNCC: The New Abolitionists.* 2nd ed. Boston: Beacon, 1965.

Zizek, Slavoj. "How Did Marx Invent the Symptom?" In idem, ed. *Mapping Ideology.* New York: Verso, 1994.

Zolberg, Aristide R., et al. *Escape from Violence: Conflict and the Refugee Crisis in the Developing World.* New York: Oxford University Press, 1989.

Zuberi, Tukufu, and Akil Khalfani. "Racial Classification and the Census in South Africa, 1911–1916." Working Paper 7, African Census Analysis Project, University of Pennsylvania, March 1999.

Index